Industrial Behavior Modification

(PGPS-107)

Pergamon Titles of Related Interest

Goldstein/Sorcher CHANGING SUPERVISOR BEHAVIOR
Moses/Byham APPLYING THE ASSESSMENT CENTER METHOD
Work in America Institute PRODUCTIVITY THROUGH
WORK INNOVATIONS
A Work in America Institute Policy Study
Zager/Rosow THE INNOVATIVE ORGANIZATION: Productivity
Programs in Action

Related Journals*

BEHAVIORAL ASSESSMENT
BEHAVIOUR RESEARCH AND THERAPY
EVALUATION AND PROGRAM PLANNING
TECHNOLOGY IN SOCIETY
WORK IN AMERICA INSTITUTE STUDIES IN PRODUCTIVITY

*Free specimen copies available upon request.

Industrial Behavior Modification
A Management Handbook

Edited by
Richard M. O'Brien
Hofstra University

Alyce M. Dickinson
New York State Office
of Court Administration

Michael P. Rosow
Work in America Institute

Published in cooperation with Work in America Institute

Pergamon Press

New York   Oxford   Toronto   Sydney   Paris   Frankfurt

Pergamon Press Offices:

U.S.A.   Pergamon Press Inc., Maxwell House, Fairview Park,
                     Elmsford, New York 10523, U.S.A.

U.K.   Pergamon Press Ltd., Headington Hill Hall,
                     Oxford OX3 0BW, England

CANADA   Pergamon Press Canada Ltd., Suite 104, 150 Consumers Road,
                     Willowdale, Ontario M2J 1P9, Canada

AUSTRALIA   Pergamon Press (Aust.) Pty. Ltd., P.O. Box 544,
                     Potts Point, NSW 2011, Australia

FRANCE   Pergamon Press SARL, 24 rue des Ecoles,
                     75240 Paris, Cedex 05, France

FEDERAL REPUBLIC Pergamon Press GmbH, Hammerweg 6
OF GERMANY   6242 Kronberg/Taunus, Federal Republic of Germany

Copyright © 1982 Pergamon Press Inc.

Library of Congress Cataloging in Publication Data
Main entry under title:

Industrial behavior modification.

    (Pergamon general psychology series ; v. 107)
    Published in cooperation with Work in
America Institute.
    Bibliography: p.
    Includes index.
    1. Organizational behavior--Addresses,
essays, lectures. 2. Behavior modification--
Addresses, essays, lectures. I. O'Brien,
Richard M. (Richard Michael), 1943-
II. Dickinson, Alyce M. (Alyce Muzette),
1953-   . III. Rosow, Michael. IV. Work
in America Institute. V. Series.
HD58.7.I53   1982   658.3'001'9   81-19877
ISBN 0-08-025558-2   AACR2

Printed in the United States of America

To:
Eleanor and Vincent O'Brien and Annette, Elena and Janine   R.O'B.
George and Vera Dickinson   A.M.D.
Rayna, Lori and Alison   M.R.

Contents

Foreword

"Hey, this stuff really works!" That's what industrial behavior modification is all about – applying basic principles of behavior analysis to the very practical world of business. And that's what this book is all about.

Behavior theory has been around for a while. And the principles of applied behavior analysis have been known to work for some time. That is, they have been shown capable of producing dramatic and lasting changes in behavior. So why aren't they known and used by everyone? One of the most common reasons advanced by critics of behavior analysis and technology is that "it's fine for controlled environments, but it won't work in the real world." To some extent, the critics have been right. Many early effective applications of behavior analysis were in situations where the analyst had a high degree of control – or were so costly as to be prohibitive for general use.

The use of behavior analysis has been increasing, however. Practitioners have been learning how to apply it in more and more complex and "natural" environments. The articles in this book are a sign that we've arrived. We have evolved a technology of behavior analysis and management to the point where it can be applied cost-effectively to the demanding, complex and competitive world of private industry.

This maturation of behavior technology is particularly timely. We are living in an environment of rapid change, diminishing resources, and continuing inflation. Events over the past decade have intensified the business community's traditional focus on profits and productivity. We are approaching the limits of what can be done to maintain or increase organizational productivity through investment in technology or natural resources. More and more, we are realizing that organization health requires intelligent investment in people and their performance.

Among the factors that make industrial behavior modification especially relevant to today's environment are these:

- It can be tied to the "bottom line." Behavior technology is a measurement-based approach to behavior change.
- It's testable. The focus on objective measurement of change allows a realistic assessment of the success of an intervention.
- It can be used at any level in an organization. The principles and concepts can be applied by a foreman in managing a three-person work unit, or by the human resources department in planning an organization-wide information and feedback system.
- It can be incorporated into the organization's operating system. We're not talking about one-shot interventions – or even a series of interventions by outsiders. Rather, an effective application of behavior technology in an organization will result in an employee-operated system – one that allows internal monitoring and revision in response to change.

Perhaps one of the most valuable features of industrial behavior modification is its broad applicability. It doesn't require that one be committed to a particular philosophy or set of organizational goals. Instead, it requires that individuals or organizations first carefully define goals and offer diagnostic and perscriptive tools for achieving them – whether they deal with profits or employee satisfaction, or both.

The editors have put together a series of papers that offers something for both the old hand at behavior technology and the newcomer. There are articles providing both a conceptual framework for the application of behavior analysis to business management, and a wide range of practical applications. The authors are some of the best in the business. They represent both academicians and researchers who have successfully moved into the business world, and business managers who have successfully integrated behavior theory with business management practices.

Donald Tosti
The Forum Corporation

Preface

Behavior modification has been defined as the application of the techniques of experimental psychology to problems of behavior (Mikulas, 1978). In recent years that definition has been extended to include the industrial manager and the organizational psychologist as well as those in the clinical areas. Applied behavior analysis is a specific variant of behavior modification which focuses on the techniques of response specification, recording and contingent positive reinforcement that have developed out of research in operant learning (see Catania, 1968; Honig & Staddon, 1977; Millenson & Leslie, 1979; Sidman, 1960; Skinner, 1938; 1953; 1974).

Like clinical and educational psychology, early industrial psychologists were cast into a psychodiagnostic role. Their functions were generally in the area of measurement, assessment, and prediction rather than intervention. Recently, managers have become more concerned with human behavior in increasing productivity; thus psychology's contribution to industry has begun to shift away from the selection model. As behavior change, i.e., increased productivity, becomes the goal, the behavioral model with its stress on objective measurement, observable responses, and positive reinforcements offers an appealing alternative to the traditional motivation systems. It is simply easier to tell when one is rewarding task-oriented activity with positive attention than it is to tell if one is helping the employee to self-actualize. The laboratory evidence that such rewards serve to increase desired behavior is axiomatic (see Honig, 1966) while the relationship between increased productivity and self-actualization, democratic leadership style or even improved working conditions has been more difficult to establish. Nevertheless, the earlier motivational paradigms of Maslow (1943) and Herzberg (1959) have provided a useful descriptive framework for organizational behavior. Before they are abandoned or even modified in favor of the new behavioral procedures, the industrial manager and the student of industrial psychology should take a hard look at the efficacy of applied behavior analysis as specifically demonstrated in organizational settings. Since behavior analysts pride themselves on their on-line recording, the evidence should be plentiful. The aim of the present work is to provide the best examples of behavioral programs in industry so that readers can reach their own decisions with regard to the potential of this approach.

The reports of behavior modification programs implemented in industrial settings are scattered through a broad variety of technical and popular publications. The behavioral scientists designing these programs come from business, government, and academia. Attempts to evaluate the efficacy of industrial behavior modification programs or to gain background knowledge for one's own program are hampered by the lack of a central source book in this area. The present volume represents an attempt to fill this void for the student of management and/or industrial psychology who wishes to learn these techniques as well as for the on-line manager to use as a guide for implementing behavior modification programs. Whenever possible the editors have chosen to focus on industrial experiences rather than interventions in nonprofit settings. This decision was based on the special problems of business management for profit that are not shared by hospitals, educational institutions, or mental health centers. Nonetheless, the reader should be aware of the significant behavior modification projects that have been completed in these nonprofit organizations (compare Frederiksen, 1978; Prue, Krapfl, Noah, Cannon, & Maley, 1980).

To fulfill our broad goals, the editors have attempted to bring together experts in applying behavioral techniques to a variety of industrial problems. In this way a handbook was compiled so that the reader would not have to search out the work of authorities in the field through the literature in management, training, personnel, psychology in general, and behavior analysis in particular. The skills involved in implementing behavioral programs and the effects that can be achieved are described by those who have actually developed industrial behavior modification projects. The consulting firm of Edward J. Feeney Associates has contributed five chapters, including projects on increasing sales by airline reservationists at SAS by Mr. Feeney and the firm's vice president, John Staelin, increasing retail sales by Bill Crawley, and improving productivity in manufacturing by Fred Bushhouse. They also report agency-wide applications by Dan Brand at HUD to increase clerical productivity and by Bill Abernathy throughout the Virginia National Bank. Richard Carlson and Bill Sperduto of Behavior Dynamics report on their success with the difficult problem of absenteeism, and Bill Brittain breaks ground with a behavioral approach to outplacement representing a leading assessment firm in that field, Caress, Gilhooly, and Kestin. The successes that can be achieved by in-house consultants are described by Robert Mirman of General Mills.

To provide the appropriate theoretical context for these case studies, leading exponents of industrial behavior analysis were asked to provide the reader with basic behavior modification techniques. For the professional, Tom Mawhinney presents a sophisticated review of operant theory as applied to industry. Dale Brethower, a pioneer in behavioral systems analysis was solicited to present the extension of behavior change techniques to the interactions of a whole organizational network while Howard Berthold outlines ethical concerns for the reader to address before implementing a program. Ted Ayllon, who was involved in some of the early industrial behavior modification studies with Richard Carlson, gives the reader a view of schedules of reinforcement in industry from the perspective of one of the first applied behavior analysts. Judi Komaki has been a leader in the modification of employee support behaviors such as maintenance, customer service, and safety. She offers her expertise to help managers deal with perhaps the most costly of these potential problem areas in a behavioral approach to preventive maintenance.

American management has come under increasing attack in recent years as national productivity has decreased in comparison to other industrialized nations (Bluestone, 1979; Jones, 1981). It is the editor's view, based on the available data, that the first step toward solving the American productivity problem is to implement the behavioral programs described in this volume.

Readers who complete the book should gain a current and reasonably thorough grasp of the area of industrial behavior modification. They should be able to see both the organizational advantages and limitations of applied behavior analysis. For industrial managers, the book should provide enough information to allow them to decide if they wish to implement a behavior modification project. Although it is recommended that a consultant who is trained in industrial behavior modification or at the very least in the general uses of applied behavior analysis should be employed wherever possible, managers who do not have such resources available should not be discouraged from initiating a program. If they remember the basic rules of feedback and positive reinforcement the only things that can happen are that their records will become more accurate and their interactions with employees will become more positive. Managers must remember, however, that in order to produce a change in employee behavior, they must first modify their own responses to the worker. They are likely to find that becoming a positive stimulus to the employee is much more enjoyable than the other roles they have often had to play. One really does catch more flies with honey than with vinegar as long as the honey is dispensed only for appropriate behavior.

REFERENCES

Bluestone, I. Emerging trends in collective bargaining. In C. Kerr & J. M. Rosow (Eds.), *Work in America the decade ahead*. New York: Van Nostrand Reinhold, 1979.

Catania, C. A. *Contemporary research in operant behavior*. New York: Scott, Foresman, 1968.

Frederiksen, L. W. Behavioral reorganization of a professional service system. *Journal of Organizational Behavior Management*, 1978, **2**, 1-9.

Herzberg, F., Mausner, B., Snyderman, B. The *motivation to work*. New York: Wiley, 1959.

Honig, W. K. (Ed.) *Operant behavior: Areas of research and application*. New York: Appleton-Century-Crofts, 1966

Honig, W. K., & Staddon, J. E. R. (Eds.) *Handbook of operant behavior*. Englewood Cliffs, N.J.: Prentice Hall, 1977.

Jones, R.H. How do we revitalize our technological infrastructure? In J. M. Rosow (Ed.), *Productivity prospects for growth*. New York, Van Nostrand Reinhold, 1981.

Maslow, A. N. A theory of human motivation. *Psychological Review*, 1943, **50**, 370-396.

Mikulas, W. L. *Behavior modification*. New York: Harper & Row, 1978.

Millenson, J. R., & Leslie, J. C. *Principles of behavioral analysis*. (2nd ed.) New York: Macmillan, 1979.

Prue, D. M., Krapfl, J. E., Noah, J. C., Cannon, S., & Maley, R. F. Managing the treatment activities of state hospital staff. *Journal of Organizational Behavior Management*, 1980, **2**, 165-181.

Sidman, M. *Tactics of scientific research*. New York: Basic Books, 1960.

Skinner, B. F. *The behavior of organisms: An experimental analysis*. New York: Appleton-Century-Crofts, 1938.

Skinner, B. F. *Science and human behavior*. New York: Macmillan, 1953.

Skinner, B. F. *About behaviorism*. New York: Knopf, 1974.

Acknowledgments

Through the long process of editing this volume, we have received support from many people both individually and as a group. The existence of this book owes much to Edward J. Feeney Associates, particularly John Staelin and Ed Feeney who provided encouragement since the very beginning of the project.

Our institutions have also been significant contributors to the completion of this work. Dr. Hadassah Paul, Chairperson of the Department of Psychology at Hofstra University has been particularly supportive among the many colleagues who aided our endeavors. The book was also influenced by the work of Dale Brethower at Western Michigan University, and the editors would be remiss if they did not thank Julia Vane of Hofstra for bringing them together in the initial stages of this undertaking. The interest and encouragement of Vito Soranno and Neal Charity of the New York State Office of Court Administration were instrumental in helping the second editor to fulfill her professional goals. In addition gratitude must be expressed to O.C.A. for providing both time and financial support for professional development toward the completion of this manuscript. The staff at the Work in America Institute provided editorial help and was largely responsible for the index of the book. These support services are gratefully acknowledged. The typing help provided by all three institutions was very much appreciated.

To put the manuscript in its final form required editorial, graphic, and typing services. Elaine Duffy put in many hours assisting in the final editorial writing. The editors also benefited from the graphics expertise of Hofstra University's Jack Ruegamer and Robert Noble, and we are also in their debt. The typing of a number of fine secretaries was employed in this project and the editors appreciate their work. Particular thanks must go Lynn Siconolfi, Cecelia Sokolowski, Stella Sinicki, and most of all Marion Anthony who did much of the rough typing from the editors' illegible drafts.

A measure of gratitude must also go to those who have had to endure the editors' lost personal lives as this book developed over the past three years. Foremost among these are the first editor's wife (Annette) and daughters (Elena and Janine). Their patience is appreciated.

Finally we would like to thank Jerry Frank of Pergamon Press for his editorial help. From beginning to end he provided support, criticism, nagging, and handholding that should not go unnoticed.

Industrial Behavior Modification

(PGPS-107)

Part I:
The Behavioral Model

Introduction

A manager is someone who organizes a group of people to achieve a given objective. It may be as exotic as winning the pennant or as mundane as making sure that all of the garbage is picked up, but it remains a job of controlling behavior to achieve an end. The manager's role is one of managing people's behavior so that both they and the organization prosper. The manager is responsible for scheduling behavior, prompting it, rewarding it, setting goals for it, measuring it, and evaluating it. The same scientific method that resulted in all of the sophisticated technology that today's manager has at his command, has also been applied to these questions of how to manage. Yet, as often as not, managers receive little training in the principles of behavior change or measurement. The purpose of this first unit is to present these techniques and the theories and findings that support them so that managers can begin to become technologically refined about how to manage behavior. This new technology may be identified as industrial behavior modification, organizational behavior management, organizational behavior analysis, positive management, or any of a number of other behavioral rubrics. In essence, these labels are interchangeable. They all stand for applied behavior analysis in industrial-organizational settings.

Through research, scientists concerned with increasing or decreasing behavior have uncovered a number of general rules about evoking and measuring behavior change. For example, we know that the correlation between attitudes or verbal statements and behavior is less than ideal so the most accurate measures of behavior must be sought in direct observation of responses (Rosenbaum, 1979). Similarly, it has been found that ratings of people tend to be so biased by extraneous variables that they fail to reflect the behavior that they were intended to measure. The manager who is aware of these facts is unlikely to spend an exorbitant amount of company dollars to develop an attitude survey or base his personnel decisions on the ratings of supervisors. He will begin to look for more direct measures of the behaviors that concern him. As Deurr (1974) has indicated, "It is not the function of the manager to pass value judgements on whether or not those with whom he deals have "proper" attitudes. His function is to see that his behavior, and those aspects of his company's systems over which he has control, give people a positive incentive to do what is desired [p. 893]."

Deurr's point about attitudes is well taken, but his view that the manager should manage through the presentation of incentives or rewards is even more important. When one reviews the research findings that compare the efficacy of reward to that of punishment in managing behavior one finds that positive reinforcement has been shown to be the more effective technique as well as being less disturbing to the subject (Azrin & Holz, 1966; Luthans & Kreitner, 1975).

In industry, however, the traditional punitive approach to management is still dominant (Kreitner, 1975; Mayhew, Enyart, & Cone, 1979). From factory worker to farm-hand the news that the boss wants to see you usually gives rise to grim forebodings. Yet nowhere is it etched in stone that managers and employees must be adversaries. It is not a sacrilege for a manager to call an employee into his office just to praise him. After all, they are both on the same team, working for the same goals.

Unfortunately, the history of labor-management relations has rarely highlighted the

3

congruent interests of worker and boss (Horvitz, 1981). As noted, management, by definition, involves controlling employee behavior in order to reach organizational goals. All too often management and labor assume that the employee does not have any interest in those goals. This assumption is most often translated into a carrot and stick management approach with so much emphasis on the stick that the employee gets only the short end. The employee gets no extra pay, no praise, no attention, and no status for doing a job well, so he does it only well enough to get by. His salary is at best unrelated to his performance and at worst used to maintain a level of mediocrity.

How does one begin to use rewards to change employee behavior? How does one directly measure important work behaviors rather than attitudes or by ratings? Finally, is there a technology that can make management more positive, its assessment more accurate, and its outputs more effective? Applied behavior analysis is the branch of psychology that has been attempting to answer these questions about how to manage behavior. In Chapter 1 behavior modification is introduced as a management tool. The behavioral approach of direct behavior change is contrasted to earlier psychological theories that focused on the employee's needs, values, and traits. The theoretical foundation for this new, empirical approach is explained and guidelines for the use of positive reinforcement, behavior change programs are presented. The aim of Chapter 1 is to help correct what Kalish (1981) has noted as the two basic mistakes that managers and industrial psychologists have made in dealing with organizational behavior. First, the reader should learn to substitute measures of external events and behavior for inferences about unmeasurable attitudes and drives. Second, the chapter should help the reader correct the choice of behavior to be measured so that the unit of work behavior that is chosen is small enough for functional analysis. Finally, Chapter 1 presents a brief historical account of the progress of behavioral programs in industry over the last decade.

The basic interrelationship of behavior and environmental events is presented in Chapter 1, but there is considerably more complexity to this interaction than can be digested in a simplified overview of functional analysis. Consequences usually do not occur just once nor do they occur every time the individual makes a response. Having been introduced to the effects of changing the consequences of work behaviors, the reader should now be prepared to learn more about the most effective ways to implement positive reinforcement programs. A critical issue in extending program life and cutting project costs is the schedule of reinforcement on which rewards are delivered. In Chapter 2 Ayllon and Kolko examine both contingent and non-contingent reward schedules in industry. Productivity effects are discussed for everything from strict fixed ratio schedules such as piecework to non-contingent fixed interval or fixed time schedules such as the weekly salary. The effects of reinforcement schedules within organizational settings is a question of continuing research interest (Pritchard, Hollenback, & De Leo, 1980).

Applied behavior analysis is not a static intervention system. It demands on-going data collection and evaluation, but the data must be the actual behavior that is of concern to the manager. The rationale and methods for behavioral assessment in business are presented in Chapter 3. With these skills a manager can determine if an intervention is warranted or evaluate the progress of a project as it unfolds. The reader is given tools for behavioral rather than statistical measurement.

By the end of the first three chapters the reader will probably be convinced that a behavior modification approach to organizational management is a theoretically sound idea in limited situations. This is sometimes called the "that sounds great but it would never work in my company" philosophy. It is usually supported by appeals to logical arguments such as "Our people don't care about their work," "The machines set the pace in our company so productivity can't be increased," and "With our unions you couldn't possibly set up any kind of incentive or recognition system." The best response to these concerns is to present an actual case history or two in order to demonstrate how common sense behavior modification theory can be turned into real world productivity gains.

The two case studies that Fred Bushhouse and his coauthors report in Chapter 4 are two of the latest projects of the Edward J. Feeney Associates consultation group. The first case report depicts the straightforward application of feedback, positive reinforcement, and improved contingencies to bring a company into the black from a large deficit. The second study explores more conceptually complex problems. The behavioral intervention in this instance dramatically improved machine paced productivity which is generally considered to be independent of organizational reinforcement factors. Of particular interest in this report is the parceling out of rewards to support personnel based on overall on-line performance. Evaluating and contingently rewarding managerial productivity is one of industry's most thorny problems (Sweetland & Rosow, 1978). This percentage based reward system represents an innovation that could have a significant impact on the managerial productivity problem in a variety of settings.

In industry the schedule of reinforcement is most often embodied in some form of contractual agreement. But the contract of the lawyers and courts is not quite the same animal that behaviorists talk about when they discuss contingency contracting. Howard Berthold presents the principles of contingency contracting as a specification of the response to reinforcement requirements in Chapter 5. In this instance the contract serves to bridge the gap of time between the behavior and its consequences. It can be viewed as a written statement for what Skinner (1974) has called rule governed behavior – responses that are under the control of instructions and delayed reinforcement.

Berthold also examines another reinforcement technique in Chapter 5. The Premack Principle, sometimes called Grandma's Rule, represents a program for using activities as reinforcers based on their baseline probabilities. The opportunity to engage in a high probability behavior such as playing baseball or calling on a preferred customer can be used as a reward for low probability behavior such as practicing the violin or visiting an obnoxious client. Due to the fact that such activity reinforcers involve no cost to the organization, they represent a valuable asset to any industrial behavior modification program.

The next chapter in this part follows closely on the theme of contingency contracting introduced in Chapter 5. Chapter 6 examines a real world example of what happens when reinforcement contingencies become disconnected from the response that they are meant to reward. Using archival data, decreases are uncovered in the most significant performance measures for baseball pitchers following the introduction of guaranteed, high salary contracts.

To conclude Part I, Tom and Renee Mawhinney give the reader an in-depth overview of behavior analysis as applied to industry. Chapter 7 should help the reader to understand the derivation of industrial behavior modification techniques. As a step toward implementing these procedures, this chapter will allow the reader to become competent in the use of operant terminology. The theoretically oriented reader will find the Mawhinney's presentation particularly intriguing.

At the conclusion of this unit the reader should have a good grasp of the general methodology of applied behavior analysis and be prepared to study behavioral approaches to a variety of topic areas. Such specific behavioral programs that have been developed in response to typical management concerns are presented throughout the rest of this volume.

Richard M. O'Brien
Hofstra University

REFERENCES

Deurr, E. C. The effect of misdirected incentives on employee behavior. *Personnel Journal*, 1974, **53,** 890-893.

Horvitz, W. L. Labor-management committees: Their impact on productivity. In J. M. Rosow (Ed.), *Productivity prospects for growth*. New York: Van Nostrand Reinhold, 1981.

Kalish, H. I. *From behavioral science to behavior modification*. New York: McGraw Hill, 1981.

Kreitner, R. PM-A new method of behavior change. *Business Horizons*, 1975, **18,** 79-86.

Luthans, F., & Kreitner, R. *Organizational behavior modification*. Glenview, Ill.: Scott, Foresman, 1975.

Mayhew, G. L., Enyart, P., & Cone, J. D. Approaches to employee management: Policies and preferences. *Journal of Organizational Behavior Management*, 1979, **2,** 103-111.

Pritchard, R. D., Hollenback, J., & DeLeo, P. J. The effects of continuous and partial schedules of reinforcement on effort, performance and satisfaction. *Organizational Behavior and Human Performance*, 1980, **25,** 336-353.

Rosenbaum, B. L. Common misconceptions about behavior modeling and supervisory skill training (SST). *Training and Development Journal*, 1979, **33** (8), 40-44.

Skinner, B. F. *About behaviorism*. New York: Knopf, 1974.

Sweetland, J. & Rosow, M. *Managerial productivity*. Scarsdale, N.Y.: Work in America Institute, 1978.

1

Introduction to Industrial Behavior Modification

Richard M. O'Brien and Alyce M. Dickinson
Hofstra University   *New York State Office of Court Administration*

Behavior is a function of its consequences. That is the heart of the behavioral approach. If, as a manager, you have some employee behavior that never seems to get done, the most likely culprit is that there are no rewards for doing it. On the other hand, if you spend all of your time nagging and criticizing a particular employee, you are likely to find that he comes to work less frequently and avoids you when he is present. Work is punishing to that employee and he will escape it whenever possible. Work behaviors that lead to rewards will increase. Those that lead to discomfort will decrease. So it is for every organism including your workers.

If the relationship between the act and the results is the heart of behavior management, it's life blood is data. Accurate observations of employee behavior is the evidence that is required before earned rewards can be appropriately delivered. It provides the feedback that an employee must have in order to know that he is performing satisfactorily.

Industrial behavior modification is based on the work of B.F. Skinner (1938, 1953) and the broad area of psychology called learning theory. Beginning with Thorndike (1911), learning theorists have focused on the law of effect: that behavior that leads to positive consequences is likely to increase while behavior that leads to aversive or punishing consequences is likely to decrease. While this principle has obvious implications for managers in terms of increasing or decreasing worker performance, the law of effect implicitly holds within it an even more basic point that many management theorists have ignored. As Watson (1924) pointed out many years ago, the appropriate field of study for psychologists is behavior: that which can be observed and quantified. It is not job involvement, job satisfaction, self-actualization, attitudes toward authority, or personality traits, all of which must be inferred from behavior or verbal behavior. While behaviorists are not diametrically opposed to these concepts (or Mom's apple pie for that matter), they do insist that concepts such as these can only be understood as they are reflected in behavior. Thus, it is the behavior not the inferred construct that is of importance.

Behavior modification or applied behavior analysis is the application of the techniques of experimental psychology to applied problems. It is an attempt to bring the precise data collection methods of the laboratory behavioral scientist to bear on real world problems. As sciences go, psychology is a fledgling, yet the techniques of monitoring, charting, feedback, and positive reinforcement (in the form of attention and more tangible rewards) have produced some remarkable successes in a wide variety of settings. Behavior has been changed, improved, initiated, and eliminated in a predictable fashion at reasonable cost.

As might have been expected those with the most intractable problems were usually the first to adopt the new methods of behavior change. Early successes came in mental retardation (Thompson & Grabowski, 1972), childhood autism (Lovaas, Bergerich, Perloff & Schaeffer, 1966), adult psychotic behavior (Ayllon & Azrin, 1968; Lindsley, 1956), education (Ulrich, Stachnik & Mabry, 1974), and juvenile delinquency (Phillips, Phillips, Fixen & Wolf, 1971). More recently, psychologists have expanded the application of behavior modification principles to problems of self-control such as smoking (O'Brien & Dickinson, 1977) and obesity (Stunkard, Craighead & O'Brien, 1980), community interventions such as control of littering (Kohlenberg & Phillips, 1973), and sports (Simek & O'Brien, 1981).

While many industrial problems certainly involved increasing or decreasing behavior, the industrial manager was not nearly as devoid of effective techniques as his behavior modifying colleague on the back ward of a state hospital. He had incentive plans, wages, bonuses, disciplinary procedures, and at last resort the threat of termination as behavior change techniques. Even if these did not work perfectly, they worked well enough to be rewarding to the manager. It was not until the late sixties and early seventies that a number of behavioral scientists (Brethower, 1972; Luthans & Kreitner, 1975) began to extrapolate the principles of applied behavior analysis from other areas into the workplace.

It is probably impossible to attribute the birth of industrial behavior modification to any one individual, school, or even area of the country. The first publications on positive reinforcement (Brethower & Rummler, 1966) can be attributed to the programmed learning and behavior change workshops conducted at the University of Michigan under George Ordione. At the same time researchers like Tom Gilbert, Paul Brown, and Robert Presbie in New York, Aubrey Daniels and Milton Blood in Georgia and Donald Tosti on the West Coast were beginning to impact industry with innovative programs in applied behavior analysis. Individuals such as Dan Grady, Karen Brethower, and Don Bullock were also implementing applied behavior analysis programs within their respective companies even though these programs were not identified specifically as such. Programs that employed behavior modification principles began to appear in advertising (Nathan & Wallace, 1965, Winters & Wallace, 1970) training (Sorcher, 1971, Goldstein & Sorcher, 1973) absenteeism control (Lawler & Hackman, 1969, Nord, 1970) sales (Gupton & Lebow, 1971) and quality control (Adam, 1975; Adam & Scott, 1971; Verhave, 1966).

In addition to data based reports from industry and other organizational settings (Hollander & Plutchik, 1972), theoretical discussions and reviews of the use of behavior modification in industry began to appear (Aldis, 1961, Jablonsky & DeVries, 1972, Mawhinney, 1975, Nord, 1969 and Schneier, 1974). The works of Nord and Mawhinney were particularly influential in extending the audience for operant intervention through their translation of management problems and theories into the terminology and perspective of applied behavior analysis. The publication of behavioral books for managers by Mager & Pipe (1970), Brethower (1972), and Luthans & Kreitner (1975) added further resources for the manager who was looking for effective behavioral tools.

With these books and reviews there were also some critics of industrial behavior analysis (Fry, 1974, Whyte, 1972). The most telling of these has been Edwin Locke who has argued forcefully that goal-setting rather than knowledge of results is the crucial variable in the effectiveness of feedback based interventions (Komaki, 1981; Locke, 1980; Locke, Cartledge & Koeppel, 1968). This question remains unresolved, but the limited literature suggests that while goal-setting is an effective technique to improve performance (Latham & Baldes, 1975) it is not sufficient to account for feedback effects (Kim & Hamner, 1976; Luthans, Paul & Baker, 1981).

While it is difficult to identify the first admittedly "operant" approach in industry, it is far easier to say who is most responsible for bringing the positive results of industrial behavior management programs to the attention of the general public. Ed Feeney's success at Emery Air Freight inspired three influential reports (At Emery Air Freight Positive Reinforcement Boosts Performance, 1973, Laird, 1971; Performance Audit, Feedback and Positive Reinforcement, 1972) and a widely distributed film (Business Behaviorism and the Bottom Line). In addition to the developments at Emery, reports of other large scale programs by internal consultants became known. In particular, Douglas Bray at AT&T, Roger Bourdon at J.P. Stevens, Melvin Sorcher at General Electric and a number of operant managers at General Motors established training and productivity programs based on a behavioral model.

True to the laboratory derivation of this approach, a number of academicians have continued to provide advances on the application industrial behavior management. Mawhinney and Scott at Indiana, Latham, Yukl, and Wexley at Akron, Dale Brethower at Cleveland State and later at Western Michigan University, Fred Luthans at University of Nebraska, Lincoln, Robert Kreitner at Western Illinois University, and Judi Komaki at Georgia Tech have been particularly influential in demonstrating the efficacy of applying behavioral techniques to industrial problems.

Industrial behavior management is not really a theoretical approach as much as it is a new methodology for managers. It represents a concrete, practical program for changing employee behavior through changes in management behavior. For the manager to achieve organizational goals he must change his behavior so that it is possible for the employee to gain something in exchange for competent work. He must provide rewards and collect accurate data so that the rewards follow behaviors that he wants to increase. That's really all there is to it!

Psychological approaches to management, however, have eschewed such a common sense approach. The history of psychology's contribution to management theory has been a series of very theoretical, abstract, and impractical ideas. From ethereal discussions about the nature of man to endless lists of "needs" to be fulfilled, the manager has come to expect a psychologist to identify a large number of areas where he is failing his employees but be unable to suggest feasible alternatives to improve the situation. At best the psychological consultant will encourage more "democratic management style" which the manager is told will lead to increased self-actualization, feelings of achievement, and better attitudes toward the job; none of which can be measured in any reliable way.

In the following section we will review some of the theories of motivation that have been most popular in the management literature. The reader who is already familiar with the difficulties inherent in applying these theories may wish to skip this section by going directly to page 13. Others who have not encountered Maslow, Herzberg, Vroom and Porter, and Lawler should read on to familiarize themselves with this material. But be warned! You may find it tough sledding. The same weaknesses that make these theories too academic and abstract to fruitfully apply, also make them impossible to concisely explain.

Maslow

The need hierachy of Abraham Maslow (1943) is perhaps the most widely discussed and researched motivational theory. According to Maslow's theory, individuals are motivated to act by internal forces which Maslow labels as needs. These needs when activated produce tension within the individual who will then act in a manner to reduce this internal tension, or in Maslow's terminology "satisfy the need." Once a need has been satisfied, it ceases to be a motivator and another need becomes activated. This need then acts as a motivator. These needs spiral us through life, each taking precedence as another wanes.

Maslow postulates that these needs exist in a hierarchy, and that we all progress through the same order of needs. The most prepotent needs are the physiological needs, followed successively by safety, social, ego, and self-actualization needs. Each of us may behave in different ways to achieve the same end-satisfaction of our most urgent need. Some of us may be stalled at a lower level need state and, for example, spend our entire lives attempting to satisfy social needs. Indeed, Maslow hypothesizes that very few of us ever reach the highest pinnacle – the self-actualization need state.

Generally, results from empirical investigations of Maslow's theory are discouraging (Wahba & Bridwell, 1972). But even if the research did support it, imagine how difficult it would be to apply the theory to an actual work situation. We have no way to observe need states, measure need states, activate need states, or predict behavior if the need states could be identified. While being able to describe the needs of a worker, we have been given no practical tools to directly influence a worker's behavior – the very thing a manager wants to do. Needs do not explain the cause of behavior but merely provide an easy way to summarize observations of an employee's behavior. Therein lies the danger. As Skinner (1953) argues.

> When we say that a man eats *because* he is hungry, smokes a great deal *because* he has the tobacco habit, fights *because* of the instinct of pugnacity, behaves brilliantly *because* of his intelligence, or plays the piano well *because* of his musical ability, we seem to be referring to causes. But on analysis these phrases prove to be merely redundant descriptions. A single set of facts is described by the two statements: 'He eats' and 'he is hungry' [p. 31].

In other words, needs are inferred from behavior. There is no other evidence for them. So let's stick to the observables instead of complicating the issue by creating the hypothetical construct of a need. Inferring a hypothetical construct is redundant, but as Skinner suggests, it has even more troublesome properties. After a while need states seem to take on a life of their own and instead of being viewed as simply a summary of behavior observations they begin to be seen as the *cause* of the behavior. Need states thus tend to obscure the variables that are immediately available for analysis by the manager – the event which precedes the response, the behavior, and the event which follows the behavior.

If an employee is not productive, you can either suggest that the work environment is not satisfying one of his prepotent needs or you may hypothesize that his behavior does not lead to appropriate rewards. As a follower of Maslow, you would search for an internal, unfulfilled need while as a behavior manager you would simply change the reward structure to make productive behavior more likely to occur.

Herzberg

The difficulties in applying Maslow's theory have not gone unnoticed. Herzberg (1966) attempted to tailor Maslow's approach to the work environment by identifying organizational factors that corresponded to Maslow's needs. For example, Maslow's physiological, safety, and social needs took on the Herzbergian look of pay, job security, company policy, and supervision. Maslow's ego and self-actualization needs were transformed into the organizational factors of achievement, recognition, and responsibility. If Herzberg had stopped at this point, we could have lauded him for identifying some of the organizational and environmental events that can and do influence worker behavior (under appropriate conditions, of course). Unfortunately, as theorists are prone to do, he went a few steps too far. He divided the organizational factors into two distinctly different groups. The one group of factors (pay, job security, company policy, and supervision) were labeled, hygiene factors, while the other group of factors (recognition, achievement, advancement) were labeled motivators. Herzberg proposed that when the hygiene factors existed in an organizational setting above some acceptable level, employee dissatisfaction was prevented. These factors, however, were totally unrelated to either satisfaction or motivation. On the other hand the motivators, when present in the organization, lead to increased job satisfaction and motivation.

Motivators, Herzberg maintained, were totally unrelated to dissatisfaction. Essentially, satisfaction/motivation and dissatisfaction are viewed as discrete concepts with one set of organizational factors influencing satisfaction/motivation and an entirely different set influencing dissatisfaction.

Herzberg's theory has not stood the test of empirical validation (House & Wigdor, 1967; Hulin & Smith, 1967; Lindsey, Marks, & Gorlow, 1967; Schneider & Locke, 1971). Two major criticisms are aimed at Herzberg. The first is that there is little support for the dichotomy of organizational factors. Secondly, his theory is method-bound. That is, his two factor theory is only borne out when researchers use the exact experimental procedure that Herzberg used.

From a more practical viewpoint, imagine as a manager attempting to determine when the organizational factors "existed above some acceptable lever." Herzberg further maintained that all workers responded in the same manner to the organizational factors. Our common sense eschews the notion that all our friends and acquaintances would respond in the same fashion to these factors.

Herzberg did identify several factors that can be used as rewards for behavior change. What he failed to recognize is that employees will work to gain that which is in short supply and that this may vary from employee to employee, and that the timing and frequency of the presentation of the organizational factors is critical if one is to change behavior in a desired manner. Still, Herzberg's theory hangs on in the management literature. Perhaps it has survived as an academic exercise to test an individual's "ability to conceptualize and deal with abstract ideas." Theories, like snowballs, tend to gain momentum and density over time eventually ending up as abominable snowmen.

Expectancy Theories of Motivation

Expectancy theorists, rather than attempting to classify and label factors which influence worker behavior focused exclusively on examining the process of motivation. Vroom (1964) and Porter and Lawler (1968) tried to specify how organizational factors interact with individual variables to influence a worker to behave in a certain manner.

Based on Lewin's (1947) hypotheses about motivation, expectation and behavior, Vroom suggests that motivation is a function of the person's perception of the desirability of the outcomes of a given behavior (valence) and the perceived probability that these outcomes will be forthcoming (expectancy). According to Vroom, individuals add up the pros and cons of various outcomes as weighted by the probability that each will occur and then act in the manner which will provide the greatest payoff. Vroom presents his theory in a mathematical model:

The force on a person to perform an act is a monotonically increasing function of the algebraic sum of the products of the valences of all outcomes and the strength of his expectancies that the act will be followed by the attainment of these outcomes [p. 18].

Mathematically, $F_i = \sum_{j=1}^{n} (E_{ij} V_j)$ $(i = n = 1, \ldots, m)$

F_i = the force to perform act i
E_{ij} = the strength of the expectancy that act i will be followed by outcome j
V_j = the valence of outcome j
n = the number of outcomes.

The mathematical model is appealing because of its apparent precision. All of us have been taught to associate mathematical models with scientific credibility from our chemistry and algebra classes. However, the foreman trying to predict the behavior of his workers would be required to sit for hours with his calculator or else be an expert in computer technology if he was going to use Vroom's approach. The apparent precision of the formula is also misleading. The variables of an algebraic equation or a chemical formula are quantifiable. The variables in Vroom's formula cannot be observed, measured, or quantified. Vroom has taken a precision tool – math – and applied it to the imprecise. The only way of determining hypothetical valence and expectancy for an individual is to analyze the individual's past behavior. Since these constructs must be based on observations about behavior, there is no need to flail around in the abstract. A manager can observe a worker's behavior and analyze the events that precede the response and follow it. When those same conditions exist in the work setting it is probable that the worker will behave in the same manner. More concisely, the best predictor of future behavior is past behavior.

Porter and Lawler (1968) spurned the mathematical model but added more elements to Vroom's theory. They suggest that an individual's performance is influenced not "only" by the perceived valences of outcomes and the perceived probabilities that the outcomes will follow a behavior, but also by an individual's abilities, traits, and role perceptions. They distinguish between an individual's effort to perform an act and the successful performance of the act itself, emphasizing that effort does not necessarily result in successful performance. Further, performance is influenced by how the individual defines the job or his role perception. If the individual perceives his job differently than his supervisor, the employee may expend a great deal of effort that is misdirected and thus perform poorly from the supervisor's viewpoint. In essence, Porter and Lawler maintain that if an individual is to perform a job effectively, he must have an accurate concept of what his job is, and the abilities and traits that are required to perform the job. He must also perceive a high probability that his efforts will lead to specific, predictable outcomes and believe that the positive outcomes will outweigh the negative outcomes.

Porter and Lawler's performance model exists in a parallel cognitive universe to industrial behavior modificaton. The model is a future-oriented theory based on internal thought processes. In contrast, industrial behavior modification relies on observable environmental events and the reinforcement history of the individual. There is no need for the creation of this cognitive universe. Porter and Lawler's concepts can be readily transformed and redefined in behavioral terms.

Their theory maintains that an individual's behavior is influenced by subjective feelings (valences) about the outcomes that will follow a behavior. Since an individual's feelings about an outcome cannot be directly observed, these feelings must be inferred through past behavior. The behaviorist rather than dealing with unobservable and unmeasurable feelings, simply determines how a specific outcome or consequence affects the frequency of the behavior. If a particular consequence increases the frequency of a certain behavior, the consequence is a reinforcer. If an outcome presented contingently upon a response, decreases the frequency of the response, the outcome is a punisher.

A second major component of Porter and Lawler's theory is an individual's perceived probability that certain outcomes will follow certain behaviors. The perceived probability can only be developed through prior association of the response and the outcome or outcomes. Therefore, it is easier to measure this association directly than to refer to the concept of perceived probability. Behaviorists analyze the relationship between the antecedent stimuli that precede the behavior, the behavior, and the consequences that follow the behavior. If the behavior consistently occurs in the presence of the same antecedent stimuli and/or is followed by the same consequence, it is reasonable to predict that, given these circumstances in the future, the behavior will most likely occur.

Porter and Lawler maintain that an individual must perceive a high probability that his efforts will result in a behavior that leads to positive outcomes. Whether or not this effort results in appropriate behavior depends on an individual's abilities, traits, and role perceptions. Applied behavior analysts deal with the concept of effort in a different manner. Effort is not measurable but the resulting response is. If the response is not the desired response, the behavior analyst reinforces successive approximations to the desired response. You start where the individual is and continually shape the desired response. It is recognized that individuals must have the physical and intellectual ability to perform the response if shaping is to be effective.

A person's role perception is based on the feedback he has received for prior responses and the responses that have been reinforced will be "perceived" as appropriate responses. While a manager cannot directly alter a person's "role perception," he can alter the consequences that follow the response.

Porter and Lawler's performance model refutes the traditional notion that satisfaction causes good performance. Instead, they suggest that if good performance results in the attainment of equitable and desired rewards, the attainment of the desired rewards causes satisfaction. The key variable for both good performance and satisfaction is the receipt of desired rewards. The assumption that satisfaction causes good performance is one that has long plagued industrial psychology. Satisfaction is a feeling or attitude that results from the receipt of a desired reward; it does not influence performance. In a similar vein, behavior managers view satisfaction as an accompanying feeling which results from reinforcement of behavior. It does not help us explain behavior.

THE BEHAVIORAL MODEL

While industrial psychology was off studying the psyche, most of the rest of psychology has been engaged in a scientific quest for ways to quantify and change behavior directly. Through the years this approach progressed to analyzing behavior in terms of the situation in which it occurred and the environmental impact that it had on the organism once the behavior had been performed. In the work of Skinner and his colleagues, the methodology for examining the interrelationships between behavior and the environment became known as a functional analysis.

According to the Skinnerian view, any behavior consists of a three term contingency relationship: the antecedent stimuli, the behavior or response itself, and the consequences that follow that behavior. For example, as you are sitting at your desk, the telephone rings (antecedent stimulus), you pick up the receiver and say hello (response), and the information or conversation of the caller is the consequence of this response. In the phone example, the act of picking up the receiver is the response (R). The consequence is the response of the caller, a rewarding stimulus or positive reinforcer (S^{R+}). This contingent relationship is symbolized $R->S^{R+}$. But favorable consequences (positive consequences) are not the only possibilities that can occur when we make a response. There are five other possibilities.

Suppose for example that when you pick up the phone, there is no one there. This represents nonreinforcement for the behavior. Should such nonreinforcement continue the response will eventually cease. This is called extinction and is symbolized:

R	-------X------->	S^{R+}
picking up the phone	does not lead to	positive reinforcement

The third possible consequence for any response is encountering an aversive or punishing consequence. This is punishment. Suppose that you picked up the phone and due to some unfortunate crosswiring received an electric shock. It is likely that your phone answering behavior would decrease. This contingency is symbolized:

R	------------>	S^-
picking up the phone	leads to	shock

Assuming that the crosswiring was not soon corrected each time you picked up the phone, you would quickly withdraw your hand in order to end the shock. This is called escape behavior and is symbolized:

R	-->	$\cancel{S^-}$
withdrawing hand from phone	leads to	end of shock

(Note that the elimination of a painful stimulus increases the frequency of the behavior and thus is reinforcing.) This is one form of negative reinforcement.

As the situation of the shocking phone continued, you might be tempted to put on a rubber glove when handling the phone. The response of putting on the glove serves to prevent the occurrence of the punishing stimulus. This is called avoidance behavior because it allows the individual to eliminate the aversive stimulus before it actually appears. Avoidance behavior is symbolized:

R	-------X------->	S^-
putting on the glove	does not lead to	shock

This is also called negative reinforcement because the response frequency increases as a result of the response's ability to postpone the aversive stimulus. The difference between escape behavior and avoidance behavior can be most easily exemplified by reference to a common aversive stimulus, the alarm clock. If you find the ring of your alarm clock aversive when it goes off and you quickly shut it off, you are engaging in escape behavior. On the other hand, if you wake up before the alarm clock goes off and fix it so that it doesn't ring, you have made an avoidance response. Both avoidance behavior and escape behavior are negative reinforcement since they increase the probability that the response will occur in the future.

Finally, engaging in a behavior may result in a loss of positive reinforcement. This is symbolized   R ----> $\mathcal{S}^{R+}$ and is called by two different names depending on the nature of the lost reinforcement. Suppose that you are working on a report that you are eager to complete. Yet each time you begin to work on the report, the phone rings making you take time out from your task. In this situation answering the phone is keeping you from obtaining the reinforcement that you get from finishing the report. Appropriately enough this contingency is called time-out from positive reinforcement. The reader should note that suspending a person from a job he hates is not time-out from positive reinforcement. Time-out is only effective if it represents a loss of the opportunity to gain reinforcement. A response that leads to time-out decreases in probability as a result of the lost possibility for accruing reinforcement.

While time-out limits the possibility of being rewarded it is also possible to make responses that lead directly to the loss of previously accrued reinforcement. This is called response cost. Let us suppose that your employer allows no more than five dollars a month for personal long distance phone calls. If at the end of each month an employee exceeds this amount he must pay the additional charge. In this situation each call over the $5.00 limit results in a loss of a reinforcer (money). Response cost in the form of fines and deductions is the most frequently used disciplinary procedure in the business environment. Although most industrial behavior modification projects have employed positive reinforcement, Marholin and Gray (1976) reported a very effective group response cost intervention to decrease cash shortages.

The contingencies between behavior and consequences do not occur in a vacuum. Rather antecedent stimuli set the occassion for a response through previous association with a given response-consequence relationship. Our office worker does not answer the phone unless it rings. Picking up the phone and listening for the conversation in the absence of ringing is rarely rewarded. The ringing of the phone is an S^D or discriminative stimulus because it tells the employee that the response of picking up the phone will now be rewarded by conversation. Let us suppose that you have an intercom line with one or two other people in the office. Two buzzes is the signal for you to answer the intercom while three buzzes is the signal for one of your associates to pick up the phone. The two buzzes represent an S^D (discriminative stimulus). If you continually picked up the phone on three buzzes you're unlikely to speak to anyone who wishes to talk to you. In this instance the three buzzes would be as an S^Δ (ess - delta), signalling that the response of picking up the phone would not be rewarded. Eventually the behavior of the office worker will come to correspond almost perfectly to the nature of the discriminative stimuli. He will answer the phone on two buzzes and ignore it on three buzzes. When this occurs it is said that his response has been brought under stimulus control. Many times the problems that beset the manager are a function not only of inadequate and noncontingent rewards but also of discriminative stimuli that signal off task behavior. The day before a holiday serves as a relatively harmless S-delta in that it signals that work is unlikely to be rewarded by one's associates. The office worker who is constantly talking about fishing, the hunks or babes of the office, or Monday night football, is a more costly S-delta in terms of lost work hours. In summary, if you want to improve employee performance provide conditions that encourage on task behavior (appropriate discriminative stimuli) and rewards that are contingent upon productivity (S^{R+}).

If you are a traditionally trained manager you are very likely at this point to be on the verge of a great outcry. "But what about job satisfaction, motivation, and leadership style? And then there's job involvement, job enrichment and self-actualization, not to mention personality traits, attitudes and the need hierarchy of the employee. Why, you don't even know if you're dealing with the employee's child, parent, or adult ego state!" Well, what about them? They are all very interesting and impressive and probably unrelated to employee productivity except as they provide rewards for on task behavior.

Many of the traditional "solutions" to worker productivity, such as job enrichment, democratic leadership styles, and satisfaction, evolved from Douglas McGregor's proposed management styles (1960). Using Maslow's need theory as a starting point, McGregor summarized management styles into two categories which he labeled Theory X and Theory Y. Theory X was based on observations of current day management practices. These management practices evolved from the scientific management school of psychology which maintained that employees work solely for money. Man was presumed to be machine-like, unconcerned with rewards such as recognition and praise. When employee productivity did not meet management expectations, management responded with strict controls over behavior, controls that were primarily negative. Management viewed employees as either passive or resistant to organizational needs, inherently lazy, lacking ambition, disliking responsibility, and self-centered. With these beliefs about the nature of man, it is small wonder that adversarial relationships grew between management and labor. Employees were subjected to punishing controls and responded with output restriction, antagonism, and sabotage.

McGregor, assuming that Maslow's theory was accurate, maintained that employees were not inherently passive or indifferent to organizational goals but grew to be so through past experiences within organizations. Theory Y states that man will work hard to satisfy the needs outlined by Maslow if given the opportunity to do so. It is thus management's responsibility to structure the organizational environment so that employees can satisfy their needs while achieving organization goals. A manager should remove organizational barriers, create opportunities for responsibility, encourage self-development, and provide guidance. McGregor believed that if organizations were to survive in the future, they would have to decentralize and delegate responsibility, enlarge jobs, and promote participative management.

McGregor recognized that employee behavior was influenced by the organizational environment. Management controls, he stated, were responsible for inappropriate employee behavior. Unfortunately, McGregor did not distinguish between the "carrot" and the "stick." *Punishing* management controls were responsible for inappropriate employee behavior, not management controls per se. His failure to analyze the difference between positive and negative controls led him to rely on Maslow's need theory to construct Theory Y. Theory Y is flawed as Maslow's need theory is flawed.

As Nord (1969) has observed, McGregor's contribution was that he recognized that the worker was not management's natural enemy. Unfortunately, he and his followers failed to recognize the contingent relationship between rewards and productivity.

McGregor's theories have had a considerable impact on management style. They have led employers to venture far afield in their efforts to promote job satisfaction and indirectly job performance through more "democratic" leadership. Let us compare how a behavioral and a sophisticated "democratic" manager might solve a typical performance problem.

Suppose that we have two fast food restaurants whose managers are both concerned that their employees are not behaving pleasantly enough in their interactions with customers. Sophisticated manager Y's first reaction to this problem might be to try to determine why his employees aren't happier by measuring job satisfaction through the use of some standardized attitude survey instrument. The sophisticated manager might also begin by attempting to measure his employees' attitudes toward the customer and designing a program to reeducate his staff. This program might include lectures on the importance of affability in relating to the customers with appropriate films and perhaps a slide presentation showing how good the customer feels after a pleasant interaction with the employee. In particular, lectures would stress the profit and loss import of proper customer relations. The aim of such a program is to educate. It is felt that once the employee understands the importance of interacting positively with the customer he will change his behavior and will become more pleasant and cheerful.

Should this educational program prove insufficient, Manager Y might then suspect that it was some employee dissatisfaction that was producing his sour workers rather than simply ignorance of the importance of a positive attitude. Once having identified areas of job dissatisfaction, the manager may then take steps to correct these problems based on the assumption that satisfied workers will be more pleasant in customer interactions. As a corollary step the sophisticated manager would be likely to identify and recruit happier people as prospective employees and hire only those who score above the mean on some personality test measure of a happiness or pleasantness trait.

From his measure of job satisfaction Manager Y would be in a position to analyze the employee's motives in terms of Maslow's need hierarchy. As noted earlier, Maslow (1943) theorizes five sets of needs in hierarchial order with the physiological needs being prepotent. In this hierarchy each lower group of needs must be satisfied before the next higher one becomes a motivating force. The manager might then reason that if he told his employees that no matter what, no one was going to get fired, he would get better hamburgers and more positive customer relations. Manager Y might believe, for example, that fear of being laid off (security need) was blocking the motivational effect of social needs which would result in more positive customer-employee relations.

In spite of Manager Y's analysis of his employee's need hierarchy and job satisfaction surveys he might still feel that lack of employee involvement was a factor in the workers' poor attitude toward the customer. One traditional way to attack this problem is to give the employee a greater role in decision making. In this case such participatory management might involve seeking out the employee's analysis of the problem, and requesting employee input as to possible solutions. In this particular instance the clerks might report that an eight-hour shift of serving hamburgers and french fries was less than intellectually stimulating – that such boring work naturally led to sour expressions. The manager and the employees could then jointly design a program of job enrichment to enliven work on the fast food front. For example, the clerks might not only take orders and payment but also become involved in the whole hamburger process. Thus, they would take the order, select the patty, toast the bun, grill the burger, mix the sauce, assemble the burger, hold the pickles, and even deliver the finished product. There would be a feeling of accomplishment for the employee who made the complete burger, and although the customer may have to wait longer for his "fast food," it would be presented with pride. One might even want to establish work groups who all made the completed burgers together in order to enrich the job through interpersonal interactions or provide educational breaks where the employees could learn the fast food business, perhaps for college credit. If having each employee make the whole burger proved impractical, rotation from burgers to fries to shakes might be instituted, and shifts might be alternated. All of these steps might lead to happier employees or they might not. Happier employees might then be more affable with the customers or they might not. In any case, even if Manager Y does get an increase in friendliness he will have no idea what produced such a result.

Manager S^{R+}, unjaundiced by years of leadership training, is likely to take a more common sense approach. Instead of changing the attitudes or personality traits of his employees he would address the problem more directly. An example of such an intervention was recently provided by Komaki, Blood and Holder (1980). In conjunction with management they began by operationally defining "friendliness" as smiling and talking with customers. Once they had pinpointed what to measure they allowed a thirteen-week base rate period to collect data on the frequency of these behaviors prior to intervention. Observations were taken five to seven times a week at the cash register and in the dining area. Intervention followed the three term contingency model: (a) employees were provided with four S^D's (e.g., giving change) to serve as antecedents for the response; (b) the behavior was operationally defined and rehearsed; (c) three consequences which seemed likely to be rewarding to the employee were made contingent on the response. These consequences involved natural or interpersonal rewards (of no cost to management) such as employee self-monitoring, returned smiles from customers, and interpersonal reinforcement (praise) from the manager.

This intervention produced a 26% increase in friendliness behaviors at the cash register but was ineffective in the dining area. The authors attempted to correct this deficiency by increasing the value of the reward. A 5-minute coffee break was now made contingent upon talking with at least five customers in the dining area. Although this doubled the frequency of the target behavior, it proved unworkable due to "implementation problems." Our Manager S^{R+} might have resolved the scheduling problems associated with numerous breaks by instituting a lottery in which the opportunity for a chance at an extended coffee break was substituted for the 5-minute break. For every five times that an employee talked with a customer he could drop his name into a hat. Each morning and each afternoon the manager would draw the name of one employee who would receive the extended break.

If these implementations were successful, Manager S^{R+}'s employees would be as affable and cheerful as Manager Y's, if not more so, at a fraction of the cost. And they will remain affable and cheerful as long as the reinforcers continue to follow such behaviors unless the employees tire of that particular reinforcer.

But what about Manager Y's program? Do such things as job enrichment, education, and increased job satisfaction have any effect on performance? Of course they do, at least in some cases. Training programs, for example, can be very useful if the employee is unaware of the appropriate response that the manager wishes to reward. Providing rewards for a response will increase the probability of that response. Telling people how important a response is will only increase the response if you also provide rewards for that response. By providing knowledge of the response-reinforcement contingency educational programs will increase the frequency of the rewarded behavior. But if rewards are not provided such educational programs are likely to lead to only very brief improvements in behavior.

METHODS OF BEHAVIOR MANAGEMENT

At this point the reader has probably recognized that the principles of behavior management are what has always been done to effectively change employee behavior. The problem is that it is usually done so haphazardly that the desired behavior change rarely occurs. There are rules that must be followed if one is going to productively embark on a program to modify work habits.

Applied behavior analysis, behavioral systems approaches, and contingency management are highly complex terms dependent on one simple premise: that behavior is a function of its consequences. Managers have developed various step-wise systems for implementing this approach. Feeney (Murphy, 1972) for example, uses a six-step approach toward increasing the likelihood that positive consequences will follow appropriate on task behaviors. Rotondi (1976) also talks about six steps, while Murphy (1972) breaks the process down even further. The simplest outline of steps to successful behavior modification was originally proposed by Lindsley (1966). Although it has been revised many times (Luthans & Kreitner, 1975; Malott & Hartlep, 1972; Miller, 1978) it remains the most concise intervention cookbook yet developed. Unfortunately, Lindsley's program was not specifically designed for industry. In presenting our outline for implementing a behavior management program we have retained the theme of Lindsley's program with variations based on our experience and those of other behavioral consultants (Feeney, 1978; Hammond, 1975; Murphy, 1972; Rotondi, 1976).

How Does One Implement a Behavioral Contingency System?

Obviously the first thing to do is find out if there is a performance problem. As simple as this sounds, it may be the most difficult step in the entire process. Being able to identify the problem assumes an ongoing feedback system that includes both qualitative and quantitative data on specific work behaviors (one must know what the employee is to do and how well and how often he is doing it).

From the executive board room to the company mail handler, most employees think that they are doing the job as well as they can, and their supervisors are likely to believe them. The first revelation of a good behavioral measurement system in industrial settings is often the discovery that the data do not support these optimistic appraisals. Whether you call it a performance audit as Feeney (Performance Audit, 1972) and Gilbert (1978) do or simply collecting a baserate, one must begin by observing behavior, not just asking about it.

Now let us take a detailed look at how to implement Lindsley's four step procedure.

GUIDELINES FOR IMPLEMENTING A BEHAVIOR MANAGEMENT PROGRAM

Step 1 – Observe

Try to identify the crucial productivity behaviors that occur at your place of business. Don't rush this process or assume that you already know! Give some time to just observing what actually goes on. Avoid just looking for problems. You should also be attending to behaviors that are being done well but are going unrewarded or under rewarded. As Feeney (1978) suggests, look for the payoff. Find out what behaviors are most directly connected to the bottom line: profits and losses.

Step 2 – Pinpoint

Your goal at this step is to identify those behaviors that may require change. The keystone of this process is to uncover performance standards for these behaviors if they exist.

Step 3 – Record

Take a baseline or baserate to establish the preintervention level of the behavior that you have pinpointed. Record not only the activity itself but the stimulus conditions under which it occurs, as well as the consequences that follow it for the employee. Remember that behavior is a function of its consequences and those consequences are usually signalled by some sort of discriminative stimulus or cue. You can alter the frequency of that behavior either by changing the consequences or by eliminating the cues that call forth that response.

Your system of recording should be nonreactive. That means that the mere collection of the data should not affect the frequency of the behavior. If this is impossible in a given situation, remember that it is better to have reactive measures than no measures at all. In fact the reaction is likely to be in the desired direction, i.e., the behavior will improve just by being recorded. Reactive recording provides feedback to the employee that he can use to improve performance.

If the behavior that you have chosen is immeasurable, go back to Step 2. There is no more sacred rule in the behavioral approach than the truism that "if you can't measure it you can't work with it" (Laird, 1971). Fortunately, the creative manager will find that most significant profit and loss activity can be quantitively recorded if he can overcome his tendency to ask people's opinions rather than collect real data. This point cannot be made too strongly! If your evaluation program is committed to supervisor's ratings over direct measures of employee output, you will be left to reap what you have sown in misdirected rewards and unreliable feedback. If you want your workers to respond so that the supervisor likes them, you should use some system of supervisory ratings. If on the other hand you are interested in increasing the employee's productive work behaviors, you better directly measure those behaviors. The weaknesses of traditional performance appraisal have been well documented (McMillan & Dorel, 1980; Yager, 1981).

Once you have a baseline on the behavior that you have pinpointed, it is necessary to put those figures into some organizational perspective. The first thing that you need to know is if the performance matches company standards for that activity. In order to answer that question you must find out if the company has any standards for that response. If the company has quantified standards, and this is the exception rather than the rule, it is worthwhile to inquire into whether or not the employee is aware of what the standards are supposed to be. If he knows the standards, does he have any way of knowing how well he is doing in comparison to them? Can he find out if his performance is up to par as he goes along, instead of 6 months later? The employee himself must know how well he is doing in order to change or even maintain performance (Kirby, 1980). Feedback or knowledge of results has been shown to be an absolute necessity for learning (Ammons, 1956). Simek and O'Brien (1978) have recently demonstrated that as little as 2 minutes of feedback for head steadiness was enough to enable golfers to significantly improve their putting. For an employee to adequately perform the tasks assigned to him he must: (1) know what the appropriate response is; (2) have the skills to do it; (3) find it rewarding to engage in the behavior; and (4) most importantly, be able to recognize when he has performed adequately. Without feedback the fourth step is impossible. Seybolt and Pavett (1979) have shown that type of feedback is a significant moderating variable for expectancy theories of motivation.

Researchers in a variety of fields have shown that feedback alone is enough to change behavior, but feedback is most effective when it is most explicit and least threatening. These criteria are most easily fulfilled when employees themselves are encouraged (rewarded) for collecting data on specific response components of their work behavior. This can only be done if the employee feels secure in the knowledge that the data he collects will not be used against him. Suppose that we want to know how many new customer sales calls a sales representative makes. One must praise the sales representative for recording the number of calls but not criticize the number of calls or increase the quota of calls based on the data without providing rewards for increased behavior. Even if the sales representative does not do the recording, punishment should be avoided and rewards dispensed for activities that may lead to recording. The manager must identify the specific behavior to be rewarded but also recognize that the behavior is part of a chain of responses. For example, recording behavior consists of developing a record keeping sheet, taking the sheet along on calls, etc.

The positive effects of self-monitoring on performance have been demonstrated in a variety of settings (Burg, Reid, & Lattimore, 1979; Lamal & Benfield, 1978; O'Brien & Sperduto, 1981), although in most instances self-monitoring has been only a part of the intervention (Andrasik, Heimberg & McNamara, in press). Attitudinal studies (Greller, 1980) suggest that direct feedback from the task as is provided by self-recording is highly valued by workers, and peer comments are also highly rated sources of feedback.

Individual feedback can effectively produce worksite behavior change (Brown, 1980; Dick, 1978; Nadler, 1979), but the more common industrial use of feedback has been in terms of group performance (Komaki, Heinzmann, & Lawson, 1980; Rhoton, 1980; Runnion, Johnson, & McWhorter, 1978). In fact, productivity improvements have even been demonstrated through feedback to a supervisor on the behavior of a group of employees (Chandler, 1977).

A final and crucial variable in feedback effects is the choice between positive and negative approaches to providing the employee with data on his performance. As noted earlier feedback is most effective when it is least threatening and is perceived as least threatening when it is positive and supportive (Nemeroff & Wexley, 1979). The notion that a supervisor can effectively slip in a little negative feedback as long as he ends up on a positive note has not been supported in recent experimentation (Tosti & Jackson, 1981).

There is one final piece of information that you must gather before you can proceed to Step 4, changing the consequences. You must systematically analyze the rewards and sanctions that are maintaining the current behavior or keeping the desired behavior from occurring. In simple terms, what happens when the employee takes the correct action? If your answer is nothing or, worse yet, something aversive, you are going to have to change the effects of that behavior if you want it to increase or even continue at the same level. Similarly, if the consequences for an undesirable behavior are positive, you are going to have a tough time getting rid of it until you eliminate the rewards that follow it (Piamonte, 1980).

A simple example that occurred in the consulting work of the first author may help to illustrate the self-defeating reward structures often present in industry. A well-known New York area bank responded to teller shortages by having all of the tellers work together after hours to find the difference. All of the tellers got paid overtime while they worked to find the shortage. Observations suggested that this activity involved considerable interpersonal reinforcement as well, since difference finding became a social occasion for the employees. In effect, the company was providing more pay and the opportunity for social interaction contingent on somebody coming up short. To make matters worse the bank encouraged the tellers who came up short most frequently to close their windows early so that they could check for differences before the end of the day. Thus if you regularly failed to balance you got to go home early most of the time. It should come as no surprise that teller shortages were a major problem for this financial institution.

The questions that a good recording system has to answer have been nicely outlined by Murphy (1972) from the work of Feeney and his associates at Emery Air Freight. Table 1.1 presents Feeney's step by step approach to seeking data on performance contingencies.

Step 4 – Change the Consequences

The first consequence that you should change is to correct the feedback deficiencies discovered in Step 3. Remember, knowledge of results is a reward if the employee is allowed to collect his own data and/or he has no fear of reprisals for substandard performance. In many instances (Emmert, 1978; Ford, 1980; Lamal & Benfield, 1978; McCarthy, 1978; Nadler, 1979; Prue, Krapfl, Noah, Cannon, & Maley, 1980), correction of the feedback

TABLE 1.1. Questions for Analyzing Current Performance Contingencies.

1. What is the standard of performance?
2. Does the employee know the standard?
3. How well does the employee think he is doing?
4. How well does his supervisor think he is doing?
5. What aversive consequences of the desired behavior may be suppressing it?
6. What is reinforcing the undesired behavior?
7. What natural or contrived reinforcers are at hand in the immediate work environment to begin reinforcing the desired behavior?
8. What aversive consequences of the undesired behavior are at hand?
9. What learner responses are already available in embarking on a program of progressive approximation to the desired behavior?
10. What schedule of reinforcement is most efficient for developing and maintaining the desired behavior?
11. What reinforcers are available to reward the worker's supervisor for reinforcing the worker's new behavior?

Source: Reprinted from John R. Murphy, Is it Skinner or nothing? by special permission from the February, 1972 *Training and Development Journal*. Copyright 1972 by the American Society for Training and Development, Inc.

program has significantly improved performance so that more complicated procedures were unnecessary. Unfortunately, inadequate feedback is not the only reason for poor performance. When your baserate suggests that a lack of rewards rather than a lack of feedback is creating the problem, it may be time to implement a positive reinforcement program.

In order to justify such a program, there are other questions that you should answer from your baserate data. To begin this procedure you must find out if the employee ever makes the correct response. In the rare case where he does not, you may be dealing with activity that the employee has simply never learned how to do. In this case no amount of increased reward is going to improve performance. This situation requires training not a change in contingencies. If the employee either cannot make the correct response or has never learned it, you will have to teach new behaviors rather than simply increasing the frequency of already existing ones. While the most appropriate methods for training and shaping new behaviors are similar to the behavior management techniques used to increase performance, instructions and modeling offer effective antecedent based interventions for initiating new response. Giving goals, providing instructions, and modeling a behavior are all examples of providing discriminative stimuli (S^D's). They identify responses to be rewarded. They also act as reinforcers in that individuals will make responses so that they can ascertain the goal, hear the instructions, or see the model. A number of studies have shown that modeling is a potent training technique (Kraut, 1976; Moses & Ritchie, 1976) but as with goal setting (Erez, 1977) and many reports of instructional training (Brown, Malott, Dillon, & Keeps, 1980; Geller, Eason, Phillips & Pierson, 1980; O'Brien & Sperduto, 1981), feedback is crucial to the effects (Tosti, 1980). Specific training concerns are addressed in a later chapter by Duncan and Lloyd (Chapter 20).

IMPLEMENTING A POSITIVE REINFORCEMENT PROGRAM

If your data reveal that the worker makes the correct response at least once in a while, you need to design a program that will increase the percentage of correct responses. As in anything else there are some basic, general rules that you must master before you implement such a program.

Rule 1 – Reward Selection

The only way to increase behavior without alienating the employee is to make it more rewarding to perform effectively. Before you can change the contingencies in favor of the desired behavior, you must identify what the employee finds reinforcing. You can only discover this by observing what the employee prefers to do and how he reacts to various rewards. The greatest danger at this point is in the head of the manager and the language of the employee. If you think that you can assume that money, praise, attention, recognition, time-off, or any other common reward is necessarily a reinforcer for an individual employee, you are probably overgeneralizing your way into failure as a behavior manager. Remember that by definition a reinforcer increases the probability of the preceding behavior. If the frequency of the behavior doesn't increase, your reward wasn't a reinforcer. The kind of manager who is likely to be reading this book is also the kind of manager who would have trouble accepting next week off as an extra paid vacation because he would believe that the lost time would interfere with his performance. For such a manager both money and time-off fail to function as reinforcers. Put another way, for the worker who is afraid of being viewed as a "brown-noser," praise and recognition are unlikely to increase performance.

The language of the employee leads a behavior management project astray when the supervisor decides that he can ask the employee what would be reinforcing rather than directly observing the effects of various rewards. Verbal behavior is never a substitute for ac-tual observation. At best the questionnaire approach can waste time and create paper work. At worst, it can lead the manager to punish the very behaviors that he wishes to reinforce by using the wrong opportunities as rewards for the right behavior. Asked in the abstract, our hard-working manager might say that he would love an extra paid week off but this conse-quence might not be reinforcing when it came down to taking the time. In the search for rewards, attitude surveys may point a manager in the appropriate direction, but only direct observation of behavior will identify specific effective reinforcers.

The baserate will tell you which consequences have led to an increase in productivity for that specific employee in the past. Nonetheless, if each manager had to start from scratch to identify unique rewards for every employee it would be a monumental task. Fortunately, a number of consequences have been identified that are likely to serve as reinforcers for most workers. Approval, social recognition, money, feedback on their performance, in-dependence, participation, time-off, and increased responsibility offer a good place to start looking for possible rewards. You must remember though, that for any individual employee none of these rewards may be reinforcing. The variety of rewards at a manager's disposal is quite extensive.

Finding out what the employee finds reinforcing is not the only trick to reward iden-tification. There are two other rules that are helpful in reward selection.

Rule 2 – New Rewards Should be Identified

Introducing new rewards works better than trying to get more work for the old ones. When you put in a new program that utilizes reinforcers that had previously been freely available, you are inviting disaster. If you have always given everybody who worked for you a Christmas bonus but now decide to make them earn it based on some productivity figures, you are actually removing the rewards that were in effect for just showing up. You have put the response of attending work on extinction because it is now necessary to make additional responses in order to gain that same reward. Extinction is known to produce emotional behavior. Your workers will get upset if something that they could take for granted is now restricted so that it must be earned. If you watch the union reaction to give-backs at contract time, you know how emotional these reactions can be. It really is not necessary to risk this emotional reaction in most cases of reward selection because there are plenty of potential rewards that go unused. In most organizations praise is so rarely offered that there is no reason to believe that employees will feel bad about being given the opportunity to earn it.

The second limitation in choosing reinforcers reflects the need to establish a lasting program.

Rule 3 – Look for Naturally Occurring Rewards

Rewards that occur naturally are more effective in the long run than artificial rewards (Collins, 1981). Industry has an abundance of natural rewards to choose from. Everything from praise to profit-sharing can be made available naturally. Several systems have been developed in which a fraction of the savings over anticipated expenditures is distributed to the workers for improved performance. This kind of system is preferable to one time, tangible reinforcers offered as short-term productivity incentives. If you want brief effects or a boost to get the program going, short-term artificial rewards can be quite useful. The sales competition for the proverbial cruise to Bermuda gives the employees something to work for until the more natural reinforcers take over. Most companies would be hard pressed to give out a trip to the islands for every competent performance every week. If your interest is in enduring, high-level performance, you must have a program of on-going, naturally available rewards.

Rule 4 – Give Out Enough of the Reward so that it is Worthwhile for the Employee to Respond

For a reward to really be a reinforcer there must be enough of it to justify the employee's activity. Most of us would find $10 rewarding, but if we had to walk 10 miles for it, it would probably not be enough of a reward to increase the probability of that behavior. In other words, it would not be a reinforcer. It is often the case that when someone suggests providing rewards for appropriate employee behavior, a manager will report that the company already provides incentives. Closer inspection reveals that the worker can, for example, earn a certificate for perfect attendance or a commendation for a suggested improvement. The simple truth is that these rewards are not large enough to justify much effort by the employee. When the company makes thousands off a suggestion for which the employee got $15, you are not effectively reinforcing innovative suggestions. Some years ago Jones and Azrin (1973) noted that a job locator fee of $100 netted the Illinois State Employment Service eight times the number of jobs that were reported when a firm hand clasp was the only reward.

Providing reinforcers is probably a necessary condition for producing behavior change but it is not sufficient to be effective in and of itself.

Rule 5 – Provide Rewards Contingent Upon Performance of Appropriate Work Behaviors

A major problem in many organizations is that the primary reward – salary – is based on presence rather than performance. As a result of this arrangement, many employees appear to see taking up space at their desk as their primary function. One might indeed ask: Why shouldn't they feel that way? After all that is what they get paid for. The only time they don't get paid is if they don't show up, so the positive consequence (salary) is obviously contingent only on the response of being present. No reward is useful if it is contingent on the wrong behavior.

How do you improve this situation? Well it is probably a little late to put everyone on commission or piece work. But you have plenty of other rewards from bonuses to praise that you can make contingent on performance. The key is to make sure that you don't give them away!

A good example of the noncontingent use of a potent reinforcer has occurred in tipping. The gratuity could be a potent reinforcer for good service if it were contingent on that behavior. Unfortunately, most customers tip a standard amount whether the service was superb, adequate, or perfunctory. The net effect is that the waiter, porter, or paperboy expects a tip regardless of performance. The provider will view the size of the tip as a trait of the customer ("a good tipper") rather than as feedback on his work.

Rule 6 – Set up Reinforcers for a Behavior so that They Follow that Behavior as Quickly as is Practical

It is not only the gold watch at the end of fifty-years service that violates this principle. Any delayed reward is likely to be perceived as unconnected to the work behaviors for which it was delivered. For the salesman on commission or the factory piece worker the only way extra money can continue to function as a reinforcer is if the employee keeps some count of how much he is earning. If he is keeping track of his production, each time that he adds to his count is a reinforcing event. The pay at the end of the month makes such record keeping rewarding, but the immediate knowledge of increased income on the horizon is the reward for the actual work behaviors. Obviously then, if you provide such employees with immediate feedback on how much they have earned, you should get increased productivity. Miller (1977) illustrated this point nicely in a program designed to increase the performance of sales representatives for a chemical company. By changing from a system in which bonuses were paid yearly to one in which monthly feedback was delivered on the amount earned for specific work behaviors, he found that performance increased dramatically.

Rule 7 – Make Sure that Your Rewards Follow Rather than Precede the Behavior You Wish to Increase

The immediacy principle (Rule 6) holds within it this second obvious necessity for administering rewards. On the face of it, the notion that the reward must follow the desired behavior seems so simple minded that it is not worth mentioning. It would indeed be a trivial point if managers didn't so often violate it. As a simple example of this kind of backward conditioning take the college faculty member who is granted tenure or promotion after promising his chairman that he will spend more time on campus and give more preparation to his classes. Of course, the professor's habitual behavior does not undergo a miraculous change after the reward is delivered. Having thrown away his reinforcers noncontingently, the department chairman finds that the professor's behavior gets even worse and finds himself bitterly muttering something about the faculty's lack of "gratitude." It is interesting to note that in both of the cases in which we have observed this phenomenon, the chairmen were industrial psychologists. You would have expected them to know better, but they didn't. No organism works for rewards that it already has. Rewards must be earned before you give them out, not afterward. The interested reader can find another example of what happens when this principle is violated in Chapter 6.

Rule 8 – Make Your Rewards Contingent on Behavior not Outcomes

The most common contingent reward systems in industry are those commission arrangements that reward sales personnel. Such programs represent a highly successful use of
contingency principles, but they could be even more effective. The key to behavior management through contingent reinforcement is to reward appropriate behavior. The usual sales
commission system rewards not behavior but the results of the salesman's actions (see
Chapter 10). Like early management by objectives theory, it gives the salesman feedback
on where to go but no information on how to get there (Ritschl & Hall, 1980). With such a
system the salesmanager is able to identify who gets results but not what behaviors are effective. As a result salesmanagers are forever searching for born salesmen, but they are unable
to teach good sales behaviors. The cure for this problem is embodied in Rule 8.

       Once you know what you want to reinforce with what kind of reward, you have to
know how you are going to do it. The first mistake that most people make is to decide what
behavior it is that they wish to increase and simply offer a system of rewards for that
response. Typically the manager will offer a handsome bonus for a 100 percent increase in
productivity or a spotless shop and wonder why he has no takers. The reason that this approach does not work is that the manager has failed to follow the next guiding principle of
contingency management.

Rule 9 – Start at the Current Level of Performance

An employee who shows up on time once a month is not likely to gain a reward that is offered for a year of being prompt. Such a reward might just as well not exist for that
employee. On the other hand, if he is rewarded for being on time once a week, you are likely to produce a significant increase in punctuality. Both the manager and the employee must
recognize that these rewards are but a step on the road to acceptable levels of performance.
Yet this is a step that cannot be skipped. It is of the utmost importance. If the manager in-
stitutes a program of rewarding only perfect behavior, he better not hold his breath waiting
for it to develop.

       Starting at the current level of the employee is not only absolutely necessary if you are
going to have any effect, it is a practical guide for improving what otherwise would appear to
be hopeless behavior (Brethower, 1972). It forces the manager to uncover what the
employee is doing correctly so that he knows where to begin his reward system. In so doing
it provides the grey area between the manager's white of perfect performance and his black
of "that guy never does anything right." Even the terrible employee does some part of his job
better than he does other parts. Starting to reward at his current level you begin by reinforcing him when he performs less poorly than he usually does. As Brethower notes, you can
tell him that it is exceptionally good performance that is being rewarded because for him
even minimal improvement is exceptionally good.

       Just as you must begin to reinforce behavior that the employee is currently doing well,
it is most appropriate to increase the behavioral demands for rewards very slowly.

Rule 10 – Reward Small Steps of Improvement Toward a Final Goal

Rule 11 – Establish a System that Will Overreward Rather than Underreward Behavior

These two principles are based on the fact that you are trying to correct a deficiency. The
employee who has been doing poorly is not likely to have been receiving much in the way of
rewards for his efforts. He has in fact been on extinction because his work performance has

not been good enough to get reinforced. He is likely to have given up any hope of being rewarded. Any large increase in what is demanded of him will result in extinction occurring again because he will quit before he accomplishes enough to get rewarded. The manager must make sure that correct work behavior does not go unrewarded. If he is too stingy with his rewards or trys to move too quickly in bringing the employee's behavior up to criterion, the empoyee will fail to get enough reinforcement to keep him going.

The early Emery Air Freight manual *Positive Reinforcement* (1971) makes a strong case for the importance of rewarding early and often. Emery's managers are told that "any response the individual makes, however slight, toward the goal should be recognized as very important and should be strongly reinforced. This is true even if there are many steps on the behavioral scale yet to be exhibited. (You may appear to be a long way from the results goal, but you really are not). The behaviors listed in Table 1.2 are examples of rewardable efforts that often go unnoticed (Positive Reinforcement, 1971).

Table 1.2 exemplifies the direction that a manager must pursue if he is going to improve employee behavior. It emphasizes the need to find and reward adequate work and efforts to improve the quality of performance. In order to implement this approach the manager must know the right questions to ask when he observes substandard work. In Table 1.3 (Positive Reinforcement, 1971) the manager is provided with guidelines for finding reinforceable behavior even in the worst of situations. These questions are intended to identify a starting place for delivering rewards. They offer a way of responding to inadequate performance without hammering the worker and making things worse.

Memorize these questions! They are the most direct route to improving performance because they provide a way to reward employees without waiting for perfect performance.

The steps that we have described so far have dealt with reinforcers and when to apply them. We have done little with the all important topic of what to reward. The simple answer is to reward the behaviors that you want to increase. The key concept is to look for the behaviors that you want and stop looking for the behaviors that you don't want. The late Buddy Parker who coached the Detroit Lions to two National Football League titles in the early fifties put this point best when he said "I didn't want to tell them (his players) what not to do, I wanted to stress what they had to do [Herskowitz, 1974]."

Rule 12 – State Your Objectives in Positive Terms

Lists of "Don'ts" are the most obvious incorrect example at this step, but they represent only

---

TABLE 1.2. Examples of *FIRST* Behaviors that Should be Reinforced.

1. Talks about performance problem even though he doesn't do anything.
2. Admits there is a problem.
3. States he was thinking about a solution even though no solution was conceived.
4. Tries, but fails.
5. Does it right one time out of a hundred.
6. Measures performance and finds it is poor.
7. Asks a question about how to do it.
8. Offers a solution that couldn't possibly work.
9. Reduces the amount of degree of negative behavior.
10. Completes it or does it correctly even though late.
11. Does part of it correctly.
12. Merely mentions the subject matter.
13. Recognizes he made a mistake.

Reprinted by permission from *Positive Reinforcement*, Emery Air Freight, 1971.

TABLE 1.3. Finding Out What is Being Done Well.

1. In the problem area (even when it makes you spitting mad), was it ever done *right once* out of many attempts?
2. What *parts* of it were done well?
3. Which results were *closest* to, though short of, the goal?
4. Were *attempts* made (even though unsuccessful)?
5. Were attempts planned?
6. Knows a problem exists?
7. Completes it, though late?
   On time, but incomplete?
   Accurate but incomplete?

Reprinted by permission from *Positive Reinforcement*, Emery Air Freight, 1971.

the tip of the iceberg. Everytime you only notice who's late, make only corrections on a report, or speak to only the low man on the sales chart, you are attending to poor performance and ignoring good work. By now you probably know that at least as far as behavior is concerned, if you ignore it, it may very well go away. You want to stop putting adequate performance on extinction. You accomplish that by rewarding those behaviors that are done well and attending to small instances of improvement. You have to tell the employee what you want, not what you don't want, and establish a list of "Do's" rather than a list of "Don'ts." Every behavior change that you wish to make should be stated in positive terms. Employees should be told to "arrive on time" rather than "not to be late," to "produce up to a certain goal" rather than "not to goof off," and to "work carefully" rather than "not to make errors."

A helpful way of checking on whether you are stating your requirements positively is Ogden Lindsley's "Deadman's Rule." If a dead man can do it, you probably stated it incorrectly. A corpse is not likely to make errors or goof off. If those rules were the basis for getting rewarded, the dead body would fulfill the requirements every time. On the other hand a real "graveyard shift" would have a difficult time working carefully or producing up to a set standard.

There is another reason for focusing on positive rather than negative behavior. When you reward someone for a response, you communicate exactly what you want them to do. When you criticize or punish you only tell them what you don't want them to do. You eliminate one wrong response, but you don't do anything to make sure that it isn't replaced by another wrong response rather than the right one. If you think verbal instructions to "do it this way" solve this problem, consider the number of times that you have described how to do something and had little or no effect. If you reward the correct response, you identify it for the worker through his experience not through your verbal description.

Punishing the wrong behavior is the indirect way to teach the right behavior, but that is not the only thing wrong with the negative approach. Punishment, criticism, nagging, fines, disciplinary procedures, and reprimands may well help you to change employee behavior, but they are expensive. The negative approach leads to hostility, aggression, and withdrawal (Azrin & Holtz, 1966; Thompson, 1978). All of these methods are based on punishment, and punishment is associated with negative emotional behavior. It keeps the employee working through fear of what happens if he stops. Behavior motivated by fear is rigid, uncreative, and inconsistent. Nonetheless, control by sanctions is the most common management technique currently employed in industry (Mayhew, Enyart, & Cone, 1979).

If punishment worked, it might be worthwhile to endure the sabotage, absences, and hostility. But it doesn't work! For punishment to be successful in the long run requires that the aversive stimulus be severe. The punishment must be aversive enough that it is really worth avoiding. In almost no case in industry is such a punishment available to managers, which is probably just as well. The mild negative consequences that the manager does have at his disposal will produce the same negative side effects as more severe punishment but only minimal improvements in performance. A wide variety of research approaches have demonstrated that criticism and punishment in its various forms provide gains that are at best short-lived. The manager finds himself having to nag, criticize, and punish over and over again. To complicate the picture further, people habituate to punishment. The more you use it the less effect it has, so that even the small increase in performance that you initially get from punishment will require more and more nagging. Unfortunately, the negative approach works just well enough to be reinforcing to the manager. It works well enough to keep him using it, but not well enough to solve the problem so the manager can stop using it.

There are many managers who believe that they must be tough on their subordinates. It is the repeated experience of the authors of this book that presenting rewards for good performance is a great deal more effective than trying to motivate good performance through fear of management reprisals. The experiences at Emery Air Freight (Performance Audit, 1972) and much of the research reported here demonstrates that positive reinforcement works. Yet many managers spend years in the shop with nary a positive word crossing their lips. An acquaintance of one of the authors manages a drugstore in a large chain. Of the over 200 stores in the company this manager had the second best profit ratio despite a major remodeling project which inflated the store's costs. His supervisor's only response to his performance was to inquire why he hadn't done as well as the store with the best record. As a natural reaction to extinction, the store manager was looking to change companies.

Many managers complain that they too find that criticism and threats have no lasting positive effects, but that they have also had difficulties trying to use rewards to control behavior. If they have followed the other rules that we have described, the most likely fault in their programs is a lack of consistency. The program that you develop must be applied systematically and unswervingly. Those who perform adequately must be consistently rewarded while those who fail to improve must forego the reinforcement. The manager who rewards almost achieving the goal is undermining the system. You must reward steps approaching the goal, but you can not be manipulated into rewarding inadequate effort. The simplest example of this error is the college professor or manager who rewards people for getting their reports in early. If he also gives the same reward to the student who hands a paper in late but has a good excuse, he is teaching how to make good alibis not how to hand in reports early. If he wants to set up contingencies for creative excuse making, that's his business, but he is undermining his attempt to get papers in on time. When it comes to delivering reinforcement you must rigidly adhere to the contingencies that you have developed or your program will have no effect.

At this point you may think that all this sounds pretty good in theory but wonder how practical it is. The results that you will read in the rest of this volume suggest that it is very practical indeed. It is currently being employed by many of the nation's major corporations.

In 1976 Hammer and Hammer reported an extensive list of corporations that had implemented behavior modification programs. Included in this group were AT&T, General Motors, B.F. Goodrich, General Electric, Weyerhauser, American Can, IBM, Proctor and Gamble, Upjohn, Ford Motor Company, Chase-Manhattan Bank, Westinghouse, and Wheeling-Pittsburgh Steel to name just a few. In the years that have passed since the publication of their report, the number of companies that have initiated behavior analysis projects has continued to expand. Successful behavior modification projects have been reported throughout the airline industry, in each of the big three automotive manufacturers, and in a variety of retail applications.

Yet the surface has been barely scratched. Primitive management strategies still abound while rewards are delivered noncontingently or too late to have any meaningful effect. Ineffective management techniques remain the rule rather than the exception. Direct learning of specific skill segments through shaping with positive consequences has still not replaced our overdependence on verbal instructions in learning complex behaviors, despite the success of programmed instruction (Babb & Kopp, 1978; Nash, Muczyk & Vettori, 1971). If you are a typical manager you have probably already realized that you do not get enough individual data to objectively evaluate your employees and that your employees lack feedback and realistic standards to evaluate what feedback they get.

While the industrial giants have begun to implement behavior management programs with notable success, in a tight economy small businesses remain concerned with day-to-day survival and crises management abounds. The techniques of applied behavior analysis can improve the productivity, quality of working life, and profit margin of any business if the management is willing to commit itself to a planned program of data collection and contingent rewards for productivity.

REFERENCES

Adam, E. E., Jr. Behavior modification in quality control. *Academy of Management Journal*, 1975, **18**, 662-679.

Adam, E. E., Jr., & Scott, W. E. The application of behavioral conditioning techniques to the problems of quality control. *Academy of Management Journal*, 1971, **14**, 175-193.

Aldis, O. Of pigeons and men. *Harvard Business Review*, 1961, **39**, 297-300.

Ammons, R. B. Effects of knowledge of performance: A survey and tentative theoretical formulation. *Journal of General Psychology*, 1956, **54**, 279-299.

Andrasik, F., Heimberg, J. S., & McNamara, J. R. Behavior modification of work and work-related problems. In M. Hersen, R. M. Eisler, & P. M. Miller (Eds.), *Progress in behavior modification*. New York: Academic Press, in press.

At Emery Air Freight: Positive reinforcement boosts performance. *Organizational Dynamics*, 1973, **1** (3), 41-50.

Ayllon, T., & Azrin, N.H. *The token economy: A motivational system for therapy and rehabilitation*. New York: Appleton-Century-Crofts, 1968.

Azrin, N. H., & Holz, W. C. Punishment. In W. K. Honig (Ed.), *Operant behavior: Areas of research and application*. New York: Appleton-Century-Crofts, 1966.

Babb, H. W., & Kopp, D. G. Applications of behavior modification in organizations: A review and critique. *Academy of Management Review*, 1978, **3**, 281-292.

Brethower, D. M. *Behavioral analysis in business and industry: A total performance system*. Kalamazoo, Michigan: Behaviordelia, 1972.

Brethower, D. M., & Rummler, G. A. For improved work performance: Accentuate the positive. *Personnel*, 1966, **43** (5), 40-49.

Brown, M. G. Behavioral engineering in the sewn products industry. *Journal of Organizational Behavior Management*, 1980, **2**, 267-268.

Brown, M. G., Malott, R. W., Dillon, M. J., & Keeps, E. J. Improving customer service in a large department store through the use of training and feedback. *Journal of Organizational Behavior Management*, 1980, **2**, 251-265.

Burg, M. M., Reid, D. H., & Lattimore, J. Use of self-recording and supervision program to change institutional staff behavior. *Journal of Applied Behavior Analysis*, 1979, **12**, 363-375.

Business, behaviorism and the bottom line. Del Mar, CA: CRM Educational Films.

Chandler, A. B. Decreasing negative comments and increasing performance of a shift supervisor. *Journal of Organizational Behavior Management*, 1977, **1**, 99-103.

Collins, S. R. Incentive programs: Pros and cons. *Personal Journal*, 1981, **60**, 571-575.

Dick, H. W. Increasing the productivity of the day relief textile machine operator. *Journal of Organizational Behavior Management*, 1978, **2**, 45-57.

Emmert, G. D. Measuring the impact of group performance feedback verses individual performance feedback in an industrial setting. *Journal of Organizational Behavior Management*, 1978, **1**, 134-141.

Erez, M. Feedback: A necessary condition for the goal-setting performance relationship. *Journal of Applied Psychology*, 1977, **62**, 624-627.

Feeney, E. J. Personal Communication, 1978.

Ford, J. E. A classification system for feedback procedures. *Journal of Organizational Behavior Management*, 1980, **2**, 183-191.

Fry, F. L. Operant conditioning in organizational settings: Of mice and men. *Personnel*, 1974, **51** (4), 17-24.

Geller, E. S., Eason, S. L., Phillips, J. A., & Pierson, M. D. Interventions to improve sanitation during food preparation. *Journal of Organizational Behavior Management*, 1980, **2**, 229-240.

Gilbert, T. F. *Human competence: Engineering worthy performance*. New York: McGraw-Hill, 1978.

Goldstein, A. P., and Sorcher, M. Changing managerial behavior by applied learning techniques. *Training and Development Journal*, 1973, **27**, 36-39.

Greller, M. M. Evaluation of feedback sources as a function of role and organizational level. *Journal of Applied Psychology*, 1980, **65**, 24-27.

Gupton, T., & Lebow, M. Behavior management in a large industrial firm. *Behavior Therapy*, 1971, **2**, 78-82.

Hammond, P. F. Increasing productivity through performance audit, feedback, and positive reinforcement. Unpublished paper. Emery Air Freight, Wilton, Conn., 1975.

Hamner, W. C., & Hamner, E. P. Behavior modification on the bottom line. *Organizational Dynamics*, 1976, **4** (4), 2-21.

Herskowitz, M. *The golden age of pro football*. New York: MacMillan, 1974.

Herzberg, F. *Work and the nature of man*. Cleveland: World Publishing Company, 1966.

Hollander, M. A., & Plutchik R. A reinforcement program for psychiatric attendants. *Journal of Behavior Therapy and Experimental Psychiatry*, 1972, **3**, 297-300.

House, R. J., & Wigdor, L. A. Herzberg's dual factor theory of job satisfaction and motivation. *Personal Psychology*, 1967, **20**, 369-390.

Hulin, C.L., & Smith, P.A. An empirical investigation of two implications of the two-factor theory of job satisfaction. *Journal of Applied Psychology*, 1967, **51**, 396-402.

Jablonsky, S. F., & DeVries, D. L. Operant conditioning principles extrapolated to the theory of management. *Organizational Behavior and Human Performance*, 1972, **7**, 340-358.

Jones, R. J., & Azrin, N. H. An experimental application of a social reinforcement approach to the problem of job-finding. *Journal of Applied Behavior Analysis*, 1973, **6**, 345-353.

Kim, J. S., & Hamner, W. C. Effect of performance feedback and goal setting on productivity and satisfaction in an organizational setting. *Journal of Applied Psychology*, 1976, **61**, 48-57.

Kirby, P. G. Performance improvement the adult way. *Personnel*, 1980, **57** (6), 35-43.

Kohlenberg, R., & Phillips, T. Reinforcement and rate of litter depositing. *Journal of Applied Behavior Analysis*, 1973, **6**, 391-396.

Komaki, J. A behavioral view of paradigm debates: Let the data speak. *Journal of Applied Psychology*, 1981, **66**, 111-112.

Komaki, J., Blood, M. R., & Holder, D. Fostering friendliness in a fast foods franchise. *Journal of Organizational Behavior Management*, 1980, **2**, 151-164.

Komaki, J., Heinzmann, A. T., & Lawson, L. Effect of training and feedback: Component analysis of a behavioral safety program. *Journal of Applied Psychology*, 1980, **65**, 261-270.

Kraut, A. I. Behavior modeling symposium: Developing managerial skills via modeling techniques: Some positive research findings – A symposium. *Personnel Psychology*, 1976, **29**, 325-328.

Laird, D. Why everything is all loused up, really (and what to do about it). *Training in Business and Industry*, March, 1971, 52-55.

Lamal, P. A., & Benfield, A. The effect of self-monitoring on job tardiness and percentage of time spent working. *Journal of Organizational Behavior Management*, 1978, **1**, 142-149.

Latham, G. P., & Baldes, J. J. The practical significance of Locke's theory of goal setting. *Journal of Applied Psychology*, 1975, **60**, 122-124.

Lawler, E. E., III, & Hackman, J. R. Impact of employee participation in the development of pay incentive plans: A field experiment. *Journal of Applied Psychology*, 1969, **53**, 467-471.

Lewin, K. Group decision and social change. In T. Newcomb and E. Hartley (Eds.), *Reading in social psychology*. New York: Holt, 1947, pp. 330-344.

Lindsey, C. A., Marks, E., & Gorlow, I. The Herzberg theory: A critique and reformulation. *Journal of Applied Psychology*, 1967, **51**, 330-339.

Lindsley, O. R. Operant conditioning methods applied to research in chronic schizophrenics. *Psychiatric Research Reports*, 1956, **5**, 118-153.

Lindsley, O. R. Teaching teachers to teach. Paper presented at the American Psychological Association Convention, New York, September, 1966.

Locke, E. A. Latham versus Komaki: A tale of two paradigms. *Journal of Applied Psychology*, 1980, **65**, 16-23.

Locke, E. A., Cartledge, N., & Koeppel, J. Motivational effects of knowledge of results: A goal-setting phenomenon. *Psychological Bulletin*, 1968, **70**, 474-485.

Lovaas, O. I., Berberich, J. P., Perloff, B. F., & Scaeffer, B. Acquisition of imitative speech by schizophrenic children. *Science*, 1966, **151**, 705-707.

Luthans, F., & Kreitner, R. *Organizational behavior modification*. Glenview, Illinois: Scott Foresman, 1975.

Luthans, F., Paul, R., & Baker, D. An experimental analysis of the impact of contingent reinforcement on salespersons' performance behavior. *Journal of Applied Psychology*, 1981, **66**, 314-323.

Mager, R. F., & Pipe, P. *Analyzing performance problems*. Belmont, CA: Fearon, 1970.

Malott, R. W., & Hartlep, P. *Contingency management in education and other equally exciting places*. Kalamazoo, MI: Behaviordelia, 1972.

Marholin, D., II, & Gray, D. Effects of group response-cost procedures on cash shortages in a small business. *Journal of Applied Behavior Analysis*, 1976, **9**, 25-30.

Maslow, A. H. A theory of motivation. *Psychological Review*, 1943, **50**, 370-376.

Mayhew, G. L., Enyart, P., & Cone, J. D. Approaches to employee management: Policies and preferences. *Journal of Organizational Behavior Management*, 1979, **2**, 103-111.

Mawhinney, T. C. Operant terms and concepts in the description of individual work behavior: Some problems of interpretation, application, and evaluation. *Journal of Applied Psychology*, 1975, **60**, 704-712.

McCarthy, M. Decreasing the incidence of "high bobbins" in a textile spinning department through a group feedback procedure. *Journal of Organizational Behavior Management*, 1978, **1**, 150-154.

McGregor, D. *The human side of enterprise*. New York: McGraw-Hill, 1960.

McMillan, J. D., & Dorel, H. W. Performance appraisal: Match the tool to the task. *Personnel*, 1980, **57** (4), 12-20.

Miller, L. M. Improving sales and forecast accuracy in a nationwide sales organization. *Journal of Organizational Behavior Management*, 1977, **1**, 39-51.

Miller, L. M. *Behavior management: The new science of managing people at work*. New York: John Wiley and Sons, 1978.

Moses, J. L., & Ritchie, R. J. Supervisory relationships training: A behavioral evaluation of a behavior modeling program. *Personnel Psychology*, 1976, **29**, 337-343.

Murphy, J. R. Is it Skinner or nothing? *Training and Development Journal*, 1972, **26** (2), 2-8.

Nadler, D. The effects of feedback on task group behavior: A review of the experimental research. *Organizational Behavior and Human Performance*, 1979, **23**, 309-338.

Nash, A. N., Muczyk, J. P., & Vettori, F. The relative practical effectiveness of programmed instruction. *Personnel Psychology*, 1971, **24**, 397-418.

Nathan, P. E., & Wallace, W. H. An operant behavioral measure of TV commercial effectiveness. *Journal of Advertising Research*, 1965, **5** (4), 13-20.

Nemeroff, W. F., & Wexley, K. N. An exploration of the relationship between performance feedback interview characteristics and interview outcomes as perceived by managers and subordinates. *Journal of Occupational Psychology*, 1979, **52**, 25-34.

Nord, W. R. Beyond the teaching machine: The neglected area of operant conditioning in the theory and practice of management. *Organizational Behavior and Human Performance*, 1969, **4**, 375-401.

Nord, W. R. Improving attendance through rewards. *Personnel Administration*, 1970, **33** (6), 37-41.

O'Brien, R. M., & Dickinson, A. M. Contingency factors in negative practice of smoking. *Psychological Reports*, 1977, **40**, 495-505.

O'Brien, R. M., & Sperduto, W. A. An undergraduate course in OBM: Course description and practicum outcomes. In A. M. Dickinson & R. M. O'Brien (Chairs), *Organizational behavior management: Procedures, problems and progress*. Symposium presented to the Association for Behavior Analysis, Milwaukee, 1981.

Performance audit, feedback, and positive reinforcement. *Training and Development Journal*, 1972, **26**(11), 8-13.

Phillips, E. L., Phillips, E. A., Fixen, D. L., & Wolf, M. M. Achievement place: Modification of the behaviors of pre-delinquent boys within a token economy. *Journal of Applied Behavior Analysis*, 1971, **4**, 45-49.

Piamonte, J. S. An employee motivational system that leads to excellent performance. *Personnel*, 1980, **57** (5), 55-66.

Porter, L. W., & Lawler, E. F. III. *Managerial attitudes and performance*. Homewood, Illinois: Irwin-Dorsey, 1968.

Positive reinforcement. Wilton, Conn.: Emery Air Freight, 1971.

Prue, D. M., Krapfl, J. E., Noah, J. C., Cannon, S., & Maley, R. F. Managing the treatment activities of state hospital staff. *Journal of Organizational Behavior Management*, 1980, **2**, 165-181.

Rhoton, W. W. A procedure to improve compliance with coal mine safety regulations. *Journal of Organizational Behavior Management*, 1980, **2**, 243-249.

Ritschl, E. R., & Hall, R. V. Improving MBO: An applied behavior analyst's point of view. *Journal of Organizational Behavior Management*, 1980, **2**, 269-277.

Rotondi, T., Jr. Behavior modification on the job. *Supervisory Management*, 1976, **21** (2), 22-28.

Runnion, A., Johnson, T., & McWhorter, J. The effects of feedback and reinforcement on truck turnaround time in materials transportation. *Journal of Organizational Behavior Management*, 1978, **1**, 180-191.

Schneider, J., & Locke, E. A. A critique of Herzberg's incident classification system and a suggested revision. *Organizational Behavior and Human Performance*, 1971, **6**, 441-457.

Schneier, C. E. Behavior modification in management: A review and critique. *Academy of Management Journal*, 1974, **17**, 528-548.

Seybolt, J. W., & Pavett, C. M. The prediction of effort and performance among hospital professionals: Moderating effects of feedback on expectancy theory formulations. *Journal of Occupational Psychology*, 1979, **52**, 91-105.

Simek, T. C., & O'Brien, R. M. Immediate auditory feedback to improve putting quickly. *Perceptual and Motor Skills*, 1978, **47**, 1133-1134.

Simek, T. C., & O'Brien, R. M. *Total golf: A behavioral approach to lowering your score and getting more out of your game*. New York: Doubleday, 1981.

Skinner, B. F. *The behavior of organisms*. New York: Appleton-Century-Crofts, 1938.

Skinner, B. F. *Science and Human Behavior*. New York: Macmillan, 1953.

Sorcher, M. A behavior modification approach to supervisor training. *Professional Psychology*, 1971, **2**, 401-402.

Stunkard, A. J., Craighead, L. W., & O'Brien, R. Controlled trial of behaviour therapy, pharmacotherapy, and their combination in the treatment of obese hypertensives. *The Lancet*, Nov. 15, 1980, 1045-1047.

Thompson, D. W. *Managing people influencing behavior.* St. Louis: Mosby, 1978.

Thompson, T., & Grabowski, J. (Eds.) *Behavior modification of the mentally retarded.* New York: Oxford, 1972.

Thorndike, E. L. *Animal intelligence.* New York: Macmillan, 1911.

Tosti, D. T. Behavior modeling: A process. *Training and Development Journal*, 1980, **34** (8), 70-74.

Tosti, D., & Jackson, S. Formative and summative feedback. Paper presented at the annual meeting of the Association for Behavior Analysis, Milwaukee, May 1981.

Ulrich, R., Stachnik, T., & Mabry, J. (Eds.) *Control of human behavior: Behavior modification in education.* Glenview, Illinois: Scott, Foresman, 1974.

Verhave, T. The pigeon as a quality control inspector. In R. Ulrich, T. Stachnik, and J. Mabry (Eds.), *Control of human behavior: Expanding the behavioral laboratory.* Glenview, Illinois: Scott, Foresman, 1966, 242-246.

Vroom, V. H. *Work and motivation.* New York: John Wiley and Sons, 1964.

Wahba, M. A., & Bridwell, L. G. Maslow reconsidered: A review of the research on the need hierarchy theory. *Proceedings of the Academy of Management*, 1973, **33**, 514-520.

Watson, J. B. *Psychology from the standpoint of a behaviorist.* (2nd ed.) Philadelphia: Lippincott, 1924.

Whyte, W. F. Pigeons, persons and piece rates: Skinnerian theory in organizations. *Psychology Today*, April, 1972, 66-68; 96-100.

Winters, L. C., & Wallace, W. H. On operant conditioning techniques. *Journal of Advertising Research*, 1970, **10** (5), 39-45.

Yager, E. A critique of performance appraisal. *Personnel Journal*, 1981, **60,** 129-133.

2

Productivity and Schedules of Reinforcement in Business and Industry

Teodoro Ayllon and David J. Kolko
Georgia State University

One of the emerging trends in the world of business and industry concerns the shift in emphasis from internal to external variables as the predominant means of motivating worker productivity and satisfaction (Miller, 1978). A variety of theories of internal causation have, until recently, provided management with the direction for improving human performance problems (Luthans, 1973; Luthans & Kreitner, 1975; Connellan, 1978). As Miller (1978) has aptly pointed out, this internal approach is marked by an equivocal relationship to performance, difficulty in direct application or translation, and only modest outcome results. In its place has developed an approach based upon scientific principles and analyses rather than alleged internal processes (Beech, 1978).

Paralleling the recent surge of interest in the application of behavioral strategies to clinical practice and other areas (Redd, Porterfield & Anderson, 1979), greater attention has been paid to the use of behavioral principles in the resolution of problems encountered in the work arena (Connellan, 1978; Hampton, 1978). This approach to business management derives largely from the pioneering work of B.F. Skinner in the area of operant conditioning (1938, 1953, 1969). In particular, the operant conditioning literature provides the manager with the fundamental tools by which organizational behavior can be directly influenced to more fully realize specified objectives and goals.

The operant technology for analyzing and modifying human performance is characterized by several notable elements. The variables most directly affecting performance are considered external to the individual (Miller, 1978). Hence, an emphasis is placed upon the observable variables which ultimately control the worker's behavior in the setting where the behavior is demonstrated. The behavioral approach attempts to improve performance by systematically manipulating the antecedants and consequences of which the behavior is a function. These environmental conditions become the focus of analysis and intervention. The approach is scientific in that its success is determined on the basis of empirical, data-based outcome results. Quantitative documentation of changes in performance is a necessary tool in the evaluation of any strategy applied in the work setting, consistent with the rigorous scientific methodology of operant research (Kazdin, 1977; Luthans, 1973).

The control of behavior by its consequences has long been a basic operational guideline in the remediation of human problems that can be profitably applied to organizational behavior (Luthans & Kreitner, 1975; Miller, 1978). This is most typically illustrated by the principle of reinforcement which the operant literature indeed suggests plays a principal role in human motivation (Skinner, 1938; Luthans & Kreitner, 1975). In recent years, the utility of positive reinforcement has been documented in various business applications (At Emery Air Freight,

1973; Conversation with B. F. Skinner, 1973; Where Skinner's Theories Work, 1972). These initial, optimistic results have given rise to further application of the principle of reinforcement in a host of business and industrial settings (see: *Journal of Organizational Behavior Management*).

The judicious use of reinforcing consequences or events to maximize performance requires attention to certain technical considerations (Beatty & Schneier, 1974; Lawler, 1973). While reinforcement in the laboratory has involved the use of food, sounds, and other sensory stimuli, the application of reinforcement to human behavior requires the identification and management of naturally occurring reinforcers in the applied setting. To accomplish this end, the manager can systematically analyze worker reinforcement histories, and employ self-report inventories or trial and error applications to determine effective positive reinforcers (Luthans & Kreitner, 1975; Miller, 1978). Two major classes of reinforcement have been so identified: social and monetary. In actual application to the job setting, these reinforcers have included job status or security, opportunity for personal growth, professional achievement, and monetary rewards.

A contingent relationship between worker performance and the delivery of positive reinforcers must be specified as well (McCormick & Ilger, 1980). Worker productivity increases most when reinforcing consequences reliably and immediately follow a desired performance. The establishment of performance-reinforcer relationships has become a predominant strategy guiding the management of behavior in various work settings (Cherrington, Reitz & Scott, 1971; Hermann, de Montes, Dominquez, Montes & Hopkins, 1973; Lawler, 1971; 1973; Nord, 1969).

Finally, as explicated by Ferster and Skinner (1957), the rules by which reinforcers become available (i.e., schedules of reinforcement) ultimately determine the maintenance and persistence of behavior (Zeiler, 1977). A variety of specific effects produced by different schedules of reinforcement have been well documented in experimental laboratory investigations (Skinner, 1938; Reese, 1966; Reynolds, 1968) and applied research (Hutchinson & Azrin, 1961; Krasner, 1971; Sulzer & Mayer, 1972).

The rules that govern the availability of reinforcement can be divided into two major types: continuous reinforcement (CRF) and intermittent reinforcement (IMT). In a continuous schedule, a one-to-one correspondence exists between a response and the delivery of reinforcement. In an intermittent schedule, reinforcement is delivered after some responses but not others. There are four primary types of intermittent schedules:

1. Fixed Ratio (FR): An FR schedule specifies a systematic relationship between a fixed number of responses (or units of behavior) and the presentation of reinforcement. For example, payment for every three dresses sewn represents an FR 3.

2. Variable Ratio (VR): A VR schedule specifies a systematic relationship between a variable number of responses (or units of behavior) and the presentation of reinforcement. Therefore, the actual number of responses required for reinforcement varies around an established average. For example, payment for growing an average of nine bushels per acre of food represents a VR 9.

3. Fixed Interval (FI): On an FI schedule, the first response that occurs once a fixed amount of time has elapsed is reinforced. While we do not typically employ a true FI schedule, we frequently provide reinforcement at the end of a particular time period. The difference here is that work (i.e., responding) within the hour is expected to take place in order for the individual to get paid, whereas in the technical, laboratory-based FI schedule, reinforcement is delivered if the individual works right after the interval has elapsed. For example, the closest approximation to this schedule involves payment delivered weekly (FI 1).

4. Variable Interval (VI): On a VI schedule, the first response that occurs once a variable amount of time has elapsed is reinforced. Here, the time requirement (interval) is stated as an average time interval. For example, payment delivered every 4 weeks, on the average, would represent the VI 4 schedule.

In addition, within intermittent schedules there are combinations of ratio and interval requirements at the completion of which reinforcement is delivered. For example, a salesman may receive a basic minimum wage or floor pay of $5 per hour (similar to FI) plus a bonus for every 30 units of goods sold (FR 30). The salary can be viewed as a fixed interval schedule in which attendance at work functions as the response which is reinforced. As noted earlier, this represents a departure from the usual laboratory requirements of a fixed interval schedule since it depends on the worker to recognize that performance of the job is assumed when his presence is rewarded. Within these limitations, a salary may be viewed as a type of fixed interval schedule in applied settings but since reinforcement is not actually response contingent, one may not always obtain fixed interval effects on the productivity of salaried workers. In any case, the very fact that schedules can be combined suggests that they offer considerable flexibility in the design of suitable financial payment systems.

Each of these major schedules, continuous and intermittent reinforcement, has a distinctive effect on behavior. Characteristically, continuous reinforcement is suitable when the concern is to build or generate behavior. The major limitation of this schedule is that it does not provide for long-term maintenance of behavior. On the other hand, intermittent reinforcement is suitable when the concern is to maintain behavior. Its major limitation, however, is that it requires that the behavior be already in strength for it to be maintained through intermittent reinforcement (Ferster, Culbertson & Perrot-Boren, 1975).

These empirical findings (Zeiler, 1977) bear implications for industrial and organizational behavior. As recommended by Porter (1973), for example, worker performance improvements can be maintained through the effective employment of an intermittent reinforcement schedule. Furthermore, Miller (1978) has documented the following benefits to the use of intermittent schedules: (1) practical efficiency, (2) avoidance of satiation, and (3) improved maintenance of performance under external conditions. These and other advantages to intermittent schedules have been discussed by others (Aldis, 1961; Hamner, 1974). For the manager with limited resources, intermittent schedules can provide for essential conservation of reinforcers in that rewards need not be delivered after each correct response.

The use of reinforcement schedules has particular relevance to the establishment and maintenance of job-related behaviors through monetary incentives. The durability of money as a reinforcer has long been recognized (Bijou & Baer, 1966). What is needed is an understanding of the optimal schedule by which it is delivered. The objective of this paper is to review the evidence bearing upon the use of different reinforcement schedules in simulated and actual work tasks, and to analyze the major variables governing their effectiveness.

CRF (FRI) VS. VR SCHEDULES OF REINFORCEMENT

Simulated Analogue Tasks

The practical difficulties attendant to conducting research on schedules of reinforcement in the work place have led to studies that have minimized these problems by employing brief analogue rather than long-term actual work tasks. The emphasis in this type of research has been on determining methodological solutions rather than practical ones to the implementation of reinforcement schedules. Therefore, at times, arbitrary but well defined and measured responses have characterized these efforts. In avoiding the unwanted influence of variables such as the level of difficulty of the task, the degree of familiarity with it, the social cohesion of the workers, and other work-related variables, these studies attempted to bridge the gap between the operant laboratory work with lower organisms and the applied setting.

The earliest experimental investigation of the effects of intermittent schedules in a simulated work setting was conducted by Yukl, Wexley and Seymore (1972). Fifteen females were hired through the university placement office to score answer sheets using a key. They worked for one hour per day for between 2 and 4 weeks, receiving $1.50 an hour as basic hourly pay. The subject simply wrote the test score on a computer printout. All subjects worked for 1 week in a no-incentive period. They were then assigned to one of the three experimental groups based upon the time constraints of their individual schedules. In the 25¢-CRF condition, a 25¢ bonus was given for each completed sheet. In the 25¢-VR2 conditions, bonuses of 25¢ and 50¢, respectively, were given provided that the subject correctly guessed the result of a coin toss after finishing each sheet. Therefore, the probability of receiving a bonus in the latter two conditions was 50%.

The results indicated greatest productivity improvement over baseline in the 50¢-VR2 group (45%), followed by the 25¢-CRF group (37%), and the 25¢-VR2 group (31%). While all three groups found the task relatively dull, the 50¢-VR2 and 25¢-CRF groups expressed significantly greater satisfaction with the incentive pay received.

Berger, Cummings and Henneman (1975) conducted a similar study designed to address certain methodological difficulties associated with the Yukl et al. (1972) investigation and replicate their findings. Fifteen female subjects also worked one hour a day coding attitude questionnaires onto coding sheets. They were paid $1.60 per hour. For 3 days, all subjects worked in a no-incentive condition. The remaining 6 days constituted the incentive condition. Subjects were randomly assigned to the same three conditions as in the Yukl et al. (1972) study: 25¢-CRF, 25¢-VR2, and 50¢-VR2. Those in the VR2 groups received the bonus payment for half of the questionnaires they finished.

For all three groups, performance increased in the incentive conditions relative to the baseline condition ($\bar{X} = 40\%$). The overall effects of the schedules, however, were not significant, but they were in the appropriate direction. That is, although the incentives produced performance increments there were only modest differences between the magnitude of the effects produced by each schedule. The relative ineffectiveness of the variable schedules used in these two experiments may be due, in part, to the uncertainty of the availability of reinforcement. Reinforcer delivery in this case was only possible if the coin toss was guessed correctly. Conceivably, several subjects may have received their bonus on a schedule much thinner than that described by the experimenters.

The effects of additional intermittent schedules were examined by Pritchard, Leonard, Berger and Kirk (1976). The task involved learning self-paced lessons on electronics, electricity, and transistors. In preliminary pilot research, the task material was broken up into one-half hour work units. Sixteen subjects were then selected who upon initial testing showed little knowledge of arithmetic and electronics. They were told that their hourly payment would be approximately $2.

After studying each work unit, subjects were tested at one of four different computer consoles, each of which was associated with a particular reinforcement schedule. The console indicated among other things the number of items correct and the amount of money earned for passage of the test. According to a Latin Square design, the subject worked for 1 week under each of the four schedules on a random basis: Hourly ($2/hour); FR3 ($3 for every three tests passed); VR ($3 for an average of three tests), and VR-VA (average of $3 for an average of three tests). On the performance measures (number of tests taken and passed, earnings), significant differences were found between the three schedules and the hourly condition, though none were found between the schedule conditions. Forty-six percent more tests were passed in the schedule conditions than the hourly one. Greatest overall satisfaction was expressed for the VR-VA condition on Monday and the FR condition on Friday. The FR condition was also associated with greatest satisfaction with the pay received. Finally, subjects preferred to work under the FR schedule than the other schedule conditions.

An extension of this research was recently reported by Pritchard, Hollenbeck and DeLeo (1980), this time employing a group design to eliminate order effects. The same programmed test course as described previously was employed here. The test, however, was scored by an instructor. Once the subject completed six tests, a comprehensive test covering all of the material was given. Sixty male and female subjects, mostly high school students, were randomly assigned to one of the following groups for a total of four days: Hourly ($2/hour); FR ($2 × number of hours to complete each test), and VR-VA (0, 1, 2, 3, 4, or 6 dollars × mean number of hours to complete the test). The subject was told how much each test was worth after it was passed.

The authors reported two measures of work effort: time-on-task and the number of times the subject changed from working to not working or vice versa (reversals). The FR group showed the most time-on-task, followed by the VR-VA group. Fewer reversals were observed for the FR group than for the other groups. Similar results were reported for the performance indices. The mean number of tests passed was 17.3 for the FR group, 16.8 for the VR-VA group, and 9.7 for the Hourly group. The Hourly group registered the highest mean passing score (94.4), followed by the VR-VA (93.0), and FR (91.6) groups. This finding is in part due to the greater number of appraisals taken per unit for the hourly group. The overall comprehensive test scores indicated that all three groups retained comparable levels of material. Finally, regarding attitudinal variables, the subjects were generally satisfied with all three schedules. Across six variables (job and pay satisfaction, equity, control, interestingness, and valence of pay), no significant differences among schedules were found.

Based on the overall pattern of results from the preceding studies, it appears that a CRF or FR schedule of reinforcement enhances performance relative to a payment system based on an hourly rate. While both schedules increase work-related performances, so do VR schedules. One possible reason for the equivalency of their effectiveness is the fact that the ratio requirements with respect to payment on CRF and VR schedules have been both low and similar to one another. Therefore, the two schedules have produced effects which are functionally equivalent. To obtain differential effects with these two schedules under these conditions, it may have been necessary to have the VR schedule value be sharply different from that of a CRF (or FR) schedule (e.g., VR10 vs. FR3). In our summary, this consideration will be more fully addressed.

Actual Work Tasks

Several studies investigating the effects of schedules in actual work tasks parallel those involving simulated or analogue tasks. Yukl and Latham (1974) employed a quasi-experimental group design with four company crews of tree planters. The subjects were generally young, uneducated male and female marginal workers who had a high turnover rate. Each planter received a minimum of $2 an hour basic pay and, for the most part, worked each 8-hour day in pairs. After a 3-week baseline period, subjects were assigned to one of the experimental conditions. In the CRF group, a $2 incentive for each bag was earned provided the planter correctly guessed the outcome of a coin toss. An $8 incentive was given to subjects in the VR4 group contingent upon guessing correctly on two coin tosses. A control group was also assessed for comparison purposes.

Productivity over baseline improved most for the CRF group (33%), compared with the VR2 (8% decline) and VR4 (18%) groups. In terms of cost-effectiveness, the same pattern of results was found. These findings cannot be unambiguously interpreted because of the nature of the design employed and it was later learned that certain planters and the supervisor disapproved of the operation of the schedules in the form of gambling.

A subsequent experiment by Yukl, Latham and Pursell (1976) attempted to remediate these limitations using a repeated measures design with another population of pine seedlings planters. The planters were 28 semi-literate workers, mixed by race and sex, who had received good productivity ratings. Only eight planters, however, were exposed to all five of the experimental conditions. After a no-incentive (baseline) condition, subjects worked under a CRF incentive condition in which they received a $2 bonus for each bag planted. They were then exposed to a VR4 condition in which an $8 bonus was earned only after correctly guessing the color of a marble twice in a row. Next, the planters worked under the CRF condition a second time. The last condition, VR2, was modified as such because the planters expressed considerable disinterest in the VR4 condition. Here, a $4 bonus was given for each bag and correctly guessing the color of one marble.

Because of the continuous attrition rate across the experimental conditions and different durations of exposure to each schedule, the results can only be interpreted with reservation. In general, the findings indicated that productivity was highest in the CRF conditions, even though a slightly higher percentage of reinforcement was obtained under the VR4 schedule. The preferences registered by the planters were coincident with this pattern as 77% preferred the CRF condition over the other conditions. They disliked the VR4 condition mainly because of the unpredictability of the delivery of the bonus.

Such findings have been corroborated using a within-subjects design in a later study by Latham and Dossett (1978). The participants were 14 male, unionized trappers having high school or college educations. Each received a basic salary of $5 an hour. In addition, following a 1-week baseline period, they were exposed to two different incentive conditions after random assignment to one of two groups. In group A, a CRF schedule was in effect in which they earned $1 for each rat trapped, followed by a VR4 schedule in which $4 was earned for each rat only if the color of a marble was correctly identified before drawing it from a bag of four marbles. For group B, the same schedules were in effect but in reverse order.

The introduction of the incentive conditions resulted in reductions in the cost of catching a rat. In terms of productivity, a 20% increase in the number of rats caught per hour was found with exposure to the first schedule in both groups relative to the baseline condition. Further increases in productivity resulted when the second schedule was imposed. In group A, a 20% increase was observed under VR4 relative to the preceding CRF condition. For group B, a 44% increase was found under the CRF schedule relative to the preceding VR4 schedule. Overall, the CRF condition led to a 16% increase in productivity over the VR4 condition. The authors indicated that experienced workers caught more rats on the VR4 schedule while inexperienced workers showed greater productivity on the CRF condition. Interestingly, 71% of the trappers (10/14) preferred the VR4 schedule over the CRF schedule.

Despite differences in design and certain methodological variables, these studies indicate that worker performance improves when bonus payment is delivered on either a CRF or VR schedule in comparison to baseline (i.e., no-incentive) conditions. However, all three investigations point to the relative superiority of payment according to a CRF schedule, particularly when task familiarity and experience is low. In line with these conclusions, workers in general expressed a greater preference for the CRF than VR schedule although this preference was reversed in one study where workers were fully informed of the relationship between their performance and reinforcer delivery (Latham & Dossett, 1978).

Schedules of reinforcement involving a form of payment resembling gambling (e.g., lotteries) have also been employed to reduce attendance and tardiness problems. Pedalino and Gamboa (1974) worked with five groups of blue-collar, unionized employees, ranging in size from 30-215 workers, in different plants in a manufacturing and distribution center. One group of assembly line workers constituted the experimental group, while those in the four comparison groups worked in assembly line, picking, loading, and unloading and meat processing operations. The employees received $4.86 per hour on the average and were paid weekly.

The experiment was implemented in four phases. Baseline data was collected in the first phase. A poker game incentive system was then implemented in which the employees received a playing card for each day of the week on-time. For each of the eight departments, the employee with the highest hand at the end of the week won $20 (FI-1). In the third phase, the poker game was scheduled for every other week. Finally, the lottery was removed in the fourth phase. With the introduction of the weekly lottery system, absenteeism was reduced by 26% for the experimental group. Absenteeism rose 5% when the incentive system operated every other week. However, there was no significant difference between the absenteeism rates for these two phases. Absenteeism was reduced 18.27% overall for the experimental group while a 13.8% increase was recorded for the comparison groups.

A similar weekly lottery system was used by Ayllon and Carlson (1973) to improve on-time attendance in a medium-sized distributing company. Baseline assessment revealed that between 10 and 30% of the employees arrived at work on time. In the lottery, a ticket was given to each employee who arrived on time for the entire week (5 days). A drawing was held at the end of the week for four prizes, ranging from $5 to $25, for those who received a lottery ticket. On-time attendance increased to between 47 and 80% approximately after the incentive program was introduced. The employees indicated that they enjoyed the lottery and, in fact, looked forward to lottery day.

The reduction in absenteeism produced by the operation of a lottery system is consistent with Skinner's original recommendation (Conversation with Skinner, 1973). It appears beneficial to implement a lottery system on a weekly basis and then to thin out the schedule so that it operates on a more intermittent basis. It is premature, however, to assert from these two studies that a lottery would have such effects indefinitely. Further research is required to determine the optimal schedule for its implementation as well as the long-term effects of a lottery system, especially once it has been terminated.

A recent study has examined the use of intermittent schedules in increasing transportation usage. Deslauriers and Everett (1977) studied the effects of intermittent and continuous token reinforcement on bus ridership. The participants were riders on a university bus from a population of students, faculty and staff, and townspeople. The tokens were small cards worth about 10¢ which were presented as the passengers boarded the bus. The experimental bus was in operation from 11-2. Ridership was measured across five phases: Baseline, VR3 (tokens given to every third passenger on the average), CRF (every passenger received a token), VR3, and Baseline. Ridership was also measured for two control conditions: the 11-2 operation of a second bus (control A) and the average of the ridership for all other times of operation for both buses (control B).

Nonparametric statistics indicated no significant differences between the experimental bus and both control conditions in the baseline phases. However, ridership for the experimental bus increased during token reinforcement phases relative to the control conditions. Ridership in the first VR3 phase increased 30% over the first baseline phase, continued to increase slightly in the subsequent CRF and VR3 phases and decreased abruptly with the reintroduction of the baseline phase. Furthermore, the VR3 condition resulted in a considerably lower net loss in revenue (5%) than for the CRF condition (75%). These results suggest that the CRF and VR schedules produced comparable levels of bus ridership while the VR schedule appeared more cost-effective in the long run. Such findings are consistent with those of studies reported previously in which the values of the reinforcement schedules were functionally similar.

CRF (FR1 OR PIECE-RATE) VS. FI (HOURLY RATE) SCHEDULES

Simulated Analogue Tasks

Only a few laboratory studies of the relative effectiveness of piece-rate (CRF) payment or incentive systems have been reported. One laboratory study reported by Farr (1976) investigated the utility of individual and group incentives. The participants were required to sort computer cards in two, 20-minute periods. One hundred and forty-four undergraduates working in groups of three were randomly assigned in a factorial design to one of the following experimental conditions: (1) No individual incentive, no group incentive (hourly – $1.80); (2) Individual incentive, no group incentive (piece-rate); (3) No individual incentive, group incentive (equal distribution – total group pay determined by piece rate and divided equally); (4) Individual incentive, group incentive (differential distribution – total group pay differentially divided according to individual performance).

Both individual and group incentives significantly influenced productivity independently in the two experimental periods relative to their respective no-incentive conditions. Goal setting scores reflecting estimates of the subject's own performance were also higher for the two incentive conditions. Individuals in the hourly condition indicated greater satisfaction with their productivity than those in the individual incentive condition. Productivity was highest in the individual incentive-group incentive condition, although they perceived the pay scale as unfair.

On another brief experimental task, sixty subjects, mostly college students, were recruited to assemble a complex model having moving parts made from Tinker Toys (Terborg & Miller, 1978). A 2 × 3 crossed design (Pay × Goal) was employed. Half of the subjects were paid an hourly rate ($2.50), while the other half received piece-rate pay (40¢/model). In addition, subjects were assigned to one of the three goal conditions (quantity, quality, or no assigned goal). On the performance measures, the piece-rate system resulted in a statistically significant increase in quantity of performance above that found in the hourly condition. No significant differences were found for production quality. On two measures of work effort (self and supervisor ratings), higher ratings were noted for subjects in the piece-rate condition. Goal setting was found to have an effect on quality and quantity of performance as well.

In conclusion, the findings here indicate that individual payment on a CRF schedule (i.e., FR1 piece-rate) improves performance relative to that found with traditional hourly pay. Furthermore, the research conducted by Farr (1976) suggests that productivity on an individual CRF schedule can be enhanced when employed in conjunction with a group CRF schedule. Unfortunately, it is not possible to analyze the effects of the group incentive condition alone in that study. Nonetheless, the potential benefits accruing to the use of both individual and group contingencies of reinforcement should be investigated in subsequent research, particularly in light of the difficulties associated with individual CRF plans (Lawler, 1973). Caution must be exercised in evaluating these studies, however, because of the extremely short task duration, arbitrariness of the task, and the fact that statistical significance may be found for what appear to be minimal differences in task performance.

Actual Work Tasks

The majority of research examining the effects of performance-pay contingencies has been conducted in industrial settings. Reported here are some of the rudimentary findings from early piece-rate applications as well as more recent, substantive research investigations.

Burnett (1925) studied four girls, aged 17, who were selected from a school for unemployed young people. Each was engaged in a monotonous cross-stitching task for six hours per day. The girls worked on an hourly system for 8 weeks, followed by a piece rate system for 5 weeks which was based on their average output from the last 3 weeks of the hourly condition. A 6-month period intervened between the two experimental conditions. Piece-rate payment increased output over the average output of the hourly condition by 12.8%. Roethlisberger and Dickson (1939) report similar results working with three groups of experienced workers at a Western Electric Plant. One group of relay assembly workers showed a 30% increase in output when switched from hourly to piece-rate employment. A 12.6% increase in output occurred for a second group of assembly workers when the basis of payment was changed from output by a large group (i.e., mean performance of 100 workers) to output by a small group of workers (mean performance of five workers). Output decreased 16.2% when the basis of payment in terms of the large group was reintroduced. Finally, output for a group of mica-splitting workers increased on an individual piece-rate system relative to a preceding period in which pay was based upon the large group incentive described above.

The effects of a specific contingency between performance and reinforcement on productivity has also been investigated when the basis of payment is switched from a CRF to an FI-like salary schedule. The output rates of workers in a repair and special order shop in a metal company were measured after the payment system was changed from piece-rate to hourly rate (Jacques, Rice & Hill, 1951). Shop achievement in terms of the number of hours worked dropped 18% with the changeover. Interestingly, however, both management and the workers expressed greater satisfaction with the flat, hourly rate. The workers preferred the fixed weekly income associated with an hourly payment system. The decline in output due to removal of a long-term incentive system was also reported by Rothe (1970). Performance data for a group of welders indicated a drop in productivity of 25% across a 48-week period following termination of the system.

Large scale surveys of worker productivity have provided supplementary evidence bearing upon the effectiveness of piece-rate wage incentive systems. Results from three surveys were summarized by Viteles (1953). One government survey of 514 incentive plans in the United States found that production increased 39% on the average. In a second survey of 48 manufacturing companies in the New York area, wage incentives resulted in an average increase of 28%. Furthermore, an average production increment of 16% was reported by a company manufacturing steel frames for motor vehicles. Dale (1959) provides similar findings in a report of the results of a study of 2,500 wage incentive plans from 29 various industries. Productivity increased an average of 64% while the average increase in earnings was 20.6%.

One of the most comprehensive investigations of piece-rate payment on productivity and worker satisfaction was reported by Wyatt (1934). Five pairs of young females in a candy manufacturing company had experience with each of the following operations: unwrapping, packing, weighing, wrapping, and weighing and unwrapping. The employees worked for two 3 3/4-hour shifts per day. For 9 weeks, they earned a fixed weekly wage. A bonus system was added for 15 weeks in which the employees were ranked and differentially paid an incentive according to individual output. This phase was followed by a flat piece-rate system which was in operation for 12 weeks.

The results indicated that payment method significantly influenced work rate. Productivity increased by 46% with the introduction of the hourly incentive system. The piece-rate system led to a further increase of 30% in productivity over that measured during the bonus system. The hourly condition was least likely to prevent boredom within each shift while the piece-rate system was associated with a progressive decline in work due to fatigue. The greatest amount of time lost through absence from work was recorded during the hourly and piece-rate systems, respectively. Observational ratings of the employee's behavior suggested that the piece-rate system stimulated competition and other objectionable forms of behavior, whereas friendly relations characterized the hourly system. Finally, the workers' opinions indicated greater dissatisfaction with the hourly and bonus systems. On the other hand, the piece-rate system was considered fair in that rewards were directly proportional to an individual's work output.

Pierce and Risley (1974) investigated a form of piece-rate payment with seven adolescent recreation aides using a single-subject design. The aides were initially given job descriptions which specified where each worker should be, what task was to be completed, and by when it should be completed. In the second phase, the aides were threatened with the loss of their jobs if no improvements were observed. Next, they were informed that payment would be based on the percentage of daily tasks actually completed. A short reversal involving a return to the full pay hourly condition was programmed in the fourth phase. Finally, in the last phase, the employees were again paid according to the percentage of tasks completed.

The overall results indicated that between 50 and 75% of the tasks were completed when the aides were given job descriptions. Threats to fire the aides resulted in some improvement, but for three of the aides these were only temporary. When pay was given contingently upon the percentage of tasks completed, the aides completed near 100% of their work tasks. The introduction of the full pay condition resulted in the completion of about 35% of the tasks. Performance rose immediately when pay was again given contingently upon task completion.

A further study compared both individual and group piece-rate payment systems with hourly payment (Saad & Barling, 1977). The participants were 33 students in a training college for the clothing industry. Each was employed to sew skirts in a textile factory after assignment to one of the following groups (1) FI (hourly – $1.10); (2) FR1 (individual incentive – 50¢ per hour and 50¢ bonus for each adequate skirt completed); (3) FR1 (three-person group incentive – 50¢ per hour and 50¢ for the group for each skirt completed).

Output was measured in terms of the number of units produced. The figures for the hourly condition and the individual and group conditions were 9.61, 12.17, and 13.22, respectively. The differences between the hourly and both incentive conditions were statistically significant, though no significant differences existed between the individual and group conditions. Additionally, the authors suggest that the group incentive condition eliminated some of the difficulties associated with individual incentive conditions (Lawler, 1973).

It appears quite clear from the results of extensive surveys and both early and recent work-setting applications that considerable increments in productivity occur when pay is delivered according to a CRF (FR1 or piece-rate) rather than an FI (hourly rate) schedule. Tying pay to performance by specifying a contingent relationship between specific units of output and reinforcement is a consistently well-documented and effective means of motivating workers. The research conducted by Wyatt (1934) is especially noteworthy in illustrating this conclusion.

Recent research also sheds light on additional variables which might be considered in the design of financial incentive systems. For example, Pierce and Risley (1974) demonstrated the relative inefficacy of job descriptions and threats of the loss of one's job in boosting productivity, which may frequently be employed by management. Saad and Barling (1977) found that individual and group CRF schedules resulted in comparable increases in performance when compared to an hourly payment schedule. The latter finding is in line with the data reported by Farr (1976) in providing preliminary evidence of the utility of group CRF (i.e., FR1) contingencies.

SUMMARY AND CONCLUSIONS

The application of reinforcement schedules to work-related performance reflects an interest that has only recently been investigated. This may account for the rather limited aspects of schedule-controlled behavior studied in most of the research. For example, one of the major concerns of applied researchers has been to extend the laboratory findings documenting the power of an intermittent schedule in maintaining behavior when compared to a CRF schedule (Reynolds, 1968). The question has been raised, is an intermittent (e.g., VR) schedule more effective than a CRF schedule in maintaining performance? The studies reviewed here show these two schedules to be functionally similar with simulated work tasks, while the CRF schedule has proven somewhat more effective in improving and maintaining performance with actual work tasks. This functional similarity of the VR and CRF schedules has also been pointed out by Pritchard et al. (1980). However, they explain this equivalence as being due to the inferiority of the VR schedule in applied settings since a clear superiority of intermittent schedules in maintaining performance was expected.

Alternative explanations for this unexpected equivalence can be raised, one of which may lie in the schedule requirements that have been examined. Specifically, the choice of values for a VR schedule has typically been too low to generate the high response rates and maintenance characteristic of the schedule (Ferster & Skinner, 1957). An intermittent schedule requires that responses go unreinforced which results in decrements in performance and satisfaction when the schedule is imposed. This undesireable feature of intermittent schedules has been obviated in the work setting by using low values so that periods of nonreinforcement cannot be easily discriminated.

Differences in the amount of task experience may also influence productivity. A worker having little familiarity with a work task and requiring considerable time to acquire the skills necessary for mastery of the task would not be expected to show improvements on a VR schedule. On the other hand, when the task can be quickly mastered by the worker, improvements should be found under the VR schedule. Studies reporting the superiority of the CRF schedule (Yukl & Latham, 1974; Yukl et al., 1976) have employed tasks which were novel to the workers and required much time for learning. Moreover, the operant literature suggests that the behavioral requirement for reinforcement should be systematically increased so that the worker is accustomed to working under periods of nonreinforcement. The use of this shaping procedure is of particular importance in facilitating maintained responding when the worker is unfamiliar with the task.

The relative superiority of CRF with actual work tasks seems related to issues that are of a pragmatic nature. An intermittent schedule would be very difficult to implement in an applied setting because of the uncertainty associated with the delivery of reinforcement. The worker is not able to predict the availability of reinforcement on the basis of the amount of work he has completed. For example, being told that reinforcement would be available every nine items, on the average, does not inform the worker of the range of values or the behavioral requirement for the next reinforcer. This unpredictability of reinforcement as an undesirable aspect of the implementation of intermittent schedules has been reported by workers in a study reviewed here (Yukl et al., 1976).

Furthermore, if a worker were informed of the range of values for reinforcement on a VR schedule, for example, between 1 and 19 items on VR10, he would probably request that his payment be delivered for every 10 items. Of course, if one granted his request, the schedule would no longer be a VR, but rather a straight FR (FR10). A methodological procedure that avoids fixing the schedule values for reinforcement consists of providing bonus payment on the basis of guessing of color of a marble or the outcome of a coin toss (Yukl & Latham, 1974; Yukl et al., 1976; Latham & Dossett, 1978). By using a quasi-gambling schedule of payment which appears to have face validity to the worker, applied investigators have further circumvented the difficulties associated with a VR schedule. In the animal laboratory, however, such a procedure does not have its counterpart. There the experimenter simply determines *a priori* the values of the VR schedule to which the subject will be exposed, and then gradually increases the behavioral requirements of the schedule to avoid the effects of abrupt periods of nonreinforcement.

Finally, as noted in the introduction, an intermittent schedule may specify the delivery of reinforcement following the completion of a fixed or variable number of responses (Ferster et al., 1975). The majority of studies reported in the literature have investigated VR schedules, while only a few studies have examined the effects of a low value FR schedule (Pritchard et al., 1976, 1980). Since the latter studies found the FR and VR schedules to be comparable in improving worker productivity, it would appear desirable to compare worker performance under CRF and low FR schedules. Use of the FR schedule may eliminate the problem of reinforcer availability associated with the VR schedule as well as the practical difficulty involved in its implementation, while capitalizing on the fact that reinforcement is still delivered on an intermittent basis.

The studies reviewed in this paper also bear upon another question regarding the use of reinforcement schedules: Is a CRF (i.e., FR1 or piece-rate) more effective than an attendance based (i.e., hourly) FI schedule in maintaining performance? A host of experimental work from both analogue and actual work tasks consistently points to the relative superiority of a payment system based on a specific piece-rate requirement. In particular, studies have demonstrated significant improvements in productivity and task satisfaction when a CRF reinforcement schedule has been implemented following the use of a salary-based FI schedule. Furthermore, changeover from a CRF to a salary-based FI schedule of payment has resulted in decreases in productivity. These schedule effects in the work setting parallel those found in the experimental operant laboratory indicating a higher level of response for CRF (FR1) schedules (Reese, 1966; Reynolds, 1968), highlighting the superiority of ratio over interval schedules. The answer to the above question, therefore, is in the affirmative.

A final issue which was partly addressed in this paper concerns the relative effectiveness of individual versus group contingencies in maintaining performance. While this is probably one of the more important and contemporary questions regarding schedule applications to work settings, there were only three studies that addressed this issue. Given the limited results reviewed here, one can conclude that payment based on performance of a small group of workers (e.g., three to five) leads to a higher output than payment based on performance of a large group (e.g., 100 workers). Furthermore, when the behavioral requirement for reinforcement is identical for a small group of workers as it is for a single individual, their level of work output is comparable. This conclusion must be tempered by the fact that only a few studies have investigated the relative effectiveness of group mediated contingencies. Still, it appears that the employment of a group contingency may prove advantageous in facilitating worker performance while concomitantly neutralizing some of the negative side effects associated with traditional individual incentive plans (Lawler, 1973).

BUSINESS AND INDUSTRIAL APPLICATIONS: A LOOK TO THE FUTURE

The studies reviewed here suggest that FR and VR schedules of reinforcement may prove beneficial when properly employed in the work arena. It is to be noted that the powerful controlling properties of the chosen values were such that the performances under each schedule were comparable, despite obvious differences among studies in experimental tasks, level of difficulty and experience with the task, duration of exposure, worker characteristics, as well as form of payment. Therefore, the well documented schedule equivalence found in these studies represents a highly robust phenomenon. The following recommendations are directly derived from an analysis and review of the current literature:

1. It would appear desirable to tie pay or the delivery of other reinforcers to performance. While simple piece-rate payment may not suffice as the sole means by which workers are paid, making reinforcement contingent upon performance, to some extent, would increase productivity relative to that found with simple hourly payment.
2. Both CRF and VR schedules can be employed to enhance productivity relative to that found with an hourly payment schedule only. At low values (e.g., 2-4), the VR schedule may result in equivalent levels of performance as found with CRF, though at times the CRF schedule is shown to be more effective. When little time is required for learning the task, the VR schedule can be directly applied and may be preferable to CRF because it is less time-consuming and expensive. If considerable learning is required, the CRF schedule may be preferable because it facilitates response acquisition and eliminates the unpredictability of reinforcement found with the VR schedule. It may then be advantageous to gradually shift the requirements for reinforcement to approximate those of a low VR schedule.
3. Whenever possible, the establishment of an individual payment system based on the performance of a small group of workers (e.g., 3-5) may be a feasible means of facilitating productivity. Such an arrangement may improve group cohesion and on-task behavior while removing many of the problems associated with straightforward individually-based incentive plans.
4. When using an intermittent schedule in which the values permit long periods of nonreinforcement (i.e., with high schedule requirements), every effort must be made to explicate the conditions under which payment can take place. Workers should be informed of the relationship between their performance and the delivery of reinforcement to prevent a disruption in the level of productivity due to the intermittency of reinforcement. This is an expedient means of facilitating maintenance and one which easily makes contact with the worker's repertoire. In point of fact, the studies reviewed here have varied significantly in the extent to which workers have been informed of the relationship be-

tween their performance and reinforcer availability. This suggests that some workers were more adequately prepared to continue working in the face of nonreinforcement than others. It is to be noted that Latham and Dossett (1978) were keenly aware of the imminent cessation of work performance when placed on an intermittent schedule. They cleverly minimized the effects of nonreinforcement (e.g., reduced responding) by formally and explicitly stating the relationship between the amount of work required for reinforcement.

5. Preliminary evidence suggests that the implementation of low value FR schedules may improve response maintenance relative to that found with payment based on an hourly rate. Furthermore, the FR schedule specifies the delivery of reinforcement on a more predictable basis than the VR schedule.

In sum, the issue of the vaunted superiority of intermittent schedules over CRF awaits further experimentation in the applied setting. The greatest limitation in so doing may be found in the unsuitability of a method of payment that is based on keeping the worker uninformed as to when reinforcement (e.g., pay) is to occur. This difficulty may be obviated by using low value FR schedules. Future research is required to further investigate the differential effects of CRF, FR, and VR schedules in the work setting if this area of interest is to reach fruitful application.

REFERENCES

Aldis, O. Of pigeons and men. *Harvard Business Review*, 1961, July-August, 59-63.

At Emery Air Freight: Positive reinforcement boosts performance. *Organizational Dynamics*, Winter 1973, 41-50.

Ayllon, T., & Carlson, R. Instilling responsibility through incentives. *World Trade Journal*, 1973, **1**, 41-42.

Beatty, R., & Schneier, C. A case for positive reinforcement. *Business Horizons*, April 1975, 57-66.

Beech, H. Learning: Cause and cure. In C. L. Cooper & R. Payne (Eds.), *Stress at work*, London: Wiley, 1978.

Berger, C., Cummings, L., & Henemen, H. Expectancy theory and operant conditioning predictions of performance under variable ratio and continuous schedules of reinforcement. *Organizational Behavior and Human Performance*, 1975, **14**, 227-243.

Bijou, S., & Baer, D. Operant methods in child behavior and development. In W. K. Honig (Ed.), *Operant behavior: Areas of research and application*. New York: Appleton-Century-Crofts, 1966.

Burnett, F. An experimental investigation into repetitive work. Industrial Fatigue Research Board, Report No. 30, H. M. Stationery Office, London, 1925.

Cherrington, D., Reitz, H., & Scott, W. Effects of contingent and non-contingent reward on the relationship between satisfaction and task performance. *Journal of Applied Psychology*, 1971, **55**, 531-536.

Connellan, T. *How to improve human performance: Behaviorism in business and industry*. New York: Harper and Row, 1978

Conversation with B. F. Skinner. *Organizational Dynamics*, 1973, **1**, 31-40.

Dale, R. Wage incentives and productivity. *Personnel*, 1959, **36**, 4-5.

Deslauriers, B., & Everett, P. Effects of intermittent and continuous token reinforcement on bus ridership. *Journal of Applied Psychology*, 1977, **62**, 369-375.

Farr, J. Incentive schedules, productivity, and satisfaction in work groups: A laboratory study. *Organizational Behavior and Human Performance*, 1976, **17**, 159-170.

Ferster, C., & Skinner, B. *Schedules of reinforcement*. Appleton-Century-Crofts, 1957.

Ferster, C., Culbertson, S., & Perrott-Boren, M. *Behavior principles*, (2nd ed.) New York: Prentice-Hall, Inc., 1975.

Hamner, W. Reinforcement theory and contingency management in organizational settings. In H. Tosi & W. Hamner (Eds.), *Organizational behavior and management: A contingency approach*. Chicago: St. Clair Press, 1974.

Hampton, D. *Behavioral concepts in management*. Belmont, Calif.: Wadsworth Publishing Co., 1978.

Hermann, J., de Montes, A., Dominquez, B., Montes, F., & Hopkins, B. Effects of bonuses for punctuality on the tardiness of industrial workers. *Journal of Applied Behavior Analysis*, 1973, **6**, 563-570.

Hutchinson, R., & Azrin, N. Conditioning of mental hospital patients to fixed ratio schedules of reinforcement. *Journal of the Experimental Analysis of Behavior*, 1961, **4**, 87-95.

Jacques, E., Rice, A., & Hill, J. The social and psychological impact of a change in method of wage payment. *Human Relations*, 1951, **4**, 315-340.

Journal of Organizational Behavior Management. Behavioral Systems, Inc., Atlanta, Ga.

Kazdin, A. Methodology of applied behavior analysis. In T. Brigham & A. C. Catania (Eds.), *Handbook of applied behavior research: Social and instructional processes*. New York: Irvington Press/Halstead Press, 1977.

Krasner, L. Behavior therapy. In P. Mussen & M. Rosenzweig (Eds.), *Annual Review of Psychology*. Palo Alto, California: Annual Reviews, 1971.

Latham, G. P., & Dossett, D. L. Designing incentive plans for unionized employees: A comparison of continuous and variable ratio reinforcement schedules. *Personnel Psychology*, 1978, **31**, 47-62.

Lawler, E. *Pay and organizational effectiveness: A psychological view*. New York: McGraw-Hill, 1971.

Lawler, E. *Motivation in work organizations*. Monterey, California: Brooks/Cole Publishing Company, 1973.

Luthans, F. *Organizational behavior*. McGraw-Hill, 1973.

Luthans, F., & Kreitner, R. *Organizational behavior modification*. Glenview, Illinois: Scott, Foresman and Company, 1975.

McCormick, E., & Ilgen, D. *Industrial psychology*, Englewood Cliffs, N.J.: Prentice-Hall, Inc., 1980.

Miller, L. *Behavior management: The new science of managing people at work*. New York: John Wiley & Sons, 1978.

Nord, Beyond the teaching machine: The neglected art of operant conditioning in the theory and practice of management. *Organizational Behavior and Human Performance*, 1969, **4**, 375-401.

Pedalino, E., & Gamboa, V. Behavior modification and absenteeism: Intervention in one industrial setting. *Journal of Applied Psychology*, 1974, **59**, 694-698.

Pierce, C., & Risley, T. Improving job performance of neighborhood youth corps aides in an urban recreation program. *Journal of Applied Behavior Analysis*, 1974, **7**, 207-215.

Porter, L. Turning work into non-work: The rewarding environment. In M. Dunnette (Ed.), *Work and non-work in the year 2001*. Monterey, California: Brooks/Cole Publishing Company, 1973.

Pritchard, R., Leonard, D., Von Bergen, C., & Kirk, R. The effects of varying schedules of reinforcement on human task performance. *Organizational Behavior and Human Performance*, 1976, **16**, 205-230.

Pritchard, R., Hollenback, J., & DeLeo, P. The effects of continuous and partial schedules of reinforcement on effort, performance, and satisfaction. *Organizational Behavior and Human Performance*, 1980, **25**, 336-353.

Redd, W., Porterfield, A., & Anderson, B. *Behavior modification: behavioral approaches to human problems*. New York: Random House, 1979.

Reese, E. *The analysis of human operant behavior*. Dubuque, Iowa: Brown, 1966.

Reynolds, G. *A primer of operant conditioning*. Glenview, Illinois: Scott, Foresman and Company, 1968.

Roethlisberger, F., & Dickson, W. *Management and the worker*. Cambridge, Mass.: Harvard University Press, 1939.

Rothe, H. Output rates among welders. *Journal of Applied Psychology*, 1970, **54**, 549-551.

Saad, L., & Barling, J. Relating pay incentives to work performance: Effects of fixed ratio (group and individual contingent) versus fixed interval reinforcement in industry. *Psychologia Africana*, 1977, **17,** 135-142.

Skinner, B. *The behavior of organisms: An experimental approach.* New York: Appleton-Century-Crofts, 1938.

Skinner, B. *Science and human behavior.* New York: The Free Press, 1953.

Skinner, B. *Contingencies of reinforcement: A theoretical analysis.* New York: Appleton-Century-Crofts, 1969.

Sulzer, B., & Mayer, G. *Behavior modification procedures for school personnel.* New York: Holt, Rinehart & Winston, 1972.

Terborg, J., & Miller, H. Motivation, behavior and performance: A closer examination of goal setting and monetary incentives. *Journal of Applied Psychology*, 1978, **63,** 29-39.

Viteles, M. Motivation and morale in industry. New York: W. W. Norton & Company, 1953.

Where Skinner's theories work. *Business Week*, 2 December 1972, 64-65.

Wyatt, S. Incentives in repetitive work: A practical experiment in a factory. Industrial Health Research Board, Report No. 69, H. M. Stationery Office, London, 1934.

Yukl, G., & Latham, G. Consequences of reinforcement schedules and incentive magnitudes for employee performance: problems encountered in an industrial setting. *Journal of Applied Psychology,* 1974, **60,** 294-298.

Yukl, G., Wexley, K., & Seymore, J. Effectiveness of pay incentives under variable ratio and continuous reinforcement schedules. *Journal of Applied Psychology*, 1972, **56,** 19-23.

Yukl, G., Latham, G., & Pursell, E. The effectiveness of performance incentives under continuous and variable ratio schedules of reinforcement. *Personnel Psychology*, 1976, **29,** 221-231.

Zeiler, M. Schedules of reinforcement: The controlling variables. In W. Honig & J. Staddon (Eds.), *Handbook of operant behavior.* New York: Prentice-Hall, 1977.

3

Performance Measurement and Evaluation

Alyce M. Dickinson   and   **Richard M. O'Brien**
New York State Office   *Hofstra University*
of Court Administration

People are working hard. Yet productivity in both the private and public sectors continues to decrease (Fabricant, 1981). Attempts to improve productivity must be based on accurate and reliable indices of performance (Mark, 1981). While all agree on the need for accurate measures, there remains much controversy surrounding how to identify critical work productivity behaviors and how they should be assessed (Feeney, 1980; Siegel, 1980; Sokolik, 1967; Teel, 1980). Managers, when faced with the dilemma of performance measurement, encounter the same questions that a good news reporter must answer – who, what, where, when, and how (Newman & Hinrichs, 1980).

WHAT TO MEASURE

Since organizations are such complex systems, the initial question that a manager must resolve is what to measure, or in other words he[*] must identify the critical accomplishments. Currently, industrial evaluations most often rely on direct measures of output or on performance appraisal rating scales (Landy & Farr, 1980). Direct measures of output while quantifiable, often reflect factors outside the control of the employee. For example, the number of merchandising demonstrations that a sales representative completes will depend, among other things, upon the sales territory, the number and types of stores he can contact, the distances he must travel, the nature of competition he must face, and the relative amount of advertising his own firm has done in comparison to their competitors. Similarly, the quality and quantity of output by the assembly line worker will depend on the speed of the assembly line belt and the quality of parts coming to him on the line. Even in those situations where outcomes adequately reflect performance, these measures tell you little about what behaviors to encourage. It is nice to know that Sue makes 200 more widgets an hour than Phil does, but if you want to increase Phil's productivity you have to know what behaviors actually differ between him and Sue. The managers who talk about born salesmen or natural workers are those who have nothing but outcome measures and therefore no way of teaching how to improve sales or productivity.

Outcome measures are at best incomplete and at worst misleading. But you can't do without them. They must be supplemented, not replaced. The last thing that you want are sales representatives being rewarded for their great interpersonal skills, even though they don't make many sales. Outcome measures suggest who is doing the job correctly, but you must measure behaviors in order to ascertain what the appropriate activity is.

---

[*]The pronouns he and his are used throughout this article in a generic sense only for the sake of readability.

Many employers have not relied on either behavioral or outcome measures. Instead they have subjectively evaluated their workers, particularly when the workers were not directly involved in hands-on production. In the "evaluation scheme" the supervisor rates the employee on his performance. Typical performance appraisal rating forms are based on the measurement of personality traits or characteristics such as initiative and judgement. Supervisors rate these traits according to a numerical rating scale, with five to seven scale points. Evaluation systems based on the measurement of these characteristics have generally not been very satisfactory (Cummings & Schwab, 1973; McMillan & Dorel, 1980; Yager, 1981). These traditional evaluation forms were constructed to apply to everyone, regardless of the type of job. It is virtually impossible, however, to link these employee traits to particular job responsibilities or achievements, and as a consequence it is hard to justify or substantiate the evaluations.

Further, employee characteristics are vague and ambiguous, causing supervisors to disagree on their meaning. For example, one supervisor may define a "good attitude" much differently than another supervisor. Because of this, evaluations of employee characteristics tend to differ from supervisor to supervisor. Employees, after being evaluated in such a manner, do not have a clear understanding of what is expected of them; they only know what a supervisor "thinks" about them. To improve performance, employees must know what they are expected to do in concrete terms and how well they are currently doing it. A good performance evaluation measures specifically what it is designed to measure – work performance.

In an attempt to reduce the subjectiveness of ratings, researchers began to include observable work behaviors on the evaluation forms in the place of personality traits (Barrett, 1966; Dunnette, 1966; Campbell, Dunnette, Lawler & Weick, 1970). Since job behaviors are more readily observed than personality traits, it was assumed that the evaluators would rate employees more consistently and accurately. When the measures obtained from these behavior-based forms were found to be subject to the same kinds of rater biases associated with personality measures (i.e., leniency, halo, strictness, central tendency) attempts were made to increase rater agreement with regard to the scale points (Smith & Kendall, 1963). Behavioral anchors were affixed to the scale points and the numerical rating points were eliminated. Despite the intuitive appeal of behaviorally anchored rating scales, researchers have found little evidence that they do in fact reduce rating biases, leniency, halo or strictness associated with the more global rating forms (Burnaska & Hollman, 1974; Dickinson & Zellinger, 1980; Hakel, 1971; Kingstrom & Bass, 1981; Landy & Guion, 1970; Zedeck & Baker, 1971). The behaviorally based rating scale is the off spring of the marriage of outcomes and behavioral assessment that would be denied by both parents. The problem may lie in the rating scale format itself, not in the form of the items.

Behaviorally anchored performance rating scales should not be confused with direct behavior measures. Behavioral measures offer many advantages. Performance is defined in terms of what an employee does in quantifiable terms. Information is specific. Knowledge of results, or feedback, has long been shown as a necessary component for learning or performance improvement (Ammons, 1956). Further, in order for feedback to be effective it must be specific, immediate, and continuous (Kirby, 1980; Simek & O'Brien, 1978).

Two major advantages of behavioral measures are that they minimize the influence of the judgement of the rater by providing operational definitions of performance and assessments scheduled at frequent intervals (Komaki, Collins, and Thoene, 1980). Rather than focusing only on end-results, behavioral indices indicate what an individual must do to achieve those ends. One fault in management by objectives is the lack of specific paths to the goals. Many MBO failures can be attributed to three things. First is the failure to set realistic objectives or objectives based on current production. Feeney (Performance Audit, 1972) has suggested that in the absence of objective measurement, 90% of employees will overestimate their performance or the performance of others. This is of particular importance if MBO objectives are being set in the absence of objective measurement, even though employees participate in the goal-setting. A second reason is the failure to provide sufficient and timely information to an employee as to how he is progressing toward the objectives. The third reason is the failure to provide the employee with guidelines for attaining those objectives. Telling a sales representative that his sales quota should be $120,000 does not indicate how the sales representative must change or alter performance. Augmenting MBO with feedback and incentives is becoming increasingly common (Pack & Vicars, 1979).

There are two overriding concerns when pinpointing crucial work productivity behaviors. First, what behaviors if improved will result in an economic payoff to the organization, and second, which critical behaviors offer the most potential for improvement? This potential for improvement or PIP, as Gilbert (1978) has called it, is central to the assessment process. It is the only way to distinguish those behaviors that require intervention from those that either offer little room for improvement or are of little relevance to organizational objectives, even though they may be rather poorly executed. As Ed Feeney has stated it, "Any organization tends to react to situations that are irritants but doing something about them may or may not have a payoff [New Tool "Reinforcement," 1971]." Before charging into an organization equipped with behavior change techniques we must first determine if what we are changing will be worthwhile. In his book *Human Competence*, Gilbert (1978) describes a system for pinpointing areas that could yield significant organizational payoffs if performance improved. He calls this system a stakes analysis which consists of the following steps: (1) Identifying the major accomplishments of the organization; (2) Obtaining quantifiable measures of those accomplishments; (3) Determining appropriate units of measures; (4) Figuring out the areas of the organization with the greatest potential for improvement; (5) Identifying ways to improve performance; and (6) Determining the stakes or economic payoffs of alternative solutions.

Perhaps the best documented example of where this performance audit was successfully applied is Emery Air Freight. After introducing several successful behavioral programs at Emery, Ed Feeney was faced with the problem of identifying the next area for improvement (New Tool "Reinforcement," 1971). After conducting a performance audit, Feeney discovered that the most fruitful area of concern was Emery's containerization operation. Emery's largest single expenditure was air freight. Since the airlines charge less to transport one large container than several small packages, the full utilization of containers could cut shipping costs significantly. While Emery's management believed that containers were being used 90% of the time that they could be used, Feeney's performance audit revealed that containers were being used only 45% of the time. Feeney introduced a checklist on which each employee recorded container utilization and trained supervisors to reinforce performance increases using praise and recognition. Through the combined use of behavioral measures and positive reinforcement container utilization increased from 45% to over 90%. Performance remained at that level over a two year period with cost savings to Emery of $650,000 a year.

Finding the critical work productivity behaviors suggests a direction for the precise interventions that are likely to impact the problem. The performance audit concept of Gilbert (1978) and Feeney (Performance Audit, 1972) which contrasts the best performance with the average performance in order to identify the performance improvement potential is an excellent strategy for uncovering the intervention that is likely to have the best bottom-line effects.

Once the program goal has been identified, measurement should change from outcome to process. Luthans and Kreitner (1975) suggest a functional analysis based on the three-term contingency of *antecedents*, *behaviors* and, most importantly, *consequences*. This model allows for the identification of the conditions present when the behavior occurs as well as providing data for an analysis of what happens to the worker when he makes the response. Since intervention is most likely to occur in the form of altered consequences or modification of the stimulus conditions under which the response occurs, a functional analysis identifies the most important variables to monitor when beginning any intervention. It also provides a baseline behavior measurement to contrast to intervention periods.

One final note on what to measure, Gilbert (1978) has justly criticized industrial behavior modifiers for ignoring potential sources of performance deficiency that lie outside the behavior of the employee or the consequences of that behavior. The wood carver who is doing poor work may not be getting adequate feedback or reinforcement, but he may also simply have dull tools. While it is possible to go the long way around and suggest that it is impossible for the wood carver to get reinforced with dull tools so his poor performance is essentially an extinction phenomenon, it is certainly more direct to identify the conditions that must be present for the individual to make the appropriate response and intervene to obtain those conditions.

WHO SHOULD MEASURE

Once a target behavior has been identified and accurate measures developed, the manager must decide who should do the measuring and who should receive the information. Since performance must be measured regularly, the supervisor and the employee are the individuals with the best access to the job information. Having the employees keep track of their own performance has some advantages. If the employee is to improve performance, he is the one who must receive the data. Further, feedback is most effective when it is presented immediately. Again, immediacy is inherent in self-recording.

The main disadvantage of employee self-recording is the possibility that the employees will alter the data to their benefit. Managers can encourage accurate self-recording by reinforcing employees for recording the data regularly and accurately. It is essential that employees are not criticized or otherwise punished for the performance that is reported or self reports will be doctored to avoid negative consequences. For example, in one instance at Emery Air Freight, an employee displayed no performance improvement. Instead of criticizing the employee, the supervisor responded, "At least you've recorded your performance honestly [New Tool "Reinforcement," 1971]." Perhaps the "at least" could have been left out, but in any case the employee was not put in a position of having to carry out an oral defense of his performance. It is important that supervisors learn to pick out the good things an employee is doing and reward such behavior even when performance is substandard. The perfect response is a two stage answer that rewards accomplishments and sets small goals for the future. Thus when a manager fails to get a report on sales calls for the month, his ideal reaction might be, "I'm glad you've been thinking about that information. Do you think you could get the first week's data to me by next Friday?" He has rewarded the smallest of steps and set an intermediate goal. Unfortunately most managers would have found nothing to reward and a long monologue of the sales representative's deficiencies would have followed.

When employees are recording their own performance, corroborative independent observations should be recorded at frequent intervals. This task usually falls to the supervisors. Supervisors may actually record employee behaviors while observing performance or compare the employee's records with direct output or performance accomplishments. Not only is this check required to evaluate the accuracy of the data, but employees will be more likely to report the data accurately, knowing that their supervisor will pick up data discrepencies (Andrasik, Heimberg, & McNamara, in press).

Some individuals may contend that the supervisors themselves cannot be objective observers since if their employees look good, they look good, and vice versa. These individuals may propose that observers be employed who are from outside the organization. While one cannot dispute the objectivity of outside observers, it simply isn't feasible to bring in outside individuals for extended periods of time. As Komaki, Collins and Thoene (1980) point out the relative biases of employers, supervisors, and outside observers have not been systematically investigated. They suggest that the organizational contingencies, specifically the way in which the information is used, are likely to determine measurement accuracy: employees who are punished if the data look bad may fudge the data. This occurs not because they are employees, but because they wish to avoid negative contingencies.

Regardless of who records the data, there is one cardinal rule with regard to who receives it: the data *must* go to the employees who do the work. While this sounds obvious, it is difficult to find an organization that doesn't have some example of performance data that never reaches the performer. Recently the authors became involved in a project to improve the quality of reports written by professional level staff in a government organization. The director of the department believed that the reports could be significantly improved. He estimated that a large number of reports were being returned to the staff for rework. Discussions with the staff revealed that they were unaware of the director's dissatisfaction with the reports and stated that reports were seldom returned. The staff further maintained that when the reports were returned, they were returned because of a shift in agency policy, not something that the staff could control. Upon closer examination, it was discovered that the director would "sign off" on the reports even though he believed that they could be improved. He would speak to the manager of the department about his concerns, but this information would rarely filter down to the staff. Since most of the reports were in fact approved, the staff naturally assumed that the quality was acceptable. The point is, if the employee does not get adequate feedback, performance cannot be improved since he does not even know that improvement is required.

Besides the employee doing the work, the data should be disseminated to all relevant levels of the organization with managers in each successive level rewarding the individual who reports to them. Supervisory behavior is just as influenced by performance contingencies as employee behavior. If appropriate behavior is reinforced, it will increase; if appropriate behavior is ignored or punished, it will disappear.

WHEN TO MEASURE

Thus far we have addressed the issues of what should be measured, who should measure the performance, and who should receive the performance information. The next issue that must be addressed is when performance measurements should be taken. Ideally, behavior should be measured when it occurs, or in other words, all the time. Performance data must be accurate since they will be used to evaluate the effectiveness of any intervention and will also provide feedback to employees regarding their performance. Very often performance varies on different days, at different times throughout the day and/or during different times of the year. Measurement systems must be sensitive to performance fluctuations if they exist. Otherwise these performance trends may obfuscate performance increases or, on the other hand, be mistaken for improvements due to intervention when they are actually due to other factors. While some behaviors lend themselves to continuous measurement, others may not. Even when employee behaviors do lend themselves to continuous measurement, it may not be possible due to organizational constraints. Behavior managers may select one of several basic methods of measurement. Before initiating a project or organizational change program the behavior manager should consider all these methods, choosing the one that is most appropriate for the type of behavior and the organizational setting.

Perhaps the most commonly used method of measurement in industrial settings is outcome measurement. In outcome measurement the results or products of behaviors are recorded rather than the behaviors themselves. Examples of outcome measures include the number of pages typed at the end of the day, the number of widgets assembled at the end of the day, and annual sales volume.

Some organizations have reams of computer printouts containing outcome measures. But data is not necessarily information, and therein lies the problem with outcome measures. Outcome measures usually fall prey to the pitfalls associated with end-result indices that were previously discussed: they often fail to reflect individual performance; they are affected by events outside the control of the employee; they fail to provide sufficient and timely feedback to the employee; and they fail to specify the behaviors that must occur in order to attain the end results. When using outcome measures, behavior managers must take care to avoid these problems. Outcome measures are extremely useful in identifying performance deficiencies but usually must be supplemented with behavioral measures.

Event sampling involves counting discrete events of short duration over a certain period of time. Discrete events have a recognizable beginning and end. Event sampling can be categorized as a continuous recording method since the observer measures the behavior when it occurs, each time it occurs. Event sampling is usually most appropriate for low frequency behaviors such as the number of sales calls made in a day, the number of papers filed within an hour, or the number of times that a supervisor criticizes or berates a subordinate.

Duration sampling is similar to event sampling in that the observer records the behavior when it occurs, each time that it occurs. The difference is the emphasis: the length of behavior is important in duration sampling, not just the number of times it occurs. The observer can note how long the behavior lasts using a stopwatch. Duration sampling may be appropriate if a behavior manager wishes to determine the amount of time that an employee spends wandering around the office each time he leaves his desk, the amount of time employees spend hovering around the coffee machine, or the length of time from when the employee arrives to work to when he begins working.

A fourth type of measurement sampling is interval sampling. In interval sampling the measurement period is divided into short consecutive segments of time and the observer records whether or not the behavior occurs within that time segment. Only one behavior occurrence is recorded regardless of the actual number of times it occurs during the interval. Depending on the frequency of the behavior and the precision which the behavior manager desires, the intervals can range from 10 seconds to 15 minutes. Ten-second intervals provide more precise data but in many cases may be rather pointless. For instance, the number of times a person initiates a conversation with a coworker can be just as accurately measured with 5-minute intervals as with 10-second intervals since once conversation has been initiated it usually lasts longer than 10 seconds. Supervisors generally do not have the time for this type of recording, but outside observers or employees can easily be taught this method of measurement. Interval recording as a general rule is useful for behaviors that occur once or more every 15 minutes. Data is reported not by counting the number of times the behavior occurs but by determining the percentage of intervals in which the behavior occurs.

Time sampling is similar to interval sampling in that observation periods are divided into time segments. In time sampling, however, the observer records whether or not the behavior is occurring at a specified time at the end of the interval. This method is useful for behaviors that occur frequently.

If continuous recording is impractical, variations of the interval and time sampling methods may be employed. After dividing the observation period into discrete time segments, the behavior manager may randomly select intervals during which measurement will be taken. For instance, when employing a time sampling procedure, a 9 A.M. to 5 P.M. work day may be divided into 32 fifteen-minute intervals, and behavior may be measured at the end of the second, fifth, sixth, ninth, thirteenth, fifteenth, twenty-first, twenty-sixth, twenty-seventh, and thirty-second intervals. When employing this type of sampling it is important to insure that the intervals during which behavior is recorded are truly representative of the work day or work week. That is, behavior should be measured on different days, during mornings and afternoons, and at different times throughout the morning and afternoon.

When selecting one of the measurement methods, behavior managers should consider the performance variable or variables of interest as well as the type of behavior. Gilbert (1978) has conveniently categorized performance variables in terms of quality, quantity, and cost. Quality variables or requirements include accuracy, class, and novelty. Accuracy represents the degree to which an accomplishment matches a standard or model; class, the comparative superiority beyond accuracy; and novelty, the degree to which an accomplishment reflects innovation. Quantity may be measured by rate, timeliness or volume. Rate is the number of accomplishments or behaviors per unit time, such as the number of widgets assembled in an hour; timeliness refers to whether or not an accomplishment or behavior occurs by a certain time; and volume relates to a large amount or bulk that is less sensitive to time than rate, such as sales quotas or number of new customers. The third category, cost, is less relevant when considering the measurement method to employ, but is useful in guiding the selection of the behavior or accomplishment to be examined and is essential for an analysis of the economic benefits of performance improvement. The cost measures include the amount of expenditures for labor including benefits, wages, insurance, materials such as supplies, tools, space and energy, and management, including the internal allocations of general and administrative cost associated with an accomplishment. In certain cases a behavior manager may wish to consider more than one of these variables, for instance rate and quality or timeliness and quality.

A common complaint of supervisors when introduced to the various methods of measurement is that they would be too time consuming and require too much attention. It is easier to rely on the measurement systems designed by personnel offices such as performance appraisals. After all, that's what the personnel staff is paid to do. However, supervisors usually come to accept that the increased accuracy and specificity of job information is well worth the time and effort. Performance appraisals, as Komaki, Collins, and Theone (1980) point out, rely on the assumption that individuals can accurately summarize performance information over long periods of time (3, 6 or even 12 months) into a single index. Most, if not all of us, are simply unable to do that. Choose a behavior and then try to remember how many times you performed that behavior within the past week. More likely than not, your memory will fail you. Yet traditional performance measurement systems rely on this type of memory.

Regardless of the way behavior is measured, observers may err. While we can never be certain that the data are absolutely accurate, steps can be taken to reduce as much doubt as possible. One of the best ways to check the accuracy of measurement is to compare two independent measures of the same behavior. If the data from two independent sources are the same or highly similar we can reasonably assume the data are accurate. This can be accomplished in two basic ways. The first is comparing the employee records to the outcome measures or products. The second is to compare the records of two observers which were taken independently. Behavior analysts refer to this comparison procedure as interobserver agreement. Interobserver agreement is reported in terms of the percentage of agreement and there are several ways to calculate this percentage.

The most desirable form of interobserver agreement is based on a comparison of data collected by two individuals who are observing the behavior at the same time. When either time sampling or interval sampling is used to measure behavior, interobserver agreement is calculated by dividing the number of intervals in which the observers agree by the number of intervals in which the observers disagree, or the total number of intervals. In shorthand; agreements/agreements + disagreements. To obtain a percentage, the resulting answer is multiplied by 100. For example, if two observers measured behavior for ten intervals and their observations agreed for eight of the intervals as follows:

INTERVALS

	1	2	3	4	5	6	7	8	9	10
Observer 1	Yes	Yes	No	No	Yes	Yes	No	Yes	Yes	Yes
Observer 2	Yes	Yes	Yes	No	Yes	Yes	No	No	Yes	Yes

Interobserver agreement would be 80% (8 agreements/8 agreements + 2 disagreements × 100). Interobserver agreement can only be reported in this fashion when both occurrences and nonoccurrences of a behavior are recorded.

This approach is less precise when used to calculate interobserver agreement for event sampling, outcome sampling, and duration sampling. In these measurement methods the behavior (or result) is only recorded when it occurs. To calculate interobserver agreement the same formula is used as with time sampling or interval sampling (A/A + D) using the number of times observers agree that a behavior occurred over the number of times the observers agree that the behavior occurred plus the number of times the observers do not agree the behavior occurred. For example, if one observer recorded that 55 papers had been filed while another observer reported that 60 papers had been filed, interobserver agreement would be 55/60 × 100 or 91.7%. Unfortunately since nonoccurrences are not recorded, one cannot be assured that one observer recorded the same 55 behaviors as the other observer and that disagreement occurred only on 5. Because of this, interobserver agreement based on observations of both occurrences and nonoccurrences is more desirable.

Since outcome measurement does not rely on constant observation, it is relatively easy to design a system so that both the supervisor and employee collect data that can then be used to determine interobserver agreement. However, when employing the various other measurement methods in an industrial environment, it is sometimes very difficult to obtain corroborative information using two independent observers. It is hard to imagine a supervisor constantly following an employee around the office in order to record behavior, or even one employee constantly following around another employee. Such recording techniques would in most cases disrupt the unit's work. It may be entirely feasible, however, to periodically request a supervisor or a fellow employee to collect data and calculate interobserver agreement. The second observer should always observe and record behavior randomly. If the second observer records behavior on the same days or at the same time, the first observer whether it be an outside observer or an employee will quickly learn the schedule and will be likely to measure behavior more accurately during those times.

WHERE TO MEASURE

Just as behavior should be measured when it occurs, behavior should be measured where it occurs: on the job. While it hardly seems necessary to address this issue, there are some organizational members, particularly trainers, who tend to overlook it. Contingencies that control behavior during a weekend training seminar in the Catskills simply differ from contingencies on the job. Since the contingencies differ, the behavior manager would naturally expect performance to differ. Off the job training can be effective particularly if a careful performance analysis indicates the need for such training. But the trainer's job does not end on the last day of training with some sort of measurement of training "effectiveness." Training can only be considered successful to the extent that performance improves at the worksite. Thus, the performance of trainees should be carefully monitored before and after training.

HOW TO MEASURE

In an organizational environment we are concerned with effectiveness – was our performance successful? Organizational behavior management stresses the evaluation of intervention strategies, or accountability. Accountability is demonstrating a cause and effect relationship between the event that was deliberately altered and changes in performance. The notion of accountability separates industrial behavior modification from traditional productivity and motivational theories.

Precise and accurate measurement of behavior is, of course, required for evaluation of the efficacy of intervention strategies. However, accurate measurement in and of itself is not sufficient to demonstrate a cause-effect relationship between altered events and changes in behavior. Work behavior is influenced by numerous factors. In the experimental laboratory, extraneous factors can be controlled or eliminated, but it is impossible to control the multiplicity of factors that exist in an organizational environment. For example, we have little or no control over business cycles, seasons of the year, rate of unemployment, or the numerous social and political organizational interactions. Thus it becomes very important to show that the events which were deliberately altered by the behavior manager caused the change in performance. Indeed, such accountability is required if we expect upper management support to continue and maintain the environmental alterations.

One way to determine if what you have done has been successful is to compare the performance data collected before intervention with the performance data obtained during intervention. This is referred to as a comparison method. This method does not, however, rule out alternative explanations for the change in performance. Some other factors in the environment may have also changed coincidentally with intervention and have been responsible for the changes in performance.

Two basic experimental designs, which rule out alternative explanations, have been frequently used by behavior analysts in applied settings: the reversal design and the multiple baseline design. By using these designs a cause-effect relationship between intervention strategies and performance changes can be established. While there are certainly other designs that serve the same function, the current discussion will be limited to these two commonly used approaches. For a more complete presentation of research strategies and experimental designs, the reader is referred to Johnston and Pennypacker (1980), Campbell and Stanley (1963) and Wolf and Risley (1971).

The reversal design, commonly symbolized ABA, is an extension of the comparison method. As in the comparison method, the data collected prior to intervention during baseline (A) is compared with the data collected during intervention (B). An additional step is added to complete the reversal design. After the intervention strategy has been implemented for a certain period of time, the behavior manager returns to baseline conditions (A) or *reverses* the conditions. If performance improves during intervention then returns to the baseline level during reversal conditions, one can reasonably assume that the intervention strategy was indeed responsible for the performance change. Increased credibility of the effect of the intervention strategy can be gained if the intervention is once again introduced and performance improves. The design with this additional step is symbolized ABAB. On the other hand, if performance improves during the intervention phase (B) and maintains that same level when the baseline conditions are reintroduced, something other than the intervention may have been responsible for the improvement.

There is a basic lesson inherent in the reversal design which managers often neglect. If, indeed, the intervention strategy is responsible for the performance improvement, you cannot abandon the strategies and expect performance to be maintained. Behavior is controlled by its consequences and if those consequences change, behavior will change. If a supervisor or manager tires for any reason of the intervention strategy, Miller (1978) suggests that the behavior manager use this to his advantage. By eliminating the intervention strategies, a reversal design can be achieved. If performance returns to a baseline level, the behavior manager can demonstrate the effectiveness of the intervention and allow the supervisor to make a decision as to whether or not to reinstitute the procedures based on the data.

In organizations it is usually difficult or impractical to return to baseline conditions. If the intervention resulted in, for example, increased employee safety, reversal to conditions that increase the number or probability of accidents would be unethical. Secondly, management is usually content with comparison designs, particularly if the improved performance yields high cost savings. Management may not be as concerned as the behavior modifier in verifying the cause-effect relationship. The philosophy of "if it works, let's stick with it" is prevalent.

In such cases, a multiple baseline design provides a good alternative to the reversal design (Brown, 1980). In a multiple baseline design the same intervention strategy is introduced at different times across different subjects, different behaviors, or different settings.

In a multiple baseline across subjects, the behavior manager would select one behavior which is engaged in by several employees. He would design an intervention to improve that behavior and introduce the intervention strategy to two or more individuals at different times. For example, if you want to increase the number of positive comments made by two supervisors to subordinates, you would as the first step collect baseline data for both supervisors. You would design an intervention strategy, let's say, graphing the number of positive comments to subordinates daily and allowing the supervisor to leave one-half hour early on Fridays when the number of positive comments exceeds a certain level. Baseline data would be collected for Supervisor 1 for 4 weeks with intervention beginning week 5. For Supervisor 2, baseline data would be collected for 8 weeks, with intervention beginning week 9. The data collected during the project may be graphed as indicated in Figure 3.1.

To evaluate the effectiveness of the intervention strategy, you would need to examine three issues. First, was there an increase in the number of positive statements for Supervisor 1 during intervention? Second, did the baseline data for Supervisor 2 remain stable for the entire 8 weeks? Third, was there an increase in the number of positive statements for Supervisor 2 during intervention? If each of these questions can be answered affirmatively, as in

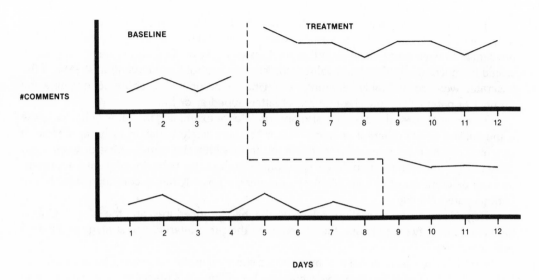

Fig. 3.1. Sample Data from Multiple Baseline Design.

our example, one can reasonably assume that the intervention strategy was responsible for the performance change. On the other hand, if Supervisor 2 increased the number of positive comments during weeks 5 through 8, we could not conclude that the intervention was responsible for the behavior changes exhibited by Supervisor 1. Some coincidental event may have occurred at the same time as intervention which could have accounted for the behavior changes for both supervisors. Similarly, if the baseline remained stable for Supervisor 2 for the entire 8 weeks, but performance did not change during intervention, we could not conclude that the intervention strategy accounted for the performance change exhibited by Supervisor 1.

The multiple baseline design can also be used with the same behavior across different subjects and settings. This variation has been used effectively in two plants of the same company (Kempen & Hall, 1977) and in several similar scientific laboratories (Sulzer-Azaroff, 1978).

Very often in industry, you may be interested in the performance of one individual if only for the reason that the employee may be the only one performing a particular job. Since most jobs are multifaceted, you may be interested in changing a number of behaviors, such as the number of papers filed within one day of receipt and the number of papers retrieved within one day of request. In this example, you would collect baseline data on both behaviors and introduce the same intervention strategy at different points in time. To evaluate the efficacy of the intervention you would examine the same issues presented earlier: Was there an increase in the first behavior to which the intervention was applied, the number of papers filed during the intervention phase? Did the baseline data for the second behavior to which the intervention strategy was applied, the number of papers retrieved, remain stable through the entire baseline period for that behavior? Was there an increase in the number of papers retrieved during intervention?

When evaluating the efficacy of the implementation strategy, one must also consider the differences in the strength of the changes in the two behaviors (Bailey & Bostow, 1979). If large performance changes occur with one behavior and only small changes with the other behavior, the cause-effect relationship must be questioned. For this reason, the baselines of the two targeted behaviors should be as similar as possible to start with. Thus it is important that the behavior manager select two behaviors that initially have approximately the same frequency of occurrence. This can usually be accomplished by identifying two behaviors that are similar to each other, such as in the previous example of filing and retrieving papers. It would be much more difficult to evaluate the effectiveness of the intervention strategy if the baserates were considerably different, which could occur if one chose to examine the number of papers filed and the number of letters typed error-free.

The multiple baseline design is also appropriate for examining the same behavior of the same subject across different settings. This is the least likely variation to be applicable in organizations as most employees perform job tasks within the same setting or work area. Nonetheless, this variation could be appropriate to the sales behavior of a sales representative in different stores or with different customers or possibly refuse collecting behaviors in various parts of a city.

Regardless of the variation selected, the basic procedures are the same. Collect baseline data on two behaviors, then implement the same intervention strategy at different points in time.

It is probably best to end this chapter with a short example. This particular case is drawn from the teaching experience of the second author. Figure 3.2 presents the weekly sales of bottles of shampoo in a beauty salon. In this project Arthur Field, an undergraduate student at Hofstra University, attempted to increase the number of bottles of shampoo sold to

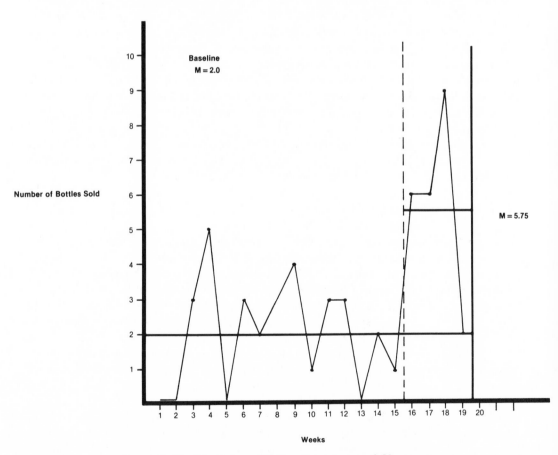

Fig. 3.2. Weekly Sales of 8 Oz. Containers of Shampoo

customers who came to the salon to have their hair cut and styled. A glance at Figure 3.2 shows that the performance improvement potential comparing the best baseline week to the average week was 5.00/2.00 or 2.5. The stakes were small at a $2 net per bottle, but the shop was stocking the item so it seemed reasonable to try to sell a few.

The sales program that was begun consisted of nothing more than adding a prompt for asking the customers if they would like to purchase the product. A small red box was drawn on the top of the standard bill. When the beauticians took the money for their services, they made a check mark in the box if they had asked for a shampoo sale. Since the red boxes (prompts) were hand drawn by the student, there was no cost to the salon. The value of the ratio of increased profit to program costs was therefore quite high.

Figure 3.2 suggests that the program was a marked success, but it is only a comparison design. The return to baseline level of sales during the fourth week did not represent a reversal to baseline conditions. Rather, it represented a decrease in the number of sales requests during this particularly busy week, as well as the fact that a number of weekly customers had already bought shampoo and reacted negatively to being asked a second and third time. Obviously, this problem could have been avoided by varying the prompt to other items on a weekly basis.

Were this study only a comparison design, it would be difficult to interpret the results. Fortunately, the presence of a second salon under the same ownership offered the opportunity for a multiple baseline. The data from this second store showed no increase in sales under baseline conditions during the time that the treatment was in effect for the first shop. Although the program was redesigned before any attempt was made to implement treatment at the second shop, this partial multiple baseline design suggests a strong relationship between the treatment and the increased sales.

In this chapter, we have tried to present some guidelines for deciding on measurement goals and procedures to implement monitoring and evaluation programs. The key concepts in these programs center on the need to develop objective measures of both accomplishments and the behaviors necessary to reach those goals, as well as the need to measure performance against its own baseline in order to evaluate programs.

REFERENCES

Ammons, R.B. Effects of knowledge of performance. A survey and tentative theoretical formulation. *Journal of General Psychology*, 1956, **54**, 279–299.

Andrasik, F., Heimberg, J.S., & McNamara, J.R. Behavior modification of work and work-related behavior. In M. Herson, R.M. Eisler, & P.M. Miller (Eds.) *Progress in behavior modification*. New York: Academic Press, in press.

Bailey, J.S., & Bostow, D.E. Research methods in applied behavior analysis. Tallahassee: Copy Grafix, 1979.

Barrett, R.S. *Performance rating*. Chicago: Science Research Associates, 1966.

Brown, M.G. Evaluating training via multiple baseline designs. *Training and Development Journal*, 1980, **34**(10), 11–16.

Burnaska, R.R., & Hollman, T.D. An empirical comparison of the relative effects of rater response biases on three rating scale formats. *Journal of Applied Psychology*, 1974, **59**, 307–312.

Campbell, D.T., & Stanley, J.C. *Experimental and quasi-experimental designs for research*. Chicago: Rand McNally, 1963.

Campbell, J.P., Dunnette, M.D., Lawler, E.E., III, & Weick, K.E., Jr. *Managerial behavior, performance and effectiveness*. New York: McGraw-Hill, 1970.

Cummings, L.L., & Schwab, D.P. *Performance in organizations: Determinants and appraisal*. Glenview, Illinois: Scott, Foresman, 1973.

Dickinson, T.L., & Zellinger, P.M. A comparison of the behaviorally anchored rating and mixed standard scale formats. *Journal of Applied Psychology*, 1980, **65,** 147-154.

Dunnette, M.D. *Personnel selection and placement.* Belmont: Wadsworth, 1966.

Fabricant, S. The productivity issue: An overview. In J.M. Rosow (Ed.), *Productivity prospects for growth.* New York: Van Nostrand Reinhold, 1981.

Feeney, E.J. Twelve ideas toward effective training. *Training and Development Journal*, 1980, **34**(9), 14-16.

Gilbert, T.F. *Human competence: Engineering worthy performance.* New York: McGraw-Hill, 1978.

Hakel, M.D. Similarity of post interview trait rating intercorrelations as a contributor to interrater agreement in a structured employment interview. *Journal of Applied Psychology*, 1971, **55,** 443-448.

Johnston, J.M., & Pennypacker, H.S. *Strategies and tactics of human behavioral research.* Hillsdale, N.J.: Lawrence Earlbaum Associates, 1980.

Kempen, R.W., & Hall, R.V. Reduction of industrial absenteeism: Results of a behavioral approach. *Journal of Organizational Behavior Management*, 1978, **2,** 11-44.

Kingstrom, P.O., & Bass, A.R. A critical analysis of studies comparing behaviorally anchored rating formats. *Personnel Psychology*, 1981, **34,** 263-289.

Kirby, P.G. Performance improvement the adult way. *Personnel*, 1980, **57**(6), 35-43.

Komaki, J., Collins, R.L., & Thoene, T.J.F. Behavioral measurement in business, industry and government. *Behavioral Assessment*, 1980, **2,** 103-123.

Landy, F.J., & Farr, J.L. Performance rating. *Psychological Bulletin*, 1980, **87,** 72-107.

Landy, F.J., & Guion, R.M. Development of scales for the measurement of work motivation. *Organizational Behavior and Human Performance*, 1970, **5,** 93-103.

Luthans, F., & Kreitner, R. *Organizational behavior management.* Glenview, Ill.: Scott, Foresman, 1975.

Mark, J.A. Productivity measurement. In J.M. Rosow (Ed.), *Productivity prospects for growth.* New York: Van Nostrand Reinhold, 1981.

McMillan, J.D., & Dorel, H.W. Performance appraisal: Match the tool to the task. *Personnel*, 1980, **57**(4), 12-20.

Miller, L.M. *Behavior management: The new science of managing people at work.* New York: John Wiley & Sons, 1978.

Newman, J.E., & Hinrichs, J.R. *Performance evaluation for professional personnel.* Scarsdale, N.Y.: Work in America Institute, 1980.

New tool: 'Reinforcement' for good work. *Business Week*: December 18, 1971.

Pack, R.J., & Vicars, W.M. MBO – today and tomorrow. *Personnel*, 1979, **56**(3), 68-77.

Performance audit, feedback and positive reinforcement. *Training and Development Journal*, 1972, **26**(11), 8-13.

Siegel, I.H. *Productivity measurement: An evolving art.* Scarsdale, N.Y.: Work in America Institute, 1980.

Simek, T.C., & O'Brien, R.M. Immediate auditory feedback to improve putting quickly. *Perceptual and Motor Skills*, 1978, **47,** 1133-1134.

Smith, P.C., & Kendall, L.M. Retranslation of expectations: An approach to the construction of unambiguous anchors for rating scales. *Journal of Applied Psychology*, 1963, **47,** 149-155.

Sokolik, S.L. Guidelines in the search for effective appraisals. *Personnel Journal*, 1967, **46,** 660-668.

Sulzer-Azaroff, B. Behavioral ecology and accident prevention. *Journal of Organizational Behavior Management*, 1978, **2,** 11-44.

Teel, K.S. Performance appraisal: Current trends, persistent progress. *Personnel Journal*, 1980, **59,** 296-301, 316.

Wolf, M.M., & Risley, T.R. Reinforcement: Applied research. In R. Glaser (Ed.), *The nature of reinforcement.* New York: Academic Press, 1971.

Yager, E. A critique of performance appraisal. *Personnel Journal*, 1981, **60,** 129-133.

Zedeck, S., & Baker, H.T. Nursing performance as measured by behavioral expectation scales: A multitrait-multirater analysis. *Organizational Behavior and Human Performance*, 1972, **7,** 457-466.

4

Increased Productivity in Man-Paced and Machine-Paced Performance

Fred E. Bushhouse Jr., Edward J. Feeney
Edward J. Feeney Associates
Alyce M. Dickinson   **Richard M. O'Brien**
Western Michigan University and *Hofstra University*

The now familiar early success of behavior modification at Emery Air Freight (Laird, 1971; Performance Audit, 1972) has been followed by increasingly sophisticated contingency systems to increase employee productivity. Behavioral Systems Engineering Training or B.E.S.T. is the training program developed by Edward J. Feeney and his associates. The effects of the B.E.S.T. application of contingency management and feedback are presented in the following two case studies as rather typical examples of applied behavior analysis to improve productivity.

The two case studies exemplify programs that were successful in increasing productivity in a labor-intensive operation and a machine-paced operation. Most of the reported applications of applied behavior analysis have occurred in labor-intensive operations where the human factor contributes significantly to productivity. If human performance can be increased there is likely to be a substantial improvement in production. The task becomes more difficult in machine-paced operations since the human component plays a much smaller role in the actual productivity rate. There would be, it seems, less potential for improvement in machine-paced processes. Most of the work is completed by machines at a standard production rate, and barring any machine breakdowns productivity should be maximized. The human components in such operations usually consist of employees who operate and troubleshoot any minor equipment problems, employees who set up the machines, employees who perform ancillary operations such as manual adjustments, shipping and packing, and maintenance personnel. Since the production rate and quality of the final product are primarily machine-controlled there is a question as to whether increased human efficiency could affect productivity to a meaningful degree. The initial case study presents a program implemented in a human-paced operation while the second case study presents a similar program based on B.E.S.T. concepts implemented in a machine-paced operation where productivity was already well within acceptable limits.

CASE STUDY 1: INCREASED PRODUCTIVITY IN A HUMAN-PACED OPERATION

The use of feedback and contingency management is probably best exemplified when the net effect brings the client company from the red to the black. The primary thrust of the program was to make a division of the company financially stable as quickly as possible. Interventions were necessarily outcome oriented rather than process oriented. Attempts to investigate the effects of specific aspects of the interventions had to take a back seat to bottom line outcomes. In the present case, a complex intervention program was introduced, some aspects of which were implemented before performance measurement was tied into the company's accounting system so that valuable time would not be lost on the road to recovery.

The client in the present case was a relatively small contractor for a huge electronics conglomerate. The contractor had two major divisions, one of which was profitable. This division was financially carrying the second division. The role of the second division, the Card Assembly Division, was to assemble and deliver circuit boards and various other related mechanical devices required by the customer. This division consisted of four units; a printed circuit board assembly unit, a printed circuit board inspection unit, a mechanical assembly unit and a substrate inspection unit. Feeney Associates developed a system-wide organizational strategy, intervening first in the substrate inspection unit. Following their success in this unit, productivity programs were simultaneously introduced in the printed circuit board inspection unit and the printed circuit board assembly unit. The project that will be presented focuses on the program initiated in the printed circuit board assembly unit which was identified as the source of the division's economic drain. While the other units of the Card Assembly Division were making a profit, the division was losing an average of $30,000 a month when the Feeney Associates program commenced in the printed circuit board assembly unit.

Setting

At the beginning of this program the card room, where the printed circuit board assembly operations occurred, employed almost 200 workers. These employees were divided into groups of ten to twelve under a leader. The leaders reported directly to the shift foreman. The operation ran on a 24-hour schedule with different foremen overseeing each of three shifts.

The work force was basically a high turnover minimum wage population. Although the company had minimal material costs since the materials were supplied by the contractor, the operation worked on a small profit margin. While the actual value of each circuit board could be hundreds of dollars depending upon the particular type of board, the added value of each board, or in other words, the average value of the work completed by the assembler, was a few dollars. Assembly time could range from 15 to 35 minutes based upon the complexity of the task and the number of component parts required to complete the printed circuit board assembly. Obviously the faster the cards were completed, the greater the profit on any individual job.

As is typical in a moneylosing operation, there was a generally negative climate. The management was justifiably concerned with the monetary losses and continually exerted pressure on the foremen to increase productivity. Although the foremen were competently completing many job requirements, management typically ignored these effective behaviors emphasizing deficiencies and pointing out the differences between the desired performance and current performance. Effective behaviors were being ignored while ineffective behaviors were being criticized and punished. This led to emotional behavior such as frustration and anger generated both by the extinction of appropriate work behaviors and punishment for ineffective work behaviors. Efforts to improve productivity were unsuccessful which added to the pressure exerted by management. Employee behaviors were also on extinction which produced similar emotional responses in employees. An atmosphere of considerable tension arose between management and foremen, between foremen and employees, and among employees themselves. This atmosphere, once established, was self-perpetuating in that each employee's emotional responses served to evoke emotional behavior on the part of the other workers.

The Task

The printed circuit board assembly unit was responsible for attaching components of integrated circuits to previously etched circuit boards. The circuit boards or cards would arrive from the contractor with a tub full of perhaps 75 different components (with a range of 50 to 100) to be attached to the card as indicated in an accompanying schematic. While there were potentially over 5,000 different printed circuit board configurations that could be requested by the customer, over 80% of the orders called for one of 1,000 common circuits.

There were six basic production steps. Following an inventory of parts conducted by a receiving clerk to insure that the company had received all the required components, a few of the components would be automatically inserted by machine. The majority of the components would then be inserted manually with an employee inserting on the average, three to four components. After assembly, the card was processed through a soldering machine which was followed by manual soldering touch-up. Any required rework that resulted from the assembly process, but not as a result of any employee error, was then performed. The final step was inspection. At this point if a card was unacceptable and the error could be linked to a particular employee, the card was returned to that employee for correction. The correction process necessarily meant removing the soldered component and reinserting it properly. The card would then be resoldered and reinspected.

Productivity Measurement

Based on the cost of previous assembly jobs, the company had developed standards that indicated the number of labor hours required to assemble a particular type of card and still generate a profit. The bid which was submitted to the customer was based on this figure. Labor efficiency was thus of prime concern as the quicker the job was completed, the more profit the company made. If the job took longer than the computed time, the company would lose money.

Prior to the initiation of the productivity program, two problems were identified by the consultants and corrected. The first concerned the manner in which work was scheduled. The foremen were provided with the time requirements for the jobs which were then divided up and given to the various group leaders. Scheduling was done by foremen primarily according to job priority with no consideration being given to the number of labor hours required to complete the job versus the number of labor hours available in any given work group. While some jobs could be completed well within the time deadlines, other jobs could not possibly be completed on schedule. Employees were sometimes placed in the position of being asked to do more than they could do, while at other times they could slack off and still complete the job in the alotted time. Eventually this type of scheduling threw the foremen into a crisis management situation where lower priority jobs already in progress were being displaced by higher priority jobs. Even if a job was proceeding on or ahead of schedule it was not uncommon for a foreman to interrupt that job for another one of higher priority although both could have been completed on schedule without such an interruption. Such disruptions were time consuming and aversive to employees and group leaders since a job that was going well was replaced with a job accompanied by deadline pressure.

A schedule control program was designed by the consultants that matched, as closely as possible, the labor demands versus the labor availability while taking shipping priority into account. This was accomplished by varying the size of the work groups according to the labor requirements of the job and scheduling jobs daily on the basis of completion requirements. Foremen were trained to spend an hour or so at the beginning of each day reviewing the labor requirements of all current jobs, their respective shipping deadlines, and the number of labor hours available. Once implemented, the schedule control program was rewarding for all concerned as production proceeded according to a consistent and realistic pace. Employee work behaviors were rewarded with job completion. Job interruptions were minimized eliminating the aversiveness associated with such disruptions. Productivity began to rise, and more jobs were completed on schedule thus relieving some of the pressure on the foremen.

The second problem encountered was a quality control problem. The customer's quality requirement was 98.2% error free work. That is, the customer would accept the job if it contained 1.8% defective parts. If this standard was not met, the entire shipment would be returned to the company. The customer's inspection process consisted of a statistical sampling method so that in a shipment of 1,000 cards, perhaps only 30 to 40 of the cards were actually inspected. While the defects in the sampled cards were identified, the defective cards in the remaining job were not specified. The contractor would then have to reinspect the unsampled cards in the shipment to determine the particular cards that were defective and to pinpoint the specific problem, which could range from an improperly inserted component to poor soldering. After discovering a defect, the card would be reworked. This was obviously a very expensive procedure for the company since the recycling process was, by necessity, a manual operation. Each repair had to be made by hand and usually resoldered by hand.

Following assembly and soldering, the cards were subjected to a double inspection process at the contractor's site, first being inspected by a contractor inspector and then being reinspected by the customer's quality control inspector. In spite of this double inspection process, the contractor's quality averaged 89 to 94% which was considerably short of the 98.2% required by the customer. Because of this the contractor was experiencing production constipation since a substantial amount of direct labor had to be diverted from production to rework. The consultant focused management's attention on this problem and assisted them to realize that demands for improvement would not result in improvement. The foremen just didn't know how to solve the problem. Management held a series of meetings and decided to implement a process inspection system whereby inspectors would examine each card at specific points in the assembly process, prior to soldering. Not only was time saved by correcting the error before soldering, but any errors could be directly linked to a particular employee. With this type of accountability, individual errors were markedly reduced. The company began meeting the contractor's quality requirement at such a high frequency that any further reduction would not have been cost-effective for the company.

After these initial problems were identified and solved, the productivity improvement program was initiated. Since the critical variable was the number of hours taken to complete a job, the overall productivity measure that was selected was earned hours: the ratio of the expected number of hours to complete the job to the number of hours actually taken to complete the job. This figure was then multiplied by 100 to obtain a percentage. For example, if the standard for a particular job was 100 hours and the job was in fact completed in 100 hours, the earned hours would equal 100%. If the job was completed in 50 hours, the earned hours would equal 200%. Similarly, if the job was completed in 200 hours, the earned hours would equal 50%.

Due to extreme weekly fluctuations in production which resulted from the type and number of assignments received from the customer, a 4-week moving average was employed. For instance, several short runs in which the number of cards was small would result in lower productivity because of greater machine set up times and employee practice effects. The 4-week moving average consisted of the current week's data plus the data from the immediately preceding 3 weeks.

The foremen participated in the B.E.S.T. training program where they were taught how to develop output requirements, to recognize good aspects of employee performance, to inform the group leaders and employees about performance and to reinforce good performance using praise. They learned to build on the strengths of employee performance by setting goals and rewarding progress toward those goals rather than emphasizing and criticizing the employees about discrepencies between the goals and current performance. A detailed account of the B.E.S.T. training program can be found in Chapter 16 of this book.

Using the productivity measures that were developed, the foremen calculated what percentage of the job should be completed by specific times throughout the day. They circulated on the floor on a regular basis checking on how production was proceeding. They would then inform the group leaders and employees whether production was proceeding according to schedule, was ahead of or behind schedule, praising employees when work was being completed on or ahead of schedule. If work was behind schedule, supervisors would observe the employees in order to determine the nature of the problem and assist employees to correct it using prompting and shaping techniques. Criticism was avoided; instead supervisors provided the necessary assistance and set goals for reaching standards in the subsequent hours.

The use of these prompting and shaping techniques by the foremen resulted in dramatic changes in the behavior of the group leaders and employees. They were no longer placed in a position of defending themselves, which sometimes occurred even when their performance problems were due to circumstances beyond their control. Performance standards were realistic and employees were receiving frequent positive reinforcement for good performance. As a result, more of their attention was focused on getting the job done rather than avoidng and disputing supervisory reprimands.

The supervisory feedback program focused mainly on group performance. Concurrently with the changes in supervisory techniques, a self-monitoring system was implemented wherein each employee measured and recorded his/her own performance. While standards had previously been developed for each assembly task, these standards had not been communicated to the employees. The employees were now given the task standards when the task was presented. These standards were stated in terms of the number of cards that should be completed in an hour. Employees recorded the time they began the job and measured performance hourly keeping track of the number of cards completed. Foremen and group leaders continued to observe and monitor progress providing praise and assistance when required.

The final step in this complex intervention program was the establishment of an incentive system. Employees received a monetary incentive for each card produced above standard in addition to the hourly pay they were already receiving. The incentive consisted of a flat amount per piece produced over standard. The direct cash payment was distributed to employees weekly and generally varied from $20 to $60. For exceptional performance the incentive occasionally exceeded $60.

Results

As can be seen in Figure 4.1, substantial performance gains were realized as the result of this program. Prior to the implementation of the incentive program which was established dur-

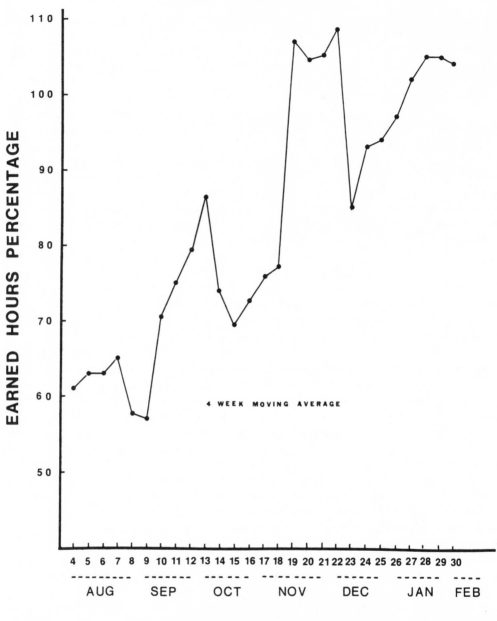

Fig. 4.1. Earned Hour Production as a Function of the Intervention Program.

ing May, the overall improvement was 72.3%. Performance has consistently remained at or above the 100% level once the complete program was installed. Financially this improvement translated into a $500,000 turn around which occurred over a period of 10 months. As the result of the applications of applied behavior analysis techniques as set forth in the B.E.S.T. model and the implementation of an incentive program, the division moved from loss to profit in a relatively short time frame.

The morale of the employees has also changed drastically. They're working as hard as ever, but the strain associated with a losing operation has been eliminated. People report that they are more relaxed and have a greater sense of job security knowing that as the result of their improved productivity the contractor is now financially stable. In addition, turnover and absenteeism have been reduced by 22% and 29% respectively.

The decline in the data during December represents a seasonal fluctuation. Toward the end of the year the customer typically does not have consistent work for the contractor. This reduction in work results in a lack of backlog so there is no control over the set up of jobs, and employees have nonproductive time through no fault of their own. The customer pays for this downtime but it does not enter into the calculations of the earned hours. A second factor which contributes to this seasonal decline concerns a higher absenteeism rate during the holiday period which reduces the total number of labor hours available.

The key to the success of this program was that the operation was almost entirely man-paced so that individual productivity gains resulted in profit increments for the contractor. The next case study that will be presented involves an almost 100% machine-paced operation. Thus the company's success is much less dependent upon the human component.

CASE STUDY 2: INCREASED PRODUCTIVITY IN A MACHINE – PACED OPERATION

The company in the present case was a very profitable organization. After becoming acquainted with the B.E.S.T. principles, management decided that they were interested in applying these principles in order to increase their profit if possible, improve the quality of their products and enhance the quality of the work life for their employees.

Setting

The company produces plastic lenses that are employed for various optical uses. The production sequence is almost completely automated, with the lenses being molded by an injection molding machine. When the part has been completed, the press operator deflashes and degates the lens clipping off any excess material surrounding the lens. The lenses are then packed in a box and sampled for quality by quality control inspectors. The labor force, which consists of approximately 85 employees, is divided into two groups: direct labor and indirect labor. Direct labor includes press operators. The indirect labor is made up of utility personnel who load the raw material into the machine, set up personnel who prepare the machine, run samples until a satisfactory piece is produced, and periodically check the machine in order to ascertain if any further adjustments are required, quality control inspectors, packers, shippers, relief operators, a receiving clerk, equipment maintenance personnel, and a janitorial staff. The operations runs on two 7-1/2 hour shifts.

Productivity Measurement

The company had very accurate records of production, and upon reviewing these historical sources it was discovered that the number of acceptable parts produced differed when the same part was produced on the same machine at different times or on different runs. In essence, since the mechanized process remained exactly the same, the productivity differences could be attributed to the people variables: the different operators, utility personnel, and set up personnel who were rotated on the basis of availability.

Production standards had previously been developed as a basis for bid submissions to customers. The production manager would first consult with the production engineer to ascertain the number of parts that the machine could produce per hour. He would then review archival production records. He would develop the bid based on these production records building in a certain degree of cushion. This meant that the bids were based on a lower production rate than previously achieved. While employees were unaware of the specific standards on which the bids were based, they did know that production rates that fell within the bid standards could be relatively easily attained. As long as bid standards were attained, employee performance was considered acceptable. These contingencies were maintaining performance at a rate that was considerably lower than what was possible rather than reinforcing optimal productivity.

For the present program, performance standards were developed for approximately 200 parts which accounted for 80+% of the company's production. Baseline production was determined by reviewing the production records for nine months of the preceding fiscal year. The performance standards for each of the 200 parts were based on these archival records. The standards were reviewed by the production engineer to insure that they were reasonable in terms of the number of parts that the machine could produce per hour. The standards were found to be goals that were well within the average operator's limits.

The productivity program consisted of three basic components. One component of the program consisted of a feedback system for operators whereby they measured and recorded their own performance comparing this performance against the production standard for each part produced. A second component consisted of supervisory feedback and monitoring that occurred on a daily and weekly basis. The third component consisted of an incentive program implemented for both direct and indirect labor using merchandise stamps which could be traded for consumer goods at a commercial store or for up to ten paid days off each year for above standard performance. Incentives were also awarded for good attendance.

Feedback and Monitoring System for Employees

When the operators were assigned a job, they were given a card with the part number and the number of acceptable or good pieces that should be produced per hour. A quality yield factor was incorporated into this figure. Thus if 100 pieces were produced per hour with 90 of those pieces being acceptable, the effective yield was 90. Inspectors checked the performance of each operator on a regular basis, separating out the scrap and informing the operator how many pieces were acceptable. The operator would record the time at which the inspector monitored the work, the number of parts produced since the last entry, and the number of pieces scrapped by the inspector. They would then subtract the number of pieces scrapped from the total number produced to arrive at the number of good pieces produced. In this manner, the operators received direct, immediate feedback by comparing actual performance against the standard for the part being produced.

Supervisory Feedback

All supervisors participated in the B.E.S.T. training program where they were taught the principles of goal setting and positive reinforcement. The foremen would circulate on the floor on a regular basis noting the production information recorded by the operators. In accordance with B.E.S.T. principles, they would reinforce operators for good performances using social praise. If any operator was having difficulty meeting the production standards they would work with the operator to ascertain what the problem was and solve it together with the employee. The following day the production records were summarized for each operator indicating the total number of good pieces produced and comparing this figure to the standard. The foremen would then give this information to each operator at least once every two days. Each operator who exceeded the standard was immediately praised by the foreman. For any operator who had fallen below the standard, the supervisor would employ prompts and shaping techniques or provide additional training to enable the employee to upgrade his or her performance.

The set up personnel were critical in the process since the time during which the machines were prepared resulted in lost production time. Standards based on historical records were established and their performance was also recorded, comparing actual performance to the set up standards. The same type of reinforcement provided to the operators by the supervisors was provided to these workers, although these data were not used as the basis for the incentive program described in the following section.

Incentive Program

Bonus points were awarded to each operator for each good piece produced over standard. The value of the bonus points was based on an economic marginal analysis, or in other words, on the calculation of the higher rate of return achieved for parts produced over the standard. Employees were awarded a percentage of this added economic value. The conversion value of each bonus point determined in this manner was 7.4 mills or $.0074. Each bonus point was worth three merchandise stamps that could be traded for consumer goods at a commercial store or for paid vacation days. To compute the number of merchandise stamps required for a paid vacation day, the value of the bonus point, $.0074, was divided into the employee's base hourly salary, multiplied by the number of hours worked daily, then divided by 3 (since each bonus point was worth three merchandise stamps). For example, if an employee was being paid $4.60 per hour and a typical work day consisted of 8 hours, the number of merchandise stamps required for a paid vacation day would be calculated by dividing $4.60 by $.0074 or 622, times 8 or 4976 divided by 3 which would equal 1658 merchandise stamps.

The press operators received 60% of all bonus points awarded for above standard performance. Fifteen percent of the bonus points went into a pool for the set up personnel and inspectors; 15% went into a pool for the utility personnel, relief operators, lead operators, lead inspectors and packers; and 10% went into a pool for the lead packer, receiving clerk, janitors, and maintenance personnel. Employees within these pools divided up the bonus points on the basis of the ratio of the hours each had worked in that particular pool to the total hours worked in the pool. This system fostered teamwork and cooperation among all the employees, and accented the role of indirect labor. Both direct and indirect labor personnel realized the extent to which the indirect labor force contributed to production rates.

Employees could earn bonus points through this positive reinforcement system in a number of ways. But employees could also lose points. An attendance procedure was developed on a response cost model in which the employees could earn extra points by avoiding absences. At the beginning of each month each employee received a 500 bonus credit. If the employee had perfect attendance or only one absence per month, no bonus points were deducted. Five hundred bonus points were subtracted for absences in excess of one a month and 250 bonus points were subtracted for each lateness in excess of one lateness up to a maximum of 500 points.

Absences were not the only way employees could lose bonus points. Employees found to be fudging performance data lost all of their points for the day. In addition to these punishment procedures, the employees were also functioning under a time out procedure for quality control. Parts that required rework were returned to the individual operators, but

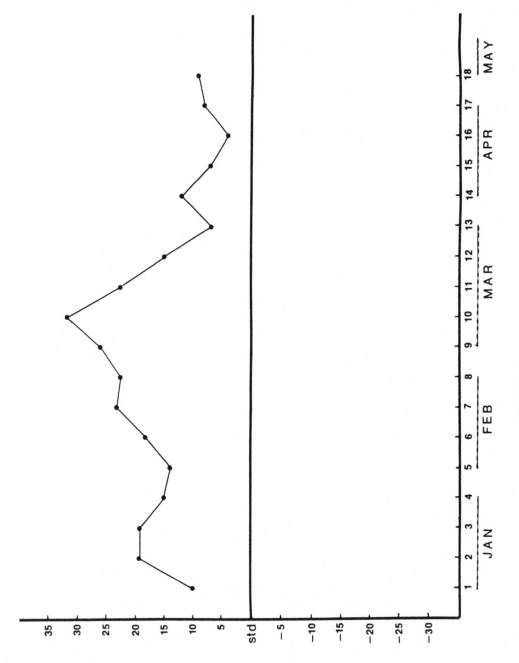

SUCCESSIVE WEEKS

Fig. 4.2. Production After the Intervention Program.

reworking did not earn bonus points. Therefore, the more time the individual spent redoing pieces, the less opportunity he or she had to earn bonus points.

The total number of bonus points earned each week was posted on an Employee Points Earned record, and the employee was informed by the forman of the total bonus points earned per week. At the end of each calendar quarter each employee could turn in the points for merchandise stamps.

Results

Performance consistently exceeded the standard as can be seen in Figure 4.2. Performance averaged 15% over standard. Since the standard was set at 5% above the previous year's productivity, production averaged 20% over the prior year's production. The additional monetary profit was approximately $400,000 a year for this 3-1/2 to 4 million dollar operation. Management also reported a 20% improvement in quality, demonstrating that quality need not be sacrificed for gains in productivity. Previous years' data suggest that the decline in the data during March can be attributed not to a change in performance but a change in the type and amount of work received by the company. Customers place major orders at the beginning of the year so that the production runs are longer, thus requiring less time for machine set up and preparation and less total training time for operators than that required on the shorter production runs. Nonetheless, even for the worst week, the data still represent a 9% productivity improvement over baseline.

Substantial productivity and quality gains were achieved in spite of the fact that the operation was almost entirely machine-paced. This indicates that machine-paced operations can benefit greatly from the application of behavior analysis principles as set forth by the B.E.S.T. program. In addition to the productivity and quality increments, management has reported being surprised and pleased at the intensity of the positive climate generated by this program. The formen emphasized and rewarded positive aspects of employee performance utilizing nonfinancial reinforcers such as praise, recognition, cups of coffee, etc. Further, the incentive program was designed in such a manner to increase the teamwork and cooperation among direct labor and indirect labor personnel, thus fostering improved interpersonal relations among the staff.

GENERAL CONCLUSIONS

Taken together these two case studies demonstrate the positive productivity effects that can be achieved through relatively brief behavior management programs. These case studies are not presented as examples of rigorous scientific research but represent the systematic application of various behavioral techniques. In Case Study 1, it was demonstrated that a relatively unobtrusive program of feedback and praise can help a company turn the corner from loss to profit. The second case study shows that positive and negative contingencies can have a significant effect in performance areas that have generally been viewed as unresponsive to human performance incentives. The project led to a 20% increase in machine-paced productivity resulting in improved worker morale and increased profits. The old argument that increases in productivity result in decreases in quality is clearly repudiated in each of these case studies. Substantial quality improvements accompanied productivity gains. This resulted from the development of performance standards that incorporated both quality and quantity requirements and contingencies that were arranged to reinforce above standard performance. These two case studies have effectively demonstrated that providing employees with performance data and appropriate consequences for their behavior leads to meaningful increases in productivity and quality.

REFERENCES

Laird, D. Why everything is all loused up, really (and what to do about it). *Training in Business and Industry*, March, 1971, 52-55.

Performance audit, feedback and positive reinforcement. *Training and Development Journal*. 1972, **26**(11), 8-13.

5

Transitional Contingency Contracting and the Premack Principle in Business

Howard C. Berthold, Jr.
Lycoming College

One of the more frequently-heard criticisms of the application of behavioral principles to industrial/organizational settings is that the approach requires constant, external control (Argyris, 1971). Critics argue that such control is probably impossible, and certainly undesirable, since it is antithetical to current notions that people should be given greater responsibility for directing their own work (McGregor, 1960; Likert, 1967; Myers, 1970). As one of my former colleagues was fond of saying, "People don't live in Skinner boxes!"

Behaviorists have several ways of responding to this criticism. These critics and others who adhere to the "Human Resources Model" of management often advocate shifting control to the worker as a management goal (Miles, 1965). Rather than defend the behavioral model, this paper will demonstrate how it can be used to accomplish their objective. The specific approach was developed by Homme and Tosti (1971) in a set of materials which, sadly, are now out of print.

The first section of the paper will contain a brief overview of the Homme and Tosti approach. This will be followed by two examples.

CONTINGENCY CONTRACTING

As the name implies, contingency contracting is a technique that entails clearly specifying all of the responsibilities and elements in a program of behavioral change. Homme and Tosti (1971) provided ten essential rules for conducting a successful program in contingency contracting:

1. The contract must provide for immediate reinforcement.
2. Initial contracts must call for and reinforce small approximations.
3. Reinforce frequently with small amounts.
4. The contract must call for and reward accomplishment rather than obedience.
5. Reward the performance after it occurs.
6. Attempt to impose a criterion of quality as well as of quantity.
7. The contract must be fair in the sense that the amount of reinforcement and the amount of performance bear a reasonable relationship to one another.
8. The terms of the contract must be clear.
9. The contract must be positive, avoiding the threat of punishment.
10. Contracting as a method must be used systematically.

Transitional Contingency Contracting

In Transitional Contingency Contracting, people proceed through several types of contingency contracts. They move from the point of having no involvement in designing the terms of contracts to having total responsibility for the contracts.

Many human resource theories of management seem to imply that workers harbor innate tendencies toward higher levels of performance and the assumption of greater responsibility. All that is required is the freedom to exercise these instincts. Behavioral theories also imply that workers can achieve higher levels of performance and assume greater responsibility, but these behaviors must be learned. Transitional Contingency Contracting is a method for teaching workers these skills.

Homme and Tosti (1971) suggest that workers proceed through five levels of contracting in their journey from total dependence upon a manager's instructions to personal responsibility for their own contracts. Some of the levels have several forms, all of which must be completed before progressing to the next level. These are shown in Table 5.1.

EXAMPLE 1 OF TRANSITIONAL CONTINGENCY CONTRACTING: THE TECHNICAL COLLEGE SETTING

Since Homme and Tosti used an educational setting to illustrate their approach, the first example is taken from this kind of organizational environment. It is based upon an actual application by Ronald Stark (1972) who used the technique in a human factors design drafting course for second year college students. Stark was confronted with the problem of low student involvement and motivation in his course. He felt that if students could be taught to take their own initiative in selecting tasks and reinforcers, this situation might improve. He decided to try the Homme and Tosti approach.

One difference between Stark's approach and that of many people who advocate contingency contracting in the classroom (including Homme and Tosti) is that tasks and reinforcements were not individualized for each student as a function of the student's level of competence. While individualization is clearly a more sophisticated and effective method, it requires considerably more skill, time, and preparation than a group approach.

One advantage of the group approach is that it can circumvent problems of perceived

TABLE 5.1. The Five Levels of Transitional Contingency Contracting.

Form	Level				
	1	2	3	4	5
1	R – M	R – MW	R – MW	R – W	R – W
	T – M	T – M	T – MW	T – MW	T – W
2		R – M	R – W	R – MW	
		T – MW	T – M	T – W	
3			R – M		
			T – W		

R: Reinforcement
T: Task
M: Manager
W: Worker
MW: Manager and Worker
Source: Adapted from Homme & Tosti, 1971.

inequity which sometimes haunt the inexperienced behavioral practitioner. Suppose, for example, that the following contract is made with a messy worker: "If you clean up your work area to a specified level of neatness, then you can leave work 10 minutes early and avoid rush hour traffic out of the plant." This is an extremely effective contract for changing the behavior of a messy worker. Unfortunately, it can cause open rebellion on the part of other workers who have always maintained a neat work area but aren't allowed to leave early.

One further observation about Stark's approach is in order. Before beginning his program, he explained transitional contingency contracting to his class of 22 students so that they understood the levels through which they would be proceeding. One of the positive features of the contracting method is the clarity and openness of both goals and methods. We will now look at how Stark took his class through the various levels.

Level 1

In Level 1, the Manager selects both the Task and Reinforcement. As a task, Stark told students to draw a cartoon which illustrated a population stereotype. He assigned a different population stereotype to each student. Some of the population stereotypes were: a light switch (up is on), hot water (left tap), green (safe), red (danger), and octagon sign (stop). The cartoons were then to be taped to the wall and the class was to vote upon which was best. Reinforcement was recognition by the class for one's efforts.

Level 2

Form 1. Here the Manager selects the Task and the Worker and Manager select the Reinforcement. As a task, Stark told the class to furnish an example of a poor human factors design on campus. Through class discussion, he and his students agreed that an acceptable reinforcement would be for each student to have the opportunity to discuss his or her example in class. This capitalized on the fact that complaining about conditions on campus is a well established reinforcing event for both professors and students almost anywhere one goes! Some of the examples that were furnished were: stairways (too narrow), classrooms (no left hand desks), rest rooms (no shelf on which to place books), doors (no window to see people on opposite side), and black boards (too low).

Form 2. In the second form of Level 2, the Manager and Worker jointly decide upon a Task, and the Manager determines the Reinforcement. Through class discussion, it was agreed that the next task would be to draw examples of poor human factors design in the automobile. Stark decided that the reinforcement would be using the second hour of class time to survey opinions of students outside the class on the furnished examples. Some of the examples furnished by students were: speedometer (poor spacing in the main driving range; poor positioning such that it was concealed by the hands or steering wheel), headroom (low), bumper jack (unsafe), and idiot lights (too dim during daylight).

Level 3

Form 1. In Form 1 of Level 3, the Manager and Worker jointly decide upon the Task and Reinforcement. Class discussion led to agreement that student groups of three would spend two class sessions designing four different automobile dashboards and four different interiors. The reinforcement would be spending a class period questioning non-drafting students about their preferences.

In theory, the agreed upon reinforcement seemed a good one. There was considerable enthusiasm and competition within and between the groups. When the projects were completed, however, the drafting students were disappointed to discover that non-drafting students were so unsophisticated about human factors principles, no consistent agreement was reached about which designs were superior. This would come as no surprise to a human factors engineer, who consistently watches the automobile industry produce, and the American public buy, automobiles that are poorly designed from a human factors point of view. This was an important fact for the students to learn in this kind of course, but it failed to accomplish its intended role as a reinforcement. For this reason, Stark stepped in and provided his own praise for the various designs. The students learned something besides the ignorance of the non-drafting public, however. They learned that opinions by non-drafting students would not necessarily serve as an appropriate reinforcement. Since they had participated in the selection of the reinforcement, they felt personal responsibility for the failure, and *they* began to think of different kinds to use in the future. This is an important step in shaping the shift of control to workers. Had they not participated in selecting the reinforcement, they might simply have blamed the manager for a poor decision and taken little interest in trying to decide upon how to improve upon it. This didn't happen. The process of shifting control from Manager to Worker was taking hold.

At this point, the manager might have decided to repeat Form 1 of Level 3 until it was completely successful. Instead, he decided to proceed to Form 2 because it appeared that the class had learned its lesson and was in fact ready to continue its journey toward complete control.

Form 2. In Form 2 of Level 3 the Worker has complete control over the Reinforcement while the Manager selects the Task. Stark made the task finding an example of a design that could be considered part of the consumerism movement. The students, having learned their lesson, decided that the reinforcement would be a 15-minute coffee break to caucus and select candidates (by themselves) for the "Ralph Nader Award."

Some of the examples that were furnished were deposit bottles, gas mileage design since the addition of pollution control equipment, enzyme and aromatic blunders, and deception in packaging. Students agreed that both the task and reinforcement were fair and worked well.

Form 3. In Form 3 of Level 3 the Reinforcement is selected by the Manager and the Task is selected by the Worker. The students decided they would work in groups of three to select a product and define an audience for it. Stark decided to fall back upon a typical reinforcer in the academic setting, the assignment of a grade for their work. He added a twist, however, in that he asked the students to grade their own work. After they had done so, he reasserted his role as manager with control over the reinforcement and raised each of their self-assigned grades by pointing out positive aspects of their work. This was greeted with considerable enthusiasm by the students.

Level 4

Form 1. In Form 1 of Level 4 the Manager and Worker jointly decide upon the Task, and the Worker selects the Reinforcement. Through class discussion it was agreed that the students would select some examples from their current social science or humanities elective courses (General Psychology, Economics, and Technical Writing) and indicate how the principles could be applied to designing for the human element. The students decided that an appropriate reinforcement would be the granting of credit for presenting their work in the other courses. It turned out that this was easily arranged. The success of this project was succinctly described by Stark: "This one was great!"

Form 2. In Form 2 of Level 4 the Worker selects the Task and the Manager and Worker jointly select the Reinforcement. In discussing the task, the students decided they would like to try to do some actual research in the human factors area. They decided to divide into small groups, attempt to identify three areas in which research could be done, and outline where and how they would collect data on these problems. As a reinforcement, the students said they would simply like to be able to sit down with the professor and discuss which of the ideas had the greatest merit and why. The professor, as manager, readily agreed.

Three rather extraordinary things had happened up to this point in the transitional contingency contracting program. First, the students had come to the point where they preferred working as a team rather than as individuals. Second, the students were becoming increasingly creative in their selection of tasks, rejecting routine problems for the opportunity to do original research. Third, the students were moving away from external reinforcement like coffee breaks and praise from students outside the class, and were instead satisfied with the opportunity to ponder and discuss their ideas among themselves and with an expert (the professor/manager) who could help them in their effort to do better work. In a sense, they were finding reinforcement in the knowledge that they had done a task well, and in learning how to do it even better. It is a superb example of what Blake and Mouton (1964) term "Team Management," with all the positive characteristics inherent in such an approach. The behaviorist, of course, would simply say it is an example of how people can learn self-control through a gradual shaping process.

Level 5

In Level 5 the Worker is responsible for both the Task and the Reinforcement. The students quickly decided that the task would be collecting and analyzing data for the best of the three projects they had designed during the previous level. The discussion about an appropriate reinforcement was an interesting one. Initially, the students said they didn't feel that any reinforcement was necessary, they simply wanted to go ahead with the task. If they had been somewhat more sophisticated in behavioral theory, they would have realized that the feeling of accomplishment from doing a job well is a valid reinforcement, and one that lies at the heart of many personalized systems of instruction. As Skinner has said, they are reinforced by their success.

The students weren't aware of this resolution to their problem, however, and continued their discussion about a proper reinforcement. In point of fact, their problem went beyond lack of knowledge about behavioral theory. Anyone who has operated a successful PSI program within a traditional educational setting quickly discovers that even though administrators may claim that the purpose of grades is primarily to motivate better performance, a second function is to categorize people for future employers and admissions officers at graduate and professional schools. It would seem that in order to serve such people outside the college, most institutions would rather see grades follow a normal curve than have students attain complete mastery of subject matter. While the students in the present class didn't articulate the dilemma in this way, the discussion reflected it in that they eventually began to focus on the instructor's obligation to grade their work. In the end, they agreed that the reinforcement would be to present their work to the other students in the class and have the instructor grade it. One couldn't help but feel, however, that the real reinforcement was the work itself, and the rest was simply a condescension to the constraints of the educational system. The fact that students who were not "internally" motivated were willing on their own to incorporate such external constraints into their program to aid their professor shows just how far they had come in taking over full, realistic control of their work. Incidently, some of the projects were: a study of the anthropometric dimensions of 28 3 to 5-year old children, determination of counterbore hole socket clearances for #10 to 1-inch bolts, determination of the minimum cut-out (swing) for wrenches to tighten or loosen #4 to 1-inch nuts and bolts, and calculation of optimal chair dimensions for 15 subjects over 6 feet 2 inches in height.

It should be noted that not only did the students in this program learn to assume control over their own education, they also developed a strong interest in the subject matter. This in turn proved to be a strong reinforcement for the manager/instructor, who prior to this approach had been unable to generate student interest in the topic.

TRANSITIONAL CONTINGENCY CONTRACTING IN THE INDUSTRIAL/ORGANIZATIONAL SETTING

The idea of applying transitional contingency contracting to educational settings isn't new (Homme & Tosti, 1971), although the number of actual attempts, like the one in the first example, is fairly low. Applications to industrial/organizational settings outside of education are even rarer. The second example of transitional contingency contracting will describe a program in the personnel office of a large research and development center. It is doubly interesting because it makes frequent use of the Premack Principle, another technique with great potential but little application in the industrial/organizational setting (Luthans & Kreitner, 1975). Because of this, it seems wise to divert our attention for a moment to the Premack Principle and to provide a relatively straightforward example of its effectiveness before seeing how it was used in a second major example of transitional contingency contracting.

The Premack Principle

The Premack Principle states that behaviors having higher probabilities of occurrence will reinforce behaviors having lower probabilities of occurrence if the higher probability behaviors immediately follow the lower probability behaviors. For example, if school children are more inclined to run around than sit quietly in class, then running around can be used as a reinforcer for increasing the amount of quiet sitting (Homme, deBaca, Devine, Steinhorst, & Rickert, 1963). Likewise, if male schizophrenics spend more time sitting than engaging in productive work, then sitting periods can be used as reinforcers for specified amounts of work (Mitchell & Staffelmayr, 1973). Thus, in order to utilize the Premack Principle, one simply reverses the order in which activities would normally be selected in the absence of external constraints.

In order to utilize the Premack Principle in the Industrial/Organizational setting it is necessary to have two or more distinct activities that can be ranked in accordance with their probability of occurrence in the absence of external constraints, and it must be possible to arrange them in the opposite order of their natural occurrence. Fortunately, many businesses have tasks that meet these criteria and could take advantage of the Premack Principle. Unfortunately, managers frequently ignore this principle and are confronted with the predictable consequences. One well-known example occurs when different shifts are utilized to keep a business operating for more than the traditional eight hour work day. An oft heard complaint is that people on the previous shift fail to complete their work and leave (usually the less desirable) work for the next shift. This behavior eventually erodes morale among even the most conscientious employees and leads to similar behavior on each subsequent shift. Eventually the organization may be confronted with a serious problem. Given a choice, people will do the more desirable work first and leave the less desirable work for someone else. The Premack Principle not only predicts this result, but provides a solution. The following example demonstrates this phenomenon.

An Example of the Premack Principle in a Small Business Setting

Terri Lyons (1973) was a student enrolled in my Industrial/Organizational Psychology course at the State University of New York at Albany. After classes, Terri worked the 4 to 9 P.M. shift at a local drugstore. As a part-time clerk, she occupied the bottom rung of the organizational ladder. She had little opportunity to influence work activity except through informal persuasion, but this did not prevent her from observing some of the behavioral laws that operated in her organization.

Terri had noticed that she seldom completed a task in the same amount of time from one day to the next. The quality of work remained relatively constant since the store manager was a stickler for detail and had a consistent criterion for completed work. On the other hand, within reasonable limits, the manager did not pay particular attention to how rapidly tasks were completed. Terri wondered if the variations in completion times which she had noticed were related to the Premack Principle. To find out, she questioned other employees about their preferences for doing different tasks. She discovered a consensus among all the employees, a fact which simplified data collection. She observed that sometimes employees were told which tasks would follow other ones and sometimes they were not. Over the course of several weeks, she timed how long it took other employees to complete tasks under three conditions, when they: (1) knew a more preferred task would follow, (2) knew a less preferred task would follow, and (3) did not know what task would follow.

Terri needed an efficient method of collecting data which wouldn't interfere with her own work or alter the typical behavior of the other employees. She devised a small data sheet on which she simply had to place a few checks in appropriate boxes every five minutes. After several weeks of data collection, she merely lined up the data sheets and found the modal five minute time period for each combination of task and condition.

The data in Table 5.2 show the average amount of time each task took under the three conditions. The tasks are listed in order of preference from least to most preferred. The numbers are modal values for several employees over several weeks of work. Considerable time was saved on each task and on all tasks combined when employees knew a more preferred task would follow rather than a less preferred task. The percentage improvement tended to be greater the less preferred the task.

TABLE 5.2. Average Time in Minutes to Complete Tasks Under Three Contingencies.

Task	High Probability Behavior To Follow Low	Low Probability Behavior To Follow High	Subsequent Task Unknown
Stock Candy Shelves	20	35	30
Stock Cigarette Shelves	5	15	15
Vacuum Floor	5	15	10
Dump Trash	5	10	10
Clean Store	45	90	60
Check in Orders	30	60	45
Aid Pharmacist	50	60	60
Deliver Orders	50	60	60
Total	210	345	290

In a second phase of her project, Terri tried to intervene in the system to improve work performance. Although she was not in a position to formally arrange work schedules, she tried some informal alterations during the last week of her project. Whenever possible, she agreed to change jobs with people to ensure that they would have higher probability assignments following those with lower probabilities. Collecting time data during this phase proved to be impossible, but she did demonstrate the effectiveness of her intervention in another way. In the weeks before she initiated her program, the evening employees never finished all of their assignments. Several tasks always remained for the morning shift to complete (the typical shift problem). During the week that she attempted to alter tasks according to employee preferences, all of the tasks were not only completed before closing, but time remained at the end of each evening during which there was no work to be done.

One major advantage of this simple approach was that it required little extra effort or attention on the part of anyone. It might be argued that the project failed to meet many of the demands of strict experimental design. This is true. For example, no attempt was made to equalize the number of data points for each person, task, or group. Nevertheless, observations were made over a sufficiently long period and the assignment of work among employees was such that there is no a priori reason to suspect that such factors could account for the differences between conditions. Moreover, the data are consistent with previous findings based upon the Premack Principle.

Knapp (1976) correctly pointed out the need to continually question the validity of theoretical constructs like the Premack Principle and to try to isolate the real factors that produce such results. The present study does little to help in this regard. Nevertheless, our friends in the business community can't wait for the final resolution of our controversies. They have problems to solve and people to manage right now. In addition to their intuitive instincts, a few of them will also use the principles recommended by psychologists, provided these principles are simple to comprehend, easy to apply, and likely to produce positive results. In this respect, the Premack Principle seems to be of genuine value. One need not be a specialist in learning theory to know how to apply this technique. All that is required is the knowledge that tasks should be ordered in accordance with employees' preferences, and that employees should be informed of that order. In this way, the tasks themselves become the reinforcers.

Although there is a need for more sophisticated tests of the Premack Principle, the widespread tendency for businesses to utilize precisely the opposite contingencies than those dictated by the principle may explain some of their long-standing problems. The success of this study as well as those in other settings suggests that the Premack Principle deserves greater attention and application by organizational consultants and people in the business community.

The Premack Principle can be utilized in conjunction with more traditional forms of reinforcement, like praise and recognition, and it fits nicely into programs involving transitional contingency contracting. The next example provides a good illustration of both.

EXAMPLE 2 OF TRANSITIONAL CONTINGENCY CONTRACTING: PERSONNEL ADMINISTRATION

The second example is based upon an actual application by Judi Arendos (1973) who was Personnel Administrator for Physical Engineering at a large research and development center. She and two clerks who worked under her served approximately 450 managers, scientists, engineers, and technical and support personnel in the areas of recruiting, salary and wage administration, job classification, equal opportunity/minority relations, manpower development and education, and new employee orientation.

A major problem in this kind of setting is the huge volume of routine paperwork that must be handled on a weekly basis. The obvious solution is to mechanize the process. Unfortunately, here as elsewhere, the clerical workers strongly opposed mechanization. Their stated reason was that they feared the "machines would abolish their jobs."

For 2 years, Arendos wrestled with the problem of how to mechanize her unit without generating unnecessary ill will. This illustrates an important principle of good management. Many managers behave as if finding solutions to problems is their only task. As Elbing (1978) has noted in his Decision-Making Process Model, however, finding a solution is only one of five steps a manager needs to go through in adequately coping with sources of disequilibrium. The last step, which follows finding a solution, is devising a good way to implement the solution. Many times "perfect" solutions fail because of inadequate methods of implementation. Arendos recognized this, and bided her time until she could devise an effective strategy of implementation. Two events finally occurred which gave her the opportunity she sought. One was exposure to Homme and Tosti's materials in a graduate course I was teaching, and the other was an attitude survey conducted by her company which gave her a natural opportunity to begin discussing transitional contingency contracting with her clerical support personnel.

The attitude survey was prompted by unionization of clerical and technical support personnel at another of the Center's locations. The Center's management wanted to be sure it had an accurate reading on any discontent at its other non-union locations lest they too decide to unionize. The results of the attitude survey indicated many people felt "belittled, exploited and isolated," and that they were unable to establish self-identity in the organization. In discussing these feelings with the clerks, they indicated that they desired more responsibility and wanted to participate more in the decision-making process. At this point, Arendos told them about the Homme and Tosti method of transitional contingency contracting which could accomplish this goal. The clerks agreed to participate in such a program.

Before the program could commence, Arendos had to select appropriate reinforcers. She decided to utilize the Premack Principle, by having behaviors with higher probabilities of occurrence follow (and therefore reinforce) behaviors with lower probabilities of occurrence. One of the easiest ways to determine probabilities is to ask employees to list tasks they like to do (high probability behaviors) and tasks they find boring (low probability behaviors). Table 5.3 is an example of some of the behaviors listed by the clerks when Arendos asked them to do this.

At this point, we will follow the progress of only one of the clerks, who will be called Mary. The other clerk was reassigned half-time to another person during the course of the project. In a sense, it might appear that the clerk's fear of losing her job to the machines was

TABLE 5.3. Low and High Probability Behaviors

Low Probability Behaviors	High Probability Behaviors
1. Typing job descriptions	1. Orienting new employees
2. Setting up meetings	2. Meeting candidates
3. Checking expense accounts	3. Interacting with higher levels of staff
4. Typing budget charts	4. Doing statistics on salaries
5. Other routine typing of a technical nature	5. Suggesting solutions to problems in personnel relations
6. Typing routine letters	

justified, given this reassignment. In fact, however, her newly acquired skill of self-direction made it possible for the Center to assign her different kinds of work which were much more interesting than her previous duties. We will now look at how the various levels of the transitional contingency contracting model were utilized by Arendos (the Manager) and Mary (the Worker).

Level 1

In Level 1, the Manager selects both the Task and Reinforcement. The task Arendos chose was sending Mary to IBM School to learn the operation of an IBM mag-card selectric typewriter and memory unit. This machine would allow them to mechanize the many long, routine letters that were taking so much time to type. Arendos realized that this was a large task, and that in order to satisfy Rules 2 and 3 of the contingency contracting process, it would be necessary to provide frequent reinforcement for small gains. She decided to use earshotting. Arendos began informing management and staff that Mary was enrolled in the IBM program and would be the resident expert in the use of such equipment. The technique worked, and Mary who was an out-going person and enjoyed interaction with people at all levels soon found that many people were commenting to her about how impressed they were with her gradually increasing skills. By this time, Arendos had purchased the machine, giving Mary the opportunity to demonstrate her skill and knowledge to others. Fortunately, the IBM School was well run, and they too provided Mary with considerable reinforcement for her progress. Mary, too, found the operation of the machine to be interesting and was reinforced by her success.

Level 2

Form 1. The first form of Level 2 requires that the Manager select the Task, and Manager and Worker jointly determine the Reinforcement. The task selected by Arendos was for Mary to place two of the more frequently used routine letters on magnetic cards for immediate use. Using the previously obtained list of High Probability Behaviors (Table 5.2) as a guide, they decided a suitable Reinforcement would be to allow Mary to explain the organization of the Physical Engineering Sector and present brochures on the Center to candidates for employment.

Form 2. Form 2 of Level 2 reverses the responsibilities in Form 1, hence the Reinforcement is selected by the Manager and the Task is determined jointly. Since Mary had begun to place letters on magnetic cards in Form 1 of Level 2, they decided to continue the task until all the routine letters currently on file had been transferred to magnetic cards. They devised a specific schedule whereby the number and complexity of letters increased on each successive day. Arendos decided that immediately after Mary completed the required typing on each day, Mary could work on calculating percent change in salaries and keeping the statistics on a component basis. This fit nicely into Arendos' schedule, since she was currently preparing the annual exempt salary plan for her Sector and needed these data. Arendos viewed the statistical calculations as routine work (low probability behavior), but Mary enjoyed doing them. Thus, the high probability behavior of doing salary computations was used as the Reinforcement for the low probability behavior of typing routing letters (see Table 5.2).

Level 3

Form 1. The initial form of Level 3 calls for joint selection of both Task and Reinforcement.

Arendos and Mary met to discuss where they should go next. Mary had learned the operation of the machine and completed the file of cards during Levels 1 and 2. Now they decided that an appropriate task would be to do one final investigation to make sure all possible letters and forms had been placed on cards, including the "boiler-plate" of position guides so that they wouldn't have to return to this later. As a reinforcement, they decided to begin preparing for the next sequence of tasks Mary would undertake, namely the orientation of new employees. Specifically, the reinforcement was to allow Mary to observe Arendos during the orientation of new employees.

Form 2. In Form 2 of Level 3 each person bears sole responsibility for one part of the contract. The Manager selects the Task and the Worker the Reinforcement.

Arendos decided that is was time for Mary to tackle the task of learning the benefit plans in some depth. Arendos devised a schedule whereby Mary had to learn a new plan every three days. Arendos arranged progress checks to ensure that Mary understood each one well enough to explain it to new employees. Since assuming less routine duties and acquiring greater responsibility was a high probability behavior for Mary, she decided that her reinforcement would be answering incoming questions on plans she knew, and then checking with Arendos to see if she had given accurate information. Arendos, of course, provided positive feedback to Mary for her correct answers. As Mary's ability to answer a wider range of questions grew, so did her self confidence. She found she had to check with Arendos less and less. The reinforcement changed from being told by someone else that she was correct to the personal satisfaction of knowing for herself that she was correct. She completed the task of learning all the benefit plans in less than a month.

Form 3. Form 3 reverses the responsibilities of Form 2. The Worker selects the Task and the Manager selects the Reinforcement.

Mary was aware of the fact that Personnel had overrun its recruiting budget by $20,000 the previous year, and that a system had to be devised that would permit a more realistic prediction of expenses for the coming year. When asked to select a task for Form 3 of Level 3, Mary offered to go through all expense accounts for the previous and current year and set up a record sheet for each candidate. Arendos realized that this was a big task and would require a comparable reinforcement if the contract was to satisfy the rule of fairness. Returning to the list of high probability behaviors (Table 5.2), Arendos decided to draw upon Mary's interest in interacting with higher levels of staff. Arendos had recently been asked to sit on a task force to update the secretarial procedures book. Arendos offered this assignment to Mary, knowing that as a clerical person, she would have good ideas to contribute, that she would not be intimidated by the other members due to her outgoing manner, and that she would find it very rewarding to be able to interact with upper level staff.

Level 4

Form 1. At Level 4, the Worker participates in selecting both Task and Reinforcement. The Task is jointly determined, and the Worker has sole responsibility for selection of the Reinforcement.

Arendos and Mary decided to turn to the task of keeping better records on personnel changes so that when the time came for compiling annual reports, they wouldn't have to spend so much time searching their files for bits and pieces of information. When asked what she would like to do as a reinforcement. Mary said she would like to draw upon the knowledge she gained in Form 2 of Level 3 by compiling a booklet which summarized all the benefit plans, checking it with their benefits' expert, and jointly issuing copies to the other personnel offices.

Form 2. Form 2 of Level 4 reverses the responsibilities in Form 1. The Worker selects the Task, and both Worker and Manager select an appropriate Reinforcement.

By now, Mary had become aware of the many major projects awaiting completion by the Personnel Office. She decided to tackle the task of setting up new personnel folders for a component of the firm in another city for which they had recently assumed responsibility. By now, also, other groups at the Center had become interested in the IBM equipment. Arendos and Mary decided that Mary would begin formal demonstrations for small groups to assist in the training of new users of the equipment. Once again, this drew upon Mary's original list of high probability behaviors (Table 5.2), which included interacting with other employees.

Level 5

In Level 5, the Worker assumes full responsibility for both the Task and Reinforcement. Mary had come a long way from when she spent most of her day typing routine letters. She now took the initiative in selecting a wide variety of tasks and ordering them so that less desirable ones were followed by more interesting ones. As one reads through the levels, it is also apparent that the tasks themselves gradually changed in character. They required increasing amounts of responsibility and self-direction. In one sense, this was a fortuitous occurrence made possible by the acquisition of machinery which eliminated much of the dull, routine work. On the other hand, there are many companies and departments where new equipment and more efficient procedures could be adopted but aren't, due to employee fear and resistance. Technical advances in hardware require parallel advances in behavioral management if such equipment is to achieve its potential.

Through the transitional contingency contracting program, Mary had become a much happier, involved, self-directed employee. She required considerably less supervision. It should be noted, however, that the organizational chart had not been modified. Mary and Arendos did not share equally in all the tasks coming into the office. Mary had taken over many of the tasks that Arendos once assumed, but Arendos did not in turn have to take over any of the lower probability tasks Mary once did. They were still Mary's responsibility, and she recognized this, placing them in the correct order so that interesting tasks followed less interesting ones. Moreover, on occasion Arendos still had to take the lead in pointing out what had to be done, a regression to earlier levels of the transitional contingency contracting program. Nevertheless, they seldom regressed all the way to Level 1, but instead went to a level where Manager and Worker jointly discuss Tasks and the Worker selects the Reinforcement (Form 1 of Level 4). Moreover, the number of occasions where this occurred became markedly reduced. Mary simply performed the tasks as they arose without being told to do so.

One might ask what the Reinforcement is for management to engage in transitional contingency contracting. Is it merely the knowledge that one has increased participation by employees, a goal espoused by many current management texts? Certainly this is part of it, but the preceding example illustrates the fact that it goes far beyond this. Many of the tasks that Arendos originally had to perform were actually low probability behaviors for her, but high probability behaviors for Mary. By shifting these tasks to Mary, both people were able to engage in higher probability behaviors than they had previously. Moreover, freed from these tasks, Arendos found she had the time to do what most managers merely dream about, engage in long-range planning. Most managers are kept so busy with immediate problems, they seldom have the luxury of being able to adequately plan for the rapidly changing future events that are bound to overtake them. Arendos was freed from her routine tasks so she could begin, for example, to devise long-range planning on manpower development, seek better ways to find highly qualified people, devise new ways of rating staff for the salary administration process, and plan seminars for other managers so that they too could learn behavioral principles that would help them become more effective and enhance the attitudes of their employees.

SUMMARY AND CONCLUSIONS

Many current theories of management note that employees want greater control over their work. Few of these theories suggest programmatic methods for achieving this goal. Instead, they assume that if management simply abdicates control, workers will automatically begin to exhibit appropriate behaviors. The behavioral approach agrees with the goals of these management theories, but suggests that responsible and independent behaviors must be learned just like any other behaviors. This requires systematic training. One such method, transitional contingency contracting, has been discussed and illustrated.

One might ask how we know such a program of gradually shaping appropriate behaviors is necessary. Perhaps the two managers in the examples cited could have achieved the same result in much quicker fashion by merely announcing one day that hereafter the workers would be responsible for devising their own work schedules. Obviously, neither Stark nor Arendos ran an appropriate control group to check this possibility. This remains an area for future research.

In the absence of appropriate controls, one can only ask whether the positive results outlined above are consistent with principles that have been empirically tested. Obviously, they are. Moreover, there are examples where the principles were not applied and the desired results weren't achieved.

During the last decade or so, educational theory was heavily influenced by the notion that greater control should be shifted to students. The result was disappointing. Distribution requirements disappeared, high school transcripts began to look like wastelands of nonacademic trivia, and basic reading, writing, and quantitative skills declined almost as rapidly as SAT scores. The argument here isn't that shifting control to the students was misguided. Rather, it is argued that the students needed guidance in learning how to cope with this responsibility.

The same is true in the business setting. Another of my students provided a rather interesting example of what can happen when control is shifted to workers without adequate training in handling it. Porteus (1973) devised a carefully planned program for applying transitional contingency contracting for a group of mechanical technicians. The details are interesting, but unimportant for present purposes. Suffice it to say, the employees began at Level 1 where the manager determined both the tasks and reinforcements. As the manager began to institute Level 2, the company was suddenly confronted with a marked increase in orders. It responded by hiring more highly experienced workers, but keeping only one manager. The manager had to cope with the situation by immediately shifting to level 3 of the transitional contingency contracting system so that workers could assume more of the responsibility that management no longer had time to handle. The number of orders continued to increase, and although theoretically there were enough workers per order received to handle the orders based upon their initial level of efficiency, the manager now had to move to Level 5, giving workers complete responsibility for determining their own tasks and reinforcements, since the manager simply had no time to work with them. Porteus described the result as "total confusion" with a "growing sense of resentment among workers."

It would be folly to suggest that the examples of failure in schools and the work place or the two examples of success outlined above provide unequivocal support for the method of transitional contingency contracting. Nevertheless, the successful examples do demonstrate that such a system can work, and the failures point to the need for questioning any assumption that control can be shifted to the worker without a systematic method for preparing them to cope with it.

REFERENCES

Arendos, J. Unpublished term paper, Union College, 1973.

Argyris, C. Beyond freedom and dignity by B. F. Skinner (an essay review). *Harvard Educational Review*, 1971, **41,** 550-567.

Blake, R., & Mouton, J. *The managerial grid*. Houston, Texas: Gulf Publishing Co., 1964.

Elbing, A. O. *Behavioral decisions in organizations* (2nd ed.) Glenview, Illinois: Scott, Foresman, 1978.

Homme, L. E., deBaca, C., Devine, P., Steinhorst, J. V., & Rickert, E. J. Use of the Premack Principle in controlling the behavior of nursery school children. *Journal of the Experimental Analysis of Behavior*, 1963, **6,** 544.

Homme, L., & Tosti, D. *Behavior technology: Motivation and contingency management*. San Rafael, California: Individual Learning Systems, 1971.

Knapp, T. J. The Premack Principle in human experimental and applied settings. *Behavior Research and Therapy*, 1976, **14,** 133-147.

Likert, R. *The human organization*. New York: McGraw-Hill, 1967.

Luthans, F., & Kreitner, R. *Organizational behavior modification*. Glenview, Illinois: Scott, Foresman, 1975.

Lyons, T. *An application of contingency management*. Unpublished term paper, The State University of New York at Albany. 1973.

McGregor, D. *The human side of enterprise*. New York: McGraw-Hill, 1960.

Myers, M. S. *Every employee a manager: More meaningful work through job enrichment*. New York: McGraw-Hill, 1970.

Miles, R. E. Human relations or human resources? *Harvard Business Review*, 1965, **43** (4), 148-163.

Mitchell, W. S., & Staffelmayr, B. E. Application of the Premack Principle to the behavioral control of extremely inactive schizophrenics. *Journal of Applied Behavioral Analysis*, 1973, **6,** 419-423.

Porteus, C. *Applications of contingency management in business*. Unpublished term paper, Union College, 1973.

Stark, R. Unpublished term paper, Union College, 1972.

6

The Performance of Major League Baseball Pitchers on Long-Term Guaranteed Contracts *

Steven R. Howard, Robert W. Figlerski, and Richard M. O'Brien
Hofstra University

Sports in general and professional sports in particular provide a fertile field for evaluating management strategies. The direct competition for high payoffs has led to the development of better performance measures in sports than are available in other fields of endeavor. There are a number of truths about performance improvement in the sports literature that could be useful to managers in any area. For example, some of the best demonstrations of the effects of feedback and self-monitoring come from the clear performance improvements noted in a variety of sports behaviors such as football (Komaki & Barnett, 1977), golf (Simek & O'Brien, 1981), soccer (Luyben, Hansen, Hardy, Leonard, & Romero, 1980), swimming (McKenzie & Rushall, 1974), tennis (Buzas & Ayllon, 1981) and bowling (Kirschenbaum, Ordman, Tomarken & Holtzbauer, in press).

Another advantage to studying management through athletics is the reliance on behavioral outcome data that typifies such performance. In sports, verbal behavior and attitudes are given little attention when it comes to rewards. Managers attend to who hits homeruns, not who says they will, and the team with the best record wins the pennant regardless of alibies. There is no way to take back the bad pitch or verbally convince a pin that it should have fallen down. The rewards follow deeds, not words or personality traits.

Compensation for performance in sports mirrors many of the problems that managers face in other organizations. The rewards in professional sports range from being completely dependent on performance to being unrelated to productivity. The weekly tournaments for professionals in golf, bowling, and tennis represent contingent reinforcement systems. At the other extreme, the guaranteed purse of a boxer is dependent only on being present for the fight. Between these extremes are the guaranteed contracts of baseball, basketball, football, and hockey which function as noncontingent reward systems augmented with bonuses for individual and team performance. Given the magnitude of the noncontingent rewards (salaries) present in professional sports, the effects of these relatively small performance bonuses remain open to question. For managers who are faced with numerous compensation decisions, the relationshp between rewards and performance is crucial to developing contracts that will lead to the greatest productivity.

---

*The authors are indebted to Joanne Caggiano and Ray Grebey for help in data collection. This study was not funded by The Major League Baseball Player Relations Committee which bears no responsibility for the content of this report.

In the operant model of behavior, responses are learned and maintained according to their consequences (Keller, 1954). A schedule of reinforcement is a specification of the relationship between the responses to be made and the reinforcers to follow (Millenson & Leslie, 1979). A contract is a verbal or written statement of the relationship between pay and performance. It may also identify the conditions under which these reinforcers will be delivered in return for the prescribed behavior. Taking Skinner's (1969) three-term relationship as a starting point, the contract may be viewed as a statement of the contingencies of reinforcement and the discriminative stimuli that set the occasion for the response. The contract thus represents a verbal shortcut to bring the response under stimulus control and identify the contingent relationship between response and reward.

Work behaviors such as safety, job performance, and loyalty are learned (Costello & Zalkind, 1963). They occur as a result of prior consequences experienced with the particular response in question. The importance of establishing a contingent relationship between reinforcers and work performance has been recognized for many years (Elbing, 1970; Fitts, 1966; Luthans & Kreitner, 1974; Siddall & Balcerzak, 1978; Tosi & Hamner, 1972; Wiard, 1972). Nicolai Lenin was bemoaning the lack of contingent rewards for increased productivity among factory workers as early as 1914 (Lenin, 1972), while more recently President Ronald Reagan asserted that taxation had eliminated the rewards for work in the United States. In fact, a number of studies have demonstrated that contingent reinforcement systems produce increases in performance (Farr, 1976; Johnson, 1975). Johnson's simulation study of quality control is of particular importance because it compared the effects of actual contingent reinforcement to both persuasion and announcements of reinforcement without actual contingency change. The results indicated that only the actual change in contingencies produced the desired increase in quality.

There have been numerous examples of improved productivity through contingent rewards (Andrasik, Heimberg & McNamara, in press; Miller, 1978). In addition to money, contingent praise and recognition have been found to provide a simple, effective, and humanistic approach to increasing productivity (Cloud & O'Brien, 1981; Employee Recognition, 1981; Feeney & Staelin, 1981; Montegar, Reid, Madsen & Ewell, 1977). It should be noted that immediate feedback on performance is of crucial importance to these effects. The time lag between performance and reinforcement can have great consequences on behavior. Even when the same reward is available, variation of time and accessibility can effect productivity (Farr, 1976; Fiedler & Mahar, 1979; McNamis & Dick, 1973; Rothe, 1978; Terborg & Miller, 1978).

Once the relationship between the environment and the response (i.e., the contingencies) breaks down, performance can be expected to deteriorate. When reward is dispensed noncontingently, deleterious effects occur not only in the acquisition of a response, but also in its maintenance. Leeming, Blackwood, and Robinson (1978) for example, investigated the effects of noncontingent rewards on learning an instrumental response using college students. Their subjects received either contingent reinforcement alone or a combination of both contingent and noncontingent reinforcement. The subjects who received both types of reinforcement performed at much lower levels than those in the exclusively contingent group. Similar results following the introduction of noncontingent reinforcement have been reported in a number of other studies (Calder & Staw, 1975; Gamzu, Williams & Schwartz, 1973; Kruglanski, Friedman & Zeevi, 1971; Levine, 1962; Redd, 1969; Welker, 1976).

If one were to review current management practices in the United States, one would get the impression that the relationship between performance and rewards was a very well-kept secret. The contingencies are often unclear for salaried employees, and the rewards are quite delayed. In many cases, for example, tenure for teachers, the contingencies between rewards and performance have been completely abrogated. The current movement is away from rewards for merit, i.e., performance, toward "equality" of compensation, but there are few real world opportunities to observe the productivity effects of shifts in the basis of compensation.

Recently the salary and contract system in professional baseball has undergone a dramatic change. Beginning in 1977, multi-year, guaranteed contracts, in some cases for over one million dollars, began to be awarded to many players (Lord & Hohenfeld, 1979). Prior to this time most players negotiated contracts at the end of each season on the basis of the previous year's performance. In essence, what has occurred in major league baseball is that top players are now being paid in a way that they perceive as more equitable, yet the contingency between pay and performance has been removed. Since prior to the institution of long-term contracts, players were awarded contracts annually, the yearly renegotiation presented reinforcement contingent on performance. In fact, those teams who were out of pennant contention were often described as playing for next year's contract. Contingency theory suggests that noncontingent pay will lead to abrupt deterioration in both the quality and quantity of performance. Equity theory (Adams, 1965) would predict that those players not on long-term, guaranteed contracts who are playing at the same time as the guaranteed contract players, should perceive an inequity between their input-output ratio relative to their contemporaries, i.e., social referents. Therefore, these players should also show a decay in performance.

The sudden change from a contingent system of reinforcement to a noncontingent one for some but not all of the players in major league baseball provides a real-world opportunity to study predictions from both equity theory and contingency theory. The presence in baseball of a variety of relatively objective, quantitative performance measures that are publicly available is an advantage that is often lacking in other organizational settings as well as in simulation studies. Since it is impossible to compare hitting statistics with those from pitching or defense, it was decided to limit the current research population to pitchers. This provided a smaller, more workable sample and stressed the importance of pitching, which most authorities consider upwards of 75% of the game.

The present research took advantage of the change in baseball's compensation system by examining the effects of replacing relatively performance contingent, 1-year contracts with long-term, guaranteed (3 years or more), high pay ($100,000 or more) contracts. These effects were assessed through within group comparisons of performance among major league pitchers. The effects of guaranteed contracts on the performance of pitchers whose contracts were not guaranteed was also investigated for issues of equity from a social-referent perspective. Their performance was examined through within group comparisons over the same time period as the guaranteed pitchers. In addition, 6-year performance of a control group of pitchers from 10 years earlier when such guaranteed contracts were nonexistent was also examined.

Method

Subject. The experimental group of subjects comprised the population of 76 pitchers awarded high salary (minimum of $100,000) long-term contracts (minimum of 3 years). Contracts ranged in length from 3 to 10 years as follows: 3 years, N = 25; 4 years, N = 18; 5 years, N = 20; 6 years, N = 7; 7 years, N = 2; and 10 years, N = 2. All contracts began with the onset of the 1977 baseball season. Mean subject age was 28.40 years with a standard deviation of 5.30 years and a range of 22 to 37 years.

Subjects' names and contract lengths were supplied by the Baseball Commissioner's

Players Relations Committee. However, the experimenters were not informed of specific salaries, such information being kept confidential by the above office. For later comparisons, all pitchers who did not have major league pitching records for 3 years before and 3 years after signing the guaranteed contract were eliminated from this group leaving an N of 38.

A control group of 38 contemporary pitchers was chosen from the population of pitchers not on long-term contracts who played major league baseball in each of the seasons from 1974 to 1979. Mean subject age was 30.70 years with a standard deviation of 5.53 years and a range of 23 to 38 years.

A second control consisted of 40 pitchers from 10 years earlier who pitched in the major leagues during the 1964 through 1969 seasons. This group was drawn alphabetically from the 1970 edition of "Who's Who in Baseball" (Roth, 1970), to compare the consistency of present baseball pitchers to a time in the game's recent history when long-term contracts were unknown. Mean subject age for this group was 30.7 years with a standard deviation of 3.8 and a range of 22 to 38 years.

Procedure. Data for the experimental and contemporary control groups were collected from the 1979 and 1980 Baseball Register (Balzer, 1979, 1980). The register is a comprehensive raw data compilation of relevant performance measures of all players in the major leagues. Data compilation for the past control was drawn from the 1970 edition of "Who's Who in Baseball" (Roth, 1970), a publication similar to the Baseball Register. Eight dependent measures were analyzed, selected in accordance with what the experimenters believed to be a broad cross-section of pitching performance. These included (1) the average number of earned runs given up by the pitcher per nine innings (ERA), (2) wins, (3) losses, (4) innings pitched, (5) pitching appearances per season, (6) strikeouts, (7) hits, and (8) walks. The latter three measures were also examined as ratios per inning by dividing the total number of innings pitched per season into the season's total hits, walks, and strikeouts.

Initially, a general comparison was carried out to determine whether an overall deterioration in pitchers' performance occurred during their first year on contract when compared to the previous year.

Next, two Pearson correlations were performed to assess the relationship between performance 1 year prior to contract with the length of that particular contract and the relationship between contract length and the first year of on-contract performance.

Following this, a trend analysis was carried out over a 6-year period beginning 3 years prior to the onset of contracts. Since all contracts assessed began with the onset of the 1977 season, analyses began with the 1974 season. It was hypothesized that an overall increase in performance would occur for the first 3 years of play, followed by a marked decrease in performance for the 3-year period after the onset of contracts, since at this point, pay was no longer contingent on performance. A similar trend analysis was performed for the same 6-year period on the contemporary control group. Likewise, a trend analysis was performed on the past control group for the 6-year period of 1964 through 1969 as a means of comparison with present pitching performance.

Ancillary trend analyses were performed for the same period in the experimental group for starters, relief pitchers, and those pitchers not appearing on a disabled list over the 6-year period assessed. Correlational matrices for all three groups were examined over all eight dependent variables. This was done to assess any differences in the predictive validity of these measures between the groups over 6 years of performance.

RESULTS AND DISCUSSION

The means and standard deviations for each performance measure for the year immediately prior to the long-term guaranteed contract and for the first year after signing the contract are reported in Table 6.1. Correlated t-tests (df = 73) comparing these measures revealed significant increases in both ERA and hits per inning. In addition, a significant decline occurred in wins while the decline in innings pitched approached significance. Differences between walks, strikeouts, losses, and games were not significant. These probability values are also presented in Table 6.1.

Given the limitations of multiple t-tests, these results support the hypothesis that a deterioration in performance would occur upon removal of contingencies between pay and performance. The general comparison of performance 1 year pre- to 1 year post-onset of guaranteed contracts, shows a deterioration across three measures and a noticeable decline in a fourth. This deterioration was not only found in measures of quality (ERA, hits per inning, wins), but also in quantity (innings pitched).

Pearson correlations carried out between performance the year prior to contract and length of contract indicated little if any relationship between these variables. For example, wins pre-contract correlated .12 with contract length. Similarly, contract length and performance the first year on contract also correlated poorly. In this instance, contract length correlated .02 with wins post-contract. These two correlations are representative of correlations between other performance measures and contract length.

The fact that no dependent measure the year prior to the onset of contract correlated with length of contract suggests contract length was not dependent on the quality of pre-contract performance. It appears that variables other than performance such as management needs, interteam competition, and the skills of the player's agent were the crucial variables in determining contract length for each player. These nonsignificant correlations indicate a breakdown in the contingent relationship between performance and reinforcement at the very onset of negotiations. Further, the lack of correlation between performance first contract year and contract length indicates that predictability of performance is in no way enhanced by the length of contract. Theory would suggest that the predictability of performance would be enhanced by introducing continent relationships between performance and contract length when such contracts are initially awarded.

TABLE 6.1. Means, Standard Deviations, and t-values of Pre-Contract and Post-Contract Performance Comparison Over Eight Measures for 74 Pitchers.

Variable	Pre-Contract		Post-Contract		t	p (two-tailed)
	Mean	SD	Mean	SD		
ERA	3.10	.65	3.48	.95	−3.15	< .002
Hits per inning.	.89	.13	.94	.13	−3.13	< .002
Wins	13.04	4.90	11.70	5.50	2.72	< .002
Innings pitched	193.00	69.00	183.00	76.00	1.84	< .07
Games	42.00	13.60	40.00	16.30	1.66	< .10
Losses	9.50	4.20	9.4	4.00	.16	< .87
Strikeouts per inning	.61	.19	.61	.18	.05	< .96
Walks per inning	.34	.09	.33	.09	.83	< .41

Performance measures over a 6-year period for from 3 years before to 3 years after contract for pitchers with long-term guaranteed contracts (N = 38) are reported in Table 6.2. A trend analysis of these measures revealed a number of significant quadratic trends in which performance improved each year up until the guaranteed contract was signed and deteriorated for each year thereafter. Following this quadratic pattern were ERA, innings pitched, wins, and games. Significant quadratic trends were also found for walks, hits, and strikeouts per season, although the trends were absent on per inning measures of these variables. There was also no significant trend for losses.

Performances measures for pitchers without long-term contracts (N = 38), playing simultaneously with the guaranteed contract group, are presented in Table 6.3. A completely different pattern of trends was found with this group of pitchers. Significant linear trends for innings pitched, wins, and hits per inning were uncovered. Season totals for walks, strikeouts, and hits showed a similar linear performance decrease. Only ERA, games, losses, and per inning ratios for walks and strikeouts failed to show a linear decrease in performance.

Means and standard deviations for pitchers playing 10 years prior to 1979 are reported in Table 6.4. Though the majority of the significant trends were linear, there was more variability in the 1969 sample of trends. For example, ERA followed a cubic trend, while

TABLE 6.2. Means, Standard Deviations and Trends for All Dependent Measures for 38 Pitchers with Major League Records for Three Years Pre Long-Term, Guaranteed Contract and Three Years Post Contract.

		Pre-Contract Years			Post-Contract Years				
		1st	2nd	3rd	4th	5th	6th	Trend	Prob.
ERA	X	3.66	3.19	2.91	3.38	3.52	4.04	Quadratic	< .0001
	SD	1.12	.55	.56	.83	1.1	1.12		
Innings pitched	X	153	179	198	185	165	140	Quadratic	< .0007
	SD	92	84	73	80	80	78		
Wins	X	9.3	12.1	13.8	12.2	10.8	8.2	Quadratic	< .0001
	SD	5.9	5.8	4.9	5.7	5.9	5.6		
Games	X	33	39	43	42	41	37	Quadratic	< .003
	SD	17	13	13	16	17	17		
Walks per season	X	60	68	74	67	60	48	Quadratic	< .02
	SD	52	43	48	43	41	25		
Hits per season	X	149	165	176	173	162	137	Quadratic	< .008
	SD	84	78	67	71	77	70		
Strikeouts per season	X	101	124	128	125	104	87	Quadratic	< .002
	SD	73	63	61	64	63	65		
Walks per inning	X	.43	.46	.44	.44	.44	.45	None	
	SD	.52	.53	.59	.6	.6	.54		
Hits per inning	X	1.3	.95	.91	.99	1.06	1.06	None	
	SD	.43	.34	.35	.41	.52	.47		
Strikeouts per inning	X	.7	.75	.7	.74	.66	.63	None	
	SD	.35	.52	.51	.47	.35	.27		
Losses	X	9.1	8.8	10	9.3	8.9	8.2	None	
	SD	5.2	3.9	4.1	4.	4.2	4.2		

TABLE 6.3. Means, Standard Deviations and Trend for All Dependent Measures Over a 6-Year Period Those Pitchers in the Major Leagues without Guaranteed Contracts (N = 38).

		Years						Trend	Prob.
		1st	2nd	3rd	4th	5th	6th		
ERA	$\overline{X}$	3.70	3.88	3.68	3.96	3.76	4.10	None	–
	SD	.74	.96	1.15	.77	.87	.99		
Innings	$\overline{X}$	179	181	162	154	145	124	Linear	<.0001
pitched	SD	75	74	67	52	67	61		
Wins	$\overline{X}$	10.9	10.5	9.6	8.5	7.8	7.5	Linear	<.0004
	SD	5.6	5.5	5.3	3.9	4.9	4.6		
Games	$\overline{X}$	35	38	38	36	35	39	None	–
	SD	12.0	9.8	10.4	10.5	11.8	13.4		
Walks	$\overline{X}$	64	65	51	53	48	44	Linear	<.0001
per season	SD	28	22	22	23	22	19		
Hits	$\overline{X}$	172	180	159	156	145	130	Linear	<.001
per season	SD	73	73	66	51	68	63		
Strikeouts	$\overline{X}$	103	103	83	83	70	65	Linear	<.0001
per season	SD	51	46	35	39	37	32		
Walks	$\overline{X}$	.37	.39	.34	.35	.35	.38	None	–
per inning	SD	.12	.14	.15	.14	.13	.16		
Hits	$\overline{X}$	.97	.99	.99	1.03	1.00	1.10	Linear	<.02
per inning	SD	.14	.11	.14	.12	.11	.16		
Strikeouts	$\overline{X}$	.57	.59	.53	.54	.50	.54	None	–
per inning	SD	.14	.17	.18	.17	.13	.17		
Losses	$\overline{X}$	9.2	10.7	9.6	8.2	7.7	6.8	None	–
	SD	4.9	4.9	4.1	4.4	4.8	4.0		

walks per inning were quadratic. Innings pitched, wins, walks, hits, and strikeouts per season followed a significant linear trend over the 6 years. Games and losses as well as hits and strikeouts per inning showed no significant trend.

Performance variations for each group can be readily seen in Figures 6.1 through 6.4. Figure 6.1 presents ERA over a 6-year period for each of the three groups. The contract group allowed fewer earned runs per each nine innings on the average for each year until a guaranteed contract was signed. At that point, a steady increase begins in earned runs allowed. This pattern over 6 years is not present in either of the other groups. By the sixth year, performance of the guaranteed contract group has deteriorated past initial year performance and almost equals the record of the older non-guaranteed contract pitchers.

Figure 6.2 presents wins for each group. The same improvement can be seen for the guaranteed contract group up until contract date. Once on contract, a steady decrease in wins begins. The linear trend for the other two groups is apparent over the 6-year period.

The quadratic patterns for the guaranteed contract group for innings pitched and games is apparent in Figures 6.3 and 6.4. A linear decline is also evident for the noncontract groups in innings pitched but not in games.

The quadratic trends that occurred over these four crucial measures of pitching performance among the guaranteed contract group represent consistent performance deteriora-

TABLE 6.4. Means, Standard Deviations and Trend for All Dependent Measures Over a 6-Year Period for Pitchers in the Major Leagues Playing 10 Years Prior to 1979 (N = 40).

		Years						Trend	Prob.
		1st	2nd	3rd	4th	5th	6th		
ERA	X̄	3.32	3.21	3.45	3.20	2.86	3.57	Cubic	< .009
	SD	.79	.74	.82	.85	.85	1.04		
Innings	X̄	187	195	180	159	165	161	Linear	< .02
pitched	SD	68	68	78	75	83	88		
Wins	X̄	11.6	12.1	10.9	9.4	9.5	9.8	Linear	< .02
	SD	5.6	5.5	6.0	5.2	6.1	6.2		
Games	X̄	38	40	37	35	36	38	None	–
	SD	10	12.5	9.5	10.1	10.2	8.8		
Walks	X̄	60	61	53	49	47	55	Linear	< .05
per season	SD	27	26	27	27	24	28		
Hits	X̄	167	173	165	143	144	148	Linear	< .03
per season	SD	66	62	71	66	71	74		
Strikeouts	X̄	133	139	122	111	109	110	Linear	< .01
per season	SD	59	60	63	62	65	71		
Walks	X̄	.33	.32	.31	.31	.30	.37	Quadratic	< .04
per inning	SD	.11	.10	.11	.11	.10	.16		
Hits	X̄	.88	.89	.92	.91	.88	.96	None	–
per inning	SD	.12	.10	.14	.14	.13	.23		
Strikeouts	X̄	.72	.72	.67	.69	.65	.68	None	–
per inning	SD	.18	.15	.16	.17	.16	.18		
Losses	X̄	9.3	10.1	8.9	8.8	8.7	7.9	None	–
	SD	4.9	5.2	4.8	4.6	4.3	4.1		

tion after signing the guaranteed contract. Each of the four trends is extremely unlikely to have occurred by chance. For example, the weakest trend would have occurred only three times in one thousand by chance. The odds of getting chance quadratic trends of a similar nature over all four measures becomes truly astronomical. Regression toward the mean might explain the deterioration from years 3 through 6, but a group of top ERA pitchers from 1966 showed no consistent regression although they were selected to maximize regression effects.

The picture of steady improvement until the guaranteed contract and steady decline following it is even more striking when the guaranteed contract pitchers are compared to the two control groups. (Figures 6.1-6.4). While the experimental groups showed quadratic trends for the four measures discussed above, pitchers without long-term guaranteed contracts and those from 1969 showed either a linear deterioration, no trend at all, or in one case, ERA for the 10-year group, a cubic trend. While initially a sizeable difference in performance was observed between groups, after guaranteed contracts were awarded, little if any practical difference existed by the sixth year. This was most notable for wins, ERA, innings pitched and games.

Referring to Figures 6.1 through 6.4, it is apparent the guaranteed contract group performed at their highest level during the third, or precontract year of play. From reinforcement theory, these pitchers could be viewed as playing at their peak level when

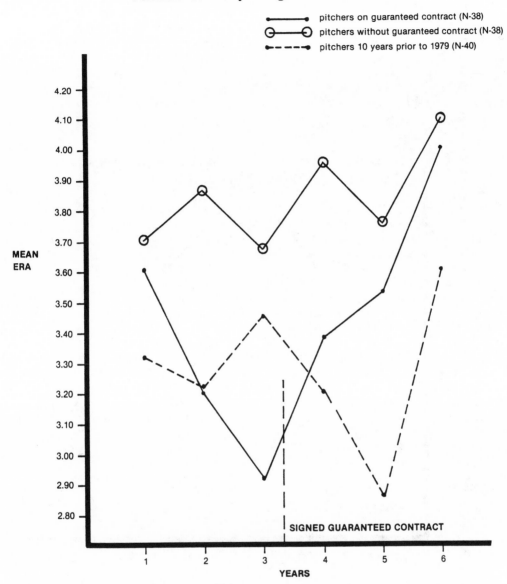

Fig. 6.1. Mean Earned Run Average Over Six Years for Pitchers by Group

rewards of considerable magnitude were most directly contingent on their performance. Once the contract is signed, however, rewards are earned regardless of performance. Ironically, the owners, in anticipation of several years of peak performance, awarded the contracts in such a fashion that both the contingency and motivating force of the contracts were lost. While one cannot attribute cause and effect from a trend analysis, the steady decline in years 4, 5, and 6 and the abrupt sharpness of this decline following the removal of contingencies eliminates many alternative explanations for the trend.

In analyzing the performance variation of walks, hits, and strikeouts per season, a fluctuation occurs that seems directly attributable to playing time (See Tables 6.2, 6.3, and 6.4). Such confounding prohibits any inferences about variations in the quality of performance. When these three variables are analyzed per inning, no change occurs across the 6-year period for pitchers on guaranteed contracts. When assessing these variables in the noncon-

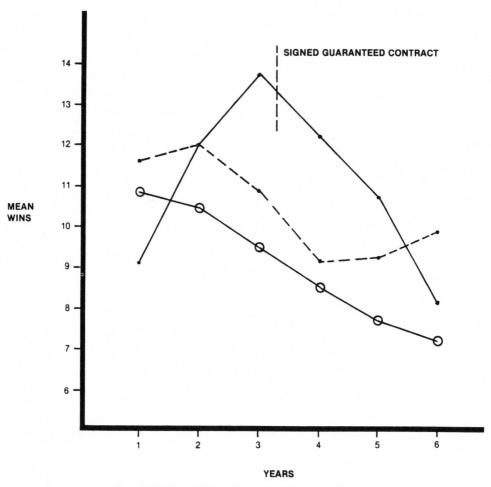

Fig. 6.2. Mean Wins Over Six Years by Group.

tract group, there is no change for walks or hits, but as mentioned above, there is a decline in strikeouts.

These between-group differences are quite striking, but there remains a good deal of uncontrolled variance that could be cited as problematic in the interpretation of these results. For example, it could be argued that injuries played a major part in the performance decay noted for the long-term quaranteed contract pitchers over the 3 post-contract years. Lehn (1981) has reported that professional baseball players on multi-year guaranteed contracts spent 153% more time on the disabled list than they had prior to signing guaranteed contracts with pitchers accounting for a substantial portion of that increase. Lehn, in fact, found that the number of remaining years on the guaranteed contract was the only significant predictor of days on the disabled list in a multiple regression analysis.

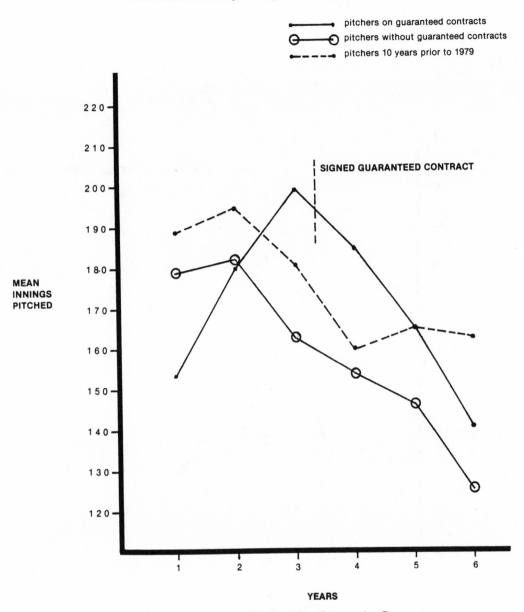

Fig. 6.3. Mean Innings Pitched Per Season by Group.

Table 6.5 reports the means and standard deviations for pitchers on long-term contracts excluding those appearing on the disabled list during that 6-year period. The exclusion of this data had little effect on the outcome of the trend analysis. The trend analysis on contracted pitchers minus injuries (Table 6.5) followed the same pattern of previous results for contracted pitchers, even with a reduced subject population (n = 29). It can be concluded that the previous results were not related to injuries among the guaranteed contract group. The random variation of injuries over 6 years appears to have masked a trend for one of the more precise measures of performance, hits per inning which now shows the same quadratic performance decay as the other four measures for the guaranteed contract pitchers (See Figure 6.5).

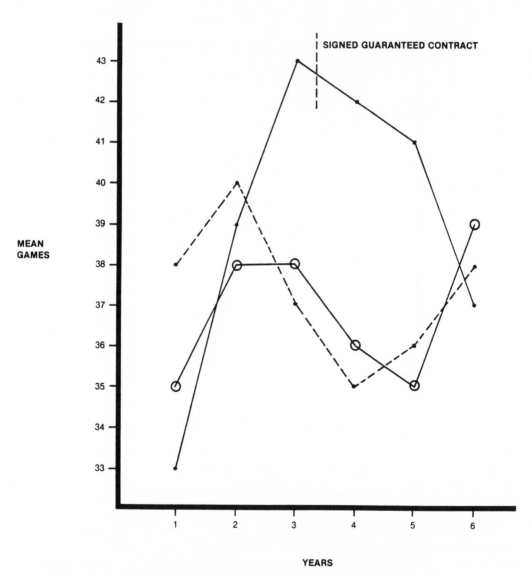

Fig. 6.4. Mean Appearances for Pitchers by Group

Another challenge to these results could come from the rather global definition of pitching that was adopted in this report. Pitching is not just one skill. Rather it has evolved to the point where each pitcher occupies a rather specific role on his team. To lump relief pitchers with starters ignores the differential demands of these two roles. Further, the de-

TABLE 6.5. Means, Standard Deviations And Trend for All Dependent Measures Over a 6-Year Period for All Those Pitchers in the Major Leagues with Guaranteed Contracts Excluding injuries.

| | | Pre-Contract Years | | | Post-Contract Years | | | | |
		1st	2nd	3rd	4th	5th	6th	Trend	Prob.
ERA	$\overline{X}$	3.64	3.13	2.88	3.22	3.39	3.83	Quadratic	< .0001
	SD	1.19	.53	.55	.62	.92	1.03		
Innings	$\overline{X}$	162	187	207	200	173	147	Quadratic	< .001
pitched	SD	95	87	73	71	77	80		
Wins	$\overline{X}$	9.5	12.5	14.0	13.1	10.7	9.0	Quadratic	< .0001
	SD	6.1	6.0	4.8	5.3	5.8	5.6		
Games	$\overline{X}$	33	39	44	44	41	38	Quadratic	< .006
	SD	18	14	14	16	16	18		
Walks	$\overline{X}$	56	63	70	65	58	49	Quadratic	< .01
per season	SD	41	30	34	34	31	25		
Hits	$\overline{X}$	151	168	177	179	164	139	Quadratic	< .02
per season	SD	83	82	69	65	76	72		
Strikeouts	$\overline{X}$	108	126	132	136	110	96	Quadratic	< .01
per season	SD	78	58	60	65	66	70		
Walks	$\overline{X}$	.34	.38	.35	.33	.35	.37	None	–
per inning	SD	.11	.15	.12	.11	.12	.13		
Hits	$\overline{X}$	.96	.89	.84	.90	.96	.99	Quadratic	< .0004
per inning	SD	.18	.11	.11	.12	.17	.16		
Strikeouts	$\overline{X}$	.67	.70	.65	.68	.63	.63	None	–
per inning	SD								
Losses	$\overline{X}$	8.8	8.7	10.2	9.4	9.2	8.3	None	–
	SD	4.7	4.1	4.3	3.6	4.3	4.1		

pendent measures that may be all important in evaluating a starting pitcher such as wins or innings pitched may have little relevance to the short relief pitcher who comes out of the bullpen to retire one batter. It could be argued that the performance decay seen in the guaranteed contract pitchers is an artifact of mixing starters and relievers so that performance on unimportant dependent measures for each group adds up to an artificial overall deterioration. In order to account for these different pitching demands, separate trend analyses were performed for starters and relievers.

The means and standard deviations for starting pitchers on long-term guaranteed contracts over the same 6-year period are reported in Table 6.6. As in prior analyses, the guaranteed contract group's performance followed a quadratic pattern. Significant quadratic trends were found for ERA, number of innings pitched, wins, games, and losses. Walks, hits, and strikeouts per season also showed a quadratic trend. However, these three measures were not significant on a per inning basis. The significant variation in pitching appearances (innings pitched and games) is presented in Figure 6.6.

Considering only starting pitchers reveals a pattern of improvement before the guaranteed contract and deterioration following it over four of the most significant variables in evaluating starting pitchers. These pitchers appeared less often, for shorter periods of time, while winning fewer games and allowing more earned runs per nine innings.

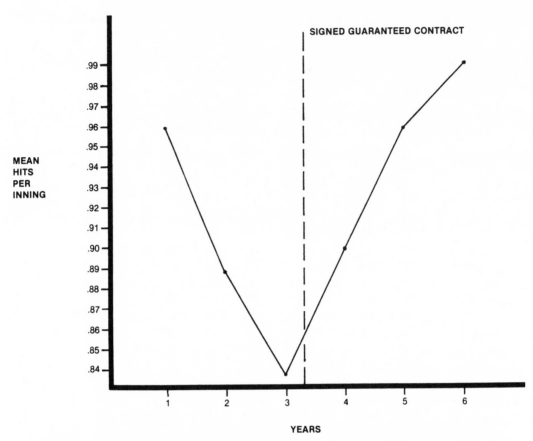

Fig. 6.5. Mean Hits Per Inning for Pitchers with Guaranteed Contracts Excluding Those Who Appeared on the Disabled List Between 1974 and 1979 (N-29).

When relief pitchers were eliminated, making the contract group more homogeneous, losses also showed significant quadratic trend. This makes sense since the system of assigning losses makes it more likely that a loss will be attributed to the starter than to a relief pitcher. It is no accident, for example, that relief pitcher Elroy Face of the Pittsburgh Pirates once won 22 games without a loss. This variation in losses over the 6-year period for starters is probably attributable to playing time, i.e., the more appearances and innings pitched the more chance of a loss. More important in this comparison is the significant deterioration in number of games played and innings pitched per season. Since starting pitchers are expected to pitch every 4 or 5 days, hopefully for nine innings, such a decrease in playing time can have a disasterous effect on management's planning for the season by placing extraordinary demands on other pitchers to take up the slack.

Performance means and standard deviations for relief pitchers (n = 13) with long-term guaranteed contacts are presented in Table 6.7. Variables that followed a significant quadratic trend over a 6-year period were ERA, games, hits per inning, and strikeouts both per inning and season. Measures that failed to reach significance were innings pitched, wins, losses, walks per inning, and walks and hits per season. The performance variation of ERA, hits and strikeouts per inning are presented in Figures 6.7 and 6.8, respectively.

As can be seen in Table 6.7, relief pitchers on guaranteed contracts did not vary significantly over a 6-year period for a number of measures that typically followed a

TABLE 6.6. Means, Standard Deviations and Trend for All Dependent Measures for All Starting Pitchers in the Major Leagues with Long-Term Contracts.

		Pre-Contract Years			Post-Contract Years				
		1st	2nd	3rd	4th	5th	6th	Trend	Prob.
ERA	X̄	3.58	3.15	3.11	3.38	3.57	3.96	Quadratic	< .002
	SD	1.14	.56	.47	.74	1.21	.88		
Innings	X̄	175	221	240	228	199	166	Quadratic	< .0001
pitched	SD	101	64	51	62	79	84		
Wins	X̄	10.6	14.9	16.5	14.8	12.6	9.2	Quadratic	< .0001
	SD	6.5	4.8	3.1	5.0	6.3	6.2		
Games	X̄	29	34	35	33	32	27	Quadratic	< .0002
	SD	13.6	4.5	3.4	4.5	9.1	10.0		
Walks	X̄	70	83	90	82	72	56	Quadratic	< .02
per season	SD	60	45	51	46	46	26		
Hits	X̄	170	203	218	216	199	164	Quadratic	< .0001
per season	SD	88	52	28	42	69	70		
Strikeouts	X̄	119	153	153	151	124	105	Quadratic	< .003
per season	SD	83	54	60	64	68	74		
Walks	X̄	.47	.47	.47	.47	.48	.48	None	-
per inning	SD	.64	.65	.73	.73	.74	.66		
Hits	X̄	1.05	.98	.97	1.03	1.12	1.12	None	-
per inning	SD	.52	.41	.41	.49	.62	.56		
Strikeouts	X̄	.72	.77	.71	.73	.65	.64	None	-
per inning	SD	.41	.62	.62	.58	.40	.31		
Losses	X̄	9.8	10.3	11.9	11.0	10.0	9.4	Quadratic	< .03
	SD	5.6	2.9	3.2	3.2	4.4	4.4		

quadratic trend for the group as a whole. It must be considered when viewing the data for relief pitchers that they are used in a completely different fashion than starting pitchers. Relief pitchers typically throw hard for a few innings and are usually not awarded wins or losses. Measures that become important for such pitchers are those that assess per inning performance. When looking at these measures, ERA followed a significant quadratic trend as did strikeouts, hits per inning, and appearances. The deterioration in performance quality after contract is prominently seen for ERA (Figure 6.7) and hits and strikeouts per inning (Figure 6.8). Contrary to the view that unimportant variables for each different type of pitcher might have been contributing to the overall trend, these data show that it is exactly those variables that are most significant in evaluating a relief pitcher that show the post-contract deterioration. Although the quadratic trend for games is marginal (p < .04), even with the small number of subjects, significant deterioration is seen for crucial quality variables such as hits per inning and strikeouts as well as for the less meaningful variable of earned run average.

Finally, Table 6.8 reports the correlations between the first year of performance and the 5 successive years for pitchers with long-term guaranteed contracts, pitchers without such contracts, and those pitching in 1969. The correlations over 5 years for innings pitched, wins, games, hits per season, and losses indicate more predictable performance for pitchers 10 years ago than for those playing in the major leagues today, regardless of contract. The

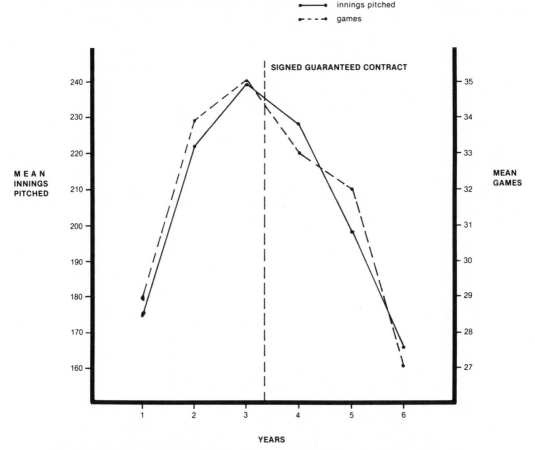

Fig. 6.6. Mean Innings Pitched and Mean Games Over 6 Years Per Starting Pitchers with Guaranteed Contracts.

correlations for walks and strikeouts per season were similar for each group. The correlations across year for ERA were surprisingly poor, indicating little predictive accuracy for future performance in this measure.

The year to year ability to predict performance is obviously important to management. It has also been cited as a major factor in fan interest in the game. While long-term guaranteed contracts are certainly not the only change to take place in baseball from 1969 to 1979, it is clear that, at least for pitching, it has become more difficult to make long-term predictions based on current performance since the introduction of long-term, guaranteed contracts. For innings pitched and wins where a sizeable correlation existed over 5 year's performance 10 years ago, there is now little or no relationship.

Theoretical Implications

One possible explanation for these results could be derived from Deci's (1975) work on intrinsic motivation. It could be theorized that the noncontingent reward situation of guaranteed contracts represents a change from extrinsic reward conditions in which pay was contingent on performance to a condition in which intrinsic motivation would have to maintain performance. Deci (1972a; 1972b; 1975) has argued that externally mediated rewards

TABLE 6.7. Means, Standard Deviations and Trend for All Dependent Measures for All Relief Pitchers (N = 13) in the Major Leagues with Guaranteed Contracts.

| | | Pre-Contract Years | | | Post-Contract Years | | | | |
		1st	2nd	3rd	4th	5th	6th	Trend	Prob.
ERA	$\overline{X}$	3.81	3.25	2.54	3.37	3.44	4.19	Quadratic	< .0003
	SD	1.12	.54	.54	1.02	.89	1.52		
Innings	$\overline{X}$	111	100	118	103	99	89	None	–
pitched	SD	54	57	31	30	14	21		
Wins	$\overline{X}$	6.77	6.69	8.61	7.15	7.15	6.31	None	–
	SD	3.2	3.4	3.4	3.0	3.6	3.4		
Games	$\overline{X}$	41	49	57	58	58	55	Quadratic	< .04
	SD	22	18	13	18	13	14		
Walks	$\overline{X}$	40	40	43	38	37	34	None	–
per season	SD	26	16	14	14	11	13		
Hits	$\overline{X}$	109	92	95	91	92	84	None	–
per season	SD	62	65	36	38	20	27		
Strikeouts	$\overline{X}$	67	69	81	76	65	54	Quadratic	< .02
per season	SD	26	34	22	26	24	18		
Walks	$\overline{X}$	.35	.45	.38	.39	.38	.37	None	–
per inning	SD	.10	.14	.12	.12	.11	.10		
Hits	$\overline{X}$	.98	.89	.79	.89	.93	.94	Quadratic	< .009
per inning	SD	.17	.13	.11	.12	.15	.19		
Strikeouts	$\overline{X}$	.64	.72	.69	.76	.67	.61	Quadratic	< .05
per inning	SD	.17	.20	.18	.16	.22	.18		
Losses	$\overline{X}$	7.7	5.8	6.2	5.8	6.8	6.1	None	–
	SD	4.4	3.7	2.8	2.9	2.9	3.0		

destroy the intrinsic motivation for the task in question. If this were to be true, it would have great significance for managers in almost every field. Money, praise, recognition, and gifts are all extrinsic reinforcers which management might have to consider discontinuing for fear of decreasing the "intrinsic" motivation of the worker. Before each and every manager junks his bonus system, the dichotomy between extrinsic and intrinsic motivation warrants closer scrutiny.

In a critique of the intrinsic motivation literature, Scott (1975) concluded that the meaning of intrinsic motivation is obscure and that there is no acceptable evidence that extrinsic reinforcers inevitably disrupt "intrinsically motivated behavior." Farr, Vance, and McIntyre (1977), for example, failed to find deleterious effects from external rewards. Calder and Staw (1975) have raised serious methodological questions about the intrinsic motivation literature, and Scott and Erskine (1980) have questioned the generality of this phenomenon. Mawhinney (1979) reanalyzed the performance of the individual subjects over the various conditions in Deci's (1971) original data. He found that the decrease in intrinsically motivated behavior following exposure to extrinsic rewards was not evident for 58% of the subjects.

Scott (1975) suggests that intrinsically motivated behavior is really behavior that is maintained by other, but perhaps less obvious, reinforcers. If one views the difference be-

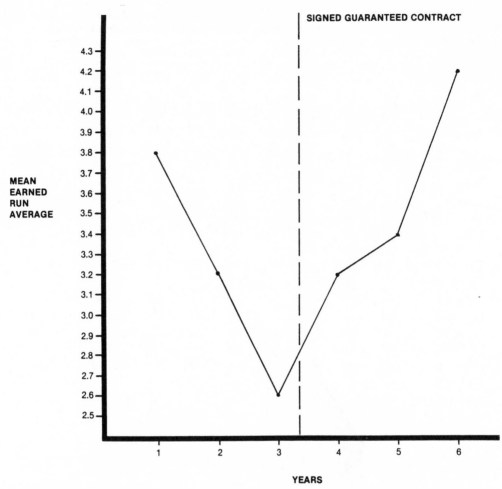

Fig. 6.7. Mean Earned Run Average Over 6-year Period for Relief Pitchers on Guaranteed Contracts.

tween intrinsic and extrinsic rewards in this light, one can reexamine the observed negative effects of extrinsic rewards on "intrinsically motivated" behaviors from a behavioral contrast (Catania, 1961; Reynolds, 1961) perspective. Levine, Broderick, and Burkhart (1980) recently investigated this explanation by presenting the opportunity to do puzzles and get noncontingent money in the opposite order to groups of subjects. They found both positive (money rated more highly following puzzles) and negative (puzzles rated less favorably following money) contrast effects even though doing puzzles was never rewarded with money. Like Tinklepaugh's monkeys (1928) for whom lettuce was reinforcing following nothing and not reinforcing following banana chips, Deci's (1971) subjects may have simply found puzzles less reinforcing in contrast to money. Without being able to identify the other reinforcers operating on the pitchers in the present study and given the poor empirical support for Deci's hypothesis, it does not seem to be helpful in explaining these results.

One effect that researchers (Kruglanski, Stein, & Riter, 1979) have found in studying the relationship between extrinsic rewards and performance is that when reinforcers are contingent on performance, subjects maximize task requirements viewed as integral in attaining rewards and minimize irrelevant task demands. If this is the case, studies of intrinsic

TABLE 6.8. Correlations and Explained Variance Between 1 Year and 5 Successive Years for All Dependent Measures for Pitchers on Guaranteed Contract (Beginning in Year 4), without Guaranteed Contracts and 10 Years Prior to 1979.

		2nd			3rd			4th			5th			6th		
		Con.	No Con.	10 yr.	Con.	No Con.	10 yr.	Con.	No Con.	10 yr.	Con.	No Con.	10 yr.	Con.	No Con.	10 yr.
ERA	r	.37*	.19	.23	-.14	.05	.15	.24	-.22	.07	-.04	.12	-.03	.00	-.19	.11
	r²	.14	.04	.05	.02	.00	.02	.06	.04	.00	.00	.01	.00	.00	.04	.01
Innings pitched	r	.56*	.68*	.80*	.39*	.55*	.83*	.32*	.29*	.67*	.20	.12	.57*	.33*	.25	.46*
	r²	.31	.46	.64	.15	.30	.69	.10	.08	.45	.04	.01	.32	.11	.06	.21
Wins	r	.42*	.44*	.53*	.29*	.40	.65*	.16	.15	.62*	-.02	.31*	.50*	.20	.13	.41*
	r²	.18	.19	.28	.08	.16	.42	.03	.02	.38	.00	.10	.25	.04	.02	.17
Games	r	.31*	.49*	.69*	.23	.59*	.28*	.43*	.29*	.55*	.26	.40*	.54*	.21	-.05	.45*
	r²	.10	.24	.37	.05	.35	.08	.18	.08	.30	.07	.16	.29	.04	.00	.20
Walks per season	r	.44*	.45*	.30*	.48*	.43*	.65*	.55*	.34*	.63*	.34*	.17	.43*	.55*	.26	.42*
	r²	.19	.20	.09	.23	.18	.42	.30	.12	.40	.12	.03	.18	.30	.07	.18
Hits per season	r	.57*	.69*	.78*	.37*	.55*	.77*	.29*	.39*	.66*	.26	.20	.47*	.32*	.31*	.39*
	r²	.32	.48	.61	.14	.30	.59	.08	.15	.44	.07	.04	.22	.10	.10	.15
Strikeouts per season	r	.53*	.72*	.62*	.69*	.70*	.67*	.56*	.40*	.63*	.41*	.20*	.45*	.51*	.30*	.40*
	r²	.28	.52	.38	.48	.49	.45	.31	.16	.40	.17	.04	.20	.26	.09	.16
Losses	r	.43*	.16	.69*	.25*	.30*	.39*	.06	.29*	.39*	.29*	-.12	.40*	.28*	.17	.25
	r²	.18	.03	.48	.06	.09	.35	.00	.08	.15	.08	.01	.16	.08	.03	.06

*p < .05.

109

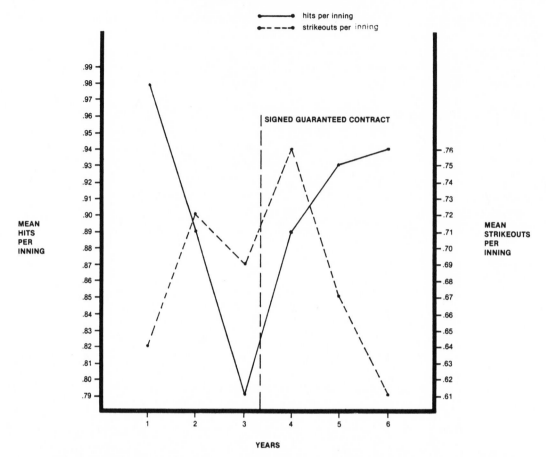

Fig. 6.8. Mean Hits Per Inning and Strikeouts Per Inning with Guaranteed Contracts for Relief Pitchers

motivation in contingent reward settings may demonstrate a decline of performance in areas that the subjects view as irrelevant to attaining rewards and not necessarily a decline in what they call intrinsic motivation. Thus, the worker does what he is paid to do and decreases irrelevant behaviors. This would suggest declines in performance can be avoided if the reinforcement contingencies are clearly stated and consistently followed. That is, the contract must be enforced so that the worker knows what responses will be rewarded. Obviously no one can identify the behaviors that are being rewarded if reinforcement is not contingent on any performance.

An issue related to, yet distinct from, reinforcer contingency is that of equity theory (Adams, 1965). Basically, equity theory maintains that individuals attempt to establish ratios of outcome (pay) and input (amount of work) equivalent to those of their coworkers. It is essentially a theory that specifies conditions under which various stimuli will act as reinforcers. Equity is established by the worker adjusting his performance in relation to the perceived equity of his rewards. Thus, if an employee feels over- or underpaid relative to his coworkers, he will adjust his efforts accordingly. Equity theory predicts and has found a direct relationship between pay and productivity (Folger, Rosenfield & Hays, 1978).

Lord and Hohenfeld (1979) posited that following the dramatic increase in compensation for players in professional baseball, some players "would perceive themselves as undercompensated" compared to those who received guaranteed, high salary, contracts. Some players who had announced that they would become free agents actually received salary cuts in the contract option year with their present club. According to equity theory, these players would also see themselves as undercompensated compared to their previous ratio of pay to performance. Lord and Hohenfeld predicted that the productivity of those players who experience inequities in comparison to the compensation of others (social referents) or their own previous salary (self-referents) would decrease. Their predictions from equity theory were supported.

For managers, equity theory highlights the difference between rewards and reinforcers. A $100 bonus for reaching quota may be a reward but is unlikely to function as a reinforcer if the salesman had been promised $1,000. The manager should be aware that it is not unusual for feelings of inequity to arise as rewards become noncontingent. The hard working employee who gets the same standard raise as the laggard experiences feelings of inequity and a breakdown in the relationship between productivity and rewards.

The case of pitcher Vida Blue (Lineberry, 1973) presents an excellent case of equity problems as well as a breakdown in response-reinforcement contingencies. During his first full year with the Athletics, Blue's salary was $14,750, although he had other benefits totaling another $13,500. During that season, Blue's performance was outstanding. Attendance at home and on the road increased substantially, thereby increasing the revenue of the team.

At this time, players were typically paid a traditional first year minimum salary with an average annual salary increase of 20% if performance increment occurred. This set rate minimized the contingent relationship between pay and performance and provided for perceptions of inequity between the player's performance and contribution to increased team revenue and his salary. Thus, the player's performance and value to the team may increase drastically while he receives only a 20% increase in pay. Then Athletics owner, Charles Finley, offered Blue $50,000 the following season, while Blue in turn requested $75,000. When no compromise could be reached, Blue prematurely retired from baseball. It is likely that a contigent system of pay and performance that had been specified before his first season would have been effective in satisfying both the player and the needs of the team management.

The current data offer little support for equity theory. The guaranteed contract pitchers experienced a significant increase in the reward half of the response to reinforcement ratio. Equity theory would predict that such increases should result in simultaneous increases in employee (pitcher) performance. However, the present results indicate this did not occur. It is hypothesized that the severence of contingencies between performance and reinforcement overrides the equity effects that might be expected from this increase in the magnitude of rewards. In other words, for increased reinforcement to effectively increase productivity, contingencies between pay and productivity must be maintained.

The decline in performance in the no-contract group also can not be justifiably attributed to issues of equity for two reasons. First, performance steadily decreased from year one rather than with the onset of contracts where an inequitable distribution would occur. Second, a similar deterioration occurred in the past control group again starting with year one without any equity issue being involved. Perhaps the best explanation for this finding would be an age effect. Overall, players in both control groups were older than those in the guaranteed contract group. As a result, deterioration may be attributed to the aging process. This is most evident when looking at the trends for strikeouts per inning. Pitchers who attempt to strike batters out rely heavily on the prowess of their throwing arm (i.e., throwing power). The contract group, being younger, remained consistent in strikeouts per inning across the 6-year period, while the older control group showed a significant decline. This would be expected, since power pitchers would be apt to show the effects of age more rapidly. It is interesting, however, that by the sixth year the guaranteed contract group, which is 2 years younger than the two other groups, begins approaching the same performance level.

The current findings suggest that pitchers signed under high pay, long-term guaranteed contracts show an overall decrease in performance once the contract takes effect. It is possible that this effect could be lessened in a system of contingently-based contracts which emphasized the attainment of performance goals. Unfortunately, the current noncontingent rewards are of such large magnitude that performance-based consequences might have little effect. It should be noted that a contingent contract based on accomplishment would not necessarily decrease the magnitude of reinforcement available for the player. There is also no reason that contingent performance contracts could not be established with fluctuating goals over a several year period. Such a contract system would also be inclusive of the average player who has not performed well enough to attain a long-term, high salary contract. In this instance, achievement goals can be negotiated that would allow equitable reward for productive seasons for all players.

In summary, removal of contingencies by giving out guaranteed, high pay, and long-term contracts has been shown to consistently coincide with significant deteriorations of major league pitchers' performance over several measures. This has occurred in spite of remarkable increases in pay. These results suggest that the contingent relationship between performance and reinforcement plays an integral part in maintaining both quantity and quality of performance for these athletes. This relationship is so crucial that even substantial increases in salary are rendered ineffective if they are not contingent upon attaining performance goals. Glen Chico Resch, the popular hockey goalie of the New York Islanders and Colorado Rockies, stated in a recent television interview (March 21, 1981) that long-term contracts may be fine for some players but you can see when most players are in their option year trying for a better contract. The present data suggest that this observation may also be applicable to members of major league baseball's pitching fraternity.

REFERENCES

Adams, J.S. Inequity in social exchange. In L. Berkowitz (Ed.), *Advances in experimental social psychology*. Vol. 2. New York: Academic Press, 1965.

Andrasik, F., Heimberg, J.S., & McNamara, J.R. Behavior modification of work and work-related problems. In M. Hersen, R.M. Eisler, & P.M. Miller (Eds.), *Progress in behavior modification*, New York: Academic Press, in press.

Blazer, H.M. (Ed.) *Official baseball register* St. Louis: The Sporting News, 1979.

Blazer, H.M. (Ed.) *Official baseball register* St. Louis: The Sporting News, 1980.

Buzas, H.T., & Ayllon, T. Differential reinforcement in coaching tennis skills. *Behavior Modification*, 1981, **5**, 372-385.

Calder, B.J., & Staw, B.M. The interaction of intrinsic and extrinsic motivation: Some methodological notes. *Journal of Personality and Social Psychology*, 1975, **31**, 76-80.

Catania, A.C. Behavioral contrast in a multiple and concurrent schedule of reinforcement. *Journal of the Experimental Analysis of Behavior*, 1961, **4**, 335-342.

Cloud, D.A., & O'Brien, R.M., *The effects of social reinforcement and feedback on cash register drawer neatness and accuracy.* Paper presented at the meeting of the Association for Behavior Analysis, Milwaukee, May 1981.

Costello, T.W., & Zalkind, S.S. *Psychology in administration; A research orientation; Text with integrated readings.* Englewood Cliffs, New Jersey: Prentice Hall, 1963.

Deci, E.L. Effects of externally mediated rewards on intrinsic motivation. *Journal of Personality and Social Psychology*, 1971, **18,** 105–115.

Deci, E.L. Intrinsic motivation, extrinsic reinforcement and inequity. *Journal of Personality and Social Psychology*, 1972a, **22,** 113–120.

Deci, E.L. The effects of contingent and non-contingent rewards and controls on intrinsic motivation. *Organizational Behavior and Human Performance*, 1972b; **8,** 217–229.

Deci, E.L. *Intrinsic motivation.* New York: Plenum Press, 1975.

Employee recognition: A key to motivation. *Personnel Journal*, 1981, **60,** 103–107.

Farr, J.L. Task characteristics, reward contingency, and intrinsic motivation. *Organizational Behavior and Human Performance*, 1976, **16,** 294–307.

Farr, J.L., Vance, R.J., & McIntyre, A.M. Further examinations of the relationships between reward contingency and intrinsic motivation. *Organizational Behavior and Human Performance*, 1977, **20,** 31–53.

Feeney, E.J., & Staelin, J.R., The use of tangible and intangible reinforcers in industry. In A.M. Dickinson & R.M. O'Brien (Chairs), *Organizational behavior management: Procedures, problems and progress.* Symposium presented at the meeting of the Association for Behavior Analysis, Milwaukee, 1981.

Fiedler, F.E., & Mahar, L. A field experiment validating contingency model leadership training. *Journal of Applied Psychology*, 1979, **64,** 247–254.

Fitts, P.M. Cognitive aspects of information processing. *Journal of Experimental Psychology*, 1966, **71,** 849–857.

Folger, R., Rosenfield, D., & Hays, R.P. Equity and intrinsic motivation: The role of choice. *Journal of Personality and Social Psychology*, 1978, **36,** 557–566.

Gamzu, E.R., Williams, D.R. & Schwartz, B. Pitfalls of organismic concepts: "Learned laziness?" *Science*, 1973, **181,** 367–368.

Johnson, G.A. The relative efficacy of stimulus versus reinforcement control for obtaining stable performance change. *Organizational Behavior and Human Performance*, 1975, **14,** 321–341.

Keller, F.S. *Learning: Reinforcement theory.* New York: Random House, 1954.

Kirschenbaum, D.S., Ordman, A.M., Tomarken, A.J. & Holtzbauer, R. Effects of differential self-monitoring and level of mastery on sports performance: Brain power bowling. *Cognitive Therapy and Research*, in press.

Komaki, J., & Barnett, F.T., A behavioral approach to coaching football: Improving play execution of the offensive backfield on a youth football team. *Journal of Applied Behavior Analysis*, 1977, **10,** 657–664.

Kruglanski, A.W., Stein, C., & Riter, A. Contingencies of exogenous reward and task performance: On the "minimax" strategy in instrumental behavior. *Journal of Applied Social Psychology*, 1977, **7,** 141–148.

Leeming, F.C., Blackwood, H.D., & Robinson, K.D. Instrumental learning in the presence of non-contingent reward. *Journal of Experimental Psychology: Human Learning and Memory*, 1978, **4,** 266–273.

Lehn, K. *Property Rights, Risk-Bearing and Player Disability in Major League Baseball. Working Paper #64.* St. Louis, MO, Washington University-Center For the Study of American Business, 1981.

Lenin, V.I. The Taylor System – man's enslavement by the machine. In G.E. Stein (Ed.), *Broken image.* New York: Random House, 1972.

Levine, F.M., Broderick, J.E., & Burkart, M.R. *Attribution vs. Contrast: A reinterpretation of the effects of externally mediated rewards on intrinsic motivation.* Paper presented at the American Psychological Association meeting. Montreal, Aug. 1980.

Levine, M. Cue neutralization: The effects of random reinforcement upon discrimination learning. *Journal of Experimental Psychology*, 1962, **63,** 438–443.

Lineberry, W.P. (Ed.) *The business of sports.* New York: H.W. Wilson, Co., 1973.

Lord, R.G., & Hohenfeld, J.A. Longitudinal field assessment of equity effects on the performance of major league baseball players. *Journal of Applied Psychology*, 1979, **64,** 19–26.

Luyben, P., Hansen, R., Hardy, J., Leonard, T., & Romero, J., *Behavioral athletics: Improving shooting accuracy on a college varsity women's soccer team*. Paper presented at the meeting of the Association for Behavior Analysis, Dearborn, Michigan, May 1980.

Mawhinney, T.C. Intrinsic and extrinsic work motivation: perspectives from behaviorism. *Organizational Behavior and Human Performance*, 1979, **24,** 411–440.

McKenzie, T.L., & Rushall, B.S. Effects of self-recording on attendance and performance in a competitive swimming training environment. *Journal of Applied Behavior Analysis*, 1974, **7,** 199–206.

McManis, D.L., & Dick, W.G. Monetary incentives in today's industrial setting. *Personnel Journal*, 1973, **52,** 387–392.

Millenson, J.R., & Leslie, J.C. *Principles of behavioral analysis*. New York: Macmillan, 1979.

Miller, L.M. *Behavior management: The new science of managing people at work*. New York: Wiley, 1978.

Montegar, C.A., Reid, D.H., Madsen, C.H., Jr., & Ewell, M.D. Increasing institutional staff to resident interactions through in-service training and supervisor approval. *Behavior Therapy*, 1977, **8,** 533–540.

Redd, W.H. Effects of mixed reinforcement contingencies on adults' control of children's behavior. *Journal of Applied Behavior Analysis*, 1969, **2,** 249–254.

Reynolds, G.S. Behavioral contrast. *Journal of the Experimental Analysis of Behavior*, 1961, **4,** 57–71.

Roth, A. *Who's Who in Baseball* (55th edition). New York: Who's Who in Baseball Publishing Co., 1970.

Rothe, H.F. Output rates among industrial employees. *Journal of Applied Psychology*, 1978, **63,** 40–46.

Scott, W.E. The effects of extrinsic rewards on "intrinsic motivation." A critique. *Organizational Behavior and Human Performance*, 1975, **15,** 117–129.

Scott, W.E., & Erskine, J.A. The effects of variations in task design and monetary reinforcers on task behavior. *Organizational Behavior and Human Performance*, 1980, **25,** 311–335.

Siddall, J.W., & Balcerzak, W.S. A behavioral model for welfare reform: the volunteer incentive system. *Behavior Therapy*, 1978, **9,** 243–247.

Simek, T.C., & O'Brien, R.M. *Total golf: A behavioral approach to lowering your score and getting more out of your game*. Garden City, N.Y.: Doubleday, 1981.

Skinner, B. F. *Contingencies of reinforcement: A theoretical analysis*. New York: Appleton-Century-Crofts, 1969.

Terborg, J.R. & Miller, H.E. Motivation, behavior and performance: A closer examination of goal setting and monetary incentives. *Journal of Applied Psychology*, 1978, **63,** 29–39.

Tinklepaugh, O.L. An experimental study of representative factors with monkeys. *Comparative Psychology*, 1928, **8,** 197–236.

Tosi, H.L. & Hamner, C.V. *Organizational behavior and management: A contingency approach*. Chicago: St. Clair Press, 1974.

Welker, R.L. Acquisition of a free operant appetitive response in pigeons as a function of prior experience with response – independent food. *Learning and Motivation*, 1976, **7,** 394–403.

Wiard, H. Why manage behavior? A case for positive reinforcement. *Human Resource Management*, 1972, **11,** 15–20.

7

Operant Terms and Concepts Applied to Industry

Thomas C. Mawhinney and **Renée R. Mawhinney,** *Associate*
Indiana University   *Barnes & Thornburg*

The operant paradigm has been employed to discover and describe mechanisms or principles which relate behavior variations to the history of the individual organism and the environmental consequences of behavior, past and present (Ferster & Skinner, 1957; Honig, 1966; Skinner, 1938, 1956). In order to isolate these principles, the histories and environments of organisms phylogenically lower than man were manipulated in highly controlled laboratory settings. Many of these principles have been replicated with human subjects in laboratories and in constrained field settings such as schools and mental hospitals (Bandura, 1969; Catania, 1968; Ulrich, Stachnik & Mabry, 1966, 1970). Successful replications with human subjects piqued the interest of some industrial/organizational psychologists concerning the paradigm's implications for theory development (Adams & Romney, 1959; Hamner, 1974; Joblansky & De Vries, 1972; Mawhinney & Ford, 1977, Mawhinney, 1979b), applied laboratory experimentation (Mawhinney, 1981), and the practice of management (Mawhinney, 1975).

Although interest in application, theoretical extension, testing, and contrasting operant conditioning and cognitive theories of individual behavior determination has grown rapidly throughout the decade of the 1970s, the operant paradigm is still not well understood or appreciated by many applied industrial/organizational psychologists.

These psychologists typically fail to appreciate the complexity of the operant account of human behavior determination and the attention to detail required in its application when describing individual work behavior and its environmental determinants. Heiman (1975) reminded us that "operant terms are not as simple-minded as they may appear [p. 169]" while correcting a misinterpretation of negative reinforcement made by Joblansky and De Vries (1972). Yet Locke (1980) has perpetuated the notion that operant theory is not an adequate theory of work behavior by characterizing it in *simple minded terms*. His representation of the paradigm is, of course, simply incorrect and certainly incomplete (Mawhinney, 1980).

Locke (1980) contends that behaviorists deny the existence of cognitions, purposiveness, and intentions (Skinner, 1974). Although behaviorists in the operant tradition believe that cognitions, as cognitive theorists characterize them, are by-products of physiological brain mechanisms (Skinner, 1975), they also consider the essence of operant behavior to be purposiveness. (If one believes that Locke (1980) has accurately portrayed the operant model of individual behavior, however, one is not likely to look for operant terms and concepts that describe purposive behavior or behavior which appears to result from cognitive processes in spite of the fact that terms and concepts for their description are included in the operant paradigm.)

Given these misunderstandings regarding the operant paradigm, readers should not be surprised to learn that industrial/organizational psychologists tend to employ only two of the three terms of a functional analysis when they describe reinforcement contingencies. They note only the response and schedules of reinforcement, punishment, or extinction. Although operant theorists (Skinner, 1953, 1969) consider individual *reinforcement histories* to be essential elements in describing and understanding individual reactions for work environments, *reinforcement histories* are typically omitted when industrial/organizational psychologists describe reinforcement contingencies (Mawhinney, 1975).

The purpose of this chapter is, therefore, to present the operant paradigm in a manner that focuses attention on its relation to purposiveness in behavior and how the paradigm may be employed to help one understand and control, within limits, one's own behavior and the behavior of others for which one may be responsible in a work environment. Achievement of this objective may be facilitated by recounting some of the more common problems of interpretation and application of operant terms and concepts (Mawhinney, 1975). Thus, the chapter includes elements of review, criticism, and commentary regarding the current value of the operant paradigm.

TWO-TERMED OPERANT CONTINGENCIES: SOME ISSUES OF INTERPRETATION

The most fundamental problems related to interpretation and understanding of the operant approach to behavior description and explanation are conceptual in nature. However, there are a number of technical problems of interpretation that contribute to the many misunderstandings about operant psychology. For these reasons we begin our examination of the paradigm by considering some of the technical problems and then shift to consideration of conceptual problems related to interpretations of the paradigm.

The dependent variable, or the one to be explained or controlled in the operant paradigm, is rate of responding or performance rate. The responses, behaviors, or performances must be observable ones because an operant analysis requires that response rate be measured in terms of number of occurrences over some period of time, i.e., responses per minute, responses/hour, responses/day, responses/week, and so on. The dependent variable is one that is influenced by many independent variables including the effortfulness of the response itself, consequences that depend upon the response (reinforcers and punishers), deprivation/satiation for the response consequences, schedules of reinforcement (consequences), alternative reponses, and a host of other environmental variables, not the least of which is the reinforcement history of the behavior and its consequences in the situation wherein the response is (or is to be) observed (Honig, 1966; Honig & Staddon, 1977; Ferster & Skinner, 1957; Skinner, 1938).

Of the independent variables known to influence response strength or rate of response, reinforcement schedules appear to have captured the greatest attention by industrial/organizational psychologists because they appear to be powerful and controllable determinants of behavior strength (rate). However, utilization of reinforcement schedules presumes that one can accurately isolate what are reinforcers and punishers that can be made contingent upon a response by a schedule. Psychologists have exhibited some difficulty with the task of accurately identifying and defining reinforcers in both theoretical discussions and in field tests of operant principles of reinforcement. For these reasons we begin our review of technical problems of interpretation by considering the issue regarding what reinforcers and punishers are as the terms are employed in the operant paradigm.

DEFINING RESPONSE CONSEQUENCES FUNCTIONALLY: TAUTOLOGIES

No doubt because of the association of "positive" with increases and "negative" with decreases in the values of things when the terms "positive" and "negative" are employed in everyday conversation, the scientific term "negative reinforcement" is often confused with another scientific operant term, "punishment." The term *reinforcement*, however, *always* refers to *increasing* (or maintaining) the strength or rate of a response by manipulation of its consequences.

Reinforcement of a response can be achieved in two ways. Both involve alteration of the environment in which behavior occurs or *stimulus consequences*, S_cs, of the response (where $R \rightarrow S_c$ is read R is followed by or produces a stimulus alteration as a consequence, S_c, of R). The environment in which a response occurs can be referred to as antecedent stimuli of the behavior or the ambient stimulation. This is because some stimuli, represented here by S_a, are always present when the response occurs. This environment can be changed by adding something to it as a consequence of the response, as when food is added to an animal's cage following its execution of a lever pressing response. Thus, before R occurred one would observe S_a, and after R occurred one would observe $S_a + S_c$ (where S_c represents addition of food to a cage). Of course, the situation returns to S_a quickly if our animal is deprived of food because the food is consumed by the animal. Suppose, on the other hand, that an animal's S_a includes a metal floor grid that is electrified so that its feet are shocked if it stands upon the floor. If a lever is pressed, however, the electrical current is removed from the grid for a short period of time so that before R we have S_a, and after (for a short period of time) we have $S_a - S_c$ (where S_c is termination or removal of electric shock in S_a if R occurs).

In the former procedure the stimulus consequence contingent upon the operant response was presentation to or an *addition* of some stimulus to the situation, while in the latter procedure a stimulus was *terminated* or *removed* from the situation. The reader has no doubt guessed that presentation of food and removal of electricity from the floor grid of a food deprived animal have common effects upon rate of the lever pressing response. In both cases response reinforcement (response rate increase) occurs. Reinforcement effected by contingent presentation of a stimulus consequence is termed *positive reinforcement*, and the stimulus consequence is termed a *positive reinforcer*. Reinforcement effected by contingent *withdrawal* or *removal* of a stimulus (or stimuli) as a stimulus consequence is termed *negative reinforcement* and the S_c is termed a *negative reinforcer*.

Punishment, conversely, refers to the *reduction* of response rate or strength by contingent presentation or withdrawal of stimulus consequences; that is, response rate reduction due to application of *positive punishers* and removal of *negative punishers* contingent upon the response. Joblansky and De Vries (1972) described positive reinforcement of performances by one's manager and negative reinforcement of performances by one's peers as conflicting reinforcement contingencies. They clearly confused punishment and negative reinforcement. Their error serves, however, to highlight the importance of distinguishing between everyday language usages and the scientific language which characterizes the operant reinforcement paradigm.

Figure 7.1 provides a scheme for organizing and defining these relationships among response rate and consequences. In addition, it provides us with a way to write two-termed contingency relationships. For example, $R \rightarrow S^+$ refers to positive reinforcement; $R \rightarrow -S^+$ refers to negative reinforcement; $R \rightarrow S^-$ refers to positive punishment; $R \rightarrow -S^-$ refers to negative punishment, and so on.

	Stimulus Consequence of Operant (R)	
Effect on Rate of R	$R \rightarrow$ Presentation $(S_a + S_c).$	$R \rightarrow$ Withdrawal $(S_a - S_c).$
Increases	Reinforcer/Positive $S_c = S^+$	Reinforcer/Negative $S_c = -S^+$
Decreases	Punisher/Positive $S_c = S^-$	Punisher/Negative $S_c = -S^-$
No change	Neutral Stimulus $S_c = S°$	Neutral Stimulus $S_c = S°$

Fig. 7.1 Defining Consequences by Their Effects on Operant Behavior

Extinction is the discontinuance of a contingency following one of these conditioning procedures. It can be represented by the following sentence, $R \rightarrow \phi$.

Positive and negative reinforcers are functional tautologies employed in the operant paradigm to unambiguously classify stimuli on the bases of their effects on rate of response when made *contingent* upon a response in a particular situation, S_a. Although no reference is made to the subjective experiences of the individual whose behavior may be the focus of such stimulus definition, it is reasonable to assume that positive reinforcers are relatively more attractive and satisfying to the individual than are negative reinforcers. This inference is based upon what people do with respect to the two types of stimuli. They will exert effort to acquire or make contact with positive reinforcers and exert effort to avoid negative reinforcers. Given complete freedom, people tend to approach the former and avoid the latter. It would be incorrect to assume, however, that what we typically consider rewards, e.g., tasty foods, drinks, money, and the like, are reinforcers because they typically result in subjectively experienced satisfaction or pleasure.

Premack (1971) has shown that a positive reinforcer in one circumstance can be made to function as a positive punisher in another circumstance. The controlling factor is relative deprivation/satiation for the stimulus consequence as Allison and Timberlake (1974) have demonstrated. When one is satiated with food and deprived of water, food can be employed to punish a response, while water reinforces the response and vice versa when the deprivation/satiation relationship is reversed. Thus relative deprivation/satiation for a stimulus can determine whether the stimulus will function as a reinforcer, punisher, or have no effect (neutral stimulus) when made contingent upon a response (Mawhinney, 1979a).

When it is assumed that any *reward* is also a *reinforcer*, the risk of making a potentially serious error is great. For example, the money *rewards* made contingent upon performance in one field experiment actually *reduced the performance* upon which the *rewards* were contingent (Yukl & Latham, 1975). And while Schneier (1974) concluded that "rewards can be effective in controlling . . . behavior only if they are closely linked temporally to the behavior [p. 259]", a reward which is not also a reinforcer will not benefit from a temporally short linkage to behavior. Further, as we have noted with respect to negative reinforcement, the type of linkage, presentation versus withdrawal, is an equally important element in accurately *describing* reinforcement procedures. If misunderstanding and misuse of operant terms and concepts are to be avoided, one must take care to respect the distinction between the nonscientific term *reward* and the scientific term *reinforcer* as Joblansky and De Vries (1972) have graphically demonstrated.

ENVIRONMENTAL RULES OF RESPONSE/CONSEQUENCE RELATIONS: SCHEDULES OF REINFORCEMENT

Unlike reinforcers and punishers, which are tautologically defined in terms of their effects upon response strength, schedules of reinforcement are defined independently of any effect upon response rate. Yet they have, under certain conditions, *predictable effects upon response rate*. A schedule of reinforcement (or punishment) is a role that specifies a relationship between occurrences of a response and its stimulus consequences, positive and negative reinforcers and punishers.

Reinforcement schedules are either continuous or intermittent. A continuous schedule of reinforcement specifies that every time a certain response occurs, if it occurs at all, that response will be followed by a reinforcer (presentation of a positive reinforcer or withdrawal of a negative reinforcer). It is often referred to as a CRF schedule.

Intermittent schedules are of two types, those that specify a number of responses that must occur between each reinforced response, and those that specify that some interval of time must elapse before a response may be reinforced. The former are termed *ratio schedules* and the latter *interval schedules*.

The ratios of responses occurring between reinforced responses may be fixed or variable. The fixed ratio schedule (FR) specifies a fixed number of responses N which must occur between each Nth response that is followed by a reinforcer, FR-N. The variable ratio schedule of reinforcement (VR) specifies that the value of N vary over some range of values and occur in such a way that the average ratio of responses to reinforcements equals N, VR-N. Flipping a fair coin after each response and giving a reinforcer each time a head is observed results in a VR-2 schedule.

The fixed interval schedule (FI) specifies that the first response that occurs after an interval of time (T) has elapsed since the last reinforced response be followed by a reinforcer FI-T. The variable interval (VI) schedule specifies that the intervals vary in such a way that the average interval of time between reinforced responses is T, VI-T.

Ratio schedules typically produce rates of response that are appreciably higher than those produced by interval schedules for reasons that will become apparent as we proceed. Every response to a ratio schedule contributes to progress toward the response that will produce a reinforcer, while only responses that occur after a certain time period has elapsed contribute to reinforcement on an interval schedule. Consider the following example: The maximum rate of a response a hypothetical person can achieve is 60 per hour. Now suppose this person works at the rate of 30 resp./hr (responses per hour). If s/he is working on an FR-5 reinforcement schedule, s/he will receive 6 reinf./hr. (reinforcements per hour). If s/he slows to 15 resp./hr. on this schedule, then rate of reinforcement *also* slows to 3 reinf./hr. And, if s/he accelerates on this schedule to say 45 resp./hr., then rate of reinforcement will rise to 9 reinf./hr. The maximum rate of reinforcement which can be achieved by our hypothetical person on this schedule is fixed by the value of N (here N = 5) and the upper limit on response rate (here 60 resp./hr). Thus, maximum possible reinf./hr. in the example is 12 reinf./hr. Notice too that the probability of a response being reinforced does not vary with response rate variations; it is always 1/N.

Now consider another example: Let maximum response rate remain at 60, but let our subject work on a fixed interval schedule with a value for T equal to 10 minutes or T = 10. If our subject has a way to measure intervals of time between responses and responds every 10 minutes, a rate of 6 reinf./hr. should be obtained. If the subject slows down, fewer reinforcers will be obtained. However, even if our subject speeds up by responding with two additional responses within each interval, rate of response will rise to 18 resp./hr., but rate of reinforcement will remain fixed at 6 reinf./hr. When responses are spaced at 10-minute intervals or greater, the probability of a response being followed by a reinforcer is one, but the probability of reinforcement for each single response falls as responses occur in addition to the minimum required to obtain all possible reinforcers. If organisms generally employ rules of effort allocations that serve to minimize the ratio of *effort output* (responses) to reinforcement *returns to effort* (reinforcements received), they should never respond at a rate higher than the minimum required to obtain all reinforcers possible on an interval schedule, for example, 10 resp./hr. on an FI-6 min., 12 resp./hr. on an FI-5 min., and so on.

The senior author has obtained empirical evidence for this theory of effort allocation in a trigger squeezing task situation with monetary reinforcement for work at trigger squeezing (Mawhinney, 1979b). Needless to say, in the absence of better alternative sources of reinforcements, ratio schedules produce as many as 100 more responses per reinforcement than do interval schedules (Mawhinney, 1981).

Given these facts about the relative effectiveness of ratio and interval schedules, confusion of the two types may represent a serious error. Schneier (1974), in arguing for the superiority of VR schedule efficiency and effectiveness as performance reinforcers, erroneously cited an experiment by Schmitt (1969). However, Schmitt (1969) compared effectiveness of FI and VI schedules only, not ratio versus interval schedules. Schneier confused interval schedules with ratio schedules. Although VI schedules do produce higher response rates than do FI schedules, both interval schedules are inferior to ratio schedules in terms of the rates of response they will produce with the same number of reinforcers.

The term operant response is typically used to refer to the effect of a response upon its environment, often without reference to its "topography." To say that a lever is pressed says nothing about the pattern of movements or the force that is exerted in achieving the response or its *topography*. Perhaps because no distinction is made between response effects and topography in the typical discussion of operant behavior in organizational settings, the continuous reinforcement schedule (CRF) has been confused with *response shaping*, a procedure that is employed to change response topography.

The topography of a response typically varies along a number of dimensions; for example, force applied by an animal when pressing a lever varies from not enough to register a response to force levels much greater than that required to operate the lever. When an animal works on a CRF schedule, every response with enough force to operate the lever produces a reinforcer. An experimenter can alter the force employed so that eventually force levels (topography) not currently exhibited by the subject can be observed with some regularity. The change is accomplished by shaping this particular aspect of response topography by *raising the force level required* but still keeping it *within the range of force levels initially exhibited* by the subject. The result of raising the force level requirement will be to raise the mean level of force exerted in responding *and* initiation of some responses with force levels *greater than any observed in the initial distribution of force levels*. Successive increases in requirements can eventually raise the level of the typical response to a level greater than the greatest force level observed before shaping began.

Response shaping or shaping is a way of introducing into a behavioral repertoire responses with topographies that would never occur otherwise. A practical and humorous example of shaping an employee's physical hygiene and dress (appearance) may be found in Brethower's (1972) comicbook approach where shaping is termed *building on strengths*. In the example an employee is described as appearing "bad" on some occasions and "worse" on others. When the employee arrives at work one day with one shined shoe the superior remarks, not sarcastically, about the worker's unusually nice appearance. Subsequently both shoes appear shined, another remark is made, and so on until the worker attains an attractive appearance. Neatness improvement represented a strength, ergo the idea of building on strengths.

In the absence of a contingency between a behavior and a reinforcer it makes little sense to speak of a reinforcement schedule. In this regard, inaccurate references to hourly wages and salaries as FI schedules of reinforcement for performance in organzations are simply too numerous to list. As has been pointed out by Skinner (Conversation with B.F. Skinner, 1973), these contingencies more accurately represent relationships between attendance on the job and pay, not contingencies between performance and pay. People frequently do work at some minimum acceptable level, however, in order to *avoid* the loss of job and necessities for living that are purchased with income from remaining on the job. But when there is no actual relationship between job performance and hourly rate of pay, it cannot be said that hourly pay constitutes an FI schedule of reinforcement.

In order to appreciate how it is that people "know" about such relationships we must consider how the operant paradigm deals with the issue of purposiveness in behavior and what appears to most people to be behavior guided by some cognitive information processing ability. The two termed contingency, $R \rightarrow S^+$, does not adequately address the issue, however.

Conceptual Issues/Problems

Because it is often assumed that operant conditioners deny the fact that people subjectively experience cognitive processes, intentions, and purposes, operant terms and concepts which describe their overt manifestations have been ignored or misunderstood by industrial/organizational psychologists (cf. Locke, 1980 and Skinner, 1974). In fact, the basic subject matter of operant psychology is *purposive behavior* (Skinner, 1969), and the human is considered a highly complex *information processor* (Millenson & Leslie, 1979). However, because the subjective experiences of people are not considered reliably observable, and because subjective statements about such experiences are not considered sufficiently reliable descriptions of the physical processes assumed to produce them (Skinner, 1974, 1975), they do not produce adequate data upon which to construct a science of behavior (Skinner, 1974, 1975). The operant paradigm, therefore, represents an attempt to describe the determinants of purposive behavior from the point of view of an objective third person observer. At the same time, subjective experiences are evident in observed behavior as we shall see.

Although the simple two-termed contingency of reinforcement (response and reinforcer) suggests what relations between behavior and environment may be employed to control behavior, it is difficult to account for complex human behavior solely in terms of its consequences (or $R \rightarrow S^{+, -, o}$). If work behavior varied in terms of topography and frequency only when its consequences were changed, much time would be spent by managers in attempts to manipulate behavior consequences. And Locke's (1980) assertion that evidence of an operant conditioning process is manifest only when "Response frequency increases in small increments as a function of the number of reinforcements. . . . [p. 17]," would be valid. But a person does not enter the work place as a tabula rasa. People bring with them a rather extensive history of reinforcement and the ability to describe with verbal behavior their reinforcement contingencies, experiences, and *some* events occurring "within their skin" (subjective experiences).

Histories of reinforcement account for much of the phenomenon termed *stimulus control*, or the effects of certain stimuli on response probability, due to their historic association with a two-termed reinforcement contingency. In the classic stimulus control experimental arrangement, one value of a stimulus (for instance, shade of light color on a screen or button) is always present at the same time that a two-termed contingency is operational, i.e., when $R \rightarrow S^+$. The stimulus correlated with $R \rightarrow S^+$ is termed a *discriminative stimulus* (or S^D). When any other value of the stimulus is present (say all other shades of light color other than the S^D value), no reinforcement follows the response, i.e., $R \rightarrow \phi$. These other stimuli, in the presence of which the response is *not* reinforced, if it occurs, are collectively termed the *ess delta*, (or S^Δ). It should not be difficult to predict the effect of alternations among S^D and S^Δ conditions (i.e., $S^D: R \rightarrow S^+$ is read if S^D then $R \rightarrow S^+$ and $S^\Delta: R \rightarrow \phi$ is read, if S^Δ then $R \rightarrow \phi$) even on the behavior of the lowly pigeon (Guttman, 1959; Herrick, Myers, & Korotkin, 1959; Jenkins & Harrison, 1960).

Initially R occurs with about equal frequency in the presence of S^D and S^Δ. However, as the reader no doubt has predicted, after repeated exposure to these contingencies, rate of R increases in frequency in the presence of the S^D and decreases in frequency in the presence of the S^Δ. Eventually, R all but ceases to occur in the presence of S^Δ and occurs at a rate governed by the schedule of reinforcement operating in S^D. This effect is termed *discrimination*, that is, *responding differently in the presence of different stimuli or in different situations*. Discrimination may be contrasted with *generalization*, which is characterized by *similar responding in the presence of different stimuli*.

The importance of the ability to discriminate should be clear, as should its explanation. The S^D is a stimulus which is correlated with situations in which R will be *effective* in producing S^+, and S^Δ indicates occasions when R will *not be effective* in producing S^+. Thus, once discrimination learning has occurred, R increases in rate *abruptly* when the S^D appears (or the situation changes) and all but ceases just as quickly when the S^Δ takes the place of the S^D (Herrick et al., 1959). If people and other animals failed to make discriminations of this type, i.e., which behavior will be effective in which situation(s), their behavior would appear to be random or "aimless" until in each new situation, an R which resulted in S^+ was reinforced. Even in relatively novel situations, *people do not behave randomly*. They tend to behave in ways that have been effective in *situations similar to*, even if in some ways different from, their present situation. That is to say, their responses *generalize* from one situation to other similar situations. Thus, both generalization and discrimination serve to facilitate adaption of behavior choices to the environment.

Contrary to the popular misconception which asserts that "the contingency of reinforcement . . . refers to a relation between a behavior and its consequences [Schneier, 1974, p. 529]," Skinner (1969) defines a *contingency of reinforcement* in the following terms: (a) the occasion of a response; (b) the response per se; and (c) the consequences of the response. It is a three-termed, not a two-termed contingency statement. In our shorthand it may be written: $S^{D,\ \Delta} \rightarrow R \rightarrow S^{+,\ -,\ o}$.

Luthans and Kreitner (1975) have employed the acronym A-B-C to refer to antecedents-behavior-consequences as a three-termed contingency. In order to appreciate what antecedents of behavior(s) comprise a *constellation* of S^Ds and S^Δs for a person, one must either construct or have extensive knowledge about the individual's reinforcement history, since effects of S^Ds and S^Δs on R result from such a history.

It is difficult to conceive of operant behavior in terms of "purposiveness" and "intent" if one considers only the two-termed contingency of reinforcement when describing behavior-environment relationships, since it provides no connection between past and present circumstances and experience. When the terms and concepts which join the elements of the *three-termed contingency* are considered, however, an appealing account of apparently

	Situations or Stimulus Antecedents	Response Consequence Relations or Reinforcement Contingencies	Three Termed Contingencies
Undifferentiated Environment	S_a S_a	$R \rightarrow S^+$ $R \rightarrow \phi$	$S_a \rightarrow R \rightarrow S^+$ $S_a \rightarrow R \rightarrow \phi$
Differentiated Environment	$S_a + S^D$ $S_a + S^\Delta$	$R \rightarrow S^+$ $R \rightarrow \phi$	$^*S^D \rightarrow R \rightarrow S^+$ $^*S^\Delta \rightarrow R \rightarrow \phi$

*When situational antecedents differ only by virtue of the informative S^Ds and S^Δs, the S_a need not be elaborately described.

Fig. 7.2 Differentiated and Undifferentiated Contingencies.

future oriented behaviors may be rendered from the operant paradigm. And when verbal behavior is considered in addition to other types of behavior, one may account for highly complex human activities using operant terms and concepts.

Millenson and Leslie (1979) note that we may employ two ways to represent purposive behavior in our language, but that only one is appropriate for a scientific analysis of behavior. The two ways are: (a) "the purposive, in which we use the term *to* (or, *in order to*) and imply the future tense;" or (b) "the descriptive, in which we state the present behavior and conjoin it with what happened in the past [Millenson & Leslie, 1979, p. 27]."

Mentalistic goal setting theory employs the first approach according to Locke (1968). "For [Locke's] purposes the terms goal and intention [are] used in their vernacular meaning as 'what the individual is consciously trying to do' [p. 158]." Thus, in goal theories, our attention is focused upon the individual's view of the future. Millenson and Leslie (1979) suggest we consider an example from Skinner (1956) before deciding which perspective to adopt, future (goal theory) or descriptive (operant theory). The example is the following:

> During the war the Russians used dogs to blow up tanks. A dog was trained to hide behind a tree or wall in low brush or other cover. As a tank approached and passed, the dog ran swiftly alongside it, and a small magnetic mine attached to the dog's back was sufficient to cripple the tank or set it afire. The dog, of course, had to be replaced [Skinner, 1956, p. 228].

The dog's behavior can be explained in terms of past events, such as reinforcements received for approaching tanks in the manner described, but not by reference to its purpose unless we alter what is meant by the term purpose. The dog did not run to the tank in order *to be* blown up. Thus, the future does not determine behavior, as this extreme example demonstrates.

Our use of "purposive language" reveals our knowledge of the effects of our behavior on earlier occasions. It is these *past effects of behavior that determine behavior in the present*. Utilizing the mentalistic approach, we would say that the dog's *intention* was to behave in the present circumstances in ways that had historically been effective in producing reinforcers in similar circumstances, i.e., tanks were S^Ds for approaching them and receiving reinforcers, i.e., S^D = Tank → R = Approach → S^+ = food, attention, etc.

The mentalistic approach recognizes that "in the last analysis the content of a particular individual's goals and intentions must be inferred from his verbal report (based on introspection) [Locke, 1968, p. 159]." The content of these verbal reports (or verbal behavior) essentially constitutes the individual's history of reinforcement to the extent that it is known to the individual, i.e., to the extent it can be verbalized. The operant approach to purposiveness is thus descriptive in that it focuses upon *actual histories* rather than verbal generalizations about a nonexistent future state of affairs held in some mental content.

The operant position is further clarified by distinguishing between "so called" or "futuristic purposes" of behavior and their actual consequences (Millenson & Leslie, 1979). Table 7.1 provides several examples of this distinction.

To the extent that one succeeds in obtaining consequences of behavior which have historically followed the behavior, one's purposive behavior is essentially defined by its consequences. That is, the purpose of behavior is its historic consequences. We should, therefore, be able to predict what "goals" will be adopted by people if we know something about their reinforcement history and current level of deprivation, satiation, and other circumstances.

A person who has had nothing to drink for a long period of time and sees a water fountain (S^D) will likely approach and use the fountain (Rs) and obtain water (S^+) as a result.

**TABLE 7.1. Actual Consequences Contrasted to
So-Called Purposes of Behavior**

Behavior	So-Called Purpose	Actual Consequence of Behavior
Tie a shoelace	*To* keep shoe on	Shoe stays on
Turn on faucet	*To* get water	Water appears
Raise umbrella	*To* keep rain off	Rain is kept off

Adapted from *Principles of Behavioral Analysis*, 2nd Edition, by J. R. Millenson &
J. C. Leslie (Copyright © 1979, J. R. Millenson)

Another person might go to a bar for a beer. And a third person might avoid bars and beer because of a history of religious training. To summarize, we note that purpose is found in behavior consequences or "in past instances in which similar behavior has been effective [Skinner, 1969, p. 105]." And the past is observed in the present when behavior antecedents are examined, $S^{D, \triangle}$s.

Behavior may change abruptly as a result of interpersonal communications which are termed *verbal behavior interactions*. A person who has experienced the contingencies of reinforcement in a given environment (e.g., the work place as it relates to supervisor behavior, see Mawhinney and Ford, 1977) may be able to verbalize the contingencies there. This verbal behavior may function to instruct another person with no experience in the situation regarding which behaviors (Rs) will be effective (produce S^+ and prevent S^-), and what conditions are correlated with these opportunities for reinforcement (or avoidance of punishment) (S^Ds). When a person behaves in response to such instruction, the behavior is termed *rule governed*, whereas the behavior of the instructor is *contingency shaped*. Rule governed behavior may, but need not necessarily, duplicate contingency shaped behavior (Ayllon & Azrin, 1964; Baron, Kaufman, & Stauber, 1969) depending on individual histories of reinforcement (Weiner, 1964). As Mawhinney and Ford (1977) have suggested, rules will be adopted (instructions followed) which come from sources that are found by experience to be credible, and not from those that one's experiences have discredited (Galizio, 1979).

The operant paradigm can comprehend complex human behavior often referred to as goal directed or purposive behavior. Abrupt changes in behavior rates, e.g., a change in response rate upon announcement of a reinforcement schedule change and before receipt of reinforcers from the schedule, are accommodated by the paradigm when the paradigm is properly employed. Proper employment of the paradigm requires analysis of reinforcement histories of individuals and groups. Failure to give due consideration to these histories ($S^{D, \triangle}$s) can have serious consequences as subsequent examples demonstrate.

Once the operant view of purposiveness and the roles of $S^{D, \triangle}$s, discrimination, generalization, and rule governed behavior are comprehended, one is prepared to consider how the operant paradigm deals with cognitive processes, intention, and purposes on the part of people. These descriptive operant terms provide for a fairly rigorous account of the overt manifestations of such internal processes. Skinner (1974), for example, describes thinking as behavior under weak stimulus control and covert verbal behavior by the individual (i.e., talking to oneself about past experience in the situation, similar situations, or similarities and differences between the present circumstances and ones past experiences). In almost every case, however, the covert behavior (thinking) is acquired in overt form, "and no one has ever shown that the covert form achieves anything which is out of reach of the overt [Skinner, 1974, p. 103]." Thus, while not denying individual experiences of cognition (covert verbal behavior), operant behaviorists prefer to deal with them as they are made manifest in overt observations rather than inferring them from these observations.

It is important to note in this regard the striking similarity between operational definitions of expectancies, instrumentalities, positive and negative valences, and schedules of reinforcers and punishers in one's past experience with them. Such experiences are evidenced in reactions of S^Ds and S^Δs or discriminations and generalizations observed in the presence of $S^{D, \Delta} \rightarrow R \rightarrow S^{+, \circ}$ contingencies. Operant rules set by reinforcement schedules and the $S^{D, \Delta}$s which can serve to predict them are purely properties of the individual's objective environment. Expectancies and instrumentalities, on the other hand, are rooted in the individual's history in the environment, which leads him/her to believe that certain cause-effect relationships exist between alternative behaviors and their consequences in that environment. Individual subjective experiences of purpose and intention are related to these beliefs which arise, as we have seen, out of experiences with the outside environment. Subjective expectations, instrumentalities, and valences are evident in actual behavioral responses in terms of type and rate of behavior and discrimination and generalization one exhibits in the presence of S^Ds, S^Δs, and the $R \rightarrow S^+$ and $R \rightarrow \phi$ relations with which they are correlated.

If, for example, a supervisor (A) gives praise to a subordinate every time he or she is observed performing well ($R \rightarrow S^+$) and another supervisor (B) does not ($R \rightarrow \phi$), and whenever B is in charge the subordinate's performance decreases abruptly and increases just as rapidly when A returns, we know that, objectively, A is an S^D for $R \rightarrow S^+$, and B is an S^Δ for $R \rightarrow \phi$. Because R varies drastically in rate in the presence of S^D and S^Δ, we say that discrimination of R has occurred. In cognitive terms, we would say that the subordinate believes or expects that a valent outcome (verbal praise as a reinforcer) results from good performances if A is supervising, but expectation of praise for good performances in the presence of B is low. If supervisor C replaces A, and the subordinate behaves similarly in the presence of C as in the presence of A, generalization has occurred. The subordinate would be said in cognitive terms to expect C to behave like A. If C behaves like B, however, the subordinate's generalization may not be functional. Of course, C could describe his/her rules *verbally*, "I shall recognize good performance," and then follow up by doing so. The subordinate could then test this proposition (S^D) for validity by performing well in the presence of C and then either experiencing confirmation ($R \rightarrow S^+$) or disconfirmation ($R \rightarrow \phi$). As Mawhinney and Ford (1977) have noted, leaders/supervisors/managers set up or fail to set up environmental contingencies ($S^{D, \Delta} \rightarrow R \rightarrow S^{+, -, \phi}$) in which good performances are facilitated or inhibited. Individual cognitions (if they exist at all) do not arise out of nothing; they arise out of the interaction of past experiences and current environmental contingencies ($S^{D, \Delta} \rightarrow R \rightarrow S^{+, -, \phi}$ relations).

Although schedules of reinforcement are objectively defined environmental contingencies that relate behavior (R) and consequences ($S^{+, -, \phi}$) which have highly predictable effects on choice of R type and R rate, in the field we are dealing with people who have an extensive history of reinforcement and opportunities for reinforcement from sources *other* than those set up by leaders/supervisors/managers. Joblansky and DeVries (1972) correctly noted that one's peers may punish behaviors that supervisors reinforce. Thus, management efforts to improve performance may be competing with peer efforts to inhibit improvements. Mawhinney and Ford (1977) have employed the matching law or relative law of effect to discuss the effects of such competition.

Expectancy theories (Vroom, 1964) also deal with this competition by noting how positives and negatives can cancel one another. Many alternative ways of quantitatively representing how these sources of S^+s and S^-s are balanced may be suggested. But we shall not go into the issue. Rather, suffice it to say that in operant labs subjects often face "Hobson's Choice" (Mawhinney, 1979b) i.e., assignment of a reinforcement schedule and no other alternative sources of reinforcers or punishers either monetary or from peers (e.g.,

Yukl, Wexley, & Seymore, 1972). In the field, however, employees face *real choices* and multiple sources of reinforcement/punishment other than management's formal contingencies. In addition, groups develop and maintain rules of interpersonal conduct. The equity norm, for example, is conditioned by past experience and current situations. Pairs of friends tend to behave equitably in dealing with one another, while strangers are less likely to do so when they interact (Marwell & Schmitt, 1975). Of course, failure to maintain equity in exchanges with friends has likely resulted in lost friends or less reinforcing interactions historically. Interactions with strangers, being more temporary, do not provide for punishments contingent on violating the equity *norm* or *rule* of interpersonal relations. What sort of rule one adopts or exhibits in observable behavior suggests something about past experiences carried forward into the present.

History of reinforcement is a critical behavior antecedent. The discriminations and generalizations people make in the presence of S^Ds and S^Δs and $R \rightarrow S^{+, \phi}$ relations are heavily dependent upon past experiences. Thus, we accept a limited view of operant behavior at great risk. This is evident in the following review of problems applied psychologists have experienced when attempting to deploy operant principles.

Application Issues/Problems

There are two potential sources of error when the operant paradigm is employed to account for and guide development of applied behavior change programs in the field. One is related to the accurate description of an intervention based upon operant approaches. The other relates to the actual application of operant principles for predictable alterations of behaviors. As has been noted, industrial/organizational psychologists tend to neglect behavior antecedents in the description and application of operant procedures. This practice has certain undesirable consequences both for the practitioner who would employ the paradigm and for academics concerned with judging the generality of operant principles.

Describing Antecedent Conditions. The work performances of subjects in studies by Yukl et al. (1972) and Berger et al. (1975) were attributed to one of three reinforcement schedules: 25¢CRF, 25¢VR-2, or 50¢VR-2. In neither of these studies did subjects receive any money reinforcements before the end of the experiment. Receipt of money based upon performances was obtained only after the experiments had been terminated. Thus, the two-termed contingencies the researchers employed to describe the three treatment conditions $(R \rightarrow S^+)$ do not account for the performances that were observed.

Locke (1980) would like to argue that some cognitive process must be invoked to adequately describe what occurred. However, we know now, having considered the roles of reinforcement history, verbal communication of contingencies of reinforcement, discrimination/generalization, and rule governed behavior, that the promise of money for work performed and the rules applicable to performance-money relationships set the occasion for rule governed behavior or generalizations based upon past experiences in work-for-money (or other outcome) situations. It was the promise of money-for-work relationships ($S\overset{D}{v}$s, where subscribe vs refers to the verbal statement about when or where $R \rightarrow S^+$) that produced the observed responses or $S\overset{D}{v}$s $\rightarrow$ R (Scott & Cherrington, 1974). If these verbal $S\overset{D}{v}$s had not accurately reflected the true $R \rightarrow S^+$ contingencies and subjects had been paid throughout the experiment, very different results are likely to have been observed (Galizio, 1979). The observed results would have conformed to actual $R \rightarrow S^{+, -, \phi}$ contingencies following initial behavior in accord with the rule(s) stated in the $S\overset{D}{v}$s. And on subsequent occasions the experimenter's $S\overset{D}{v}$s would not produce predictable or consistent responses since the experimenter's verbal behavior would no longer function as an $S\overset{D}{v}$. In everyday language we advise "Don't believe a word s/he says!" to describe people whose S_{vs}^{D} do not correspond to reality or actual R $\rightarrow$ S$^+$ relations in the environment.

Similarly, Pedalino and Gamboa (1974) described an incentive lottery designed to control absenteeism as an FI schedule of financial reinforcement. Although there was a significant reduction in the absence rate, the reduction occurred abruptly in the first week of the intervention before anyone could have received a reinforcement ($20 lottery prize), and the reduction was maintained even though only one worker per department received a cash prize each week. Again, either some antecedents in the form of S_{vs}^{D} were operating to produce generalizations (e.g., past histories of reinforcement with playing lotteries and gambling include the experience of working or playing for extended periods of time without reinforcements accruing to all investments or gambles), or something other than the $20 prizes reinforced the attendance behavior.

Unlike the other two experiments in which the reinforcement contingencies (as described by experimenter verbal behaviors) were evident, any one of a number of contingencies could account for the observed effectiveness of the intervention. A critical question in this case concerns definition of "the reinforcer(s)." If playing the lottery to obtain a chance to win was "the reinforcer," then eligiblity required completion of an FR of 5 days attendance (a card for a poker hand was drawn each day, and at the end of the week the winning hand in each of several departments was awarded the $20 cash prize). However, there was also a time limitation on completion of the FR-5 days attendance since 4 days attendance during 1 week could not be carried over into the next week. If the lottery prize of $20 was "the reinforcer" then one had to complete an FR-5 within a single week and then participate in a VR-? each week (the ratio would depend upon how many department members participated and how many cards were issued per week). This complex arrangement is more like a "tandem" or "chained" schedule (Ferster & Skinner, 1957).

If "the reinforcer" was the card drawn at the beginning of each work day only for those workers who arrived to work on time, then the schedule would be more like a CRF for each working day. In addition, the intervention could have been altered by workers making side bets on who would draw high card for each day. In this case, conditioning could have been the direct result of experiencing a CRF schedule. With these latter two exceptions, however, each of the potential descriptions of what happened requires some terms or concepts to relate history of reinforcement to the current circumstances. The additional terms required are the discriminative properties of the intervention provided by the experimenters' verbal behavior describing the lottery, S_{vs}^{D}, and generalization of behavior from other experiences with such gambling to the present case by subjects in the experiment, i.e., their reaction to S_{vs}^{D} or $S_{vs}^{D} \rightarrow R \rightarrow S^+$. In addition, appropriate description of what actually occurred depends upon accurate identification of the reinforcer(s).

Applied operant conditioners have attempted to avoid some of the problems associated with reinforcer identification by using a feedback-control-system paradigm (Brethower, 1972; Luthans & Kreitner, 1975). Whatever behavior is observed in a situation, it is assumed to be either intrinsically reinforcing (Mawhinney, 1979a), to be reinforced by extrinsic reinforcers in the environment, or to occur as the result of some antecedent (S^D) which signals a reinforcement opportunity. For example, notice how as students we tend to begin to pack books to leave a class when the clock (S^D) nears the time of class termination, no doubt because aversive verbal remarks by teachers regarding such behavior do not occur near the end of class. Similarly, workers gather about the time clock or washroom as the clock shows times closer and closer to quitting time.

Alternative stimuli in an environment can be tested for reinforcement/punishment effects. However, such testing assumes an opportunity to observe and quantify rate of reinforced/punished behavior. So behaviors not easily observed and behaviors designed to hide other behaviors may preclude such analyses. If measurement and quantification is achieved, however, the experimenter or manager is then in a position to more accurately describe and evaluate whatever intervention is employed (shaping, modeling, schedules, etc.) to control behavior, since the procedure is not begun until the situation is clearly analyzed in terms of what is reinforcing which behavior and when. (Komaki et al. (1978) provide an excellent example of how observable technology can be improved in a work setting.)

Applications to Control Behavior. Theoretically, when reinforcing stimuli in an environment are known to the behavior modifier or change agent, a behavior control system can be designed to obtain or increase desired behaviors and reduce undesired behaviors based on known regularities between behavior rates and schedules of reinforcement and punishment. In laboratory experiments, for example, FR schedules produce high steady rates of response if the ratio value (N in FR-N) is small. High rates of behavior can be maintained even when the value of N is increased (i.e., when ratio of responses to each reinforcer received is increased) up to some limit (whereupon extinction occurs).

Although not apparent, Pedalino and Gamboa (1974) could have used the logic described here to guide the development of their experiment. First, it would be assumed that the lottery would reinforce attendance on time and that 5 days of on-time behavior would not be too large a ratio for humans (i.e., would not result in extinction). Making the reinforcer contingent upon satisfying an FR schedule of 5 days on-time within a single week would then be expected to reduce absenteeism among group members if lottery play was a reinforcer for most of them. Using this logic, we would predict that the intervention would be effective in spite of the fact that its expected value would be at most $1.40 per week for any one player. This is an unintuitive result from the point of view of subjective expectation theory in which the only value considered is monetary. Yet it follows logically from the operant analysis.

The analysis above was predicted upon an assumption regarding what was "the reinforcer(s)," and neglected critical consideration of subjects' reinforcement histories and the discriminative properties of the intervention ($S^{D, \triangle}$ s). Among some groups of people, a lottery represents a gamble and group members who gamble may be punished by peers for such behavior because it deviates from the group moral code of conduct or violates a taboo. Thus, the a priori assumption that what one personally believes will function as a reinforcer, and construction of seemingly sound reinforcement contingencies based upon such an assumption without a thorough analysis of antecedent stimuli and individual and group histories, is a risky procedure as evidenced by the following example.

Yukl and Latham (1975) attempted to replicate the Yukl et al. (1972) experiment by flipping a coin to establish a VR schedule of "reinforcement" for a group of women who were tree planters. The combination of coin flip and incentive pay determined by it were viewed as a gamble which was contrary to religious beliefs and norms held by these women. The net effect of the intervention was an 8% reduction in performance following implementation of the VR schedule of "reinforcement." Although money may have functioned as a reinforcer under other circumstances, it was a negative discriminative stimulus ($-S$, i.e., one associated with $R \rightarrow S^-$, or punishment) in the Yukl and Latham study.

From the point of view of the experimenters, the coin flip was simply a means to insure fairness of the VR system of reinforcer distribution. Their subjects, however, failed to make the same discrimination. Rather, the subjects' behavior can best be described as generalization. They behaved in the presence of the coin flip in the same way they would with a gambling event, by trying to avoid it. Use of the feedback-control-system model would have helped the experimenters in this case by identifying the norms and values of the community from which subjects were drawn.

Values and norms may be thought of as discriminative properties of a system which arise out of historic reinforcement contingencies maintained by a community or group (see Brown & Herrnstein, 1975). Failure to give them due consideration in the design of reinforcement contingencies aimed at performance improvement can have even more serious consequences.

One would look foolish proposing to employ a performance improvement system in an economic system if a proposed system was perpetuated when it failed to cover its costs either in improved employee satisfaction (if it is a criterion of success or a benefit) or economic profit for the system. Cost-benefit analyses, although rarely reported for such interventions, were reported by Yukl and Latham (1975). Successful maintenance of systems such as incentive pay systems may depend upon such analyses in economically rational systems and are therefore recommended. Measurement of satisfaction among those exposed to such systems is another viable benefit which may be measured by those systems that place value upon its development among employees. And satisfaction with work places is known to have desirable effects on absenteeism and turnover and thus is ultimately of economic as well as humanistic value. Continuous monitoring of these behavioral correlates of job satisfaction may also indicate when workers in a system are not satisfied with a system that is more or less effectively reinforcing high performance. People will exhibit high performance and experience low satisfaction when there are few or poor alternatives available (Mawhinney, 1979b). Behavior modifiers should be sensitized to this possibility, i.e., low verbal reports of satisfaction and high performance, since it may predict future withholding of effort and performance when the system requires it. Low reported satisfaction in survey measures ought to be a signal for management to examine current contingencies of reinforcement/punishment in a system (Smith, 1977).

Adequate evaluation of an operant intervention requires an unambiguous identification of reinforcers, punishers, ess deltas, and discriminative stimuli in a situation. Failure to correctly identify them can lead to invalid conclusions regarding operant principles as in the Yukl and Latham (1975) experiment or inability to accurately isolate the operant process involved as in the Pedalino and Gamboa (1974) experiment. An equally important element of an adequate evaluation of an applied operant principle is selection and utilization of an appropriate research design. Other critical components are the method of data gathering within the design and methods of observation and control in the field setting.

Design of adequate data gathering methods, behavior observation, and recording techniques are common problems in field experiments. Neither Yukl and Latham (1975) nor Pedalino and Gamboa (1974) utilized trained-on-site observers to record behavioral responses to their interventions. In the first case, this prevented early notice and reaction to the coin flip problem. In the second case, it prevented the experimenters from learning which of several alternative reinforcement contingencies produced the observed effects.

There exist two equally difficult alternatives for adequate evaluation of such interventions. One is complete control of the environmental situations (impossible); the other is complete continuous observation of all behavior in the environment (possible but economically unfeasible). However, an approximation to continuous observation is possible. This is accomplished by conducting on-site observations aperiodically or randomly and using multiple observers. Komaki, Barwick, and Scott (1978) provide a good example of the use of these methods in a field experiment. She and her colleagues have employed methods of observation, recording, and analysis suggested by Bijou, Peterson, and Ault

(1968), Hamerlynck, Handy, and Marsh (1973), and Baer, Wolf, and Risley (1968). If such methods had been employed by Pedalino and Gamboa (1974), they could have identified the precise behavioral processes which led to the observed effects. In order to draw any conclusion from the study, however, one must assume that the lottery as a whole was "the reinforcer" and that workers did not continue to gamble during the weeks when it was not officially employed.

Although these gross evaluation methods permit one to judge the practical significance of an intervention, they fail entirely to serve as *tests* of the behavioral principles purported to be responsible for observed effects. That is, we still do not know whether or not it was a weekly lottery or daily side-betting that produced the effects observed by Pedalino and Gamboa (1974).

Schneier (1974) suggested that operant researchers in organizations concentrate on field experiments using analysis of variance (ANOVA) to compare groups under various conditions of reinforcement. Although ANOVA may be appropriate for evaluation of different behavior control systems, it may be inappropriate for *testing* the efficacy of a specific operant principle. Operant principles have been validated and their generality established using systematic replications in the ABAB reversal design with the individual serving as both unit and level of analysis (Sidman, 1960). The Pedalino and Gamboa (1974) lottery intervention could have been implemented with each of three groups at different times to form a multiple baseline design. Then, if attendance improved for each group at just the time the intervention began, one would be confident that it, and not some other factor, produced the effects observed. For an excellent example of this design as employed in a working setting, see Komaki et al. (1978).

As the above review suggests, operant researchers rely primarily upon within-subject and within-group analyses of reinforcement contingency effects. It is important for field researchers to respect this convention. This is recommended because as Dunham (1968) has noted, significant differences in behavior responses to treatments are evident when different designs, between-subjects versus within-subjects, are employed by researchers. For example, an increase in rate of response has often been observed when the value of N in FR and VR schedules had been increased for subjects working in within-subject design experiments. However, the effects have not been replicated in between-subjects experiments, e.g., Yukl, Wexley, and Seymore (1972). This could very well by attributable to the difference in designs.

However, a potentially more important difference exists. In the typical operant lab an animal or person is given one alternative source of a highly salient reinforcer at a time. Thus when the value of N increases and no other schedule with a smaller value of N is available, the only adaptive response is to increase rate of response, or if one's limit has already been reached, to continue at a constant rate. If people try to maximize the ratio of reinforcers to responses, they should reduce rate of response to a ratio schedule as N increases if there exists some alternative source of the reinforcer governed by an interval schedule (Staddon & Motheral, 1978). The "relative law of effect" (Herrnstein, 1970; Mawhinney & Ford, 1977) makes the same prediction. And the senior author (Mawhinney, 1979b) has demonstrated the phenomenon with a human subject.

The absence of choices or alternative sources of reinforcement is called "Hobson's Choice" as opposed to real choices that occur when there are alternative sources (schedules) of reinforcement. It should be evident that operant lab results regarding stretching (maintenance or increased response rate even when N of an FR or VR schedule is increased), have been established under conditions of Hobson's Choice, i.e., no real choice. In the real world of the field people do have choices. Therefore, we ought not be surprised if stretching fails to succeed in many field settings. Practical importance of this point is found in labor market statistics. For example, 80% of worker turnover is accounted for by the business cycle (U.S. Department of Labor Manpower Monograph, 1974).

When the economy is healthy and growing, people have choices and express a desire to increase the ratio of reinforcers to work behaviors by moving among organizations with different pay rates. When the economy is poor, workers are essentially faced with Hobson's Choice. Workers in the auto industry have accepted pay reductions or stretching. Continued constant rate of working for less pay is similar to an increased N with no decrease in rate of R. The explanation of this phenomenon is similar to that for a lab experiment. Given no better alternatives or no choice, one makes the best of a bad situation by continuing to maintain a good work rate for less pay. Inflation has the same effect on people who do not receive adequate pay increases. (Thus, we should not be surprised to find that people who would leave an organization or work less hard if they had a real alternative, under these circumstances continue to work hard while verbally expressing "dissatisfaction with work.")

We can draw two conclusions from recognition of the lack of isomorphism between operant labs and sites of field interventions. First, to the extent that a lab finding requires Hobson's Choice as a precondition (as does stretching), it will not be likely to be replicated in field settings. Second, to the extent that people are facing Hobson's Choice, or no viable alternative to present conditions of employment, certain operant contingencies of reinforcement can be imposed upon them which may increase their rate of work behavior while raising the probablility of turnover as soon as alternative employment is available. Thus, while the authors do not subscribe to some of their other professional values and beliefs, they agree with Lawler and Hackman (1969) in their estimation of the value of participative approaches to the design of reinforcement systems aimed at improving worker productivity.

CONCLUSIONS

Many of the problems encountered by those who attempt to utilize and evaluate operant principles, terms, and concepts spring from the rigor with which the paradigm has been stated and thus the methods required to conduct adequate evaluations (Argyris, 1971). Industrial/organizational psychologists (e.g., Locke, 1980) are either unaware of terms and concepts more complex than the simple two-termed contingencies characterized by reinforcement schedules or, for whatever reason, are reluctant to use such terms and concepts when describing work behavior. Although these terms and concepts may not provide the sence of *Verstehan* one seems to feel when using terms like "expectations" or "beliefs," the environmental stimuli and behavioral phenomena to which they refer must be appreciated if one is to fully exploit the operant approach to understanding and controlling the behavior of one's self and others. Traditional methods of data gathering are simply not adequate to the task of evaluating the efficacy of this paradigm, and the alternatives discussed here should be adopted for use. With respect to both implementations and evaluations we must more carefully consider the nature and implications of the differences between the lab origins of operant based knowledge and the field settings in which we hope to employ and evaluate them.

People live in social systems that are at least in part subject to change by the people who comprise the system (Skinner, 1971). And when people are not free (lack alternative sources of reinforcers of job mobility), reinforcement contingencies which shape and maintain high rates of performance may do so at the individual's expense. That is, "satisfaction" with the contingencies of reinforcement and performance produced by them need not be positively related. Thus verbal expressions of this "satisfaction" may well predict future turn-over in systems that produce performance by use of punishment and negative reinforce-ment. However, the relationship will only be evident when people have real choices (Mawhinney, 1979b; Smith, 1977). This issue of freedom, attitude, and behavior (perfor-mance and turnover) was broached because the authors see an advantage to practitioners who can appreciate and employ both approaches to work environment analysis. More work must be done in the area of learning what affect operant interventions in work organizations have on verbal behaviors, i.e., responses to attitude surveys.

Finally, it should be recognized that people who comprise the social systems we call work organizations may be in as good or better positions to suggest reinforcement con-tingencies that aid their own performances. The operant approach to behavior control does not preclude participation or more democracy in organizational life. As a method of descrip-tion and analysis, however, it suggests how we might evaluate the contingencies such an ap-proach may foster and performance it might maintain. Recognition of these complexities and possibilities, we believe, is a first step to a fuller and more accurate utilization of the operant paradigm.

REFERENCES

Adams, J. S., & Romney, A. K. A functional analysis of authority. *Psychological Review*, 1959, **66**, 234-251.

Allison, J., & Timberlake, W. Instrumental and contingent Saccharin licking in rats: Response depriva-tion and reinforcement. *Learning and Motivation*, 1974, **5**, 231-247.

Argyris, C. "Beyond freedom and dignity by B. F. Skinner." A review essay. *Harvard Educational Re-view*, 1971, **41**, 550-567.

Ayllon, T., & Azrin, N. H. Reinforcement and instructions with mental patients. *Journal of the Experi-mental Analysis of Behavior*, 1964, **7**, 327-331.

Baer, D. M., Wolf, M. M., & Risley, T. R. Some current dimensions of applied behavior analysis, *Journal of Applied Behavior Analysis*, 1968, **1**, 91-97.

Bandura, A. *Principles of behavior modification*. New York: Holt, Rinehart, and Winston, 1969.

Baron, A., Kaufman, A., & Stauber, K. A. Effects of instructions and reinforcement on human oper-ant behavior maintained by fixed-interval reinforcement. *Journal of the Experimental Analysis of Behavior*, 1969, **12**, 701-712.

Berger, C. J., Cummings, L. L. & Heneman, H. G. III. Expectancy and operant conditioning predic-tions performance under variable ratio and continuous schedules of reinforcement. *Organizational Behavior and Human Performance*, 1975, **14**, 227-243.

Bijou, S. W., Peterson, R. F., & Ault, M. H. A method to integrate descriptive and experimental field studies at the level of data and empirical concepts. *Journal of Applied Behavior Analysis*, 1968, **1**, 175-191.

Brethower, D. M. *Behavior analysis in business and industry: A total performance system*. Kalamazoo, Michigan: Behaviordelia, 1972.

Brown, R., and Herrnstein, R. J. *Psychology*. Boston: Little Brown, 1975.

Catania, C. A. *Contemporary research in operant behavior*. New York: Scott, Foresman, 1968.

Conversation with B. F. Skinner. *Organizational Dynamics*, 1973, **1**, 31-41.

Dunham, P. J. Contrasted conditions of reinforcement: A selective critique. *Psychological Bulletin*, 1968, **69**, 295-315.

Ferster, C. B., & Skinner, B. F. *Schedules of reinforcement*. New York: Appleton-Century-Crofts, 1957.

Galizio, M. Contingency-shaped and rule-governed behavior: Instructional control of human loss avoidance. *Journal of the Experimental Analysis of Behavior*, 1979, **31**, 53-70.

Guttman, N. The pigeon and the spectrum and other complexities. *Psychological Reports*, 1956, **2**, 449-460.

Hamerlynck, L. A., Handy, L. C., & Marsh, E. J. *Behavior change: Methodology, concepts, and practice.* Champaign, Ill: Research Press, 1973.

Hamner, W. C. Reinforcement theory and contingency management in organizational settings. In H. L. Tosi & W. C. Hamner (Eds.), *Organizational behavior and management: A contingency approach.* Chicago: St. Clair Press, 1974.

Heiman, G. W. A note on "Operant conditioning principles extrapolated to the theory of management." *Organizational Behavior and Human Performance*, 1975, **13**, 165-170.

Herrick, R. M., Myers, J. L., and Korotkin, A. L. Changes in S^D and S^Δ rates during the development of an operant discrimination. *Journal of Comparative Physiological Psychology*, 1959, **52**, 359-363.

Herrnstein, R. J. On the law of effect. *Journal of the Experimental Analysis of Behavior*, 1970, **13**, 243-266.

Honig, W. K. (Ed.) *Operant behavior: Areas of research and application.* New York: Appleton-Century-Crofts, 1966.

Honig, W. K., & Staddon, J.E.R. (Eds.) *Handbook of operant behavior.* Englewood Cliffs, New Jersey: Prentice-Hall, 1977.

Jenkins, H. M. & Harrison, R. H. Generalization gradients of inhibition following auditory discrimination learning. *Journal of the Experimental Analysis of Behavior*, 1962, **5**, 435-441.

Joblansky, S. F., & DeVries, D. L. Operant conditioning principles extrapolated to the theory of mangement. *Organizational Behavior and Human Performance*, 1972, **7**, 340-358.

Komaki, J., Barwick, K. D., & Scott, L. R. A behavioral approach to occupational safety measurement and reinforcement of safe performance. *Journal of Applied Psychology*, 1978, **63**, 434-445.

Lawler, E. E. III, & Hackman, J. R. Impact of employee participation in the development of pay incentive plans: A field experiment. *Journal of Applied Psychology*, 1969, **53**, 467-471.

Locke, E. A. Toward a theory of task motivation and incentives. *Organizational Behavior and Human Performance*, 1968, **3**, 157-189.

Locke, E. A. Latham versus Komaki: A tale of two paradigms. *Journal of Applied Psychology*, 1980, **65**, 16-23.

Luthans, F., & Kreitner, R. *Organizational behavior modification.* Glenview, Ill.: Scott Foresman, 1975.

Marwell, G., & Schmitt, D. R. *Cooperation: An experimental analysis.* New York: Academic Press, 1975.

Mawhinney, T. C. Operant contingencies of leadership: An experimental analysis of reciprocally causal relations in the Superior-Subordinate dyad. *Journal of Applied Psychology*, in press.

Mawhinney, T. C. Operant terms and concepts in the description of individual work behavior: Some problems of interpretation, application and evaluation. *Journal of Applied Psychology*, 1975, **60**, 704-712.

Mawhinney, T. C. Intrinsic x extrinsic work motivation: Perspectives from behaviorism. *Organizational Behavior and Human Performance*, 1979 a, **24**, 411-440.

Mawhinney, T. C. Individual decision making in the context of Hobson's Choice and Real Choices. Unpublished manuscript, Indiana University, 1979b.

Mawhinney, T. C. Polemics and progress: A reply to Locke's tale. Unpublished manuscript, Indiana University, 1980.

Mawhinney, T. C., & Ford, J. D. The path-goal theory of leader effectiveness: An operant interpretation. *Academy of Management Review Journal*, 1977, **2**, 398-411.

Millenson, J. R., & Leslie, J. C. *Principles of behavioral analysis.* (2nd ed.) New York: Macmillan, 1979.

Pedalino, E., & Gamboa, V. U. Behavior modification and absenteeism: Intervention in one industrial setting. *Journal of Applied Psychology*, 1974, **59**, 694-698.

Premack, D. Catching up with common sense to two sides of a generalization: Reinforcement and punishment. In R. Glaser (Ed.), *The nature of reinforcement.* New York: Academic Press, 1971, 121-150.

Schmitt, D. R. Punitive supervision and productivity: An experimental analog. *Journal of Applied Psychology*, 1969, **53**, 118-123.

Schneier, C. E. Behavior modification in management: A review and critique. *Academy of Management Journal*, 1974, **17,** 528-548.

Scott, W. E., & Cherrington, D. L. Effects of competitive, cooperative, and individualistic reinforcement contingencies. *Journal of Personality and Social Psychology*, 1974, **30,** 748-758.

Sidman, M. *Tactics of scientific research: Evaluating experimental data.* New York: Basic Books, 1960.

Skinner, B. F. A case history in scientific method. *American Psychologist,* 1956, **11,** 221-233.

Skinner, B. F. *The behavior of organisms.* New York: Appleton-Century-Crofts, 1938.

Skinner, B. F. *Science and human behavior.* New York: Free Press, 1953.

Skinner, B. F. *Verbal behavior.* New York: Appleton-Century-Crofts, 1957.

Skinner, B. F. *Contingencies of reinforcement: A theoretical analysis.* New York: Appleton-Century-Crofts, 1969.

Skinner, B. F. *Beyond freedom and dignity.* New York: Knopf, 1971.

Skinner, B. F. *About behaviorism.* New York: Knopf, 1974.

Skinner, B. F. The steep and thorny way to a science of behavior. *American Psychologist*, 1975, **30,** 42-49.

Smith, F. J. Work attitudes as predictors of attendance on a specific day, *Journal of Applied Psychology*, 1977, **62,** 16-19.

Staddon, J. E. R., & Motheral, S. On matching and maximizing in operant choice experiments. *Psychological Review*, 1978, **85,** 436-444.

Ulrich, R., Stachnik, T., & Mabry, J. *Control of human behavior: From cure to prevention.* Glenview, Illinois: Scott, Foresman, 1970.

Ulrich, R., Stachnik, T., & Mabry, J., *Control of human behavior: Expanding the behavioral laboratory.* Glenview, Illinois: Scott, Foresman, 1966.

U.S. Dept. of Labor, Job Satisfaction: Is there a trend? Manpower Research Monograph No. 30, Washington, D. C., U.S. Government Printing Office, 1974, p. 17.

Vroom, V. *Work and motivation.* New York: John Wiley & Sons, 1964.

Weiner, H. Response cost and the aversive control of human operant behavior. *Journal of the Experimental Analysis of Behavior*, 1963, **6,** 415-421.

Yukl, G. A., & Latham, G. P. Consequence of reinforcement schedules and incentive magnitudes for employee performance: problems encountered in an industrial setting." *Journal of Applied Psychology*, 1975, **60,** 294-298.

Yukl, G., Wexley, K. N., & Seymore, J. E. Effectiveness of pay incentives under variable ratio and continuous reinforcement schedules. *Journal of Applied Psychology*, 1972, **56,** 19-23.

Part II:

Increasing Sales

Introduction

There is no greater area of concern to industry than marketing its product. Even increased productivity is of little worth if somebody else is getting all of the business. Marketing the product involves, among other things, advertising it, distributing it, and selling it. It is probably no accident that some of the earliest examples of behavioral influence in business occurred in these areas. When the popularizer of behaviorism, J. B. Watson, left psychology in the mid-1920's, he began a very successful career in advertising (Bolles, 1979). Marketing people have spent a great deal of energy searching for what makes a product attractive, so reinforcement theory did not sound foreign to them (de Groot, 1971; Staunton, 1967). Those in direct sales were even more aware of the effects of their behavior and the need to sell the client satisfaction, i.e., reinforcement, rather than merchandise (Kirkpatrick, 1971).

Despite the focus on behaviors that increase sales, the implicit assumption that good salesman are born, not made, has dominated the marketplace (Ivey, Horvath & Tonning, 1961). Selling has been viewed as an art (Huttig, 1973) based on a specific set of traits and attitudes that the sales representative brings to the task. Training in specific selling skills is seen as helping to compensate for some sales representatives' weaknesses and maximizing the abilities of the top people (Ivey et al., 1961). If it is true that specific behaviors need to be learned in order to increase successful selling, than applied behavior analysis would seem to have a natural role in identifying successful selling behaviors and teaching those responses.

The number of articles and books on how to sell is legion. Several specific selling behaviors have been identified as being productive through observation and experience. Among the most frequently cited of these are: learning to recognize sales opportunities, emphasizing the benefits to be gained from buying the product, and attempting to close the sale by directly suggesting that the client make the purchase (Huttig, 1973; Roth, 1970). Yet many of these field observations remain to be tested through empirical research (Holder, 1967). The first chapter in this unit presents the results of a sales training project with telephone reservation personnel for a major international airline. It explores the potential benefits of implementing a sales training program in what is often perceived as an order-taking role. The sales coaching program that is outlined serves as a model, positive reinforcement, management intervention.

In Chapter 9, Robert Mirman of General Mills considers the bigger sales picture as he reports on a total performance sales system. This program stresses increasing the frequency and quality of selling behaviors rather than training new sales responses. The emphasis is on encompassing principles of reinforcement, goal-setting, feedback, and accountability within the extant sales management system. As in each of these chapters, the focus is on improving sales behaviors while measuring the effects of the program on sales outcomes rather than simply setting goals for increased sales.

The final chapter in this unit concerns selling at the retail level. Retail selling has been defined as the art of "selling goods that do not come back to customers that do [Ivey et al., 1961]." Retail sales personnel are likely to receive less training and less pay than those in other marketing functions (Holder, 1967), yet they are closest to the customer and may have the greatest impact on increasing sales.

Chapter 10 presents a complete behavioral training package for retail sales personnel.

This program is based on a precise, segmental behavioral assessment of the performance of the company's best sales personnel. Successful selling behaviors were identified through observing the actions of top sales people and pinpointing those responses that discriminated their performance from that of the average sales representative. In this way an empirically-based sales training program was developed that specified the exact responses that each sales representative should make. The program includes everything from how close one should stand to the customer at the first meeting to what responses should be made to follow-up the sale. Pilot experiments and the nationwide results of the training program reveal substantial sales increases.

While the importance of selling behavior has long been recognized, there have been relatively few experimental studies on this crucial topic. Obviously, producing buying responses from "just looking" responses is a behavior change task. Unfortunately, the typical approach to increasing sales behavior has been to educate employees on the importance of general customer service responses. This approach usually has less than durable effects (Connellan, 1978). Applied behavior analysis is just beginning to impact this important area. The early interventions have generally been small studies aimed at increasing specific behaviors by clerks (Bardenstein, 1979; Komaki, Blood, & Holder, 1980; Komaki, Waddell, & Pearce, 1977; O'Brien & Sperduto, 1981; Rettig, 1975) or changes in the reward systems for sales personnel (Gupton & Lebow, 1971; Kreitner & Golab, 1978; Miller, 1977; Weitz, Antoinetli, & Wallace, 1954). Only very recently have any large scale controlled studies of increasing sales behaviors appeared in the literature (Brown, Malott, Dillon, & Keeps, 1980; Luthans, Paul & Baker, 1981). These successes and the comprehensive programs reported in this unit suggest that sales behaviors can be dramatically increased through response specification and reinforcement procedures.

Richard M. O'Brien   and   Michael P. Rosow
Hofstra University   *Work In America Institute*

REFERENCES

Bardenstein, J. Improving customer service in a retail setting. In. B. L. Hall (Chair), *Behavioral management procedures in sales organizations*. Symposium presented at the meeting of the Association for Behavior Analysis, Dearborn, Michigan, 1979.

Bolles, R. C. *Learning theory* (2nd ed.) New York: Holt, Rinehart & Winston, 1979.

Brown, M. G., Malott, R. W., Dillon, M. J. & Keeps, E. J. Improving customer service in a large department store through the use of training and feedback. *Journal of Organizational Behavior Management*, 1980, **2**, 251–265.

Connellan, T. K. *Performance improvement in business and industry*. New York: Harper & Row, 1978.

de Groot, G. Motivational principles. In T. Dakin (Ed.), *Sales promotion handbook*. Epping Essex, Great Britain: Grover Press, 1974.

Gupton, T., & Lebow, M. Behavior management in a large industrial firm. *Behavior Therapy*, 1971, **2**, 78–82.

Holder, E. J. Sales training research. In R. F. Vizza (Ed.), *The new handbook of sales training*. Englewood Cliffs, N.J.: Prentice-Hall, 1967.

Huttig, J. *Psycho-Sales-Analysis*. Totowa, N.J.: Littlefield, Adams & Co., 1973.

Ivey, P. W., Horvath, W., & Tonning, W. A. *Successful salesmanship*. (4th ed.) Englewood Cliffs, N.J.: Prentice-Hall, 1961.

Kirkpatrick, K. C. *Salesmanship*. (5th ed.) Cincinnati: South-Western Publishing, 1971.

Komaki, J., Blood, M. R. & Holder, D. Fostering friendliness in a fast foods franchise. *Journal of Organizational Behavior Management*, 1980, **2**, 145-164.

Komaki, J., Waddell, W. M., & Pearce, M. G. The applied behavior analysis approach and individual employees: Improving performance in two small businesses. *Organizational Behavior and Human Performance*, 1977, **19**, 337-352.

Kreitner, R., & Golab, M. Increasing the rate of salesperson telephone calls with a monetary refund. *Journal of Organizational Behavior Management*, 1978, **1**, 192-195.

Luthans, F., Paul, R., & Baker, D. An experimental analysis of the impact of contingent reinforcement on salespersons' performance behavior. *Journal of Applied Psychology*, 1981, **66**, 314-323.

Miller, L. M. Improving sales and forecast accuracy in a nationwide sales organization. *Journal of Organizational Behavior Management*, 1977, **1**, 39-51.

O'Brien, R. M., & Sperduto, W. A. An undergraduate course in OBM: Course description and practicum outcomes. In A. M. Dickinson & R. M. O'Brien (Chairs), *Organizational behavior management: Procedures, problems, and progress.* Symposium presented at the meeting of the Association for Behavior Analysis, Milwaukee, 1981.

Rettig, E. B. How to reduce costly "mis-takes" in a steak house. *Work Performance*, 1975, **1**, 4-8.

Roth, C. B. *Secrets of closing sales.* (4th ed.) Englewood Cliffs, N. J.: Prentice-Hall, 1970.

Staunton, J. D. Applying the principles of learning. In R. F. Vizza (Ed.), *The new handbook of sales training.* Englewood Cliffs, N.J: Prentice-Hall, 1967.

8

Increasing Sales Performance Among Airline Reservation Personnel

Edward J. Feeney, John R. Staelin
Edward J. Feeney Associates

Richard M. O'Brien and **Alyce M. Dickinson**
Hofstra University   *New York State Office
of Court Administration*

Up until the early 1970s nearly all airlines viewed their telephone reservationists as fulfilling booking and informational functions. The reservation agent was considered to be someone who took orders and answered questions rather than someone who influenced sales.

At Scandinavian Airlines, management began to question the old view. They wondered if the percentage of inquires that ended in bookings could be increased if proper training and reward systems were introduced. As Edward J. Feeney Associates had been successful in improving human performance in SAS's cargo area, they were commissioned to investigate the company's reservations sales effort. This report will present the program developed at SAS.

Airline management throughout the industry has always wanted to increase sales. However, in the early 1970s there was no consensus that much of a sales increase could be achieved by the reservationists. Airline scheduling and advertising were considered to have the biggest impact on sales. This view was so widely held that the computer system shared by SAS and several other airlines was not programmed to provide individual sales figures for the reservationists. Since all bookings were entered directly into the computer, the operator had no forms or records of what had been booked. After each reservation was made the display screen went blank in preparation for the next call. The computer recorded many items, from the flight number to the name of the passenger, but it did not total data by the code of the agent who made the booking. The only performance data available on an individual basis was the number of calls that each agent took per day. This measurement system was appropriate only as long as the airlines concept of the reservation agent's job was oriented toward order taking and information giving. As SAS began to question this role, it began to see the problems in the way that performance was being measured. The natural correction for this problem was to rewrite the computer program so that it gave booking figures for each agent. Incredibly, the other airlines that shared the computer facilities expressed no interest in obtaining such information. SAS was informed that it would have to fund the modification of the computer read-out itself. One can only conclude that these airlines did not believe that booking agents could have any effect in bringing in more customers or did not understand the importance of attaining individual performance data.

Although it was too expensive for SAS to go it alone in modifying the computer, management remained interested in obtaining the data on its agents. The current system seemed to be rewarding the wrong behaviors, but no one was sure that this problem was affecting sales or profits. The question that remained to be answered was "Can we increase bookings on SAS based on the responses of our telephone reservationists, or has the customer already decided to book or not to book before he picks up the phone?" The consultants designed a research program to answer this question.

TESTING THE EFFECTS OF OFFERING TO BOOK

One of the most basic sales techniques since Eve and the serpent has been to offer one's services to the client. Over a period of 5 weeks, a base rate of offers made by the agents was collected by listening in on randomly selected incoming calls. Although the agents knew the listening was going on as preparation for a sales training program, no one knew what the consultant was listening for, and no individual agent could ascertain when she specifically was being monitored. It was found that the agents offered to book a flight for the caller on only 34% of the sales opportunities sampled (935 calls, 321 opportunities, 110 offers). Of course, if the client has made up his mind before he dials, the offer to book is academic. On the other hand if the client actually needs to be sold, he is more likely to book if you offer to serve him.

In order to test the effects of making offers on sales, six reservationists were randomly divided into three equal groups. The two subjects in Group 1 were instructed not to make an offer to book a flight. Of course, if the caller specifically asked to make a reservation this group did so, but they did not offer returns on other flights unless these too were specifically mentioned. In Group Two, the agents were told to continue their normal telephone responses. The reservation agents in Group Three were given instruction in sales techniques. They were told to offer to book a reservation whenever possible and were taught how to back up their offer with benefits or other positive reasons for making a reservation at that time. For this group the consultant provided not only verbal directions but modeling and feedback on the performance of these new skills.

For a period of 4 weeks, data was collected by having each of these six agents record the outcome of each call received. The reader should note that this system provided feedback for these six reservation agents that was not previously available to them. As Parsons (1974) has noted in his analysis of the "Hawthorne Effect," it is this kind of improved feedback that could account for the general increases in performance noted at Hawthorne. Regardless of what was done to the employees, at least they knew how well they were doing and could pace themselves. The provision of such additional feedback should have improved the performance of all the reservation agents in the study regardless of their offering behavior.

In setting up this research it was discovered that the simple number of passengers booked was a poor dependent measure. Since tickets can represent more than one flight, the outcome data for this research are presented in segments. A segment is defined as any actual flight on SAS. Thus, the customer who books a ticket on TWA from New York to Rome and on SAS from Rome to Copenhagen would have booked one segment, whereas someone who flies SAS to Copenhagen and then boards another SAS flight to Rome has booked two segments. The latter flight round trip would be four segments if all flights were SAS.

The results as depicted in Table 8.1 represent more than a general increase. Making offers had the effect of adding one segment per hour over the no offer group and a half a segment per hour over the usual pattern of agent responses. This large difference occurred in spite of the notorious reactivity of recording that could be expected to boost the performance of the regular pattern group above the norm. Anectodal reports suggest that the

TABLE 8.1. Sales by Groups in Increased Offer, Regular Offer and No Offer Conditions.

Elements	No Offers	Regular Offers	Good Offers
Calls surveyed	1055	1017	734
Segments per hour	2.19	2.83	3.37
Calls per hour	7.84	8.32	7.96
Segments per call	.28	.34	.42
Eastbound bookings per hour	1.52	1.82	2.20
Other SAS flights booked per hour	.41	.45	.51
% Eastbound flights with return booked	16.60%	17.50%	29.10%
% First class	6.10%	5.50%	5.80%
First class per hour	.13	.16	.20

group that was instructed to make its normal response to calls did indeed perform above expectations while the subjects in both control groups requested training in making offers as the study progressed because they "didn't like the other people getting all the sales."

The results of this study demonstrated that the reservation sales agents could influence sales. Different telephone approaches accounted for differences in total bookings, but are these differences worthwhile? At the time that this study was completed SAS estimated the average segment at $190 in additional revenue. Given a half a segment increase per hour over forty reservation agents over the course of a year, you would expect a seven figure increase in income. Even if 99% of those who did not book when offers were not made were to call back a second time to book, the 1% increase would more than cover the cost of a sales training program or any other behavior modifiction techniques the company might consider.

Table 8.1 indicates that in telephone sales what you say affects what you get. In every category save one, the offer group outstripped the other agents. Only the percentage of first-class bookings seemed unaffected. The first-class comparison is misleading, however, as the good offer group obviously sold more "shoppers" than the regular offer group. These shoppers tend to be tourist class passengers, so the first-class percentage of the good offer group was lowered. Other data indicated a 3 to 5% increase in the number of first-class sales by the good offer group.

Any lingering doubt about the desirability of sales training and behavior modification for the telephone agents was overcome by this data. Management's doubts about past theories were right! The agents could sell more effectively. But how does one help forty reservation agents change into sales representatives? The remainder of this chapter will outline the behavior modifiction program that accomplished this goal.

THE GENERAL SALES IMPROVEMENT MODEL

Developing a sales program involves a great deal more than simply telling the company representatives what to say. In order to establish the sales improvement program at SAS, a consultant from Edward J. Feeney Associates became a full-time fixture in the reservations department for six months. The consultant was introduced as someone who was going to help with sales. He was given an office and established an open door for questions about the program. Every effort was made to defuse any possible anxiety about his role by making him available to the agents and by running the program as openly as possible.

The forty telephone reservationists at the SAS New York office handled most of the inquiries from across the nation. Simply writing prescriptions for new behaviors was not going to solve the variety of problems presented by this large staff with this much volume. A lecture or two wasn't going to do the job. A full program of training, coaching and feedback was required.

The sales training that was developed at SAS is most easily presented in the model of the three-term contingency of Antecedents, Behavior, and Consequences. Selling involves not only Behavior but Consequences for that behavior. Further, neither changes in behavior nor the modification of its consequences will have much effect unless the individual can recognize the appropriate Antecedents for making the desired sales response. From the ABC model the program at SAS had three goals:

1. Improve the recognition of sales opportunities by the reservation agents (Antecedents).
2. Provide new sales techniques for the agents to use (Behavior).
3. Increase the recognition and rewards available to the agents for improved sales performance (Consequences).

MEASURING SALES BEHAVIOR

As in any program of behavior modification the SAS project had to begin by establishing a system of data collection. Employees are not going to be able to change their behavior unless they have some knowledge of the results of their responses. They must know how well they are doing, and management must have some measures in order to evaluate performance.

Figure 8.1 presents the daily record form filled out by each reservationist. Each call represents a separate line on the form. The column headings across the top of the form represent caller questions, agent responses, and outcome for the call on that line. As each item on the form occurs it is checked off by the agent. The first three columns are for requests for information on fares, schedules, and miscellaneous matters, respectively. Columns 4 through 9 relate to calls about previously arranged bookings. Numbers 5, 6, 8, and 9 are to be checked on the basis of customer action. For example, if a customer were to cancel a reservation, column 6 would be checked while a caller who wanted to add another stop on his trip would be marked off in column 5. The behavioral data in this section is in columns 4 and 7. These columns note the reservation agent's offers to the caller. Column 4 would be checked if an additional segment was suggested, and column 7 would be ticked if a rebooking of a cancelled reservation was recommended. The reader should note that these columns (4 and 7) are checked only if an offer is made by the agent and regardless of whether that offer is accepted. The customer who volunteers that he wants to add a flight to his itinerary would be checked off as an add but would not qualify as an offer to add.

Columns 10 through 21 contain the data on new sales in terms of offers made and number of persons booked for each SAS service. Proceeding left to right across the form these transactions represent: eastbound flights from the United States to Scandinavia, westbound flights to the United States, SAS flights not originating or terminating in the United States and SAS hotel service. Columns 16 through 19 count first class (F) and tourist (Y) ac-

Name				Existing Records						East Bound SAS		West Bound SAS		Other SAS		Class F		Y		SAS Hotel		Weekday Agents Sign. Remarks
Number	Fare	Sched.	Misc.	Offer Add	Add	Cancel	Offer RBK	Rebook	RCFM	Offer	Segments Booked	Offer	Segments Booked	Offer	SEG booked	Offer	SEG Booked	Offer Up	SEG Booked	Offer	Bed Nites Booked	
	1 2 3			4 5 6 7 8 9						10	11	12	13	14	15	16 17		18 19		20	21	
1	X	X								X	4	X	4	X			X		8	X	10	
2																						
3																						
4																						
5																						
7																						
8																						
9																						
10																						
11																						
12																						
13																						
14																						
15																						
16																						
17																						
18																						
19																						
20																						
21																						
22																						
23																						
24																						
25																						
Subtotal 1																						From / To / Hours
Subtotal 2																						
Total																						Total hours

Fig. 8.1. Sales Call Analysis Form

commodations and must be checked for each flight booked. A final column under the heading of "Remarks" provides space for the agent's idiosyncratic comments ranging from good sales ideas to complaints about being disconnected.

As an example of how this form is to be used, note call number 1 in Figure 8.1. Mrs. Brown inquired about the fare and schedule to Copenhagen from New York. The agent offered to book her on a flight 3 weeks hence. She accepted for herself and her three sons at tourist rates (four segments booked eastbound). The agent offered-up explaining the advantages of first class, but Mrs. Brown preferred to save money. The agent then offered to book a return and was again accepted. The agent then asked if Mrs. Brown would be traveling to any other cities and reminded her that if she was she should book these flights now to save time. Mrs. Brown reported that she wanted to remain in Denmark. The sales agent then noted that the SAS hotel in Copenhagen would be a good central headquarters for her tour of Denmark, but Mrs. Brown wished to spend no more than the first week in the capital. She did book two rooms for the first five nights after her arrival, however. This represents two rooms for five nights or ten bed nights.

At the end of the day each agent was to enter his or her hours worked and total bookings. Then the agent was to transfer his totals to the weekly-monthly Performance Rating Form (Figure 8.2). The daily form would then be submitted to the Group Section Leader for review and comment. Each Section Leader was responsible for eight agents. At the end of

Agent

Section Leader

WEEK 1

DAY

	Types	W	TH	F	SA	SU	M	TU	Subtotal	Elements	Rating	Der.
A	Eastbound	12		18	10		19	19	78	EB/Hour	2.38	A/H
B	Westbound	2		2	3		8	5	20	% Return	25.6%	B/A
C	Other	6	O	5	3	O	8	6	28	Other/Hour	.86	C/H
D	F-Class	1	F	0	1	F	6	2	10	% F-Class	7.9%	D/D + E
E	Y-Class	19	F	25	15	F	31	26	116	Segm./Hour	3.85	ABC/H
F	Hotels	2		1	0		1	0	4	Hotels/Day	.8	F/5
G	Calls	61		55	41		65	59	281	Calls/Hour	8.58	G/H
H	Hours	6.75		5.75	6.75		6.75	6.75	32.75	Segm./Call	.45	ABC/G

Fig. 8.2. Weekly/Monthly Performance Rating Form.

each week the Section Leaders would total the efforts of their agents and have a statistical clerk calculate the percentage ratings on the right hand side of the form according to the formula in the last column. For example, eastbound Flights booked per hour are calculated by dividing Row H into Row A. Similarly, the rating for percent return shows the number of return trips booked as a percentage of the trips to Europe. The number of segments in elements E and H represent the total bookings on SAS flights, that is eastbound, westbound, and non-transatlantic. The critical measure for evaluation purposes turned out to be segments per hour because an agent must be taking many calls and selling hard in order to raise this figure. In slow periods, however, segments per call becomes the most significant variable since it corrects for fewer sales opportunities.

This form was used for both monthly and weekly summaries. For comparison sake, a composite standard was made up based on the average of all the agents. This composite was included with the feedback to each individual reservationist. In order to avoid individual discomfort and build camaraderie the agents were divided into teams of four agents each. At the end of each week the team performance rating for all teams was posted in the working area. In this way team competition was fostered and cooperation within teams began to emerge, but since individual performance was not posted, poor individual performance did not receive undue attention.

Introducing record keeping is often a thankless task. In order to avoid antagonisms it is best to keep the process simple. The use of check-off forms worked well at SAS, but such forms must be accompanied with detailed directions for data recording. Of even greater importance is the need to justify the data collection to the employee. At SAS these forms provided the employees with their first real knowledge of how well they were performing. By adding monthly tabulations to the report the agent was able to see the more stable aspects of his performance. The danger of overreacting to a bad or slow week was countered by instructions to base one's self-analysis on long-term performance. The employees never objected to the forms because their purpose was well explained, and they all wanted to see how they were doing.

The recording form provided feedback to the agents, but that is not the only benefit that resulted from the new forms. By analyzing the weekly and monthly measures it was possible for management to develop individualized training programs tailored to the strengths and weaknesses of each agent. An agent who consistently fell below standard in selling hotel space could be trained on the virtues of spending the night with SAS while a coworker who made many hotel bookings did not have to waste time on instructions that were not needed. Similarly, an agent who always seemed to get return bookings could be employed in slow periods to train those who have difficulties with returns. The ongoing data collection provided a direction for behavior change as well as a tool for evaluating changes as they occurred. SAS now had a way of measuring the accomplishments of the sales force. Attention could, therefore, be focused on teaching the reservation agents the behaviors that would produce better sales outcomes.

THE FIRST STEPS IN CHANGING SALES BEHAVIORS

Once the measurement system was in place, a behavior modification program to develop new sales behavior was instituted. Historically, the reservationists had received very limited sales training. They were trained in how to work the computer terminal and familiarized with SAS procedures, but there had been no major effort to produce salesmanship. In fact, the initial step in sales training was to convince the agents that management was right in its view that selling was not alien to the agent's role of helping the flying public.

Much of the training was to be conducted by the supervisors so prior to the agent training, the supervisors were given a 1-day program which explained the instructional-coaching approach. It showed the supervisors the advantages of having short classroom training sessions at intervals interspersed with on-line coaching and supervision. The 1-day session was to develop a rationale and materials for the other classroom experiences as well as to teach coaching skills to the supervisors. Role plays, case-study materials, and lecture presentations were used.

The new behaviors that the reservation agent had to learn can be divided into general goals and specific skills. The lecture and role-play presentations were oriented toward a redefinition of the agent's role. In order to accomplish this goal, the agent's expectations about selling and the need to change old behaviors had to be addressed.

Selling is a percentage business, but in operant terms it is also an extinction business. The agent who is doing a great job booking 25% of his calls is still being "rejected" 75% of the time that he offers to book. On the other hand, the agent who makes offers only when he is sure of a booking does not get rejected at all but books only 10% of his opportunities. Yet the 15% difference in their overall sales performance could be a major factor in the company's overall success. The first thing that the agents had to learn was to continue to swing the bat even though they were only hitting .250. Where large expenditures are involved a 5% increase in sales represents a major revenue supplement. Although most of the time the agent does not get rewarded (with a yes answer) for offering to book he cannot allow that behavior to extinguish.

Having learned to make offers even though they often get turned down, the agents also had to get over another discomfort that they could feel with the new system. They had to begin to accept the importance of sales as a measure of performance rather than judging themselves on how many calls they had taken. Speed is the enemy of salesmanship. One cannot make a sincere effort to sell a caller if one is worrying about making a daily quota of calls or making sure there is no backlog. The agents had to recognize that the half-hour call that resulted in a booking is well worth the time it takes no matter how many calls are waiting. They had to see that the important call was the current one; that selling tickets paid the bills and speed in taking calls did not. Since their past reinforcement contingencies had rewarded speed, the agents were being asked to adjust to a reversal of contingencies. The rationale for this change was explained as an upper management concern. As long as the agents were selling tickets, SAS could always hire more people to make sure there was no backlog of calls.

These concepts were not difficult to teach, but they did require a foundation in terms of modifying many of the agents' definitions of their jobs. Program material had to be developed to increase their consciousness of their role as sales agents. They had to fully grasp that they were more than just booking agents. They had to recognize that they had an area of expertise (airline travel to Europe) that the customer did not possess. Even the travel agent does not specialize in transatlantic airlines. He has a thousand other things to arrange, and he will appreciate the agent's assistance. Since the agent is perceived as the expert, the caller is not going to be offended if a better route is suggested or if the agent offers to book a flight. After all, if they weren't interested in SAS they wouldn't have called in the first place.

In order to alleviate some of the discomfort associated with trying out new behavior, the reservation agents were reminded first that there really are benefits to flying SAS, and second that what the customer wants is a pleasant trip with as few complications as possible. As the air travel expert working for a quality airline, the reservationist is in a better position than anyone to assure a pleasant journey for the client.

Specific Sales Behaviors

The behaviors that needed to be increased were those that typically lead to sales in any business. Any client is more likely to buy if it can be shown that it is in his best interests to do so. The sales behaviors that the agents had to learn were those that would lead to this result.

The sales training program centered on increasing the frequency of the following three verbal responses to callers:

1. Compares airlines
2. Outlines the benefits of SAS
3. Offers to book so that the caller will make at least a tentative reservation.

If these behaviors could be mastered, it would represent a major change in reservationist activity. The experiments presented earlier demonstrated that these responses increased sales. Such a change in reservationist behavior, therefore, had tremendous value to SAS.

As an example of the new behaviors that the agents had to learn, take the case of the caller who requests a flight from Washington to Copenhagen. The reservationist with no sales training and a reward system based upon calls per hour is likely to state that SAS has no direct flights out of Washington and wait for the caller to say goodbye. With a program of rewards for sales, the agent could be trained to respond more affirmatively. He could tell the caller that if he flies Pan-Am out of Washington he will have to carry his luggage over to the Copenhagen flight when he has to change planes in London, whereas if he books a domestic carrier from Washington to Kennedy, his luggage can be checked right through to Copenhagen on SAS. The agent still may not get the booking, but at least he is in the running.

In almost every situation a potential benefit can be found for the client. A 10 hour layover in Copenhagen can be presented as a chance to see the city rather than as a horrible connection. Similarly, the hour between planes in Copenhagen can be seen as an opportunity to put yourself back together before an important meeting that would not be available if one made a direct transatlantic flight.

The idea of this approach was not to create flim-flam artists who made every SAS connection the best connection. The stress instead was on honesty. If the customer was not interested in the benefit he could try some other carrier. The main thing was to let the customer see what SAS had to offer. This is impossible without comparisons and benefit statements. The caller made the final decision.

The rationale for this sales model is quite simple. If agents make decisions without the client's approval, the client is likely to resist, if not on this trip then on the next. If the agent misleads the potential passenger by booking a trip that is not convenient, the client will avoid SAS in the future. The long-range effects of chicanery will be a decrease rather than an increase in revenue. Further, deceit is not necessary in an industry where there is great similarity of service such as equipment and fares. The agents knew that given the basic equality of major service factors, SAS still offered distinct advantages that could be presented without gilding the lily. Finally, the agent's knowledge of SAS flights and the airline industry as a whole justified making recommendations to a public that could be confused by advertising and informal advice on how to make the best world-wide flight plans.

The air traveler is presented with a confusing picture of costs, special plans, hotels and rental cars, time and travel packages and restrictions, tours and idiosyncratic concerns. The reservation agent can make recommendations to solve these problems as well as extol the benefits of SAS.

TELEPHONE SALES TECHNIQUES

It is one thing to outline goals for the reservationists and quite another to teach them specific means to those ends. The general statement that one should try to book every flight first class says nothing about how to accomplish that goal. The plan to actually change the responses of the telephone reservationists embodied two steps. First, there was classroom training to teach the new behavior, then a coaching program of feedback and positive reinforcement was designed to maintain the use of appropriate sales responses on the job. The classroom sales training was based on teaching specific responses to the most common inquires. The general model of the reservationist as the air travel expert who would provide the benefits of traveling SAS and seek a booking was expanded to include a step-by-step approach to each potential passenger.

Initial Elements of the Call

1. Relax the Passenger
2. Determine the Passenger's Needs

The individual who is calling to book a transatlantic flight is usually on very unfamiliar ground. He is also facing a larger than average expenditure. The reservationist who expresses an interest in his concerns and takes the time to reduce his apprehension will be perceived as sincerely interested in helping him. Once such rapport is established and the agent has become a reinforcing stimulus, the caller is much more likely to respond affirmatively to suggestions to fly SAS.

The airline reservationist role is as the expert resource for the client. Yet, it is impossible to help the client maximize his trip without a basic knowledge of the caller's goals. In the case where a caller begins with a request for the fare and schedule to Oslo, the agent cannot even answer his questions until he knows much more than what the caller has volunteered. He must obtain the technical details of the flight such as date of travel, length of stay, number of people in the party, and ultimate destination, since all of these could influence the fare and flight possibilities. The technical details are the minimal data required before a flight can be booked. Previously most reservation sales agents had simply asked questions of the customer such as, "When will you be leaving?" and "How long are you planning to stay?" Unfortunately, many customers reacted adversely to these questions and felt pressured because they did not understand the need for such inquiries when they simply wanted to know a fare. The SAS agents were taught to get around this problem by stating, "I will be happy to give you fare and schedule information but in order to get you the best fare I must first ask you some questions."

The general tenor of the agent's responses in completing the first two steps of the call are information gathering in nature. The techniques to be employed involve active listening, questioning, and positive reinforcement of the client's inquiries and tentative plans. Responsiveness is demonstrated by restating vague answers to confirm the agent's understanding of the request as well as decisive, affirmative responses to the customer's questions. The client who seems confused by all the rigamarole should be reassured that everyone feels a little uncertain planning these long trips while the client with the well organized itinerary is congratulated on his foresight.

Planning the Flight

3. Make Recommendations
4. Give Benefits
5. Focus on the Positive

Once the customer's goals have been established, it is time for the air travel expert to take over. The reservation agents were taught to make recommendations at every opportunity. When the client seems unsure or requests aid, the agent must be prepared to offer SAS alternatives. If the client comes prepared with an itinerary but SAS has a better flight, a recommendation is appropriate.

The key to making successful recommendations is knowledge of the potential benefits for the customer. In order to help the reservationist with this task, lists of potential benefits were developed for each of the most common sales recommendations. As examples, Table 8.2 presents the advantages of connecting through Copenhagen and Table 8.3 gives the benefits of staying at SAS hotels. Since it is often impossible to know which benefits will strike home with a particular caller, agents were trained to support their recommendations with as many benefits as possible. Training focused on matching the benefits to the client's goals and bringing the benefits into the conversation as early as possible. The benefits were, therefore, used to lead to the recommendation rather than to justify it. The agents were instructed to mention the benefits and recommendation before the customer had made a decision so that commitment to his own verbalizations did not interfere with the client's ability to accept the course of action recommended by the agent.

As part of portraying the advantages of flying SAS, the agent was trained to emphasize the positive in every situation. For the potential traveler who requested direct service to Munich, the agent was instructed to respond, "We have daily service to Munich through Copenhagen. For about the same cost you can visit both cities." A benefit has been presented leaving the option to fly with SAS still viable for the client. Obviously this is superior to "We don't have direct service to Munich. You'll have to call TWA." Benefits are a highly individual phenomenon. By expressing the positive aspects of a situation the reservation agent is likely to strike a responsive chord in at least some callers.

TABLE 8.2. Benefits of Connecting Through Copenhagen Airport.

Clean, comfortable, and convenient
Baggage checked through to destination
No customs clearance required (except Domestic Denmark)
Showers and rest cabins available
Beauty shop and barber shop
Baggage lockers and check room
Hotel reservation and rental car desks
Bank, post office, and cable & telegraph offices
Coffee shop and bar
Nursery
Duty free shop
First class lounge
Highly rated gourmet restaurant
Twenty minute bus ride to town for sightseeing

TABLE 8.3. Benefits of SAS Hotels

Instant confirmation
Prices guaranteed
Prices include taxes and service
Modern hotels
All conveniences
Good restaurants
Airport bus usually stops at SAS hotels
English-speaking personnel

Responding to the Client

6. Overcoming Objections

No matter how much one emphasizes the positive aspects and benefits, there are also going to be obstacles that must be overcome in any sales opportunity. The next step in the training regimen stressed positive steps to overcoming these difficulties while at the same time maintaining rapport with the caller. The foundation of this approach was in empathizing with rather than confronting the customer. In reality, the telephone agent cannot change most of the things that people object to about a flight. He can't bring the price down, make the layover shorter or magically produce a direct flight. What he can do is accept the caller's concern and provide comparisons, alternatives, and benefits to balance against them. The agent was taught to provide the facts of a situation and any potential benefits to the customer without arguing. He was also trained to try to quickly correct problems that could be overcome.

Closing the Deal

7. Reinforce the Caller
8. Ask for the Booking
9. Get Some Action from the Caller

Training in positive reinforcement was an integral part of the sales package for reservation agents. The caller is investing a great deal in SAS service. He is more likely to be shaped into making the desired end response (booking a flight) than he is to make the response all at once from scratch. The successive approximations that can be reinforced include any positive statement about SAS or the potential benefits described. In addition the agents were instructed to agree with and support potential booking statements. Thus, the caller who said "Maybe I should make a reservation now, I can always change it later" received an affirmation of the ease of changing bookings without obligation and information on the benefits of doing so. An immediate offer to book was then made before the opportunity was lost.

If there is little difference in basic service, the customer who is comparison shopping by phone is likely to sign with the airline that he talks to last. If the reservation agent can make the comparisons for the client he negates the need for a series of information requests and puts the customer in a position to book immediately. Still, the caller may be hesitant for a number of reasons, so the benefits of making an immediate reservation (See Table 8.4) should be presented with a suggestion for a specific booking.

A major goal of the sales training was to eliminate the use of general, open-ended responses by the reservation agents. Agents were instructed to replace "Is there anything else I can do for you?" with specific alternatives for the customer to evaluate. Similarly, they

TABLE 8.4. Benefits of Making Tentative Booking.

You can still go to travel agent for ticketing and advice
There is no obligation
You can cancel or change at any time
You can book hotel now
You will be guaranteed a seat at the time you wish to travel
When you call in later, we will have a record of your plans
You don't have to pay now
You can order cars now
You can give me your seat selection (First Class)
You will have better choice of domestic connections
You will have time to arrange tours and other packages
If requests are necessary, there will be more time to use for this
Our ticket office can prepare your ticket in advance
TBM is possible if you book now
You can order Businessman's Special now
You can order Day on the Danes now
We can submit your special meal request now

were told to avoid advice to book early in favor of offering the benefits (Table 8.4) of making the reservation before the current call was completed.

The final step of the booking progression was to get some commitment from the caller. Ideally this was a reservation, but it didn't have to be. An address where literature could be sent or permission to return the customer's call were viewed as commitments to remain in contact with SAS. Such contacts offer another chance to book the client and in some cases overcome the obstacle of booking with the airline that the client happens to call last.

Recommended Selling Phrases

The sales program would not be really complete until it had identified the actual responses that the reservationists were to use. But what are the best things to say to a potential customer? Suppose, for example, that a caller states that he would like to fly from New York to Helsinki on August 18th. The reservationist responds that there is a flight at 9:30 A.M. and offers to book SAS flight 938. The caller concurs. The agent's next task is to sell the customer on traveling first class, but just what approach is most likely to produce more first-class bookings? The sales agent has many possible ways of phrasing this question. He could say "First class or tourist?" or "Will that be first class?" or "That's a long flight. You might be more comfortable in first class" or "For the price differential our first-class service is excellent" or any number of other tempting prompts. Which of these will be the most effective?

There is no need to try to choose among these phrases by rational argument. The question is an empirical one which is amenable to data collection. Before the training program was created, experiments were conducted to determine what the reservationists should say. A wide variety of statements were tested in the real world. In each instance reservationists were given a form with the phrase to be evaluated. Each time the phrase was used a check would be placed on the form and the outcome associated with that phrase was recorded. At the end of a 3-week trial period, the results of using various phrases were compared for positive outcomes.

The results of these experiments produced a list of phrases that seemed to maximize sales. The most potent form of request appeared to be statements that began with "May I suggest" or "May I recommend." Questions that asked for booking dates rather than whether or not to book were also very successful. In general those questions that assumed that the caller was flying SAS but questioned what day or how many seats produced the greatest number of bookings.

This research also showed that particular benefits could be potent sales tools. For example, "Since you have a business meeting the moment you arrive, why don't you fly first class? You'll be able to spread out your papers and get some last minute work done." Personal endorsements by the reservation agents also scored well. When the agents indicated that they had recently stayed in and enjoyed a given SAS hotel, bookings increased. Finally, inquiries as to first class or tourist did not do nearly as well as a first-class recommendation that included a statement of the potential benefits of the more expensive accomodation.

THE COACHING-FEEDBACK PROGRAM

Once everyone knew which behaviors would increase sales, one might expect those responses to immediately become the predominant behaviors in the sales agent's repertoire. Unfortunately, that is not the way behavior change works. It just isn't that easy. The classroom experiences and handouts were effective in teaching new skills, but task interference continued to cause problems. Paper and pencil tests showed that the agents' knowledge of the concepts was outstanding, but unobtrusive monitoring of calls revealed that many sales opportunities went by the board. In particular the problem seemed to be one of stimulus recognition. In the ABC model, antecedents or discriminative stimuli that set the occasion for making a selling response were not always recognized. This continued to occur despite the fact that situational training had been employed in the classes. Covert monitoring showed a lack of transfer in that agents still missed some selling situations in actual calls after they had reacted well to those situations during class testing.

The difference between the correct responses of the test situation and the poor performance on actual calls appeared to be related to situation-specific problems on the line. While the reservationists could think through the appropriate response in the classroom tests, the situation changed with a caller on the line. With a customer the agent had to type, look up rates, and monitor the computer as well as sell the client. Neither the new behavior nor the stimulus recognition skills had been learned well enough to compete with these other demands. The long history of reinforcement for taking calls as quickly as possible seemed to be interfering with the practice of new sales behaviors. The agents were not taking the time to consider how a given inquiry (Antecedent Stimulus) could be a cue for a sales response. A particularly telling instance of this occurred as the consultant was sitting with a particular reservationist. She received an inquiry about whether SAS allowed a dog to fly in the cabin if it was in a container that would fit under the seat just as one would place any carry-on luggage. The agent replied, "Yes, we do," and the caller terminated the call with a word of thanks. The agent then turned to the consultant and said, "See what I mean, I'm not getting any sales opportunities today." Of course, the agent could have asked where and when the client was traveling, extolled the benefit that SAS provided in allowing the animal to ride in the cabin, and attempted to book a flight. Unfortunately, none of this was accomplished because the antecedent stimulus for a sale was not recognized.

To investigate this issue a test was given in three different ways to the same group of agents. First, actual calls were monitored with the consultant sitting right next to the reservation sales agent. As the agent knew the consultant was there to see how well he or she was selling, one would expect that they would try to sell whenever possible. In this situation 62% of the sales opportunities led to some offer to book. Later the consultant role played exactly the same situations with the agent involved. This time, however, the agent did not have the burden of using the computer, although it was still necessary to respond quickly. Under these conditions 84% of the sales opportunities led to an offer to book. Finally, the same responses were written out in the form of a paper and pencil test. When this test was taken without a time limit, 97% of the opportunities led to a booking offer.

The classroom training had been successful, and it was continued intermittently for hour to half-day sessions, but something more was required. The solution was supervisor monitoring while sitting with the agent as a means of rewarding and prompting the new sales behaviors. The supervisors had been trained in how to do this, but they were not doing side-by-side monitoring frequently enough. Somehow they thought that training alone would be sufficient. Although the data from the experiment mentioned earlier helped to change this view, implementation of the monitoring program was not left to chance or good intentions. Monitoring goals were established, and each supervisor was asked to keep track of his or her performance.

The monitoring model for the supervisors was based on prompts, shaping, and positive reinforcement as exemplified in Table 8.5. The consultant was used as a model and instructor in helping the supervisors to adapt to this monitoring program. All negative comments were eliminated. In the face of a mistake, the supervisor was trained to note the error and prompt the next call before the error could be made again. Using this method the employee had no reason to ever feel threatened or defensive. By replacing the supervisor's negative comment about a mistake with a prompt for the correct behavior on the next call it was possible to avoid alibis and rationalizations about an error.

A typical supervisor-agent interaction on a call would go something like this:

Caller: I'm interested in your schedule to Stockholm.

Agent: Yes, we have excellent service to Stockholm. In order to give you an accurate schedule, I must know when you are planning to fly.

Supervisor: Nods Approval

Caller: I think around the 17th or 18th of August

Agent: Good, we have an afternoon flight on both those days. Let me see what is still available.

Supervisor: Thumbs up sign!

Agent: Yes, we can make a reservation for you on either day.

Caller: Book me on the 18th.

Agent: Fine, will that be first class or tourist?

Supervisor: (Notes inappropriately phrased question for prompt on a future call. Notes are made in writing on a simple supervisory form so that prompts for future calls are not forgotten.)

Caller: Tourist.

Agent: This is a busy time of the year. I'd recommend that you make a return reservation at this time so that you don't get shut out.

Supervisor: Smiles and makes OK gesture. (This suggestion had been absent in an earlier call and therefore warranted enthusiastic reinforcement.)

Caller: Yes, that's a good idea.

Supervisor: Writes "Hotel" in front of the agent. (Prompt)

Agent: (Makes return reservation and then states) We have a very attractive SAS hotel in Stockholm. To simplify things for you I could make a reservation there for your stay.

Caller: That's not a bad idea. Does it have. . . .

TABLE 8.5. Supervisor's On-Line Monitoring Hints for Feedback to Agents.

Concepts

1. In the beginning, performance will probably not be what you would like.
2. Even on good calls not everything will be good (and on bad calls not everything will be bad).

Do's

1. *Do mention things done well.* Especially
   a. when an individual missed an important step before but does it now
   b. when an unusual or difficult situation is performed well
2. *Do be specific*, e.g., "It was good that you mentioned alternatives. When you told the passenger he could either leave through Chicago or New York, he became ready to book."
3. *Do relate specific items to concepts learned in class*, e.g., "The benefits you mentioned worked. The more you mention "no obligation" and "this way you will be guaranteed to have a seat," the more bookings you will get."
4. *Do be brief.* Zero in on the important points.
5. *Do postpone mentioning a problem area.*
6. *Do prompt desired responses for the future.*
   a. use stories
   b. write notes during the call
   c. tell the Reservation Sales Agent what to try on the *next* call (do not review the bad points of prior calls).
   d. ask agents for their own opinions, e.g., "How can we handle a situation like – – – ."
7. *Do tell the agent to keep doing the good things.* "If you ask for the bookings like that on every call, you will get much more business."
8. *Do talk about topics other than SAS business.*

Don'ts

1. *Don't just say "excellent."* That reinforces the good *and* bad points.
2. *Don't review past problems.* Remember these points and prompt desired actions after a pause.
3. *Don't forget about problems.* We are not ignoring problems, we are trying to attack them in a positive way.
4. *Don't talk business the entire time* (unless the phones are extremely busy).
5. *Don't say too much about one call.* Comment on the most important areas. Do not try to mention every slight detail.
6. *Don't prompt every action if it doesn't come when you expect it.* Wait for the agent to act. Many times his/her timing will be different than yours, but the end result will be attained.

Feedback To You

1. If someone offers an excuse, you have probably punished them in some way.
2. If you say "but" very often you are probably punishing people.

At the conclusion of the call the supervisor would praise the agent for seeking the booking and mentioning the hotel. He might go on to ask the agent if he is familiar with SAS hotels in other cities and discuss the advantages of these. He will not address the poor phrasing of the class of flight request but on a future call he will prompt: "Will that be First Class?"

Each supervisor was expected to monitor and coach at least two of their eight agents a day. In addition, the consultant was employed as a monitor-trainer on an intermittent basis and supervisors paired agents to monitor each other during slow periods. Since the posted data was presented for teams of four agents each, the better salespeople on each team often served as models for those whose skills were less well developed.

Of course, coaching was not the only responsibility of the supervisors. They were also responsible for reviewing the sales calls analysis forms and compiling the data for their group. They had a major role in providing favorable comments on performance and reinforcing the agents for taking the time to note their observations on the "Remarks" section of the form. Yet for a truly successful program, reinforcement must come from more than just the immediate supervisors. Upper management at SAS had been seen by the employees as being concerned about the performance of the workers only when there was a problem. This was an inaccurate perception, as in fact upper management did more in direct interpersonal reinforcement of employees than most companies. Nonetheless, the reservation agents wanted more recognition, so top management responded. They visited the reservation center more frequently and made a point of asking for sales data. They also increased the number of positive comments on improvement in performance. In addition, top management presented physical and task-oriented reinforcers. The top performers and those showing improvements were given gifts, allowed special freedoms, or assigned to favorable tasks such as problem-solving sessions. Verbal reports suggest that the agents found these to be quite reinforcing.

RESULTS

The results of the sales program at SAS can be viewed individually or for the group as a whole. Since a variety of behaviors were treated, it seems most appropriate to present the outcomes based on the program goals.

At the beginning of the project a study was undertaken to demonstrate the effectiveness of asking for orders as a selling tool. A random sampling of calls at that time demonstrated that only 34% of the potential offer opportunities actually resulted in offers being made. At the completion of the program that figure had risen to 84%. The offer percentage through the 6 months of the intervention is presented in Figure 8.3. One can only conclude that, if as demonstrated earlier, increased offers lead to increased sales, this change was going to increase business.

Figure 8.3 also presents the percentage of return bookings for the groups as a whole for each month of the program. The data indicate a meaningful increase in the number of people booking their returns on SAS at the time that they booked their eastbound flight. This addition in round-trip bookings is a valuable increase in company revenue, although it could be argued that most of these people would have flown back on SAS anyway. In fact, if even a tiny percentage would have returned on another airline, the increased income at $190 a segment is quite substantial.

This program represents a systematic application of behavior technology to sales problems that can be duplicated in almost any business. In outline form it employed:

1. Baserate collection of data on behavior and consequences before treatment.
2. Development of simple recording forms.
3. Collection of data on consequences and potential consequences for the employee.
4. Survey of desired employee consequences which proved most frequently to be those things that would increase their productivity, e.g., improved headsets so that they could hear the caller more clearly.
5. Empirical studies to ascertain the impact of behavior change in a sample before a full program was adopted.
6. Lecture and classroom material that was empirically tested before being used.
7. A positive reinforcement, on-line monitoring system that led to improved performance and employee-management relations.
8. Outcome data that measured employee behavior as well as increased income.

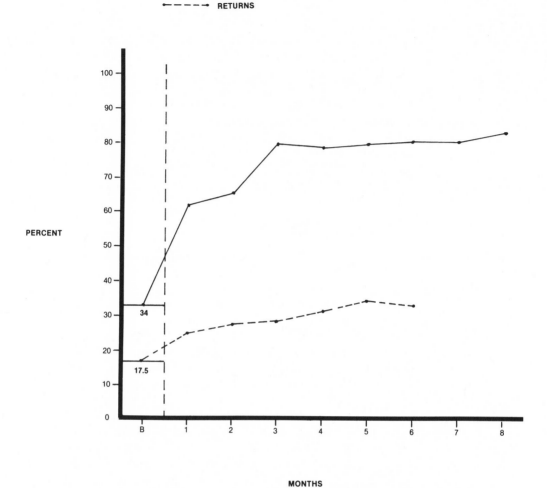

MONTHS

Fig. 8.3. Percent of Offers Made Out of Opportunities and Percent of Flights Booked With Return Baseline Through 8 and 6 Months of Treatment Respectively.

The program has been running for 5 years and continues to produce useful feedback to the staff and productive training material for management. It represents the first systematic attempt to empirically evaluate sales techniques at the phrase-by-phrase level as well as the most sophisticated regimen for training managers in how to shape and reward their sales force.

REFERENCES

Parsons, H.M. What happened at Hawthorne? *Science*, 1974, **183,** 922-932.

9

Sales Management: An Effective Performance System

Robert Mirman
General Mills, Inc.

"You, Sir! That's right, YOU! No need to walk any further down that boardwalk. Bring your lovely wife a little closer and look at something which will make her life easier. That's right, step right up and see the miracle invention of our time! Son, how much time do you think your wife spends in your kitchen each week peeling potatoes, carrots, and other vegetables? What's that – 1 hour? Why, no sir! Today's housewife spends 2½ hours each week ruining her delicate little fingers on such drudgery. But with this new miracle "Peel-O-Matic", she'll spend less than 4 minutes a day peeling vegetables! Isn't that amazing! Now, I'll tell ya' what I'm going to do. . . . "

The popular image of the boardwalk barker selling pots, pans, and other necessary kitchen paraphernalia to passers-by is far removed from the reality of today's computer-age salesperson who uses techniques unheard of just a decade ago: psychological profiles of customers, sophisticated marketing analyses, and minute-to-minute computer reports showing everything from projected sales volume to out-of-stock conditions. The increasing sophistication of client accounts' data systems and purchasing skills demand continual upgrading of the salesperson's skills if a successful business relationship is to be maintained.

To sustain a competitive edge in the marketplace, sales organizations have depended heavily on a myriad of sales training regimens, the purpose of which has ostensibly been to provide an adequate amount of product knowledge and "how-to-sell" skills for sales personnel. The underlying assumption in any training program, of course, is that skills developed in such sessions will be utilized by the salespeople upon their return to the field. The accuracy of such an assumption is certainly open to question. In fact, there is a paucity of data available to support the long-term effectiveness of most sales training programs (Hahne, 1977). This is not to say that such training has not been effective, but that controlled verification of training effectiveness has only rarely been conducted. The majority of reports describing the results of sales training efforts are anecdotal and most often report either high participant ratings for the training or overall increases in sales without the use of common verification strategies such as control groups, reversal or multiple-baseline designs, etc.

If all we had to do to increase sales was provide proper training to our salespeople, we certainly would not need as many sales managers. However, the common experience of sales managers indicates that salespeople don't always do what they have been trained (or paid) to do (Weitz, Antoinetli & Wallace, 1954). The effects of sales training can be somewhat transitory, and as a result sales organizations have become reliant on corporate systems of control to ensure continual high levels of performance by their sales force. These corporate controls include sales commissions, incentive pay, merchandise credits, bonus payments, and sales contests. In essence, the organization is saying "We've provided our salespeople with the proper skills to make the sale; now we must provide them with sufficient reason to *use* these skills." Apparently, sales organizations pessimistically believe that *training* employees to sell and *getting* them to sell are separate issues which must be separately addressed.

Recent studies using sales incentives by Krietner and Golab (1978), Neider (1980), and an excellent review of incentive programs in various industries by Spector and Hayes (1979), confirm the effectiveness of incentives in stimulating high performance. The pessimistic philosophy inherent in any incentive system lends credence to the argument that salespeople do not consistently work to their potential, otherwise why would performance improve under incentive contingencies?

Moreover, the successful use of sales contests to increase sales by many firms is a further indication of the gap that exists between actual and potential performance. These contests, usually of short duration, very often result in increased sales volume during the contest period, although it is debatable that the long-term sales picture is at all brightened by these short bursts[1] (Haring and Myers, 1953). Nevertheless, the fact that sales performance normally increases (sometimes dramatically) during contests provides additional support to the thesis that salespeople could perform better under the right conditions.

The "Compleat" Sales Manager

As demonstrated by the effectiveness of incentive programs and sales contests, it appears that failure to maintain consistently high sales performance is only infrequently caused by a lack of knowledge but most often by a lack of action in the *application* of this knowledge. One of the basic responsibilities of sales managers, therefore, is to get their salespeople to do what they have been trained to do. To accomplish this task, the sales manager must at the same time play the role of a statistician, psychologist, trainer, marriage counselor and, sometimes, a Mississippi riverboat gambler. He or she has to be a Dale Carnegie, Vince Lombardi, Sigmund Freud, Florence Nightengale, and Norman Vincent Peale all wrapped in one. Wearing all these hats, the sales manager must construct the sales and management environment to ensure continual strong performance by the sales force.

The "compleat" sales manager, i.e., one who has strong technical and sales competencies and can, more importantly, ensure that his people completely *utilize* their many skills, is a critical figure in any organization. One of the first people to earn a mega-salary as president of a large national firm was Charles D. Schwab, President of U.S. Steel, in the heavy growth period during the first part of this century. His salary, astronomical according to the standards of the times, created a furor among the stockholders and management community. Once, when asked why he was worth that much money, he frankly admitted he knew little about steel. "However," he added, "I'm worth it because I know how to get people to do what they're paid to do".

While not yet relegated to the 'extinct species' list, "compleat" managers are the exception, not the rule. Unlike J. P. Barnum's 'suckers' who were born every minute, "compleat" managers apparently have a longer latency period between births.

The Performance System

Sales managers have many tools at their disposal which can be utilized to improve sales performance. The corporate structure provides organizational control systems such as a standardized performance evaluation format, incentive pay systems, sales contests, and salary administration. These corporate controls are effective change agents, but they are for the most part beyond the control of the district level sales manager. For example, these managers can certainly influence the manner in which the performance evaluation is completed, but they are probably required to follow the standardized evaluation format which may not allow for tailoring to meet the specific needs of individual sales people and differing account conditions. They also have a voice in salary administration but are, once again, limited by rigid corporate policies governing frequency and amount of salary increases.

The sales manager does, however, have much more flexibility and control in other important areas. These include the following systems:

- Goal Setting
- Performance Measurement
- Data Feedback
- Reinforcement
- Performance Review

The above systems, in combinations with the corporate control systems, are the elements of every sales organization's *PERFORMANCE SYSTEM*. These factors directly affect performance of salespeople and managers alike and must be fine-tuned if the firm is to prosper. The elements of the manager's Performance System provide stimuli for initiating action (e.g., goal setting) and, most importantly, also provide consequences contingent upon performance.

Proper utilization of these systems is done on an ongoing basis by the "compleat" sales manager and will inevitably influence sales performance to an even greater extent than the corporate controls previously described.

That these systems are important components in any management approach that hopes to maximize performance should come as no surprise to any manager. Most managers use these systems as a matter of course. Too often, however, managers who determine to improve the performance of their salespeople decide to do *more* of what they've already been doing: they set *more* objectives, hold *more* meetings, criticize *more* often, and do *more* store audits. They apparently feel that the situation will improve if they simply do it harder. They have yet to learn that doing it *more* is not as effective as doing it *better*!

Many organizations, realizing the need "to do it better," have found great success using the performance improvement model known in different circles as Behavior Modification, Organizational Behavior Management (OBM), Contingency Management, or Performance Management. Used almost exclusively by manufacturing firms in the late 1960s and early 1970s, (Schneier, 1974) the application of these procedures has recently become increasingly popular in a wider variety of organizations. Although, in theory, the application of behavioral technology seems well suited to the area of sales management, this application has been infrequent and confined to small retail stores or pilot studies within small units of larger organizations. Until recently, no firm has undertaken the full-scale development and utilization of a behavioral program within a large national sales division. The remainder of this chapter will be devoted to a description of such an endeavor within General Mills, Inc., a $4 billion company headquartered in Minneapolis, Minnesota.

The Sales Organization

The Grocery Products Sales Division of General Mills, Inc. is responsible for over $1 billion in food sales to grocery stores of all sizes, from small "Mom and Pop" independents to national chains. The 550 salespeople and 145 field managers are spread out nationally across 20 sales regions, each containing three to five districts, with six to ten salespeople per district. Regions are divided geographically into three Zones, each headed by a Zone Director who reports directly to the Vice President, General Manager of Sales (See Table 9.1).

The Sales Division is not a profit center, but is responsible for sales volume, (i.e., cases of product). Recent years have seen case volume in excess of 70 million, averaging over 120,000 cases per salesperson. Best sellers such as Gold Medal Flour, Wheaties, Cheerios, and Bisquick make up some of the 250 food products sold by the sales force.

Sales Force Priorities

The basic responsibility of the grocery products salesperson is to convince the store manager or chain store (i.e., "account") buyer to purchase promotional items offered at a reduced price by the manufacturer in exchange for in-store displays or newspaper advertisements of the product at its regular or reduced priced during the promotional period (several weeks). The salesperson has two priorities:

1. Convince the buyer to purchase sufficient quantities of product at a reduced price during the promotional period.
2. Convince the buyer to pass along these savings to the consumer.

For example, if the account is offered an allowance of 10 cents for every package of Betty Crocker Super Moist Cake Mix purchased during the promotional period, the salesperson will (in many accounts) actively attempt to convince the buyer to pass this entire 10 cent savings along to the consumer by reducing the price of the cake mix an equal

TABLE 9.1 Organizational Chart of Sales Division Detailing Typical Region Structure.

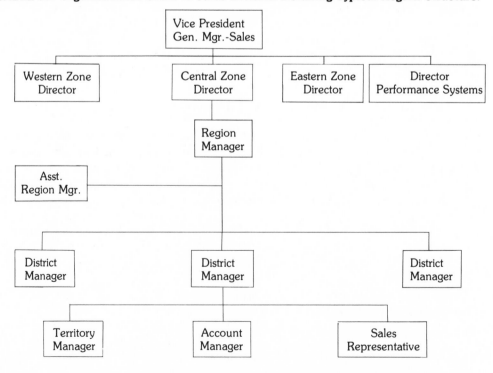

amount. This represents 100% "pass-through" of the promotional allowance and will have a positive impact on sales volume. In addition, the salesperson tries to convince the accounts to advertise these promotional items in local newspapers to further stimulate sales volume.

The salesperson also has accountabilities in such areas as sales of new products, increased distribution of established products, additional facings (shelf space) for established products, and submission of required administrative reports in such areas as competitive activity, sales calls, and performance against sales objectives. Performance in these areas is formally evaluated semiannually using a format established by the corporate headquarters. This format lists specific accountabilities, weighted according to importance. Although regional autonomy allows for infrequent and minor changes to this format, it has most often been followed.

The overall yearly evaluation rating is used to determine frequency and amount of salary increases, promotion potential, and yearly cash incentive award. This yearly incentive award is based on a combination of factors, including total region sales, individual performance rating, and position title. Turnover within the sales force has averaged approximately 10% each year for the past 5 years, which is slightly more than half the industry average.

Application of the Performance System

In 1976 the Grocery Products Sales Division of General Mills, Inc. initiated an assessment of its operation to determine if sales performance could be improved through adjustments to incentive and evaluation approaches, goal setting, feedback, and performance measurement systems. This assessment, conducted through questionnaires to sales personnel, personal interviews, and extensive systems analysis, confirmed management's perceived need for such adjustments, and in early 1977 a test program was begun in two of the twenty national sales regions (65 sales personnel). The purpose of the 6-month test was to determine if measurable improvements in sales performance could be obtained by adjustment to these elements of the organizations.

The data resulting from this test revealed that these procedural changes directly influenced overall sales performance by affecting both outcome measures (sales volume) and process or behavioral measures (sales calls per day, number of displays sold, number of facings gained, etc.). As a consequence, a Performance Systems Department was established within the Sales Division and given the responsibility of upgrading all organizational/management systems and behaviors which influenced sales performance.

It should not be inferred that this program was initiated as a result of top management's fear that the Sales Division was being poorly managed or in danger of imminent failure. To the contrary, the General Mills sales force had consistently done well in the face of increasing competition in a flat market. In fact, the same aggressive corporate thinking that allowed George Odiorne to develop the MBO concept within General Mills in the late 1950s (Odiorne, 1965) and in 1942–43 provided B. F. Skinner with the funds, laboratory space, and engineering assistance to develop the ill-fated "pigeon-guided" air-to-ground missile (Skinner, 1960), had also built one of the most highly regarded and sophisticated sales/marketing organizations in the country. Viewed as one of the top three marketing organizations for graduating MBA's, General Mills has consistently maintained a competitive edge in a highly competitive market. The Performance Systems program was viewed as a means of sharpening that edge.

Program Objectives

The Performance Systems Department was established in 1978 to fulfill several major objectives.

1. To improve sales performance by improving managers' utilization of the elements of their *Performance System:*

MANAGER-CONTROLLED SYSTEMS
- Performance Reviews
- Objective Setting
- Performance Measurement
- Performance Feedback
- Reinforcement

CORPORATE-CONTROLLED SYSTEMS
- Incentive Pay
- Compensation Plan
- Sales Contests

Primary emphasis was given to those Manager-Controlled Systems that directly affect day-to-day performance.

2. To increase salespeople's perception that a strong relationship exists between performance and consequences.

3. To provide sales managers with the behavioral skills necessary to improve the performance of their people and ensure they *use* these skills.

4. To develop the concept of a "Positive Accountability System" (P.A.S.) in which objectively measured accountabilities were specified and positive consequences (recognition, feedback, salary increases, improved ratings, etc.) awarded as these accountabilities were achieved and negative consequences (warnings, memos, probation, termination) provided following unsatisfactory performance. This was somewhat different than most "accountability" models which have earned a negative connotation due to an over-reliance on the use of negative consequences.

Process

The application of the Performance Sysems program to the twenty Sales Regions followed this basic pattern:

1. *Region Assessment*

   Purpose: To allow the program director to analyze the operation, style, and philosophy of the Region's management team. Management systems and effectiveness were also evaluated.

   Process:
   a. Individual interviews were held with key management personnel and, in some instances, sales personnel. Managers were asked to describe and show examples of their systems for objective setting, performance measurement, feedback and reinforcement.
   b. All management reports, performance evaluations, incentive pay structures, and other control systems were analyzed.
   c. A 75-question survey was sent to each salesperson in the Region asking for opinions on such issues as frequency of management feedback, equity and frequency of performance evaluations, effectiveness of sales training, satisfaction with salaries, perception of relationship between performance and salary/incentive pay/promotions, etc.

d. Managers were also asked to identify specific sales performance areas in need of improvement. These areas would serve as preliminary targets during the first phase of the program.

2. *Region Management Workshop*
   A 3-day workshop was held in each Region for the entire management team. Participants included the region sales manager, assistant region sales manager, district sales managers, region office manager[2], and the region sales assistant (i.e., manager-in-training).

   Purpose: To present participants with guidelines for maximizing the effect of the Region's performance systems on sales performance.

   For example, managers were given guidelines showing how to set sales objectives in such a way as to increase the likelihood these objectives would be met. Managers were then given the opportunity to compare their current objective-setting procedures to these guidelines and develop improved performance objectives during the workshop.

   Most importantly, managers were shown how to use data feedback, recognition, and other positive consequences to improve sales performance. These procedures were discussed in light of the great geographic distances between managers and their salespeople. Emphasis was placed on providing increased feedback through improved written and telephone communication.

   Process: Other topics included in the workshop:

   - Accountability models
   - Performance Analysis (Mager & Pipe, 1970)
   - Performance Evaluation
   - Pinpointing
   - Reinforcement
   - Punishment

   The final day of the workshop included a detailed review of the questionnaire completed by the Region's salespeople, and an identification of pinpointed objectives by managers. Rather than simply provide information on behavioral procedures and hope the managers would follow these guidelines on their return to the field, each sales manager was required to identify at least one targeted performance concern for each of his/her salespeople. To identify this area of concern, the sales manager frequently reviewed the salesperson's most recent performance evaluation and selected the lowest rated category as the targeted performance. An "Action Plan" for improving this target area was then developed.

3. *Follow-Up Consultation*
   The program director returned to the Region 3 to 4 weeks following the workshop and met individually with each participant to review progress since the workshop. For this session, each manager was to have:
   a. finalized selection of performance targets for each salesperson.
   b. collected baseline data to show past and current levels of performance for each targeted area.
   c. established preliminary performance objectives for each targeted performance.

d. reviewed steps a-c with the region sales manager.

Purpose: To provide guidance and feedback on the initiation of this program in each Region, District, and Region Office. Reinforcement, normally via memos to region and zone Managers, was provided for district sales managers who demonstrated any proficiency in accomplishing the first steps of this program.

4. *Program Maintenance*
   Each district sales manager was accountable to the region sales manager for the progress of his/her salespeople on the specific target performances assigned to each (Note: Although the targeted performance areas were selected by the district sales manager, the objective or goal for this performance was most often *negotiated* between the manager and salesperson). The district manager was also responsible for providing the region manager with monthly status reports summarizing progress of each salesperson. The purpose of these reports was to provide an accountability framework as well as stimulate feedback from the Region's management team. Copies were frequently sent to the zone director.

District managers were also accountable for increasing the frequency of feedback

TABLE 9.2. Sample of Measurable Performance Targets Successfully Improved by Sales and Office Personnel. This List Represents a Small Sample of Total Number of Areas Improved. Note That Most Sales Force Targets are *Activities* Which Lead to Sales Volume.

Performance Targets

SALES FORCE: SALES TARGETS

	Open-Ended Questions Asked
Sales of Displays	During Presentation
Shelf Share vs. Market Share	Facings vs. Competition
Cases Sold per Call	New Product Acceptance
Calls per Day	Distribution
Adherence to Planned Coverage	Promotions Sold
Ad Features Sold	Suggested Selling
Pricing Parity	Order Filing Speed
Pass-Through of Allowance	

SALES FORCE: ADMINISTRATIVE TARGETS

Sales Forecast Accuracy	Expense Report Timeliness
Quality of Business Review	Contract Timeliness
# Negative Comments	Orders Meeting Guidelines
Quality of Sales Presentation	Unitized Shipments
Competitive Reports	Expense Reductions
	Performance Proofs Submitted

OFFICE STAFF: ADMINISTRATIVE TARGETS

Accounts Receivable-($)	Overdue Contracts
(30 and 90 days)	Expense Report Errors
Accounts Receivable- # Items	
(30 and 90 days)	
Invoice Corrections	
Order Errors	

given for performance improvement. Some Regions required managers to track the number of occasions in which positive feedback was given, although most Regions simply required district managers to frequently send copies of reinforcing memos to the region manager. (This "copy" procedure was already being utilized in all Regions on a very limited basis prior to this program.) These reinforcing memos were extremely effective because (1) they reinforced specific behaviors or sales outcomes, (2) they let the salesperson know that his/her performance was important enough to inform the region manager, and (3) they helped to bridge the gap created by the lack of personal contact time between manager and salesperson.

Although less of a problem than in most conventional performance improvement designs, program maintenance in behaviorally-based programs has traditionally been a major concern. Once the consultant rides off into the setting sun, and the novelty has died away, performance gains will often fade along with management's enthusiasm. Maintenance of effect has been difficult because too often the program was directed entirely at changing the behavior of people without also making corollary adjustments to the *systems* that direct and maintain the behavior of these people (i.e., performance evaluations, incentives, etc.). The program must be accepted as a part of the current system, as a way of managing, and not just as another "here today, gone tomorrow" motivational program. As evidence of this danger, the author of the only published report of a behavioral sales program that failed (Miller, 1978) admonished that the likelihood of program success is greatly improved if "the program procedures are incorporated into the routine management practice [p. 238]."

Integrating The Program Within the System

After the Performance Systems program had been introduced in the first few Regions, it became apparent that it was perceived as something apart from the normal management systems, and as a result maintenance of the initial successes would most likely be difficult. As an example, sales managers often sent memos to their salespeople listing progress on "*Performance Systems* Objectives," rather than "District Sales Objective." Salespeople were not told how their performance against these objectives would affect their performance ratings, and therefore, their incentive pay and salary increases. Too much emphasis had been placed on informal consequences such as recognition and data feedback, without integrating the process into the accepted formal system of consequences.

To correct this perception and improve the likelihood of long-term success, sales managers were urged to tie their targeted performance objectives directly into the performance evaluation system. Not only did this step alter the long-term prognosis of this program, but it had an immediate, often dramatic, effect on current levels of performance.

At least one-half day of each Region workshop was then devoted to the performance evaluation process. Each Region's current evaluation format was scrutinized and improved in four major areas:

1. *Performance standards were objectified.* Although measures for performance variables often existed, performance standards had not always been developed. Qualitative standards were added to those quantitative measures already in existence.

2. *Performance standards were individually established on the basis of the account's history and sales potential.* Previous Region standards were most often based on a universal standard for all accounts, regardless of account conditions or merchandising philosophy. (Note: Volume quotas, however, had always been set differentially.) For instance, the

Region might establish '100 products in distribution' as the "satisfactory" performance level for all accounts. Therefore, a salesperson in an account that stocks only 65 items would get a below-average rating for this accountability even though he/she might have recently increased the distribution base from 59 to 65 (i.e., + 10%). The punishing aspect in such a rigid system had been felt by most managers and salespeople, but managers had been concerned about the time and effort necessary to convert to a more equitable system that evaluates each person on recent performance within his/her account, rather than against a Region-wide standard.

3. *Performance standards were most often negotiated with each salesperson.* Although sales volume quotas continued to be assigned to each territory, individual performance standards for sales activities such as distribution, promotion sales, shelf share, etc., were negotiated with sales personnel. It was felt that this negotiation process would increase the salesperson's commitment and sense of accountability for the accomplishment of the objective. The salesperson, therefore, became an active agent, rather than a passive object in the performance evaluation process.[3]

4. *The relationship between potential performance levels and the eventual evaluation rating was specified prior to the performance period.* In an effort to increase the perception of a relationship between performance and consequences, it was necessary to change the nature of the evaluation process. Prior to this change, performance ratings were assigned to each sales representative by the district manager at the end of the 6-month evaluation period. This allowed for too much subjectivity, uncertainty, and anxiety for managers and subordinates.

To eliminate most of this uncertainty, it was decided that the goal of the performance evaluation process was: *under no circumstances should a salesperson be surprised by any aspect of his/her performance evaluation.* As reviewed above, the likelihood of surprise was reduced by establishing measurable standards that were objectively set on the basis of territory conditions and required input from each salesperson. The final element in this process was to pre-specify the relationship between potential performance outcomes and evaluation ratings. For example, rather than telling salespeople that their objective was to "control expenses," specific expense parameters were assigned to potential performance ratings *at the beginning of the 6-month evaluation period* (See Table 9.3).

This final element allowed each salesperson to evaluate his/her own performance on an ongoing basis. It also removed much of the 'judicial' responsibility from the shoulders of

TABLE 9.3. Effect of Objective Setting Format on Performance

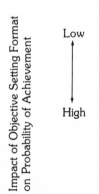

Impact of Objective Setting Format on Probability of Achievement — Low ↑ High

Objective:	"Do the best you can on expenses"
Objective:	"Keep your expenses down"
Objective:	"Bring your expenses in at or under budget"
Objective:	Expense Control

Standard	Rating
More than 6% over budget	1 (Poor)
3-6% *over* budget	2
0-3% *over* budget	3
0-3% *under* budget	4
4% + under budget and 100% of sales quota	5 (Excellent)

the Sales Manager and placed the responsibility and accountability right where it belonged: on the salesperson.

After convincing several Regions to experiment with this evaluation approach on one or two major accountabilities, it became relatively easy to sell this concept to the remaining Regions. Performance improvements from these first Regions were often so dramatic that the data were unbelievable. Consequently, managers of these first Regions were asked to provide a written summary of their programs which could then be distributed at other Region workshops.

The major advantage of this evaluation system, other than its effect on performance, was that it allowed the performance evaluation system to become the focal point of the program rather than focus only on the series of individual projects initiated by each manager. It also helped absorb the program's behavioral procedures and principles into the ongoing management system. Most importantly, this focus provided a framework in which to cover the basic behavioral procedures of objective setting, measurement, feedback, and reinforcement. In essence, the development of a behaviorally-oriented evaluation process helped to ensure the continued high levels of performance identified as the overall goal of the Performance Systems program.

Performance Systems: Summary

The Performance Systems program was established to improve sales performance by tightening the accountability system in the Grocery Products Sales Division. By training managers to more effectively utilize the elements of their Performance System, consistent changes in sales performance have resulted.

The "Positive Accountability System," established as the structural backbone of the Performance System, relied heavily on the development of a behaviorally-oriented performance evaluation system. The Positive Accountability System followed this basic pattern:

1. A list was developed of every performance area for which the salesperson would be evaluated.
2. A measurement system was developed and agreed upon for each area.
3. Accountability was established by defining the standards for each area; potential performance parameters were assigned to evaluation ratings prior to the evaluation period (i.e., negotiated between manager and salesperson).
4. Each salesperson was responsible for maintaining records of performance in each measured area and submitting a summary and performance graphs to the sales manager on a monthly basis.
5. Optional mini-reviews of performance were held quarterly. These were informal, brief sessions in which the salesperson reviewed the performance data for the manager.
6. Major performance reviews were held twice each year. The sales manager directed a review of the individual's performance and finalized the evaluation ratings.

In addition to establishing the Positive Accountability System, managers were given a model to use in dealing with performance problems. Following the same approach as the P.A.S., managers encountering persistent performance problems were trained to:

1. Pinpoint the problem in measurable terms.
2. Collect performance data (baseline).

3. Communicate this performance concern to the salesperson and establish negotiated goals for improvement.
4. Tie-in to the evaluation system, if this was a major performance concern.
5. Arrange for self-measurement by salesperson (as a means of stimulating performance and feedback for improvement).
6. Provide increased positive feedback via memos, telephone calls, mail-o-grams, calls from Region and Zone managements, etc., for *any* improvement.
7. Evaluate the data. If improving, maintain the procedure. If still at a low level of performance and not improving, change to an alternative procedure.

The remainder of this chapter will describe the results from specific programs designed as a consequence of the Performance Systems program.

PROGRAM RESULTS

During the past 2½ years, the Performance Systems program has been introduced in all twenty Sales Regions and Offices. Although all Regions experienced measurable success in improving performance on a multitude of sales behaviors and actions, this success has been most dramatic in those Regions entering the program following the introduction of the integrated performance evaluation approach discussed earlier. As a function of this adjustment in emphasis from a single manager-oriented "project" approach to a total systems philosophy, region managers generated programs which at once affected the performance of entire Regions.

A major part of the recent follow-up consultation has been to return to the initial Regions and present the total "Positive Accountability System" concept to these managers. The utilization of this improved structure, in combination with the original program presented to these Regions over 2 years ago, has resulted in additional performance gains.

In most instances, performance improvements were generated for sales behaviors and activities rather than dollar sales or numbers of cases sold (See Table 9.2). This was in keeping with the Sales Division's philosophy of emphasizing those activities which led to case volume. As recently as 7 years ago, the performance evaluation format was adjusted so as to reduce the emphasis then placed on sales volume. Actual sales volume versus quota now accounts for less than 10% of each individual's performance rating.[4] The premise of this approach is certainly debatable, for it is difficult to verify the differential effectiveness of either procedure, (i.e., one which provides consequences for sales activities leading to volume versus another which simply evaluates the salesperson's ability to meet volume quota).

Sales managers in this organization were, however, convinced that a direct relationship existed between sales volume and success in such activities as gaining additional distribution of products, increasing the number of shelf facings of a given product, increasing speed in gaining the initial order on a new product, and convincing the buyer to "pass-through" the manufacturer's promotional allowance to the consumer. The responsibility of the sales force was only to *increase the probability of sales* by successfully engaging in these sales activities. The likelihood of increased sales volume was certainly improved when such activities were appropriately completed, but never guaranteed. Marketing and sales data have confirmed the effect of these activities in stimulating consumer purchases. Therefore, in most cases, no attempt was made to collect data confirming increases in cases sold as a consequence of improvements in sales activities.

The case studies reported here are indicative of the literally hundreds of documentable single-subject and group performance improvements resulting from the introduction of the Performance Systems program. Data and program descriptions are presented for the following sales activities:

1. Quality of advertising support given by grocers to major product promotions (Cases I and III: Group Data).
2. Timely reports submitted by sales personnel on competitive activity (Case II: Individual and group data).
3. Timeliness of initial orders on new product introductions (Case IV: Group Data).

CASE STUDY I: THE DYNAMIC DOZEN

As stated earlier in this chapter, the primary responsibility of the salesperson is to convince the wholesaler or retail grocer to accept a promotional allowance on a given product in exchange for promoting this product via newspaper advertising or 'cents-off' coupons, through reductions in the regular shelf price, or end-aisle displays. In most cases, the only contractual obligation by the grocer is to advertise the product and, often, to reduce the advertised or shelf price by a minimum of 1 cent. Therefore, to receive the monies offered by manufacturers, the grocer must only place a small ad (called a "liner") in the newspaper. Such an ad has virtually no effect on sales volume, but it does allow the grocer to collect the manufacturer's allowance. This is a perfectly legal and well-accepted practice in a business where the profit margin of the average store is *less than 1%!*

It is in the manufacturer's interest, of course, to stimulate sales by having their products advertised in the largest possible ads, at the lowest possible price. For this reason, as the salesperson presents the grocery buyer or store manager with promotional information, he/she also presents suggested ad prices along with a breakdown of resulting profit margins, potential earnings per case, and suggested order quantities. The buyer or buying committee must then decide to accept or reject the promotional offer; if accepted, an advertised price is also determined. Although the salesperson will frequently receive an immediate accept/reject decision from the buyer, the pricing decision normally takes place in the 2 weeks following the presentation. In fact, many accept/reject decisions are also made by buying committees, and as a result the salesperson will not receive *any* immediate feedback on the sales presentation.

Prior to the initiation of this program, salespeople in this Region were evaluated at the end of each 6 months on their success in selling promotions. "Success" was defined as the percent of promotions accepted by the buyer. A specific standard for this performance had not previously been determined, nor were there any measures available for the qualitative aspects of the acceptance. That is, salespeople were evaluated on the quantitative issue only; a salesperson could receive a high rating for this accountability by selling 100% of available promotions even though 95% were "liner" ads which generated little additional volume. Sales managers had always stressed that salespeople were responsible for convincing their accounts to provide increased "pass-through" of allowances, but *this responsibility was never directly tied to an accountability for achievement.*[5]

The following steps were taken by the sales managers of this Region to increase the percent of promotions accepted at a "quality level":

1. A "quality ad" was defined as one which met specific characteristics. These characteristics differed from account to account due to the advertising philosophy of the specific

account. In general, the following factors were rated by the District Manager for each ad:

a. *Price* – This was the critical factor. A low or "hot" price would probably guarantee that that the ad would meet the remaining criteria. Knowing that his/her profit margin was reduced due to the hot ad price, the grocer would probably need to place a large ad in a prominent spot on the page to ensure high consumer traffic.

b. *Size* – Large size ads draw consumer attention.

c. *Placement* – Depending on the advertising style of the account, "hot" features are generally placed in a consistent and prominent place on the page. Consumers are used to looking at the ads in these spots.

d. *Stated Regular Price* – It is supposedly more effective to provide the regular price along with the featured price to allow for accurate comparison by the consumer.

e. *Picture of the Product* – For increased product identity and attention.

2. Region management identified the top twelve products (designated as the "Dynamic Dozen") which had the strongest impact on the Region's sales volume picture. Performance on only the "Dynamic Dozen" products was included in this program, but sales on these products covered approximately 60% of the Region's volume.

3. Since it was normal practice for salespeople to submit actual newspaper ads to their district managers as "proof of performance," the manager had easy access to a permanent product record of the accounts' promotional support histories. Prior to the initiation of this program, each manager reviewed the past year's ads for the "Dynamic Dozen" and established a baseline for "percent of quality" (i.e., number of ads meeting quality criteria plus total number of promotions) for each account. District and Region baseline totals were also computed.

4. Ads were rated according to each account's advertising style. An ad considered "quality" for Food King Stores might not have met the standards set for Safe Town Stores. Managers did not use a point system for evaluating quality; their determination was done subjectively, based on factors a-e above, but was frequently checked by the region manager. Disagreements were almost nonexistent. Moreover, once the program started, quality criteria were so well accepted that some salespeople began to rate their own ads prior to submission, and once again their judgments were sustained in virtually every instance.

5. Baseline data were presented by the district manager to each individual. The measurement system was reviewed, and performance objectives negotiated and tied into specific potential evaluation ratings.

In Table 9.4, the salesperson for Food King Stores has agreed with his/her district manager that a quality performance of 45-53%, for example, would be rated "4"

TABLE 9.4. Example of Performance Contract Identifying Objectives and Potential Ratings.

Account	Last Year's Baseline "% Quality"	% Quality Performance Necessary to Receive Rating (1-5)				
		1	2	3	4	5
Food King Stores	34.6	20	28	38	45	54
Safe Town Stores	68.2	50	58	68	76	85

(i.e., "Superior Performance"). This "Performance Contract" would then be passed up to the region manager for final approval. The evaluation was based on an improvement over past performance rather than on a comparison with a universal standard.

6. Each salesperson tracked his/her performance on a graph used to track monthly progress against objectives. This self-monitoring process was critical to the success of this program as it provided immediate visual feedback to the salespeople. The salespeople knew at the end of each month what their updated rating was on this important accountability.

7. In addition to the extensive and immediate feedback resulting from self-monitoring and graphing, monthly reports on individual, District, and Region "Quality" performance were circulated to all personnel. The extensive involvement by the region

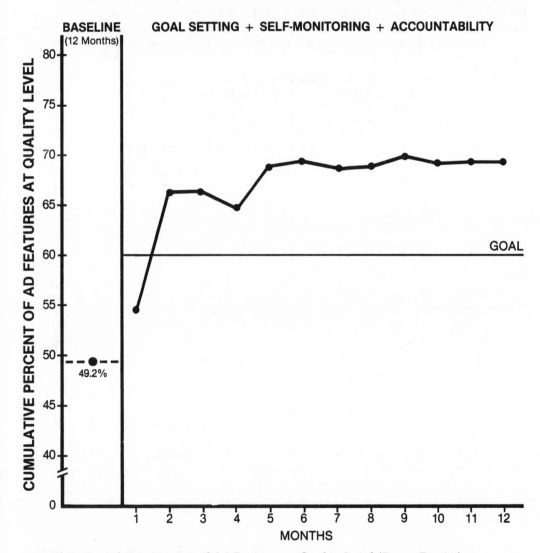

Fig. 9.1. Cumulative Percent of Ad Features at Quality Level (Entire Region)

Baseline (12 months) $\overline{X}$ = 49.2%.
Intervention = 69.5%.

manager in sending congratulatory memos to people demonstrating improvement was a strong factor in the program's success.

Results

During the 12-month baseline period, a total of 57 sales promotions were presented to 26 major accounts (1,482 opportunities); 729 or 49.2% of these opportunities were converted into quality ad features.

In the 12 months following the introduction of goal setting, self-monitoring, and increased accountability, 1,069 of 1,538 promotions (69.5%) met the quality standards. This 69.5% represented a 41% increase in ad quality level. Although such factors as differential levels of marketing support and the competitive environment played a role in this improvement, the region manager stated that this program was "the major factor in earning one of the highest incentives in the country." In fact, during the 4 years prior to this program, this Region had never ranked higher than 9th of 20 Regions on sales versus quota (Table 9.5). At the end of the first year of the program's operation, this Region was ranked second in the country.

TABLE 9.5. Region Based on Sales Versus Quota. This Improvement in Sales Volume Was the Result of a Complex Series of Sales, Marketing and Environmental Factors, Including the Performance Systems Program.

	Year	Region Ranking (of 20 Regions)
BASELINE	1975-76	13
	1976-77	13
	1977-78	9
	1978-79	16
PROGRAM	1979-80	2

This Region's program is now nearing the end of the second full year of operation. Quality performance is 71.4%, slightly ahead of last year.

Salespeople stated they were much more "aware" of the need to sell quality promotions, but, interestingly, also claimed they were not selling any differently than during the baseline period. Managers, however, have seen evidence of increased assertiveness by salespeople when suggesting ad prices to buyers. Several managers also noted salespeople's increased reluctance to "take no for an answer," resulting in many additional sales. An indication of salespeople's heightened awareness was the numerous occasions they called the Region Office to correct or question data reported in the Region Manager's Monthly Summary on quality performance.

Although it is difficult to identify with any certainty what salespeople did differently, it is certain that they changed *something* and were apparently reinforced for doing so. Most importantly, in the nine Regions implementing similar programs for improving quality performance, all have shown a minimum 12% improvement in the first year of program operation (See Case Study III).

CASE STUDY II: EYES ON THE AISLES, EARS TO THE GROUND

Although successful completion of sales activities increases the likelihood of improved sales volume, there is not a 1:1 correlation because of the numerous confounding variables inherent in the sales environment. The most critical of these extraneous conditions is the unpredictability of the competition.

The purpose of the Marketing Divisions is to develop new products, devise advertising and promotional strategies, develop appropriate timing of promotions, and provide support to the sales force. These tasks could not be completed appropriately without considerable input from the sales force, particularly in the area of Competitive Activity Reporting. An ongoing responsibility of all salespeople was the communication of information to the Region Office regarding evidence of competitive activity. This includes rumors of new products or test markets and evidence of dates and rates of upcoming competitive promotions. The food business is fiercely competitive, particularly on flour items, and a Region's early morning report of a price reduction in flour by a major competitor might stimulate a reciprocal reduction by late morning. Salespeople were supposed to keep their eyes on the store aisles, but their ears to the ground.

Although it was absolutely imperative that salespeople continually feed this information to the Region Office for transmission to the Marketing Divisions, very few actually provided such information. In one Region, a baseline survey revealed that during a 2-month period, only 58% of the sales personnel had submitted any competitive reports, and most of these were submitted too late to be of any use. There were several explanations for this poor performance level:

1. The salesperson had to go out of his/her way to ask about competitive activity. These questions frequently met with resistance from buyers.
2. They felt someone else had already submitted the information.
3. Although responsible for this activity, they were not held accountable.
4. There was no direct or immediate benefit to the salesperson for submitting this information.
5. Salespeople only rarely learned how their report was *used*.
6. Management feedback was most often directed at those who were *not* submitting information. Reinforcement for timely submission was practically nonexistent.
7. Most Regions did not include this activity on the performance evaluation, and in those rare cases in which it was included, performance was not measured.

Clearly, it did not appear to matter if salespeople performed poorly. There were no immediate or strong consequences for appropriate performance.

The data presented in Figure 9.2 represent the results of an early study (II-A) completed by a district manager interested in increasing competitive information flow from one key salesperson. Data on submission frequency had been kept by the Region Office, but no feedback had even been offered to the sales force. During a 5-month baseline period, this salesperson had submitted a total of five reports of competitive activity.

After again explaining the need to submit this information, the manager helped this individual set up a graph which the salesperson used to track his monthly report frequency. An updated copy of the graph was sent to the manager each month, and reinforcement provided if any improvement was noted. At this point, a Region-wide program had not yet been initiated and, thus, this accountability had not been integrated within the performance evaluation system. Occasional copies of the graph were sent to the region manager.

Results (II-A)

From an average of 1.0 reports per month during baseline, the number of reports increased to 7.3 per month once the salesperson began to monitor his own performance and receive

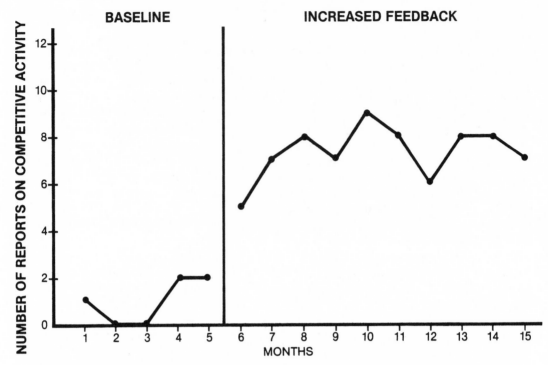

Fig. 9.2. Frequency of Individual Sales Representative's Submission of Reports on Competitive Activity.

Baseline $\overline{X} = 1.0$ per month
Invervention $\overline{X} = 7.3$ per month

increased feedback for improvement. Instrumental in this improvement was a letter sent to this individual by the region manager specifying that one of his recent competitive reports was the first such report in the country and was extremely valuable to the Marketing Division. Competitive reporting had begun to "matter" to this salesperson.

Although the data presented here on competitive reporting came from only two Regions, at least fourteen Regions have initiated specific accountabilities for competitive reporting. The following steps were generally followed:

1. Reports submitted by salespeople were tracked by the Region Office. These reports were normally phoned in to one person in the office; this individual was trained to reinforce callers for submitting information.
2. Reports were categorized as "on-time" if they were submitted within 2 weeks prior to the start of the competitive promotion.
3. A monthly summary of group and individual performance was sent to all salespeople.
4. Reinforcing memos were distributed by managers on an intermittent basis to those salespeople showing improved performance.
5. The name of the salesperson submitting the competitive information was included in the usual telegram sent to marketing headquarters. A copy of the telegram was also sent to the salesperson.
6. Several Regions identified specific performance goals based on improvement over previous performance levels.

Data for an entire Region's competitive reporting activity (II-B) is presented in Figure 9.3. Since historical data were not available with which to establish an adequate baseline and due to management pressure to begin the program, baseline measures were taken during one month only. This was not a long baseline period, but all those managers involved felt this was an accurate representation of typical performance. Therefore, the 25% baseline represents an 'estimate' of actual performance based on one month's observation. Records were kept on frequency and timeliness of reports.

Results (II-B)

Immediately following the initiation of performance measures and contingent feedback, the frequency and quality of reports improved dramatically. In the first 12 months of this program, the percent of reports submitted on time increased from 25% to 59%. Frequency of submission more than doubled. Most importantly, information was now being submitted by an average of 88% of the sales force during any given month, versus 58% during the 1-month baseline.

There was a common perception among sales managers that good salespeople are horrible administrators. Very often, the best salespeople had developed terrible administrative habits: reports were often late, sloppy, inaccurate, incomplete or forgotten. These deficits were often tolerated if the salesperson was doing an acceptable job (i.e., "Where do you want me to spend my time: selling, or on paperwork?") Administrative responsibilities are normally given low weighting on the performance evaluations of most sales organizations. In light of this lack of consequences for administrative competency (in fact, salespeople were

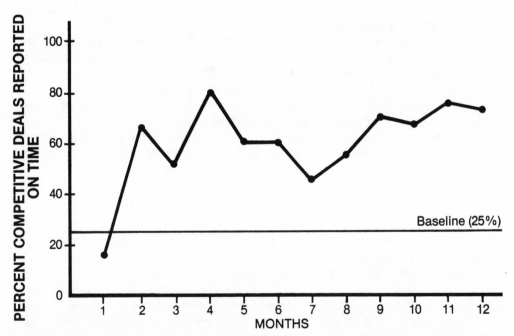

Fig. 9.3. Percent of Competitive Reports Submitted at Least Two Weeks Prior to Start Date of Competitive Deal. (Entire Region)

Baseline $\overline{X}$ = 25%
Feedback Intervention $\overline{X}$ = 59.6%

often negatively reinforced for avoiding paperwork), it was not surprising that competitive reports were only rarely submitted on time, if at all. The addition of immediate consequences demonstrated to salespeople that their performance was important. Rather than relying on a training procedure that simply explained *why* this activity was important, managers demonstrated this importance through their actions. Surprisingly enough, good salespeople are not genetically inferior administrators.

CASE STUDY III: QUALITY PRICE OBJECTIVES: "YOU CAN'T SCORE IF YOU DON'T GOT A TARGET!"

While visiting with a veteran district sales manager several years ago, I casually asked how much emphasis he placed on objective setting within his district. Displaying a wisdom which made me smile, he told a brief little tale, the punchline of which was "You can't score if you don't got a target!" He clearly understood the motivational value of the objective-setting process and used it to facilitate the performance of his staff.

This case study is similar to Case Study I which reported on a regionwide program to increase ad feature quality. In this case, quality of ad features was also the dependent variable, but the "advertised price" was the sole criterion used to determine quality. Instead of continuing to measure only the percent of promotions accepted, the Region decided to also measure the "percent of promotions accepted with quality ad features." The major ingredient in this program was the negotiated agreement of a 'target feature price' for each major promotion. The following steps were taken:

1. Each promotion of the top 26 products was included in this program. These products covered over 80% of the Region's volume.
2. Prior to the beginning of each promotion period, the district manager and the salesperson determined a price which the salesperson would try to convince the buyer to place in his ad. This target price was entered on a monthly form. If the *actual* ad price equaled or was less than this target price, the ad was rated as a 'quality' ad.
3. Although some salespeople kept informal records of their success in meeting price targets, monthly reports were issued by district managers.
4. Reinforcement was provided by District, Region and Zone Managers for improvements in the quality data. Results were displayed at District and Region meetings. This program was not integrated into the normal performance evaluation procedures.

Results

Historical records supplied the advertised price, regular price, and size of promotional allowance for every promotion during the previous year. District managers used this information to determine the quality/non-quality rating for each promotion. Sample checks by the region manager yielded over 99% reliability on these ratings.

For the entire Region, 44.2% of all promotions on the 26 products received quality prices during the 12 baseline months. Following the initiation of "target prices" and increased feedback, cumulative performance during the next year 51.1%. This represents over a 15% increase in the occurrence of quality prices.

This Region's gain of 15% was modest compared to the 41% improvement noted in Case I and was primarily due to the Region's initial failure to integrate this program within the regular performance evaluation program. This transition is, however, currently under way.

The critical factor in each of the Region programs on ad quality appeared to be tightened accountability through *measurement of quality*, rather than just quantity. Regardless of the definition of quality, and each Region had a different definition, *the fact that something called quality was being measured has improved that quality in every instance.*

CASE STUDY IV: SEARCHING FOR ANOTHER GOLD MEDAL

One of the primary ways consumer food manufacturers grow is through the development and sale of new products. Although grocers are always looking for unique products, these items are still difficult to sell because:

1. They have, at best, a limited track record in a test market. Grocers want to stock products with predictable sales patterns.
2. In order to find room to stock the new item on the shelf, an established item must be

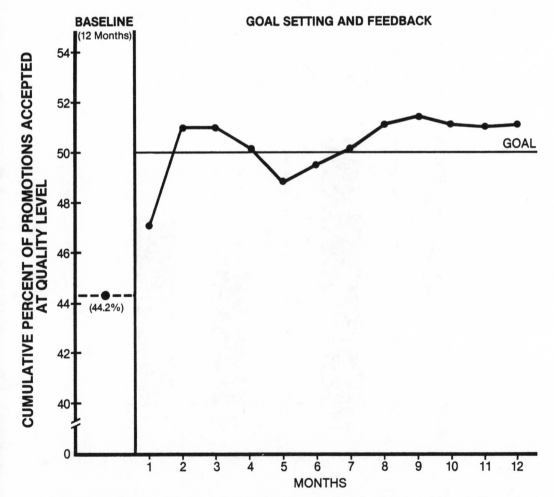

Fig. 9.4. Cumulative Percent of Promotions Accepted at Quality Level (Entire Region).

Baseline (12 months) $\overline{X}$ = 44.2%.
Intervention = 51.1%

discontinued. Not only is this a time consuming and expensive step to take, but it is often difficult to identify a product to eliminate.

3. Gold Medal Flour has been available for 100 years, but most products on the grocers shelves today were not in existence 5 years ago. The new item which initially succeeds and has holding power is a rare exception. New products, therefore, represent expensive gambles for the grocer. Approximately four to ten new products are introduced each year. In addition to these unique products, extensions of current lines (e.g., new flavors) or new package sizes are also presented to grocery buyers.

The marketing plan used to introduce these new products followed the same general pattern in every case. A 6-week Introductory Promotional Period (IPP) was established during which grocers could purchase the new product and qualify for the promotional allowance. Items purchased prior to the IPP or during the first 2 weeks of the IPP were shipped to the grocer to be on the shelf within 2 to 3 weeks. If this initial purchase was sold out, the grocer still had enough time to purchase an additional order prior to the end of the IPP.

Due to this potential of a second order in the latter weeks of the IPP, it was to the

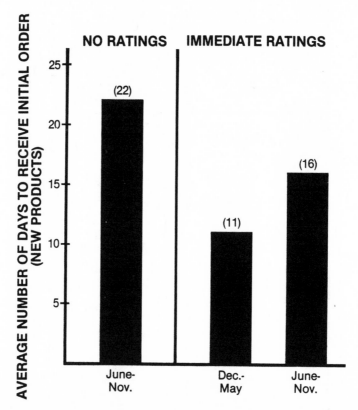

Fig. 9.5. Average Number of Days to Receive Initial Order on Sale of New Products (Entire Region)

Baseline $\overline{X}$ = 22 Days
Immediate Ratings:
  Dec.-May $\underline{\overline{X}}$ = 11 Days
  June-Nov $\overline{X}$ = 16 Days

salesperson's advantage to acquire the account's initial order by the second week of the IPP. Occasionally, salespeople would wait until the second or third week of the IPP to make the initial presentation to the buyer. On other occasions, buyers would postpone a decision on the new item. On the other hand, many large accounts made decisions through buying committees and this process was structured to take several weeks. Therefore, there were both controllable and uncontrollable events which affected the timeliness of the account's initial order. One Region, concerned that the average initial order was submitted on the 22nd day of the IPP, felt that a great deal of sales volume was being lost due to controllable reasons.

The Region established a measurement system for order timeliness and integrated this measure into the performance evaluation system. Salespeople received a rating (See Table 9.6) for timeliness of each new product order ranging from "0" for 'No Order' to a "5" for an order during the first week of the IPP. These ratings were totaled for each evaluation period and divided by the number of new products offered during that period. Performance records and ratings were maintained in the Region Office and sent to salespeople each quarter.

TABLE 9.6. Region Performance Contract for Rating Speed of New Product Orders.

Rating	Order Filed During:
5	1st Week
4	2nd Week
3	3rd Week
2	4th or 5th Week
1	6th Week
0	No Order

Results

As with similar programs in other Regions, managers reported that salespeople were "much more assertive" in asking for decisions on the 17 new products and line extensions available during the first year of the program. They also made appointments with their buyers earlier in the selling period. Frequent calls to the Region Office by salespeople with questions like, "If I get the written order on Friday, but it takes until Monday to arrive at the Region Office, do I still get credit for a sale in the first week?" verified that salespeople really felt accountable.

From the 22-day average during the 6-month baseline, order timing during the first 6 months of the program was reduced to 11 days (50% improvement). During the next 6 months, performance averaged 16 days. Most importantly, this early sell-in allowed for multiple orders from many accounts and made it possible for the Region to receive the highest possible volume rating on every new product. This was the first time a perfect volume rating had been accomplished in this Region.

Once again, it was apparent that *training* salespeople to file orders quickly during the IPP and *getting* them to do this were separate issues. The "PAS" model worked well to place this responsibility on the shoulders of the salesperson: salespeople earned access to the consequence (i.e., high rating) by getting a quick order and were given a low rating for failure to do so. These ratings took on additional significance due to the integration within regular performance evaluation system.

SUMMARY

In one of the few articles describing behavioral applications in a sales organization, Miller (1977) described several inherent difficulties in dealing with a large sales force:

1. Geographical distribution prevents frequent observation of actual sales presentations.
2. Feedback on selling skills, therefore, occurs all too infrequently.
3. Sales performance cannot be compared across territories due to market differences in each territory.
4. Market and account differences limit or exclude establishment of uniform goals or standards.
5. Uniform evaluation guidelines are, therefore, almost impossible.

In addition, salespeople can often successfully complete all those sales activities which should result in strong sales volume, but negative external conditions may exert a stronger control over consumer behavior. Too often, the lack of observation time by managers places too much emphasis on evaluation of sales volume, rather than on the performance of sales activities.

With these constraints in mind, the Performance Systems approach emphasized more effective use of those managerial procedures and control systems which affect sales performance. The success of this program verified that managers could be taught to control the performance of their salespeople through better objective setting, measurement, feedback and reinforcement. However, maximum effectiveness was gained as these procedures were tied into the regular performance evaluation and incentive pay systems.

As an indication of the overall success of this program, the Performance Systems concept has been extended company-wide and is being introduced throughout all operating divisions and subsidiaries, including Marketing, Manufacturing, Purchasing, Retail Stores, Restaurants, and Coupon Processing areas. In addition, this success has also stimulated the development of a behavioral training program which General Mills, Inc. is now providing for retail grocery managers called "Make Performance Matter" (Mirman, 1981)[6].

Clearly, the Performance Systems approach offered little in the way of startling or unique procedures, but was presented to sales managers as a program that could be used to 'fine tune' those managerial skills already in their repertoire. The success of this program was due as much to the "common sense" of the approach as it was to these managers' skills in making it work.

NOTES

1. Customers whose stores and warehouses are often "packed to the rafters" with product pushed during the contest will, therefore, order less than normal during the "trough" period immediately following the contest. The 'peak and trough' effect of sales contests is typical of contests based primarily on sales volume. This can be avoided by basing the contest on performance areas other than sales volume, such as number of new accounts sold, new items in distribution, additional shelf facings, percent of promotions sold at a predetermined quality level, etc. Improvements in these areas will result in smaller, but sustained, volume improvements over time. Variations, including awards contingent upon weighted performance in several areas (perhaps including volume) can also be effective in ensuring consistent improvement.
2. Region office managers fully participated in this program and developed procedures for improving many areas of office performance (see Table 9.2). In some cases, an office supervisor also attend-

ed the workshop with the office manager. The success of these office programs was often dramatic, particularly in the area of accounts receivable reductions.

3. A concise analysis of the importance of participatory performance reviews can be found in McGregor, D. "An uneasy look at performance appraisals," *Harvard Business Review*, Sept.-Oct. 1972, pp. 132-138.

4. Additional weight is given sales volume by making it a large factor in the formula used for determination of incentive pay.

5. For an excellent discussion of the responsibility-accountability model, see Schleh, E. C., *Management by Results*, McGraw Hill, 1961, pp. 62-74.

6. "Make Performance Matter," a behavioral training program for retail grocery managers, was based on an idea by, and developed for, Mr. Howard L. Ross, Vice President and General Manager, Grocery Products Sales Division. This package includes a 20-minute, 16MM film with three manuals for group or self-instruction.

REFERENCES

Hahne, C. E. How to measure results of sales training. *Training and Development Journal*, 1977, **31**, 3-7.

Haring, A., & Myers, R. H. Special incentives for salesmen. *Journal of Marketing*, 1953, **18**, 155-159.

Kreitner, R., & Golab, M. Increasing the rate of salesperson telephone calls with a monetary refund. *Journal of Organizational Behavior Management*, 1978, **1**, 192-195.

Mager, R. F., & Pipe, P. *Analyzing performance problems*. Belmont, Ca.: Fearon, 1970.

McGregor, D. An uneasy look at performance appraisal. *Harvard Business Review*, 1972, **50** (5), 133-138.

Miller, L. M. Improving sales and forecast accuracy in a nationwide sales organization. *Journal of Organizational Behavior Management*, 1977, **1**, 39-51.

Miller, L. *Behavior management*. New York: John Wiley & Sons, 1978, pp. 232-239.

Mirman, R. *Make performance matter*. Minneapolis, Minnesota: General Mills, Inc., 1981.

Neider, L. L. An experimental field investigation utilizing an expectancy theory view of participation. *Organizational Behavior and Human Performance*, 1980, **26**, 425-442.

Odiorne, G. S. *Management by objectives*. Belmont, Ca.: Fearon, 1965.

Schneier, C. E. Behavior modification in management: A review and critique. *Academy of Management Journal*, 1974, **13**, 528-548.

Skinner, B. F. Pigeons in a pelican. *American Psychologist*, 1960, **15**, 28-37.

Spector, B. I., & Hayes, J. J. *Productivity improvement through incentive management*. Report prepared by C.A.C.I. Inc. for Cybernetics Technology Office, Defense Advanced Research Projects Agency, Sept. 1979.

Weitz, J., Antoinetli, J., & Wallace, S. R. The effect of home office contact on sales performance. *Personnel Psychology*, 1954, **1**, 381-384.

10

Making Salesmen: Behavioral Assessment and Intervention

William J. Crawley
Edward J. Feeney Associates

Beverly S. Adler, Richard M. O'Brien and Elaine M. Duffy
Hofstra University

Behavioral sales programs are rare in the literature. The few successful programs that have been reported (Gupton & LeBow, 1971; Luthans, Paul & Baker, 1981; Miller, 1977; Weitz, Antoinetli, & Wallace, 1954) have focused on reinforcement techniques to increase the act of selling rather than attempting to teach specific selling behaviors. While there is clearly a profit to be gained from increasing the motivation of sales personnel through goal-contingent reinforcement, it should not be assumed that this is the most appropriate type of sales intervention program. Direct behavioral intervention to obtain successful selling responses has also been demonstrated to be a viable alternative (Brown, Malott, Dillon, & Keeps, 1980; Collins, Komaki, & Temlock, 1979; Komaki, Waddell, & Pearce, 1977).

As Edward J. Feeney has pointed out (Performance Audit, 1972), when developing a performance program within any organization, one must identify what are likely to be the most profitable areas of intervention through what is called a "performance audit." The performance audit not only indicates the areas in which the largest potential payoffs exist, but also quantitatively demonstrates to skeptical managers that improvement is needed.

As a basis for comparing potential opportunities to improve performance, Gilbert (1978) utilizes a theoretical tool called the "PIP" (*Potential for Improving Performance*), while Feeney talks about *Performance Improvement Opportunities*. The "PIP" is computed by examining the ratio of the best level of performance to the level of typical performance; similarly, the "PIO" subtracts average performance from exemplary performance. The larger the "PIP" or "PIO," the greater the potential for improvement. When taking the goals of an organization into account, the "worthiness" of the performance goal is measured by assessing the cost of the performance improvement in comparison to the money generated by improved performance. In computing the performance audit, the performance goal is measured in terms of quality, quantity, or cost. When working with sales personnel, *quantity* is often the most appropriate measure.

When obtaining a measure of quantity on sales, one can measure the *rate*, the *volume*, or the *timeliness* of performance. After taking into account the number of sales personnel and the potential performance rate, volume, or timeliness, the economic potential is assessed, and the performance improvement program can be implemented.

The present sales project was implemented in a national retail store chain which has a primary commitment to furniture and accessory sales. The responsibility of salespeople within this organization is to sell furniture and accessories. This is done either within the store or in the customer's home. Archival data suggests that visiting the customer is by far the more profitable approach. When servicing the customer through "in-home calls" (visiting the customer's home), the "close ratio" (ratio of sales to customer contacts) is 60% versus 22% for customers served within the store. The average sale for in-home calls is $2,700 versus $600 for walk-in sales. Although in-home calls are profitable for the organization, the sales people experience negative consequences for working away from the store. These include phone calls missed from prospective customers, the inability to promote sales to prospective customers walking into the store, and travel costs. Therefore, when computing a performance audit, increasing the frequency of in-home calls would be a profitable area of intervention, provided the negative consequences for performing this service are changed.

When a performance audit was conducted before implementing the present sales performance improvement program, the output areas shown in Table 10.1 were indicated as having the greatest economic potential for the retail stores.

As can be seen, the net gains from improved performance in these outcome areas outweigh the program costs by as much as 295 times. Program costs include the cost of rewards, procedure and form costs, and, in the case of in-home calls, costs of travel from the store to the customer's home.

The overall goal of this sales program was to increase the sales growth by 15% per year (5% real growth over 10% inflation). In order for the total sales force to produce this 15% increase, each sales representative needed to increase his sales by 15%. Since it would be difficult to expect that all sales representatives could meet this new standard due to variability in their comparative sales performance, the hiring of additional staff becomes a consideration. If one assumes an average close ratio of 20% for sales within the store, one out of every five unseen customers should be a sale. This is equivalent to a loss of the average sale sum of $600. At this ratio, one can see the added worth of hiring additional staff. In fact, when quantified, the potential added worth of additional staff was found to be $1,100,000 per year! As a result, additional sales representatives were hired.

In assessing the type of program one would design to accomplish the goal of improving performance, the term "performance" must be more clearly defined. Gilbert (1978) has proposed that performance is comprised of both behavior and accomplishment, but it is the accomplishment *alone* that has direct value. Therefore, one may never need to focus on the behaviors that lead to the desired outcome. In other words, it is only the accomplishment that can be translated into dollar return.

Yet, this dichotomy is somewhat artificial. It is hard to imagine more than a few examples in which the performance involved in attaining these accomplishments requires improvement, but the behavioral repertoire remains unmodified. Although Gilbert is correct in assuming that the impact of performance is in the accomplishment, deficient behavior will negatively affect the reward value of the accomplishment. When taking the view that *both* the accomplishment and the behaviors are equally important in affecting outcome performance, one can concentrate on changing the essential behaviors comprising a particular performance.

In the present sales project, the accomplishment measure of "close ratio" is directly affected by the selling skills of the stores' salespeople. Although it used to be believed that "salesmen are born, not made," (World Book Encyclopedia, 1960) it has been demonstrated that many specific methods of salesmanship can and must be learned in order for a salesperson to be successful. But, what makes a good sales representative? The first thing the consultants did was identify what made some of the salespeople more effective in selling furniture. Initially, surveys of the top salespeople in the company were attempted in order to answer this question. When attempting to obtain this kind of data through self-report

TABLE 10.1. Selected Performance Improvement Opportunities (PIO) in Furniture Sales.

Output	Quantity Measure	Percent of Opportunities		"PIO"	Annual Cost of Solution	Annual Net Payoff
		Typical Perf.	Exemplary Perf.			
1. In-home calls	rate	0.7%	5%	4.3%	$2,840	$647,860
2. Customer name & address obtained	rate	50%	94%	44%	$3,000	$332,172
3. Referrals obtained	rate timeliness	25%	96%	71%	$ 200	$282,300
4. Following the furniture delivery truck with accessories	rate timeliness	20%	95%	75%	$4,657	$305,842
5. Additional products & services suggested	rate	2%	18%	16%	$ 200	$329,800

186

measures, the investigators frequently obtained responses such as "I'm just friendly" or "It's genetic . . . my parents were salespeople." When asking salespeople about their selling techniques, they frequently responded with nebulous advice, such as "be aggressive" or "be up." However, what behaviors are really involved in being "friendly," "aggressive," or "up"? Does the person smile, make eye contact, shake hands, or perhaps just have an opening line? Although these top sales representatives knew how to perform with a high degree of expertise, they found it difficult to analyze exactly what it was that they did. The result is that the behaviors they described are difficult to specify in behavioral terms. They tended to attribute success to such "superstitious" behavior (Skinner, 1953) as wearing a "lucky jacket."

The reason for assessing the specific behaviors involved in being a good sales representative is to reproduce these same behaviors in other salespeople (Feeney, 1980). In the present sales project, asking their best sales representatives just didn't provide the investigators with any data. Therefore, the investigators began to directly observe their top salespeople in order to assess the behaviors involved in good salesmanship.

The development of the performance improvement program was based on the sales behavior of the most successful sales representatives. The top producers selected were 65 salespeople whose sales ranged from $400,000 to $800,000 per year. These top dollar salespeople were observed during 4 months for 1,000 hours, as they worked with actual customers in stores and in homes. Observers took notes based on a stimulus-response analysis of the sales interactions. An additional 50 hours were spent interviewing customers. Based on this data, a tentative Behavioral Sales Model was developed.

The Behavioral Sales Model was then tested against the sales behaviors of the top sales representatives in additional stores throughout the retail store chain to check the validity of the instrument. The result of the cross-country observations of 450 salespeople demonstrated that the behaviors necessary for successful selling are the same, although regional language style differences are evident.

Using behavioral assessment to identify critical sales responses is unusual in the business world. It allowed the consultants to develop a sales model based on those behaviors engaged in by the most successful sales representatives and bolstered by customer feedback.

Once the sales model was developed, one store was selected to test the program. Out of seven salespeople, three were chosen to participate as the experimental group and the remaining four served as a control group. In terms of the previous sales totals, the experimental group included a top, an average, and a low producing salesperson, while the control group included one top sales representative, two who were average, and one low "writer." The two top "writers" were within $5,000 of each other's sales, while the two low "writers" were within $2,000 in total sales. The program was implemented for 1 month. The results clearly demonstrated the effectiveness of the intervention. The three sales representatives in the experimental group showed an average increase of 45% in their sales, compared to the control group who decreased an average 3% for the month from the previous year.

An essential element of the sales program was on-line coaching provided by the consultant. In a second test store, transferring the training role of the coach from a consultant to a store manager was examined. Baseline data were collected for one month. The stores' eight sales representatives were all involved in the program. The results dramatically demonstrated the success of the intervention, as well as indicating that coaching by supervisors was as effective as coaching by the outside consultants. Sales for 1 month were up an average of 28% over the same month in the previous year. However, sales increased an average of 99% over the previous month. In prior years, sales for these 2 months had been about the same.

To begin to implement the sales program nationally, baseline data were collected on each of the 450 sales representatives. The importance of the behavioral baseline should not be underestimated, for it is the key to this sales program. It provides the "base" from which improvement can be measured as well as data to customize the program for each salesperson. The baseline procedure involved being observed by the coach during ten sales presentations. After ten complete observations, the coach had a clear understanding of the strengths and weaknesses of the representative's selling behavior. At that time, the coach reviewed the results confidentially with the individual concerned. The results were not known by anyone else.

The presence of the coach was explained to customers in the following manner: first, the coach was introduced to the customer, since the customer was curious about the presence of the coach. It was then explained that the company was "developing" a training program for new employees, and the way they were doing it was by observing the most experienced sales representatives. Often the customers expressed pleasure that "their" sales representative was selected as a "model" for the training program. The coach did not interfere with the sales presentation by talking to the customer. If the customer spoke to the coach, the coath remained silent and looked directly at the sales representative. Customers quickly understood that the coach would not engage in conversation. In previous behavioral assessments, sales had been carefully measured. The results showed that they did not decrease during observation.

The intervention involved providing feedback to the sales representatives on the behaviors observed during the baseline phase. They received feedback on their selling behavior and their sales totals. Based on the baseline data, the sales manager coached the sales representatives on how to improve their performance. High payoff behaviors that were below standard were prompted before each sales presentation. However, no more than three such behaviors were prompted on any given sale. Immediately after the correct behavior occurred, the sales representative was reinforced by the coach with a smile, an okay gesture, or another pre-arranged signal. No coaching was deemed necessary on a behavior when its occurrence was within ten percentage points of the standard. Sales representatives were observed intermittently and without prior announcement. The feedback/coaching phase was followed by the post-call learning cycle. This involved the sales representatives in continual review of their own performance. An observation-coaching check list was used as a guide for preparation as well as for feedback in the post-call learning cycle (See Fig. 10.1). To insure accuracy and timeliness, the sales representatives reviewed their own behavior within 5 minutes after a customer left the store.

The coaches were also observed as they coached the sales representatives. The coaches' behaviors were evaluated on a checklist as they were observed by fellow coaches, such as the manager. These observations occurred randomly, although they were sometimes preannounced. The frequency was faded from twice a week to a variable schedule averaging once every 3 weeks. The observation checklist for the coach (See Fig. 10.1) was divided into three phases: pre-observation, sales contact, and post-observation. Coaches were responsible for prompting desired behaviors, reinforcing the occurrence of those behaviors, and providing feedback – both positive and negative – after the sales contact. The coaches were also provided with feedback after their observations, in order to insure that there were no weak links in the corporate monitoring chain. A post-coaching learning cycle was used for self-review in the same way the sales representatives used their post-call learning cycle.

An additional indicator of success that the sales representatives received was their commission. Commissions, based on sales, were automatically built in and given every month.

However, these commissions were not likely to function as effective reinforcers for selling, since there was a delay of sometimes up to 3 months before the paycheck reflected the performance. For reinforcement to be most effective, it should be given immediately, contingent upon the occurrence of the specified desirable behavior. The commissions were not provided immediately and the specific set of behaviors that led to the sale were not identified.

In order to increase the probability of productive selling, reinforcers were provided contingent upon reaching a set behavioral goal. Behavioral goals were based on the standards achieved by the top producers. High payoff areas such as using the customer's name and collecting follow-up information were identified for each sales representative. A contingent reward system was implemented to increase these behaviors. This part of the program employed secondary reinforcers (tokens) which could be turned in for large, back-up reinforcers. The tokens, a dollar-like bill with the manager's picture on it, had no value in themselves but were rewarding through their connection with other reinforcers such as money. Such conditioned or "once removed" reinforcers can effectively provide a bridge to intermittently available, high cost rewards. These secondary reinforcers can also serve as tangible signs of progress to bolster behaviors that might extinguish before natural reinforcers take effect.

The potential reinforcers that were employed can be divided into three groups: activities, personal items, and items of monetary value. Activities in the first category were normally tangible and often available at no cost to the company. In order to insure that the activities were actually rewarding, efforts were made to increase schedule flexibility so that these new activities would not be perceived as additional chores. Activity reinforcers were further subdivided into two sets. The first set included tasks that were desirable to the individual and normally outside their current job specification. Examples include attending local meetings, co-signing a report, being left in charge for a day or week, and/or joining a committee or advisory group, etc. The second set of reinforcing activities included tasks that were desirable to the individual and within the current job specification. Examples include writing a status report or being assigned to those preferred aspects of the individual's role that had the most authority, visibility, or responsibility.

The second category of potential reinforcers, personal items, were normally intangible to the individual, but also involved little cost. Examples include being mentioned on a sales honor roll, given a choice of hours to work, being made salesperson of the week, and, of course, receiving concurrent praise from the manager. Reinforcers within the third category included items of monetary value, such as money in the form of bonuses or savings bonds, free meals with the regional manager or store manager, a free car wash, a magazine subscription, drinks after work, flowers, free tickets to sporting or cultural events, and/or a contribution to a charity in the employee's name.

At least four potential reinforcers were selected for each individual. These were based on the following fact-finding questions:

1. Can it be used with a high frequency?
2. Is it readily available?
3. Is it inexpensive?
4. Is the reinforcer desired by the performer?
5. Can it be used without the performer tiring of it?
6. If added, will it make the consequences of the behavior positive to the performer?
7. Can it be given or withheld dependent upon performance?

DSP _____   TIME: Start _____ End _____
Date _____

TYPE OF CONTACT (circle one):   CUSTOMER CONTACT HISTORY (circle one):
  Walk-in   First Contact
  Appointment in store   Previous contact—no sale
  In-home call   Previous sale to customer
  Store presentation   Referred by another customer
  Telephone (SR called cust.)   Other
  Telephone (Cust. called SR)
  Other

BEFORE STARTING, CIRCLE BEHAVIORS YOU HAVE PROMPTED FOR THIS OBSERVATION

	YES	NO	N/A
CUSTOMER GREETED:	YES	NO	N/A
1. Customer approached in prescribed manner			
2. Customer welcomed to store			
3. Customer reinforced for coming to store			
4. SR introduced self using first & last name and title			
5. Customer's first & last name obtained			
6. Customer asked if working with another SR			
7. Customer told reasons for needs probe questions			
8. Feedback obtained to insure reasons for needs probe understood			
Smiling Eye Contact Natural Voice Cust. Name Used Yes No Yes No Yes No Yes No			
CUSTOMER NEEDS IDENTIFIED:	YES	NO	N/A
1. General probes used first			
2. Specific probes used when general probes fail to identify needs			
3. Respect shown for customer's opinions, ideas, feelings			
4. Meaning of all customer questions identified			
5. Feedback obtained to verify each need that can be met with store benefit			
6. Reinforcement given each time customer identifies need that can be met with store benefit			
7. In-home call asked for			
8. Product needs identified			
9. Personal needs identified			
10. Additional products and services suggested			
11. Product and personal needs summarized (only needs that can be met with store benefits)			
Smiling Eye Contact Natural Voice Cust. Name Used Yes No Yes No Yes No Yes No			
NEEDS MATCHED TO STORE PRODUCT AND SERVICE BENEFITS:	YES	NO	N/A
1. Specific benefit matched to specific need			
2. Feedback obtained after each benefit statement			
3. Reinforcement given for each favorable comment about store products and services			
4. Reinforcement given each time store benefit is accepted			
5. Accepted benefits summarized			
Smiling Eye Contact Natural Voice Cust. Name Used Yes No Yes No Yes No Yes No			

Fig. 10.1. Sales Representative (SR) OBSERVATION/COACHING CHECKLIST.

OBJECTIONS IDENTIFIED AND OVERCOME:	YES	NO	N/A
1. Objections responded to each time encountered 2. Meaning of all questions identified 3. Respect shown for all customer's opinions, ideas, feelings 4. Feedback obtained to verify objections 5. Customer reinforced for stating objections 6. Objections overcome with store benefits 7. Feedback obtained to verify objections overcome 8. Customer reinforced for accepting benefits Smiling Eye Contact Natural Voice Cust. Name Used Yes No Yes No Yes No Yes No			
DECISION-MAKER IDENTIFIED:	YES	NO	N/A
1. Decision-maker and those who will influence decision are present 2. Appointment made to meet with decision-maker and those who will influence decision Smiling Eye Contact Natural Voice Cust. Name Used Yes No Yes No Yes No Yes No			
CLOSE MADE:	YES	NO	N/A
1. Sale asked for 2. SR remained silent until customer responded to request for sale 3. Objections to close identified and overcome 4. Customer reinforced for making purchase Smiling Eye Contact Natural Voice Cust. Name Used Yes No Yes No Yes No Yes No			
RESULTS OF SALES CONTACT:	YES	NO	N/A
1. Gifts presented 2. In-home call appointment made 3. Store presentation appointment made 4. Sale made 5. Other (specify):			
FOLLOWUP ACTION TAKEN:	YES	NO	N/A
1. Followup card updated 2. Referral obtained 3. "Thank-you" note sent 4. "Follow-the-truck" appointment made 5. Other (specify):			

COACHING FOLLOWUP

Specific selling behaviors improved:	Specific selling behaviors needing improvement:	Specific selling behaviors you will prompt for next observation:
1.	1.	1.
2.	2.	2.
3.	3.	3.
4.	4.	
5.	5.	

CIRCLE THOSE BEHAVIORS YOU PROMPTED FOR
THIS OBSERVATION

DSP _____   TIME: START _____

DATE _____   FINISH _____

TYPE OF OBSERVATION BY COACH

☐ Preannounced   ☐ Unannounced

	YES	NO	N/A
PRE-OBSERVATION PHASE			
1. Prompted desired behaviors			
2. Prompts stated in specific stimulus (when) response (do this) terms			
3. Benefits of prompted behavior to SR stated			
4. Feedback obtained from SR to insure prompts understood			
5. SR reinforced for stating willingness to accomplish prompted behaviors			
OBSERVATION PHASE			
1. Coach introduced to customer by SR			
2. Coach redirected all questions, etc., from customer to SR			
3. Reinforced SR for performing prompted behavior by using positive gesture, nod, smile, etc.			
4. Remained with SR throughout sales contact			
*State specific reason for each interruption of Coach			
POST-OBSERVATION PHASE			
1. Emphasized what was done well			
2. Showed approval of what SR did well by smiling, positive gesture, voice level, etc.			
3. Used numbers and/or percentages to make statements specific			
4. Recreated specific situations in stimulus response terms			
5. Stated goal			
6. Prompted desired behavior for future			
7. Obtained feedback from SR to insure each point is understood			
8. Reinforced self-review by SR			
9. Coach stated benefits to SR of performing desired behavior			
10. Applied positive consequences			
11. Applied negative consequences			

Fig. 10.2. Checklist for Observing Coach Working with SR and Customer

In addition to these four reinforcers, praise was used throughout the program since it is almost universally applicable and effective.

THE BEHAVIORAL SALES MODEL

The Behavioral Sales Program is a sequence of clearly defined behaviors and interrelated steps for selling. It includes those behaviors that have been shown by observation to be the most effective responses to use in this particular sales situation. Each step in the program was empirically developed based on the results that it produced. Every point relevant to making the sale is covered and presented within a reinforcement model; that is, what behaviors the sales representative should emit in order to increase the probability of being reinforced with a sale. Within the Behavioral Sales Model each sales episode is divided into eight segments beginning with the initial customer welcome and concluding with follow-up action. The choice of the response in each section is based on direct observation of the most successful sales people and customer feedback gathered through interviews.

Greeting the Customer

The program begins as the customer enters the store. Observations suggest that customers should be *approached within 120 seconds*. The salesperson stands *within 3 to 4 feet* of the customer, *smiles*, and *maintains eye contact*. Customers reported that a smiling sales representative was seen as "friendly" and eye contact was seen as "paying attention." The walk to greet the potential customer is at a *normal pace*, and the sales representative maintains a *natural and relaxed posture* while *welcoming the customer to the store*.

The welcome is the first step in closing the sale. In a natural voice, the sales representative acknowledges the effort the customer put forth to come to the store. The salesperson then introduces himself or herself using his/her first and last names, and identifies his/her function. Giving one's name is an important step in obtaining the customer's name, which is a high payoff area. Obtaining the customer's name is also essential for the follow-up process. Once the customer's name is obtained, it is used throughout the sales interaction. At this point, the customers are asked whether they have been working with another salesperson, as the sale would belong to the "sales representative of record." Assuming they are not working with another sales representative, the next step is to determine the customer's knowledge of store products and services through probing questions. The purpose of these probing questions is explained in terms of understanding the customer's needs. Verification of their perception of the sales representative's role is obtained through customer feedback. Such feedback assures that the customer understands exactly what has been said and why. The eight steps of the greeting can be observed and checked during performance evaluations using the stimulus-response observation checklist in Figure 10.1.

Identifying Customer Needs

The next task in the program is to identify the needs of the customer. The quickest way to uncover customer needs is general probing statements that encourage the customer to speak freely. General probes strengthen the role of the salesperson as a problem solver by allowing him/her to offer potential answers to the customer's problems in the form of benefits from the store's products and services. Specific probes are helpful when the customer has been totally unresponsive to a series of general probes or when the sales representative wants to direct the customer to a new subject area.

It is important to show respect for the customer's opinions and feelings. In this way the sales representative becomes a source of reinforcement for the customer. The verbal behaviors that are most effective are those that exhibit understanding, acknowledge the importance of a point raised, show sympathy or concern, compliment, and/or agree in part with the customer's statements. All these responses suggest that the sales representative is there to help solve the customer's problems. When customers identify those needs that can be satisfied with benefits of the store's products and services they should be verbally reinforced. Reinforcing customers will measurably increase the frequency of this desirable behavior. Obtaining feedback from customers to verify their needs insures agreement in order to match specific needs to specific product and service benefits.

Matching Needs and Benefits

The key to selling is the process of satisfying customer needs with the specific benefits of the store products and services. A benefit is an actual advantage the customer will gain from using the products and services. From an operant view, a customer buys a product because of the positive consequences he or she anticipates from it based on past experience with similar products. One "sells" product features as evidence of the anticipated benefits the customer will gain. When matching the customer needs to product benefits, feedback should be solicited on each benefit statement to determine its acceptance. Customers should be reinforced for each favorable comment about store products and services and for accepting product benefits. Accepting product benefits is the first step toward accepting the sale.

Customers' needs can be expanded by suggesting additional, related products and services. Suggestive selling of additional services should include probing for in-home call opportunities.

Overcoming Objections

Expanding customer needs also includes seeking out objections. It is important to identify objections and overcome them, since undetected objections are a primary cause of lost sales and cancellations. While objections are most often stated directly, customer questions are often a less direct expression of an objection. The meaning behind all questions should be probed to reveal possible reservations about the product. The goal at this point is to acknowledge the customer's objection without punishing him for raising it.

Objections should be handled immediately. When objections are based on a misunderstanding about the products or services due to lack of information, rephrasing the objection into question form helps clarify and isolate it in the customer's mind. However, it is important when rephrasing not to imply agreement with the objection. Answering the question directly should clear up the misunderstanding.

Once the objection is overcome, the benefits accepted by the customer should be summarized. This reminds the customer of the benefits they have accepted throughout the sales discussion. Since the sale may take many hours over several meetings, the customer should not be expected to remember all the benefits that have been mentioned. When the benefits have been summarized, feedback should be obtained to verify that the customer accepts the benefits. Feedback directly from customers is the only way one can be certain that they accepted the benefits of the store's products and services. Responding to objections is summarized in Figure 10.1.

Locating the Decision-Maker

The next task is to identify not only the decision-maker, but those who will influence the decision as well. A sale cannot be made if one is not working with the person who will make the final decision to purchase or if input from others involved in the decision has been ignored. If an important decision-maker is not present, another specific appointment should be formally scheduled to include the absent source of information and influence.

The Close

Everything in the sales process leads to the close. The sale is a complex series or chain of responses in which the acceptance of each benefit is a reinforced segment leading to the final act of making the purchase. The close is the test of whether or not the customer's needs have been uncovered and met. If the decision-maker is present, one should ask for the sale in a way that reflects the sales representative's belief that agreement has been reached. Assuming the belief that agreement has been reached serves to remind the customer that he or she has accepted the benefits already presented. Nothing the sales representative says should express doubt, hesitation, or uncertainty. After the request for the sale is made, the sales representative should stop talking and wait for the customer's response, even if it takes as long as 3 minutes. This tells the customer that an answer is expected and allows the customer time to make a considered response. If the close is not accepted, previously unanswered questions or objections must be solicited. A five-step program was established to isolate and clarify obstacles to the sale. First, the salesperson should restate the question or state the objection as a question. Second, the question or objection should be isolated by identifying it as the only obstacle to the purchase. Once this is accomplished, the third and crucial step is to get the customer's commitment to buy if the question or objection is answered satisfactorily. Obviously, step four requires that the salesperson effectively answer the question or objection and in step five request the sale again.

If the close is not accepted due to some specific fear or doubt, further evidence can often be offered to reassure the customer. For example, if the customer is concerned that the item will not be delivered on time, a phone call to the warehouse may be made in the customer's presence to confirm that the piece is in stock and that the delivery date is set. On the other hand, if the close is not accepted due to a lack of perceived need for the benefits, additional benefits should be provided. The customer's decision can be made easier by focusing on the most important previously agreed upon benefits of the item. If the close is not accepted because the customer is reluctant to say "yes," have the customer make a decision on a minor point or detail. It is easier for some people to say "yes" to a minor point even though they recognize that they are saying "yes" to buying the item. Once any of these questions are resolved, the sales representative should again ask for the sale.

Sometimes the customer will offer no reason for not buying, but will choose to abstain for the time being. If the close is not accepted because the customer wants to "think it over," every item which previously received positive agreement should be recapped. Any objections should be answered and the request for the sale made again. If the close is not accepted because the customer must confer with someone else before making the decision to buy, the items to be checked should be reviewed and a written summary should be provided to the customer. It is important to make a specific appointment of the date and time for the next meeting in the store. Then it should be made clear, without any implied criticism of the customer, that the purpose of the next meeting is to make decisions, and that it is best if all decision-makers could be present.

Results of the Sale Contact

The customer should be thanked when he or she accepts the sale. Follow-up action to the sale should be outlined for the customer before goodbyes are said. When the sale has been made, it can be classified as a perfect success and the sales representative should feel a sense of accomplishment. Even if the sales approach could have been better, this is not the place to try to improve it. The manager should praise the success and at all costs avoid criticizing any specific behaviors at this time. The self-analyzing attempt to improve sales behaviors should not be allowed to detract from the reinforcing effects of a successful effort.

Follow-up

Once the customer leaves the store, follow-up action should begin. This is most important in establishing and maintaining the sales relationship, since this is the time when the necessary information on the sale is most easily remembered. A follow-up card is started or updated. It includes information such as: name, address, telephone number, date, type of contract, product, and personal needs. It also includes a date to check on delivery information. If the contact resulted in a sale, a thank-you note should be composed immediately. The sales representative's enthusiasm is at its highest point at this time and the note should reflect these feelings. The customer should also be called 3 weeks after the sale with delivery information. This demonstrates that the salesperson is concerned about the customer's needs and will follow through to be sure that committed services are provided.

If the contact did not result in a sale, it is worthwhile to phone the customer 3 to 5 days after the contact. This allows the customer time to formulate plans from the ideas developed in the store and gives the salesperson the opportunity to continue the sales process. If the telephone call does not result in further sales contact, a thank-you note should be written to the customer 3 to 5 days after the phone contact to express appreciation for the visit to the store. This provides another opportunity to make an additional contact with the customer. Extending the role of salespeople beyond the actual buying of the product was shown to be a very high payoff behavior in the assessment that led to the development of the Behavioral Sales Model. The accomplishments that are most responsive to this behavior are accessory sales and gathering referrals.

When the purchases are delivered, the sales representative should *follow the delivery truck with accessories*. The data suggest that this is the most successful method of selling accessories. It provides an opportunity to develop the sale into a total interior appearance that the customer will find even more reinforcing. Once the customer is completely satisfied, *referrals should be obtained*. Satisfied customers are the most valuable sources of new customers and this step is most crucial.

The most successful sales representatives use the following additional follow-up steps: calling regular customers on new arrivals of merchandise, notifying customers of sale items, personally inviting customers to in-store events, calling every customer in the follow-up file once every 6 months to maintain contact, and sending greeting cards on New Years and the 4th of July reminding customers of the winter and summer sales.

RESULTS OF THE BEHAVIORAL SALES MODEL

There are presently over 100 retail stores in the program. Results have shown rapid increases in sales. Due to seasonal fluctuations in the furniture business, all data comparisons were made to archival records for the same month of the previous year. A comparison of a big sales month like February to a relatively slower month like December only 2 months earlier would be meaningless. Compared to the previous year, stores in the program have increased their sales an average of 30%, with a range from 18% to 63%. The data from one store in Maryland exemplifies the success of the program. When coaching began in November, sales increased 40% for the month over the previous year. In December much of the reinforcement program was suspended while the sales manager was on vacation. During this time sales dropped to baseline. Upon the manager's return in January, sales increased 60% over January's total for the previous year. During February, which had historically been their biggest month, there was a 25% increase in sales. Given the large volume of this month in the previous year, this represents a very significant increase.

A store in Kentucky offers a similar success story: Sales were up 20% in November, 12% in December, 33% in January, and 17% in February. Another successful store, this one in Connecticut, reported an increase of 47% in sales for December, 35% in January, and 11% in February. The high point of these early results was reached in Florida, where one store reported sales up 58% in December and 63% in January. Although the examples reported are few and selected, the results are the same across the country: increased sales. While this represents only comparison data for the most part, there is really no general factor across every store nationwide that could account for these effects except adherence to the steps and framework of the sales program and the resulting increase in the selling effectiveness of the salespeople.

The close ratio is a measure of sales based on the opportunities to sell. In a declining economy or when the store is faced with increased competition, the close ratio represents the most valid measure of on-line sales efficacy. It compares the number of successes and the number who got away in terms of the potential buyers who actually begin to shop. If one can estimate the number of people who come into the store, the close ratio can be computed to provide the number of sales needed to get to the set sales goal.

Stores across the country increased their close ratios after implementing the Behavioral Sales Program. In one instance, a store in Minnesota upped its close ratio from 18% to 28% for a 2-month period. A close ratio increase from 28% to 39% was reported in a New York store, and in Connecticut, over 3 months, a below average close ratio went up to 26%. Average dollar sales in that store were up 30%, while average dollar sales in a store in Maryland increased 33% following a similar increase in the close ratio.

The performance audit conducted at the beginning of this sales intervention project identified a number of areas with large potential for bottom-line gains. Some examples of how the sales improvement program impacted these high payoff outputs are presented below.

The in-home call is one of the most effective selling tools available. As noted earlier, the close ratio for in-home calls was 60% with an average sale of over $2,700, compared to 22% and a sale of approximately $600 for store sales that did not include an in-home call. Yet, there were negative consequences attached to in-home calls from the salesperson's perspective. For example, most stores employed a system in which the salespeople took turns approaching each new customer who entered the store. If there were eight sales representatives, the person who got the last customer went to the end of the line and each of the others moved up a position. Of course, if the salesperson's name came up while he or she was out on an in-home call, they would go to the end of the line. This represents a potent negative consequence because it serves as time-out for the opportunity to gain a sale. The salesman or woman who was out on call was also likely to miss calls from regular customers and, with gasoline prices being what they are, was faced with an outlay of cash that would not be repaid for a month or more.

One way of countering the negative reinforcement connected to staying in the store was through providing substantial rewards for the incompatible response of going out on in-home calls. This kind of solution is called differential reinforcement of other behavior (DRO). The large advantage in commissions associated with in-home calls certainly could be viewed as differentially reinforcing that behavior, yet the long delay between response and reinforcers made other approaches necessary. Systems changes were employed to directly counter the negative consequences of in-home calls. To avoid losing one's turn in the sales line, a rule was made that held a person's place in line so that if they were number two when they left for an in-home call, they were also number two when they got back. Message arrangements were made, and immediate reimbursement for gas money was provided when the salesperson returned from the in-home call. The results of these changes in the consequence for visiting the customers' homes were quite significant. In-home calls increased by 40% in one Maryland store, and the increase reached 75% in one New York location.

Obtaining and using the customer's name is another high payoff behavior. One store in Kentucky reported an increase from an 18% baseline to 79%, and a New York store increased their frequency from 30% to 95%. One store in South Carolina tested the importance of obtaining and using the customer's name. Results of their observations showed that 94% of all sales were made when the customer's name was known and used by the salesperson.

Another high payoff behavior identified in the behavioral assessment was greeting the customer. One store in New York reported the desired behavior up from 30% during baseline to 70% following intervention. A store in Ohio reported an increase from a baseline of 30% to a maintained frequency of 90%.

Customer referrals represent another potential improvement area of profit significance. A good example of the impact of the intervention in this area was one of the Maryland stores where referrals obtained increased by 300%.

These percentages indicate the success of the Behavioral Sales Program, as well as the performance improvement analysis. The results are consistent across the country. The comparison to baseline data on specific sales behaviors revealed substantial increases in the responses that had been previously demonstrated through empirical investigation to be the key responses for successful salesmanship in this field.

There can be no question that the eventual outcome measure of any intervention in a business setting must be improvement in the profit column. In that sense, all behavior management is aimed at what Gilbert (1978) calls an accomplishment measure. But like MBO before it, Gilbert's engineering model cannot be maximally effective if it stops at the outcome level. To change the outcome or the accomplishment, one must often modify behavior directly. Nowhere is this more clearly evident than in sales. Every sales manager and all of the sales personnel know what the objective is. The desired outcome or goal is as much of the market as one can possibly obtain. Setting specific goals or objectives is the norm in sales organizations. Often these goals are established in terms of a percentage of the available market. Commissions, prizes, recognition, and numerous other rewards are frequently connected to these accomplishments. Unfortunately, making a sale requires more than just desire. In this report, sales were increased in a large number of stores with over 450 sales personnel by directly changing the behaviors of the sales representatives. The accomplishment remained sales, and it's true that reinforcement techniques were used to make the sales more reinforcing. But the key to this successful intervention was true behavior modification. Program development was based on finding those behaviors that discriminated top from average sales personnel. Once these specific responses had been identified, a program was implemented to teach each response to every sales representative. The accomplishment remained sales, but the people on the floor had learned the behaviors necessary to reach those goals.

REFERENCES

Brown, M. G., Malott, R. W., Dillon, M. J., & Keeps, E. J. Improving customer service in a large department store through training and feedback. *Journal of Organizational Behavior Management*, 1980, **2**, 251–265.

Collins, R. L., Komaki, J., & Temlock, S. Behavioral definition and improvement of customer service in retail merchandising. Paper presented at the annual meeting of the American Psychological Association, New York, September 1979.

Feeney, E. J. Twelve ideas toward effective training. *Training and Development Journal*, 1980, **34** (9), 14–16.

Gilbert, T. F. *Human competence: Engineering worthy performance.* New York: McGraw-Hill, 1978.

Gupton, T., & LeBow, M.D. Behavior management in a large industrial firm. *Behavior Therapy,* 1971, **2,** 78-82.

Komaki, J., Waddell, W. M., & Pearce, M. G. The applied behavior analysis approach and individual employees: Improving performance in two small businesses. *Organizational Behavior and Human Performance,* 1977, **19,** 337-352.

Luthens, F., Paul, R., & Baker, D. An experimental analysis of the impact of contingent reinforcement on salespersons' performance behavior. *Journal of Applied Psychology,* 1981, **66,** 314-323.

Miller, L. M. Improving sales and forecase accuracy in a nationwide sales organization. *Journal of Organizational Behavior Management,* 1977, **1,** 39-51.

Performance audit, feedback, and positive reinforcement. *Training and Development Journal,* 1972, **26** (11), 8-13.

Skinner, B. F. *Science and human behavior.* New York: Macmillan, 1953.

Weitz, J., Antoinetli, J., & Wallace, S. R. The effect of home office contact on sales performance. *Performance Psychology,* 1954, **1,** 381-384.

World book encyclopedia. Chicago, Illinois: Field Enterprises, 1960, p. 55.

Part III:
Personnel

Introduction

Management involves more than just productivity and marketing. There are personnel and support functions that must be performed if the organization is to survive and prosper. The most well-engineered system for producing the product is useless if the employees don't come to work or turn over so quickly that recruitment and training become major expenditures. Similarly, even a management program based on applied behavior analysis cannot succeed if debilitating stress sidelines a significant portion of the organization's management staff. In manufacturing settings, it is not only the staff that can break down. Equipment must be kept functioning if products are going to continue to roll off the end of the assembly line. It is generally agreed that the key to decreasing equipment down time is preventive maintenance. Yet, despite their financial impact, maintenance functions are often given only perfunctory attention. A final source of down time for both man and machine is accidents. Increases in safety can have direct financial benefits to the company in both increased productivity and decreased compensation costs. All of our technological advances in management assume that there is a workforce to manage. In fact, hiring and firing remain major problems for most managers, while a signficant portion of the population remains unemployed. In this part, various authors address themselves to these personnel and support issues. They describe a number of behavioral programs for improving management's care of its resources.

In Chapter 11, Carlson and Sperduto present their experiences with programs to increase the amount of work time employees actually spend at their jobs. Absenteeism has been identified as a particularly difficult problem for American business. According to Business Week (Absenteeism won't quit, 1970), absenteeism represents a major cause of low industrial productivity. In one survey of 100 large and medium-sized companies (The nagging problem, 1967), over 50% readily admitted that absenteeism and tardiness present either production or economic strains on the organization. Faced with their inability to solve absenteeism and tardiness problems, many companies have been lulled into complacency. Supervisory Management (Curbing absenteeism, 1970) found that most management authorities would accept a 3 to 4% absenteeism rate. In the past, American industry has tolerated a $15–20 billion dollar yearly price tag for absenteeism and tardiness (Cruikshank, 1976) or an average cost of $100 to $300 per employee per year (Reid, 1963). This figure has no doubt risen in the last decade.

The reason organizations have been willing to accept these high costs and concurrent production problems is that most attempts to control such behavior have met with little success (Cruikshank, 1976). The traditional methods of dealing with unjustified days off and lateness have been to apply some sort of disciplinary procedure. Of the 100 companies surveyed by Business Management (The nagging problem, 1967), 80% used a disciplinary approach to control absenteeism and tardiness, yet many of these companies still have absenteeism and tardiness problems. Typically, disciplinary procedures have resulted in some initial curtailment of the problem. Unfortunately, many companies find that after a period of time the rate of absenteeism returns to pretreatment levels. Further, disciplinary procedures often deepen the adversary nature of manager-employee relations and alienate the employee. These problems have led to the development of other techniques designed to control absenteeism and tardiness such as the 4-day work week, flextime, and job enrichment. Again, initial results were promising, but many companies found absenteeism creeping back to prior rates (Cruikshank, 1976). With these dubious results, it is no wonder that industry generally accepts the existence of absenteeism and tardiness as just another business expenditure which must be budgeted. In fact, one company actually maintains its work force at 14% above their requirements to compensate for the high absenteeism (Reid, 1963). Such a situation clearly demonstrates the need for innovative solutions to attendance problems. The reports presented in Chapter 11 suggest that positive reinforcement programs can significantly improve the attendance picture.

Absenteeism will not always respond to positive reinforcement. There are many cases of accidents and job-related health problems that incapacitate the individual. The problems of safety, occupational health, and job stress add significantly to the cost of every item or service sold in the United States. The Bureau of Labor Statistics reported that over 34 million work days were lost due to accidents in 1972 (Monthly Labor Review, 1974). Ten times as many work days are lost annually to injuries (255 million) as are lost to strikes (25.4 million) (Gordon, Akman, & Brooks, 1971).

The picture in occupational stress is no less discouraging (Sweetland, 1979). Stress-related conditions account for substantial absenteeism. Estimates are that more than 52 million work days are lost to hypertension yearly (Penn, 1977). Heart attacks cost another 132 million work days a year (Fat people's fight, 1977). Business Week (Business dries up, 1972) estimates that the industrial tab for alcoholism could be as high as ten billion dollars. Looking at the data on just executive illnesses, the President's Council on Fitness was led to conclude that the desk and swivel chair are two of society's most serious health hazards (Fat people's fight, 1977).

Behavioral programs are beginning to cut down some of these losses. In the area of safety, the pioneering work that laid the foundation for future programs was the simulation work of McKelvey, Engen, and Peck (1973). They demonstrated that time out could be used to increase vigilance for safety signals and decrease accidents even when high productivity was heavily rewarded. This procedure keeps the employee from gaining the rewards associated with his or her productivity when the rate of the machine exceeds safe limits by turning off the machine for a specified perod of time.

Unfortunately, the time-out approach is situation specific to certain manufacturing operations. In other work areas where safe behavior is less tied to fixed industrial machinery, positive reinforcement systems that directly reward accident-free performance offer a more practical approach to increasing safety consciousness. There are numerous examples of successful positive reinforcement safety programs. By replacing the traditional disciplinary procedures (write-up, disciplinary hearing, and suspension) with an annual competitive incentive program, the Kansas City, Missouri, Public Works Department-Refuse Division obtained a 72% decrease in lost man hours and a 25% decrease in accident repair costs (Caulkins, 1971). In this project, teams were established with a $25 prize to each member of the safest team. Importantly, an extra day of vacation was given regardless of the team standing in the "Safety Sweepstakes" to anyone who went through the year accident free. Costs for the year were $277 in team rewards and $1,062 in paper and vacation time costs. Subtracting the cost of the program, the city saved over $4,000 in lost man hours alone. Theoretically, the program could have been even more effective had the reinforcers been dispensed more immediately than on an annual schedule.

Similar programs have been effective with snowplow operators in Bloomington, Minnesota, the state highway department in Utah, and sanitation workers in Lake Charles, Louisiana. The latter example is particularly interesting since the rewards were provided by distributing monies saved from workman's compensation, and the project was initiated as part of a union contract (Employee Incentives to Improve State & Local Government, 1975). More recently, behavior modification safety programs have been implemented (Komaki, Barwick, & Scott, 1978; Komaki, Heinzmann, & Lawson, 1980; Ritschl, Mirman, Sigler, & Hall, 1977; Rhoton, 1980; Sulzer-Azaroff, 1978; Sulzer-Azaroff & de Santamoria, 1980) with success rates that have reached 100% safe behavior. Even the poker game format originated by Pedalino and Gamboa (1974) for attendance has been effectively employed to minimize accidents (Halbardier, 1981).

Behavioral programs have also been developed to combat occupational stress. Although worksite programs have been reported that directly attack health problems such as hypertension (Charlesworth, Williams, & Bear, 1980; Herskowitz, 1980), stress management projects are usually designed to teach specific skills that decrease job stress and provide appropriate responses to professional demands. Self-management skills, hypnosis, relaxation training, and alternate response training for both overt and covert responses are often included (Shea, 1980; Udolf, 1981). The program that Miller and Pfohl present in Chapter 12 embodies many of these techniques from a cognitive-behavioral framework. Their analysis of the subject's responses begins with an ABC model of the relationship between an individual's thoughts and his/her emotional reactions.

Their ABC model represents an adjustment to the typical operant three-term contingency of discriminative stimuli, responses, and consequences to deal specifically with emotional reactions. The A still represents antecedent conditions, but the focus is on those stimuli that are stressors. B is the organism's response or behavior, but that includes its cognitions or self-messages about the stressful event. C represents not only the external consequences but also the bodily reactions that characterize emotional states such as anxiety or anger.

The need to present a somewhat altered model to deal with stress management stems from the physiological nature of the response. Throughout this book we have focused on voluntary behaviors and their effects on the environment. Emotional reactions, however, are not voluntary. The operant learning paradigm through which we have considered other behaviors may be incomplete for an analysis of non-voluntary, emotional responses which are generally viewed as following a classical conditioning (Pavlov, 1927) or contiguity (Guthrie, 1935) model. In simplified terms, classical conditioning may be viewed as learning in which one stimulus substitutes for another. A neutral stimulus frequently occurs at the same time as a stimulus that already elicits a reaction. Eventually, that neutral stimulus serves to elicit a similar reaction. For example, if the only time an employee sees his boss is the anxiety-arousing situation of being criticized, eventually the mere sight of the boss will serve to elicit an emotional reaction. The boss has become a conditioned stimulus (CS) for anxiety.

The effects of occupational stress as described by Miller and Pfhol may be viewed as involving both reflexive ("involuntary") and operant ("voluntary") behavior. The thoughts that they describe as eliciting an emotional response would represent a learned stimulus for the involuntary emotional reaction. Yet, the act of thinking the thought is a voluntary response that the organism has learned to emit through operant learning processes. The intervention that they recommend is essentially differential response training in which executives are reinforced for thinking about stress in such a way that it does not serve as a CS for emotional responses. While it is certainly possible, and in many cases obviously true, that an external stimulus will act as a CS for an emotional reaction without verbal mediation, it is also evident that words can act as a CS for emotional responses (Skinner, 1957), and our self-messages represent nothing more than words that we say to ourselves.

Productivity demands not only that people be at work, but that the equipment that they require to do their jobs be functional. Like safety, equipment maintenance requires temporary decreases in productivity rates to insure long-term high performance levels. In Chapter 13, Komaki and Collins present a behavioral program for increasing preventive maintenance of equipment. While it is impossible to even estimate the tremendous productivity losses and replacement costs associated with inadequate maintenance, it is clear that if the applied behavior analysis approach outlined in Chapter 13 were adopted throughout industry it would result in substantial productivity gains.

Chapters 14 and 15 address a somewhat different aspect of management – job procurement. Both through necessity and governmental urging (Desruisseaux, 1981), companies are reaching out to hire those who have formerly had difficulty finding employment (Beattey & Schneier, 1973). Yet unemployment remains a difficult societal problem, particularly for disadvantaged groups, women returning to the labor market, and those who are over forty. As Jones and Azrin (1973) indicate, gainful employment is crucial to survival in this society, yet our unemployment figures tell us that many people lack the necessary skills to succeed in the job hunt. Helping them to learn these skills provides organizations with a productive employee as much as it helps the individual to become self-sufficient. In Chapter 14, Richman provides a comprehensive program for job finding using both behavior modification and cognitive restructuring techniques. Based on her own research, which demonstrated the effectiveness of a behavioral approach to job finding, she presents a complete package for helping the hardcore unemployed find employment.

A group that has received considerably less attention than the disadvantaged but has a similar job-finding problem is the terminated executive. The individual who no longer fits into the plans of a given company requires help in finding another position where the use of his talents can be maximized. The worth of this step for the organization is more than public relations. The organization's treatment of those who are leaving the company most certainly influences the behavior of those who remain. In recent years, companies have begun to devote more attention to out-placement (Rendero, 1980) but little theory or research has developed from these programs. Chapter 15 presents a behavior analysis of the out-placement function in which Brittain makes recommendations for a more contingent approach to helping the executive regain employment and resolve the emotional response to termination.

Richard M. O'Brien
Hofstra University

REFERENCES

Absenteeism won't quit. *Business Week*, July 25, 1970, p. 66.

Beatty, R. N., & Schneier, C. E. Reducing welfare roles through employment: The changes required in society, organizations, and individuals. *Social Welfare, The Forensic Quarterly*, 1973, **47,** 379-390.

Business dries up its alcoholics. *Business Week*, November 11, 1972, 168-169.

Caulkins, M. D. A municipal safety program that works. *The American City*, August 1971, 67-68.

Charlesworth, E. A., Williams, B. J., & Bear, P. E. A worksite stress management program for essential hypertension. Paper presented at the annual meeting of the Association for the Advancement of Behavior Therapy, New York, November 1980.

Cruikshank, G. E. No-shows at work: high priced headache. *Nation's Business*, 1976, **64** (9), 37-39.

Curbing absenteeism. *Supervisory Management*, 1970, **15** (1), 10-12.

Desruisseaux, M. D. This month – Incentives for hiring disadvantaged workers. *Personnel Journal*, 1981, **60**, 264-269.

Employee incentives to improve state and local government productivity. Washington, D.C.: National Commission on Productivity and Work Quality, 1975.

Fat people's fight against job bias. *U. S. News and World Report*, 1977, **83** (23), 78-80.

Gordon, J. B., Akman, A., & Brooks, M. *Industrial safety statistics: A re-examination*. New York: Praeger, 1971.

Guthrie, E. R. *The psychology of learning*. New York: Harper, 1935.

Halbardier, L. This month – Motivate like a marketer. *Personnel Journal*, 1981, **60**, 358-361.

Herskowitz, J. M. *Behavior modification to improve drug compliance in hypertension*. Unpublished doctoral dissertation, Hofstra University, 1980.

Jones, R. J., & Azrin, N. H. An experimental application of a social reinforcement approach to the problem of job-finding. *Journal of Applied Behavior Analysis*, 1973, **6**, 345-353.

Komaki, J., Barwick, K. D., & Scott, L. R. A behavioral approach to occupational safety: Pinpointing and reinforcing safe performance in a food manufacturing plant. *Journal of Applied Psychology*, 1978, **63**, 434-445.

Komaki, J., Heinzmann, A. T., & Lawson, L. Effect of training and feedback: Component analysis of a behavioral safety program. *Journal of Applied Psychology*, 1980, **65**, 261-270.

McKelvey, R. K., Engen, T., & Peck, M. B. Performance efficiency and injury avoidance as a function of positive and negative incentives. *Journal of Safety Research*, 1973, **5**, 90-96.

Pavlov, I. P. *Conditioned Reflexes*. Translated by G. V. Anrep. London: Oxford University Press, 1927.

Pedalino, E., & Gamboa, V. U. Behavior modification and absenteeism: Intervention in one industrial setting. *Journal of Applied Psychology*, 1974, **59**, 694-698.

Penn, A. C. Your personal management: The silent killer. *Supervisory Management*, 1977, **22** (5), 37-42.

Reid, P. C. Absenteeism – Industry's high-priced headache. *Supervisory Management*, 1963, **8** (10), 9-13.

Rendero, T. Consensus: Outplacement practices. *Personnel*, 1980, **57** (4), 4-11.

Rhoton, W. W. A procedure to improve compliance with coal mine safety regulations. *Journal of Organizational Behavior Management*, 1980, **2**, 243-249.

Ritschl, E. T., Mirman, R. I., Sigler, J. T., & Hall, R. V. Reduction of lost-accident rates in an industrial setting. In M. R. Blood (Chair), *Behaviorism in the post-industrial revolution: Where the action is*. Symposium presented at the annual meeting of the American Psychological Association, San Francisco, August 1977.

Shea, G. F. Cost effective stress management training. *Training and Development Journal*, 1980, **34** (7), 25-33.

Skinner, B. F. *Verbal Behavior*. New York: Appleton-Century-Crofts, 1957.

Sulzer-Azaroff, B. Behavioral ecology and accident prevention. *Journal of Organizational Behavior Management*, 1978, **2**, 11-44.

Sulzer-Azaroff, B., & de Santamoria, M. C. Industrial safety hazard reduction through performance feedback. *Journal of Applied Behavior Analysis*, 1980, **13**, 287-295.

Sweetland, J. *Occupational stress and productivity*. Scarsdale, NY: Work in America Institute, 1979.

The nagging problem of absenteeism. *Business Management*, 1967, **33** (1), 12-22.

Udolf, R. *Handbook of hypnosis for professionals*. New York: Van Nostrand Reinhold, 1981.

U.S. bureau of labor statistics. Monthly Labor Review, 1974, 97.

Improving Attendance and Punctuality Within a Behavioral Consultation Model

Richard M. Carlson and William A. Sperduto

Behavior Dynamics, Inc.

Absenteeism saps American industry. Each year it is estimated that over 400 million working days and perhaps as much as $26 million dollars are lost due to absenteeism and tardiness (Cruikshank, 1976; Hedges, 1973; Steers & Rhodes, 1978).

To date no specific program has gained widespread acceptance in successfully dealing with this problem. Everyone agrees that absenteeism is a complex phenomenon with multiple causes (Kempen & Hall, 1977; Muchinsky, 1977; Forrest, Cummings & Johnson, 1977; Yolles, Carone & Krinsky, 1975). But until Steers and Rhodes (1978) formulated a conceptual model for examining attendance behavior, research although voluminous, lacked a cohesive frame of reference. Steers and Rhodes based their model on evidence gathered from over one hundred articles on the subject. The model suggests that "an employee's attendance is largely a function of two important variables: (1) an employee's motivation to attend and (b) an employee's ability to attend." Each variable is broken down into components. Motivation includes job situation, satisfaction, attendance motivation, job level, leader style, co-worker relations, opportunities for advancement, role of employee values, job expectations, pressures to attend, economic and market conditions, incentive/reward system, work group norms, personal work ethic, and organizational commitment. Ability to attend includes illness and accidents, family responsibilities, and transportation problems.

Although "ability to attend" with its concomittant components plays a definite role in job attendance and punctuality, these factors appear to be beyond the scope and control of most industrial managers. In addition, the evidence points to more structural considerations that must be attended to in efforts to control absenteeism and tardiness (Wallin & Johnson, 1976; Nicholson, 1976). The basic principles of operant conditioning emphasize that people will be most likely to engage in desired behaviors if they are rewarded for doing so. Behavior which is not rewarded or is punished is less likely to be repeated. Although the behavior of employees in organizations is subject to these same laws, many of our personnel policies are inconsistent with this idea. Current personnel policies often reward people for not coming to work (Hinrichs, 1980). Sick pay and paid holidays are obvious examples of this. Current sick leave programs not only provide an acceptable excuse for employees not to come to work, but also actually reward them through monetary benefits for being absent (Nord, 1970; Wallin & Johnson, 1976). As Nord (1970) has pointed out, in many cases the rewards for attending are not sufficiently great to counterbalance rewards for not coming to work. Control of absenteeism and tardiness needs to focus largely on these structural characteristics.

Many managers in attempting to alleviate employee problems have relied upon punishment tactics. In its broadest sense, punitive control includes a variety of punishing behaviors ranging from fines and threats to more verbal acts such as criticism and ridicule. "While it is possible to influence behavior through the systematic application of punishment, such an approach can precipitate a variety of dysfunctional consequences, e.g., employee anxiety, negative attitudes toward the punishing agent, etc. [Johnson & Peterson, 1975]." A few studies have examined the role of punitive sanctions by management in controlling absenteeism and tardiness. The results of such studies have been mixed. Two studies found that the use of stringent reporting and control procedures (e.g., requiring medical verifications for reported illnesses, strick disciplinary measures) was related to lower absence rates (Baum & Youngblood, 1975; Seatter, 1961), while one found no such relationship (Rosen & Turner, 1971). Moreover, Nicholson (1976) found that such controls did not influence average attendance rates and actually led to fewer but longer absences. Such contradictory results suggest that positive reward systems might be more effective than punishment (Johnson & Peterson, 1975; Herman, de Montes, Dominguez, Montes, & Hopkins, 1973).

A wide variety of field experiments have investigated the effectiveness of positive reinforcement, i.e., the employee receives positive consequences for coming to work, on attendance behavior, and punctuality. It has been found that small incentives can be used effectively to increase employee attendance. The earliest applications of this principle (Lawler & Hackman, 1969; Nord, 1970) focused on providing small prizes for perfect attendance. Nord (1970), for example, described a case study of a leading hardware company that used a lottery and a bonus incentive system to decrease absenteeism and tardiness. All employees with perfect attendance and punctuality for the past month were eligible for a drawing at the end of the month held in each of the stores. Prizes consisted of appliances worth about $25. In addition, at the end of 6 months, all employees demonstrating perfect attendance and punctuality were eligible to take part in a separate drawing for a major award such as a color TV set. This lottery system was highly successful. The personnel department estimated a 62% reduction of sick-leave payments. During the first year of the program, absenteeism and tardiness was reduced to one-fourth its prior level. Although the data are retrospective reports from a manager and not actual controlled recording, they suggest that rewarding desired behavior by the power of a lottery can be an effective tool for industry.

Wallin and Johnson (1976) report on the successful application of a cost-effective lottery for decreasing employee absenteeism in an electronics firm. In order to qualify for the monthly drawing, employees were required to have perfect attendance and punctuality records for the month. Thus eligibility was contingent upon emission of the desired behavior, work attendance. A $10 cash prize was awarded to the winner. In addition, the names of all employees who qualified were posted on the bulletin board providing social reinforcement in the form of recognition. The authors report a 30.6% decrease in sick-leave expenditures for 88 employees over the 11-month period the lottery was in effect as compared with the previous 11 months. The total expense to the company was $110. In sick leave alone this represented a savings of over $3,000, not to mention the increased productivity obtained by having employees at work more often.

One of the reasons that Wallin and Johnson's intervention is so cost effective is that it is not necessary to reward every response in order to increase the number of appropriate responses. The principle that intermittent reinforcement, i.e., rewards delivered for every so many responses, produces a higher rate of behavior than is obtained by rewarding each correct response (continuous reinforcement) has been amply demonstrated in learning research (Ferster & Skinner, 1957). It is also obvious in many real world settings. Any track tout or slot machine player will tell you that the chance of winning is enough to maintain a high rate of responding. It is for these reasons that lotteries have frequently been the intervention strategy used in studies aimed at increasing attendance and/or punctuality (Nord, 1970; Wallin & Johnson, 1976; Pedalino & Gamboa, 1974).

Pedalino and Gamboa (1974) treated both attendance and punctuality by giving a $20 prize to the employee who had the best five card poker hand each week. The catch was that the employee had to be present and *on time* each day in order to draw a card. While this early study does not present estimates of costs or savings, an absenteeism reduction of 18.2% occurred over 4 months for 215 unionized employees. Also of interest is the fact that the absence rates were maintained when the incentive system was switched to a biweekly game.

Kempen and Hall (1977) increased attendance in two factories of a large manufacturing company (7500 hourly-rated employees). The intervention consisted of an Attendance Management System (AMS) designed by plant management with experimenter consultation. The AMS provided nonmonetary privileges to reinforce good and improving attendance plus progressive disciplinary warnings for excessive and worsening absence. The experimenter consultant recommended that disciplinary action focus on time lost rather than frequency of absences, that a review period of several years be used rather than the traditional 12 months, and that "discipline" be limited to a series of warnings and interviews. Salaried employees at the two plants and hourly employees at eleven equivalent plants served as comparison groups. Despite encountering the kind of highly complex problems that a modern industrial manager typically faces such as layoffs, the contingency management program significantly decreased the rate of absenteeism below the rate observed during a baseline condition when another type of absence control was in effect. No significant decrease in absence was observed in any of the comparison groups during the study. It is worth noting that at Plant A absenteeism decreased to below 3.0%, a rate more than 50% below the baseline mean and lower than any rate achieved at the plant during its 18 year history. This study is particularly important because it demonstrates the constructive use of punishment as a behavior change technique in industry.

Continuous positive reinforcement has also been demonstrated to be effective with punctuality problems. Herman, de Montes, Dominguez, Montes, and Hopkins (1973) modified excessive tardiness through small monetary rewards among Mexican factory workers. Employees were given a daily bonus slip by the company guard each time they arrived at work before 7 A.M. This bonus slip provided positive reinforcement of two pesos (.16 US) for each day the employee was on time, and at the end of the week the slips could be cashed in. While the low wages and Mexican tax structure eliminated some of the drawbacks inherent in using monetary incentives in the United States, the results are compelling even if it may require ingenuity to replicate these effects. A tardiness rate of 15% per day was significantly reduced to 2% at minimal cost. The authors present data on individual employees, demonstrating that even the employee for whom the treatment was least effective was substantially more punctual during the contingent reward system. Herman et al. report that contingent monetary consequation for punctuality also proved superior to reinforcing punctuality with an annual bonus and punishing tardiness with mandatory time off without pay. Orphen (1978) has recently reported a similar program for absenteeism among U.S. textile workers. A $.50 bonus was paid to workers for perfect attendance each week. This minimal contingency proved to be effective in reducing absenteeism while it was in effect, but as is often the case, the absenteeism rate returned to baseline levels upon withdrawal of the system.

One of the simplest and least expensive behavior change interventions that can be implemented in business settings is a feedback system (Emmert, 1978; Feeney, 1980; Panyan, Boozer, & Morris, 1970). One major advantage of such a system is the likely possibility that it can be built upon the performance data that are already being collected as part of normal business procedures. The development of a feedback system usually requires very little change in the normal day-to-day routine. Given this advantage, a feedback procedure was chosen by Anthony and O'Brien (1980) as a means of reducing work tardiness among female camp counselors. Following a two week baserate, feedback and public charting on group punctuality were instituted. Praise and a preferred activity (Premack Principle) were made contingent on being on time. Group punctuality increased from 36% to 81% during treatment but decreased to 66.6% on a partial return to baserate conditions. The authors report however that when the contingencies were fully reinstated, on-time performance climbed to 90%.

The systematic implementation of visual feedback and social reinforcement also proved effective in improving attendance among 84 factory employees at a sheltered workshop (Keelin, 1980). A specialized chart was placed in the work area which contained both weekly absence rates (feedback) and positive comments on any improved performance (reinforcement). Attendance increased from a baseline average of 93.77% to an average of 95.48% during the 7-week intervention period. A dependent t-test revealed that this increase was significant ($p < .05$). These two reports (Anthony & O'Brien, 1980; Keelin, 1980) are noteworthy for they illustrate the cost effectiveness of feedback systems. Cost considerations are one of the realities of applying behavior management in work settings to which every manager is well accustomed. Many potential reinforcers cost money – money that the company may not have at its disposal to spend. Information on past performance however is often available to the manager at no additional expense. Systematic feedback and social reinforcement delivered to employees can serve as powerful reinforcers if used properly.

Case Studies in Attendance and Punctuality

The three case studies that follow bear witness to the cyclical nature of the absenteeism problem. In only one instance (Case 1) was the problem of absenteeism *per se* the obvious identifiable problem. Here the consultant was called in to specifically remediate an absenteeism/tardiness problem. But in Cases 2 and 3, absenteeism/tardiness was not the ostensible problem. The consultant was engaged to resolve employee attitude and performance problems (Case 2) and low productivity (Case 3). In both cases, as the consultant explored the total job situation and offered recommendations for resolving them, he found that improved attendance and decreased tardiness was a positive by product. Though the consultant could not fully realize it at the time, he was corroborating Steers and Rhodes' suggestion that attendance is the product of a set of variables and not necessarily a singular element. There is no common root. Each situation must be critically analyzed for its own peculiarities.

In each of the three cases the consultant utilized behavior modification techniques. In Case 1, a lottery was employed to provide an incentive to increase attendance. In Case 2, a management training program was set up in order to end labor strife. Although it was not expected, the by product of ending labor strife was improved attendance and increased productivity. In Case 3, a basic work measurement study was transformed into a management training program which not only resulted in increased productivity but improved attendance and reduced tardiness. The management training programs in Cases 2 and 3 were behavior management programs utilizing positive reinforcement as a means for rewarding positive performance.

CASE STUDY 1

The problem was a high rate of tardiness and absenteeism and related poor employee morale. The client, a shipping distributor based in Atlanta, Georgia, was concerned because productivity was declining. The company was small and consisted of five managers and twenty staff, all of whom were hourly day laborers. The company was profitable, but labor unrest was making the management apprehensive. In an attempt to abate a potentially destructive situation, management approached the consultant.

Because the consultant was assigned to resolve a specific problem (tardiness, absenteeism, and turnover) management did not request a work measurement study. This would have been useful, but management was impatient and looking for immediate results. Through functional analysis it became clear to the consultant that management's pattern of reinforcement left much to be desired and probably contributed significantly to the high absenteeism and turnover rate. The functional analysis also included face-to-face interviews with each staff member, completion of an anonymous questionnaire, and an open staff meeting. Management was not asked to participate in any of these activities, and staff was assured that their comments would be held in confidence. Baseline data on tardiness and absenteeism were taken.

What the consultant learned from the information gathered was that management focused mainly on mistakes rather than accomplishments, and that this was perceived by the workers as aversive. Feedback was mainly negative and even antagonistic. Staff believed that management cared only about results and had no regard for the individuals doing the work. It was learned, for example, that there was no lunch room and no area for the employees to interact socially.

The consultant proposed that the rate of tardiness and absenteeism could be reduced by implementing an incentive program. In this instance, an internal lottery was considered the appropriate format similar to that used in earlier studies (Ayllon & Carlson, 1973; Nord, 1970; Pedalino & Gamboa, 1974; Tjersland, 1972; Wallin & Johnson, 1976). Each staff member was rewarded with a lottery ticket at the end of the week if he was not tardy or absent. Each recipient of a lottery ticket was also eligible for a weekly prize which was given away at a drawing held each Friday during working hours. The weekly cost of the lottery tickets was $50. This was a small price to pay when compared to the increase in production time the lottery generated. The consultant also recommended that a lunch room and lounge area be constructed. Management complied with this request and construction began soon after.

Staff attendance improved demonstrably throughout the 8 weeks of interaction. The consultant's activities among the staff and the rapidity with which management responded to his suggestions and recommendations mollified the staff. On-time attendance increased to 80% from 55% as shown in Figure 11.1. The consultancy was considered a success by management and staff. Management was particularly pleased that the rate of shipments was increasing, and that the previous trend of performance deterioration had been reversed. At this point, after 5 months of working with the consultant, management decided to go it alone.

Follow-up

For a period of 7 months immediately following the termination of the project, the consultant maintained contact with management and key staff. At first, the positive trend continued as before. Management and staff were pleased with each other's performance. But the residual effects did not last. A decline set in when management resorted to its previous

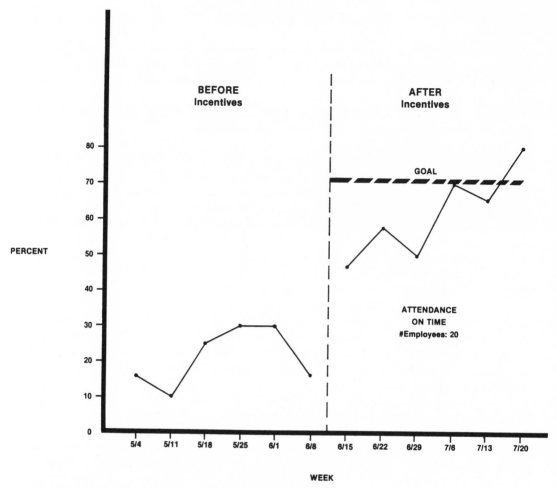

Fig. 11.1 Attendance Baseline Through Treatment.

non-reinforcing (results-oriented) behavior pattern. After 3 months, the lottery incentive/ reward program began to appreciably lose its effectiveness. Staff reported that it once again felt management was resorting to negative consequences. At the end of 7 months, tardiness and absenteeism increased, though not to previous levels. Here the consultant lost touch with the company.

On reflection, the consultant concluded that his role was an important factor in keeping the program alive. He had functioned as a catalyst and a facilitator. When he departed, the management could not or would not assume this role. They ended the lottery. Absenteeism returned to its old levels. The conclusion drawn was that for incentive/reward programs to continue to be successful, praise and attention for positive performances must continue to be present. The staff at this company increased its productivity voluntarily when it saw that management rewarded their performance. Unfortunately, management never really understood the reinforcement value of contingent praise and recognition. It looked only for results, and this produced a mutually unworkable situation. The continued employment of the consultant or the training of an on-site consultant might have alleviated this stalemate and maintained the mutually rewarding environment that existed during his consultancy.

CASE STUDY 2

The client, a laundry business based in the Southeast, was concerned about mounting union grievances, a wildcat strike, and rising absenteeism. The business, a plant of a national corporation, had 200 workers and 30 managers. Plant absenteeism was high and the plant ranked in the lower third of national productivity; job performance was not adequate and the employees appeared sullen. Management recognized that things could be better. At the time that they contacted the consultant a wildcat strike had just ended, and another seemed imminent.

Initially the consultant was called upon to improve management/labor relations. It was hoped that an improved communications feedback system would improve the situation. It was agreed that management would participate in a behavior management training program that would focus on four areas: (1) ways of measuring job performance, (2) developing positive reinforcement skills and implementing feedback systems, and (3) improving interpersonal relations (Glaser, 1976). Periodic and final evaluation was built into the program. It was essential that management keep in close touch with its new activities. Since the program was expected to last 1 year, the first major evaluation was planned at the end of 3 months. A final evaluation was to be completed at the end of 12 months, at which time a decision was expected to be made on the value of the consultancy and its continuation.

Two management training groups were set up. Group membership consisted of middle and lower production management staff. Top management, although they wanted the program and gave it their blessing, attended sessions infrequently. Group size was 12 or 13, and meetings were held once a week for 2 hours a session, for 6 months. Each group was a cross-section of the production management staff. Two groups were scheduled with attendance at the A or B group depending upon meeting times. Switching from one group to another was discouraged.

Measuring job performance and productivity was the first task that the consultant presented to the members of the training program. From the beginning it was clear that this was not a topic that had been carefully thought out at the company. Participants admitted that no one had ever realistically measured job performance, or if job performance was measured it was never used positively for management's advantage. It was usually utilized threateningly at the expense of both labor and management. The only feedback ever given to a worker was negative. Workers were seldom if ever given positive commendations. During the first month (four meetings), a formula for measuring performance was developed and implemented. It was decided to use the rate measurement of pounds of laundry processed through the plant per man hour since this information was readily available. Baseline production level was 44.5 pounds per man hour (See Figure 11.2). Archival sources showed that this level of productivity had remained relatively constant for the previous year with little seasonal fluctuation.

Once baseline data were collected, the groups began to formulate particular job expectations for individuals and departments. Participants were asked to keep detailed records of their activities. In turn, the production workers were asked to keep records of what they did, and they complied because they were following management's example. Organizational commitment is an important factor in this process because it provides visible evidence of management's desires. It sets a climate for sharing common goals and working for their achievement (Porter, Steers, Mowday, & Boulian, 1974; Smith, 1977; Steers, 1977).

The second task for the groups consisted of training the production management staff to develop and implement the positive reinforcement aspect of the program. Sessions now focused more on individual needs of management and worker. Under the consultant's

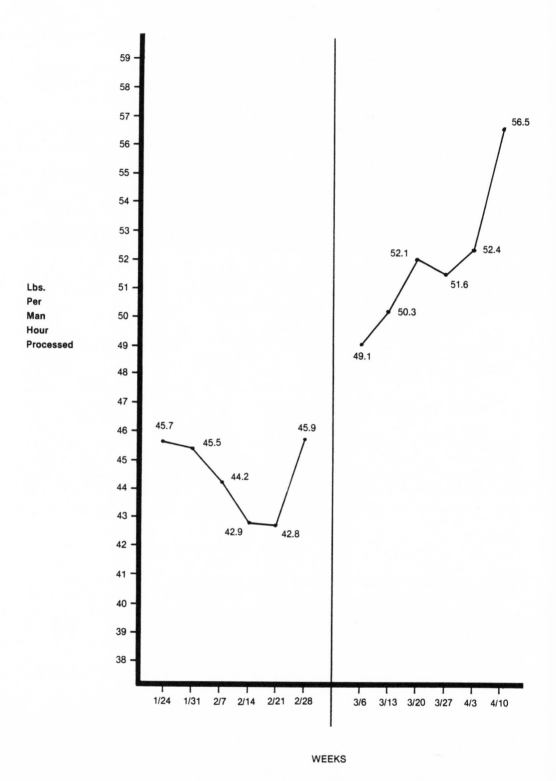

Fig. 11.2. Mean Pounds of Laundry Processed Baseline Through Treatment.

guidance additional lessons were conducted on topics such as listening, stress management, assertiveness, and "reality management." No fixed schedule was established, and topics were treated on a demand basis. Time was allotted as needed. Topics were often reviewed as situations developed. This flexibility suited the climate of the plant and enhanced the value of training sessions (Wexley & Nemeroff, 1975).

The managers took what they learned in class and generalized it to the actual work setting. Absenteeism and turnover decreased while worker morale improved. Productivity increased. At the end of the first 6 months everyone involved – production management, workers and the consultant – reacted favorably to the program. Management participants, polled (publicly and anonymously) in the training sessions reported that the workers' tensions had eased and that fewer grievances were being reported by shop stewards. Management admitted for the first time that they felt confident when dealing with workers. They were enthusiastic about how they were able to promote cooperation and settle potentially harmful disputes. Someone remarked that he had never before realized how much of his production supervision job was "peacemaking" or "coaching." He said he worked hard to get team spirit and that his efforts were not lost on the workers in his department. Confidence is infectious, he said. Another manager was particularly pleased with his newly developed ability to deal with other managers, including the top management, utilizing the same positive feedback techniques. He had originally looked to the program as a means for improving his relationship with workers, but he soon realized that he was learning much about his peers and superiors. For example, before the sessions began and the managers began openly sharing information, it was rarely possible for the production managers to disagree with top management and not get fired. The training sessions created an open communications network, allowing for more reinforcement up and down the managerial ladder.

During the first 6 months grievances decreased roughly 80%. This was better than expected during what is considered a start-up period. For the next 6 months union grievances decreased to an average of about two per month. Of course problems did not disappear. But the management was able to resolve disputes efficiently. This ability instilled confidence in the workers who no longer used the grievance procedure as a means to antagonize the management. A productive status quo was reached.

Most importantly, the plant's productivity improved and absenteeism and tardiness declined. Management calculated an impressive yearly savings. According to a high level manager:

> Productivity gains have provided opportunities to expand and improve our current marketing strategies. In the plant the pounds of linen produced per man hour has risen from an average of 44.5 pounds per man hour to 52 pounds per man hour which is translated into a $3,000 per week or $156,000 per year saving. In another facility the difference in two comparable weeks of operation revealed a $9,000 per week saving. Absenteeism had dropped significantly as well as a marked decrease in union grievances and labor strife. Of more significance to the future of our company is the drastic change to a positive attitude by both management and employees. The team concept of management is now a reality.

Follow-up

At the end of 12 months, the plant was rated in the upper third of productivity nationally. The parent corporation was pleased; the local plant management was enthusiastic. The production staff was confident that they could maintain the gains achieved, and they expressed the desire to keep the training groups functioning on their own. The consultant agreed that his services were no longer required, and his consultancy was amicably terminated.

On reflection, the consultant was pleased with the results of this behavior management training program. During the year he spent at the plant, he observed a marked growth of confidence in the participants. For one thing, it was clear that the production management staff was ready for training. They were professionally competent to perform the technical portions of their jobs, but they were woefully unprepared to perform as people managers. The excessively high volume of union grievances was due to management's inability to perceive its own shortcomings. For the most part they had taken as their model the plant manager who was autocratic and aloof from the daily production work flow. Once the production managers were shown alternative role models utilizing positive reinforcement as an important managerial tool, they began working out more individual styles of management. They were better able to deal with the plant manager and the workers. In the give and take of the training sessions the production managers shed inhibitions and gained confidence in their own ability to work out problems and take responsibility for command.

A key ingredient in the training process was the participation of the production manager, who was the highest ranking member of the staff to attend training sessions on a regular basis. His presence and enthusiasm strongly motivated the others. As is usual in training situations, group solidarity protected and abetted individual members. But having an immediate superior work out his problems with his subordinates on an equal footing made the whole experience realistic. At the end of 6 months it was the production manager who commented that he was learning more about dealing with the upper level managers, especially the plant manager, then he ever realized was possible. This new-found ability had so reduced his levels of stress that he was now clearsighted about how to handle his subordinates and workers. His example stimulated the other trainees, who in turn stimulated the workers.

Work-related grievances fell off as the managers became more adept at solving problems. The concept of providing immediate and, when appropriate, positive feedback satisfied the needs of the workers. In fact, the workers wanted attention; they were not solely complaining about economic unfairness though this seemed to be the case at first. Money seemed to be less reinforcing than recognition. Once the production managers positively acknowledged the people who worked for them, the behavioral climate of the plant improved. As problems arose, the managers helped to resolve them by talking things over with the training group under the guidance of the consultant. The immediate feedback process in the training group set a pattern of behavior that was then transferred to the actual work sphere. This set the stage for a positive mutual reinforcement cycle to develop. When the consultant left, this was firmly in place.

CASE STUDY 3

The problem was low productivity. The client, an insurance company located in the Southeast, thought that the way to increase productivity was to initiate a work measurement program. The company had three upper level managers, fifteen middle level managers, and 85 clerical staff. When upper level management approached the consultant, they were concerned only with rising overhead costs to which absenteeism and tardiness were a contributing factor. They had no true idea of the avoidance climate in which most employees worked and were unaware that this management approach was sapping productivity.

The consultant's initial task was to determine how many jobs could be eliminated. For this he was allotted 9 months. It was supposed to be a rather straight work-measurement operation, but management indicated that it would listen to the consultant's recommendations for attempting alternative behavior management strategies. With this in mind, the consultant asked for and received management's assurance that during the period of his consultancy all jobs would be guaranteed. This precondition was necessary in order to make everyone feel less threatened by what the program would reveal. This agreement subsequently had much to do with the extensive scope of cooperation the program elicited. It also enabled the consultant to work in an atmosphere that was relatively free from fear and suspicion. The idea was to set up a mutually rewarding situation. Often it is the case that the consultant meets with hostility because he is perceived as a "hatchetman." This must be dispelled at the start of a program or else much of the consultant's time is wasted on declaiming or self-justification. A good consultant will avoid this trap (most of the time).

First, the level of productivity was observed. The consultant interviewed all of the managers and several key clerical workers. Interviews were conducted in groups and privately, but what the consultant observed was discussed in group meetings. The consultant requested detailed job descriptions to help formulate a standard work measurement study. With the baseline data this provided, he installed short interval scheduling (SIS). SIS determined the expected level of productivity by scheduling work to be completed in short segments, usually 1 or 2 hours. Second, along with the SIS a set of individual job objectives was developed. Third, department work objectives and productivity levels were set. Forth, all middle managers were requested to attend a series of behavior management training courses including reinforcement strategies, interpersonal relations, time scheduling, and evaluation. Fifth, the effects of the consultancy were to be evaluated at stated periods.

Baseline figures indicated that productivity was 62 to 65% of the developed work standards. Gathering this data took 9 months after which time new productivity levels of 90 to 95% were set. This level was agreed upon by the managers and the clerical staff. No positions were eliminated.

During the work measurement period, the consultant analyzed employee feedback and determined that management focused on mistakes and performance problems even though such incidents were in the minority. The attention devoted to these deficiencies was deemed a probable cause of the continuing sloppy work habits and low productivity. In order to create a positive behavioral climate, the consultant convinced upper management to enter a new phase of development. He recommended that the managers take part in a behavioral training workshop and that an incentive/reward program be installed for the clerical workers. Under the consultant's guidance the middle managers began earnestly working on mastering techniques and strategies for giving positive reinforcement and developing confidence (Hamner & Hamner, 1976). The group was especially interested in contingency management training because they had come to realize that absenteeism, tardiness, and productivity could be improved utilizing positive reinforcement rather than by eliminating jobs. While the managers learned to be more efficient, the clerical staff was participating in the work/incentive scheme that was implemented with the new work standards. This was based on a point system that rewarded clerical help for attaining new productivity levels. Points were given for on-time attendance, as well as for not being absent during a one month period. Points were also awarded for individual productivity as well as meeting departmental productivity standards. As points were being accumulated the employee could redeem them for various rewards. A catalogue was used for a variety of prize choices, allowing each employee to choose according to their own preference.

As soon as the incentive/reward program was installed significant declines in absenteeism and tardiness and increases in productivity were observed. At the end of 30 days productivity was up to 88% from 65%. Work volume increased, too, but the clerical help did not complain. In fact they were enthusiastic about both their own newly found abilities to produce more and the points they were earning. They worked harder to get points and enjoyed their rewards. Work group norms reinforced good attendance leading to improved productivity. Workers received more points for good attendance and increased productivity (on work group norms see Cartwright & Zander, 1968; Gibson, 1966; Ilgen & Hollenback, 1977; Lawler, 1971; Shaw, 1976). The management was also pleased because absenteeism and tardiness were decreased while productivity increased. There was a salary savings of $85,000 per year projected, and the staff was "happy." The consultancy was evaluated positively.

Follow-up

At the end of 12 months, the consultancy moved into a maintenance phase. For the next year it was agreed that the consultant would visit the company once a month. During his visits he would moderate workshops and conduct training sessions. To replace the consultant, a staff member was selected to be trained as an "in-house" consultant. This position was full time and was continually supervised by the original consultant. Both upper and middle management agreed that as long as productivity remained in the 90 to 95% range, the program could be controlled in house. This situation remained in place for four years, at which time the consultancy was finally terminated. During this entire period productivity remained in the 85 to 95% range.

On reflection, this consultancy was successful on two levels: the managerial and the human. Management was pleased that it was able to increase attendance and productivity and reduce labor costs. They found out that they had to revise their work measurement standards. And, most importantly, they realized that their managerial style had to change. Management learned to be more capable of administering positive reinforcement. They learned that to accomplish goals they had to know how to set realistic standards. In order to do so, management had to redefine their managerial objectives and develop new responses to their employees. In essence, the management of this insurance company learned that performance is related to the consequences for the worker, and when people are positively reinforced, they work more productively (Katzell & Yankelovich, 1975). It was the consultant's objective to help management change its behavior so that the clerical staff felt less like things or machines who were there merely to be used and discarded. With this in mind his whole approach to helping management in this instance was to get them to establish a more reinforcing but still authoritative role in determining operations.

The incentive plan instituted on recommendation of the consultant probably worked because it provided positive feedback as much as because it provided tangible rewards. Earning enough points meant that the employee was receiving acknowledgement for work done. By setting up such a contingency system, the consultant was able to bring the clerical staff and the management into a mutually reinforcing sphere of action. Management "managed," the clerical staff produced, the staff was rewarded for its productivity, management was pleased with its rate of profit – a positive work-management cycle was established. It was kept active, and in this instance successful, because the consultant continued to play a role once the program was in motion.

Perhaps the major lesson to be learned from the research on improving attendance and punctuality is that workers must find it rewarding to come to work if management expects them to do so regularly and promptly. The major obstacle to implementing reinforcement programs for attendance and punctuality is a management view that employees should want to come to work on time every day because that's what they are paid for. Unfortunately, the salaried employee can only lose rewards by failing to fulfill attendance and punctuality standards; he gains nothing over his contracted salary. This system is therefore doomed to a punishment approach. Management can alienate employees through punishment, terminate them, or put up with excessive absences and lateness while muttering about employees who don't give the company an honest day's work. Perhaps workers should come to work regularly and on time, but they don't and ranting about how they "should" is not likely to be very productive. Once management recognizes that the goal is to get the employees in, not to make pronouncements about the character of the workers, it is possible to begin an intervention to improve attendance and punctuality.

The studies from private industry reviewed in this chapter and several reports from health settings and government productivity programs (Employee Incentives, 1975; Hutchison, Jarman, & Bailey, 1980; Reid, Schuh-Wear, & Brannon, 1978; Shoemaker & Reid, 1980; Stephens & Burroughs, 1978) demonstrate that absenteeism and tardiness can be conquered by cost-effective incentive programs. Further research is required to identify maximal reinforcement to response ratios and provide guidelines for the maintenance of program gains as well as to investigate the amount of reward delay (e.g., payment for sick days not used at retirement) that can be tolerated while maintaining a reinforcing program. Building attendance incentives into the contracted salary would seem to be the most productive step to insure program maintenance.

The research completed to date has been encouraging. Enough examples of creative absenteeism/tardiness control programs appear in the literature to show that employee withdrawal can be controlled and reduced through operant procedures. While there is still a paucity of reports in the literature on long-term effects, the possibility of applying positive reinforcement to improve attendance and punctuality of employees in industry appears promising. Further research is needed to more fully evaluate the relative effects of incentive and disciplinary procedures. Replications of apparently effective strategies across diverse populations and settings will increase our confidence in the generality of the cause-effect relations.

REFERENCES

Anthony, J., & O'Brien, R. M. Improving punctuality of summer camp counselors through feedback and reinforcement. Paper presented to the Association for Behavior Analysis, Dearborn, Mich., June 1980.

Ayllon, T., & Carlson, R. Instilling responsibility through incentives. *Trade World Journal*, 1973, **1**, 41-42.

Baum, J. F., & Youngblood, S. A. Impact of an organizational control policy on absenteeism, performance, and satisfaction. *Journal of Applied Psychology*, 1975, **60**, 688-694.

Cartwright, D., & Zander, A. *Group dynamics*. New York: Harper & Row, 1968.

Cruikshank, G. E. No-shows at work: High priced headaches. *Nations Business*, September 1976, 37-39.

Emmert, G. D. Measuring the impact of group performance, feedback versus individual performance feedback in an industrial setting. *Journal of Organizational Behavior Management*, 1978, **1**, 134-141.

Employee incentives to improve state and local government productivity. Washington, D. C.: National Commission on Productivity and Work Quality, 1975.

Feeney, E. J. Twelve ideas toward effective training. *Training and Development Journal*, 1980, **34** (9), 14-16.

Ferster, C. B., & Skinner, B. F. *Schedules of reinforcement*. New York: Appleton-Century-Crofts, 1957.

Forrest, C. R., Cummings, L. L. & Johnson, A. C. Organizational justification: A critique and model. *Academy of Management Review*, 1977, **2**, 586-601.

Gibson, J. O. Toward a conceptualization of absence behavior of personnel in organizations. *Administrative Science Quarterly*, 1966, **11**, 107-133.

Glaser, E. M. *Productivity gains through worklife improvement*. New York: The Psychological Corporation, 1976.

Hamner, W. C., & Hamner, E. P. Behavior modification on the bottom line. *Organizational Dynamics*, 1976, **4** (4), 2-21.

Hedges, J. N. Absence from work – A look at some national data. *Monthly Labor Review*, 1973, **96**, 24-31.

Herman, J. A., de Montes, A. I., Dominguez, B., Montes, F., & Hopkins, B. L. Effects of bonuses for punctuality on the tardiness of industrial workers. *Journal of Applied Behavior Analysis*, 1973, **6**, 563-570.

Hinrichs, J. R. *Controlling absenteeism and turnover*. Scarsdale, N.Y.: Work in America Institute, 1980.

Hutchison, J. M., Jarman, P. H., & Bailey, J. S. Public posting with a habilitation team: Effects on attendance and performance. *Behavior Modification*, 1980, **4**, 57-70.

Ilgen, D. R., & Hollenback, J. H. The role of job satisfaction in absence behavior. *Organizational Behavior and Human Performance*, 1977, **19**, 148-161.

Johnson, R. D., & Peterson, T. O. "Absenteeism or attendance, which is industry's problem?" *Personnel Journal*, 1975, **54**, 568-572.

Katzell, R. A., & Yankelovich, D. Improving productivity and job satisfaction. *Organizational Dynamics*, Winter 1975, 69-80.

Keelin, J. Absenteeism: The utilization of visualized feedback and reinforcement to improve attendance in an organizational setting. Unpublished manuscript, Hofstra Unversity, 1980.

Kempen, R. W., and Hall, R. V. Reduction of industrial absenteeism: Results of a behavioral approach. *Journal of Organizational Behavior Management*, 1977, **1**, 1-21.

Lawler, E. E., III *Pay and organizational effectiveness*. New York: McGraw-Hill, 1971

Lawler, E. E., III, & Hackman, J. R. Impact of employee participation in the development of pay incentive plans: A field experiment. *Journal of Applied Psychology*, 1969, **53**, 467-471.

Muchinsky, P. M. Employee absenteeism: A review of the literature. *Journal of Vocational Behavior*, 1977, **10**, 316-340.

Nicholson, N. Management sanctions and attendance control. *Human Relations*, 1976, **29**, 139-151.

Nord, W. Improving attendance through rewards. *Personnel Administration*, 1970, **33**, 37-41.

Orphen C. Effects of bonuses for attendance on absenteeism of industrial workers. *Journal of Organizational Behavior Management*, 1978, **1**, 118-124.

Panyan, M., Boozer, H., & Morris, N. Feedback to attendants as a reinforcer for applying operant techniques. *Journal of Applied Behavior Analysis*, 1970, **3**, 1-4.

Pedalino, E., & Gamboa, V. U. Behavior modification and absenteeism: Intervention in one industrial setting. *Journal of Applied Psychology*, 1974, **59**, 694-698.

Porter, L. W., Steers, R. M., Mowday, R. T., & Boulian, P. V. Organizational commitment, job satisfaction, and turnover among psychiatric technicians. *Journal of Applied Psychology*, 1974, **59**, 603-609.

Reid, D. H., Schuh-Wear, C. L., & Brannon, M. E. Use of a group contingency to decrease staff absenteeism in a state institution. *Behavior Modification*, 1978, **2**, 251-266.

Rosen, H., & Turner, J. Effectiveness of two orientation approaches in hard-core unemployed turnover and absenteeism. *Journal of Applied Psychology*, 1971, **55**, 296-301.

Seatter, W. C. More effective control of absenteeism. *Personnel*, 1961, **38**, 16-29.

Shaw, M. E. *Group dynamics*, New York: McGraw-Hill, 1976.

Shoemaker, J., & Reid, D. H. Decreasing chronic absenteeism among institutional staff: Effects of a low-cost attendance program. *Journal of Organizational Behavior Management*, 1980, **2**, 317-328.

Smith, F. J. Work attitudes as predictors of specific day attendance. *Journal of Applied Psychology*, 1977, **62,** 16-19.

Steers, R. M. Antecedents and outcomes of organizational commitment. *Administrative Science Quarterly*, 1977, **22,** 46-56.

Steers, R., & Rhodes, S. Major influences on employee attendance: A process model. *Journal of Applied Psychology*, 1978, **63,** 391-407.

Stephens, T. A., & Burroughs, W. A. An application of operant conditioning to absenteeism in a hospital setting. *Journal of Applied Psychology*, 1978, **63,** 518-521.

Tjersland, T. *Changing worker behavior.* New York: American Telephone and Telegraph Company, Manpower Laboratory, December, 1972.

Wallin, J. A., & Johnson, R. D. The positive approach to controlling employee absenteeism. *Personnel Journal*, 1976, **55,** 390-392.

Wexley, K. N., & Nemeroff, W. F. Effectiveness of positive reinforcement and goal setting as methods of management development. *Journal of Applied Psychology*, 1975, **60,** 445-450.

Yolles, S. F., Carone, P. A., & Krinsky, L. W. *Absenteeism in industry.* Springfield, Illinois: Charles C. Thomas, 1975.

12

Management of Job-Related Stress

Richard Miller and William F. Pfohl, Jr.
Western Kentucky University

Stress is an inescapable fact of life which we all experience throughout our lives. Frequently our adjustments to stress bring about beneficial outcomes in our jobs or personal lives; however, it can be harmful. Consider the following examples:

John P. is a 34-year old assistant editor of a city newspaper. His responsibilities are broad and his time lines were typically short. Today he is unusually pressured. He feels faint, is very pale, and cannot get up from his desk.

Susan M., 39, is an office manager of a utilities company. Lately she reports feeling very edgy. She is frequently losing her temper and blowing up at her teen-age son. She reports having difficulty relaxing at any time.

A young salesman, Fred B., has been told he must increase his output by 30% or face dismissal. As he attempts to make the increased effort, he experiences a panicky feeling, dizziness, and disorientation.

Paul S. has been employed as a line manager for an industrial parts manufacturer for 8 years. Until last month, he had been satisfied with his job and had developed a regular routine to meet his company's production demands. Lately he has found that his paycheck has lost purchasing power to the point that he cannot pay his bills. This has necessitated his wife's taking employment to help meet their financial commitments. Their two children, aged 11 and 14, have now begun to do poorly in school, and the younger is not getting along with schoolmates.

Three months ago, Paul's company merged with a larger corporation. Paul has retained his position but finds his regular routine no longer meets the new set of production demands imposed by the merger. To further complicate matters, he cannot get a clear picture of his new job demands because instructions from his immediate supervisor are frequently contradicted by a section chief above the supervisor. When Paul attempts to clarify the discrepancies in orders from the two superiors, he is told by each to disregard the other.

Paul has now begun to experience headaches and chest pains. He seems to be quarreling more with his wife, has begun to feel uneasy about going to work, and seems depressed.

These people are experiencing stress, but they do not understand what it is. They are disturbed about their inability to adjust to changing life conditions, and consequently feel that they are sick, weak, or inadequate.

THE COST OF STRESS

The emotional and financial cost of stress-related disorders on industry is staggering. Much of the loss is not calculable; however, consider the following statistics reported by Manuso (1980).

1. One out of every four individuals in America suffers severe emotional stress (Presidential Commission on Mental Health, 1970).
2. The cost of such illness is 20 billion dollars per year to industry, which averages out to $1,600 per employee per year for stress problems.
3. Mental Health services for stress problems cost 14.5 billion dollars per year.
4. Disability payments average 10.5 billion dollars annually.
5. Loss of 3.9 billion dollars per year from the Gross National Product are incurred because of lost work days from stress-related disorders.
6. Companies experience a rise in insurance premiums which are paid as a contract benefit.
7. Industry is experiencing a steady rise in tort and litigation claims, charging unwarranted work-induced stresses contributed to physical or psychological disabilities in its employees. As an example, consider the case of Dilworth Thomas Rogers, a research chemist. After 30 years of service for a large oil company, he was forced to retire at the age of 60. Several years later, he died of cancer. His family charged the company with having reassigned Rogers to lower status tasks when he refused to resign. They further charged the company with discrimination in regard to his age, and stated that he had suffered severe emotional stress because of their actions. The jury agreed with the family and awarded them $780,000 (*The Atlanta Constitution*, page 1, col. 5, 2/7/75)!

Such statistics as these are impressive testimonials to the dollar impact of stress in industry. However, they may constitute the tip of the iceburg. We have no way to assess the many other contributors to corporate loss. These include employee turnover and lateness, absenteeism, losses due to poor decision-making, cost of termination and retraining, dissension among colleagues, lost sales to the corporation, the impact of lower morale in a stress climate, or overtime costs necessitated by reduced productivity under stress (Greenwood & Greenwood, 1979).

The cost of stress is by no means confined to the corporation. The price of constant tension is equally high on the individual. The following statistics are only a sample of this personal impact:

1. 500% increase in coronary disease in the last 50 years.
2. 30 million people with heart or circulatory disease.
3. One million heart attacks per year, of which 65% are fatal.
4. One in five heart attacks prior to age 60.
5. 25 million people suffer from hypertension.
6. One person in every eight experiences migraine-like headaches.
7. 16,000 tons of aspirin are consumed each year at a cost of 500 million dollars.
8. 230 million prescriptions for medication are filled each year of which 15 million are tranquilizers, 3 million are amphetamines, and 5 million are barbiturates.
9. 80% of people seeking medical care do so for stress-related problems (Pelletier, 1977).

WHAT IS STRESS?

All individuals are constantly confronted by events that force them to react physically or psychologically to their environment. These events might appropriately be called *stressors*.

The simplicity of such definitions, however, is deceptive because, at present, no universal meaning exists for the concept of stress. Some individuals prefer to define stress as a set of environmental characteristics which adversely affect individuals (Beehr, 1976). For example, McGrath (1976) states that the potential for stress exists in any environment in which perceived demands threaten to exceed a person's ability to manage these pressures, and stress grows stronger in situations in which more (i.e., values, goals, welfare) is at stake for the individual.

An alternate view of stress is proposed by Hans Selye (1974), who states that stress is a physical (biological) *reaction* to stressors. He views stress as a non-specific body response to any demand from our environment. Consequently, stress should not be viewed as arising from adverse reactions, but characterizes a reaction or adjustment to *any* event in our lives. It is physical tension which cannot be avoided and does not always result in damage to us. For example, when individuals react to hunger, thirst or sex needs by moving into activity to satisfy these drives, they certainly are not experiencing unfavorable personal physical consequences. Nor would persons successfully meeting professional and personal challenges which require reasonable demands on their capacities and reserves be considered to be adversely stressed. Selye refers to situations such as these as producing *eustress*, a necessary, positive physical reaction which aids individuals in succeeding in daily demands in their lives. However, bodily responses that tax our capacities and reserves (e.g., reactions to loss of loved one, dismissal, reduction in pay, etc.), are characterized by a debilitating reaction, *distress*. It is distress which is cause for concern because it most severely taxes our reserves. This is more graphically apparent when we examine Selye's General Adaptation Syndrome.

General Adaptation Syndrome

The Selye stress response is referred to as the General Adaptation Syndrome (G.A.S.) and is characterized by three stages:

1. Alarm reaction – The body shows strong arousal and its resistance is temporarily diminished.
2. Resistance – As the stressor continues, the body stiffens its resistance and then repairs itself from the impact of the alarm reaction.
3. Exhaustion – If the stressors continue, the body reserves that were installed during the resistance phase are exhausted. The subject now appears to reenter the alarm reaction phase, but cannot terminate the alarm response. Carried to its most extreme, death can ensue. Most often, what happens is that the body physically begins to break down, leading to continued physical problems.

The preceding stages of stress paint a grim picture of a person's inability to cope with pressing demands from the environment, particularly when it is realized that stress in life cannot be avoided. However, humans do not routinely perish from daily demands. An adult faces deadlines, financial responsibilities, job demands, family responsibilities, crowd-pollution, health problems, etc., and rises to challenge these demands, routinely resolving them long before exhaustion is encountered. However, when stress persists, it produces a wide variety of symptoms affecting at least three major dimensions of one's life. These are a person's physical health, psychological well-being, and the development of specific behaviors which are employed when under stress. These aggregate components form the basis of a tripartite model of stress.

Tripartite model. This tripartite model (Pfohl, 1979) of stress (physical, psychological, behavioral/social) would seem to identify three categories of symptoms, which either individually or collectively, must be satisfactorily dealt with to effectively manage pressures.

Physical. When you are placed under stress, a systematic change in physical responses takes place in the body. Each aspect of the change is designed to aid you in effectively surviving an imminent crisis. The logic of the response is straightforward. The body attempts to provide large amounts of oxygen and blood sugar only to those parts of the anatomy necessary to resolve the emergency. Consequently oxygen intake is increased, and blood pressure rises due to increased heart rate and strengthened force of heart contractions as oxygen-rich blood is pumped to critical body areas. Blood vessels on the surface of the skin shrink, and those in muscles dilate, providing needed blood to these structures. Subsequently, muscle tension rises. Blood sugar rises with the stress response, insuring an adequate supply of energy for cells of the body involved in executing the behavior selected for a reaction to the stressful event. Body functions related to food intake, digestion, and elimination of waste are temporarily interrupted as a crisis is dealt with.

Ideally, a stressful situation is promptly resolved and stress declines. Such would be the case if you had just avoided a collision with a car or survived a physical beating. However, in the constantly pressing environment of work, stress frequently persists for extended periods of time. A worker under such pressure might well complain of feeling "tense," occasionally report breathing difficulty (hyperventilation), experience irregularly fast heartbeat symptoms (tachycardia), complain of abnormally cold hands or feet in the winter due to blood redirected from skin areas to muscles, or report stomach or intestinal problems. As you will read shortly, the physical component of stress has high disruptive potential if pressure persists.

Psychological. How you react to a stressful situation depends to an extent on your own personality make up; some individuals clearly seem better equipped to handle pressure than others. However, prolonged stress tends to alter psychological well being. Workers suffering irresolvable stress frequently report such psychological reactions as frustration, anger, dissatisfaction, resentment, feelings of helplessness, impaired problem solving, excessive worry, lowered emotional response, increase in negative thoughts, lowered self-esteem, a reduction in the belief that one's life is under personal control, or depression.

Behavioral/social. Unresolved stress results in our incorporating a variety of behaviors into our lives which affect our relationship with others. Under constant pressure, a line manager might become increasingly aggressive, openly challenging others. Another individual might display frequent anger, impeding his or her interaction with colleagues. However, many persons develop an opposite tack for meeting stressors in their lives by withdrawing from the stressful environment. This withdrawal can take the form of feigned illness, changing employment, or other alternatives which relieve the stress experienced by an individual. Extreme shyness is also seen under stress. Finally, many times maladaptive behaviors are developed to cope with pressure. This tendency may express itself in diverse ways such as skillful "ducking" of responsibility when pressured, the utilization of alcohol or abuse of prescriptive medication to reduce feelings of anxiety, or poor time management resulting in procrastination.

Another aspect to consider is the environment itself. Many times the environment creates stress for individuals by increasing work loads, deadlines, ambiguous job descriptions, and faulty management methods. Other factors to consider are excessive noise, unending routine tasks, phones, interruptions, and lack of communication. (Manuso,

1980). Many environments also have individuals who are "stress carriers." These are individuals who seem immune to stress themselves, but seem to carry stress around with them for everyone else, by starting rumors, delegating responsibility without regard to its consequences, etc.

These three dimensions of stress can be separated from one another for purposes of discussion, but they are frequently interactive. For example, persistent use of alcohol to make life more livable can lead to physical problems as well as psychological difficulties.

STRESS – ITS PHYSICAL EFFECT ON PEOPLE

As stated earlier, no one is immune to stress. Driving all individuals, with no respect for sex, race, or age, pressure produces cumulative effects which can force us to rise to meet challenges or strip us of reserves, producing measurable damages that necessitate professional help. Consider the possible physical impact of prolonged stress. The following is a partial list of disabilities that are either created or can be aggravated by stress:

1. peptic ulcer
2. colitis or ulcerative colitis
3. bronchial asthma
4. dermatitis
5. arthritis, bursitis
6. headaches (a) migraine; cluster (b) tension
7. irregular heart beat
8. excessively fast heart beat
9. many forms of sexual dysfunction
10. insomnia
11. alcoholism
12. hypertension
13. cancer
14. diabetes
15. Raynaud's syndrome

It is very unlikely that you know someone who has *not* experienced one or more of these problems. Many of these maladies strike large percentages of the population (e.g., 30,000,000 people suffer from insomnia; 25,000,000 persons experience hypertension). These disorders are termed psychosomatic since psychological stresses induce debilitating physical conditions and can produce permanent damage if the stresses on the body persist.

The Role of Personality in Stress

Within a work environment many potentially stressful circumstances exist. Some are easily identified (e.g., heavy work load, forced overtime, and tasks that require speed and precision) and others are less obvious (e.g., role ambiguity, role conflict, and communication breakdowns). However, not all individuals working at a given job report feeling stressed by its demands. Stress appears to occur when the characteristics of a worker are incompatible with the demands of the work environment. One important determinant of this "fit" of the worker and his or her environment is the person's personality and attitude toward the job. Perhaps the most discussed personality dimension in recent years is that of Type A and Type B individuals.

Before examining the Type A personality, you are invited to answer the following questions about your personal life:

1. Are you satisfied with your present job?
2. Does your spouse or do your friends see you as hardworking and aggressive?
3. When you play games with friends, do you give it all you're worth?
4. When you play games with children, do you purposely let them win?
5. Do you enjoy competition?
6. Is there competition in you work?
7. Do you usually drive your car just beyond the speed limit?
8. Does it irritate you to be held up by a slower car in front of you?
9. Are there many deadlines in your work? Do you find them exciting?
10. Do you work better against deadlines?
11. Do you get bothered when you see something being done at work slower or more poorly than you think it should be done?
12. Do you attempt to continue to work while eating?
13. Do you eat quickly and get on to other activities?
14. Do you feel you have the time to get everything done you want to?

If you answered "yes" to all questions except #1, 4, and 14, you are a prime candidate for a Type A label. Type A individuals have been defined by Friedman and Rosenman (1974) and Friedman (1969) as persons prone to excessive competitiveness, aggressiveness, possessing a high sense of time urgency, easily provoked impatience, and displaying an overcommitment to their profession. These behavior patterns seem deeply ingrained in a person and persist as enduring traits (Jenkins, 1976). Due to the ambitious, competitive nature of the Type A personality, this person frequently self-selects jobs that impose high exposure to stressors and defines success in terms of extrinsic rewards, such as money, status, or professional recognition, as opposed to working for self-satisfaction or personal interest in the job (Sales, 1969). This individual tends to be perfectionistic and impatient with others who do not meet his or her expectations for performance. When questioned about relationships with colleagues, the Type A prioritizes respect from his colleagues over their friendship. This person frequently creates a mountain of personal tension from moderate workloads by imposing unnecessary rigid timelines and perfectionistic work standards on his or her job. Not surprisingly, the Type A individual is a prime candidate for cardiovascular heart disease (CHD). This person runs twice the risk of clinical coronary disease, is five times as susceptible to a second myocardial infarction, and has twice the rate of fatal heart attacks as does an individual not possessing these personality characteristics (Rosenman, Brand, Jenkins, Friedman, Straus, & Wurm, 1975). When told by a physician to take time away from work to relax and unwind, the Type A person may be found playing golf, pressuring himself to shoot a new personal low score, or running in the park with a stopwatch in his hand. In other words, relaxation is approached with the same competitive, aggressive nature as work.

Type A behavior appears to be more prevalent in men than women; however, it is associated with increased coronary disease in both sexes (Blumenthal, Williams, Kong, Schanberg, & Thompson, 1978; Waldron, 1978). There appears to be a higher incidence of Type A behavior in women who are full-time employed or not employed outside their home, and those who are occupationally successful in the age range of 40 to 59. Typically, these women are not married to high status, successful husbands (Waldron, 1978).

Garfield indicates that the Type A workaholics seldom reach their potential in a corporation. While the sheer volume of work can be valuable to the company, the mounds of detail smother them making them candidates for divorce or cardiac-arrest. Garfield further states "Workaholics are addicted to work, and not results. They work for work's sake and tend not to make a major impact. The workaholic never makes the discovery, writes the position paper or becomes the chief executive officer (Why Workaholics Work, 1981)."

The Type B individual is a study in contrast with a Type A. This person is characterized by easy-going behavior patterns such as a lack of time urgency, selection of work for its ability to provide personal satisfaction, low hostility, realistic goal setting, reflectiveness, future-oriented planning, and the ability to relax and enjoy leisure time. Lazarus (1978) provides a graphic comparison of the two personality types in the following example where two individuals are on a fishing trip together. The Type A has five rods in the water, each of which has two baited hooks. He is constantly checking each. On the other hand, the Type B has one pole in the water and doesn't know (or care) if the bait is still on the hook. He is enjoying the weather and scenery.

Although the Type A and B personalities are discussed as dichotomized categories, seldom does one find pure A's or B's. Frequently an individual will appear to possess Type A characteristics, but these behaviors are situation-specific. That is, the driving, aggressive tendencies displayed in one aspect of the working environment will not generalize to all aspects of one's life. This individual might be characterized an A-B since components of both types are visible.

Stressors – Where Do They Come From?

Since most adults spend approximately half their waking lives in work-related activities, it would benefit us to know how this environment can influence our physical and mental health. Beehr and Newman (1978) provide an excellent overview of job-related stressors organized by job demands, role demands, and organizational characteristics and demands. A sample of these factors is presented below.

Job demands. Pressing work schedules, deadlines, pace of work, difficulty of tasks, high degrees of job responsibility, unwanted overtime, shift work, travel within a job, and distractions such as meetings and phone calls are all examples of job-related stresses.

Role demands. In satisfactorily performing one's job, it is expected that an individual will meet the requirements of a position in a manner satisfactory to the employer. When a specific position demands more of a person than can be provided by background or expertise, that person suffers from *role overload*. Such would be the case in a work environment where role demands shifted transiently, such as that experienced by the air traffic controller in early morning, or a bank teller just prior to closing each day. A related problem is role underload, in which the demands of a job are minimal, leaving the worker with little or nothing to do. Job dissatisfaction as well as boredom and inefficiency are common in this circumstance. Even if the individual provides a good "fit" for a role, the possibility exists of experiencing *role conflict*. Such would be the case if a middle management person were asked to satisfy two superiors, each of which possessed different management objectives. In an attempt to satisfy one superior, the manager would meet one set of goals and suffer the wrath of the other boss. A foreman might feel similar pressures when attempting to meet company demands for increased productivity and labor demands to maintain current employee requirements.

Few elements of a job produce as much stress as *role ambiguity*. This label implies either a lack of clarity in what is required to satisfactorily perform a given task or inadequate feedback to determine the quality of one's work. Kahn, Wolf, Quinn, Snock, and Rosenthal (1964) report that men who worked in conditions of role ambiguity experienced lower job satisfaction, higher employment-related tension, and reduced self-confidence. French and Caplan (1970) report similar findings for a sample of aerospace engineers, scientists, and administrators.

Ambiguity is also found in the complexity of large organizations in which managers might understand the requirements for their specific roles but cannot determine their departments' interrelationship with others. This problem is further compounded when an organization is in rapid change, either expanding or contracting. In each case, roles frequently change with major reorganization forcing subsequent readjustment by employees dependent upon organizational characteristics.

Organizational characteristics. The specific structure of a job and the company for which one works will determine organizational stressors for an individual. It appears important for the employee to affect the organization. Margolis, Kross, and Quinn (1974) report that nonparticipation of managers in the decision-making process in a corporation is the most significant factor in producing job-related stress. Nonparticipation was found to be significantly related to overall reduced physical health, problem drinking, depression, lowered self-esteem, reduced life and job satisfaction, intentions to leave present jobs, and increased levels of absenteeism from work. Additionally, employees who feel that they cannot communicate openly with superiors, peers, and those over whom they have responsibility are higher stress candidates than those employees who work in an atmosphere of openness (French & Caplan, 1970). If an individual is working in a corporate environment in which there is distrust among colleagues and poor social support from superiors, that person typically reports high levels of role ambiguity (Kahn et al., 1964).

Dual careers. Today's employment patterns for couples reflect changing life styles as husbands and wives, spurred on by economic necessity and personal needs for professional growth, both opt for careers. Faced with choices between career, home, and children, these couples are selecting life styles and goals which differ significantly from the traditional pattern of the male single wage earner who provides for his homemaker wife and children. With the exception of the unique "two person career," in which one member possesses a high profile position which requires his spouse to provide public support for his career (e.g., politicians, ministers, etc), most dual careers constitute individualized professional fields for each person. Often in dual careers, both adults suffer overload, particularly if children are present in the family, because the combined demands of home and work become excessive. Successful adjustment to dual career demands seems tied to several factors (Hall & Hall, 1980). They are:

1. Children – Couples with no children in the household experience less stress than those with children at home.
2. Professional Development – Couples at different stages of professional development in which the more advanced partner is feeling successful, suffer less stress than couples in different styles of development with a dissatisfied advanced partner (e.g., a husband feeling stagnant at a high professional level may resent his wife's rapid rise at lower levels).
3. Professional Fields – Couples in related professional fields experience less stress than do those individuals working in jobs in which there are no common interests.
4. Mutual Support – Perhaps the most important factor in controlling stress for working

couples is their ability to provide mutual support for each other in their work and home activities. This includes a willingness to adjust life styles to share household responsibilities and provide mutual respect for each other's professional involvement.

Marriages with one partner working. In many marriages involving males in managerial positions, a "hidden contract" exists between the man and woman in which the wife agrees to act as a support team for her husband as he attempts to fulfill his career aspirations. Handy (1975) suggests that this is a typical marital pattern and a necessary condition for managerial success. When the spouse fails to provide the domestic support to her husband, stress arises which spills over into the working environment. Common to these couples are frequent relocations as the husband climbs the corporate ladder. Constant moving has a pronounced psychological effect on their life style, frequently resulting in the "mobility syndrome," in which individuals treat their environment as temporary, refuse to become involved in local community activities, and orient themselves toward the present, rather than the future. Such people develop a facade of "instant friendliness" which allows them to superficially interact with their present location (Packard, 1975). It should be noted that the wife invariably draws the brunt of the stress of relocation since she is expected to quickly recreate the stable household within which the relocated employee can find security as he seeks to resolve role ambiguity and conflict in his new job. As might be expected, single employees feel much more stressed in their personal lives during relocation than do married employees (Marshall & Cooper, 1976), since no partner is available to provide constancy of stimulus conditions.

Stresses of the single parent. With divorce rates at all time highs, many individuals with children are finding themselves faced with fulfilling both the breadwinner and homemaker role. This situation poses unique stresses as the single parent attempts to coordinate a job, the children's school activities, scouts, music lessons, sports, clothing purchases, and vacations. Time, money, and privacy are frequently this person's most elusive commodities. Clearly, the potential for stress in this circumstance is high.

Other stressors. No attempt to identify job-related stressors can be confined solely to the working environment because all outside stressors interact with the demands of a professional position. Any attempt to itemize all outside stressors could result in an endless list of factors; however, notable recurring stressors are financial concerns, marital problems, difficulties with children, incurred illness or injury, loss of sleep, excessive coffee, poor diet, lack of exercise, and lack of meaningful leisure activities.

OVERCOMING STRESS

Recognition that one is under stress is a necessary first step toward managing it, however, most individuals who seek help for stress-related problems lack any real insight into the specifics of the stress-causing elements in their environment. They are unaware of (or ignore) the cues that trigger their stress responses. Any successful stress management program must aid persons in identifying specific physical, psychological, and behavioral signs of a stress response within themselves and also locate the cues within their environments which precipitate these responses. Then, and only then, can an intervention strategy be proposed to reduce stresses to an optimum level. Please note that a stress management program does not attempt to eliminate all stress response to a person's environment. If that were done, an individual would have pulled the physical and psychological plug on himself, creating an unproductive unemotional organism. Rather, what is intended in a stress management program is to adjust one's physical, psychological and behavioral response to stress to an optimum level for healthy personal and professional productivity.

Stressors – How to Identify Them

At any given moment, you are forced to cope with a variety of stressful events, some temporary, and others recurring daily. Major life stressors can be assessed by means of the Holmes and Rahe (1967) Social Readjustment Rating Scale (SRRS).

This chart includes major and minor social life changes events that force readjustment. Note that stressful events need not be negative dimensions of one's life. Marriage, birth of a child (not the childbirth itself), promotion, etc., all impose substantial stress on the persons involved in these events. Take the time to total the points associated with events in your life in the prior twelve months. If your total exceeds 150 points you run a 50/50 risk of experiencing some form of stress-related illness in the next year. If your total exceeds 300 points, your risk rises accordingly. Approximately 70% of individuals who score in this range report resultant illness.

The SRRS has enjoyed considerable success with the public and has been modified for use with unique populations of individuals. One such form allows college students to assess stressors in their environment. Students who scored in the high range reported high incidents of pimples, rashes, chest pains, and headaches. The reader is cautioned, however, to recognize that, regardless of stressors in a person's life, an individual's personal susceptibility to illness will be affected by predisposing factors such as long-established behavior patterns and physical resistance toward stress which raise or lower personal risks.

Handling Daily Hassles

While major life crises are clearly identifiable, day-to-day stress poses more of an obstacle to each of us. To master daily hassles, such as those found in a work environment, requires pinpointing sources of stress in that environment and determining our specific reactions to those stresses. This can be accomplished by the A-B-C method suggested by the Rutgers *Handbook of Techniques for Dealing with Stress* (Galano, Carr-Kaffashan, Etten, Lehrer, & Rothberg, 1978) which was adapted from Ellis' rational emotive therapy approach (Ellis & Harper, 1975). The *A* represents *antecedent* conditions which represent the stressor, *B* is your *behavior*, and *C* represents the *consequence* or bodily sensations and emotional reactions which are faced when the stressful situation is encountered.

A – the first step. When you begin to understand the events which precede such feeling as anxiety, tension, anger, or helplessness, you are taking the first step toward stress management. Feelings have a meaningful context in your life. You need to determine that context. Answers to questions such as, "What was the specific date of the stress?" "What time of day did it occur?", and "Where was I and what was I doing?" begin to provide specifics in our minds where ambiguity had previously existed.

B – thoughts and actions. Thoughts and actions provide the mediation between the stressful circumstances and the resultant bodily consequences. These interpretations of the stressful events must be accurately assessed to manage stress. Quite often our appraisal of a situation may not reliably represent the actual event. This is an important fact because our emotional response will be based upon our appraisal, not on the external event itself. Questions to be answered here are: (1) What was I expecting to happen? (2) What images or memories were called up? (3) What worries, concerns, or doubts come to mind? (4) What was I saying to myself? (5) Are certain core beliefs relevant to this situation?

TABLE 12.1. Stress Ratings of Various Life Events*

Events	Scale of Impact
Death of spouse	100
Divorce	73
Marital separation	65
Jail term	63
Death of close family member	63
Personal injury or illness	53
Marriage	50
Fired at work	47
Marital reconciliation	45
Retirement	45
Change in health of family member	44
Pregnancy	40
Sex difficulties	39
Gain of new family member	39
Business readjustment	39
Change in financial state	38
Death of close friend	37
Change to different line of work	36
Change in number of arguments with spouse	35
Mortgage over $10,000	31
Foreclosure of mortgage or loan	30
Change in responsibilities at work	29
Son or daughter leaving home	29
Trouble with in-laws	29
Outstanding personal achievement	28
Wife begins or stops work	26
Begin or end school	26
Change in living conditions	25
Revision of personal habits	24
Trouble with boss	23
Change in work hours or conditions	20
Change in residence	20
Change in schools	20
Change in recreation	19
Change in church activities	19
Change in social activities	18
Mortgage or loan less than $10,000	17
Change in sleeping habits	16
Change in number of family get-togethers	15
Change in eating habits	15
Vacation	13
Christmas	12
Minor violations of the law	11

*Adapted from Holmes, T. S., & Holmes, T. H. Short-term Intrusions into life style routine. *Journal of Psychosomatic Research.* 1970. *14*, 121–132. Reprinted with permission of Pergamon Press, Ltd. Copyright © 1970 by Pergamon Press, Ltd.

C – body sensations and emotional reactions. In this phase of the program, you attempt to define the severity and nature of your reaction. Are you nervous? Shaky? Do you have sweaty palms? What words best describe the specific characteristics of your response?

An alternative way to chart daily stresses and their impact on you is the plotting of these events on paper. This instrument can be easily constructed with nothing more than a ruler and a piece of graph paper. At equal intervals along a horizontal line at the bottom of the page write down the hours in your waking day. Now draw a vertical line at the far left of your horizontal line and number it between zero and 100 beginning at the bottom. This scale represents the intensity of your symptoms when stressed; where *zero* reflects the least intensity of the symptom that you have ever experienced and *100* represents the most intensity. This measurement device, frequently called the Subject Units of Discomfort Scale (SUDS), can be used to plot your daily routines, noting the specific circumstances surrounding your stress and your SUDS rating of its intensity (Goldfried & Davison, 1976). Look at the following example:

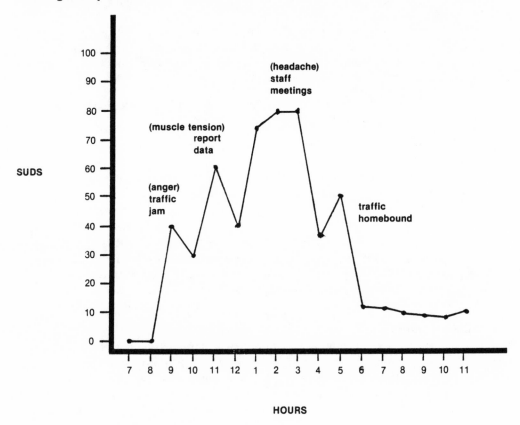

Fig. 12.1. An Example of Daily SUDS Levels.

The purpose in logging and charting the specific details of external events and internal thoughts which surround an emotional response is to create a clear picture of the relationship between antecedent events and resultant behavior. When an intervention program is undertaken to reduce stress, either or both events can be modified. Effective coping can alter the external stressful environment, change cognitive processes which trigger negative emotional reactions or restructure the behavioral response to avoid an aversive reaction.

COPING – HOW TO OVERCOME YOUR PROBLEM

When you are pressured by work or personal matters, what do you do to relieve tension? In other words, how do you cope? Perhaps you tend to talk to yourself, goading yourself into action. Many different modes of behavior are seen in people under stress as they try to manage their pressures. Note the use of the term *manage* here. Coping is managing stress, not mastering it. Additionally coping does not always result in healthy outcomes for its users. In a general sense, you can develop good coping techniques and bad ones.

The bad coper. The diversity of bad coping styles is too broad to describe. However, consider some of the following behaviors that are commonly seen when people are pressured.

Behavioral/social. Increases in smoking, drinking, abuse of medication such as tranquilizers or amphetamines, overeating, avoidance of a stressful task by engaging in low priority, nonstressful jobs, etc.

These behaviors become established in a person's behavioral repertoire because they lead to reduction of the physical signs of stress (e.g., drugs, alcohol, smoking) or remove the individual from the environmental demands which are stressful (e.g., low priority work requires attention to nonthreatening external events).

Psychological. Angry confrontation, disengagement in which you opt for isolation to avoid the stress, denial of your stress ("I have no problem here!") etc.

Effective coping. Good copers engage in actions that improve their relationship with a stressful event. This person: (1) attempts to anticipate potential stressors before encountering them and prepares appropriate plans of attack for the various outcomes, frequently rehearsing each strategy, (2) reduces physical arousal when the stressor is encountered by separating the facts from emotions. (You might engage in intellectualization, treating the situation as if you were an outside observer or utilize a physical relaxation process to calm bodily turmoil), and (3) increases positive feelings under stressful conditions. You will find it almost impossible to display physical signs of stress when you see humor in a situation. We know of one person who, when engaged in disagreements with his boss, routinely creates images of that person standing naked in a crowd carrying on an emotional tirade. This personally relieves his tension and allows him to deal more rationally with his superior.

Psychological coping

Problem solving. When individuals are confronted with stressful situations for which no effective response alternatives are immediately available, they must satisfactorily generate solutions which result in discovery of responses or patterns of responses that can alter the stressful events, maximizing positive consequences and minimizing negative ones (D'Zurilla & Goldfried, 1971). A systematic approach such as the following can facilitate the problem solving task:

1. Clearly define your problem. Employ the A-B-C method described earlier to help pinpoint your stressor and stress response.
2. List all the alternatives that could potentially resolve the problem.
3. Carefully assess the strengths and weaknesses of each alternative, considering each one at a time.
4. Choose one alternative and implement it in the stress situation.
5. Evaluate your outcome. Did you achieve the end result you desired? If not, repeat the procedure, taking care to insure that you have adequately defined your problem. (This is where most people have difficulty defining what is wrong.)

Cognitive restructuring. A recurring topic in conferences on stress has been the major impact of cognitive factors in the experience and control of stress. McGrath (1970) has noted that a person's emotional, physiological, and behavioral reactions are partially due to perceptions, expectations, or cognitive appraisals made of the stressful situation. Numerous researchers have noted that subjects will respond with a broad array of different responses to stimuli that are objectively identical (Ax, 1964; Glass & Singer, 1972; Schachter, 1966). Clearly, some factors other than the characteristics of the physical stimulus influence judgements concerning external events. Meichenbaum (1975) proposes that the mediating factors are cognitive in nature and can be conceptualized as specific sets of self-statements that an individual makes when encountering these external events. Presuming that a person's self statements lead to emotional reactions considered undesirable, it is feasible to train that individual to modify this self-talk. Meichenbaum suggests that an intervention program should identify self-statements which exacerbate the adverse emotional reactions, and train an individual to substitute positive statements in the place of negative ones.

To accomplish this goal, Meichenbaum and Cameron (1972) suggest a stress inoculation procedure which utilizes the following steps.

1. Educate the anxious person as to the specific characteristics of that individual's fear. This would include pinpointing specific physical arousal symptoms, such as increased heart rate, respiration increase, sweaty palms, etc., as well as identifying negative thoughts and self-statements.
2. The person is then taught several coping skills which could be employed to reduce physiological arousal. These skills are extensively rehearsed so that they are readily available when stress is encountered.
3. The individual then practices positive self-statements which might prove useful when confronted by stressful circumstances. Typically, these statements encourage a person to look rationally at a situation; control negative, anxiety provoking thoughts; acknowledge and use anxiety which is experienced; "psych" oneself up to perform under pressure; cope with potentially overwhelming levels of anxiety; and reinforce oneself for successful coping.
4. These skills are then tested under stressful conditions. In Meichenbaum and Cameron's program, clients are exposed to random one-second electrical shocks, ranging in intensity between .5 MA and 3 MA. Their clients would try various physical relaxation techniques and positive self-statements which maximized their anxiety reduction. The net effect of such stress inoculation training has been the production of individuals who are significantly better at managing anxiety in their lives.

Communication

Consider your reactions when challenged in a discussion with a superior at work. You need to bring to bear your maximum verbal and nonverbal communication abilities and appropriately assert your position. As tension rises, you might find the stress you experience hindering this communication. A few specific skills would help here. As confrontation occurs, you may find yourself making statements about the other person. While you attempt to remain objective in your comments, most likely accusations and rebuttals will occur as tempers flare. A first suggestion toward more effective communication is to state your feelings to the other person. This may prove difficult. Are you angry, hurt, annoyed, happy, disgusted? Try to verbally label this emotion and communicate it. Then be as specific as possible and describe your observations and perceptions. Avoid suppositions and guesses about the other person's motives and behaviors and attacking them personally. To facilitate this communication, try to initiate the conversation with a statement about your desire to resolve the conflict. For example, you might approach a colleague who has been negatively discussing your work when you were not present by saying, "John, I have a problem that I would like to resolve with you so that we can continue to work well together. I am angry with you for your derogatory statements about my work when I am not present."

An additional key to effective communication is listening. Most certainly, the content of what is being communicated is important, but equally so is the feeling or emotion behind the content. Listen to the other person's mood. When you realize the feelings behind the speaker's words, you may be less upset by the objective content. If you were to hear a person who is working under you refuse to carry out an assignment, his or her motivation might be one of fear of the task. In such a case, you might react differently than had the mood behind the refusal been one of defiance or indifference. Before engaging in a lengthy monologue, sense the position of the other person.

Asserting yourself. In any working environment you have certain rights and privileges to which you are entitled. When engaged in conflict, these rights may be challenged. When you actively and appropriately defend your ideas, opinions, feelings, and needs, you are asserting yourself. If you are deficient in this skill area, consider that the assertive person:

1. is able to express both positive and negative feelings (e.g., "Your report was excellent" or "Your production unit is not meeting its quarterly goals, you need to provide closer supervision.")
2. can make direct requests of others, is able to refuse others' requests if they are not desired, and can begin and end a conversation (e.g., "Mary, would you stay late so that we can catch up on those management reports?" or "I'm sorry, John, I can't do that this evening, even though I know you are pushed by a dealine. I have another commitment that I can't reschedule" or "Bill, I am pushed for time today so I can't talk longer. Can I call you later?")
3. speaks openly and directly, making eye contact with the other person.
4. speaks loudly and clearly enough to be understood by the other person. His non-verbal cues (facial expressions, postures, etc.) are consistent with his verbal content.
5. selects an appropriate time to assert his feelings and accepts assertiveness from the other person without adverse reaction.

If you would like to assess situations in which you feel you could be more assertive, see Gambrill and Richey's assertiveness inventory in *Behavior Therapy* (1975). (See Lange and Jakubowski, 1977, and Jakubowski and Lange, 1979, for further information.)

Time Management

Sometimes it appears that the more we do, the more there is to be done. This observation seems equally valid in a school environment or at work. What are the signs that time is getting away from you? Examine the following questions.

1. Do you chronically rush?
2. Do you frequently vascillate between unpleasant alternatives?
3. Do you find yourself physically and emotionally drained with many slack hours of non-productive activity?
4. Are you chronically late on deadlines?
5. Do you feel overwhelmed by demands and details?
6. Do you feel you are constantly doing unpleasant tasks?
7. Do you find that you don't have time for rest or personal relationships?

If your answers to these questions are yes, your problem may be one of time management. Here are several suggestions for coping with time demands.

1. Establish daily priorities listed in a "to do" format. Then keep a daily log of what you accomplish.
2. Realistically schedule or eliminate low priority tasks.
3. Estimate your completion time realistically. (In most cases, figure your completion time and double that figure.)
4. Learn to say "NO!" to new, nonessential tasks. (See the assertiveness training section for a guide to doing this.)
5. Delegate low priority items. (Do you really *have* to open your mail or could a secretary do it?)
6. Cut down on socializing time.
7. Try getting up one-half hour earlier.
8. Stop trying for perfection on every task. Ask yourself, "Is it necessary?" [Davis, Eshelman, & McKay, 1980].

Do you procrastinate? Procrastination is a double-edged sword which occurs time and time again in most of our lives. When faced with an unpleasant task, you delay tackling it. In most cases, you are not objectively considering the impact of procrastination. If you delay a job, ask yourself the following questions:

1. Am I creating more unpleasantness for myself by delaying? Won't I have to rush to complete it when it *has* to be done?
2. Why am I delaying? Am I afraid of failure?

If you are answering "yes," then seek ways to overcome your procrastination. Perhaps one of the following suggestions would help: (1) *Assume responsibility for the delay.* Tell yourself, "I'm wasting time." Make a list of your procrastinations. How long did it take you to complete it? Are you surprised at how many there were? (2) *Make decisions now.* Don't put them off. (3) If you can't face a large, unpleasant task, divide it into a series of smaller ones and work toward them sequentially, completing one at a time. This is a subtle coercion of yourself, but is effective. (4) Finish the task. Don't begin a new job until you have completed the one you are on. Decision-making and action are rewarded by successful completion of tasks.

Reducing Physical Tension

While the previous suggestions may help in dealing with psychological and behavioral aspects of stress, you still may be confronted with a rash of physical symptoms from stress. What are the most appropriate means of reducing muscle aches, chest pains, throbbing head, or blotchy skin? A variety of alternatives are available. All are designed to bring about that balanced physical state known as homeostasis, in which the body may optimally operate.

Active involvement techniques. If you are a sports enthusiast, keep up your activity. *Make time* for involvement in activities such as tennis, golf, racquetball, swimming, walking, jogging, or running. However, use discretion when deciding how much activity you can tolerate for your present health and conditioning. The right amount of exercise is excellent; excessive exercise can be dangerous, particularly if you have neglected your conditioning for some time. *Avoid* setting demanding goals and schedules. It is supposed to be relaxing. Mental games, such as chess, backgammon, cards, can be relaxing as well.

Palliative techniques. Many programs for relaxation have become available to the public in the past several years. Progressive relaxation programs such as those suggested by Jacobsen (1938) teach systematic relaxation of muscle groups in the body, helping you to develop skills to reproduce these relaxed states on command. Transcendental meditation techniques similarly allow you to block out external stressors and produce a body state conducive for relaxation by repeating a word or sound (mantra) without specifically concentrating on it. Benson's Relaxation Response (1974) suggests a technique in which a person either repeats a word or fixes his gaze on an object, while maintaining a passive attitude and ignoring external intrusions. This is accomplished while sitting comfortably in a manner which minimizes demands on muscles, and in a room which provides very few environmental distractions. Such an approach, practiced for short periods of time, leads to a significant reduction of tension for many persons.

The final training technique to be suggested is that of biofeedback. Since its inception in the 1960s, the use of biofeedback to manage stress has continued to expand. This technique accomplishes stress management in a straightforward way. It operates under the premise that you are basically unaware of the internal body states that signify tension and relaxation. If you were given a clear indication of when you were reducing tension, then you could reproduce that pattern of bodily actions in the future. For example, an electromyograph (EMG) provides you with a tone which changes frequency or a dial which shifts when you relax. Your task in biofeedback is to identify the body cues which accompany this relaxation. The best success often occurs when combined with a relaxation method.

SUMMARY

This concludes our brief overview of stress management. We would like to reemphasize several points in summary:

1. Stress is an individual matter. What stresses you may not stress another person. It can be a positive as well as negative aspect of your life.
2. Stress is multifaceted. It can cause physical, psychological, and behavioral problems.
3. The key to stress management is clearly identifying your stresses and your responses to them.
4. Implement a program of management that deals with all aspects of the stressful situation. Change the stressful environment if possible. If not, alter your response to it. Your goal is to control and use stress to help you, not to eliminate or escape from it.
5. Organize your life in such a way that you have time for your job, friends, family, and leisure. You owe it to yourself to enjoy life.

REFERENCES

Atlanta Constitution, February 7, 1975, p. 1.
Ax, A. Goals and methods of psychophysiology. *Psychophysiology*, 1964, **1**, 8-25.
Beehr, T. A. Perceived situational moderators of the relationship between subjective role ambiguity and role strain. *Journal of Applied Psychology*, 1976, **61**, 35-40.
Benson, H. *The relaxation response*. New York: Avon Books, 1974.

Blumenthal, J. A., Williams, R., Kong, Y., Schanberg, S. M., & Thompson, L. W. Type A behavior and angiographically documented coronary disease. *Circulation*, 1978, **58,** 634-639.

Davis, M., Eshelman, E., & McKay, M. *The relaxation and stress reduction workbook*. Richmond, CA.: New Harbenger Publications, 1980.

D'Zurilla, T. J., & Goldfried, M. R. Problem solving and behavior modification. *Journal of Abnormal Psychology*, 1971, **78** (1), 107-126.

Ellis, A., & Harper, R. A. *A new guide to rational living*. Englewood Cliffs, N.J.: Prentice-Hall, 1975.

Galano, J., Carr-Kaffashan, L., Etten, M., Lehrer, P., & Rothberg, M. *Handbook of techniques for dealing with stress*. JSAS, 1978, Manuscript 1730.

Friedman, M. D. *Pathogenesis of coronary artery disease*. New York: McGraw-Hill, 1969.

Friedman, M. D., & Rosenman, R. H. *Type A behavior and your heart*. New York: Knopf, 1974.

French, J. R. P., Jr., & Caplin, R. D. Psychosocial factors in coronary heart disease. *Industrial Medicine and Surgery*, 1970, **39,** 383-397.

Gambrill, E., & Richey, C. An assertion inventory for use in assessment and research. *Behavior Therapy*, 1975, **6,** 550-561.

Glass, D., & Singer, J. Behavioral aftereffects of unpredictable and uncontrollable aversive events. *American Scientist*, 1972, **60,** 457-465.

Goldfried, M., & Davison, G. *Clinical behavior therapy*. New York: Holt, Rinehart, and Winston, 1976.

Greenwood, J., & Greenwood, J. *Managing executive stress*. New York: John Wiley and Sons, 1979.

Hall, D. T., & Hall, F. S. Stress and the two-career couple. In Cooper, C. L., and Payne, R. (Eds.), *Current concerns in occupational stress*. New York: Wiley, 1980.

Handy, C. Difficulties of combining family and career. *The Times* (London) Sept. 22, 1975, p. 16.

Holmes, T. H., & Rahe, R. H. The social readjustment rating scale. *Journal of Psychosomatic Research*, 1967, **11,** 213, 218.

Jacobsen, J. E. *Progressive relaxation: A physiological and clinical investigation of muscle states and their significance in psychological and medical practice*. Chicago: University of Chicago Press, 1938.

Jakubowski, P. & Lange, A. *The assertive option: your rights and responsibilities*. Champaign, Ill.: Research Press, 1978.

Jenkins, C. D., Zyzanski, S. J., & Rosenman, R. H. Risk of new myocardial infarction in middleaged men with manifest coronary heart disease. *Circulation*, 1976, **53,** 342-347.

Kahn, R. L., Wolfe, D. M., Quinn, R. P., Snock, J. D., & Rosenthal, R. A. *Organizational stress: Studies in role conflict and ambiguity*. New York: Wiley, 1964.

Lange, A., & Jakubowski, P. *Responsible assertive behavior: cognitive/behavioral procedures for trainers*. Champaign, Ill.: Research Press, 1976.

Lazarus, R. Coping with stress: effects on somatic illness, morale, and social functioning. New York: *Biomonitoring* Applications, Inc., 1978.

Manuso, J. *Stress management training in large organizations*. Workshop presented for Biofeedback Society of America, Atlanta, GA, May 1980.

Margolis, B. L., Kross, W. H., & Quinn, R. P. Job stress: An unlisted occupational hazard, *Journal of Occupational Medicine*, 1974, **16,** 659-661.

Marshall, J., & Cooper, C. L. The mobile manager and his wife. *Management Decision*, 1976, **14,** 179-225.

McGrath, J. (Ed.) *Social and psychological factors in stress*. New York: Holt, Rinehart, and Winston, 1970.

McGrath, J. E. Stress and behavior in organizations. In M. Dunnette (Ed.), *Handbook of industrial and organizational psychology*. Chicago: Rand McNally, 1976.

Meichenbaum, D. A self-instructional approach to stress management: A proposal for stress inoculation training. In C. Spielberger and I. Sarasan (Eds.), *Stress and Anxiety*. Vol. I. Washington, D.C.: Hemisphere Publishing, 1975.

Meichenbaum, D., & Cameron, R. Stress inoculation: *A skills training approach to anxiety management*. Unpublished manuscript, University of Waterloo, Ontario, 1972.

Packard, V. *A nation of strangers*. New York: McKay, 1975.

Pelletier, K. *Mind as healer, mind as a slayer: a holistic approach to preventing stress disorders.* New York: Dell Publishing Co., 1977.

Pfohl, W. Children's anxiety management program: a broad-based behavioral program teaching children to cope with stress and anxiety. (Doctoral dissertation, Rutgers-The State University, 1979). *Dissertation Abstracts International,* 1979, **40,** 7 3905-A, (University Microfilms No. 8002178).

Rosenman, R. H., Brand, R. J., Jenkins, S., Friedman, M., Straus, R., & Wurm, M. Coronary heart disease in the Western Collaborative Group Study: Final follow-up experience of 8½ years. *Journal of the American Medical Association,* 1975, **233,** 872-877.

Rosenman, R., & Friedman, M. Neurogenic factors in pathogenesis of coronary heart disease. *Medical Clinics of North America,* 1974, **58,** 269-279.

Sales, S. M. Organizational role as a risk factor in coronary disease. *Administration Science Quarterly,* 1969, **14,** 325-336.

Schachter, S. The interaction of cognitive and physiological determinants of emotional states. In C. Spielberger (Ed.), *Anxiety and behavior.* New York: Academic Press, 1966.

Selye, H. *Stress without distress.* New York: Lippincott, 1974.

Waldron, I. The coronary-prone behavior pattern, blood pressure, employment, socioeconomic status in women. *Journal of Psychosomatic Research,* 1978, **22,** 79-87.

Why workaholics work. *Newsweek,* April 27, 1981, p. 71.

13

Motivation of Preventive Maintenance Performance

Judi Komaki and Robert L. Collins
Georgia Institute of Technology

The benefits of preventive maintenance (PM) have been widely acknowledged in both civilian and military settings (Higgins & Morrow, 1977). In firms where downtime is expensive, preventing equipment breakdowns becomes crucial. In military settings, maintenance plays a significant role in operational readiness. Unless equipment is kept in satisfactory operating condition, mobilization efforts will be severely impaired. Preventive maintenance also plays an important role in ensuring the safety of workers and consumers. Just how critical PM practices can be was illustrated in a recent airline crash purportedly caused by a failure in preventive maintenance ("Up, Up, and Away," 1979).

UNIQUE NATURE OF PM AND RESULTING DIFFICULTIES

Although preventive maintenance is readily acknowledged as important, the unique nature of maintenance makes it difficult to ensure that it is done in a timely and regular manner. Several characteristics of PM work set it apart from the typical production line job. First, there is no tangible product. Inspected vehicles look virtually the same as uninspected ones. Second, its effects are delayed. Evidence of maintenance neglect often does not surface for months or even years. Because PM efforts are invisible and its effects are delayed, it is difficult to measure it accurately.

The lack of a sensitive, ongoing, and accurate index of PM practices has significant implications. When no one can judge whether maintenance is done or not, it automatically takes lower priority than other more visible tasks. PM activities, for example, are among the first to be dropped from already packed schedules.

Moreover, favorable consequences are rarely provided when it is difficult to determine when, how, and if persons are performing maintenance. There is little recognition on a day-to-day basis, and it is rarely noted on formal appraisals. At the same time it is also difficult to rectify omissions. It is difficult to motivate personnel when they have reason to believe that it makes little difference whether they perform one way or the other.

*This research was supported by the Organizational Effectiveness Research Program, Office of Naval Research (Code 452), under Contract No. N00014-79-C-0011; NR170-8818-25-78 (Judi Komaki, Principal Investigator). Many thanks to Drs. Hayles and King and Col. Clark, Office of Naval Research, Arlington, Virginia; Lt. Col. Shaw, Development Center, Quantico, Virginia; Lt. Col. Noland, Lt. Cols. Browning and Mikkelson, Camp Lejeune, Jacksonville, North Carolina; Majs. Chacto, Herman, and McCulley (Ret.), Jacksonville, North Carolina; and Ms. Hutcheson and Dr. DeCurtis, Georgia Institute of Technology, Atlanta, Georgia.

In addition to being invisible, delayed, and difficult to monitor and motivate, maintenance is relentless. That is, it must be done regularly. *The challenge becomes one of designing a system for an area, with few immediate or dramatic effects, that needs to be done week in and week out.*

STATE OF THE ART

A review of the PM literature reveals few documented ways to ensure that maintenance is done in a regular and timely fashion. Many PM reports deal with cost issues, such as the relative benefits of replacing or repairing equipment (e.g., Corder, 1976; Knight, 1977; Mc-Carty & Moore, 1977; Wilkinson, 1968). Although this information is certainly important, it does not directly address the problem facing persons in charge, i.e., how to guarantee that maintenance is, in fact, done.

Short shrift is given to worker motivation when attempts are made to improve PM practices. Typically, the emphasis is on training programs and employee scheduling systems. Numerous reports describe PM training programs (e.g., Biersner, 1975; Carpenter-Huffman & Rostker, 1976; Smith, 1961), discuss how to set up training (e.g., Hora, 1978; Johnson & Storr, 1977), or examine reference materials (e.g., Foley, 1976; Post, 1975; Shriver, 1975). The focus of another large group of reports is scheduling, in which forms are described outlining what task is being completed by which worker during what time slot (e.g., Hannon, 1977; Murphy, 1977). The assumption is that if management can train employees thoroughly enough and can structure work schedules efficiently, maintenance will be ensured (e.g., Drake, Goto, & Crooks, 1979; Schwartz, 1976).

Other evidence, however, suggests that even if employees know what to do and when to do it, they may not be motivated to perform (Pierce & Risley, 1974; Quilitch, 1975). A recent comparison of training and feedback (Komaki, Heinzmann, & Lawson, 1980) found that on-the-job performance improved only slightly when employees were trained. Not until feedback was provided did performance improve significantly. It was concluded that more attention should be devoted to the provision of consequences for desired performance. *While proper training is essential, it is also important that the proper motivational environment be established so that personnel actually do on the job what they have been trained to do.*

POTENTIAL OF THE BEHAVIOR ANALYSIS APPROACH

The behavior analysis approach is a particularly suitable strategy for facilitating preventive maintenance for three reasons. First, the emphasis of the behavioral approach is on making meaningful improvements in actual settings. The approach has been demonstrated to be effective in a variety of work settings (see the recent review by Andrasik, Heimberg, & McNamara [in press]).

Second, the behavioral approach focuses on the consequences of performance as a source of motivation. Consequences ranging from nonmonetary reinforcers, such as feedback, to activity reinforcers, such as time off, have been arranged following desired performance. The first author and her associates, for instance, successfully used the behavioral approach to improve safety in two industrial sites in the private and public sectors (Komaki, Barwick, & Scott, 1978; Komaki, Heinzmann, & Lawson, 1980). Following the specification and communication of desired performance, employees were reinforced by feedback

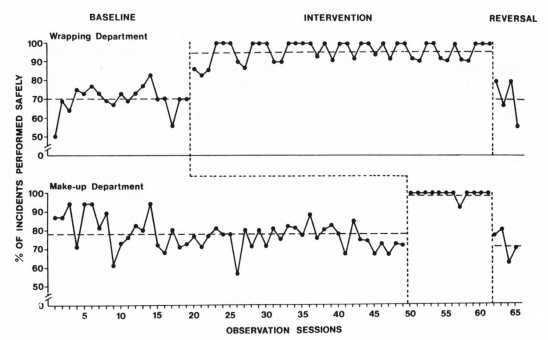

Fig. 13.1. Results of a Behavioral Safety Program Introduced in Two Food Manufacturing Departments.

Source: From "A behavioral approach to occupational safety: Pinpointing and reinforcing safe performance in a food manufacturing plant" by J. Komaki, K. D. Barwick, and L. R. Scott, *Journal of Applied Psychology*, 1978, **63**, 434-445. Copyright 1978 by American Psychological Association. Reprinted by permission.

indicating their level of desired behaviors several times a week. The results were successful in both increasing safe practices on the job (Figure 13.1) and reducing accidents.

Third, measurement techniques of the behavioral approach make it possible to analyze areas that traditionally have not been investigated in depth (Komaki, Collins, & Thoene, 1980). The first author and her associates have designed measurement systems to reflect such elusive and uncharted areas as customer service in a retail merchandising firm (Komaki, Collins, & Temlock, 1980) and the quality of care in hospital emergency rooms (described in Komaki, Collins, & Thoene, 1980). These measurement systems were direct and frequent: performance was assessed on the job by trained observers at least once a week. They were objective: desired practices were defined and redefined until two persons, recording independently, agreed with one another a substantial amount (80-100%) of the time. These behavioral measurement systems, therefore, not only helped clarify desired practices but also provided direct, objective information about the level of service – two prerequisites to improving and maintaining performance. For a further description of behavioral measures and the steps involved in developing the present measurement system, refer to Komaki, Collins, and Thoene (1980).

Although there had been no demonstrations of the effectiveness of the behavioral approach in improving preventive maintenance practices prior to the initiation of this study, the potential of the approach could be seen through its documented improvements in work settings, its successful use of performance consequences as a source of motivation, and its direct observational measurement techniques.

ARRANGEMENTS FOR PILOT PROGRAM

Arrangements were made to conduct a pilot program based on the behavior analysis approach and designed to improve organizational (preventive) maintenance in a Fleet Marine Force unit at Camp Lejeune, North Carolina. Preventive maintenance had been identified as a recurring problem in the Marine Corps, particularly with the lowest level (first echelon) personnel who do not engage in maintenance full-time. The focus was on the performance of approximately 60 Marines in the Ordnance and Motor Transport sections of a heavy artillery Battery. The primary equipment in Ordnance consisted of six 8-inch self-propelled Howitzers (M110). Equipment in Motor Transport included four jeeps, three radio jeeps, and nine 5-ton trucks. The Battery was one of three in a Battalion. Battalion personnel report to Regimental personnel, who in turn report to Division personnel.

THE CHALLENGE

At the outset, it was assumed that the work environment would not change dramatically. In analyzing the ongoing PM system in the Marine Corps, it was found: (1) that equipment was supposed to be inspected once a week by first echelon personnel; (2) that Weekly PM Checklists, noting items to be inspected, were available; (3) that time was supposed to be set aside each week and these times were scheduled in advance and noted on a Weekly Training Schedule; and (4) that identified discrepancies were supposed to be corrected by first echelon personnel or that further action, for example ordering parts or sending the vehicle to the next echelon for repair, was supposed to be initiated on Equipment Repair Orders. These procedures for inspecting, detecting, and repairing discrepancies seemed to be well thought out and firmly established. Thus the procedures were assumed as given. Likewise, it was assumed that reducing the turbulent nature of the work environment with its many nonmaintenance commitments, significantly upgrading the work force, or altering the design, age, or use of the equipment would be impossible. *The challenge was to design a system that would work well within the existing system.*

PROCEDURES

First, the current PM system was analyzed to see whether it contained the components essential to effective performance. In line with the behavioral approach, it was determined whether personnel knew what to do; whether their performance was measured directly, frequently, and objectively; and whether there were consequences for their performance. Based on this initial analysis of the system, a measurement instrument and a motivational program were then designed.

Clarity of Performance

Analysis. Questions were raised about whether first echelon personnel knew what to do, a prerequisite to performance:

- Are desired practices clear?
- Is training adequate?

Many persons expressed concern about the technical expertise of maintenance personnel. Personnel generally noted either the minimal number of persons with technical training, the fact that training was not available for the maintenance of track vehicles, and the deficiencies in the PM manuals.

Knowledge Appraisal. As a result of this finding, a decision was made to assess the technical knowledge level of maintenance personnel. Two types of questions were devised to assess their knowledge:

1 . Identification, e.g., Can you identify the fill plug on the steering gear box?
2 . Activity, e.g., What do you do when checking the oil level in the engine compartment? What do you look for?

Three individuals from Motor Transport and three from Ordnance were selected randomly each week. Each was asked three Identification and three Activity questions. The percentage of questions answered correctly was calculated for each section.

The content area of the questions was limited to top-ranking items on the Weekly PM Checklists. The Weekly PM Checklists in Motor Transport and Ordnance contained 64 and 41 items, respectively, ranging from brake fluid levels to the conditions of seats. To ensure that items judged to be more important were emphasized, items were assigned priorities. On-site personnel rated the importance of all items on the Weekly PM Checklists, using a 7-point scale. Each item was then rank ordered. The questions devised included the top-ranking 25 items on the Weekly PM Checklists. In the Motor Transport section, for instance, select items were rank ordered as follows:

  1. Brake fluid
 10. Steering gear assembly
 20. Starter/accelerator
 30. Instrument panel
 40. Air cleaner/breather cap
 50. Cargo bed/dropsides
 60. Seats

The information obtained during the knowledge appraisal was used to assess whether personnel were technically qualified to conduct weekly PM checks.

Measurement of Performance

Analysis: Next, it was determined what information was currently used by on-site personnel to judge maintenance performance. The following questions were then raised:

- Do the indicators reflect performance directly?
- Is the information collected at least monthly?
- Is the information objective?

In an area such as preventive maintenance, it is important that the measure be: (1) direct, so that it assesses personnel performance; (2) frequent, so that it captures what personnel are doing on an ongoing basis; and (3) objective, so that it reflects the actual performance of personnel.

Three primary indicators were noted. One frequently mentioned indicator was the *deadline rate*, i.e., the percentage of inoperative combat essential equipment. Unit personnel continually feed information about inoperative or unsafe equipment into the management information system. This information is then summarized from all units and subsequently used to calculate the readiness rating. The readiness rating is distributed weekly to the Commandant of the Marine Corps and other intermediate levels of management; an extract of this information is presented on a monthly basis to the Joint Chiefs of Staff. When the readiness level takes a downward trend, efforts are immediately begun to rectify the situation. Rectification generally consists of one of two functions: ordering authorized vehicles (a supply function) or repairing inoperative vehicles (a maintenance function).

The deadline rate was found lacking, primarily because it does not directly reflect performance. Instead, it reflects vehicle condition. While preventive maintenance practices do affect vehicle condition, so do other factors: age, use, and design of the vehicles; supply system; and the availability of funds and personnel. More importantly, evidence of maintenance neglect often does not surface in vehicle condition for months and even years. As a result, it is not possible to determine current PM practices by relying solely on information about present vehicle condition. Since the deadline rate is weighted heavily by factors other than PM practices and consequently does not necessarily reflect current PM practices, it is not a sensitive measure of a unit's ongoing PM performance.

A second index is the yearly evaluation of a unit's field supply and maintenance efficiency (*FSMAO*). During this evaluation an analysis team spends a week on-site talking with Battery and Battalion personnel and sifting through records. This analysis is meant to determine whether the unit is complying with Marine Corps directives and publications. After the analysis, the team writes a report which outlines all deficiencies. The FSMAO report is forwarded to both higher level personnel (Regimental and Division), who use it to evaluate the performance of unit personnel, and to unit personnel, who are expected to correct all discrepancies immediately.

The FSMAO report, while it more directly reflects the performance of a given unit, is not sufficient as an ongoing measure of performance because it is done only annually. One problem with an annual, preannounced evaluation is that it is time specific and may not accurately reflect how personnel perform the rest of the year. A second problem with an annual assessment is that it necessarily emphasizes those aspects with tangible products, e.g., submitted tool kit requisitions, established pre-expended bins, properly prepared equipment records. Unfortunately, finding the paperwork, tools, and repair parts in proper order does not mean that maintenance was accomplished during the previous year. Personnel could complete what are euphemistically referred to as "paper PMs" without ever touching a vehicle.

The third indicator is the Limited Technical Inspection, generally referred to as the *LTI*. LTIs are performed to determine the extent and level of maintenance required to restore the equipment to a specified condition. Standard forms are used. LTIs are always done prior to equipment being dispatched, and, on occasion, are done when there are indications that maintenance is being neglected. When "excessive" discrepancies are found, they are brought to the attention of higher level personnel who, in turn, notify unit personnel. These unit personnel are expected to rectify the situation.

The LTIs were also found to be lacking as a measure of PM performance. Like the deadline rate, they reflect vehicle condition, which is weighted heavily by factors other than current PM practices. Questions were also raised about the accuracy of the information being obtained during the LTIs. Items on the standard LTI form are often so briefly and vaguely stated (e.g., engine) that it becomes difficult for even well-trained personnel to agree as to whether an item should be checked satisfactory or unsatisfactory (i.e., needs repair, adjustment, or replacement). During the course of the pilot program, evidence was collected regarding interrater agreement. Of the 82 LTIs, interrater reliability was assessed 6 and 3 times in Motor Transport and Ordnance, respectively. During the interrater reliability checks, two trained personnel independently inspected a randomly selected vehicle within a 24-hour period. Afterwards, items marked as unsatisfactory were examined. An agreement was defined as any item designated unsatisfactory by one rater which was also noted unsatisfactory by the other rater. Interrater reliability was calculated as the number of agreements divided by the number of agreements plus disagreements. The results showed that the two raters were in agreement only 71% and 51% of the time in Motor Transport and Ordnance, respectively. On over one-quarter to one-half of the items they disagreed as to whether the item was unsatisfactory. These findings indicate that there are questions about the LTIs, as they are currently being conducted, as an accurate source of information regarding vehicle condition.

Behavioral Measurement System: Because of the problems noted above with the three on-site indicators, an observational measurement system was designed that was direct, frequent, and objective. Information about PM performance was collected by retired Marines who went on-site and recorded weekly in both the Motor Transport and Ordnance sections. Data sheets and observational codes, containing definitions and observational procedures, were fieldtested and refined until two independent monitors could agree a substantial portion of the time (90–100%) about the occurrence of different PM practices.

The following three performance areas were monitored:

1. *Time utilization* was defined as the number of personnel engaged in PM activities during scheduled PM periods. A monitor went to the gun park or motor transport section and recorded the number of individuals present and the number of individuals on-task in each section. "Present" was defined as being "within 1 meter of a vehicle (including extension of a vehicle or disassembled part) *and* stationary for 5 seconds." "On-task" was defined as "manipulating equipment, vehicle, or disassembled part with hands or tools for any length of time." A monitor observed five times (approximately once each hour) during the scheduled PM period for a given day, as noted on the Weekly Training Schedule. So as not to establish a predictable pattern, the six guns in Ordnance and the three types of vehicles in Motor Transport were observed in a different random order during each observation. In Motor Transport, time utilization was calculated as the mean number of persons on-task (the total number of persons on-task divided by the number of observations [usually 5]). In Ordnance, time utilization was computed as the mean number of persons on-task per gun (the mean number of persons on-task was calculated for each gun, then these means were summed and divided by the number of guns).

2. *Supervision* was defined as the percentage of time a supervisor was present when personnel were on duty during scheduled PM periods. During each observation (described above), the monitor also recorded whether a supervisor (Battery Motor Transport Officer, section chief of gun) or higher ranking officer (e.g., Battery Commanding Officer) were present. "Present" in this case was defined as being within 10 meters of the vehicle or gun being worked on; interior areas (e.g., the Motor Transport hut) were excluded. In Motor Transport, supervision was calculated as the number of times a supervisor or higher ranking officer was present divided by the total number of observations during which at least one other person was present. In Ordnance, supervision was computed as the percentage of supervision per gun (the percentage of supervision was calculated for each gun, then these percentages were summed and divided by the number of guns with at least one other person present).

3. *Action taken* was the extent to which items identified as needing attention were either corrected, or the paperwork initiated to order parts or enable further repairs. A total of

18 items, all identified as needing repair on the Weekly PM Checklists, were selected for further analysis in each section. Three items were selected from each of the six guns in Ordnance and from six vehicles selected randomly in Motor Transport. To ensure that the more important items would be examined, items with the highest priority ranking were selected. For each item selected, a determination was made as to whether either of two appropriate remedial actions were taken. First, it was determined whether the item had been corrected by examining the vehicle itself. If the item had not been corrected, the monitor determined if the appropriate paperwork had been initiated that would result in either forwarding the vehicle to a higher echelon repair shop or ordering the parts necessary for repair. Action Taken was computed as the percentage of items in which follow through was taken for each vehicle or gun, divided by the total number of vehicles or guns.

Interrater Reliability: Interrater reliability was assessed frequently, that is, on the average of one out of every two times data were collected. Two monitors independently observed and recorded. At the end of the data collection period, their recordings were compared to see whether or not they agreed. With Time Utilization, reliability was calculated by comparing one monitor's counts of persons on-task with the other monitor's and then dividing the smaller number by the larger number and multiplying by 100 for a percentage figure.

With Supervision and Action Taken, reliability was computed using the percentage agreement method as follows:

$$\text{Reliability \%} = \frac{\text{\# of agreements}}{\text{\# of agreements \& disagreements}} \times 100$$

With Supervision, an agreement was scored when one monitor noted that a supervisor was present and at least one other person was present during a given observation, and the other monitor recorded the same. For Action Taken, those items marked as having no action taken were compared on an item-by-item basis. An agreement was scored when any item designated as "no action" by one monitor was also noted by the other monitor.

In contrast to the interrater agreement of the LTIs, the above reliability figures were extremely high, ranging between 97% and 100%, indicating the objectivity of the observational codes and the accuracy of the information obtained:

	Motor Transport	Ordnance
1. Time Utilization	99%	100%
2. Supervision	99%	98%
3. Action Taken	100%	97%

Consequences of Performance

Analysis: The next and last step was an analysis of the work environment itself. To determine if and how personnel were being motivated to perform properly, the following questions were asked:

- Are there any consequences for performance?
- Are these consequences related to performance?
- Are organizational incentives related to performance?
- Is there a balance of consequences for desired and undesired performance?

Attention was directed to the consequences of performance, that is, those events that occur to the individual following his or her performance. Examples of consequences include the actions of superiors, peers, and subordinates, as well as organizational incentives such as promotions and salary increases. In work setting after work setting, dramatic improvements occur when consequences are frequent and related to both desired and undesired performance. When it makes little difference whether one behaves in a desired or undesired manner, it is difficult to motivate personnel to improve and maintain their performance.

The analysis of the PM environment revealed that personnel were not being motivated properly. There were few favorable consequences for desired performance. Because there were no measures of PM performance *per se*, preventive maintenance was inevitably low priority. Preventive maintenance received less attention because no one, at any level, had any accurate, ongoing information about PM activities. Consequences are rarely provided when it is difficult to judge how well personnel are performing. That was definitely the case with the area of preventive maintenance:

Desired Performance	Consequences
Correctly identify discrepancies.	Little recognition.
	No follow through.

Because of the difficulties in measuring PM performance, there was little recognition of quality performance on a day-to-day basis. It was difficult to tell if, when, and how the job had been completed. Consequently, it was rarely noted in formal appraisals. Even a natural consequence, that of keeping the equipment running, was frequently aborted. When first echelon personnel correctly identified discrepancies during weekly PM checks, follow-through action was rarely completed promptly. Minor repairs and adjustments were not made, parts were not ordered, vechicles were not sent for repair. Only when the vehicle finally broke down were these taken care of. When there are so few consequences for performing as desired, it is difficult to maintain performance for extended periods of time in this environment.

On the other hand, when preventive maintenance was not completed, there were also few consequences:

Undesired Performance	Consequences
Procrastinate doing weekly PM.	Nothing happens.
Postpone follow through.	Vehicles continue to operate

Again, it was difficult to determine when PM had not been done, so little corrective action was taken. Uninspected vehicles not only do not look different from inspected ones, but evidence of maintenance neglect often does not surface for months and even years. Little was said or done when the vehicles continued to operate. As long as there are no consequences for neglecting maintenance, PM activities will continue to be relegated to a lower status.

The only time personnel heard about the area of preventive maintenance was when a major mishap occurred (e.g., one-quarter of a unit's trucks were deadlined because of transmission problems). Then repercussions would reverberate up and down the line. Such an approach is generally referred to as management by exception. There are at least two problems with this approach in which persons only hear when problems surface. First, this approach lends itself to crisis management. When a crisis such as the one above occurs, attention is focused on preventive maintenance. However, when another crisis occurs, attention shifts to the other area and then maintenance is forgotten in the shuffle of more measurable commitments. The second problem is that management by exception by its very nature focuses on exceptional events that do not necessarily reflect performance. In the case of equipment failure, it is often difficult to trace whether breakdowns were caused by equipment design or maintenance neglect. Even if maintenance were the reason, the neglect may have occurred long before the present personnel arrived. Needless blame at any level is counterproductive to motivation. In summary, it was concluded that the PM environment with its lack of contingent consequences for desired and undesired performance was not conducive to motivating personnel.

Time-off and feedback program: Based on the above analysis, it was recommended that more frequent consequences should be arranged for desired performance, and that performance feedback should be provided. This was to ensure that personnel can recognize quality performance and rectify unsatisfactory performance.

Various potentially reinforcing events were discussed. One such event was *feedback,* which had been demonstrated to be an effective improvement strategy in many work settings. While feedback has the advantage of ready acceptability and low cost, there was some question as to its effectiveness when used alone. Of particular concern was the less than dramatic nature of maintenance and the many nonmaintenance commitments of the setting. Because of this, it was decided to combine feedback with at least one other performance consequence.

Monetary incentives were ruled out, since they were not feasible in this setting. Likewise, *token economy systems*, making use of points and privileges, were also ruled out because of their extensive recordkeeping requirements. *Time off,* on the other hand, was highly recommended. Time off had been identified as a highly desired incentive by Army personnel (Datel, 1972) and was currently being used at Camp Lejeune as an incentive to reduce the number of unauthorized absences. However, many personnel questioned the effectiveness of time off in this situation. Because maintenance needs to be performed regularly and consequences should be timely, it was important that the consequences be provided rather frequently. The amount of time assumed by on-site personnel to have any incentive value (4 to 8 hours), however, was viewed as a prohibitive amount of time in any work week. Alternatives were considered. One possibility was to drop the idea of time off altogether; another was to provide a greater amount of time off less frequently; another was to enhance its incentive value and provide a smaller amount more frequently. Eventually, it was decided to try the latter. Although only 30 to 60 minutes could be alloted on a weekly basis, its availability could be announced in advance and scheduled for Fridays. Based on all the above information, a program, referred to as the PM Liberty Call Program, was introduced in the Motor Transport and Ordnance sections.

EVALUATION OF PROGRAM

To evaluate the effectiveness of the PM Liberty Call Program, a within-group, multiple-baseline design was used. Information was collected weekly over a 48-week period, beginning the week of 1979 10, December and continuing through the week of 1979 15, January (Figure 13.2). After 16 weeks, the PM Liberty Call Program was introduced in the Motor Transport section the week of April 30. After 34 weeks, the program was introduced in the Ordnance section the week of September 4. Information continued to be collected to determine whether performance improved after, and not before, the sequential introductions of the program in the two sections.

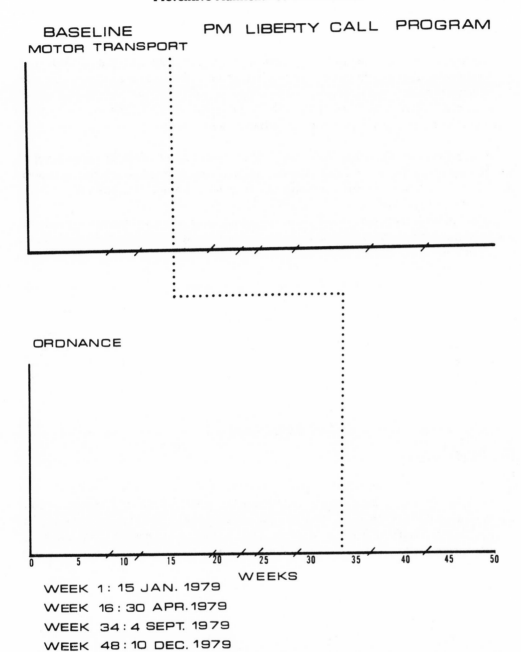

Fig. 13.2. Diagram of Multiple-Baseline Design Used to Evaluate Effectiveness of Program.

PM LIBERTY CALL PROGRAM

If all PM goals were met for the week, then an early liberty call was established for the entire Battery. Specifically:

- Monitors communicated the week's results by the close of business Friday.

- The Battery Commanding Officer announced the results no later than the Monday morning assembly.
- Early liberty was scheduled for the first available (preferably the following) Friday.
- When the Program was in effect for Motor Transport, it alone could earn the entire Battery early liberty.
- When the Program was in effect for both Motor Transport and Ordnance, both would have to meet the goals to earn the entire Battery early liberty.

Feedback was also provided each week in the form of a graph which was posted at Battery Headquarters. Figure 13.3, for example, shows a sample graph which illustrates what personnel in the Motor Transport section received as feedback after the introduction of the PM Liberty Call Program.

The PM goals were determined by on-site personnel in conjunction with project staff and in reference to previous performance levels. The goals set for each of the measures are shown below:

| | Sections | | | |
| Performance Areas | Motor Transport | | Ordnance | |
	Intermediate Goal	Ultimate Goal	Intermediate Goal	Ultimate Goal
Time Utilization	3	4.5	3.5	4.5
Supervision	50%	67%	67%	75%
Action Taken	67%	75%	75%	85%

RESULTS

PM Performance

The effects of the PM Liberty Call Program were mixed. Initially, the Program in the Motor Transport section was quite effective as can be seen in Figure 13.4. Motor Transport personnel exceeded by wide margins all PM goals (indicated by shading) during the first 4 weeks. Time Utilization doubled from an average of 2.4 Marines working during scheduled maintenance times to an average of 5.4 Marines, substantially exceeding the goal of 3.0.

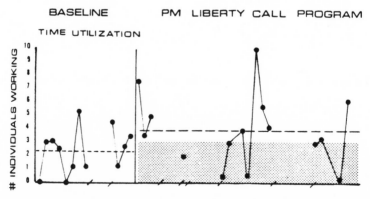

Fig. 13.3. Feedback Graph of Time Utilization for Motor Transport.

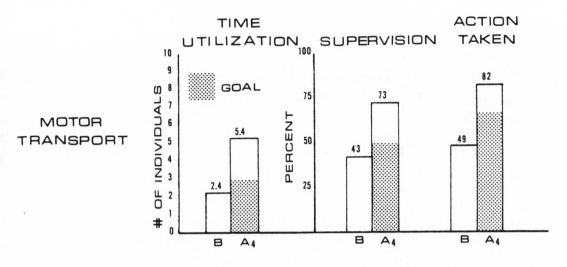

Fig. 13.4. Results in Motor Transport Before and After Four Weeks of the Program.

Likewise, the percentage of time a supervisor was present almost doubled from an average of 43% to 73%. Action taken on discrepancies also improved from an average of 49% to 82% of the items needing attention, well exceeding the goal of 67%. During this time, PM goals were met 3 of the 4 weeks and early liberty was awarded.

After the first month, however, performance in the Motor Transport section declined. By the end of the year performance had declined to such an extent that the goal was exceeded only slightly for Time Utilization and just barely attained for Supervision (Figure 13.5). Action Taken was affected most, with personnel not even attaining the goal and performing no better overall after the program (M = 50%) than before the program (M = 49%).

In Ordnance, the PM Liberty Call Program did not result in any improvements whatsoever as can be seen in Figure 13.5. For Time Utilization and Supervision, performance remained virtually the same. For Action Taken, performance actually declined over the course of the program.

Performance varied considerably from week to week as shown in Figures 13.6 and 13.7. The week-to-week changes were particularly striking in Motor Transport. During weeks 33, 34, and 35, for instance, Action Taken went from 0% to 89% and back to 0% in the space of 3 weeks time. The precipitating events for fluctuations such as this, however, were not clearly related to any particular nonmaintenance commitments nor were they consistent from one section to another.

Personnel Reactions

First echelon personnel had a positive but qualified reaction to the PM Liberty Call Program. In interviews with project staff, they noted they particularly liked the fact that the Program gave them "something to work for" and that it "gets more people down here." One Marine specifically mentioned that he liked "people observing consistently." The main problems mentioned were the frequent conflicts in scheduling and the limited amount of early liberty actually awarded (10 to 15 minutes rather than the 30 to 60 planned).

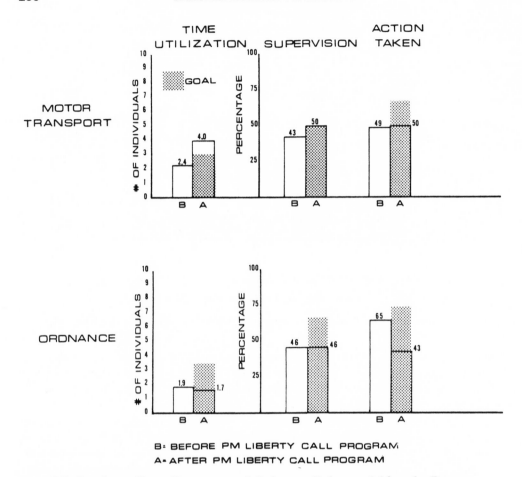

Fig. 13.5. Results in Motor Transport and Ordnance Before and After the Program.

Supervisory Support

Initially, most persons in charge readily acknowledged the importance of preventive maintenance. However, no one seemed particularly displeased with the quality of maintenance being accomplished, given the time and resources available. When asked to estimate the extent of time being spent and action taken, however, their estimates were frequently higher than warranted by the information being collected by the monitors.

In designing the Program, persons in charge discussed Program arrangements at length with the project staff. At the beginning of each phase, both the Battalion and Battery Commanding Officers personally participated in an assembly of the entire Battery during which the Program was announced and described. Immediately after the introduction of the Program in Motor Transport, personnel were reminded of PM goals and were told about their progress at formations. When Motor Transport attained all goals, arrangements were made for early liberty for the entire Battery. After a while, however, nothing much was said about the Program. When asked what had been said at formation, one Marine noted that statements about the Program had been frequent in the beginning. However, in regard to the present status of comments at formation he succinctly noted that he had heard "nothing lately."

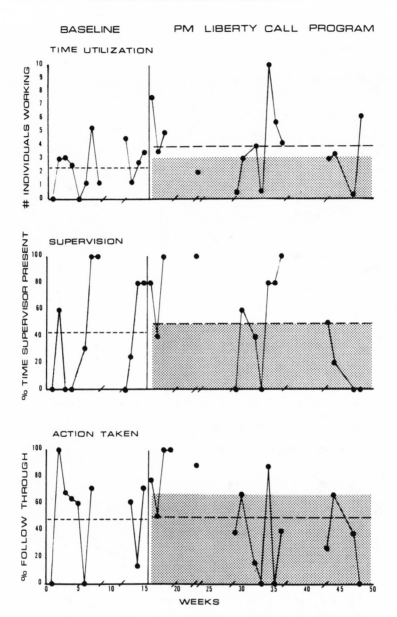

Fig. 13.6. Week-to-Week Results in Motor Transport Before and After the Program*

*The bracketed sections on the abscissa (weeks 9-11, 20-22, 24-28, 37-42) indicated the weeks during which maintenance was not scheduled and, consequently, data were not collected. Occasionally, data were collected in one performance area but not another due to changes in weather or activities.

PROMISING DEVELOPMENTS

Although the results of the pilot program were mixed, there were several promising developments:

1. A better understanding exists of why preventive maintenance is likely to be neglected. The unique nature of maintenance – the fact that it is invisible, has delayed ef-

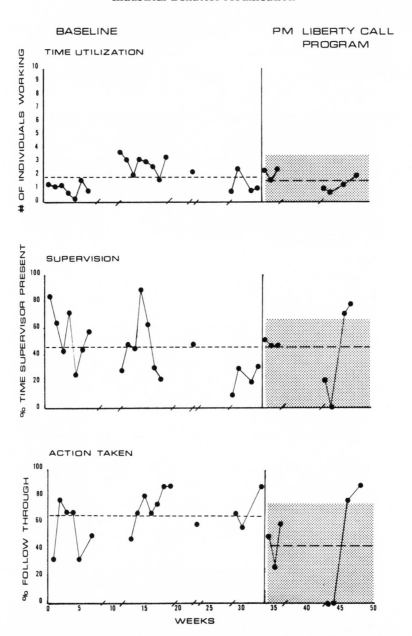

Fig. 13.7. Week-to-Week Results in Ordance Before and After the Program

*The bracketed sections on the abscissa (weeks 9-11, 20-22, 24-28, 37-42) indicated the weeks during which maintenance was not scheduled and, consequently, data were not collected. Occasionally, data were collected in one performance area but not another due to changes in weather or activities.

fects, and that it needs to be done week in and week out – and its resulting difficulties were identified. Also, the complications that arise when there is no direct, frequent, and objective indicator of PM performance and the effect this has on the recognition of performance and the rectification of omissions were indicated. By understanding the reasons for maintenance neglect, one can better design a system to improve maintenance.

2. The initial improvements in one section (Motor Transport) indicate that it is possible to upgrade the maintenance effort of a fully operational unit and to encourage personnel to devote more productive time to the upkeep of equipment. The fact that the combination feedback and time-off program was well received by unit personnel further encourages the use of these consequences in this setting.

3. An alternative measurement system in which trained monitors went on-site weekly and recorded whether specific maintenance tasks were being done was developed. It helped clarify what personnel should be doing; resulted in more sensitive, ongoing, and accurate information about maintenance performance; was the essential ingredient of the feedback component; and enabled the evaluation of the pilot program.

FUTURE DIRECTIONS

The present research also indicated that training alone, an influx of personnel, and more committed officers will not necessarily improve the quality, regularity, and timeliness of maintenance.

Persons in both Motor Transport and Ordnance demonstrated from week to week, as shown in Figure 13.8, that they knew what to do when conducting a weekly PM check. The average percentage of questions answered correctly was 99% and 94% in Motor Transport and Ordnance, respectively. *It was concluded, as a result, that maintenance was not below par because of a lack of technical expertise on the part of first echelon personnel.*

Shortage of personnel is often suggested as a reason for maintenance neglect. This implicitly assumes that if only the authorized number were on board, PM performance would be up to par. This was not the case. During the first part of the year, the total strength of the Battery (Figure 13.9) and selected positions in Motor Transport (Figure 13.10) and Ordnance (Figure 13.11) were over 100%. Yet, performance was clearly below standard. *So, the presence of an authorized number of personnel per se is not sufficient to ensure that maintenance will get done.*

A third factor sometimes mentioned concerns the individuals in charge. The implication is that if these individuals were more committed or more competent, maintenance would not be a problem. Although the evidence presented thus far does not portray this particular unit in the most favorable light, there is no evidence to suggest that it was any different from any other unit, or that the individuals in charge were any less committed or competent. At the onset, the unit chosen was judged to be representative. During the course of the project, there was the usual turnover in the Commanding Officers of the Battalion and Battery, as well as the maintenance officer (S-4) and various lower level supervisory personnel. *The presence or absence of any one individual was not responsible for the lackluster results.*

The Program simply could not overcome the crisis management environment in which higher priority was placed on more visible, nonmaintenance commitments. The way in which priorities are arranged makes it extremely difficult to conduct maintenance properly. In the press of more measurable commitments, higher level personnel indirectly encourage unit personnel to neglect maintenance. No individual, no matter how committed, could unearth maintenance from its low priority status. Even if unit personnel wished to show how additional commitments impair maintenance, they have no way of documenting their deleterious effects. Because there are no measures of PM performance *per se* and the evidence of maintenance neglect is hidden and often delayed, maintenance inevitably takes a back seat to more visible commitments.

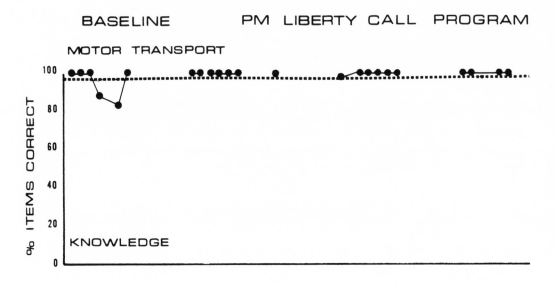

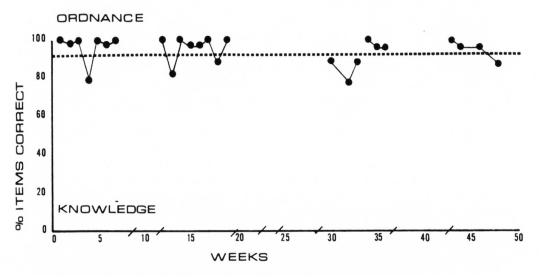

Fig. 13.8. Knowledge Level of Motor Transport and Ordnance Personnel.

Example. All personnel readily acknowledged the importance of maintenance. As one Marine simply noted: "If the trucks are not up, you can't go anywhere." However, the actual priority given to maintenance was very different. When asked what priority is placed on PM compared to other areas, personnel in Motor Transport (MT) and Ordnance (ORD) rated it as follows:

high   1   2   3   4   5   6   7   low
           Ord   MT

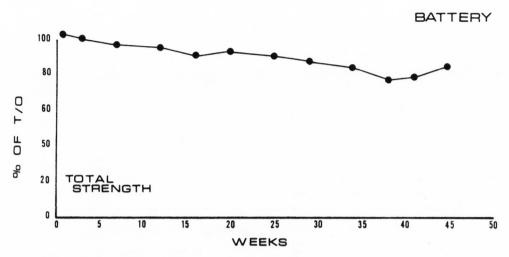

Fig. 13.9. Total Strength of Battery Throughout Year.

One Marine, identifying the problem succinctly, remarked that he would rate PM a "2" on the training schedule, but because of the many other commitments he would rate it a "6" in terms of actual practice. First echelon personnel noted that there seemed to be more emphasis on other activities such as close order drill, field days, flu shots, dental appointments, and classes.

When maintenance was scheduled, it was scheduled for a sizeable portion of the work week (15 hours on the average). However, weeks went by when no maintenance was scheduled. For a total of 17 weeks (9-11, 20-22, 24-28, 37-42), the Battery was primarily engaged in field firing exercises or preparing for a major inspection, and maintenance was never scheduled. Even during the weeks that maintenance was scheduled, maintenance activities were deleted during at least 8 weeks and other activities were added on at least one day. The net result was that the maintenance schedule was left intact for only one-half of the weeks (23 out of 48) during the year. Even if persons in charge could make maintenance their first priority, they have limited control over maintenance scheduling, in part because they have no immediate evidence to show the deleterious effects of maintenance neglect.

Another example. From one-third to one-half of unit personnel were found to be unavailable to do maintenance on any given day. On two fairly "typical" days in December 1979, for example, 40 persons of a total of 89 in the Battery were either on the rifle range, attending classes (cannoneer, driver, basic skills), assigned to guard duty (mess, regimental, light), in a working party, in the brig, or on leave. The above assignments are made first. If maintenance is scheduled for that day, the burden falls on whomever remains. Rarely, if ever, are personnel first selected for maintenance and then assignments made for working parties and so forth. Again, in the press of more measureable commitments, maintenance is typically relegated to a lower status.

If preventive maintenance is ever to be improved and sustained, steps must be taken to overcome, or at least to counterbalance, the effects of this crisis management environment.

Recommendations. The status of maintenance should be upgraded by making it more visible. Feedback about PM performance should be provided each week to persons doing the work and their supervisors. Furthermore, this information should be forwarded to mid-

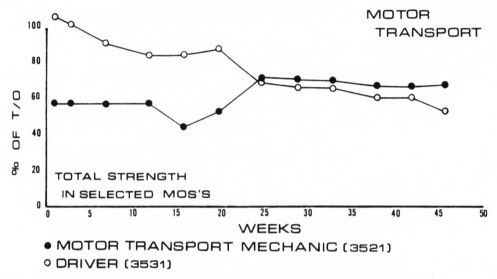

Fig. 13.10. Total Strength of Selected Positions in Motor Transport Throughout Year.

dle and upper management on a monthly and quarterly basis, respectively. By improving the adequacy and frequency of PM performance, management can make more knowledgeable decisions and persons in charge can better motivate their subordinates.

Secondly, emphasis should be placed on supervisory personnel, as well as first and second echelon personnel. Because of the hidden and delayed nature of maintenance, it is crucial that supervisors obtain direct, frequent, and objective information about the PM performance of their subordinates. By doing so, supervisors can better recognize quality performance and take care of any omissions, thus ensuring maintenance is being conducted properly.

SUMMARY

Although the importance of preventive maintenance (PM) is widely acknowledged in both military and civilian settings, there are few documented ways to improve the quality, regularity, and timeliness of maintenance. Most PM studies are not concerned with on-the-job practices; worker motivation is neglected, and there are no satisfactory measures of PM performance. One method which has been suggested as suitable for facilitating preventive maintenance is the behavior analysis approach. The potential of the approach can be seen through its documented improvements in work settings, its successful use of performance consequences as a source of motivation, and its direct observational measurement techniques.

Based on the needs identified by Marine Corps personnel, a pilot program, based on the behavior analysis approach, was designed and implemented in a Fleet Marine Force Unit. The focus was on personnel (N = 60) in the Ordnance and Motor Transport sections of a heavy artillery Battery at Camp Lejeune, North Carolina.

First, it was determined whether the current PM system contained the components essential to effective performance. In line with the behavioral approach, the PM system was analyzed to determine whether personnel knew what to do; whether their performance was

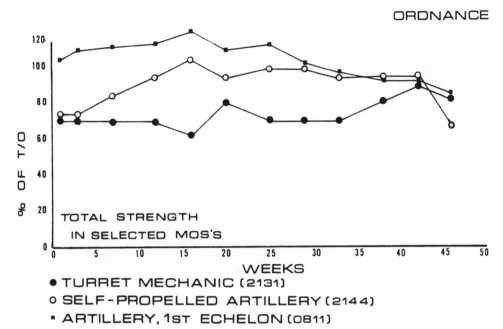

Fig. 13.11. Total Strength of Selected Positions in Ordnance Throughout Year.

measured directly, frequently, and objectively; and whether there were consequences for their performance.

Analysis of the PM system revealed the lack of direct, frequent, and objective indicators of PM performance. As a result, a behavioral measurement system was developed which consisted of the following three performance areas: (1) Utilization of time during scheduled maintenance periods, (2) supervision during these periods, and (3) extent of corrective action taken. Each of the above categories was behaviorally defined and data were collected weekly by retired Marines over a 48-week period.

Analysis of the PM environment also revealed that personnel were not being motivated properly. Because there were no measures of PM performance *per se,* and the effects of PM neglect were hidden and delayed, nothing much happened following desired or undesired performance. As a result, a motivational Program was designed which included performance consequences in the form of feedback and time-off. In this program, referred to as the PM Liberty Call Program, early liberty was awarded if all PM goals had been met. Feedback was posted weekly, announcements about the early liberty were made on Mondays, and liberty was awarded on Fridays. To evaluate the effectiveness of the Program, a multiple-baseline design was used in which the Program was introduced after 15 weeks in Motor Transport and after 33 weeks in Ordnance.

The Program was not only well received, but also initially effective in the Motor Transport section with all goals being exceeded by a substantial margin. However, the final results were mixed. Performance in Motor Transport declined to preprogram levels. No improvements were ever obtained in Ordnance.

Although the pilot program failed to obtain consistent improvements, several positive events developed. A better understanding now exists as to why preventive maintenance is likely to be neglected; the initial improvements in one section demonstrate that it is possible to upgrade the maintenance effort of a fully operational unit, and a promising behavioral measurement system was developed which resulted in more sensitive, ongoing, and accurate information about PM performance.

The present research also indicated that training alone, an influx of personnel, and more committed officers will not necessarily improve the quality, regularity, and timeliness of maintenance. Instead, it was concluded that the Program simply could not overcome the crisis management environment in which higher priority was placed on more visible, nonmaintenance commitments. To counteract its effects, it is recommended that maintenance be upgraded by making it more visible to all parties, and that equal emphasis should be placed on supervisory personnel.

REFERENCES

Andrasik, F., Heimberg, J. S., & McNamara, J. R. Behavior modification of work and work-related problems. In M. Hersen, R. M. Eisler, & P. M. Miller (Eds.), *Progress in behavior modification*. New York: Academic Press, in press.

Babb, H. W., & Kopp, D. G. Applications of behavior modification in organizations: A review and critique. *Academy of Management Review*, 1978, **3**, 281–292.

Biersner, R. J. *Attitudes and other factors relating to aviation maintenance training effectiveness* (CNETS-6-75). Pensacola, Fla.: Chief of Naval Education and Training Support, December 1975. (NTIS No. AD-A022 4 83/2 SL).

Carpenter-Huffman, P., & Rostker, B. *The relevance of training for the maintenance of advanced avionics* (RAND/H-1894-AF). Santa Monica, Calif.: Rand Corporation, December 1976. (NTIS No. AD-A047-707/5GA).

Corder, A. S. *Maintenance management techniques*. London: McGraw-Hill, 1976.

Drake, K. L., Goto, R. N., & Crooks, W. H. *Comparative studies of organizational factors in military maintenance* (PTR-1043-79-6). Woodland Hills, Calif.: Perceptronics, June 1979. (NTIS No. AD-A071-608/4GA).

Foley, J. P., Jr. Task analysis for job performance aids and related training. In T. C. Rowan (Ed.), *Proceedings of invitational conference on improved information aids for technicians* (LMI-75-10). Washington, D.C.: Logistics Management Institute, May 1975. (NTIS No. AD-A018-794).

Hannon, W. W. Work authorization and control. In L. Higgins & L. Morrow (Eds.), *Maintenance engineering handbook*. New York: McGraw-Hill, 1977.

Higgins, L. R., & Morrow, L. C. *Maintenance engineering handbook*. New York: McGraw Hill, 1977.

Hora, M. E. Five steps to follow in developing a maintenance training program. *Plant Engineering*, March 30, 1978, pp. 275–278.

Johnson, R. M., & Storr, A. Maintenance trades and supervisory training. In L. Higgins & L. Morrow (Eds.), *Maintenance engineering handbook*. New York: McGraw-Hill, 1977.

Knight, C. E. The economics of maintenance management. In L. R. Higgins & L. C. Morrow (Eds.), *Maintenance engineering handbook*. New York: McGraw-Hill, 1977.

Komaki, J., Barwick, K. D., & Scott, L. R. A behavioral approach to occupational safety: Pinpointing and reinforcing safe performance in a food manufacturing plant. *Journal of Applied Psychology*, 1978, **63**, 434–445.

Komaki, J., Collins, R. L., & Temlock, S. *A behavioral assessment of the service sector: Facilitating customer service in a retail merchandising firm*. Manuscript submitted for publication, 1980.

Komaki, J., Collins, R. L., & Thoene, T. J. F. Behavioral measurement in business, industry, and government. *Behavioral Assessment*, 1980, **2**, 103–123.

Komaki, J., Heinzmann, A. T., & Lawson, L. Effect of training and feedback: Component analysis of a behavioral safety program. *Journal of Applied Psychology*, 1980, **65**, 261–270.

McCarty, D. S., & Moore, R. L. *Aircraft maintenance cost elements* (AFIT-LSSR-17-77B). Wright-Patterson Air Force Base, Ohio: Air Force Institute of Technology, School of Systems and Logistics, September 1977. (NTIS No. AD-A047 640/8GA).

Murphy, R. Work scheduling and controls. In L. Higgins & L. Morrow (Eds.), *Maintenance engineering handbook*. New York: McGraw-Hill, 1977.

Pierce, C. H., & Risley, T. R. Improving job performance of Neighborhood Youth Corps aides in an urban recreation program. *Journal of Applied Behavior Analysis*, 1974, **7**, 207-215.

Post, T. J. Comprehensibility of technical manuals. In T. C. Rowan (Ed.), *Proceedings of invitational conference on improved information aids for technicians* (LMI-75-10). Washington, D.C.: Logistics Management Institute, May 1975. (NTIS No. Ad-A018-794).

Prue, D. M., Frederiksen, L. W., & Bacon, A. Organizational behavior management: An annotated bibliography. *Journal of Organizational Behavior Management*, 1978, **1**, 216-257.

Quilitch, H. R. A comparison of three staff management procedures. *Journal of Applied Behavior Analysis*, 1975, **8**, 59-66.

Schwartz, M. A. *Facilities maintenance demonstration study* (NPRDC-TR-76-29). San Diego: Navy Personnel and Research and Development Center, January 1976. (NTIS No. AD8009-681).

Shriver, E. L. *Fully proceduralized job performance aids: Guidance for performing behavioral analyses* (AFHRL-TR-75-38). Falls Church, Va.: URS/Matrix Research Company, June 1975.

Smith, J. P. *Briefing on performance and proficiency testing of organizational track vehicle mechanics and maintenance sergeants*. Alexandria, Va.: Human Resources Research Organization, October 1961, (NTIS No. AD-A020 0 09/7 SL).

Up, up and away. *Time*, July 23, 1979, p. 36.

Wilkinson, J. J. How to manage maintenance. *Harvard Business Review*, March-April 1968, pp. 100-111.

14

A Comprehensive Skills Program for Job-Finding With the Hardcore Unemployed

Diana R. Richman

The Institute for Rational-Emotive Therapy

DESCRIPTION OF THE HARDCORE UNEMPLOYED POPULATION

In recent years there has been an increasing amount of pressure on firms to hire the hardcore unemployed. This subgroup of jobless individuals has been typically described as being uneducated and unskilled. Most often they are of a low socioeconomic status (SES) and are recipients of public assistance. These individuals have little or no work history. What work experiences they may have is frequently sporadic, short-term, and characterized by poor work habits as reported by their employers. Often labeled as hard to place clients by employment interviewers and counselors, they continue to remain on or return to the welfare roles and maintain their unemployed status.

These economically disadvantaged individuals have been found to have a higher than average general level of self-concept problems and difficulties in relationships (Miskimins & Baker, 1973). Frequently the hardcore unemployed have social skills problems related to employment such as getting to work, developing proper attitudes towards time, and getting along with other employees (Goodman, 1969). Messer and Lehrer (1976) have emphasized the importance of recognizing the emotional conflicts of the hardcore unemployed when attempting to alleviate their vocational and related social problems. They pointed out that these emotional problems may be related to their inability to secure and maintain employment. Margolin and Goldin (1971) indicated the need for extensive vocational rehabilitation services by many public assistance clients who are designated as able to work but are in fact mentally and physically handicapped. They delineated several negative dimensions such as client motivation, attitudes, and organization procedures utilized by welfare, and stressed that many clients have learned poor work habits, experience difficulty functioning in our competitive society, and experience anxiety at the possibility of becoming employed.

Over a 9-month period, Nagle (1973) related the number of contacts with a Missouri State Employment Office to applicant success in placement and found that three to five contacts resulted in some change of status such as becoming employed. After five contacts, applicants were still in need of reevaluation or additional services in order to deal with barriers interfering with eventual employment. Normand, Fernsterheim, and Schrenzel (1967) recommended environmental intervention and the process of job finding to alleviate the depression experienced by low SES individuals. Economic change and unemployment status in itself, have been found to be related to emotional and behavior disorders (Dooley &

Catalano, 1980). Even as the minority poor begin to move upward, the increased exposure to interpersonal interactions in which their personal characteristics are misperceived becomes a source of stress. The transition of roles in the attempt to become career oriented is frequently characterized by depression (Weissman, Pincus, Radding, Lawrence, & Siegel, 1973).

Cultural and social factors may have helped these unemployed individuals maintain their disadvantaged subgroup status. Recently, Klausner (1978) suggested that provision of an economic incentive is not an effective means of weaning the economically poor from welfare and into self-sufficient status. In their comprehensive analysis of government manpower programs, Perry, Anderson, Rowan, and Northrup (1975) stated, for example, that little evidence exists on the economic effects of participating in the Work Incentive Program (WIN), a project established to provide jobs and training for individuals with children 6 years of age and over. The evidence which does exist indicates that this federal program has failed to achieve the goal of reducing welfare dependency for any given period of time.

Individuals who are designated as hard to place in jobs are those who have little or no work history and lack appropriate job skills. Due to inflation and the tightening of the job market, the number of individuals designated as hard to place has increased as more youth and women are seeking employment. While a college education has previously been a route to a job for many youth and women, a college education no longer guarantees employment after graduation. Although hard to place women and youth have traditionally come from a low SES, due to a decline in their standard of living, more women from the middle class have been seeking and failing to find employment and must be considered hardcore unemployed. With the influx of these additional individuals into the hardcore unemployed group, the necessity of developing better techniques for assisting individuals in the job search process becomes apparent.

BARRIERS TO OBTAINING EMPLOYMENT

The first step in developing a skills program which will increase vocational success among the hardcore unemployed is to identify the barriers to employment faced by this group. Employment barriers may be divided into the following four general categories: (1) lack of job qualifications, (2) social and interpersonal conflicts, (3) legal and financial problems, and (4) emotional or personal problems, although specific problems such as child care and health also should be noted (Miller & Oetting, 1977). These latter factors become even more significant for particular groups within the disadvantaged populaion. Warren and Berkowitz (1969) asked a group of employment "experts" to rate the obstacles to employment among welfare clients who were receiving Aid for Dependent Children (AFDC). Child care problems were rated first, with limited work skills, no work history, negative personality traits, and insufficient education following in that order. Studies within the federal Work Incentive Program for welfare women (WIN) have confirmed the importance of prior work history (Thursby, 1974) and education (Richman, 1979) as positive predictors for employability. On the other hand, neither length of time on welfare (Richman, 1979) nor number of times on welfare (Warren & Berkowitz, 1969) have been found to consistently predict employment potential.

For women in general and welfare mothers in particular, the barriers to employment are even more formidable (Goodwin, 1972; Niemi, 1973). Levinson (1970) lists twelve barriers to employment faced by women, including lack of self-confidence, feelings of powerlessness, poor motivation and awareness of the poor labor market, but singles out health, child care responsibilities, and lack of or dissatisfaction with day care facilities as the most persistent obstacles to employment for this population. Given their more demanding home role and the shortage of child care facilities, women have more reason to seek jobs close to home and are more likely to move in and out of the labor market (Ericksen, 1977; Niemi, 1973). Even when these women are offered job training opportunities, they are often forced to turn them down.

As can be seen from the previous lists, barriers to employment may be viewed as both societal and self-imposed. A variety of programs have attempted to reduce one or both of these types of barriers, but often the two work hand in hand toward either entry into the labor market or continued unemployment. A good example of this interaction occurs in the initial step toward finding a job. Frequently the hardcore unemployed are turned off to seeking work at the point of their interview with an employment counselor or welfare worker. The bureaucratic treatment that these individuals often receive combines with their negative perception of counselors to form a significant obstacle to productive use of the system (Goodwin, 1973; Loomis & Starry, 1975). Given the interpersonal and emotional problems noted earlier, there are likely to be problems in communication between counselors and clients and discrepancies between the clients' perception of their needs and those of the counselors (Higgins, 1976; Varga, 1974). To begin to alleviate these problems, counselors should be provided with more guidance to client needs. Greater flexibility on the part of employers and counselors and more concern for social rehabilitation have often been recommended (Burnside, 1971).

The problems of the hardcore unemployed do not end with finding work. Once placed in a job, the problem becomes finding a way to reduce external barriers related to retention. Salipante and Goodman (1976) evaluated the relationship of training and counseling to retention among trainees from 114 firms and found that content of training, rather than whether training was offered was the critical variable. Personal counseling that encouraged the trainees to attend was related to retention. The type of supervision the disadvantaged worker receives also has an influence on job success. Supportive supervision characterized by behaviors indicating two-way communication has been found to be related to job success, while structured supervision, characterized by behaviors in which the supervisor defines his own relationship to the group and organizes the group activities, has been found to be negatively associated with success on the job (Beatty, 1974).

The welfare system itself must be cited as a final societal barrier in that it has been reinforcing dependency of the unemployed poor for many years. Rein and Wishnov (1971) have pointed out that although the welfare system was established in 1935 to aid divorced, separated, widowed, and unmarried women with dependent children, the system actually serves as a barrier to employment. The financial benefits of entry into the labor market are outweighed by the advantages of receiving public assistance (Goodwin, 1972; Williams, 1975). Welfare status is viewed as supplemental income rather than a sharp break with the labor force as the theory of assistance would imply. Many individuals who receive welfare have to find part-time jobs off the books to supplement their welfare checks in order to survive economically. Often women with children avoid working for fear that they will lose their Medicaid and food stamps.

Government programs established with the goal of helping the hardcore to obtain employment cannot succeed as long as these individuals do not see the advantages of working and continue to face numerous barriers. Williams (1975) reported that the increase of welfare guarantee levels tends to have a negative income effect on work effort, while a decrease in welfare grants as family income increases tends to have a positive effect on uncompensated work effort wage. Siddall and Balcerzek (1978) have accurately described the present large welfare and unemployment roles as predictable from a reinforcement model. They point out that the welfare system nurtures the problems it was designed to resolve by providing rewards on a noncontingent basis. Thus, behaviors incompatible with self-support are inadvertently maintained. As we increase our use of behavioral techniques in counseling these clients, we might do well to apply our knowledge to the total system within which the unemployed are asked to function.

APPLICATION OF BEHAVIORAL TECHNIQUES TO THE UNEMPLOYMENT PROBLEM

Although our welfare system has not yet learned to utilize a behavioral approach for reducing the welfare roles, behavioral techniques have been successfully used to break down some of the client's personal barriers to employment. These include a lack of job skills and inappropriate job behaviors, as well as emotional barriers such as self-esteem problems. The importance of learning appropriate job behaviors becomes apparent from the work of Miskimins and Baker (1973). They found that successful job experiences had a positive impact on the self-concepts of the poor. However, they also found that unsuccessful job experiences lowered the self-concepts of the poor, suggesting that it may be better for individuals in this population to do nothing rather than to obtain employment and fail. The self-esteem of the disadvantaged has been found to be related to job success and vocational maturity (Barrett & Tinsley, 1977; Putnam & Hansen, 1972). Therefore, helping to increase the probability of successful employment is perhaps the most appropriate way to improve their self-esteem. The type of social reinforcers received when low SES clients become employed may help to produce a generally more favorable self-image (Baron, Bass, & Vietze, 1971). Employers would do well to implement schedules of very frequent reinforcement to increase job success among their low SES employees.

Group counseling and the introduction of audio-video feedback aids have provided a format for utilizing behavioral techniques in a vocational setting. Role playing, communication problem solving, and behavior self-control techniques have been effective for improving the behavior of those already working (Bonney, Parsons, Scalise, Wagner, Anderson, 1976; Roessler, Cook & Lilliard, 1977). Evidence that these approaches will help to obtain employment is still lacking.

The job interview has been conducive for stimulating the teaching of skills helpful to finding jobs. In 1973, Keil and Barbee made direct application of behavior modification to the job interview setting with the disadvantaged. Utilizing a time limited behavior change program, they defined interpersonal target behaviors to be modified as follows: responding completely to the interviewer's questions, clarifying personal circumstances and relating them to task conformance considerations, relating past work and education experiences to the job to be done, and indicating questions regarding work tasks and company policies. They found that traditional emphasis on work skills may be ineffective if it excludes interpersonal skills for the entry level disadvantaged. They demonstrated, however, that interviewee behavior rated as important by interviewers can be altered.

To improve interview skills, Barbee and Keil (1973) compared a videotape feedback and behavior modification group, videotape alone, and a no-treatment control group using disadvantaged clients enrolled in three manpower agencies. Personnel interviewers, acting as judges in randomly presented videotaped interviews, reported greater positive change from the initial to the final interview among the combined treatment group. While there were no significant differences among the three groups on job skills and personal adaptability, the combined group improved significantly on probability to hire. The combined group did significantly better on level of questions asked about job tasks and conditions and in ratings of assertiveness. Disadvantaged persons who learned specific interviewing skills in the program were potentially better prepared for actual interviews when seeking employment, presented themselves more effectively, and were better able to objectively evaluate their own performance in terms of criteria learned in training. They were able to rationally consider areas of needed improvement without blaming themselves or the interviewer or experiencing depressing feelings of failure. Although these results show that it is possible to improve the components of job interviewing, it does not demonstrate that this approach will increase job interview attendance or actual employment.

One of the few studies to demonstrate a change in employment status following social skills training was a single case design reported by Hollandsworth, Glazeski and Dressel (1978). These authors viewed social skills training as being directly applicable to the job interview setting. Through reinforcing specific social skill behaviors they were able to achieve employment of an individual who had an exceptionally dismal employment history.

Azrin (1977) has been an innovator in applying behavioral techniques to a variety of settings while measuring relevant behavioral outcomes. He believes that a major problem in treatment studies is that outcome has become secondary to form, and that unlike lab experiments in which a single variable can be isolated, outcome-oriented research, such as programs to facilitate job finding should emphasize the benefit resulting from treatment rather than a conceptual variable. By changing treatment procedures until little improvement results from additional procedure changes, he has successfully applied behavioral techniques to the job-finding situation with an outcome of increased employment.

In 1973, Jones and Azrin proposed that social factors play a major role in the job-finding process. They viewed job finding as an exchange of social reinforcers in which the first behavioral step is to locate a job opening. They designed an information reward advertisement procedure for motivating community residents to report unpublished job possibilities. Job leads were called into the Illinois State Employment Service in response to an advertisement that offered a financial reward for the information. Fewer leads were provided in response to the ad without the reward. In fact, the reward advertisement was shown to be the more cost-effective procedure. These results demonstrate the success of external incentives from the immediate environment in obtaining job leads. They also suggest that the employment process depends on factors unrelated to job skills.

In 1975 Azrin, Flores, and Kaplan designed a job counseling and finding program using behavior modification in which the central guiding concept was that the task should be a structured, supervised learning experience in which the component skills were to be reinforced. Job counseling was viewed as a learning experience to be continued until a job was obtained. Clients were referred from several sources, including a State of Illinois Employment Service Agency. Those clients receiving unemployment commmpensation were screened out because of possible lack of motivation to find work. The job-finding component required a number of complex skills to be learned in a structured situation that emphasized motivation, maintenance of behavior, feedback, and practice. The procedure included a buddy system, family support, self-help, sharing job leads, want ads, role playing, telephone contacts, constructing resumes, and contacting friends for jobs. As part of the buddy system, clients were paired off during each session to provide mutual assistance and encouragement. To increase motivation among clients, taped commentaries and statistics from past job-finding club successes were provided, and counselor and peer encouragement were an integral part of the procedure. Results indicated that 90% of those who attended the program regularly were employed within 2 months with higher salaries than the 55% of the noncounseled group who gained employment. While welfare clients were not used in this innovative project, it was suggested that hardcore populations would benefit from such a program.

The Job Factory (1976) is another job-finding type club developed in Cambridge, Massachusetts. Similar in concept to the Azrin, Flores, and Kaplan program, finding a job was viewed as daily work in itself, and jobs were to be found through the clients' own efforts. Participants were offered $2.30 an hour for 160 hours of job searching under Title I of CETA. The results suggest that at least for this select group, the quality and quantity of job-seeking efforts played a crucial role in obtaining employment.

One of the problems that occurs repeatedly with the welfare population is that as long as clients find ways to receive their payments without participating in a job-finding program, they are less likely to eventually join the labor force. Azrin, Flores, and Kaplan's results led to the development of job finding clubs in several agencies and stimulated efforts to teach job interviewing skills to other hard to place individuals, such as former psychiatric inpatients (Furman, Geller, Simon, & Kelly, 1979) and the handicapped (Rogers, 1981). In theory, the federal Work Incentive Program (WIN) is an ideal setting for a contingency management system. In reality there are no strong consequences for not participating and no strong reinforcers to motivate clients to become involved in vocational counseling or job development. The job finding club approach has been introduced to WIN, but with staff turnover and a reluctance to hire operantly sophisticated staff, the essential behavioral techniques are altered over time, and typical of agency inertia, tend to regress back to the way things were.

COGNITIVE TECHNIQUES IN VOCATIONAL COUNSELING

Systematic attempts to investigate the effectiveness of using cognitive therapy techniques in a vocational setting are lacking. Although vocational problems do occur in clients' individual and group therapy sessions, government employment programs have not systematically examined some of the newer cognitive restructuring techniques that have been found helpful to clients in other settings (DiGiuseppe, Miller, & Trexler, 1977).

Rational-emotive therapy (RET) is a type of cognitive restructuring developed by Ellis (1962) to teach individuals a more logical way of thinking by replacing irrational thoughts with more adaptive self-statements. This model is believed to reduce extreme negative emotions which interfere with an individual's healthy, goal-oriented behaviors. RET is based on the philosophy that people disturb themselves by their own irrational belief system. Ellis (1962) delineated eleven irrational beliefs that cause and sustain emotional disturbance. Since Ellis has stated that "because of its simplicity and its clarity, rational-emotive psychotherapy seems to work better with less intelligent, poorly educated, economically deprived patients than most of the . . . other therapies," it seems reasonable to conclude that a cognitive restructuring technique similar to RET might help to alter those attitudes and beliefs that inhibit the hardcore unemployed from attempting to enter the labor force.

As with behavioral techniques, counselors may be frequently and unsystematically using some cognitive techniques similar to RET either unknowingly or incorrectly, but their results are not rigorously evaluated. The inconsistencies in the evaluations of effective counseling techniques in vocational settings is exemplified in the work of Woodard, Burck, and Sweeney (1975). Twelve employment counselors and ten counselor supervisors attended a workshop on enhancing relationship skills and evaluated the counseling styles presented in the Rogers, Perls, and Ellis film, "Three Approaches to Psychotherapy." Neither counselors nor supervisors agreed among themselves on their evaluations of the relationship skills in the three counseling styles presented. A higher overall opinion of Ellis was held by counselors than supervisors. The lack of consensus suggests deficiencies in education or training among these individuals who are supposed to be fulfilling similar roles.

The only exception to the lack of evidence on systematic cognitive restructuring for vocational problems is a case study of a 39-year old chronically unemployed client reported by Mallary and Conner (1975). In this instance, lack of self-confidence was diagnosed as the vocational problem. It was found that by teaching the client to discover, challenge, and replace his irrational beliefs and by giving him training in new behaviors, he was able to reach the major objective of securing and maintaining satisfactory employment. These findings suggest as yet unexplored possibilities for using cognitive counseling techniques in job finding. They also reiterate the need for research that measures employment as the dependent variable.

Goodwin's finding (1972) that welfare women who view welfare as acceptable take fewer job-related actions than those who view public assistance negatively indicates a relationship between beliefs and an individual's functioning. Many of the employment barriers discussed earlier, such as attitudes toward welfare and anxiety about work, can be found to have a large cognitive component. The concept of rule-controlled behavior (Malott, Tillema, & Glenn, 1978) helps to explain this relationship. Our own selected self-stated rules may determine our actions. For example, the hardcore frequently tell themselves that they should be provided with job opportunities without having to learn specific job skills. This self-statement leads to maintenance of the same inappropriate behaviors and responses when going on job interviews as well as the lack of attempts to acquire the appropriate job skills. Anger is usually the emotional result. Those who have different beliefs will be more likely to obtain the job. Even if they fail to obtain the job, they will be less emotionally disturbed by the occurrence. The actual experience of being on welfare may be related to types of beliefs or self-statements. Richman (1981) found that the longer women were on welfare, the greater their endorsement of irrational beliefs as measured on an Irrational Belief Inventory (Kassinove, Crisci, & Tiegerman, 1977).

Cognitive restructuring when applied to the vocational arena can be an aid to understanding and altering the self-statements and beliefs of the unemployed as they relate to self-concept, aspirations, need for comfort, view of society and other areas associated with changing job status. The advantages of combining cognitive and behavioral techniques has been recommended (Mahoney, 1977), although this point of view is not universally accepted (Brigham, 1980; Ledwidge, 1978; Rachlin, 1977). Nonetheless, the time is certainly right for providing our employment programs with techniques that may positively impact the welfare problem.

Although behavioral skills training programs have been shown to be effective in job finding (Azrin, Flores & Kaplan, 1975) a variety of clinical observations (King & Manaster, 1977; Messer & Lehrer, 1976) suggest that emotional and self-concept variables are also important in the job-finding process. With this in mind, the current approach focuses on changing both job-finding behaviors and attitudinal concerns. Depending on the population, it is suggested that varying emphasis should be given to cognitive and behavioral techniques when counseling hard to place individuals. Throughout the literature on attempts to obtain employment for the hardcore, those with difficult barriers to employment had to be screened out and financial incentives introduced to help motivate participation in the programs. This again points out a very real barrier to finding work – you need money to get money.

A SKILLS TRAINING APPROACH TO JOB FINDING

There is a need to investigate the efficacy of cognitive and behavioral approaches to job finding both independently and as an integrated technique using employment as the outcome measure. In the only controlled examination of these techniques to date, Richman (1979) compared cognitive restructuring, behavior modification, and combined cognitive behavioral programs in a group counseling format to regular employment services within a WIN program. Subjects consisted of 76 female WIN participants who had children at least 6 years of age. Their length of time on welfare averaged 66.90 months, while aggregate time employed prior to the current unemployment averaged 34.71 months. The women were assigned to one of three treatment groups (behavioral, cognitive, or combined) or a control group that received the regular agency services. Those receiving group treatments also were provided with office services since this study was conducted in an actual job agency setting.

The behavior modification program was based on Azrin, Flores, and Kaplan (1975) but was limited to one hourly session each week for 6 weeks. Much emphasis was placed on feedback of interview responses and practice of appropriate verbal behavior using tape-recorded samples. Two telephones were used (each an extension of the other) for job interview simulation, direct contact with employers, and behavior rehearsal. Verbal reinforcement from the group leader and group members was given for appropriate job-finding behaviors. Techniques included a buddy system, progress charts, modeling, role playing, and sharing job leads. The participants were given practice in assertive behavior rehearsal. Worksheets for teaching telephone contact behaviors and following up job finding activities were modified from forms previously used by Azrin et al. (1975) [See Azrin & Besalel, 1980]. Imagery was used to rehearse behavior in a job interview situation, but the program emphasized changes in job seeking behaviors rather than changing thoughts about employment.

The group receiving the cognitive restructuring treatment was based on Ellis' theory (1962) of human disturbance as applied to a vocational counseling setting. Rational-emotive counseling was used to teach subjects that their irrational beliefs about an event lead to negative consequences. The results of these beliefs may be emotions such as anger or behaviors such as failing to keep an appointment for a job interview. The focus was on presenting and discussing the eleven irrational ideas described by Ellis (1962) and teaching subjects to dispute these views as they related to job situations and events in their lives. The cognitive components of rational-emotive counseling were emphasized, and the behavioral techniques usually used with RET were limited to focusing on attitudes about behaviors rather than on actual behavior change within the group or as homework. Worksheets were used to teach how irrational thoughts lead to disturbance. The effect of changing ideas about a vocational situation, as well as about oneself, to effect less negative emotions and more productive functioning was stressed. Rational-emotive imagery was employed with a focus on self-statements about situations rather than the actual behavior in a given situation.

The combination group utilized both the cognitive restructuring techniques and behavior modification technique during the six 1-hour weekly sessions. The first half hour of each session utilized cognitive techniques, and the second half hour added the behavioral components. The control group met with employment interviewers once a week for regular job development services.

Since the WIN population is limited to those who are certified as eligible for the Program, 17 of these women developed valid obstacles that made them unable to find a job or continue in the program. These legitimate barriers made the individual no longer eligible to obtain work through WIN. However, legitimate barriers were not equivalent to failure to obtain employment or to success in obtaining employment. Thus treatment outcome was analyzed by eliminating subjects having legitimate barriers from the analysis. Barriers that were considered legitimate consisted of child care problems, family health problems, personal health problems, loss of welfare eligibility, part-time work prior to treatment without having initially informed the experimenter, refusal of employment, and leaving the outreach community.

When excluding those who developed legitimate barriers to employment from the analysis, all of the subjects in the behavior modification group obtained jobs or entered job training programs, compared to 75% of the combination group, 53% of the cognitive group, and 35% of the control group. The number of subjects who obtained jobs or entered training programs in both the behavioral and combination groups was significantly greater than in the control group. Re-analysis considering barriers as successes because individuals were no longer on welfare, or as failures because the individuals had not obtained placement, did not meaningfully change the between group differences. There were no significant between-group differences in the number of subjects who developed barriers or in the small number of subjects (< 10%) who entered training programs rather than obtaining employment.

The results further showed that subjects in the behavior modification group obtained more jobs without agency assistance than subjects in the other three groups combined and contacted a significantly larger number of employers than subjects in the other three groups. On self-report measures, subjects in the combination group endorsed fewer irrational statements than those in the behavioral or control group.

Given the overall superiority of the behavior modification group in both job seeking and placements, it is clear that any job-finding program must focus primarily on changing applicant behavior. The Azrin, Flores, and Kaplan (1975) model of breaking the job research into segments and teaching specific skills for those segments appears to be the most effective means of increasing employability. In contrast to the Azrin, Flores, and Kaplan format, these results suggest that the 8-hour a day, 5-day a week model of job finding is unnecessary since even the hardcore unemployed of the present study obtained jobs in this once a week program. Although the behavioral techniques accounted for most of the improvement variance in the results, the clients' anecdotal reports and observations of the counselors suggested that the cognitive restructuring program was beneficial in helping the clients deal with emotional blocks to learning new behavior.

SKILLS PROGRAM FOR JOB FINDING

There are many components to the process of obtaining employment and the task becomes more problematic when working with the hardcore unemployed and a tight labor market. While there are no hard and fast rules for how to proceed in helping hard to place clients become self-sufficient, previous research and clinical observations suggest incorporting behavior modification and cognitive approaches into a job-finding package. The purpose of such a job-finding skills program is to increase economic self-sufficiency among those individuals who have experienced great difficulty in obtaining employment. This type of program is presented at the end of this chapter. It is a systematic program which can be integrated into an already functioning vocational counseling setting. The utilization of this program will provide the counselor with specific techniques to lead to beneficial changes in the behavior, thoughts, and emotions of their clients during the job-finding process.

In general the job-finding skills program is likely to be most effective if the following guidelines are adopted. First, it is recommended that individuals voluntarily participate in the program. Transportation vouchers should be provided if necessary. It seems likely that those with stated barriers to employment but a motivation to work may profit from a time-limited cognitive group to deal with their barriers before the actual job-finding behaviors are taught. The agency may also help the client by providing concrete services to take care of barriers such as child care problems.

The actual group should not exceed 10 persons, and it is preferable to have an even number of group members. The group should be conducted at least once a week for a period of 1½ hours.

To assess each client's cognitive style, the reader may want to employ an Assertion Inventory, a Rational Belief Inventory, or some measure of self-esteem prior to treatment. Some self-rating of motivation to work may also be desirable. Worksheets to be administered throughout the program are included in the following treatment plan. Ideally the groups should be conducted for eight weekly sessions but could be condensed to six as in this example or continued indefinitely if required. These sessions may be ongoing, but those who do not obtain employment after at least 16 weeks and have been following this procedure should be assessed further while continuing the program.

While the steps to take are broken down by session, it is important to understand that the presentation at each stage of the program may vary in areas such as pacing and level of teaching. This will be influenced by the group population, i.e., women, youth, welfare clients, as well as the setting in which the program is conducted, i.e., state employment service, welfare office, or private career workshop. As the group leader becomes more knowledgeable about each group member, he may find that some individuals will require more time on learning cognitive skills to deal with thoughts such as, "It is better to receive medicaid and food stamps than to obtain a low paying job." Other group members may require extra time to role play job interview behaviors before attending an actual job interview. Thus, it is recommended that the following program be utilized as an overall guide, with an emphasis placed on defining the problems of group members and frequently re-evaluating them to make sure that the session's objectives are in line with the group members' vocational problems.

There are several specific techniques that are to be used at every session. Group members should be provided with social reinforcers such as verbal praise for specific appropriate job-related behaviors and feedback about their performance as they begin to make phone calls and arrange for job interviews.

Group members should discuss their job finding experiences of the previous week and outline plans for the next week's efforts. References should be made to a centrally located bulletin board on which job leads are posted as they are obtained by group members. The following three worksheets should be discussed and reviewed at the beginning of *each* session: "Progress Chart," "My Vocational Goals," and "Behaviors I Want To Work on to Improve My Job-Finding Skills." It is important that each member make his own progress chart and that the group leader make a large progress chart with names of each group member. This larger chart should be placed in front of the room during each session. At the end of each session, members should be prompted to monitor their job-seeking behaviors and be reinforced for constructive plans for the week ahead.

JOB-FINDING PROGRAM

Session 1 – Objectives: Introduction. Teach maintenance of work sheets and begin job opening research.

    1. Orientation – explain that obtaining employment is the goal of the weekly sessions. Verbally reinforce subjects for participating. (Do this weekly.)

    2. Discuss behaviors related to finding a job, giving specific examples such as contact friends who might know of jobs, rehearse interview behavior, look up want ads, dress neatly for interview, etc.

    3. Hand out the individual "Progress Chart" to each participant and demonstrate how to fill it out. Explain the meaning of employers contacted, interviews arranged, interviews attended, and jobs obtained, show group "Progress Chart" (Figure 14.1).

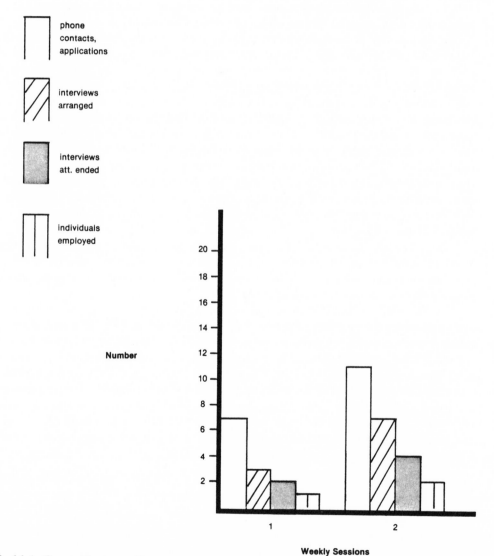

FIG. 14.1. Group Progress Chart.

4. Have the subjects fill out the worksheet, "My Vocational Goals and How I Plan to Achieve Them." Discuss realistic versus idealistic vocational goals, including type of job desired, salary range, location, and actions taken. Emphasize flexibility of goals in relation to job skills and job market.

TABLE 14.1. Vocational Goals and Plans.

My Vocational Goals and How I Plan to Achieve Them			
Date	Type Job I Want	Salary Range	Location	Where I've Looked or Plan to Look

5. Fill out the worksheet, "Behaviors I Want to Work on to Improve My Job-Finding Skills." Operationally define each term on this sheet. Help the subjects rate their current level through giving them feedback.

6. Explain importance of continuously using worksheets for monitoring job-finding behaviors as the group members look for jobs during the week.

TABLE 14.2. Selecting Appropriate Job-Finding Behaviors.

Circle the appropriate number for yourself.   Name _____

Behaviors I Want To Work On To Improve My Job Finding Skills*

Completely Inappropriate Needing a lot of Improvement	1 2 3 4 5	Completely Appropriate Needing no Improvement
Volume of Voice (soft-loud)	1 2 3 4 5	
Clarity of Voice (mumble-articulate)	1 2 3 4 5	
Assertiveness (withdrawn-expresses self appropriately)	1 2 3 4 5	
Confidence (self-downing-positive about self)	1 2 3 4 5	
Eye Contact (avoids-looks at)	1 2 3 4 5	
Content	1 2 3 4 5	
Affect (unemotional-enthusiastic)	1 2 3 4 5	
Appearance	1 2 3 4 5	

*On the actual form, the 5 point scale is presented 6 times for each behavior so that each response can be rated weekly.

Session 2 – Objectives: Set up buddy system. Present job opening location skills. Teach telephone skills. Teach discrimination between thoughts and emotions.

    1. Report on progress and fill in charts from last week. (Do weekly.)

    2. Share what behaviors have worked and not worked in the past.

    3. Set up a buddy system pairing the participants. Explain that these pairs will give each other feedback on interviews using the extension telephones.

    4. Hand out "What To Include in a First Telephone Contact with An Employer" and discuss the actions involved.

TABLE 14.3. What to Include in a First Telephone Contact With an Employer.

1. Introduce yourself.	—	—	—	—	—	—
2. Ask for Personnel or Department head.						
3. Introduce yourself to Personnel.	—	—	—	—	—	—
4. Tell how you heard of the firm. (I was referred by – – –; I found your firm in the Yellow Pages; I saw your ad for file clerk in the New York Times.)	—	—	—	—	—	—
5. Give your qualifications	—	—	—	—	—	—
6. Ask for an interview. (I would like to set up an interview with you at your earliest convenience.)	—	—	—	—	—	—
7. If the employer says no, ask for an appointment anyway. (Could I come in and talk to you anyway in case something opens up unexpectedly?)	—	—	—	—	—	—
8. Job Lead in the area. (Can you suggest any other places I could contact?)	—	—	—	—	—	—
9. Confirm date and time of interview if employer says yes.	—	—	—	—	—	—
10. Ask for name of person to speak with.	—	—	—	—	—	—
11. Ask for other positions for others.	—	—	—	—	—	—
12. Keep an organized list of appointments and contacts.	—	—	—	—	—	—

Source: Adapted and modified from Azrin, Philip, Borck, & Besalel-Azrin, 1978.

    5. Discuss resources for job finding: want ads and yellow pages, friends, relatives, previous employers, agencies. Explain that the bulletin board will be used for sharing job leads within the group.

    6. Identify and share feelings about being unemployed. Give examples of feelings: i.e., anger, joy, anxiety, depression. Help the clients to distinguish between intense and less intense feelings and between pleasant and unpleasant feelings.

    7. Teach the participants to distinguish between feelings and thoughts. Use worksheet "My Irrational Thoughts Lead to Excessive Feelings."

TABLE 14.4. My Irrational Thoughts (Ideas, Beliefs) Lead to Excessive Feelings.

Examples of Words Used in Irrational Ideas	Examples of Words Used in Rational Ideas	Examples of Extreme, Excessive feelings	Examples of Moderate Feelings
should	would be nice if	anger	annoyed
shouldn't	wish	depression	disappointed
must	want to	fear	bothered
have to	prefer	anxiety	slightly upset
can't stand it	don't like it	suspiciousness	bad
it's awful	it's too bad	guilt	sad
it's terrible	it's unfortunate		
it's horrible	it would be better if		

Self-statements About Working

Examples of Words Used in Irrational Ideas	Examples of Words Used in Rational Ideas	Examples of Extreme, Excessive feelings	Examples of Moderate Feelings
I *should* be hired without having to type 45 wpm.	*It would be nice* if I could be hired without having to type 45 wpm.	I feel *angry*.	I feel *annoyed*.
I *can't stand* having to be at work at 8:45 AM	I *don't like* having to be at work at 8:45 AM.	I feel *angry*.	I feel *annoyed*.
It's awful that I don't have a job.	*It's too bad* that I don't have a job.	I feel *depressed*.	I feel *disappointed*.

Session 3 – Objectives: Teach discrimination between productive and nonproductive thoughts. Initiate telephone contact programs. Teach skills in giving constructive, reinforcing feedback.

1. Using the Worksheet in Table 14.4, explain the difference between rational and irrational thoughts. Explain that evidence or proof can be found for rational thoughts. Fill out worksheet using irrational, and then rational self-statements about working. A chart listing the eleven irrational ideas as stated by Ellis (1962) can be helpful at this stage.

2. Tell the group the importance of recognizing their irrational or nonconstructive thoughts as these thoughts relate to job finding situations during the week.

TABLE 14.5. Job Leads – Use With Yellow Pages and Want Ads.

Who to Call	Phone Results
Name of Organization:	Date 1st call – – –
Phone Number:	Info:
Person to ask for:	Date 2nd call – – –
Address:	Info:
How to get there:	Appointment-Date – – –
	Time – – –

Source: Adapted from Azrin, Philip, Brock, & Besalel-Azrin, 1978 & Richman, 1979.

3. Hand out worksheet "Job Leads – Use with Yellow Pages and Want Ads." Using this as a guide and present vocational goals as a base, look up employers to call through want ads and yellow pages. Suggest making a list of contacts to ask for job leads during the week. Demonstrate organized method for keeping a record of the interviews that they arrange and attend and the outcome of these interviews.

4. Go over telephone contact form (Table 14.3). Play a demonstration tape of a poorly done telephone contact. Ask for feedback about the taped interview. Focus on specific behaviors previously discussed.

5. Have one pair of buddies role play a telephone interview without using the phone. Following the role play have them give each other feedback and then receive group feedback.

6. Have one subject call an insurance company while his buddy listens on the extension to evaluate initial contact skills.

7. Explain how to give positive and constructive feedback. Have five pairs give each other feedback on their phone calls using the worksheets as guides.

Session 4 – Objectives: Identify irrational thoughts about job finding. Teach flexibility in job-opening search using yellow pages and want ads. Practice interview and telephone skills with feedback.

1. Discuss the job-finding resources each member plans to use during the session.

2. Using worksheet, discuss which irrational ideas members think may hinder them in the job-finding process. Example: I need everyone's love and approval. Therefore, I can't stand the thought that an employer might reject me.

3. Teach how thoughts relate to feelings and how irrational thoughts lead to extremely negative, unpleasant feelings.

4. Demonstrate how individuals can view the same situation differently and thus experience different feelings about that situation.

5. Lead group in sharing thoughts about similar vocational situations, and ask how they felt when having those thoughts. Then ask what they did in the situation.

6. Play tape of model telephone contact. Then have a pair call while being taped. Afterwards have them listen to tape and report on the experience. Allow the caller to receive group feedback.

7. Conclude by having buddies take turns calling employers, giving and receiving feedback, and recording actions taken.

Session 5 – Objectives: Teach skills to combat negative emotions in response to job finding problems. Practice disputing negative self-evaluations. Teach skills for
combating emotional reactions in job interviews. Step-up rate of employer
calls and share job leads.

1. Distinguish between behaviors related to not working and personal worthiness. Ask
what group members think about themselves when not getting the job they desire.

2. Hand out "How I Cause My Own Disturbance as I Look for A Job." Introduce
method for disputing nonproductive thoughts. First identify activating events related to finding a job or not working and then identify feelings related to these events.

3. Ask for beliefs leading to negative feelings. Demonstrate some beliefs that come between events and emotional reactions.

4. Teach the participants disputing questions to ask after identifying the nonproductive
beliefs about the events.

5. Have group members ask disputing questions to each other and then complete the
worksheet in Table 10.6.

6. Play tape of job interview in which interviewee is withdrawn. Specify behaviors that
led to the interviewee not getting hired. Discuss feelings the interviewee might have been experiencing, the thoughts related to those feelings, and the possibility of not getting hired.

7. Call employers and share job leads.

TABLE 14.6. How I Cause My Own Disturbance as I Look for a Job.

Event *(action, experience)*	Describe the event about which you became upset. For example: The employer still hasn't called to tell me whether or not I got the job.
Rational Belief	A sensible, testable, or preferential idea about the activating event. For example: 1. *I wish* he would call me. 2. *It's too bad* he has not called me. 3. *I don't like* not knowing if I'll get the job.
Irrational Belief	An exaggerated, nonsensical idea or thought about the activating event that cannot be proven. For example: 1. *He should have* called me by now. 2. *It's awful* that he hasn't called me. 3. *I can't stand* not knowing if I'll get the job.
Emotional Consequence (emotional reaction, feelings)	Your reaction to your irrational beliefs and thoughts. For example: I feel depressed and angry.
Disputing	Questioning and challenging the irrational beliefs. For example: Why should he have called me? Where is the evidence that it is awful and that I can't stand it?
Effect	What feelings would you have if you were to think rationally? For example: I might feel annoyed or disappointed, but I can stand not knowing if I got the job.

Session 6 – Objectives: Practice responding unemotionally to job-finding problems. Practice assertive interview style. Teach rehearsal skills for job call. Collect outcome data and arrange continued programming when necessary.

  1. Ask group members what they are still telling themselves about looking for work and how they are feeling. Use the worksheet in Table 14.6.
  2. Tell the group members to imagine an event related to finding a job that they experienced during the week in which they felt negative emotions. Have them imagine changing their belief about the event and feeling better.
  3. Play tape of assertive interviewee. Identify behaviors which led to interviewee getting hired or not hired. Discuss the self-statements the interviewee was probably thinking and its relationship to his feelings and the interview outcome.
  4. Role play a job interview relating to openings that group members plan to call during the session or have appointments to attend during the week.
  5. Call employers and share job leads.
  6. Briefly review job-finding skills.
  7. Collect basic demographic data to follow-up as well as information on jobs obtained through the program.
  8. Arrange continued programming for any participants still unemployed.

REFERENCES

Azrin, N. H. A strategy for applied research: learning based but outcome oriented. *American Psychologist*, 1977, **32**, 140-149.

Azrin, N. H., & Besalel, V. A. *Job club counselor's manual: a behavioral approach to vocational counseling.* Baltimore: University Park Press, 1980.

Azrin, N. H., Flores, T., & Kaplan, S. J. Job-finding club: a group-assisted program for obtaining employment. *Behavior Research and Therapy*, 1975, **13**, 17-27.

Azrin, N. H., Philip, R. A., Borck, L., & Besalel-Azrin, V. *The job finding club as a method for obtaining employment for welfare-eligible clients: Demonstration, evaluation and counselor training.* Department of Labor Grant #51-17-76-04, 1978, National Technical Information Service.

Barbee, J. R., & Keil, E. C. Experimental techniques of job interview training for the disadvantaged: videotape feedback, behavior modification, and microcounseling. *Journal of Applied Psychology*, 1973, **58**, 209-213.

Baron, R. M., Bass, A. R., & Vietze, P. M. Type and frequency of praise as determinants of favorability of self-image: an experiment in a field setting. *Journal of Personality*, 1971, **39**, 493-511.

Barrett, T. C., & Tinsley, H. E. Vocational self-concept crystallization and vocational indecision, *Journal of Counseling Psychology*, 1977, **24**, 301-307.

Beatty, R. W. Supervisory behavior related to job success of hard-core unemployed over a two-year period. *Journal of Applied Psychology*, 1974, **59**, 38-42.

Bonney, W. C., Parsons, W., Scalise, J. J., Wagner, D. E., & Anderson, H. E. A study of group counseling with disadvantaged workers in an industrial setting. *Journal of Employment Counseling*, 1976, **93**, 86-93.

Brigham, T. A. Self-control revisited: Or why doesn't anyone actually read Skinner (1953). *The Behavior Analyst*, 1980, **3** (2), 25-33.

Burnside, B. The employment potential of AFDC mothers in six states. *Welfare in Review*, 1971, **9** (4), 16-18.

DiGiuseppe, R., Miller, N., & Trexler, L. A review of rational-emotive psychotherapy outcome studies. *The Counseling Psychologist*, 1977, **4**, 64-72.

Dooley, D., & Catalano, R. Economic change as a cause of behavioral disorder. *Psychological Bulletin*, 1980, **87**, 450-468.

Ellis, A. *Reason and emotion in psychotherapy*. New York: Lyle Stuart, Inc., 1962.

Ericksen, J. A. An analysis of the journey to work for women. *Social Problems*, 1977, **24**, 428–435.

Furman, W., Geller, M. I., Simon, S. J., & Kelly, J. A. The use of a behavior rehearsal procedure for teaching job interviewing skills to psychiatric patients. *Behavior Therapy*, 1979, **10**, 157–167.

Goodman, P. S. Hiring, training, and retaining the hard-core. *Industrial Relations*, 1969, **9**, 54–66.

Goodwin, L. *Do the poor want to work? A social psychological study of work orientation*. Washington, D.C.: Brookings Institute, 1972.

Goodwin, L. Middle-class misperceptions of the high life aspirations and strong work ethic held by the welfare poor. *American Journal of Orthopsychiatry*, 1973, **43**, 554–564.

Higgins, E. T. Social class differences in verbal communicative accuracy: A question of "which question?" *Psychological Bulletin*, 1976, **83**, 695–714.

Hollandsworth, J. G., Jr., Dressel, M. E., & Stevens, J. Use of behavioral versus traditional procedures for increasing job interview skills. *Journal of Counseling Psychology*, 1977, **24**, 503–510.

Hollandsworth, J. G., Jr., Glazeski, R. C., & Dressel, M. E. Use of social-skills training in the treatment of extreme anxiety and deficient verbal skills in the job-interview setting. *Journal of Applied Behavior Analysis*, 1978, **11**, 259–269.

Jones, R. J., & Azrin, N. H. An Experimental application of a social reinforcement approach to the problem of job-finding. *Journal of Applied Behavior Analysis*, 1973, **6**, 345–353.

Kassinove, H., Crisci, R., & Tiegerman, S. Developmental trends in rational thinking: Implications for rational-emotive school mental health programs. *Journal of Community Psychology*, 1977, **5**, 266–274.

Keil, E. C., & Barbee, J. R. Behavior modification and training the disadvantaged job interviewee. *Vocational Guidance Quarterly*, Sept. 1973, 50–56.

King, M. R., & Manaster, G. J. Body image, self-esteem, expectations, self-assessments, and actual success in a simulated job interview. *Journal of Applied Psychology*, 1977, **62**, 589–594.

Klausner, S. Z. *Six years in the lives of the impoverished; an examination of the WIN thesis*. Philadelphia: Center for Research on the Acts of Man, 1978.

Ledwidge, B. Cognitive behavior modification: A step in the wrong direction? *Psychological Bulletin*, 1978, **85**, 353–375.

Levinson, P. How employable are AFDC women? *Welfare in Review*, 1970, **8** (4), 12–16.

Loomis, R., & Starry, R. Welfare isn't working. *Journal of Employment Counseling*, 1975, **12**, 66–73.

Mahoney, M. J. Reflections on the cognitive-learning trend in psychotherapy. *American Psychologist*, 1977, **32**, 5–12.

Mallary, N. D., Jr., & Conner, B. H. An example of employment service adjustment counseling. *Journal of Employment Counseling*, 1975, **12**, 55–58.

Malott, R., Tillema, M., & Glenn, S. *Behavior analysis and behavior modification: An introduction*. Kalamazoo, Mich.: Behaviordelia, 1978.

Margolin, R. J., & Goldin, G. J. The integration of welfare and rehabilitation efforts for the rehabilitation of the public assistance client an attainable goal. *Rehabilitation Literature*, 1971, **32**, 328–331.

Messer, S. B., & Lehrer, P. N. Short-term groups with female welfare clients in a job-training program. *Professional Psychology*, 1976, **29**, 352–358.

Miller, C. D., & Oetting, G. Barriers to employment and the disadvantaged. *Personnel and Guidance Journal*, 1977, **Oct.**, 89–93.

Miskimins, R. W., & Baker, B. R. Self-concept and the disadvantaged. *Journal of Community Psychology*, 1973, **6**, 347–361.

Nagle, G. S. Number of contacts with disadvantaged applicants as an indicator of success. *Journal of Employment Counseling*, 1973, **10**, 203–207.

Niemi, B. The female-male differential in unemployment rates. *Industrial and Labor Relations Review*, 1973/74, **27**, 331–350.

Normand, W. C., Fensterheim, H., & Schrenzel, S. A systematic approach to brief therapy for patients from a low socioeconomic community. *Community Mental Health Journal*, 1967, **3**, 349–354.

Perry, C. R., Anderson, B., Rowan, R. L., & Northrup, H. R. *The impact of government manpower programs – in general and on minorities and women*. Philadelphia, PA: University of Pennsylvania, 1975.

Putnam, B. A., & Hansen, J. C. Relationship of self-concept and feminine role concept to vocational maturity in young women. *Journal of Counseling Psychology*, 1972, **19**, 436-440.

Rachlin, H. A survey of M. J. Mahoney's cognition and behavior modification. *Journal of Applied Behavior Analysis*, 1977, **10**, 369-374.

Rein, M., & Wishnov, B. Patterns of work and welfare in AFDC. *Welfare in Review*, 1971, **9**, 7-12.

Richman, D. R. *A comparison of cognitive and behavioral group counseling techniques for job finding with welfare women.* Unpublished doctoral dissertation, Hofstra University, 1979.

Richman, D. R. *Delay of gratification in relation to the rational thinking and demographic characteristics of welfare women.* Unpublished manuscript, The Institute for Rational Emotive Therapy, 1981.

Roessler, R., Cook, D. & Lillard, D. Effects of systematic group counseling on work adjustment clients. *Journal of Counseling Psychology*, 1977, **24**, 313-317.

Rogers, L. S. *A comparison of behavioral incentive systems in a job search program.* Unpublished masters thesis, Western Michigan University, 1981.

Salipante, P., Jr., & Goodman, P. Training, counseling, and retention of the hard-core unemployed. *Journal of Applied Psychology*, 1976, **61**, 1-11.

Siddall, J. W., & Balcerzak, W. S. A behavioral model for welfare reform: the volunteer incentive system *Behavior Therapy*, 1978, **9**, 243-247.

The Job Factory. Cambridge, Mass.: Office of Manpower Affairs, 1976.

Thursby, L. D. The WIN program: its success with female trainees. *Journal of Employment Counseling*, 1974, **7**, 13-15.

Varga, F. L. Employment counselors' perceptions of client needs. *Journal of Employment Counseling*, 1974, **11**, 63-72.

Warren, M., & Berkowitz, S. The employability of AFDC mothers and fathers. *Welfare in Review*, 1969, **7**, 107.

Weissman, M., Pincus, L. C., Radding, N., Lawrence, R., & Siegel, R. The educated housewife: mild depression and the search for work. *American Journal of Orthopsychiatry*, 1973, **43**, 565-573.

Williams, R. G. *Public assistance and work effort – the labor supply of low income female heads of households.* N.J.: Industrial Relations Section, Princeton University, 1975.

Woodard, W. S., Burck, H. D., & Sweeney, P. Counselors' evaluation of Rogers – Perls – Ellis's relationship skills. *Journal of Employment Counseling*, 1975, **12**, 108-111.

15

Outplacement Visited:
The New Old Personnel Function

William P. Brittain
Caress, Gilhooly & Kestin, Inc.

"O'Brien! You're fired!"
"You can't fire me! I quit!"
"You can't quit! You've already been fired!"

And so goes the termination scene as played out in soaps, dreams, movies, plays, and even once in a while in real life. Most of us at one time or another have fantasized about leaving a job and imagined the fireworks display that might accompany the event. Fortunately (or maybe unfortunately) it seldom happens this way. In fact, one of the most difficult jobs that managers at all levels have to face is the problem of terminating an employee. Most don't like to do it, and most do it badly.

Perhaps the most telling element in the scenario is the number of terms we have for describing the event. Some try to be kind. "We have to let you go." Isn't that sweet? Go? Where? Some attempt to make it sound totally mechanical: "There's been a Reduction in Force." This is known as RIF. It's kind of fun – "I've been Riffed."

If you're at the more senior level, the terms begin to change. It's embarrassing to be looking for a job as president of a corporation if you have to say that you have just been canned, fired, or excessed. To make matters worse, you just don't lay off or terminate (sounds too permanent) a vice president of corporate affairs. There simply has to be a more genteel approach. Consequently, if you've held on long enough to get to the executive suite, you probably won't be fired (except face to face). Instead, you may have to suffer the indignity of having "no place to go in the organization" or "perhaps there would be better opportunities for you elsewhere."

The terms "dehired" and "decruitment" never really caught on, but sometime in the late 1960s or early 1970s the term "outplacement" did catch on. If placement was a positive aspect of selection, then outplacement could also have positive connotations for "deselection." There might be a variety of official reasons for an executive leaving the company but the manner in which it is done and the process for making his/her departure a smooth one is becoming the province of the outplacement counselor or consultant.

A person who has been outplaced has, in fact, been fired. However, outplacement is more accurately described as a process by which an individual makes the transition from one organization to another with the assistance of professionals in the field of job changing and the marketing of individual skills. As a job change process, the outplacement approach generally cuts across several broad areas: (1) career assessment; (2) individual assessment; (3) career and personal counseling; (4) marketing and interview strategies; and (5) learning how to use the job market.

We will deal briefly with each of these facets in turn, but first let's take a quick tour of the different types of outplacement programs and approaches that are currently available.

APPROACHES TO OUTPLACEMENT

The concept of outplacement is often attributed to Thomas Hubbard of the management consulting firm THinc. Stephen Cuthrell of Fuchs, Cuthrell and Co., Inc., a New York based outplacement firm, believes the term may have been coined by David North, an early outplacement or job change consultant. In any event, the origins of outplacement are, at best, fuzzy. In the current literature (which is scant) outplacement is usually referred to as being a relatively new approach. In fact, it has been around in one form or another for 30 or so years. Bernard Haldane (Haldane Associates) received a government contract in the late 1940s to provide resumés, interview skills, and job-finding training to newly discharged servicemen moving back into the civilian job market. Perhaps this was the earliest and largest example of outplacement counselling. Many of the techniques developed during this period by Haldane have withstood the test of time and have been adopted, adapted, embellished, and refined over the years. This evolution of technique has resulted in the current process of outplacement.

Various individuals have made claims concerning the origin of certain techniques and descriptive terms. For example, Robert Gerberg of Performance Dynamics International claims to have made the conceptual connection between the marketing of consumer products and the marketing of executive talent. However, the use of "marketing plans", "sales approach", and other such terms are almost uniform within the outplacement industry. So, what's the point?

The point is this: even though different outplacement firms seem to be offering a variety of strategies and approaches to job finding and outplacement, they are really all pretty much alike in terms of the information the outplaced executive will receive regarding the "how to" of job changings. There are a limited number of ways to get inside the hidden job market, answer ads, conduct interviews and so forth. In fact, most outplacement consultants agree on the initial phases of outplacement strategy beginning with how to fire the "redundant" (another great euphemism!) person and bring in the outplacement professional.

The real difference in approach emerges in the way which the outplaced individual is handled by the outplacement firm. Even here, there are areas of functional similarity.

Nearly all outplacement consultants agree on how the termination process should proceed. For example, never fire an individual on a Friday or just before a vacation. This just serves to give the terminated person a lot of free time to stew and become bitter over the event. While most outplacement consultants would not term it quite this way, immediate intervention helps to short circuit the effects of cognitive rehearsal on the part of the terminated person. Such rehearsal can cover a lot of ground over a 4-hour period. Furthermore, the cognitive elements are not likely to be positive in nature unless guided by a counselor familiar with the situation and capable of directing the fired executive toward more positive reinforcing actions. This is why notification should be handled by a well-prepared senior executive and immediately supported by an outplacement counselor. Most consultants feel they should be the next person the terminated individual speaks to, and that the outplacement counseling should begin within 15-20 minutes of termination notice. It is in these first few minutes that the most drastic and negative alternatives will be entertained by the terminated individual. James Fuchs of Fuchs, Cuthrell and Co. has many hair raising tales concerning the irrational behavior of fired executives immediately after termination notice, including attempts to jump from the office window and the suggestion that it might be prudent to collect on a $320,000 life insurance policy to take care of the family.

Certainly, most termination situations are not this dramatic. However, they do require astute counseling skills and the ability to function effectively in a crisis intervention situation. Unfortunately, it may be the one area where outplacement consultants are least well prepared (from a professional point of view). Most rely on the tactic of reflective listening and persuasive argument to get the client to agree to participate actively in the outplacement program that is being provided. Happily, this approach works pretty well and the venting process tends to diffuse potentially difficult situations.

The next step in the outplacement process is also universally common in the various approaches. This involves giving the terminated individual a number of assignments to complete within a short span of time and setting up a series of appointments with outplacement counselors to get things rolling. This also serves to occupy the terminated individual's thought processes and time in such a way as to prevent them from dwelling on the negatives of the immediate situation related to job loss. It also helps to focus his/her attention on the positive elements of career continuation and job seeking.

Most of these assignments are focused on self and career assessment procedures which are generally oriented toward getting the terminated individual to write out personal accomplishments in a skills and bottom-line approach. In other words, what can you do, what have you done, how well do you do it, and what's your proof? This not only starts the candidate thinking in terms of successes rather than failures, but provides much of the basic data which will go into the resumé and cover letters.

The way in which the candidate will use these materials (the marketing strategy) in a job campaign to enter the hidden market and fully utilize the open job market is the backbone of the outplacement service according to the brochures. Indeed, how to go about finding a job or ensuring career continuation is something of which most executives are woefully ignorant. These tactics (though sold for a pretty penny) are really very straightforward and not very mysterious. There are several good books on the subject, some better, some worse, but all useful (Bolles, 1977; Jameson, 1978; Sweet, 1975). There are also many good references on resumé writing (Jameson. 1978; Lewis 1977; Reed, 1981; Biegeleisen, 1976; Breenan, Strand, & Gruber, 1973). There is a remarkable similarity in the quality, type, use of the resumés prepared by or under the direction of the various outplacement firms. All emphasize functional, accomplishment-oriented statements that point up the individual's skills and serve as an advertisement for the candidate. Likewise, interview techniques are very much alike in each of the different approaches.

The reason that there is so little difference in each of these programs is that they represent logical and straightforward steps toward job procurement. Unfortunately, the terminated executive is in no position to think logically or take effective action. Extinction-based emotional behavior pre-empts logical thinking. His/her self messages are dominated by avoidance responses. Like the individual who never wins contests, he/she analyzes the situation hopelessly in the following kind of way:

> "Why don't you enter the contest?"
> "Because I never win anything!"
> "How can you win if you don't enter?"
> "Can't."
> "So why don't you enter?!?"
> "Because I never WIN!!!"

This is perfectly circular logic and self-defeating behavior. What's left unspoken in this type of dialogue is the fact that you also cannot *lose* if you don't enter! If the reinforcement history has included significant elements of punishments or negative consequences for taking the initiative and being self-starting or self-motivated, then what we may be dealing with is a learned helplessness situation: I can't win so why try? Such a situation can be set up through a history of nonreinforcements for assertive behaviors as well.

Obviously, such circular logic will not stop the negative spiral. In such cases it is imperative to identify alternative sources of reinforcements that can be tied to desired consequent behaviors related to job finding in order to get the out of work executive "back in the contest."

For the executive who has had a positive reinforcement history concerning behaviors aimed at being self-sufficient and assertive, the situation may not be so serious. However, it is still important to address the problem of establishing effective reinforcement contingencies within the outplacement program in order to maintain a positive and productive behavior pattern during the job campaign.

In the former case, a more directive approach may work the best. This is true since more time must be spent in identifying and controlling the reinforcement contingencies that provide alternative behaviors to the "I can't win" behaviors which dominate the individual's job-finding attitude.

The latter situation describes an individual who may not need the same kind of redirection. As a consequence, less structure may be more effective and satisfying for the individual with a strong reinforcement history which includes behaviors consistent with an effective job campaign.

Two Basic Counseling Approaches in Outplacement

At this point in the process, divergent counseling approaches surface depending upon the individual's reinforcement history. The differences seem to fall into two categories: (Type A) "Now you know how to do it, you're on your own," and (Type B) "We've taught you how, now let's do it together."

Even the "let's do it together" type places the actual implementation of a job search campaign squarely on the shoulders of the candidate. Responsibility for generating contacts, searching out job leads, arranging interviews, and all the rest of the basic leg work must be done by the candidate. No one is going to do it for him. Of course, for the right amount of money, service can include professionally written resumés, cover letter, and printing, but the actual campaign is the sole province of the job seeker.

Type A approach. In the Type A approach, the candidate is to a large degree on his or her own very early. Working closely with a consultant is not likely to take place until after all the basic data on background, experience, and accomplishments, have been produced by the candidate and analyzed by the consultant. This information is analyzed, a marketing strategy devised, and presented to the candidate for approval and implementation. Only then, and only for a limited time, does the consultant work closely with the candidate. In fact, the goal is to minimize the amount of direct consulting time required per candidate while keeping the end result positive.

For some individuals, this system may be ideal, for others, disastrous. An individual who has a high energy level, good accomplishments, is a quick learner with intact sales skills, has maintained a strong self-image and is "rarin' to go" will thrive on this approach. Candidates weak in these areas, who are not naturally aggressive self-starters or are suffering real damage to self-esteem as a result of being fired, may find this Type A approach offensive and ineffective.

Type B approach. The Type B approach tends to be a great deal more supportive than Type A. The relationship between consultant and candidate begins much sooner in the process and continues over a longer period of time. While it is still true that the burden of the campaign is on the candidate, the consultant is likely to be more closely involved all along the route. For example, even though the candidate may be asked to independently generate the initial background data, the consultant is frequently involved in this process by probing, cajoling, listening, writing and rewriting, and working through a variety of assessment processes to arrive jointly at an appropriate marketing strategy and career goal. It is the Type B approach that best fits the description of career continuation counseling.

Clearly, this approach is designed to head off and manage many of the anxieties of the newly outplaced executive. It is highly supportive and positive in nature. By its very structure, it is a less high-pressure approach. It is slower and concentrates more on the needs of the individual, both careerwise and personally. The Type B approach would very likely frustrate the self-reliant, highly motivated individual that tends to thrive under the Type A regimen. Sometimes, the Type B approach is described defensively as hand holding or molly coddling. I have a feeling that these descriptions were coined by people who have never been fired from a position of authority on a Monday morning without prior warning and little understanding of why their life's rug has just been pulled out from under them. There is a place for both approaches to outplacement.

WHY IS OUTPLACEMENT CATCHING ON?

To quote Herbert Meyer (1977): "Next to getting the ax, there is no more dreaded experience in the corporate world than wielding it." As stated at the outset of this chapter, most executives are unprepared to handle the firing of a subordinate. It's not something that's done every day so they don't get a lot of practice. Most tend to put it off until the last minute and then just get it over with. The professional outplacement counselor can help with this chore by being there immediately after the fact to cushion the blow for both the ax wielder and the victim.

In addition, there are logical economic reasons for going the outplacement route rather than simply throwing people out into the street. In the long run, it can be less expensive than taking the traditional approach of severance pay (which could equal a year's salary or more). Instead, "bridging pay" is offered which lasts only until the outplaced person is relocated in another position.

According to the various outplacement firms, a senior executive can expect to be in the job market from 4 to 6 months. The data on this point is rather soft because outplacement consultants don't like to divulge their failures. However, the 6-month figure is probably fairly acurate. If so, then the savings to the victim's old company is rather substantial.

There is a more compelling reason for the popularity of outplacement services. Executives who have been on the job for any length of time have generally had very little experience with the problems of finding a job. If they have climbed the corporate ladder in one company, then it's a sure bet that they haven't any experience in finding a job at the senior level.

Psychologically, it's like starting over from scratch with no idea of how to begin. In other words, behaviors related to an effective job campaign simply do not exist in the individual's response repertoire. Furthermore, none of their most recent colleagues are likely to know how to help. More importantly, an individual who is abruptly canned with no offer of help and no visible means of support is likely to resist or remonstrate.

He may go away mad with revenge on his mind – the possibility of selling company secrets suddenly seems like a satisfying thing to do. A good outplacement consultant can help move the unwanted executive offstage quickly and smoothly with a minimum of histrionics. Again, the consultant's major task is to identify or provide alternative behaviors and the reinforcement to firmly establish them in the candidate's behavioral repertoire. By doing so, they can not only keep him/her from making errors of strategy early in the game, but provide a safe place to vent negative feelings, smooth out differences between the adversaries, and salve the firing organization's conscience at the same time.

Chris Welles, writing in *Esquire Fortnightly* (1978), has called outplacement a "corporate guilt trip." Perhaps it is, but in my experience and the experience of most professionals in the field, that is a minor element in the overall picture. The fact is that most fired executives are in need of some help, if even for a short time, to get themselves back into a positive mode of thinking and/or to learn or brush up on those skills that will get them back on the job and let them continue their careers.

From the corporate point of view, the positive after effects are just as important as not having to take the heat from the newly fired individual. The people who stay behind are always affected by a firing, sometimes profoundly. Problems with "post partum depression" on the part of those who were not dehired are very real. Morale is often a major problem. The fact that the company can demonstrate its human concerns by providing professional assistance can make a significant difference to those who stay as well as those who go. While this statement may seem contradictory, providing professional outplacement assistance indicates to the remaining employees that the company considers them to be important, to have personal and professional worth, and further that they will not be abandoned without help.

IN-HOUSE VS. OUTSIDE SERVICES

Up to now, I have been dealing with outplacement as a service, provided by an outside consulting organization. Many of the same services can be provided in-house. Citibank in New York and General Electric are both good examples of in-house outplacement services. Most companies either can't afford to take on the outplacement function or the turn-over rate is too small to be cost effective. The job of the outplacement counselor is a full time one, at least for the duration of the dehired executive's job search. This is true even for a single outplacement assignment. It's simply easier, in most cases, to go outside.

There are also very strong behavioral reasons to take the outplacement function outside. It is often difficult to establish a feeling of mutual trust with the in-house approach. It is a bit ironic to have the same entity that chopped off your head turn right around and offer to help you replace it in another location. It may be hard to believe in the sincerity of the offer.

Additionally, the newly fired executive really needs the opportunity to vent his/her feelings about people, the company, etc. It's safer and the fired executive is likely to work through his/her anger and frustration much more quickly with a counselor who has no real connection with the old company. It is also true that firing companies find it easier to give the real reasons for a dismissal to an outside agent than an inside person, especially if the dismissed individual is at a senior level in the organization.

Other questions which bear on this issue can perhaps best be summed up in the following guidelines for selecting an outside outplacement agent offered by Industrial Relations News (Farish, 1978):

1. What is the consultant's length of experience in the outplacement field?
2. With which companies has he worked? Were they pleased?

3. Check with companies that have seen applicants prepared by that consultant.
4. Does the consultant work with or train the person who will do the firing?
5. To what degree can or does the consultant stay with the person until he is hired?
6. How well and to what degree does the consultant work with the internal personnel staff?
7. Determine the degree to which the company is kept informed of the outplaced person's job search progress.
8. If you are considering multiple staff reductions, then be sure to check the size and experience of the consulting staff.

Each of these points is offered as a guide to selecting an outside outplacement firm. The questions should be considered when deciding whether or not to bring the outplacement function inside under the jurisdiction of the personnel department. In most cases, turnover rate and staff experience will not justify the expense of handling outplacement as an in-house function. The outplacement consultant approach will generally prove to be easier, more cost effective, and yield better results from all points of view.

WHY EXECUTIVES GET FIRED AND/OR OUTPLACED

Contrary to populat belief, most executives do not lose their jobs because they are bad at what they do. It is more often the case that the struggle for power at the top leads to disagreements in management styles or conflict over lines of control. Many times it is as simple (or perhaps complex) as a poor match in personal style (sometimes called personality differences) between top managers. There is simply not room for two "top dogs." Consequently, most outplaced executives are competent and marketable. Furthermore, if the outplacement consultants' statistics are correct, 80 to 90% will land a better job at higher pay than the one they just vacated.

Of course, it is true that executives lose their jobs because they can't handle them or because expectations all around were unrealistic. When this is the case the outplacement process can focus on the problem areas, uncover the source of the difficulty, and point the executive in a more realistic, rewarding, and potentially more productive direction.

There is another reason that has been suggested as a cause of poor performance leading to dismissal – burnout. This is really a poorly understood concept but is very real in its consequences. Burnout describes a person who has been performing well over some length of time who suddenly appears to lose interest. Traditionally, it was felt that this was simply a sign of overwork. A short vacation or relaxing weekend were recommended to straighten things out. Too often, the vacation had little positive effect, and the executive was on his way out the corporate door. There is mounting evidence that burnout is not related so much to overwork as it is to boredom, lack of challenge, or perhaps a recognition that one is not reaching expected goals.

Yet another explanation is based on simple extinction. Often the successful executive begins to feel that he/she is being taken for granted. This may, in fact, be an accurate analysis from the individual's point of view. If the hard working executive begins to feel that he/she is no longer being reinforced for performing then that perception will often be real in its behavioral consequences – non-reinforcement leading to extinction of the previously productive behavior or burnout!

It may be a necessary transition period for some people, a time to stop and take stock of goals and to regroup with more realistic expectations. It is not surprising to find that burnout seems to occur during the infamous mid-career or mid-life crisis. (Sheehy, 1976; Nelson, 1980). A lot of psychological energy can go into the process of revaluing one's career and life goals and redirecting efforts. Consequently, something has to give, and for the victim of burnout it is by definition the job.

In cases like this, the overall personal and career assessment elements of an outplacement program could be the framework within which the reconstruction and re-evaluation can take place rather quickly and positively. If so, then the outplacement burnout victim should be capable of moving back into a challenging position with a great deal of success.

Of course, there are always the standard reasons for letting go senior executives: mergers, reorganizations, major cutbacks, changes in job requirements, and strategic plans to name a few. Some have argued that only those individuals who are likely to have trouble relocating are or should be referred to outplacement. However, the trend is strongly oriented toward making such services available to all displaced personnel in one form or another. Why? Because there is a growing recognition that very good people as well as very poor executives may have a tough time securing that next career assignment, and outplacement can help (Anon., 1980).

Early retirement constitutes another situation that leads to outplacement. In this case, however, the outplacement counseling takes on a slightly different emphasis and the sense of crisis is missing. Nevertheless, many companies are turning to the outplacement consultant or internal outplacement programs to provide guidance and post-career planning services for their retiring personnel with excellent results. Increasingly, professional outplacement firms are offering special programs in the area of post-career planning to fill the need.

BEHAVIORAL CONSEQUENCES OF OUTPLACEMENT

When one works with recently outplaced or fired executives over a long period of time, one thing becomes very clear: everyone deals with being fired in his or her own way. There are no absolutes regarding the behaviors that may manifest once the ax has fallen.

In our society, the job/career that one pursues occupies a significant part of an individual's life. For many (if not most) executives, the job commands more emotional and intellectual involvement as well as time commitment than even spouse and family. In almost all organisms, the loss of a significant source of reinforcement will result in a variety of emotional behaviors including many older and often inappropriate ones. For the executive, the job and many elements connected with it provide many significant sources of reinforcement. As a result, the loss of job has the potential for the production of responses which are not unlike those following the loss of a loved one. It is a major blow.

Suddenly, a self-confident individual can become filled with self-doubt, self-pity, and overwhelming feelings of failure and worthlessness. This feeling of having failed at what could be described as a lifelong commitment can lead to a variety of severely maladaptive behaviors. It is not terribly unusual to see suicide considered as an acceptable response to being rejected by the system or corporate entity to which the individual was significantly "married." Happily, most do not respond in this fashion or continue to entertain the idea for long.

However, the assult on the ego and confidence is very real and has relatively long-term consequences if not dealt with quickly and vigorously. This is one reason why outplacement consultants prefer to start their services coincident with the termination. Giving the fired executive time to consider his/her plight and the circumstances surrounding it may simply give him/her time to dig a psychological hole that is difficult to escape from. As Kamin (1957) has shown, the mere passage of time does little to reduce the level of anxiety produced by a stressful situation. In fact, if nothing is done to replace the anxiety response with an alternative response, the level of anxiety may increase over time. Again, the role of the outplacement consultant becomes that of behavioral engineer in providing alternative behaviors to reduce anxiety and establishing reinforcing contingencies to maintain appropriate behaviors. The consulting rule-of-thumb is to avoid the "pits" if at all possible.

Writing in "Prime Time," Schuyler Chapin (1980), former general manager of the Metropolitan Opera, describes the various phases that he went through following his departure from that position at the age of 52. "Immediately following termination, the fired person experiences an instant sense of being alone and abandoned. Out of this comes both fear and anger. Anxiety mounts due to the uncertainty of the future and the feeling that his/her productive life is over."

Self-confidence begins to disappear, and it becomes very easy for the individual to convince himself that it was "really all my fault." It's during this period that the now unemployed executive gets a case of the "what ifs?" "What if I had done this?" or "What if I had said that?" It doesn't take much of this kind of failure-oriented *post hoc* analysis to produce a feeling of personal failure which can pervade the individual's outlook and sow the seeds of depression.

Quite often the behavior that is manifested by fired executives, at this point, includes many classic depressive components. They become indecisive, listless, disinterested, rife with self-doubts. I've seen talented senior executives actively resist going after a perfectly reasonable job opportunity because they had convinced themselves that they weren't capable of handling the job. This stage has many very negative effects and may last for some time if allowed to get out of control.

During this phase, it isn't uncommon to see serious marital difficulties arise leading to the break-up of what had seemed like a solid relationship. To the depressed and disheartened executive this may be seen as further proof of failure and general worthlessness. Many don't even make an attempt to repair or salvage their marriage at this juncture since they've convinced themselves that their efforts would likely end in failure anyway. The breakdown of family systems is a very complex topic and I won't pursue it here. However, it is common to people in outplacement situations and is an element that must be dealt with by outplacement consultants from time to time.

Clearly there are quite complex psycho-social interactions at work in the firing and outplacement process. There is not only a sense of loss but a frontal attack on many of the support systems that shape and sustain the successful executive. Keeping all these systems intact and operating efficiently is one of the main purposes of outplacement counseling.

As stated earlier, the behavioral area constitutes the weakest link in the outplacement consultants' armamentarium. Many are not trained in behavioral or counseling techniques. Reliance on sound knowledge of the job market and how to use it will see them through most outplacement situations.

The successful outplacement consultants seem to have adopted one or another personal styles of coping with the behavioral problems with which they are confronted. Perhaps the most common approach to counseling that I have seen utilized in the outplacement process is a form of active listening. In addition, many consultants use a kind of quasi-rational emotive approach that is very directive. The latter is sometimes effective but probably more satisfying to the consultant than effective for the client. The directive approach also has great face validity: it feels right, it ought to work! When the outplacement client falls into the inactive/depressive mode the typical consultant response seems to be a swift kick in the pants to get him/her moving again. Often times, this just serves to drive them further into the hole and reinforce their feelings of inadequacy. The circle gets tighter and a difficult case emerges. Usually the sympathetic reassuring ear works best, especially if it is combined with some other simple approaches.

One technique that appears to be universal in the outplacement business is contingency contracting. Very few consultants have a theoretical understanding of the technique. However, they recognize the practical implications of the need to elicit certain levels of personal commitment from the client. Contracting seems to be a natural. I have never seen a written contract in this context but oral agreements abound. Such agreements are usually aimed at achieving specific goals within a given timeframe. It would be interesting to compare the relative effectiveness of the written and oral approaches to contracting. I suspect the written contract would prove to be the better.

The mistake that most consultants make in the use of such contracts results from a lack of understanding of the reinforcement contingencies involved. Quite simply, they tend to contract for too much over too long a time. The behavioral goals are too far removed from the starting point. Consequently, there is frequent renegotiation of terms and a resultant weakening of the process. Nevertheless, it is a technique in wide use which has a great deal of potential in dealing with the problem of motivating an outplaced executive toward positive activity in the job market and career continuation.

There would seem to be several points at which basic operant techniques could be utilized in the outplacement process. Many of the behavioral problems common to outplaced executives are situational and should be reasonably easy to bring under behavioral control. These techniques are not being used to any significant degree at the present time. This is due mainly to the fact that very few consultants in the field have the knowledge or training to consistently apply behavioral interventions. This constitutes an area that deserves investigation, and I believe such behavioral procedures could be a powerful tool in getting outplaced executives back on their feet and functioning effectively.

Finally, a word or two should be said about assessment. One of the ways in which the outplacement process attacks the problem of low self-esteem is through careful assessment of past successes. All of the outplacement consultants I know of use some form of career assessment as the basis for evaluating the client's past work record and personal achievements. This forces the client to concentrate on positive proofs rather than failures. If this process is carried out thoroughly, many of the behavioral problems previously discussed can be avoided.

Another type of assessment used by some firms is psychological testing. This type of executive assessment is sometimes done internally by the outplacement firm. However, most who use executive assessment use an outside, independent testing organization for many of the same reasons that corporations use outside outplacement consultants.

Such testing focuses on basic personal characteristics: interests and values, reasoning ability, interpersonal skills, and traits of temperament. From this data base a fairly objective portrait of the individual can be drawn. This gives the outplacement consultant, as well as the client, outside proof of strengths and weaknesses that may have been only hinted at in other situations. Though it is not often done in any overt or controlled fashion, the assessment procedure should also include the identification of specific elements, situations, or factors which are clearly reinforcing to the person being analyzed. This information will be invaluable in developing the strategies necessary for producing effective job-finding behaviors as well as defining the most reinforcing career targets.

In short, the assessment process, whether career-based or psychological, can have a strong ameliorating effect on the insidious erosion of self-esteem that makes the outplacement situation so difficult.

CONCLUSION

Even though outplacement services in one guise or another have been around for quite some time, they are still considered newcomers on the personnel scene. The outplacement service can be handled as either an internal personnel function or at the outside consultant level. In most cases the consultant approach is more cost effective and works best for the fired executive in the long run. It seems rather clear that the majority of executives will be able to utilize professional help in working the job market.

The hard data on outplacement effectiveness, strategies, prognosis, assessment, and counseling is difficult to come by. There is very little of it, and what exists is poorly documented. Success data from outplacement firms is proudly publicized. However, if they do have a handle on their failures, they certainly aren't talking. Furthermore, this information and specific job-finding techniques are considered to be trade secrets that are not open to public scrutiny.

Psychological assessment data is also scant. Some companies use outside testing firms, while others do their own testing. Most do nothing, even though it is likely that psychological assessment contributes as a process to the management of common outplacement behavioral problems. This is an area with much potential where very little research has been conducted but is sorely needed.

The outplacement function, whether in-house or external, is becoming an important personnel area. However, perhaps because its roots are in the consulting arena, the hard data base relative to its efficacy is, at the moment, missing. Perhaps with increased acceptance as a legitimate personnel function, outplacement and its various aspects – success, failure, strategies, psychological elements, and counseling approaches – can be scrutinized more closely and understood more fully by those who need it and those who provide it.

REFERENCES

Anonymous. Easing redundant executives on to the job market. *International Management,* March 1980.

Ard, B. N., Jr. *Counseling and psychotherapy.* Palo Alto, California: Science and Behavior Books, Inc., 1966.

Bauer, D. Why big business is firing the boss. *New York Times Magazine,* March 8, 1981.

Biegeleisen, J. I. *Job resumes.* New York: Grosset and Dunlap, 1976.

Bolles, R. *The three boxes of life.* Berkeley, California: Ten Speed Press, 1978.

Bolles, R. *What color is your parachute?: A practical manual for job hunters and career changers.* Berkeley, California: Ten Speed Press, 1977.

Brennan, L., Strand, S., & Gruber, E. *Resumes for better jobs.* New York: Simon and Schuster, 1973.

Broussard, W., & DeLargey, R. The dynamics of the group outplacement workshop. *Personnel Journal,* 1979, **58,** 855-857.

Caress, R. S. Glossary of terms – Definitions of report terminology used in Caress, Gilhooly, and Kestin, Inc. aptitude test reports. Unpublished manuscript.

Chance, P. That drained-out, used-up feeling. *Psychology Today,* January 1981, **58,** 88-89.

Chapin, S. G. Surviving the ultimate slap in the face. *Prime Time,* June 1980, pp. 27-31.

Crystal, J. C., & Bolles, R. *Where do I go from here with my life?* New York: Seaburg Press, 1974.

DeVille, J. *Nice guys finish first.* New York: William Morrow, 1979.

Driessnack, C. Financial impact of effective human resources management. *The Personnel Administrator,* 1976, **21** (1).

Driessnack, C. Outplacement: The new personnel function. *Personnel Administrator*, 1980, **25** (10), 84-93.

Dyer, L. D. Implications of job displacement at mid-career. *Industrial Gerontology*, 1973 (Spring), 38-46.

Farish, P. (Ed.) Outplacement: what's ahead in personnel? *Industrial Relations News*, October 1978, **188**, 1-4.

Freudenberger, H. *Burnout – The high cost of achievement*. Garden City, New York: Anchor Press, 1980.

Fuchs, J., & Cuthrell, S. If you must fire. *D & B Reports*, July/Aug. 1980, **28** (4), 28-31.

Gallagher, J. Severence updated. *Career Management Associates*, Unpublished report, 1981.

Jackson, T. *28 days to a better job*. New York: Hawthorne Books, Inc., 1977.

Jameson, R. *The professional job changing system*. Parsippany, New Jersey: Performance Dynamics International, 1978.

Kamin, L. J. The retention of an incompletely learned avoidance response. *Journal of Comparative and Physiological Psychology*, 1957, **50**, 457-460.

Kisiel, M. *Design for change: A guide to new careers*. New York: New Viewpoints, 1980.

Lewis, A. *How to write better resumes*. Woodbury, New York: Barron's Educational Series, 1977.

Levinson, D. J. *The seasons of a man's life*. New York: Knopf, 1978.

Meyer, H. E. The flourishing new business of recycling executives. *Fortune*, 1977, **95** (5), 328-338.

Miller, J. New prestige for those in the firing trade. *The New York Times*, March 18, 1979.

Miller, K. M. *Psychological testing in personnel assessment*. New York: Halsted Press, 1975.

Nelson, J. G. Burnout – Business' most costly expense. *Personnel Administrator*, 1980, **25** (8), 81-87.

Nossiter, D. D. Success story – Some job consultants market people like soda pop. *Barron's*, February, 16, 1981.

Owens, W., & Schoenfeldt, L. Toward a classification of persons. *Journal of Applied Psychology Monograph*, 1979, **64** (5), 569-607.

Reed, J. (Ed.) *Resumes that get better jobs*. New York: Arco Pub., 1981.

Robbins, P. *Successful midlife career change*. New York: AMACOM, 1978.

Rogers, M. Outplacement specialists – Professional help for disabled careers. *MBA*, July/August, 1979.

Sheehy, G. *Passages*. New York: Dutton, 1976.

Stanat, K., & Reardon, P. *Job hunting: Secrets and tactics*. Chicago: Follett, 1977.

Sweet, D. *Decruitment and outplacement*. Reading, Mass.: Addison-Wesley, 1975.

Welles, C. Is outplacement a corporate guilt trip? *Esquire Fortnightly*, August, 29, 1978.

Part IV:
Organization-wide Applications

Introduction

The readings thus far have concentrated on the concepts of behavior analysis as applied to specific job behaviors and accomplishments. This unit emphasizes the applications of behavior management principles to entire organizations. Focus is shifted from the contingencies of reinforcement that influence the behavior of one individual to the numerous contingencies that influence and maintain the behavior of large numbers of individuals, often at several levels of an organization. Larger number of contingencies and the interactions between and among these contingencies play a more dominant role in these types of applications. Since organizations are essentially complex social systems, this movement from micro to macro applications represents a necessary trend for the field. Concern for this movement was recently reflected by OBM practitioners and researchers in a survey conducted by Andrasik, McNamara, and Edlund (1980). Organizational systems analysis was listed as one of the top three areas requiring further development. (For a detailed description of this survey readers are referred to Chapter 22.)

Before entering an organization with change techniques it is necessary to analyze the component parts of such complex environments to ascertain the value of the proposed changes as well as the ways in which the proposed changes will influence other parts of the organization. Failure to do this may result in alterations which have little impact on the operation of the entire organization, changes which maximize the performance of one part but hinder others to the detriment of the entire organization, or changes that increase the attainment of short-term goals but are likely to contribute to the eventual decay of the organization. Such considerations necessarily guide us into the realm of systems theory. While systems theory is certainly not new to business, it has only recently been fused with behavior analysis by such individuals as Brethower (1972), Gilbert (1978), and Krapfl (1980). While an indepth discussion of systems theory goes well beyond the scope of the present book, a brief overview of the systems approach and how it relates to applied behavior analysis is a necessary preamble to the upcoming chapters.

Any organization consists of interdependent systems that influence one another. One cannot change one system without affecting one or more other systems. Neither can one alter any element within a system without affecting the other elements. Stated simply, a change in the behavior of one individual affects the behavior of other individuals and thus the aggregate performance of those individuals as an organizational unit. In turn, this change in the aggregate performance of one unit may then influence the aggregate performance of one or more other organizational units, and so on. But before we get caught up in this unending spiral it may be helpful to define what a system is. While there are many different definitions of a system, Montello and Wimberly (1975) provide a concise and easily understood definition. They define a system as a multiplicity of components tied together for a common purpose. In a similar vein, Krapfl and Gasparotto (in press) have defined a system as an organization which forms a network to serve a common purpose. They emphasize the terms network and purpose because they imply that the behavior of more than one individual is involved, and that all the individuals who make up the network are ideally and ultimately under the control of the same reinforcers.

It is important to note that a system is possible at many different levels. For example, a system can consist of one individual interacting with a limited environment, such as an experimental setting, or an entire industrial organization interacting with society and the physical universe. Since systems do exist at many different levels, they are embedded in one another. Each system is contained in a larger system which is contained in a larger system, etc. This notion of embeddedness and the resulting interdependency are perhaps the most compelling reasons for the development and application of systems theory.

Systems do not exist independently of human behavior. Yet as the scope of the analysis grows, systems encompass larger aggregates of individual behavior as well as the contingencies which maintain that performance, until systems seem to take on a life of their own. The members of a system seem interchangeable at times. However, it must be kept in mind that in the final analysis a system is composed of individual behavior and the aggregate behavior of individuals. It is the individuals of an organization who maintain the contingencies of performance. Changes in group performance only occur through changes in individual performance. Conversely, changes in the aggregate performance of the individuals within one system or organization unit will influence the aggregate performance of individuals within other systems or units and thus affect the behavior of individual members.

Because of the interdependency between individual performance and group performance, applied behavior analysis and systems analysis compliment and augment each other. A systems approach allows us to organize the complexities of industrial settings and determine the links between individual performance and the aggregate group performance of organizational units. Applied behavior analysis allows us to ascertain the variables that influence individual behavior and the contingencies that are required to alter behavior and maintain behavior change.

The first chapter of this unit by Brand, Staelin, O'Brien and Dickinson exemplifies a program that was implemented in an extremely complex organizational environment, the Department of Housing and Urban Development. Government organizations tend to be viewed as well-structured bureaucracies that are impervious to change given the labyrinth of units and the legal requirements imposed upon them. These authors describe a systematic intervention program that resulted in dramatic gains in productivity as well as in the morale of employees in what would be considered a relatively short period of time. After careful examination of the organization, one department was selected for the initial intervention. The program was implemented at all levels of that department rather than horizontally across departments, the traditional intervention mode. Given the sluggishness of such hierarchial organizations, much credit is due to both the executives in this agency and the program consultants for this exemplar model of organizational change.

The Quality of Work Life (QWL) programs discussed by Rosow in Chapter 17 also represent a systems approach to organizational change. Rosow presents the historical roots of Quality of Work Life programs, the steps involved in implementing such programs, and some of the results that have been achieved by them. The thrust of these programs is embodied in the following statement by Landen (1977):

> If the quality of the outcomes of any system is a function of the overall quality of the system that produces those outcomes, then the quality of the human organization is an integral part of that overall system. Human systems cannot be separated from work systems. . . . As organizational processes are enriched, so too are the lives of people interacting with those processes. The bottom line to all of this is that the organization is qualitatively superior, human life is dignified, the enterprise is strengthened and society and civilization are the ultimate beneficiaries. . . . Productivity and quality of work life are indivisible [p. 17].

General Motors was the forerunner in the implementation of QWL programs, an approach that has been adopted by many leading companies including AT&T, Xerox, and

Honeywell (The new industrial relations, 1981). The phrase "quality of work life" defies exact definition. It is not a set of techniques or a packaged approach but a philosophy. The philosophy is a model which must be operationalized. In other words, concrete action programs must be designed and implemented to reflect this philosophy and enable its goals to be attained. The general strategy developed to achieve this philosophical approach has involved increasing employee participation, often by giving employees more control over their work environment and responsibilities. It entails the development of constructive control systems in which employees who are in the best position to affect changes receive the information, authority, and resources to do so. Employees are given the opportunity to discuss work-related problems and recommend changes. The key to the success of such programs is management's commitment in terms of providing employees with both the time needed to engage in such problem solving and the access to relevant information including internal and external constraints, as well as in implementing their recommendations.

The method by which employee participation is accomplished must vary according to the specific situation. What works in one place may not necessarily be successfully transplanted to another. An organizational analysis of the particular system must be conducted in order to ascertain the contingencies that are currently in effect and to determine how they can be effectively changed to achieve the desired results. Because of this, QWL programs have assumed many different faces. Rosow discusses some of the specific QWL programs that have been implemented within General Motors in Chapter 17.

While implementation tatics differ, all QWL programs share basic components. Employees are provided with information concerning how their work behaviors influence the performance of others at the same organizational level and the performance of others above and below their organizational level. In systems terms, internal feedback loops are established between the subsystems. Since conflicts unavoidably exist among subsystems, these conflicts can be discussed and performance objectives developed that optimize the performance of all the subsystems rather than maximizing the performance of one subsystem to the detriment of others. Through discussions with management personnel, employees come into contact with the long-term consequences of their performance. Information is received regarding what is happening in the marketplace and how their performance ultimately affects consumer behavior and consequently influences the survival of the organization itself. External feedback loops are established. This type of information enables employees to approach work problems realistically and within the framework of the whole organization. Employees who have a first hand knowledge of the day-to-day operation are given the opportunity to present problems that are barriers to performance and suggest ways to rectify them. The emphasis of group meetings is on work problems, not attitudes or feelings. Performance measures are established and implemented to evaluate the results of their efforts. Employees therefore receive direct and immediate feedback about their performance. Supervisors and managers respond by providing more frequent positive reinforcement to employees, socially, economically, or both. Employee participatory behaviors are further rewarded by management's adoption of their recommendations.

The employee-management work groups are major vehicles for changing contingencies. As a result of increased information flow, the we-they split is eliminated. Contingencies of reinforcement are altered simultaneously with the resolution of work problems. Employees establish contingencies that are consistent with the long-range consequences of performance. Peer contingencies are altered in a way that rewards good work performance rather than antagonistic behaviors toward management. Management adopts new behaviors of rewarding and recognizing effective employee work behaviors. As these contingencies are shaped and altered, employees and supervisors gradually come into contact with them, and behavior is changed accordingly. Such processes take time. All of the altera-tions may not be successful, and thus the process of forming new contingencies must begin again. Yet the benefits that result from this type of organizational change are certainly worth the time, energy, and money invested.

Continuing in the systems mode, Brethower in Chapter 18 discusses the elements that are common to all systems, thus providing a method for describing individual systems, com-paring systems to each other, and ascertaining the way in which systems influence one another. He has labeled this method the total performance system. According to Brethower, each system receives inputs from the environment, contains processes or mechanisms to transform these inputs into outputs, and creates outputs that have an effect on the environment. The environmental effects in turn influence the inputs into the original system, thus altering it in some fashion.

There is a close correspondence between the elements in the total performance system and the elements in the three-term contingency relationship of applied behavior analysis, as there must be if indeed the total performance system can be used to describe all systems (Brethower, 1980). Inputs correspond to antecedent stimuli, the processing mechanism to interim responses in a chain, outputs to responses, and, finally, the environmental effects correspond to consequent stimuli. While this correspondence is obvious at the individual level, it is much less so at the organizational level, where the correspondence is loose. For example, an individual's response immediately affects the environment, and the en-vironmental consequence in turn affects the future probability of that response. The organizational output may take a great deal of time to affect the social or physical environ-ment, and those affects may not be readily apparent or available for many years. Yet all systems adapt to their environment, or they cease to exist. This holds true for complex organizations as well as for individuals.

The total performance system permits us to examine what kinds of performance changes at the departmental and individual level would be of value to the total organization, and how the changes would impact on other departments and individuals within the organization. By first ascertaining the kinds of outputs that will be valuable to the total organization, one can then determine the types of changes that will be required to achieve those outputs. It is then possible to track those desired changes to the smaller systems, ascertaining what changes are required at the individual level. Reversing this process, the total performance system can also provide us with a method of tracing the effects of in-dividual performance changes on other systems, including the departmental level systems and the total organization.

In summary, applied behavior analysis can tell us how to achieve optimum and efficient changes in individual behavior and the types of contingencies that are necessary to maintain those changes. A total performance system analysis augments applied behavior analysis by aiding in the determination of the types of changes that are required and how the necessary contingencies can be maintained.

The concluding chapter by Abernathy, Duffy, and O'Brien provides a fine example of the interdependencies among the subsystems or units of an organization. A productivity im-provement program was initiated in one organizational unit in a large, multi-branch banking firm. While substantial gains were realized, it was ascertained that even further im-provements would be possible if the work behaviors of individuals in a linking system were improved. The outputs of this system were the inputs of the original system. The program was therefore expanded to include this additional system. Further interdependencies were uncovered among the second system and other organizational systems, and the interven-tion package slowly permeated the entire organization. This program demonstrates the old adage that success breeds success. Results of this organization-wide program are summarized for numerous departments within the multi-branch bank operation.

Taken together, the chapters within this unit exemplify the effectiveness of the fusion of behavior analysis with systems theory. The projects depict the interrelationship of behavior analysis and systems analysis – areas which compliment and augment one another. Human behavior in organizations is very complex and influenced by a multiplicity of contingencies. In order to achieve results that are of value to the organization, society, and the employees within that organization, careful scrutiny of organizational contingencies is required. Behavior systems analysis is a way to organize this complexity and successfully achieve organization-wide changes.

Alyce M. Dickinson
Western Michigan University

REFERENCES

Andrasik, F., McNamara, J. R., & Edlund, S. R. Current and future trends for behavior modification in business. Paper presented at the annual meeting of the Association For Behavior Analysis, Dearborn, Michigan, 1980.

Brethower, D. M. *A Total Performance System*. Kalamazoo, MI: Behaviordelia, 1972.

Brethower, D. M. Integrating systems analysis with behavior analysis. Paper presented at the annual meeting of the Association For Behavior Analysis, Dearborn, Michigan, 1980.

Gilbert, T. F. *Human Competence: Engineering Worthy Performance*. New York: McGraw-Hill, 1978.

Krapfl, J. The relation of systems analysis to the basic sciences. Paper presented at the annual meeting of the Association for Behavior Analysis, Dearborn, Michigan, 1980.

Krapfl, J., & Gasparotto, G. Behavioral systems analysis. In L. W. Frederiksen (Ed.), *Handbook of Organizational Behavior Management*. New York: Wiley, in press.

Landen, D. L. The real issue: Human dignity. *Survey of Business*, 12, **5,** 1977.

Montello, P. A., & Wimberly, C. A. *Management Systems in Education*. Lincoln, NB: Professional Educators Publications, 1975.

The new industrial relations. *Business Week*, May 11, 1981, 84-98.

16

Improving White Collar Productivity at HUD

Daniel D. Brand
Department of Housing and Urban Development

John R. Staelin
Edward J. Feeney Associates

Richard M. O'Brien   and   **Alyce M. Dickinson**
Hofstra University   *New York State Office of Court Administration*

The Department of Housing and Urban Development is a cabinet level branch of the Federal Government that employs 16,101 people at its own building in the District of Columbia and in regional and area offices throughout the United States and its territories. The budget for HUD in 1978 was over 38 billion dollars (The United States Government Manual, 1980). Combined with the large work force this provides a substantial management challenge.

When William A. Medina became Assistant Secretary for Administration at HUD, he discovered many of the management problems that typify large organizations. Both management and its employees expressed dissatisfaction with productivity and morale, although opinions differed on the etiology of these problems. The employees generally viewed their performance as being quite good under the circumstances. They felt under-rewarded and unappreciated. Many of the clerical workers saw themselves as trapped in unimportant, dead-end jobs. The Federal Employee Attitude Survey conducted among Federal workers indicated that: (1) they were unaware of performance goals and standards; (2) they received little feedback on their efforts, and (3) that they believed that they were often evaluated on unspecifiable, subjective attitudes and qualities.

Lower level managers – the direct, on-line supervisors – most often came from the ranks of the employees and shared many of their perceptions about the distance of upper management. While these supervisors were more likely to perceive performance problems, they usually believed that the problem was understaffing rather than underproductivity. Lower and middle management would cite budget limitations, the Civil Service System (now the Office of Personnel Management, OPM), and the lack of a trained workforce as obstacles to productivity improvement. But their usual explanation for the problem was that they just didn't have enough people to do the job.

In top management at HUD the view of current performance levels was very different. Their time studies had revealed that performance was less than 50% of what it could be. They believed that the employees could accomplish considerably more with their time, but that management had not yet developed an approach that maximized the employees performance. In late 1978 HUD requested proposals for a project to increase productivity.

Largely on the basis of its success with improving performance at the General Accounting Office (Schneier, Pernick, & Bryant, 1978), HUD awarded a $100,000 contract to Edward J. Feeney Associates. This contract called for a training and 1 year on-site consultation program beginning in January of 1979 that was to employ the Behavioral Engineering Systems Training (B.E.S.T.) program that Feeney and Associates had developed.

Management was well aware that one small consulting contract was not likely to solve all of the agency's productivity problems. Even a large program could not be implemented all at once throughout a huge corporation or governmental agency. After identifying the problem and a potential solution, Assistant Secretary Medina had to find an office of the agency which could provide a meaningful trial and model for B.E.S.T. It was decided that the approach should be a vertical one, i.e., training all of the supervisors within a given office rather than the more traditional horizontal intervention that might work with all of the first level supervisors across offices. HUD's Office of Finance and Accounting (OFA) was chosen as the test case. While it was small enough to be approached within the limits of the contract, it was representative of the agency's productivity problems as a whole. With a budget of over one billion dollars and nine hundred employees, OFA was not likely to be dismissed as inconsequential. On the other hand, management had been through numerous supervisory training and consulting programs but problems continued in terms of low productivity, backlogs, errors, poor morale, and delays. Since the office had a variety of accounting responsibilities, its difficulties represented more than just lost employee time. The potential for savings was particularly great due to the large dollar value handled by this division.

With the support of Assistant Secretary Medina, Deputy Assistant Secretary Hearing, and OFA Director Thomas J. O'Connor, Feeney Associates began a performance audit of the functioning at OFA. Under the direction of the first author, this audit aimed to uncover areas where the B.E.S.T. program could have the greatest impact on cost-relevant outcomes. The various divisions and branches of the Office of Finance and Accounting are presented in Figure 16.1. The white and gray backgrounds reflect the initial and second phase intervention programs, respectively. An asterisk on a section indicates that for logistical reasons it was eliminated from the program, while a T indicates that only the initial training sessions were completed in that section. The total number of supervisors trained to this point is 82. Post-training programs have been implemented that involve 424 employees as of this writing.

THE B.E.S.T. PROGRAM AT HUD

The units selected to initiate the project were the HUD-Held Home Properties and Mortgages Division, the branch of the Insurance Division that dealt with home mortgage receipts and deposits, and the Receipts and Deposits Branch of the Billing and Receiving Division. The B.E.S.T. Performance Improvement Project began with an initial review and diagnosis of the selected units. Several days were spent with unit managers to identify potential areas for performance improvement and to become familiar with the work and vocabulary of those units so that the workshop leaders could relate B.E.S.T. concepts to relevant situations. With the Phase I group, six half-day training sessions were held over a 7-week period (one class was snowed-out). The Phase II group held three 1-day sessions over a 5-week period. Although Phase II's full day sessions eased scheduling problems, it was generally felt that the half-day format spread over a longer period of time provided a better experience.

In both phases the program combined 24 hours of classroom training with direct coaching by the on-site consultant. This coaching allowed supervisors to examine their operations and develop behavioral interventions as part of the training. They began by identifying outputs in their sections and collecting data on these accomplishments. The on-site consultant provided aid throughout the development and maintenance of these programs.

The programs developed in the different branches shared another constant in addition to the classroom supervision and on-line coaching. Systematic positive reinforcement from the Assistant Secretary, the Director of OFA, and the various branch and division chiefs provided contingent reinforcement for appropriate supervisor behavior. These upper echelon managers also made themselves available to provide on-line praise to individual employees. In addition to providing positive feedback and status for the supervisors, this aspect of the program was aimed at correcting the employee perception that upper management only noticed employee errors.

Classroom training prepared the way for all behavioral interventions. Supervisors were instructed in setting up measurable objectives while eliminating evaluation by subjective attributes. Much time was spent on developing measurement forms and setting specific goals to replace the diffuse type of pep-talk management of "We really have to start moving on these things." The classroom examples also served to prepare the managers for potential employee resistance to measuring performance. Rather than introducing measurement as an efficiency study or another chore from the top brass, the managers learned to justify measurements by the need to have data to defend the workers. Most of the managers believed that more staff were needed in their sections. They were shown that the data they collected could be used as a selling tool to acquire more help or to determine more realistic standards. In some situations, standards were 8 years old and obsolete. Being constantly in the public and congressional eye made it necessary to have facts to counter unfair criticism. Performance data are the best evidence for this kind of defense.

Nonetheless, the notion that standards could best be set if baserate data were collected was not always easily accepted. HUD had a long history of management-employee strife which had culminated in a near revolt during George Romney's years as Secretary. Many of the first level managers had come up through the ranks. They remained very close to their employees, tending to view themselves as super workers rather than supervisors. They had little training in setting behavioral goals and even less in becoming sources of positive reinforcement for their staff. Many perceived objective measurement as a trick to increase productivity so that a new standard could be set.

These supervisory views had to be countered in training. The supervisors had to be made to realize that capriciously raising standards was not a goal of the program, although standards could be and were raised or lowered if changes in the task or work force warranted it. The fact that the system was looking for behavior to reward had to be stressed. While punishment was not disavowed in the case of continued lack of improvement, the goal of the system was to find rewards to improve performance.

The most common reservation expressed about the program revolved around the search for rewards that would indeed increase productivity. A sizable number of managers believed that a lack of training was the major productivity problem. Others were willing to accept the notion that increasing rewards would boost productivity, but they felt that only financial reinforcers would have a lasting effect. This was the only reward that they saw as meaningful to their workers.

The consultant responded to the first problem by following Mager and Pipe's (1970) dictum "could they do it if their life depended on it?" Supervisors were asked to take the "if someone put a gun to the employee's head could he do the task" test. None of the supervisors actually needed to ask this question. They knew that the employees could make the

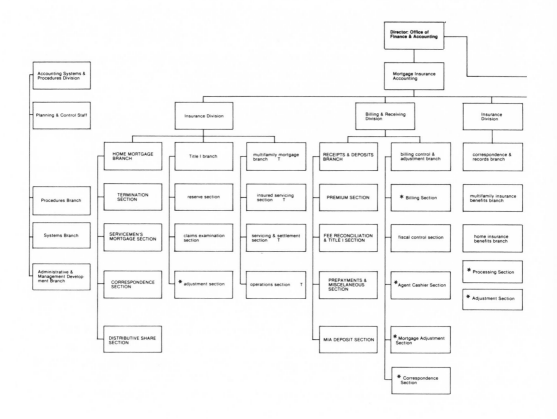

Fig. 16.1. Phases of the OFA Phase. Program 1 in Upper Case and Phase 2 in Lower Case.

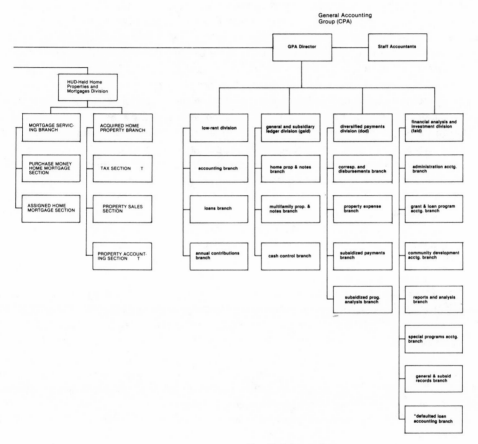

General Accounting
Group (CPA)

GPA Director

Staff Accountants

HUD-Held Home
Properties and
Mortgages Division

MORTGAGE SERVIC-
ING BRANCH

ACQUIRED HOME
PROPERTY BRANCH

PURCHASE MONEY
HOME MORTGAGE
SECTION

TAX SECTION   T

ASSIGNED HOME
MORTGAGE SECTION

PROPERTY SALES
SECTION

PROPERTY ACCOUNT-
ING SECTION   T

low-rent division

accounting branch

loans branch

annual contributions
branch

general and subsidiary
ledger division (gsld)

home prop & notes
branch

multifamily prop. &
notes branch

cash control branch

diversified payments
division (dod)

corresp. and
disbursements branch

property expense
branch

subsidized payments
branch

subsidized prog.
analysis branch

financial analysis and
investment division
(faid)

administration acctg.
branch

grant & loan program
acctg. branch

community development
acctg. branch

reports and analysis
branch

special programs acctg.
branch

general & subsid
records branch

*defaulted loan
accounting branch

T = Training only: no
onsite coaching or
program develop-
ment.

* = Not included in
program.

proper response. HUD employees, for the most part, have 20 to 30 years of service. Lack of training was not the problem.

The view that only financial rewards would be effective was more difficult to counter. Government restrictions made financial incentives nearly impossible, yet the first line supervisors saw them as crucial. Their position is similar to first line supervisors throughout industry, although many times, as was the case at HUD, upper management believes that praise is enough to produce lasting improvement. In the end the consultant could only present the data from previous successes using non-financial rewards and ask the manager to trust the consultant's judgement. For some managers this was enough to produce cooperation. Others became convinced only after the obvious success of the early projects.

Learning to give praise is not as simple as it sounds. The praise must be contingent on specific satisfactory performance. The general "You did a good job today" actually rewards both the good and bad things that the employee has done on that shift. It must be replaced by recognition for specific productive behavior such as "I like the way you got rid of that backlog." In this way the employee knows exactly what he is being praised for, and a contingent relationship is established between the proper response and the reinforcement. Further, the praise must be a shaping process that rewards individuals for improving their productivity while avoiding the punishing implication that what they had been doing previously was substandard. The supervisors had to be taught to correct positively. For example, when a form was incorrectly filled out, the supervisor would respond with, "I would like to see you do it this way." The "No, that is the wrong way to do it" that often prefaces correction is left out and the employee's defense of his previous behavior is made irrelevant. In other words, the supervisors had to learn to convey the notion that past errors are of little importance compared to future performance.

In many cases, classroom training was not sufficient to teach the supervisors to collect data and reward the employees for their record keeping. Upper management was used as the final destination for the data that were collected, so that branch and division chiefs could be employed to reinforce accurate and complete record keeping. The consultant was employed to help the supervisors get the necessary information off the data forms so that they had to go over the data. Supervisors who had difficulty in getting the records were given on-line coaching. Often the consultant and supervisor would go over the data with individual employees as a prompting and modeling exercise.

Part of teaching the supervisors to use rewards involved indentification of rewarding consequences that were available to management. Praise from direct supervisors and knowledge of performance improvement were the central reinforcers in the program, but a number of supplementary rewards were also developed. In addition to personal visits to employees, top management contributed commendations, awards, certificates, and letters for the employee's files. As office-wide newsletter was set up and produced by the consultant to highlight performance improvement in various sections, as well as individual accomplishments. Immediate supervisors also used memos and letters to top management as rewards for exceptional productivity increases. Job-enrichment opportunities such as the chance to train other staff, rotation to other jobs in order to learn new skills, promotions, and career development opportunities were used as rewards in a small percentage of cases. Following a Premack Principle approach, good performance was also rewarded with more desirable jobs and the opportunity to advise the supervisor on task problems. The latter reward often took the form of brunches with the supervisor as well as the opportunity to engage in management functions such as sitting in on higher level supervisory meetings.

In summary, the B.E.S.T. program at HUD taught performance improvement within a framework of five basic skills. First, existing accomplishment behaviors and goals were analyzed. Second, realistic standards were developed in terms of specific behaviors that reflected both intermediate and long-term goals. Third, a feedback system was created to provide managers and staff with knowledge of performance and its relation to standards. Fourth, individualized programs of rewards were specified in contingent relation to work performance. Finally, organizational models were developed to insure expansion and maintenance of the behavior improvement program. This facet of the intervention will be reviewed at the end of this report.

SPECIFIC BRANCH PROGRAMS

The basic B.E.S.T. program at HUD has been outlined above, yet each of the branch and section applications represent variations on the basic theme in response to idiosyncratic behavior problems. While space limitations do not allow a complete report on each section of all the branches involved, the strength of this project lies in the diversity of the problems that responded to the intervention. The following pages will describe, in detail, the effects of behavioral programs in specific sections. Since the overall project was administered in two phases, Phase I projects will be presented first. A major problem for various sections was the identification of measurable outputs by which individual and group performance could be evaluated. Section programs will be presented in order of complexity beginning with those in which relevant, measurable outcomes were obvious and relatively easily obtained.

Project I: HUD-Held Home Properties and Mortgages Division – Assigned Home Mortgage Section (12 employees)

Through various means, such as foreclosure on a HUD guaranteed mortgage, properties become assigned to HUD. Once this occurs, the agency incurs basic costs in maintaining these acquisitions. The Assigned Home Mortgage Section is responsible for preparation of closing statements that include all of HUD's outlay on the property so that the agency can recoup the money it has spent when it sells the property. Errors represent missed costs that cannot be recovered once the property is sold. This section has the potential to lose several million dollars through inaccurate review of agency expenses. Low productivity delays transactions and contributes to increased error rates through expenses that are discovered too late to be added to the selling price of the property.

Figure 16.2 presents the number of property reviews completed during baseline and for the 26 weeks following implementation of the program. Although data from previous years suggest that the increase to 1200 reviews completed for weeks 6 through 8 represents a seasonal increase in demand, weeks 9 through 26 represent baseline demand conditions. In any case, the increased demand had not produced a substantial increase in performance in previous years. Performance has been maintained at 600 reviews per week or over 800% of baseline in the year following the data presented in Figure 16.2.

The reader may well wonder if accuracy (which was the primary focus of the program) suffered during this increase in productivity. In this section, quantity increase clearly had to take a backseat to accuracy because each error had direct financial consequences for the agency. During the baseline period, 82% of the submissions were found to be error-free. Using baseline figures, a new goal of 92% error-free submissions was established prior to treatment. This goal was exceeded in 23 of the 26 weeks following intervention. The average error-free rate for this period of 26 weeks was 98.5%. In the weeks that have followed, it has risen to a constant 99% error-free. In fact, for the 18 months since this pro-

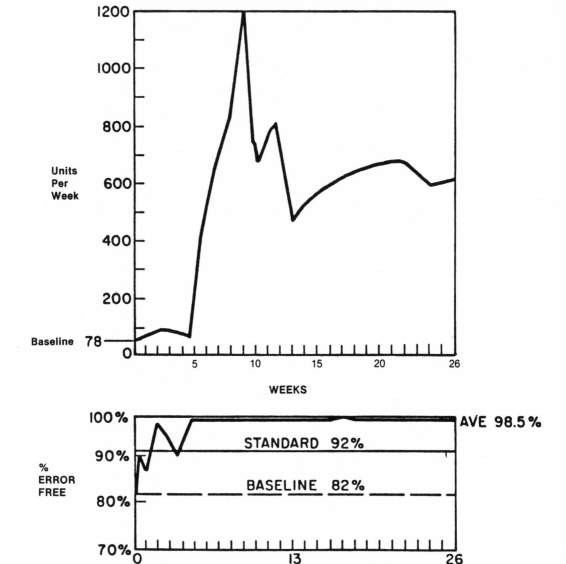

Fig. 16.2. Transactions Completed by Assigned Home Mortgage Section From Baseline Through the First 26 Weeks of Intervention.

gram began, no cost errors have been attributed to this section that were not caught on review; therefore, all financial losses from errors in this branch have been eliminated. This represents a potential seven figure savings.

These increases in accuracy and productivity were produced through problem identification, goal setting, and interpersonal reinforcement. No monetary rewards were provided for staff. The error problem was solved by identifying common error behaviors and charting their frequency. Eight common errors were noted. A ninth category was set aside for less frequent, non-monetary mistakes that often represented responses to the unique aspects of a given review. Common errors as a percentage of all errors decreased from 27 to 14.5%.

Thus, the common, careless errors were eliminated at a greater frequency than the errors made on the more difficult, idiosyncratic cases. Giving individual feedback on each of the common mistakes to each employee provided the employees with knowledge of results so that they could improve their performance.

Feedback was not limited to errors. A single chart (Table 16.1) depicted the percent of the units' workload contributed by each employee as well as each worker's accuracy figures for the week. Review of these data uncovered some outstanding performers who had previously gone unnoticed. Employee J was found to be contributing almost 20% of the work in a twelve-employee department while maintaining practically error free (99.8%) performance. The data showed that this was a truly exceptional employee, yet this man had been with the agency for 17 years without being promoted. He reported that the first time anyone had ever noticed his good work was during the current project. It would appear that he was in a high state of deprivation in terms of positive social reinforcement from his superiors. It is little wonder that a program of feedback and praise could produce such overwhelming increases in performance in this group. Obviously, the reason that this employee had not gotten rewarded in the past was that no one had collected individual performance data to find out who should get reinforced. By taking each individual's output as a percentage of the unit aggregate productivity, supervisors now had the necessary data to make praise contingent on good performance. Based on the B.E.S.T. system, the supervisors had learned how to measure the accomplishments of their staff. With the help of the consultant, they had developed specific forms that identified productive behavior as well as developing a management style that made them sources of positive reinforcement for improving employee performance.

Project 2: HUD-Held Home Properties and Mortgages Division – Mortgage Servicing Branch, Purchase Money Home Mortgage Section. (14 employees)

This section had basically the same function as the Assigned Home Mortgage Section. Although it originally had a specific task within the Agency's property selling function, the number of closing statements to be prepared had led to the necessity of employing two sections to fulfill these responsibilities.

The results of the program at the Purchase Money Section are presented in Figure 16.3. The results are quite similar to those obtained in Project 1. Errors were again the prime concern of management in this section since they represented real financial losses. Baseline reviews showed 77% of the submitted reports were error-free, and the goal was set at 95%. By the end of 5 weeks, this goal had been surpassed. Ninety-nine percent error-free functioning has been maintained for the following year of intervention. As in the Assigned Home Mortgage Section, there have been no cost errors that have gotten through review and actually resulted in lost revenue since the B.E.S.T. program was initiated.

The similarity of these programs makes the second report somewhat redundant. The reason that the Purchase Money Section intervention is reported here is that it represents an approximation of a reversal design due to a breakdown in the recording system. For a period of 3 months, the performance analysis measures were discontinued. While no data are available on these months, the number of errors had increased considerably when the program was reinstituted.

The error correction program in this section was identical to that used in Project 1 with similar effects. Over a period of 3 months, common errors were virtually eliminated. They accounted for only nine of 192 errors uncovered in review. In Table 16.2 a comparison of

TABLE 16.1. Quarterly Summary of Employee Performance in the Assigned Home Mortgage Section.

Name	Reports Submitted	% of work load	Number errors corrected	% of errors	% error-free Oct.-Dec.	% error-free March-Sept.	Reports Submitted March-Dec.	Number errors March-Dec.	% error-free March-Dec.
UNIT	6,016	100 avg. 8.33	62	1.03	98.97	98.1	18,251	301	98.4
Employee									
A	386	6.41	5	1.3	98.7	97.1	1,007	23	97.7
B	841	13.97	6	0.7	99.3	99.2	2,338	18	99.2
C	455	7.56	8	1.8	98.2	97.7	1,850	40	97.8
D	269	4.45	3	1.1	98.9	98.9	1,765	20	98.9
E	405	6.73	0	0	100.0	98.2	1,246	15	98.8
F	360	5.98	2	0.5	99.5	98.9	809	7	99.1
G	498	8.28	9	1.8	98.2	97.4	1,500	35	97.7
H	618	10.27	5	0.8	99.2	97.9	1,418	22	98.4
I	266	4.42	8	3.0	97.0	94.0	1,210	62	94.9
J	1,182	19.65	2	0.17	99.8	99.8	2,971	6	99.8
K	218	3.62	10	4.8	95.2	96.9	790	28	96.5
L	518	8.61	4	0.8	99.2	97.5	1,347	25	98.2

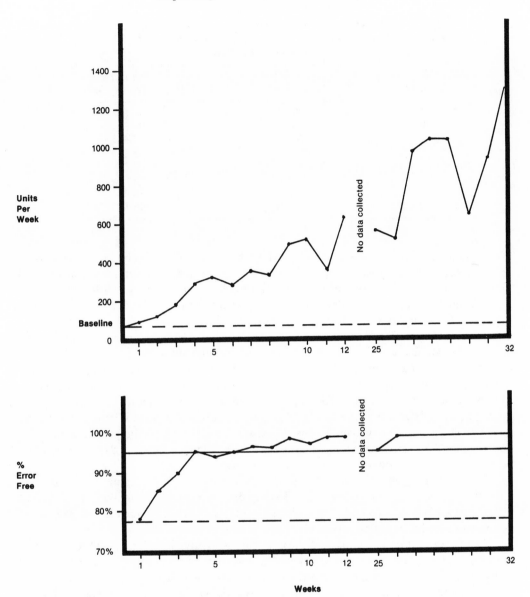

Fig. 16.3. Transactions Completed in the Purchase Money Section, Baseline Through 32 Weeks of Intervention. (Program Suspended Weeks 13-24).

individual error-free performance is presented for the baseline period as well as for the last ten weeks of the treatment year. It is obvious that workers who had been prone to making many errors were now working practically error free.

Project 3: Insurance Division – Home Mortgage Branch, Distributive Shares Section (7 employees)

At the time that the B.E.S.T. program was initiated, this section was suffering from an extensive backlog. The section had been scheduled to have many of its manual operations

TABLE 16.2. Percentage of Error-free Functioning in the Purchase Money Section During the Baseline Week and the Last 10 Weeks of the Treatment Year.

Employee	% Error-free Baseline Mean	% Error-free Post Treatment Mean
A	29	97.5
B	75	94.3
C	70	96.0
D	50	98.2
E	89	99.0
F	37	96.0
G	80	95.4
Total	61.43	96.63

taken over by automated data processing (ADP), but the ADP system had failed to perform up to expectations. The major responsibility of the section was to return money on paid-off mortgages. Part of the money paid on VA and FHA mortgages goes to insurance for the loan. When the homeowner pays off the loan, he is entitled to dividends on that insurance. These dividends or distributive shares can amount to three thousand dollars or more over a 30-year mortgage. The breakdown in this section had drawn Congressional attention because the agency would send out letters stating that the subscriber's mortgage was now paid off, and that a dividend check would follow within 30 days. Unfortunately, checks were rarely received within the time limit. Congressmen would receive indignant letters from constituents about the money that HUD had promised but failed to deliver.

As in the HUD-held Properties Section, the outputs that required improvement were obvious. In this case, however, it was timeliness – completing an output by a specified date – rather than rate or accuracy that needed improvement. Baseline data revealed that *no shares* were being delivered within the 30-day time limit.

Figure 16.4 depicts the percent of shares paid within the 30-day period from baseline through the first 5 months on the B.E.S.T. program. Following intervention, time to completion ranged between 16 and 21 days for 98% of the shares. The other 2% were held up by the need for further information.

The program that accomplished these increases involved individual self-recording of outputs in terms of daily shares distributed. These records of checks sent out were reviewed all the way up the management ladder. Again, the only reward was praise and knowledge of performance improvement. The timeliness achieved by these employees has been maintained over the following year.

Project 4: Insurance Division – Home Mortgage Branch, Correspondence Section. (4 employees)

The Correspondence Section was responsible for handling all inquiries for the Home Mortgage Branch. At the onset of the intervention, the backlog of forms to be filed on correspondence numbered 83,800. A concomitant of this backlog was that when an inquiry came in the staff member was unable to find records of previous correspondence 54% of the time that he went to the files. When records could not be found in the file, it meant that the unfiled backlog of record forms had to be searched. The reality of this task is somewhat hard to grasp, but imagine rummaging through an orderless pile of almost 84,000 forms stacked in a back room, looking for one correspondence. This search for

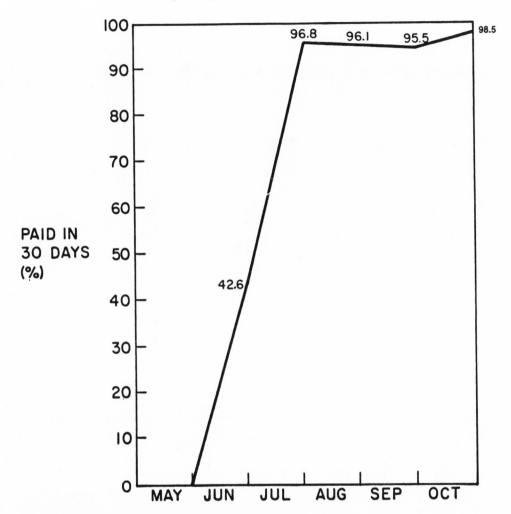

Fig. 16.4. Distributive Shares Paid Within 30 Days.

previous correspondence forms delayed agency response to the point where the person who made the original contact would call again. This meant that another correspondence form would have to be filled out and, therefore, added to the backlog. With the filing problem producing ever more correspondence, the section appeared to be on the verge of drowning in unfiled forms. Productivity had to be increased.

In this situation, the section chief did not need either training or a consultant to identify the output goal. The key was to get some individual data on performance and provide recognition for those employees who met the desired goals. A daily form was developed to be filled out by each staff member. The number of forms per inch (250) was calculated and measurement was made by the number of inches of backlogged forms that had been filed. Each individual plotted their weekly total in average number of forms filed per hour on their own graph, as well as handing in the weekly summary sheet. Baserate performance was at 201 forms filed per hour. The goal was set at 275 forms per hour. Over a 46-week period, performance reached a high of 434 forms filed per hour and averaged out at 320.3.

Reviewing Figure 16.6 shows that by the end of 9 months the backlog of forms had

**INSURANCE DIVISION ·
HOME MORTGAGE BRANCH**

NAME [   ]　　　　　　　　SECTION [Correspondence]

OUTPUT　　　　　　　　　　　　　　　　　GENERAL STANDARD
2244's Arranged/Filed　　　　　　　　　　　　Rate

Daily/Weekly Summary

Day/Date	Inches	Units/ X Inch (250)	Total = Sorted/ Filed	Hours + Worked	Units = per Hour	Goal	Goal Met Yes / No	Hours Scheduled	Hours Worked	Goal Met Yes / No
1. Monday		X 250	=	+	=					
2. Tues.		X 250	=	–	=					
3. Wedn.		X 250	=	–	=					
4. Thurs.		X 250	=	–	=					
5. Friday		X 250	=	–	=					

[ ] Week Total　+ [ ] = [ ]　[ ]　[ ]

Over	Under

Hours Scheduled during the week

Fig. 16.5. Daily Form for Recording the Amount of Filing in the Correspondence Section.

dropped to 13,500, or less than one week's receipts. It has continued to decrease. Percent of time that a form was actually found in the files rose to 96 in the first 3 months of the program. Through periodic checks, this percentage has remained virtually unchanged. It is impossible to estimate the cost savings developed by such an improvement in performance, but in man hours alone the savings in file searching has been staggering. In terms of efficiency, the program can only be termed an unqualified success.

Project 5: Billing and Receivable Division – Receipts and Deposits Branch, Mortgage Deposit Insurance Center. (24 employees)

This was a new section established shortly before the program began. It has responsibility for processing all mortgage checks that come into this branch. The staff has to verify the checks against lists submitted by the banks that send them, as well as prepare the checks for deposit. In addition, they are responsible for microfilming all incoming payments for record-keeping purposes.

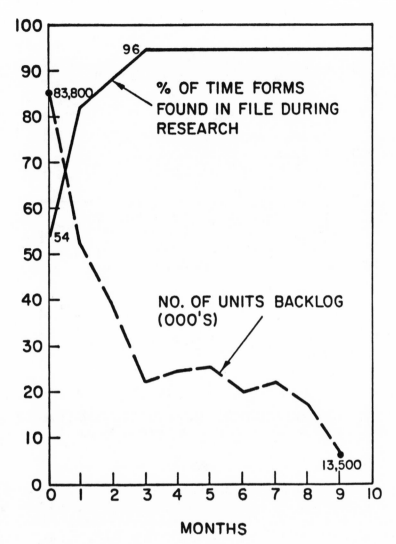

Fig. 16.6. Amount of Filing Backlog and the Percent of Time Items are Found in the Files in the Correspondence Section.

The initial program identified four different transactions that were processed by this section. Measurement was set up in terms of the outputs from each of these transactions. The varying complexity of the tasks necessitated separate baselines and goals for each transaction. As an example, one might compare regular prepayments, the most basic function in this section, to the more complex combination payments. In the former, one check covering one or a group of properties had to be processed. The latter combination payments would involve two or more checks from the same bank covering several properties.

Figure 16.7 depicts the improvement in performance for each of the section's four transactions over the first 9 months of the program. The average percentage increase was 217% of baseline in the regular prepayment area; 198% of baseline in the combination prepayments area; 149% of baseline for Title 1 payments, and 247 percent of baseline operating fees collected outside of the other categories.

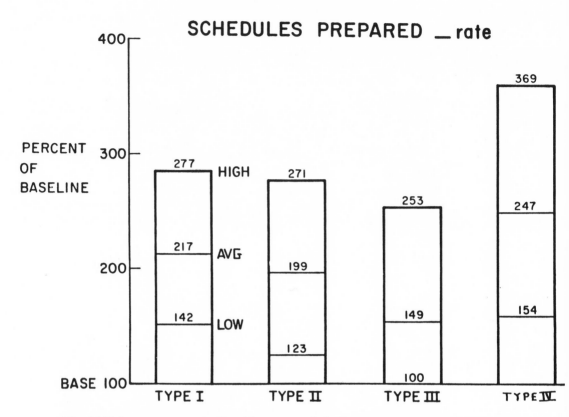

Fig. 16.7. Improvements in Four Functions of the Receipts and Deposits Branch as a Percentage of Baseline Showing High, Low, and Average Months.

PHASE II

In Phase II, the program was extended to those sections of the Mortgage Insurance Accounting Group that had not yet been involved and to the General and Program Accounting Group. The Phase I projects were most often those in which identification of meaningful outputs was easily accomplished, allowing for direct measurement of intervention effects. Phase II programs often involved more diffuse outputs requiring more complex measurement systems, as exemplified by the Fiscal Control Section of the Correspondence and Records Branch in the Insurance Benefits Division. The program in this section began with the identification of three outputs. As measurement progressed, it was soon discovered that many things were being accomplished by the workers that did not fall within the outputs that had been specified. A new measurement system was designed around seven new end functions. A brief trial of this system revealed that the products of the employee's labors were still slipping through the system. Much of the work completed by the employees was not registered within the seven factor system. A third measurement program had to be developed, expanding the number of potential accomplishments to 27. It was not until this system was instituted that overall accomplishments began to exceed goals.

Project 6: Diversified Payments Division – Correspondence and Disbursements Branch and Property Expense Branch. (9 employees)

These two branches had responsibility for basic bill paying functions. They had to process vouchers coming from within the agency, as well as bills from external suppliers. By the end of the eighteenth week of the program, the number of vouchers processed per hour had risen from 21.2 to 25.9 with no increase in error rate. However, the full magnitude of the work changes in this area are understated by simple productivity measures. As the project progressed, the work load did not keep pace. Employees began to come in early so that they could get work to meet their individual goals. In fact, competition for work developed among the staff, and the increased efficiency of the employees allowed management to shift some staff to other tasks.

Project 7: Financial Analysis and Investment Division – Administrative Accounting Branch. (5 employees).

Among the other tasks assigned to this branch was the processing of travel vouchers and vendor invoices for this division. Figure 16.8 presents the hourly rate of invoices and vouchers handled during the project's first 12 months. Shortly after the intervention began, the number of invoices processed had risen from a base rate of 1.3 per hour to 3.82 per hour. Travel vouchers followed the same pattern, rising from 2.06 to 2.70 per hour.

Figure 16.8 also shows that these initial successes were not maintained, even though

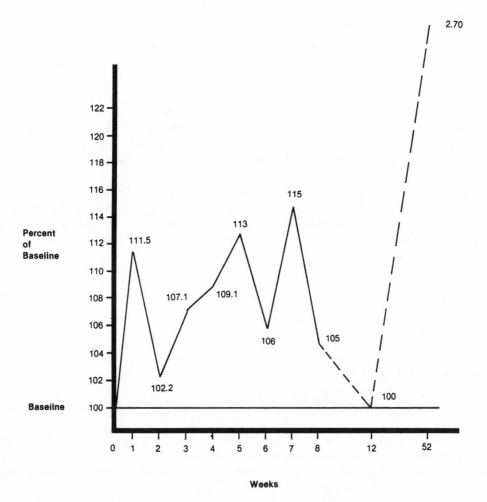

Fig. 16.8. Rate of Travel Vouchers Processed as Percent of Baseline.

the system of individual feedback and reinforcement was in full swing. Further assessment of the functioning of this branch uncovered a number of ancillary functions that were impeding productivity. In particular, poorly organized procedures, filing problems, and a constant flow of interrupting telephone contacts made productivity increases difficult to sustain. This extensive performance audit revealed that reorganizational steps were necessary.

In order to alleviate the telephone problem, a clerk was temporarily assigned the role of telephone contact person to respond to all phone inquiries. In this way, repeated interruptions of on-task behavior were eliminated. The difficulties with the filing system interacted with the telephone problem. Most of the calls were in reference to unpaid bills. Unfortunately, these bills were filed according to the date that they were due, i.e., thirty days after they were received. An invoice that came in on November 3rd was placed in the December 3rd file, but there were no cross references by name or invoice number. The person looking for the bill would simply have to guess at a date when the bill was due and then start looking through the files for that date and others close to it. To make matters worse, the bills were not filed in any order within the date files. A simple change to a name filing system was sufficient to correct the search problem.

While the telephone and filing problems were quite real, the data from the initial weeks of the intervention demonstrated that the staff could perform at an increased rate even with these obstacles. They may have made performance more difficult, but the root cause of the performance deterioration had to lie elsewhere. A review of archival records showed that in previous years a similar productivity decrease had occurred in these same weeks between the Thanksgiving and Christmas holidays. The resulting backlog had previously been alleviated through overtime work in January. It would appear that management and staff had quite inadvertently created a rather unique Christmas bonus system. The workers would receive substantial extra funds from their overtime work just in time to pay the Christmas bills that came due in January. These contingencies favored building up a backlog in December. They had to be modified before productivity would increase.

A meeting was held with staff to explain the new telephone arrangement and begin the alphabetical filing system. At this time, weekly productivity goals were set. These goals were designed to meet the seasonal demand and eliminate the annual January overtime. It was explained that overtime would not be initiated in January no matter how large the backlog became. In this way, the reinforcement for low productivity was removed. Following this new program, the number of invoices processed rose to over four per hour.

Project 8: Title I Branch – Reserve Section (12 employees).

The program for this section began during Phase I. It is presented after the case studies of all other sections, because it represents something more than a simple comparison design, although the effect came about serendipitously.

Shortly after the individualized feedback program had begun, this section was put under a new director who had not been trained in B.E.S.T. Although the new chief supported the project, he also changed a number of other procedures within the section. These concurrent programs produced substantial improvement in productivity. After several months, the section head decided to change the feedback forms that were then in use. Although he continued to collect data, the feedback system was interrupted for a period of 3 months between December and February, in preparation for the introduction of the new forms. The effects of this program change can be seen in Figure 16.9. Although the other innovations that the new chief had installed remained in effect, productivity decreased to approximately baseline levels over several of the outputs being measured.

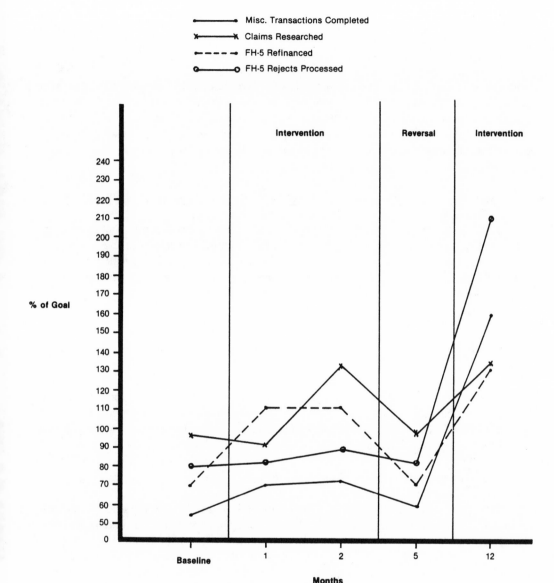

Fig. 16.9. Productivity Increases as Percent of Goal in the Title 1-Reserve Section for Baseline, Intervention, Reversal, and Second Intervention.

The Reserve Section had broad responsibilities in terms of researching claims and reconciling billing statements associated with Title 1 programs. It also must research refinancing applications on housing mortgages under Title 1 and process exceptions from the automated data processing operation. The section had a history of being a bottleneck in the system due to its large work load.

By the end of the first 6 months of the program, productivity had increased to the point that the Reserve section had no backlog for the first time in its history. In fact, all work was more than current because the staff found themselves having to keep busy while they waited for the ADP to provide them with more work. In terms of specific outputs, the number of claims researched had reached 150% of baseline, while billing statements reconciled had risen 179%. In the mortgage area, refinancing was at 132% of baseline, and the number of rejections for which the staff research had been completed was at 264% of baseline. The rate of exceptions processed from the automated data system had risen to 163% of pretreatment levels, and miscellaneous transactions were at 295% of what they had been before the project was initiated. The new chief had been skeptical of the B.E.S.T. feedback system, but his experience when feedback was withdrawn convinced him that these overwhelming increases in productivity were completely dependent on the knowledge of results and concomitant reinforcement that the employees received from their records.

OVERALL EFFECTS OF THE B.E.S.T. PROGRAM AT HUD

The B.E.S.T. Program at HUD has resulted in measurable gains in productivity, accuracy, and timeliness over a broad spectrum of accomplishments. The results of the overall program in various sections do not reveal the advantages gained from the specific segments of B.E.S.T. An examination of the steps of the program as they affected various sections at HUD offers enlightening information on program development.

Performance Audit

The intervention at HUD began with the consultant using the first few weeks of his tenure to get an overview of the agency, learn the language and procedures, and decrease the anxiety that the presence of a change agent invariably causes. As classes began, the managers and the consultant carried out an analysis of current unit performance on key activities. In many cases, this meant that unit productivity standards had to be developed or updated, although most units could provide gross measures of their output and some had already established unit performance standards. It should be noted that even where group standards existed, individual performance was not monitored systematically in any unit, and employees rarely received feedback on how well they or their unit were performing in comparison to its standard.

Once the unit standards had been identified, current overall performance was evaluated. An analysis of key activities and their production problems was then undertaken. This step was begun by evaluating the potential economic payoff to be gained from increased productivity, in comparison to the cost of correcting the performance deficiency through changing consequences, improving individual feedback, increasing staff, and/or providing further training for personnel. In order to complete this evaluation, the managers had to learn how to identify and develop measurable objectives. This is not only the first step that must be taken in any intervention, but the step that uncovers whether an intervention is possible or even necessary. A case in point is the Home Insurance Benefits Branch of the Insurance Benefits Division. The assessment of objectives and feedback that was performed on this branch revealed that standards had been in operation for several years. The major task of the unit, processing insurance benefits claims, had been identified long ago and a feedback system was in effect. Each employee regularly received data on the number of reports processed, the number of hours worked, and his average rate per hour. This branch had no backlog, and a high productivity level was being maintained with a minimal error rate. The performance audit revealed little potential for improvement, but the assessment of objectives and productivity did show when well enough should be left alone. Contrary to the myth of government operations, management in several sections like this one was so effective that intervention by the consultants was not warranted.

As noted earlier, identifying outputs was a problem of varying difficulty across branches. The Grant and Loan Accounting Branch, for example, had responsibility for reporting on 58 programs. While it was possible, after many long hours, to identify five general outputs, the data sources for these accomplishments were outside the agency and, therefore, difficult to control. A feedback system based on monthly reports was eventually implemented with favorable results, but the mere specification of the task was of central importance to productivity improvement in this branch.

Goals and Feedback

The second aspect of the training was of particular importance at HUD. The managers had to be taught how to develop recording forms for their employees, as well as feedback systems that would provide the employee and management with an estimate of how current performance compared to previous efforts. Setting goals from the baseline data was not difficult to teach, but a good form was necessary before baseline data could be collected.

A good example of the kind of forms that needed to be developed can be found in the Mortgage Insurance Accounting Deposit Center program, presented in Project 5. Figure 16.10 depicts the Daily Performance Report filled out by each employee. The upper part of the form breaks down the total work output into the different areas to which payments can be applied. Total daily performance as compared to the goal is computed at the bottom of the form. Using this format, the employee can summarize the records that he maintains as he completes each transaction. This form represents the second in a four-step process of recording and feedback that begins with the individual worker keeping a record of each of his accomplishments as they occur. At the end of the day, the daily record form is used to total these accomplishments. The data from this daily form is then entered on the weekly form presented in Figure 16.11. The weekly form serves as a performance measure for management as well as a means for the worker to compare his productivity across days. The fourth step in the measurement chain is to have the weekly results returned to the worker who then plots them on a simple graph of rate (in this case, units per hour) over time (in this case, weeks). A horizontal line at the bottom of this graph is used to denote baseline and another horizontal line further up the graph marks off the goal. The employee can immediately see the fluctuations in his performance above and below goal.

There is no overestimating the importance of developing feedback and measurement forms around relevant outputs. A major proportion of the areas in which implementation of the program was delayed or sidetracked experienced difficulty in developing appropriate forms. In some cases, for example, the Annual Contribution Branch of the Low Rent Division, where high level accountants review large scale programs and project fiscal needs, it took several months to develop appropriate measurement forms. In other cases, initial baseline data failed to pick up appropriate outputs. The problem here was not in identifying outputs, but in setting up a system that actually measured them. The intervention in the Cash Control Branch of the General and Subsidiary Ledger Division was held up extensively because of this kind of measurement problem.

Perhaps the most difficult obstacles to overcome in the area of goals and feedback were those in which the procedures of the section or branch, in one way or another, prevented direct feedback to the staff. The most common example of this type of problem was the one in the Home Properties and Notes Branch. Unit teamwork was a key concept in this branch, making it impossible to decide who actually did what in order to provide feedback. Employees regularly left their individual tasks to work on group projects or help other workers with their individual assignments. It was possible to develop unit-based feedback systems in this instance that revealed generally good performance, but the absence of in-

NAME: _____

DATE: _____

NUMBER OF CHECKS RECEIVED: _____

NUMBER OF CHECKS AND AMOUNTS DEPOSITED:

	Number Processed	Dollar Amount
Mortgage Insurance Premiums	_____	$_____
Title I Loans	_____	$_____
Fee Billing	_____	$_____
Pro Rata Premiums	_____	$_____
Title I Recoveries	_____	$_____
G. P. A.	_____	$_____
Miscellaneous	_____	$_____

TOTAL MONEY DEPOSITED: $_____

NUMBER OF SCHEDULES PROCESSED:

$$\frac{}{\text{No. Today}} \div \frac{}{\text{Hrs. Today}} = \frac{}{\genfrac{}{}{0pt}{}{\text{Avg./Hr.}}{\text{(Graph)}}}$$

◯ Goal

Goal met?
Yes | No

NUMBER OF PROGRAMS PROCESSED:

$$\frac{}{\text{No. Today}} \div \frac{}{\text{Hrs. Today}} = \frac{}{\genfrac{}{}{0pt}{}{\text{Avg./Hr.}}{\text{(Graph)}}}$$

◯ Goal

Goal met?
Yes | No

REMARKS: _____

Fig. 16.10. MIA Mail and Deposit Center Daily Performance Report.

328

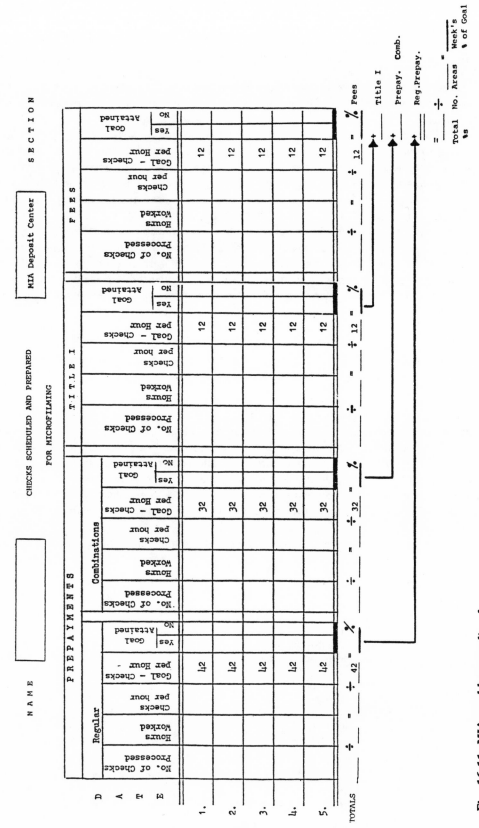

Fig. 16.11. MIA weekly recording form.

329

dividualized feedback no doubt lessened the contingent relationship between rewards and work output. However, effective measurement of group accomplishments is distinctly preferable to no measurement at all.

A second example of a feedback deficiency that is not easily corrected was encountered in the Premium Section of the Billings and Receivable Division. The procedures in this section included a "problem research group" that reviewed all individual feedback before it reached the worker. The presence of this system compromised self-recording and delayed feedback to the employee. A baseline period of 6 months yielded no useful data, and 9 months after the beginning of the program the intervention had accomplished little or nothing in this section. At that time, a new acting chief joined this section and revised the work flow so that individual responsibilities could be measured and fed directly back to the staff. It is still too early to evaluate the effects of the individualized system.

Feedback is not limited to general productivity. It can also be used to pinpoint specific problems that an employee is having. Figure 16.12 shows the type of errors made on vouchers from the Property Expense Branch. This kind of form quickly exposes the trouble spots in a particular section or procedure. It can also uncover those areas that may require direct remediation. In this instance, a performance problem was rectified by training when it was found that one employee accounted for 25% of the unit's errors by making repeated mistakes in three of the computing steps on Figure 16.12. For the quarter following training, this employee made no errors at all. In addition to telling the manager who is doing what, the feedback system indirectly suggests what the manager might do about it.

Changing Consequences

Praise and recognition in its various forms proved to be an effective reward for both managers and employees when it was delivered contingent on satisfactory performance. Some managers whose relations with their employees had been distinctly antagonistic experienced great success by becoming sources of reinforcement to their staff. They also found that this produced a very pleasurable change in their working environment. The effect of having an office director come down to congratulate a productive worker cannot be overstated. Employee reaction showed that this was perceived as very rewarding, as well as rather novel.

Yet, praise was not always enough. One employee maintained poor performance and

Type of Correction	Number Reported
1. Figure misread	
2. Accounts not balanced	
3. Voucher not verified for accuracy	
4. Justifying documents not attached	
Total Corrections _____	
(÷)	100%
Number Processed _____	−
(equals)	(Subtract % Corrections)
Percent Corrections _____	
	_____ % Error Free
	(Enter on Graph)

Fig. 16.12. Property Expense Branch Corrections Reported Form.

a great deal of absence despite the feedback-recognition program. In this case, other rewards had to be found. A program was established that gave her permission to take vacation time without prejudice any time that had accumulated if she were present and meeting standards when no annual leave was available. The importance of her efforts to the unit's performance was stressed in meeting with her. This intervention raised her performance above the group level. She attributed her improvement not to the contingent annual leave, but to the interest (attention) that she had received from management.

The intended positive consequences of the program were not the only results in some sections. One drawback of the increased productivity was that in some sections the supply of work failed to keep pace with the improved employee performance. At best, this can lead to competition between employees to obtain the little work that is available, as was reported earlier in the Diversified Payments Division. Management should be aware that the loser in this competition is on an extinction schedule, in that he will fall below standard from lack of work, no matter how productive he tries to be. Unfortunately, this was not the worst of the no-work problem. Some employees were moved because greater productivity had shifted the work to other sections. One supervisor got even more directly punished for his success after cutting his department from nine workers to two, while losing neither productivity nor accuracy. As demand increased, staff who were new to the unit were added and trained. The staff was increased to six while productivity and accuracy remained above standard. This supervisor then put in for promotion to the next level, although he feared that he was not eligible to be considered for the new post because the rules specified that he had to have spent the last year supervising at least eight employees. While top management did bend the rules to promote this supervisor, the example serves as a reminder that office procedures must be reviewed for their potential to punish productivity.

In addition to praise and recognition, managers in various sections implemented programs of small tangible rewards, such as a small celebration contingent on meeting standards. Other managers provided activity rewards such as training or special assignments. The use of these rewards was frequent and unsystematic, varying from section to section throughout OFA, making it difficult to estimate their general effects. One can only conclude that the current project offers no support for the notion that these rewards are more effective than praise and knowledge of results. However, this observation is limited to the current population which perceived itself as grossly deprived of both feedback and recognition. One veteran employee reported that in her 35 years of government employment, this program provided the first performance appraisal that she had experienced. She may have exaggerated, but a management by exception format in which employees received attention only when they made an error is likely to lead to the eventual extinction of good work habits and establish a fertile ground for a system that gives employees the opportunity to work for recognition.

Most lower level managers did not believe that feedback and praise could affect long-term performance increases without monetary back-up reinforcers. While 18 months may not qualify as long term in any absolute sense, the effects have lasted longer than many of the skeptics would have predicted. This finding is in agreement with much of the laboratory findings on the comparative efficacy of reinforcers. Recent research suggests that there may be a hierarchy of reinforcers that develops with age (Zigler & Balla, 1972). While these results are still tentative, they indicate that tangible reinforcers are most effective in early childhood. Social reinforcers such as attention and praise become more important than tangible rewards as the child matures. In adulthood, knowledge of good performance may be the most potent of all rewards. (Forness, 1972; Schultz & Sherman, 1976; Zigler & Balla, 1972). Neither the laboratory investigations nor the current applied findings suggest any reason to believe that monetary rewards would have produced more enduring or dramatic results than have been achieved at HUD through praise and feedback.

Maintaining and Extending the Program

The spectre of vanishing effects following a training program or consultant intervention is well-known in industry. Despite the fact that individual feedback provides continuous self-monitoring of performance, the effects of this intervention require an active maintenance effort. As tasks and outputs change, recording and feedback systems must be adjusted or developed anew. Supervisors and managers must attend to the performance reporting system, revise as needed, manage consequences for desirable and undesirable performance, and reinforce workers in order to maintain performance improvements. The real danger at this stage is that managers will fail to devote the necessary time to running the feedback system. When this happens, workers will conclude that data collection is no longer being rewarded, and performance levels will fall. The manager must view charts, graphs, forms, schedules, and logs as part of the general work flow, not as tasks to be completed if time is available. If workers are not asked for their performance data on a regular and continual basis, they will fail to fill out their feedback form; thus, they will be unable to see their performance levels or correct their errors. Supervisors will begin to correct worker's errors themselves in the interest of expediency and resume a crisis management, negative style. This will disrupt the work flow and make it difficult to obtain the data to schedule work efficiently and prioritize tasks for completion.

For the program to survive and prosper, the manager must monitor his workers to be sure that they continue to complete all forms thoroughly and accurately. He must continue to summarize those forms and provide feedback and reinforcement to his employees. When necessary, he must be prepared to use the forms to pinpoint performance problems which can then be solved through altering the feedback system, work schedule, or consequences, as well as by providing training or job rotation. Managing the system is truly a supervisory task, but it is also time consuming. The supervisor should delegate the day-to-day management of the feedback system to an assistant supervisor whenever possible. He should continue to assess performance and manage the workload, but he need not collect the data himself and should avoid becoming involved in the technical tasks of the unit.

There is only one sure way to keep this system functioning, and that is to establish a scheduled reporting regimen that directs performance measures throughout the management hierarchy at regular intervals. This is exactly what has been done at HUD. Data are collected and summarized from section to branch and from branch to division at monthly intervals. Quarterly reports on the data collected by the employees then go to the Director of OFA and finally to the Assistant Secretary. A copy of the monthly summary report filled out by each section is presented in Figure 16.13. These forms were designed to convey performance measures throughout the organization and to identify those individuals whose performance merits management attention. The entire monitoring program is maintained because each section has a specific date by which its reports must reach upper management.

Extension of the program is also indicated in the monthly summary form. In fact, extension has been a continuing goal of the program. In this vein, a newsletter was established which chronicled program successes as a prompt for extending the system to new areas. As the results began to become known, more sections have expedited their program interventions. As Assistant Secretary Medina said of the program, "It sells itself after a while and the cynics become believers because the results are so concrete."

ROUTING
___ 1. Section Chief to Branch
___ 2. Branch Chief to Division
Director

MIA Monthly Report

PIR-1

PERFORMANCE MANAGEMENT PROGRAM

Month of _____

Section: _____

1 Unit Results:

PERFORMANCE RESULTS

OUTPUT	BASE	GOAL	THIS WEEK	COMMENTS

2 Individual Reinforcement for Performance
(* by name indicates recommendation for Divisional or Higher Level Recognition)

NAME	ACCOMPLISHMENT	WHAT REINFORCERS HAVE BEEN USED?

3 Existing Program:
Change of goal needed (be specific – where, what output, who, why?)
Change in feedback system needed (be specific – where, what output, who, why?)
4 Projected Program:
Problem areas were performance management program may be needed.

UNIT	OUTPUT	DESCRIBE PROGRAM – what behaviors are desired which you are not getting

Fig. 16.13. Monthly Reporting Form to Upper Management.

Agency Response

In reviewing the data in this chapter, one can only conclude that the B.E.S.T. program at HUD has produced dramatic, measurable increases in productivity. But how do the employees react? Almost any traditional measure of employee morale suggests that they have reacted very positively. Attendence is up throughout OFA, while the number of grievances has decreased. Productivity has increased without adding additional staff, at the same time as overtime has decreased. Subjective supervisory judgements of improvements in employee attitudes are further supported by the lack of union objection to the intervention. The union had been briefed on the program when it began and raised no objections because the program was based on fair appraisal and provided rewards for performance. The goals of the program also fit the guidelines of the new Civil Service Reform Act, which calls for objective performance appraisal. B.E.S.T. provided management with quantitative information and objective standards for employee evaluation. At the same time, it gives the employees an evaluation that they can believe in because they collect the data themselves and can judge their own performance.

The B.E.S.T. program at HUD has been approved by the Federal Office of Personnel Management (OPM) as an Exemplary Practices Program. This program recognizes outstanding, innovative practices in federal agencies, so that they can be disseminated to other government offices. OPM has produced a film on the program components as a model for other agencies to follow. HUD plans to extend these performance management concepts into additional accounting units, other offices of Administration, and eventually into many HUD operations. Summing up the experience with the B.E.S.T. program, Assistant Secretary Medina said, "The principles of good management and human behavior are universal. Employees should know what is expected of them, they should know how well they are doing in relation to some quantifiable standard, and they should be recognized for good or deficient performance." Objective data collection, feedback and contingent consequences are the core concepts in a behavioral approach to management as exemplified in the successful performance improvement project at HUD.

REFERENCES

Forness, S. R. The reinforcement heirarchy. *Psychology in the Schools.* 1973, **10,** 168-197.

Mager, R. F., & Pipe, P. *Analyzing performance problems or 'you really oughta wanna',* Belmont, CA: Fearon, 1970.

Schneier, C. E., Pernick, R., & Bryant, D. Improving performance in the public sector through behavior modification and positive reinforcement. *Public Personnel Management,* 1978, **8,** 101-110.

Schultz, C., & Sherman, R. Social class development and differences in reinforcer effectiveness. *Review of Educational Research,* 1976, **46,** 25-59.

The United States Government Manual Washington, D.C.: The U.S. Government Printing House, 1980.

Zigler, E., & Balla, D. Developmental course of responsiveness to social reinforcement in normal and institutionalized retarded children. *Developmental Psychology,* 1972, **6,** 66-73.

17

Quality of Working Life: A Behavioral Process for Organizational Change

Michael P. Rosow
Work In America Institute

The case studies in this book focus on the specific application of behavior modification techniques to industrial organizational change. Throughout the evolution of behavior modification for purposes of specific organizational change, there has been a parallel evolution of a less direct process of change within organizations. This has included such concepts as management by objectives (MBO), human relations, sensitivity training, organizational design (OD), and many others. Very recently much of this process of change has focused on a relatively new concept called quality of working life (QWL).

The term quality of working life is perceived by many as implying improved management of human resources to bring about overall improvement in organizational effectiveness. The concept of quality of working life is seen as encompassing workplace democracy, increased worker participation, and at the same time productivity improvement through optimized human input. With some recognized successes in recent years, an increasing volume of attention and discussion has centered on quality of working life.

Quality of working life is generally seen as an outgrowth of the human relations movement of the 1950s and 1960s. But while there appears to be a logical progression from the human relations movement of the 1960s to today's quality of working life movement, the most direct predecessor of today's QWL was the sociotechnical systems approach. Conceptualized at Tavistock, England, during the 1960s, this approach promoted the redesign of work organizations through a balanced meld of human needs and goals with the technical needs and goals of the organization.

Quality of working life, together with its acronym QWL, also has roots in the ideas of the so-called youth countercultural revolution of the late 1960s and early 1970s. This era in American history represented a rejection of traditionally held values and beliefs in the pursuit of an improved environment, consumer interests, and an end to the war in Vietnam. Together these were recognized as quality-of-life issues. Consequently it was not surprising that the concern for overall improvement in quality of life spilled over into the arena of work, leading inevitably to the concept of quality of working life.

In many ways, quality of working life represents a blending of these very real concerns for human values in today's society with an awareness that all individuals devote the greater part of their mature lives to work, expending time, energy, and physical and mental resources to this endeavor. It recognizes, moreover, that work is the chief determinant of an individual's freedom, growth, and self-respect, as well as his or her standard of living. Further, the role of the breadwinner is fundamental to the survival of the family and society. Society has also begun to realize that human resources may well represent the only remaining plentiful natural resource, and that both the individual and society can clearly benefit from their full utilization. Finally, and perhaps most important, production, industrial growth, and technological advances are clearly not ends in themselves but simply a means to an end – namely, the improvement of the quality of life for all.

QWL – multifaceted and constantly evolving – has many definitions. For the purposes of this chapter, it is defined as a process stimulating attitudinal and behavioral change within work groups and organizations. The significance of this process and its impact on the workplace can best be appreciated in terms of the changes that have taken place at General Motors, perhaps the most pervasive changes that have occurred in any large organization in the world. During the past 10 years General Motors has gradually evolved a strategy for the development of quality of working life in its organization throughout the United States and the free world.

Although the exact use of, or stimulus for, change in such a large organization has not been clearly pinpointed, it obviously relates to the erosion of labor-management relations which took place in General Motors toward the end of the 1960s. These eroding relationships had clearly detrimental effects on the quality and quantity of production during that era. A growing body of evidence indicates that absenteeism, turnover, grievances, and sabotage were contributing heavily to the company's problems.

As is frequently the case in time of crisis, several bold new leaders emerged to push for change. Irving Bluestone, vice-president of the General Motors Division of the United Automobile Workers (UAW), and Delmar (Dutch) Landen, formerly director of O.D. and now director of QWL for General Motors, strongly promoted the QWL concept within their respective organizations. Bluestone led the demand in 1970 and again in 1973 for a national agreement to promote labor-management cooperation to improve the quality of working life. This agreement was signed during the 1973 national contract negotiations by General Motors and the UAW. Bluestone and Landen remain among the strongest proponents of QWL today.

Several additional facts are worthy of mention:

- Quality of working life has spread from a single experiment in one General Motors facility to experiments in over 90 General Motors plants across the country.
- The GM-UAW National QWL Agreement of 1973 became the model for the 1979 Steelworkers-Steel Industry Agreement and the 1981 agreement between the Communications Workers of America, the International Brotherhood of Electrical Workers, and American Telephone and Telegraph.
- Managerial success in General Motors today is clearly tied to the manager's attitude toward QWL.
- And perhaps most striking of all, General Motors executives consider the success of QWL critical to the company's future.

Still, the significance of General Motors' commitment to QWL cannot be fully recognized without exploring the changing role of employees within the company. These span such far-reaching changes as:

- Participation by assembly-line workers in job-related decisions.
- Direct involvement of line workers and supervisors in problem-solving activities.
- Broader skill training, with resultant interchangeability of employees in a variety of assembly jobs.
- The elimination of one or more layers of supervision in newly designed plants.

- Self-manager work teams with responsibility for decisions on:
  Production scheduling
  Daily individual job assignments
  Design and redesign of equipment, tools and products
  Budget
  Overtime
  Quality control
  Daily, weekly, annual output
- Where appropriate, such teams may also share responsibility for additional production-related decisions.
- And moving full circle from one small experiment in a single work group to today's sociotechnical systems (STS), workers are involved in the design of new facilities. In the STS approach, assembly-line workers are actively participating in the design and development of assembly facilities as well as equipment for new plants. Application of sociotechnical systems has led to manufacturing plants that pursue the optimal blending of human systems, technical specifications, production factors, and quality considerations.

Having established a pragmatic basis for considering the type of organizational process behavior change fostered through quality of working life, it is appropriate to review the QWL process itself. Quality of working life incorporates a number of critical elements including:

- A commitment at the top of the organization (in the company, the division, and the plant, and in the union, where one exists).
- Communication of this commitment throughout the organization, both vertically and horizontally.
- Volunteerism – plants, organizational entities, work groups, and individuals are free to participate in experiments or not. But few experiments, if any, proceed without a 90% or higher majority decision.
- Thorough orientation and training for all participants.
- Reinforcement in varied forms
- Review of procedures, outcomes, and effects, with appropriate programmatic change and retraining where necessary.
- Dissemination of results to participants and others throughout the organization.
- Recommitment to program goals, and new opportunities for constructive change.

The behavioral process of QWL usually incorporates most of these critical elements. In instances where one or more are absent or ignored, failure frequently results.

An exploration of the sequence of events should provide additional insight into the operation of a quality of working life program. The corporate chief executive, the plant manager, and the operations of product manager (along with union executives where one or more are present) reach a committed decision to pursue a QWL experiment or program. This decision is communicated from top management, down through the various levels of supervision, and across the organization, with provision for orientation and consultation of all employees to be involved.

In this communication process, the following review takes place:

- The rationale for change along with the justification for a QWL approach is presented.

- Desired outcomes and potential benefits are enumerated and thoroughly discussed.

If appropriate expertise does not exist within the organization, a consultant or "third party" is sought out and a selection is made with the consensus of labor and management. Consultants may be engaged at any point after the organizational commitment has been reached.

Orientation is followed by a survey of the current status of the organization, including:

- Management, supervisory personnel, and employee attitudes.
- Review of work flow, existing methods, and procedures.
- Inter- and intra-work group relations.
- Perceptions of organizational effectiveness.
- Analysis of problems and barriers to heightened effectiveness.
- Suggested approaches to greater effectiveness.
- An indication of interest in participation in the QWL program.

The survey frequently combines focused group discussions with in-depth individual interviews. It is designed to develop information on the scope of the program as well as on the "status quo" of the organizations.

Survey materials are thoroughly analyzed and a comprehensive feedback process is developed, appropriate to the needs of each level of the organization. The results and an explanation of their significance is then fed back to all participants. Additional feedback and/or orientation sessions are provided where further clarification is required.

Once the survey and feedback process has been completed and all relevant questions have been addressed, one or more work groups are selected to initiate the process. In recent experiments the tendency has been to select an interested group, because a committed group will have a high probability of success. Employees are then surveyed or a vote is held to determine their desire to participate. If participation interest is judged inadequate, usually below 90%, another vote may be taken or the project may be shelved. Where participation interest exceeds 90%, the process continues.

Endorsement of the idea to move ahead with the program is followed by the design and implementation of intensive training for all participants. Although there are many variations in QWL training, some general parameters have been established through both trial and error and actual practice, as follows:

- Groups of 10 to 12 employees are trained in problem-solving techniques, group dynamics, and interpersonal support.
- Initial training usually ranges from 3 to 5 days of paid time away from the job.
- One or two members of each group emerge as leaders and are selected as QWL coordinators or facilitators.
- QWL coordinators may be trained as trainers for future groups.
- Training may be initiated at a variety of levels within the organization.

Training can vary from place to place with initial training focus on: supervisors, lineworkers, middle managers, etc. Additional training may be provided at future intervals if necessary.

With the completion of training, employees return to their traditional jobs with a new provision for regularly scheduled problem-solving sessions. Results and outcomes are disseminated outside of the groups and the resulting change, or the rationale for no change, is fed back to the group. Reinforcement takes various forms, such as: feedback, recognition, time off, financial awards, etc. Initial successes are widely reported throughout the organization, and the effect spreads. This, as coined by one expert, is "the healthy infection principle."

The process is then gradually diffused throughout the operation. More and more groups are trained until the process ultimately has reached all interested employees. Actually, once initial successes are disseminated, there is usually a growing demand for inclusion in the experiment across the operation and throughout the organization. The schedule of training in large operations, with 3,000 and more employees, can last as long as 18 months.

All groups are provided continuous feedback on their activities, suggestions, and findings. As the process evolves, the scope of group activities is broadened to provide for increased coverage of operational procedures and increased responsibility for group members.

There are many obvious intrinsic rewards related to group participation in addition to the previously mentioned reinforcers. These intrinsic rewards are in the form of:

- Increased self-esteem
- Greater control over one's own job
- More freedom and independence in job-related decisions
- More respect from peers, supervisors, and subordinates
- Recognition
- Better understanding of one's role in, and contribution to, the organization and its goals
- Increased identification with work group, operation, and organization
- A sense of accomplishment

It is difficult, if not impossible, to determine the relative impacts of these reinforcers on this behavioral change process. In fact, from the behavioral point of view, it is only really important that the reinforcers do affect or contribute to change and that sustained reinforcement of both types clearly leads to continuous behavioral improvement.

There are a number of significant reinforcements for the organization and its management which may accompany the QWL change. These encompass such critical factors as:

- Reduced absenteeism
- Improved quality
- Increased output
- Lowered turnover
- Decreased grievances
- Bettered labor-management relations
- Improved production and service processes
- Reduced equipment downtime
- Improved overall organizational effectiveness, etc.

These factors clearly contribute to the operation and profitability objectives of virtually every organization. As positive consequences of the behavioral change through QWL, they play a critical role in sustaining the life of the program.

Although the benefits accruing to all parties involved in the quality-of-work-life process can be substantial, a failure to attend properly to any one or more steps of the process can seriously jeopardize or destroy the entire effort. Problems can arise at almost any step in the process, as follows:

- Lack of sufficient commitment at the top or any subsequent level of the organization.
- Failure to engender union and work force cooperation and commitment.
- Inadequate communication – up front or at any point in the process.
- Selection of a program inappropriate to the needs of the organization.
- Problems in consultant selection, including:
  Failure to recognize the need for a third party
  Personality conflicts, as between consultant and management, or between either of these two and the other concerned parties such as union, supervisors, employees.
  Inappropriate consultant, or one with inadequate experience.
- Lack of attention to survey results and the feedback process.
- Inadequate training of involved employees.
- Absence of sufficient feedback to groups, especially true when ideas are rejected.
- Not enough attention to reinforcement and rewards for groups.
- Failure to disseminate results.
- Resistance among supervisors.
- Inadequate focus on sustaining reinforcers.
- Somewhat surprisingly, a major problem encountered by a number of organizations experiencing success with QWL is over-publicity. The time demands for additional media and industry visits have greatly taxed many programs. In some cases success has been jeopardized, and in others publicity and visits have been terminated.

Consequently, while there have been many outstanding success stories about the QWL process, there have also been stalled and/or failed programs. It is critical to proceed cautiously and to adhere to the process, as is the case when moving into any behavior change arena.

Having reviewed the behavioral process underlying quality of working life programs and some potential gains and pitfalls, it would seem appropriate to explore several actual examples of QWL. The Tarrytown, New York, General Motors assembly plant is one of the most widely publicized quality-of-working-life success stories. The Tarrytown program, initiated in the early 1970s, is also one of the longest lived in the United States.

In the late 1960s and early 1970s, labor management relations at Tarrytown had reached an all-time low. Production costs were rising, and the quality of product was approaching a new low. The quality performance, in fact, was one of the worst among 18 GM assembly plants, and union work grievances were running about 3,000 per year.

High labor turnover in the plant led to the increased hiring of younger workers. Along with their demands for societal change, the younger Tarrytown workers also demanded some changes in their work environment. The plant manager felt that there were increasing pressures and sensed the need for change beginning in 1971. He also saw an opportunity for improvement in performance.

Despite a long history of mistrust in the relationship between management and the union and many misgivings, the plant manager began a series of overtures to the local union. Both sides expressed a genuine willingness to change the philosophy of managing Tarrytown.

At about that time, the plant was to be converted from a combination car/truck plant to total car assembly. This resulted in a variety of changes in layout, and two departments, hard trim and soft trim, were to be moved. Although the plant redesign was accomplished primarily along traditional lines, one profound change occurred. Two of the supervisors in the hard trim department suggested involving the workers in the move. It was agreed that workers should be given an opportunity to express their ideas. The departmental committeemen were told about this approach and gave it their support. As soon as the soft trim department heard about this new idea, they decided that they should try it too.

Line workers were given the plans for the new setup, and their suggestions were welcomed. The approach worked well. Many good suggestions were made and many were adopted. The move was accomplished smoothly and quickly. The following year employees became involved in the rearrangement of another major department.

These successes were widely broadcast throughout the company. Following the 1973 National Agreement, headquarters corporate and national union representatives began to extend the Tarrytown program under the aegis of this agreement.

With this approach in mind, further union/management discussion led to the decision to continue to broaden the program. A consultant was selected jointly, and management and the union each selected a coordinator to work with the consultant, supervisors, workers, and the union.

At the consultant's direction, a number of training sessions on problem solving were planned. Thirty-four workers from two shifts in the soft trim department volunteered to participate. The training began with the company agreeing to pay for 6 hours on Saturdays and the volunteers agreeing to an additional 2 hours of their own time.

The training was highly successful, and a variety of problems related to trim were solved by the groups. Suggested solutions resulted in reduced glass breakage, reduced moulding damage, and elimination of water leaks.

Despite the successes, the program was to suffer through a variety of interruptions due to drastic changes in the plant. Late 1974 saw the first gasoline shortage result in 50% layoffs at Tarrytown – an elimination of 2,000 workers, half the prior work force.

Yet the groups' efforts sustained themselves during this difficult time, and the word was spreading throughout the operation. A formal policy group, including plant manager, production manager, personnel manager, top union officials, and two QWL coordinators was established in order to provide careful planning for expansion of the program.

Union and management set up an advisory group to administer the system and to evaluate ideas stimulated by the problem-solving teams. A survey of participation interest was conducted among the remaining 600 workers in the trim department, and 95% volunteered to take part. Pairs of volunteers from management and the work force were selected and trained as trainers. A formal 27-hour off-site training program was then developed, and the 570 volunteers became participants in the program.

A second crisis developed as a speedup in production became necessary and a third when the operation returned to a second shift. Employees were shifted around due to seniority and job classification, and the QWL program was stalled again.

Early in 1977, after all necessary adjustments, the union management team committed itself to a plant-wide program involving 3,800 employees. Orientation was spread vertically and horizontally through management, supervisory ranks, and union committeemen.

Additional volunteers were selected as trainers, and a staff of 22 was thoroughly oriented to the task.

In the fall of 1977, training for the 3,800 employees was initiated. By December of the following year it was completed and the program was operating at full throttle.

There have certainly been difficult problems and stumbling blocks, but QWL is an ongoing day-to-day process at Tarrytown today and "a way of life." All parties are pleased to be a part of this process.

TABLE 17.1. Sample Outcome Data at Tarrytown.

Pre-QWL	Post-QWL

Quality Performance
    worst
	Quality Performance
	    best among 18
	    GM assembly plants

Average Daily Absenteeism
    7½%
	Average Daily Absenteeism
	    2–3%

Grievances (average annual)
    3,000
	Grievances (average annual)
	    32

Few statistics have been made in Tarrytown, but those available are quite impressive.

The Tarrytown case highlights the evolution of a significant QWL program. Born out of crisis, the program was to face one after another. Yet, as the process unfolded it developed its own momentum and substance and weathered the internal storms to emerge successfully up to the present time. In retrospect, this persistence and success under successive challenges is most probably attributable to two key factors:

• Cautious adherence to the steps outlined earlier in this chapter.
• Sufficient and consistent reinforcement.

At any rate, these factors definitely played a critical role in the long-term success of the program. Because Tarrytown represents one of the first true QWL efforts within General Motors, it would seem natural to expect it to serve as a model for all other GM programs. However, this has not been the case. There are a number of other programs which have evolved similarly, but this has been either by chance or by the free choice of the plant management and union leadership within those organizations. The major reason why Tarrytown did not become a model for all other GM programs lies in the earlier description of the behavioral process in QWL. General Motors management, along with UAW executives, hold firmly to the belief that the union and management leadership of each operating unit enters into the QWL process on a strictly voluntary basis and develops a program suited to the needs of its own organization.

Therefore, the following case of Chevrolet Gear and Axle Division, "the Gear," will reveal an altered approach to the process in a different General Motors environment – one not initiated in crisis.

Detroit Gear and Axle opened in 1934. By 1957 the operation, involving 7,000 employees, was producing a spectrum of products for Oldsmobile, Buick, Cadillac, and Chevrolet. During 1978, the team working in 2.7 million square feet produced more than 3 million axles. During 1981, major product-line changes were made to accommodate the new market demands for smaller cars.

The need for change was not completely apparent at the "Gear" during the 1960s and early 1970s. However, in the period of 1974 to 1975, "Gear" management discovered that it was no longer competitive within GM on price and quality. It recognized that change would be required in order to guarantee future survival and growth.

A clearly stated set of organizational objectives became the first step taken by management to move into the QWL process. The Gear and Axle management then proceeded to discuss its operational status with Dutch Landen's QWL group at GM headquarters. This resulted in a third-party operational diagnosis of the "Gear."

The diagnostic recommendations indicated a need to alter the traditional autocratic

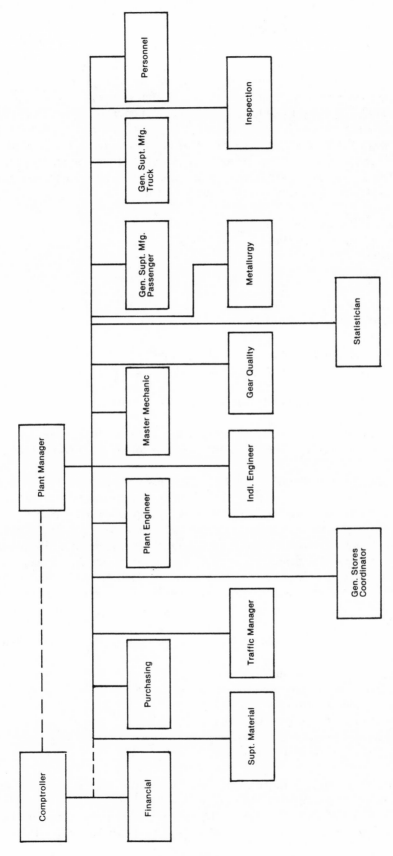

Fig. 17.1. Pre-Intervention Organizational Flow Chart.

management style. Management's time and energy were concentrated on daily operational tasks such as enforcement of standards and regulations, firefighting, etc. Issues such as productivity, employee participation, and quality were all but ignored.

Consequently, significant alteration of the organizational structure was necessary to promote vertical and horizontal communications. Figure 17.1 shows the pre-intervention organizational chart. Figure 17.2 depicts the improved communication system developed out of the QWL approach, as well as presenting a pictorial representation of the plant team concept. Figure 17.3 represents the specificity of within area responsibilities after the QWL system was implemented. Changes were made to facilitate:

- Plant-level problem solving
- Accounting information sharing
- Product teams
- Operations teams
- Plant service links
- Coordinated services
- Development of realistic budgets

QWL was treated as a major change in management's operating philosophy and style, rather than as a program. Three different approaches to change were undertaken:

- Communications to foster employee awareness of external changes as well as those within GM.
- Changes in the organizational structure to promote grassroots shop-floor participation.
- Efforts to encourage union, management, employee commitment and involvement.

Other changes were effected. Instead of sixteen people reporting directly to the plant manager, seven now reported to him. Specific functions were reorganized to improve and increase communications. Since the comptroller was not responsible to the plant manager, his cooperation had to be gained in order to facilitate broader dissemination of financial information. Once the structure was changed and new relationships refined (in 1977), management began discussions with the shop committee about costs, production, quality, and other traditionally taboo topics. Management acknowledged the inability to work toward common objectives without complete communication with employees and their understanding of all the issues. Open communication led to open policy, practice, procedures, and responsibilities across the board.

In sum, the "Gear" was able to meet the worldwide competitive challenge through:

- Improving productivity and quality levels
- Reviewing the roles and responsibilities of *all* employees
- Improving job skills and knowledge
- Reviewing and updating information systems
- Evaluating division and corporate influences
- Promoting greater union and management cooperation

The process involving the union at the "Gear" proceeded unevenly. At first, management sought only an agreement to secure union involvement.

As part of this effort, Dutch Landen and his team provided union representatives with a 2-day familiarization training session. Following the session on August 14–15, 1979, the

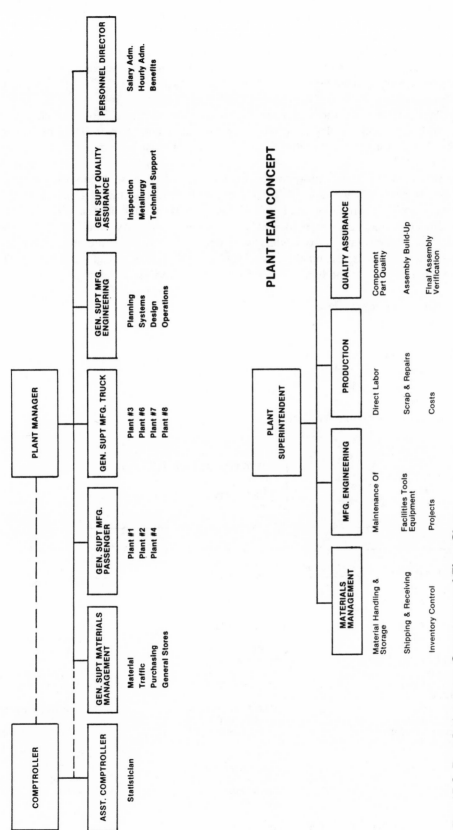

Fig. 17.2. Post-Intervention Organizational Flow Chart.

representatives agreed to commit the union to QWL. This decision led to the creation of a QWL Steering Committee of eight members, four from the union and four from management. Initial attempts failed due in part to management's attempt in 1977–79 to implement QWL by directive.

In light of that failure, the idea of employee participation circles (EPCs) was adopted in early 1980. Employee training programs were then launched. Today there are 36 circles (with 8 to 12 persons in each) at the "Gear." The number of circles is expected to double by the end of 1981.

Implementation of the program began with an EPC presentation to supervisors. Volunteer participation was sought. Supervisors contacted the hourly employees, giving them the "Gear" EPC brochure and involved them in a 10-minute discussion session. Once nonvolunteer employees observed EPCs in operation, approximately 97% of them volunteered to participate. EPC leaders were chosen by the circle members. They each received 4 to 6 hours of training in a 1-week session, with half on straight-time pay and half on over-time pay. Eight modules were included in the leadership training:

- Group-process training skills
- Teambuilding skills
- Listening skills
- Conflict resolution techniques
- Consensus-reaching techniques
- Meeting guidance skills
- Brainstorming techniques
- Problem-solving techniques

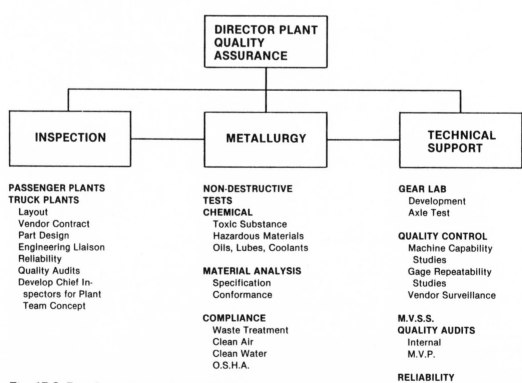

Fig. 17.3. Post-Intervention Task Breakdown.

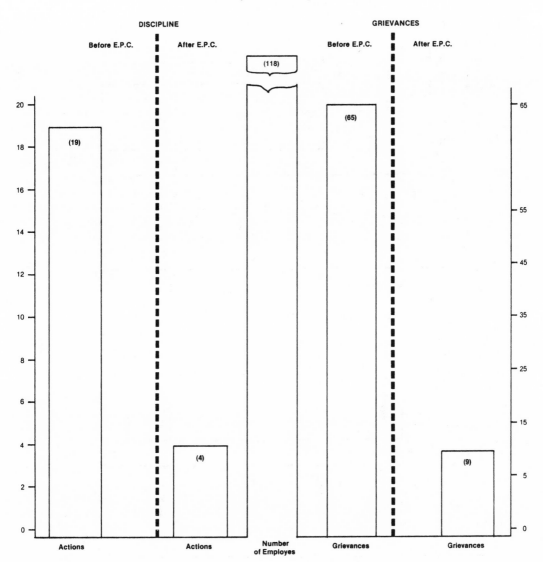

Fig. 17.4. E.P.C. Group Impact on Discipline & Grievances.

EPCs meet weekly for one-half to 1 hour on straight time, with or without a supervisor in attendance. On a weekly basis all EPC leaders meet jointly with shift supervisors to talk over problems. The supervisors' traditional role is shifting from an authoritarian to a facilitator of service for user departments. The supervisors now coordinate and nurture people, rather than giving orders.

The oldest EPCs began operating in June 1980. Some EPCs were not immediately successful; where they are working, however, results are impressive. Comparing figures for the three months ending 1980 with those for the 3 months ending January 1981 reveals dramatic changes in discipline and grievances (Figure 17.4). Similar improvement occurred in other areas (Figure 17.5).

In the case of Chevrolet Gear and Axle, a successful QWL process change was possible with a large 17,000-employee work force. Clearly, there were stumbling blocks and near

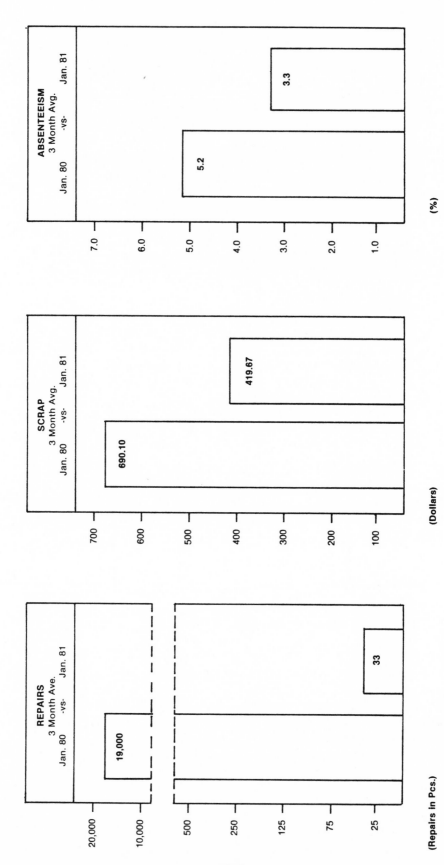

(Repairs in Pcs.)

Fig. 17.5. Group L Plt #1 Both Shifts.

failures when management coopted the program and ignored the need for voluntary participation by union and employees.

Furthermore, there were few, if any, external reinforcers employed in the process at the "Gear." It appears that virtually all reinforcement was intrinsic and related to improvements in the employee situation/job.

At any rate, these two cases illustrate one final principle applicable to both specific behavioral change and process behavioral change. This principle relates to the need for the varied application of behavior modification. The process or design of the selected behavioral approach must be tailored to the needs of the recipient, whether that recipient is an individual or an entire organization.

The successful application of QWL by GM and other organizations in a time of reduced productivity growth has led to the development of similar approaches in a wide variety of U.S. and foreign organizations within government, industry, and education.

The future of QWL does not rest on its validity in producing results for management, labor, and shareholders alike. It will actually be chiefly determined by the adequacy of design, installation, and evolution of new and future programs. The appropriate approach must be selected. The process must be followed as comprehensively as possible, and reinforcement and recommitment are essential to success. Finally, time is critical because behavioral change does not happen overnight. Results and solutions may be slow in coming (as long as 1 to 2 years), but they are long lasting.

18

The Total Performance System

Dale M. Brethower
Western Michigan University

The total performance system concept was developed to deal with difficulties encountered in organizational behavior management. The difficulties all revolve around one problem: complexity. Apparently simple problems have a way of becoming very complex when considered in an organizational context. The following incident will illustrate.

The plant manager of a job shop operation describes a recurring problem. "I've had a lot of different people in sales but they can't seem to understand an important part of their work. They've got to check with production scheduling before they bid on a job. They're always promising unrealistic delivery dates because they forget that production is already doing other jobs. They promise a delivery date and then we have to bump other jobs or run a lot of overtime. If we bump, somebody else gets mad and if we run too much overtime, we actually lose money on a job."

The salespeople could reply: "The boss just doesn't understand how we do things. We base our estimates on how long it takes to do a job. We even figure in some extra time to give production scheduling some leeway. If they can't do it on time that's not our fault. Besides, if a big customer wants a job done in a hurry we're better off doing it even if we lose a little once in a while. It's better than losing that customer's business. What the boss should do is get off our back and get production straightened out. Production is always complaining about something. If sales aren't good they complain about running below capacity and having to lay people off."

The production people could comment: "Those people in sales are a menace. They don't have a steady sales program. Instead, they go out and hustle for a while, maybe when they have some fool contest going. We run overtime and hire extra people to try to handle the demand. Then their contest is over and they go on vacation or sit around in the office telling stories. The first thing you know, we don't have enough work to do. Workers slow down to avoid lay-offs and we still have to lay-off good people who lack seniority. That produces all sorts of labor problems for us. We can't control costs – it's always overtime or slowdown. As it is we can't control costs or meet their unrealistic delivery dates. That's no way to please customers. Those turkeys in sales should know that. The boss oughta get them straightened out."

The problem is simple from the plant manager's perspective: "There are problems because sales doesn't check with scheduling! The solution is to get sales to check with scheduling before making a bid and promising delivery."

The problem is simple from sales' perspective: "The boss should recognize we are doing our job. The solution is to get production to stop *their* alibis and straighten out their operation!"

The problem is simple from production's perspective: "The boss should recognize that

350

the erratic performance of sales creates problems production can't solve. The solution is to get sales to abandon their feast or famine approach and stabilize sales!"

The differences in perspective are quite understandable in view of the differences in goals, performance evaluations, communication patterns, and specialized knowledge of the plant manager, salespeople, and production people. The interplay among simple factors makes the organizational problem *complex* even though it can appear simple from each perspective. The performance of salespeople is commonly evaluated in terms of contribution to total sales revenues generated. Salespeople communicate more frequently with customers than with production and their specialized knowledge relates to satisfying customers' real or perceived needs. A major customer can have an important and direct impact on sales revenue generated by a particular salesperson. The needs of customers can easily become more salient than those of production.

Similarly, the performance of production people is commonly evaluated in terms of meeting schedules and controlling production costs. Production people communicate with production people and others concerned with cost control. Their specialized knowledge relates to production techniques. Their interests, by training and socialization, relate directly to factors influencing production, and they are likely to view other considerations as interferences.

The plant manager should, of course, be aware of the differences between sales and production and act to balance them harmoniously. The plant manager's goals, after all, relate to the total profitability (and return on investment) for the plant. On the other hand, it's not easy to sort out the real issues from the biased arguments presented. That is especially true when we recognize that the sales versus production problem is typical of many different problems with which the manager must deal. In each instance the manager must sift through much irrelevant information to find the real issues. The real issues may be clear after the irrelevant information is swept away by an insightful analysis but until then the manager is faced with a confused clamor for attention.

I didn't know all of that twenty years ago when I first began to apply behavioral principles to organizational problems.

BEHAVIOR PRINCIPLES AS SOLUTIONS

Behavioral principles offer a very direct approach to organizational problems. The approach can be described in various ways, but aside from differences in detail, it usually goes something like this:

1 . Specify the performance desired.
2 . If it's not occurring, find out if the deficiency is due to (a) inadequate job design, tools, materials, (b) inadequate knowledge and skill, or (c) inadequate incentives (reinforcement contingencies) to sustain motivation.
3 . Correct the deficiency by changing the job, by training, or by better reinforcement contingencies.
4 . Evaluate and recycle as needed to get desired performance.
5. Once you've got it, maintain it.

Our (or at least my) initial assumption was that people in organizations knew in general what performance was desired. They might need a little help in detailed specification of performance and in job design, but the areas where behavioral principles would be of most benefit were in training and dealing with motivational problems through reinforcement contingencies. (Managers assured me there were a lot of people out there who didn't know how to do their jobs or who weren't motivated.)

Managers were often quite specific about what people should do. "Sales people should check with production scheduling before promising a delivery date." Clearly the salespeople should make realistic estimates of delivery dates. In actual practice, making such estimates for a variety of jobs, some of them "new" work, can be complex and require considerable training to learn to do well. But even then, training would not be the full solution.

Behavioral principles provide clear guidance for something else that is required: If making estimates that *consider production's problems* is to occur *such estimating must be rewarded*.

The salesperson's normal rewards come from generating sales revenues, selling well according to their standards of good sales practices, and from interaction with customers. Their rewards do not come from solving production's problems. Consequently, special rewards must be provided to encourage them to be more concerned with production problems. In some situations this would be easy to do. The plant manager or sales manager could provide occasional verbal praise for good estimating. Or a slip could be attached to each order and scheduling could make a check mark indicating whether or not the delivery estimate was attainable; the check slips could be reviewed periodically by the sales manager and commendations (or criticisms) given. The added social reinforcement contingency and management control system could solve the problem perceived by the plant manager.

Behavioral principles, properly applied, can be used to solve many training and motivational problems. Yet managers often resist using behavioral principles in the systematic fashion needed for best results. At first, the resistance to scientifically-based, practically effective principles was surprising. Why would managers resist doing something that works? If I had trouble understanding managerial behavior in that regard, it must be because I lacked important information about the managerial environment. This was the inescapable conclusion from behavioral theory, and managers assured me that it was correct. As one manager put it, "Professor, if you knew anything about what really goes on you'd know why this behavioral stuff you're telling us about is practically useless!"

Rather than abandon a life's work, it seemed appropriate to find out what the difficulties actually were. And, as stated, the problem is complexity.

THE MANAGER'S TOOL KIT

There are tools for managing complexity. Indeed, that is what management is all about. Managers bring together the tools for dealing with complex problems of organizations. *Planning, organizing,* and *directing* and related to finding the problems that need to be solved, finding or creating the tools to solve them, and bringing the tools to bear on the problems. *Control* (or administration or whatever we call it these days) is about assuring that the tools are brought to bear on the problems consistently and competently enough to achieve desired results.

Back in the mid-sixties it began to dawn on me and several colleagues at the University of Michigan that managers did not lack tools. The University's Bureau of Industrial Relations (referred to immodestly by George Odiorne, then director, as "The Thinking Manager's AMA") offered dozens of short courses to help managers acquire tools. Other universities (and the American Management Association) did the same. New tools were being invented all the time. There were hundreds of management consultants around with marvelous management tools. Managers told me, and I suppose it was true, that there were consultants out there with more tools than there were problems to solve.

The new tools my colleagues and I were offering in the mid-sixties related to very real and frequently encountered problems of training, supervision, motivation, and personnel development. Nevertheless, the tools – programmed learning, training systems design, and behavior management – were competing in the managerial market place with many other tools.

The situation hasn't changed much today. The Bureau of Industrial Relations is now called The Division of Continuing Management Education, and the director, Al Schrader, has been instrumental in adding a few more courses for the thinking manager and many more for the practicing manager. There are marketing tools, financial management tools, information handling tools, decision-making tools etc. Every self-respecting part of the organization has its special tool kit. It seemed to me in 1965, and it is even clearer in 1982, that this specialization is producing very serious organizational communication problems. The proliferation of specialized tools is converting organizations into sleek, sophisticated modern-day Towers of Babel. It's not so much that the problems faced by different parts of the organization are inherently different, as that the languages used to discuss the problems have made communication about the problems more difficult. That is nobody's fault but simply something that happens over and over in situation after situation and in organization after organization.

Each part of an organization develops better information for its own purposes. The specialized information is, by the same token, harder for other parts of the organization to understand. This is a major reason why decision makers have too much information to sift through and end up with too little information for exemplary decision making. A second major reason for having too little information is that we can get so caught up with internally generated information that we lose track of what is happening around us – outside our area and outside our organization.

The too much/too little problem is a version of the specialist/generalist problem in which specialists come to know more and more about less and less and generalists come to know less and less about more and more. It is at the heart of a number of apparently paradoxical characteristics of organizations:

1. Each organization is unique (specialist's view), yet in some ways organizations are very much alike (generalist's view).
2. No single aspect of running an organization is conceptually difficult (generalist's view), yet when examined closely most aspects of running an organization are quite complex (specialist's view).
3. The major areas of an organization can be functioning very well (from each specialist's perspective), and the organization as a whole can be running out of control and dangerously near collapse (generalist's perspective).
4. Specialists are necessary to deal with the immediate pressures of running the organization, yet whether or not the organization prospers in the long run is largely out of their control in the hands of generalists. (And in the hands of individual consumers in the marketplace.)
5. Every major aspect of the organization can be readily understood conceptually by generalists and in technical detail by specialists; nevertheless, the *interactions* among the well-understood variables can be so enormously complex that they are *not well understood by anyone.*

Each person in an organization shares the too much/too little problem. Subordinates allege that bosses have lost sight of how the work is actually done. Bosses express displeasure because subordinates know too little about the problems of the organization. In the sales versus production problem we discussed earlier, each party (boss, salesperson, and production person) would agree that the others had too little information. The plant manager could rightly argue that he had too much to keep track of to bother about such details as whether a customer occasionally pressures for a special (and costly) favor. And the salespeople could rightly argue that they had too much to keep track of without worrying about cost control problems in another department.

This problem might go on for a long time to the mutual exasperation of the individual involved and to the detriment of the organization.

The communication problem is quite real, even though pressure from customers and cost problems due to faulty scheduling are matters that are easy to talk about and understand. But if we get into more esoteric problems (e.g., "why can't Data Processing just take some Accounting data, combine it with some Marketing data and some information from Production Scheduling and Personnel to enable the strategic planning group to make an economic projection for a proposed new product?") we are involved in each area's jargon and idiosyncratic ways of compiling data. Data processing people love to talk about the complexities of taking bytes (or some such thing) out of incompatible data bases. It is possible to become bewildered by all that and hope that estimating parameters by Monte Carlo methods is really a more elegant procedure than taking a shot in the dark.

The sales versus production problem appears to be relatively easy to solve with behavioral tools. But we can't be sure that applying our behavior change tools to train and then "motivate" the salespersons to call production scheduling would be the way to go. The total system implications need to be examined.

We can't just take it for granted that the plant manager's view is correct. If we got sales to be more responsive to production and less responsive to the customer, we might "fix" the perceived problem and create a real one. If we use behavioral principles effectively we can go beyond a temporary fix that washes out later on when we stop attending to it. We can design effective control systems to maintain the changed behavior, but for all we know, this could fix (lock-in) a worse problem than the one we started with. We don't want to be in the business of using behavioral principles to solve the wrong problems.

The fear that managers will use behavioral tools to solve the wrong problems is a realistic one and a good reason for being cautious about embracing the systematic use of behavioral principles or any other powerful tools. Managers have many problems to deal with and many new tools to master. Managers need assistance in integrating new tools into the total context of their responsibilities. That is probably one reason behaviorists often try to sell humane philosophy along with behavioral techniques, urging a principled use of behavioral principles.

To use behavioral principles wisely we need to do something more than specify the desired performance. We need a way of determining why the performance is desirable from the perspective of the total performance system and from the perspective of the performer. That is a tall order. Guidance is needed in selecting appropriate tools for filling it and for finding appropriate uses for powerful tools.

THE TOTAL PERFORMANCE SYSTEM – ORGANIZING THE MANAGER'S TOOL KIT

Fundamental to managing complexity in organizations is coordinating key resources in response to changing needs and demands. That is why decision makers need both information and courage. Decision makers need information about trends and the courage to take action based on the best information they have, even though it will often be incomplete.

It seemed in the 1960s and is clear in the 1980s that each manager needs a way of organizing the complexity that comprises her or his area of responsibility. Each manager needs a way to identify the most important problems to work on. Each manager needs a way of telling whether the information available for decision making is too much of the wrong kind, too little of the right kind, or just enough to go on. Each manager needs a way of relating personal responsibility to the boss's priorities and to organization priorities. Each manager needs a way of understanding and coordinating the activities of subordinate managers. And each manager's way of organizing that complexity needs to be compatible with each other manager's way of organizing the complexity. A way of understanding the complexity of each organization and each person's job within an organization was needed. The systems approach, as fashionable then as now, provided guidance. As Silvern put it "without doubt, the 'systems approach' is a *good* thing and those who ignore it are in *bad* trouble [Silvern, 1968]."

There were some basic concepts of systems that appeared relevant.

1. Feedback (information about performance used to guide performance). Clearly managers are in the business of influencing organization, personal, and subordinate performance. Guiding those performances based upon solid information was surely the way to go.
2. Guided systems (systems guided through uncertainty by feedback relevant to progress toward goals). Once goals are decided upon it is the job of management to establish the administrative controls and performance reviews necessary to monitor progress and help maneuver along the uncertain path to successful achievement.
3. Environment (the parts of larger systems that affect what a particular system does). Clearly managers need to be aware of outside influences that are likely to affect performance within their areas of responsibility.
4. Adaptive systems (systems which modify goals, strategies, or tactics in response to both internal and environmental trends). This is a major job of top management, one that nearly all MBA's are trained for and few get to do.

We put these concepts (plus the notion that organizations have inputs and outputs) together in Figure 18.1. We grandly call it "The General Systems Diagram" or the "Total Performance System" diagram (Brethower, 1972). In lighter moments we call it "The Big Picture."

It's a General Systems Diagram because it calls attention to six of the seven key components of a very wide variety of adaptive systems. These components are inputs, a processing system, processing system feedback, outputs, a receiving system, and receiving system feedback.

Figure 18.1 lists the major inputs, outputs, etc., for the job shop operation discussed above in connection with the sales versus production problem.

The seventh component of an adaptive system is the system goal. For example, the goal of the job shop might be to produce goods ordered by customers, operating so that we achieve a substantial return on our investment and so we foster goodwill on the part of our customers, our employees, and the community.

Applications of The Total Performance System Diagram

The diagram is called the Big Picture because of its usefulness in helping people move from a specialist or nose-to-the-grindstone perspective to a broader perspective. For example, a

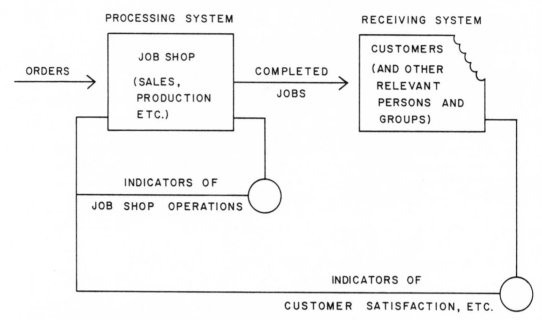

Fig. 18.1. The Total Performance System/General Systems Diagram.
Figure produced by Science Graphics, Kalamazoo, Michigan.

large multidivisional and technologically-oriented company used it as part of a project directed at getting better data on customer satisfaction. The company had excellent internal measurements. Many managers couldn't see anything to be gained by surveying customers unless it were for some nebulous PR purpose. "Our customers don't know anything about the technology involved – how could they tell us anything useful about how to run our business?" managers asked. The diagram was helpful in making managers see that whether the customers knew anything about the technology or not, their dissatisfaction meant trouble for the company. The diagram was also useful in showing managers that data from customers could be a useful form of feedback because: (a) it was a direct measure of an organizational goal of increasing customer satisfaction, and (b) the data could help validate, fine tune, and even replace some of the internal measurements.

Another example came from a management development course, Management of Behavior Change, several colleagues and I started in 1964. The purpose of the course was to equip managers with some of the basic knowledge and skill they needed to deal with human performance in their organizations.

The 3-day course is shown as a guided system (because that's the way it began) in Figure 18.2. The course went reasonable well. We were sure managers were learning, and the evaluations indicated they liked the course. We were getting repeat business and filling the course regularly. We even had a little "receiving system feedback." Graduates would sometimes call or write to tell us how well their projects went. We felt both successful and virtuous. We had set our objectives, evaluated, and found ourselves to be successfully obtaining objectives.

Carried away with our own rhetoric about evaluating management courses on the basis of on-the-job results, we began calling some of the graduates we hadn't heard from. We knew that the organizations sending managers to the course comprised the Receiving System for graduates. We wanted more receiving system feedback. We got it. A typical

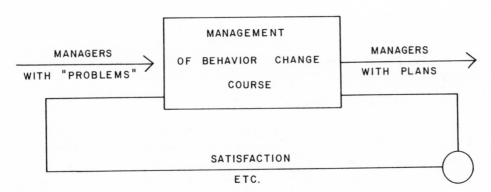

Fig. 18.2.
Figure produced by Science Graphics, Kalamazoo, Michigan.

manager said something like this: "I learned a lot from other participants and, of course, from the staff. I really liked that positive reinforcement stuff. Also, my project worked out well." But when we queried further to get specific examples of how they used positive reinforcement, the examples were few in number. Organizationally important examples were rare. The projects that had been implemented hadn't been evaluated very carefully.

We went back to the drawing board and redesigned the course. We put more advance work in to help people select good projects and to bring relevant data with them to Ann Arbor. We took out some of my favorite stories and laboratory studies and put in more time for them to work with us on problem areas in their projects. We identified check points in their projects and arranged for follow-up letters and phone calls for progress reports and consultations. Whenever possible, we got them to involve their boss in the project. (Sometimes managing their boss *was* the project!)

When we had done all that the course began to operate as an adaptive system. Instead of the *little picture* of our course, we had the *big picture* of our course in relation to their world. As a result, the quality of the course improved considerably. The internal measurements improved, and student satisfaction increased. Staff members observed definite improvements in the quality of the projects planned during the sessions. The problems became more important in terms of organizational needs, the plans for implementation became more realistic, and the use of behavior principles in the projects became more sophisticated.

The external measurements also improved. A higher percentage of the projects were successfully implemented; more managers developed and implemented additional projects after returning to their organizations: more of the projects demonstrated clearly beneficial impacts on the organizations in which they were done. In the late 1960s and early 1970s, organizational behavior management began to receive recognition in business journals, magazines, and texts. Many of the projects mentioned in those early stories had their start in or were done by graduates of the Management of Behavior Change course. We, as the course designers, would like to take full credit for that. We deserve little for our inherent cleverness but we deserve credit because we were just barely clever enough to nudge aside our expert's perspective, see the big picture, and begin to help talented managers do things that needed to be done. And managers in turn used the diagram to break out of their expert's perspective and into a results-oriented organization perspective.

The experience with the Management of Behavior Change course also led to the recognition that the diagram was a total performance system diagram. The managers brought us some really difficult human problems. Naturally, I wanted to teach them practically everything I'd learned in taking a hundred semester hours or so of graduate level psychology courses. But these managers already knew so much that they could hardly sit still when I tried to teach them anything at all, let along when I tried to lay all that on them. The diagram helped us find what information was enough.

Keeping Complexity Simple

How much information do we need in order to solve a particular human performance problem? The answer to that question is extremely important if we are to manage organizational complexity. We know that an organization is made up of enormously complex human beings. It is intuitively obvious, therefore, that we would need an enormous amount of information if we were to truly understand individuals. Freud, after all, sometimes kept clients in analysis for years before he began to understand them. We are faced with the too much/too little dilemma frequently in dealing with human performances. We need a way of getting *just enough* information.

How much information do we need? The intuitive answer is "A lot!" A more useful answer, however, is "About seven items!" Both answers are correct. We need a lot of information and we need just the right information. We need it organized into a coherent picture containing about seven items.

We can do that with seven parts of the total performance system diagram. It has seven parts because of a variety of research studies reviewed by G. A. Miller (1956) in a paper titled, "The magic number seven plus or minus two." Seven ($\pm$ 2) is the number of separate items we can readily remember or deal with at one time. Seven digit telephone numbers are easy to remember (long enough to dial), whereas social security numbers (seven + 2 or nine digits) are quite a bit harder. And dialing eleven digits to call long distance is even harder. When we try to dial 1, then the area code, and then the number we find it easier if we don't really think about the 1 at all, treating it as part of picking up the phone to call long distance. We can then remember the three digit area code as one item, the three digit exchange code as another item, and the four digit individual line code as the third item. In other words 5553836143 is *much* harder to remember than 555-383-6143.

The seven (plus or minus two) limitation holds for words, grocery lists, product lists, etc. If we have to deal with or memorize longer lists we group them into categories and subcategories. Memory experts, some data-processing people, and people who write successful reports to top management are very aware of the "magic number" limitation. "Keep it so simple that even top management can understand it" is good advice to report writers. "Get the few main ideas out front and put the supporting details in appropriately labeled appendices!"

This latter advice shows us how "a lot" of information can be conveyed while remaining within the bounds of "about seven items." We use the general systems/big picture/total performance system diagram. A company or a person's job is first described by seven items: inputs, outputs, processes, receiving system, receiving system feedback, process feedback, and goals. The big picture overview enables us to "get our head around the complexity" so that we can then pursue the details. (Top management knows that they need to read the appendices, and they also demand that people should do good staff work by organizing the report around a few salient items.)

Figure 18.1 provided a total performance system overview of one organization. "A lot" of information is presented in a coherent picture of "about seven items." Figure 18.3 shows the sales and production areas as Total Performance Systems.

The sales versus production problem described in terms of the diagram is straightforward. Both sales and production are being guided by their own standards indicated by the

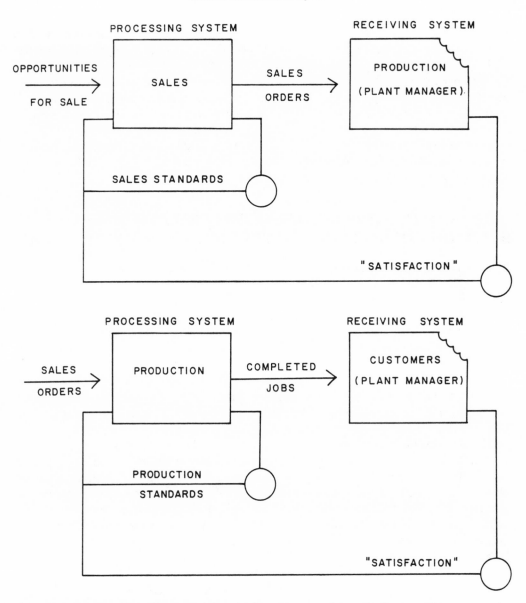

Fig. 18.3. Shows the Sales and Production Areas as Total Performance Systems.
Figure produced by Science Graphics, Kalamazoo, Michigan.

internal feedback loops. The problem is that those standards are not adequately balanced by external feedback loops.

Sales is influenced by immediate customer feedback, i.e., "I'll give you the order only if you promise me an early delivery date."

A little thought about the diagram will reveal that: (a) customer dissatisfaction will reach sales much later ("That order wasn't delivered when you promised!"); (b) the customer dissatisfaction information will come at a time when sales can't take any "corrective" action (other than blaming production); and (c) the customer satisfaction information (resulting from early delivery promises) reaches sales but not production or the plant manager.

Thus, the current system is ideally suited for maintaining the problematic behavior of sales (promising early delivery) *and* for maintaining the conflict between sales and production!

The performance problem is a direct result of the defective feedback. Both practical experience and behavioral principles indicate that such solutions as training, exhortations to be more considerate of one another's problems, and firing sales personnel will result in changes which are at best temporary. It's easy to see why. The feedback incentive management control systems would have to be changed if desired performance is to be maintained. The solution is just that simple; however, implementing the solution is complex enough that we need some supporting technology to manage the details.

JOB MODELS – LINKING THE COMPLEXITY OF JOBS TO THE SIMPLICITY OF THE TOTAL PERFORMANCE SYSTEM DIAGRAM

Any management job is made up of a formidable array of activities. The activities are rarely written down anywhere. Everyone knows (and it is probably true) that workers and their bosses often have different perceptions of what the activities are and of which activities should be given priority. It just wouldn't do to try to resolve the differences in perceptions by specifying the activities in a standard job description. Such job descriptions lead to difficulties even for repetitive hourly rated jobs. They clearly are inappropriate for managerial positions.

Instead of trying to deal with all the activities, the total performance system approach focuses on the organizationally important outputs of the manager. Job models are developed that focus on outputs or accomplishments rather than activities. Performance is valuable because it accomplishes things, not because it makes us look busy. The job model (as it was developed by Tom Gilbert, Geary Rummler, Karen Brethower, and others) is essentially an "unwrapping" of the total performance system diagram to put it in tabular form holding more detail. Two examples are shown in Table 18.1. The parts of the job models are labeled to show their relationship to the total performance system diagram. Inputs aren't shown on the form to conserve space and because they are somewhat redundant in this instance. The same is true for the receiving system; however to make it clear where the receiving system feedback/requirements come we've indicated the sources in parentheses.

Table 18.1 shows one way of using job models to resolve the sales versus production problem. The upper part shows the relevant part of the salesperson's job model, and the lower part shows part of the production person's job model. Areas above the dashed lines show the major accomplishments of each person. The areas below the dashed lines show a way of linking the job models through a properly implemented management policy. The policy had been on the books but never fully implemented by incorporating it into the jobs and the way in which the sales and the production performances are measured and evaluated.

Inspection of this table will reveal that a participative form of management by objectives is incorporated into the job models. Production and sales goals are set jointly, and "y% growth, z% plant capacity used" appear on both job models. (They would, of course, also appear on the plant manager's job model.) Each person also has a related individual goal or standard – "x% special orders" and "special order costs x% greater than regular order costs." Furthermore, the individual standards for "prospects identified," etc., and "deviation from schedule" would be set with respect to the cooperatively set growth goals.

TABLE 18.1. Partial Job Models – Sales Person and Production Person.

(Outputs) Accomplishments	(Processes) Activities	(Receiving System Feedback) Requirements	(Processing System Feedback) Standards or Goals
Orders Written	Seek opportunities Contact prospects Obtain needed information Match benefits to needs Ask for orders	Timeliness (Customer) Competitive price (Customer) Customer satisfied (Customer/Plant Mgr.) Revenue generated (Plant Manager)	X prospects identified and contacted per week y% of contacts result in orders Z dollars generated per quarter, etc.
Internal Policy Followed	Use schedule projections from production Establish short and long-term sales goals in concert with production	Orders requiring scheduling changes minimized (Production) Sales and production goals provide planned growth (Plant Manager)	X% Special orders y% Growth Z% Plant capacity used
Jobs Completed (Orders Filled)	Schedule Production Manage Production	Timeliness (Customer) Customer satisfied (Customer/Plant Mgr.) Profit margins maintained (Plant Manager)	X% Deviation from schedule y Ratio of direct to indirect labor costs Z% Down time, etc.
Internal Policy Followed	Provide schedule projections to sales Establish short and long-term production goals in concert with sales	Schedule projections updated weekly (Sales) Production and sales goals provide planned growth (Plant Manager)	100% projections on time Special order costs no more than X% regular order costs. y% Growth Z% Plant capacity used

The standards are measured quantitatively and relate closely to the requirements. The requirements are set by organizational and market considerations: they provide a reality base for the standards. Consequently, there is no doubt of the importance of the standards, a feature that makes Job Models an important tool for assuring equity and fairness in all aspects of managing and coordinating the work of managers and professionals.

Notice also that the activities are not specified in great detail as they often are in a job description. Instead, the activities are defined, in effect, as "Whatever is necessary in order to achieve the results!" The results are precisely specified by the accomplishments, requirements, and standards or goals. People are paid to achieve results, not to look busy by engaging in a lot of activities.

It should be obvious that the development of job models requires significant involvement of managers as they work to specify what each is to accomplish. That is a critical part of *planning and organizing*. The flexibility allowed for in the listing of activities allows for a great deal of self-*direction*. Self-direction is also aided by knowing the requirements and participating in setting the standards. The standards or goals provide the necessary management *controls*.

The accomplishments and standards together specify the *results* each person is to attain. The job model is, therefore, a potentially very valuable tool throughout an organization. An hourly worker ordinarily doesn't participate very much in developing the model (except through union activities and playing tricks on the industrial engineers), while high level managers often build their jobs. The job models can show *the organizationally significant aspects of jobs at any level* from CEO on down.

That is why they are so useful to persons who have other powerful tools for managing behavior. The job model specifies in quantitative and qualitative terms the critical performances to be managed. Once critical performances are identified, behavioral tools can be employed to bring them about. We need not worry so much about going off in the wrong direction. The job model identifies organizationally significant performances. And because the performances are organizationally significant, much of the reinforcement necessary to sustain performance is "intrinsic" to the job. Information about how well standards are being met can be provided and can often function as feedback. Special reinforcement contingencies can be built in if needed, but it is unlikely that they will be needed very often. This is especially true if a "team" atmosphere is built up so that there is peer support and social reinforcement for good performance.

Job models are a tool for specifying organizationally significant performances. The partial job models presented above show how they can be used to solve problems related to intra-organizational cooperation. But the partial models don't show all of the complexity of a managerial/professional job. We turn now to that task.

The Job Model as a Tool for Organizing Complex Jobs

Table 18.2 shows a job model for a manager of training and development. (The job model is a generic job model we use in a graduate level training and development course at Western Michigan University.)

A common reaction to the model by "real" training and development managers is: "That's a very interesting model. Of course, it doesn't describe my job very well. That's not a criticism, though, because my job can't really be described. . . ."

The reaction is a very normal human reaction of a specialist to any attempt to put down on paper the overwhelming complexity that is a job. The specialist is quite right to react this way. The job model leaves out a lot that *is* critical to the specialist; it leaves out a lot that the

TABLE 18.2. Job Model for a Manager of Training and Development

Accomplishments	Activities	Requirements	Standards
1.0 Performance Need and Capability Reports (Needs Assessment/Organizational Analysis)	1.1 Analyze current performance. Project future performance demands. Identify current and future performance capabilities and deficiencies. Establish short-term and long-term performance priorities. Prepare systematic communications of the results.	1.2 Data base available for identifying critical performance needs relevant to current operation and long-range planning e.g., numbers and categories of personnel/skills needed in the future, current and projected performance capabilities and deficiencies, and approximate costs of overcoming the deficiencies.	1.3 Data base organized to provide ready answers to 90% of the relevant management planning and strategy questions. Data available to establish realistic human resource development priorities. Special reports issued on a timely basis and comprehensible to a wide range of potential readers.
2.0 Training and development activities (e.g., courses, development plans, follow-up support) developed and implemented. (Program design and operation)	2.1 Assure that training and development programs and activities are designed based upon actual needs and capabilities. Assure that programs and activities are implemented for (a) key individuals and (b) the total organization. Assure that activities are scheduled to coordinate individual and organizational development. Assure that activities are designed and operated to facilitate evaluation.	2.2 Development plans, courses, and other activities designed in accordance with current and validated state-of-the-art information as well as basic principles of human learning and organizational psychology. Activities appear adequate to meet current and projected needs for human resources. Few major performance problems due to lack of adequate training and development.	2.3 Data base used in justification of all major training and development programs and at least 75% of the component activities e.g., particular courses. Personal/career development plans implemented for all persons employed three months or more. Personal/career development plans coordinated with training courses, performance reviews, etc., to form an integrated system.
3.0 Documented Performance Improvements (Evaluation)	3.1 Analyze existing data systems to identify performance measures useful for evaluation of performance. Modify existing data systems to yield more useable data. Devise new data systems. Devise temporary data collection procedures. Collect, compile, and report data to relevant persons and parts of the organization.	3.2 Programs must demonstrate that they are accepted by participants and produce beneficial results. Evaluation data relate clearly to organizational goals, time lines, and budget categories. Data demonstrate general and specific compliance with legal, ethical, and social constraints.	3.3 Evaluation data presented in the context of the performance Need and Capability Reports. All major programs and 50% of the component activities evaluated by data relevant to (a) participant satisfaction (b) acquisition of desired knowledge, attitudes, and skills, (c) on-the-job applications, and (d) organizational impact of the applications.

TABLE 18.2. Job Model for a Manager of Training and Development (Continued)

Accomplishments	Activities	Requirements	Standards
4.0 Human Performance systems improved (Systems development/performance maintenance)	4.1 Analyze incentive systems, feedback systems, appraisal systems, quality control systems, management control systems, etc., to determine their effectiveness in supporting desired organizational and individual performances. Assure that deficient systems are modified and new systems are devised as needed to achieve human resource management results.	4.2 All new performance systems designed in accordance with current and validated state-of-the-art information as well as basic principles of human learning and motivation and organizational psychology. Existing performance systems regularly reviewed and improved on a systematic basis.	4.3 Performance system reviews and modifications done prior to onset of related training and development activities. Performance maintenance systems established or discovered for all major programs and for at least 75% of the activities. Performance systems designed to yield most of the data necessary for ongoing needs assessment, evaluation, and performance maintenance.
5.0 Cooperation Achieved (Organizational Development/Internal Politics)	5.1 Identify key areas and persons whose cooperation is needed to achieve training and development goals. Identify short-term conflicts and potential, long-term conflicts that are barriers to achievement. Identify common interests. Develop strategies and tactics to overcome barriers and achieve common interests.	5.2 Strategies and tactics acceptable within the current and developing organizational culture. General balancing of organizational and individual interests rather than subsystem maximizing. Infrequent use of other-blaming to excuse deficiencies. Few major casualties of programs or persons.	5.3 An increasing percentage of major decisions made based upon data relevant to overall and balanced organizational needs. Few unexpected problems. Achievement of cooperation an explicit component of assessment, design, operation, and evaluation of training and development activities.

TABLE 18.2. Job Model for a Manager of Training and Development (Continued)

Accomplishments	Activities	Requirements	Standards
6.0 Miscellaneous Products Produced (Modeling/Organizational Development)	6.1 Identify opportunities to provide "permanent products" exemplifying good human resource management. Produce and display the products by calling attention to the value, uses, features, and benefits of the products.	6.2 Products are consistent with current and developing organizational practices. Products provide support and guidance for activities relevant to (a) application of new learning (b) performance maintenance, and (c) human resource development and management.	6.3 Approximately 90% of all permanent products are designed both to help achieve specific objectives and to provide useful models for other parts of the organization (i.e. they should be specific examples of generic products). All participants in training and development programs develop usable products.
7.0 Training and Development Function Managed (Management/Administration)	7.1 Establish specific human resource development goals and objectives for the function as a whole and for all parts of it. Establish general strategies for obtaining and using the resources needed. Implement activities so that costs can be allocated and results/benefits measured.	7.2 Training and development goals must be compatible with organizational goals. Activities must be carried out within budgetary parameters and consistent with good management practice. Training and development activities and benefits must be perceived as worth the cost.	7.3 Each training and development program is specifically directed toward identified organizational goals. All training and development programs that are continued contribute to on-the-job performance improvement likely to have organization benefits greater than their costs. The total training and development budget expenditures obtain an economic return competitive with other uses of organizational capital.

365

specialist knows and *must know* in order to perform in accordance with the model. That's good.

The purpose of the job model is to clarify the inter-relationship between performer and organization rather than to be a recipe for performance. It shows the outputs of the performance, indicates the organizational importance of the outputs, and helps in developing reasonable measurements to guide the performer in doing a job so that the work benefits performer and organization alike. That's one meaning of "total" in total performance system.

Another reaction of training and development managers is: "We don't do things that way in my organization. It wouldn't be fair to evaluate me or hold me accountable for changes in on-the-job performance after people complete one of my training courses."

They are partly right about that, too. Organizationally significant accomplishments of any manager require cooperation of others. If people aren't using what they learn in training it shows that training dollars were wasted, but it doesn't show whose fault it is. The thing to do is not to assign blame, but to keep the buck from being passed from the trainer to the trainee or to the trainee's boss. Every trainer worthy of the name has had trainees say, "I wish my boss would take this course. He won't let us do it the way (you say) it ought to be done!" That should be a problem to be solved with the boss rather than an excuse for ducking responsibility. The job model very clearly calls attention to the need for keeping such problems from falling between the cracks in the organizational chart. Doing a job model often causes rethinking and renegotiating the precise boundaries of responsibility. That is a strength of the job model, not a weakness.

Just where the boundary should be drawn must be shown by the job model and will vary according to circumstance. In one organization the trainer will be responsible for assessment of training needs. (If so, and the boss *is* the one who should have taken the course, the assessment of training needs is within the trainer's responsibility.) In another organization the trainer might be responsible only for assuring that training material is well presented. (If so, someone else should be responsible for assuring that the right material is presented to the right people so that they can use the training experience to benefit the organization.)

This feature of the total performance system approach to job models is important in any area of an organization. The interlocking job models in Table 18.1 show an example of how organizationally beneficial cooperation between two areas can be built in. In many organizations the limits to organizationally beneficial cooperation are set too narrowly by the constraints of internal politics and fed by inappropriate performance appraisals and incentive systems. The total performance system diagram is a helpful tool in reducing the deleterious impact of the resulting individually-beneficial but organizationally harmful shenanigans.

It should be obvious by now that behavioral principles are most effective in organizations when their use is guided by adequate data. The total performance system diagram emphasizes data by calling attention to the two feedback loops. The internal loop corresponds to the standards or goals part of the job model and the external loop corresponds to the requirements part. As in other areas of management, good information is vital.

RELATIONSHIP OF THE TOTAL PERFORMANCE SYSTEM TO MANAGEMENT INFORMATION SYSTEMS

Management information systems are designed to put the information managers need to make decisions at their fingertips. The systems often do that well, but there are two difficulties. First, they tend to err on the side of too much rather than too little. Second, it is very difficult to aggregate the data in a way that enables managers to break out the specific figures needed for specific decisions. Consequently, managers too often find it impossible to get the data from their fingertips into their decision-making processes.

A colleague's doctoral dissertation (Curow, 1975) showed that management information systems can be tailored effectively to facilitate special problem-solving efforts.

Curow worked in a large manufacturing company on a project designed to impact scrap costs. Curow used the total performance system concept to define the feedback needs of several different supervisors and quality assurance personnel. Improved feedback systems were designed. Curow was able to demonstrate to her doctoral committee that the total performance system concept could be used to convert general information systems into functional feedback systems. She also demonstrated to the company that doing so enabled people to control their work much more effectively saving substantial sums in scrap costs.

Returning to the sales versus production scheduling anecdote, we can see how management information systems can be designed to provide the data needed. As sales writes an order they would indicate whether it is a regular order (within normal scheduling parameters) or a "customer service" order (designed to maintain the account). Production costs and profit margins would be maintained separately for the two types of orders. Accounting data would have to be aggregated differently than usual. Some accounting departments might argue that it would be impossible or foolhardy, but the changes made would provide more accurate and useable accounting. The extra costs of the special orders would be separated out so as to not affect data needed to determine how well the production area was functioning, and the overall profitability of the special order accounts could be assessed. Dynamic pars or goals called for in the job models could be set in accordance with changes in cash flow demands, market conditions, and other variables so that the plant manager, salespeople, and production people would all know what performance would be beneficial to the organization as a whole. Sales and production could then be evaluated in terms of their contribution to current management goals rather than how "expertly" they served customers or controlled production costs.

The Total Performance System and Complexity

As stated at the outset, the problem is complexity. Complexity increases as an organization increases efficiency or productivity by incorporating advanced technology. Complexity increases as markets become more segmented. Complexity increases as market conditions become more fluid, as society expects and demands more from an organization, and as employees expect and demand more from their employer. It increases with demands and regulations for employee safety, internal security, equal employment opportunity, product safety, environmental protection, decreased energy consumption, increased productivity, and increased responsiveness to local and national social problems. Complexity also increases as an organization grows, expands, and progresses to meet the increased and conflicting demands.

The total performance system diagram (and the associated technology) helps managers integrate the conflicting demands into one coherent picture. But it is no panacea. Even when the picture is put together, there is difficulty: in spite of all the knowledge we have about any given real time problem we are very likely to lack important data. Furthermore, any important decision we make will have unforeseen consequences. We can only see dimly into the future.

We have gaps in our knowledge: some of the factors we must consider are not comensurate with other factors we must also consider, and we have neither the capability nor the mechanism for integrating all of the data we have. Such are our limitations, the limitations of our knowledge, and the limitations of our methods.

It is, therefore, not surprising that organizational behavior management techniques appear simplistic to some. They are. But only if used simplistically without considering the complexity of the context in which they are used. They are *simplistic* when used as a cure-all but *simple*, elegant, and powerful when used properly in a context of realistically assessed complexity.

It is not a criticism but a fact that persons charged with making major decisions often literally don't know what they are doing. It's inherent in the complexity of the process. The same can be said of decision making on a smaller scale. If we waited until we found out what we were doing before we did anything we would wait forever and not do anything at all.

The decision maker must sift through too much information in order to find too little information to make a rational decision. Yet (and this is the other horn of the dilemma) not making the decision would often be irrational also. There is, I believe, no real way out of this dilemma. The best one can do is attempt to slip between the horns from time to time without being gored!

Decision makers can be aided by methodology and knowledge, but such aids must be supplemented by raw courage. The problem is complexity, and there is no solution. Nor is there need to despair. The Total Performance System diagram provides a general vehicle for coordinating use of our tool kits, for coordinating the knowledge and collective energies of every person in an organization. The total performance system really is total in five very important ways. I'm sensitive to that because a reviewer of my 1972 book criticized the TPS for not being "total". He thought it would have to encompass motivational theories, such as Maslow and Herzberg, to be a *total* performance system. He had a point. I think the TPS concept is total enough to more or less engulf rather than merely encompass such motivational theories but I certainly hadn't shown that, nor will I here. My purpose here is to show totality with respect to important matters of organizational performance rather than motivational theory.

First, the total performance system concept is total in showing the critical features of a job that need to be known by performer and boss. The goals, feedbacks, and measures show the dynamics of the job so that performer and boss alike know what is being accomplished. Second, it is total in providing a common format or perspective for modeling all the complex and diverse jobs in an organization. Third, it is capable of clarifying the interlocking nature of jobs, defining boundaries of responsibility, and relating to the design of management information systems adequate for real time dynamic coordination of managerial accomplishments. Fourth, it can serve as a common unit of analysis and a building block for integrating organizational structure with organizational function. The total performance system diagram as a way of depicting adaptive systems can be a useful description of very large organizations such as AT&T or very small organizations such as the local hardware store. Perhaps as importantly, it can describe each division, each department, and each job of a large company in a common and comprehensible format. Not only can the same six or seven item format describe each part of a larger organization, but it can also help show explicity how the parts are interlocked. Fifth, those explicit descriptions are directly useful by each manager (and each managee) in doing a personally rewarding and organizationally beneficial job.

REFERENCES

Brethower, D. M. *Behavioral analysis in business and industry: A total performance system.* Kalamazoo, MI: Behaviordelia, 1972.

Curow, J. M. *Modifying management control systems to function as feedback systems.* Unpublished doctoral dissertation, University of Michigan, 1975.

Miller, G. A. The magical number seven plus or minus two: some limits on our capacity for processing information. *Psychological Review*, 1956, **63,** 81-97.

Silvern, L. C. *Systems analysis and synthesis applied to occupational instruction in secondary schools.* Education Training and Consultant, Los Angeles, 1968.

19

Multi-Branch, Multi-Systems Programs In Banking: An Organization-wide Intervention

William B. Abernathy
Edward J. Feeney Associates

Elaine M. Duffy and Richard M. O'Brien
Hofstra University

In approaching the problem of low rates of performance within any organization, one can focus on the behavior of individuals within the system or use a reductionist model to focus on the behavior of particular individuals only after examining the organization as a whole. The former approach is referred to as "behavior analysis" while the latter is termed "systems analysis." Although the systems analyst is concerned with individual behavior as a derivative of organizational contingency management, the interdependency of subsystems within the organization is the primary focus, since the "parts" are interdependent in their effect on the potential functioning of the "whole." In essence, however, the systems analyst's approach and the behavior analyst's approach are merely different paths toward common goals.

The task of the systems analyst is to design a behavioral system that will increase productivity and maintain the behavior of employees. The goal of such interventions is to develop satisfactory outputs for the organization and the recipients of its services. The employees comprising the subsystems of the organization, in effect, serve as mediators between the administrative officials, the managers, and the recipients of the organization's output. For this reason, it is essential to observe and consequate that mediating behavior (Malott, 1974). The global system of general contingencies is such that employees are held accountable to managers for their performance by being rewarded or not rewarded; managers and supervisors are subsequently reinforced for the employees' increased rate of performance; and, finally, the organization is reinforced by consumer satisfaction and improved profits. Although each department of an organization is specialized with its own purposes and contributions, the organization as a whole will best prosper when reinforcing the performance of interdependent subsystems as a means of increasing productivity. Brethower in Chapter 18 summarized this view when he stated that "to use behavioral principles wisely we need to do something more than specify the performance desired. We need a way of determining why the performance is desirable from the perspective of the total performance system *and* from the perspective of the performer."

The ideal systems analysis involves all of the subsystems of an organization. The key intervention is to improve the interaction responses of these subsystems. The current project is one of the first total systems programs to be reported in a large organization. It represents an attempt to improve organization wide functioning through the Behavioral Engineering

Systems Training (B.E.S.T.) program developed by Edward J. Feeney Associates. The organization that is attempting this progressive project is the Virginia National Bank of Norfolk, Virginia. However, before presenting this total systems program, it is necessary to review an earlier success with similar banking accomplishments.

The banking intervention which provided the ground work for much of the systems project at the Virginia National Bank was not a systems analysis at all. Rather, it was a behavior analysis program with proofing operators at the Union National Bank of Little Rock, Arkansas. This project was begun in 1978. It will be reported in detail since it lays a foundation for the later organization-wide program in Virginia, as well as because the results of the behavioral program are impressive in their own right.

The Union National Bank of Little Rock, Arkansas, is comprised of 14 branches with 350 employees, and assets of approximately 300 million dollars. The goal of this project was to improve the productivity of the bank's proving staff of eleven full-time and five part-time employees. The primary responsibility of these proof operators is to encode and proof checks and deposit slips originally received by bank tellers so that they can be fed into the computer. These are the employees who translate the amount that the draft is written for and keypunch that figure on the bottom of the check.

In order to obtain baseline data, clocks were installed in the keypunch machines utilized by the proof operators to measure the rate items were encoded per machine hour on a daily basis. It was decided that this type of measurement would be more accurate than a measurement based on rate per hours worked, since a variety of other appropriate work tasks could pull down the latter measure. The baseline mean rate was 1,064 checks and deposit slips encoded for each hour that the machine was on over a 5-week period.

Proof operators were subsequently placed on a feedback system, in which the employees themselves recorded their daily rate of performance. This feedback system enabled the proof operators to see improvement in their own performance rates, which served as continuous reinforcement for gains made. As research has shown, social reinforcement and feedback can be sufficiently rewarding to maintain high rates of employee performance (Andrasik, Heimberg, & McNamara, in press), although as will be demonstrated in the Virginia Bank Project, extrinsic reinforcers can serve to further increase high performance rates.

Following the baseline period, a new standard was set at 1300 items per machine hour. This standard was exceeded by the proof operators within the first week that the feedback system was in effect. Within an 8-month period, the proof operators were performing at the rate of 2,200 items per machine hour. This performance increment is depicted in Figure 19.1.

In order to strengthen this system and continue to reinforce high performance rates, a cash incentive system was implemented in which proof operators received one point for exceeding an hourly limit of 1,700 items, two points for exceeding a limit of 2,100 items, and three points for exceeding a limit of 2,500 items. A single point was worth $.75.

Each day each operator's total item count was divided by the hours the proof machine was operated. This daily rate was compared to the hourly standards, and points were assigned for the day's rate. The point value was then multiplied by the number of hours at the proof machine and rounded to the nearest whole number. Thus, these employees were operating under a shifting fixed ratio schedule of reinforcement in which higher levels of performance increased the point to response ratio so that more rewards could be earned. However, to improve the quality of performance, a response cost measure was also included in which proof operators were penalized for avoidable errors. Every day each operator's avoidable errors were also tallied, and points were subtracted from the running monthly

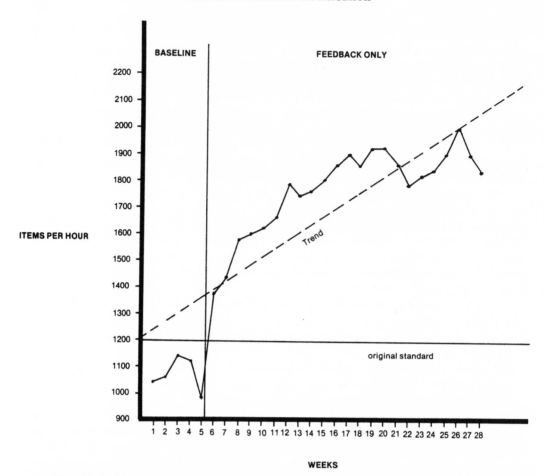

Fig. 19.1. Union National Bank Rate of Proving Checks and Deposits. Baseline Through First 28 Weeks of Treatment.

total. The more serious the error, the greater the point penalty. Encoding errors were penalized two points, balance errors were penalized four points, and incorrect error letters (miscalculating errors in customer deposits) were penalized six points.

Base pay and incentive pay for points accumulated were awarded each month or on a fixed time schedule of reinforcement. Supervisors were also awarded monthly bonuses of $2.50 per point received as a result of the daily group rates of the proof operators. This incentive system increased the item rate from 2,200 items per machine hour on the feedback system to 2,700 items per machine hour on the feedback and incentive system.

The importance of this improvement rests on more than simply a decrease in costs through increased productivity. The work of the proof operators is crucial to decreasing the time it takes for the bank to get credit for the money that it has on hand. Money that is in the bank but has not been processed is not available for loans, and the bank cannot receive federal credit for it. This "float" represents a considerable loss of revenue because the money is in the bank but not available for productive use. This intervention has now been in effect for 2½ years, and the rate for the past 8 months remains at 2,700 items per machine hour. Annual savings to the bank, calculated by man-hours saved and interest savings through reduced "float" and elimination of hold over, are estimated at approximately $700,000 annually.

Improving the performance of proof operators also played a role in the organization-wide program at the Virginia National Bank in Norfolk, Virginia. This banking organization is comprised of 165 branches and approximately 4,000 employees. Assets are approximately 2.7 billion dollars annually.

Proof operators at the Virginia National Bank were already on an incentive system before the current project began. The old system had been in effect for 4 years. It was an incentive system in which proof operators were rewarded with cash incentives for exceeding a minimum production rate of 1,000 items per hour based on rate per hours worked, similar to the measure used at the Union National Bank before intervention. Cash payments ranged from 20 to 30% of the employee's base salary, but increases could not be given that would cause the employee's salary to exceed the midpoint of her salary grade. The program was set up so that it was unlikely to exceed the maximum of the salary range for that position. Item rates for each proof operator were calculated monthly and became part of the employee's record, which was kept by the supervisors. Incentive pay was awarded monthly, based on the previous month's records. Errors were given quality ratings and were also recorded and kept as part of the records maintained by the Proof Department. These were taken into account before a final incentive pay report was submitted to Personnel for payroll adjustment. The employees themselves did not receive feedback on their performance until the end of the month, at which time the employee had the opportunity to discuss errors and item counts with her supervisor.

The management response to proof operators who failed to maintain the 1,000 item per hour rate or accumulated a large number of errors was a rather typical personnel program of disciplinary procedures. Any proof operator who failed to meet the minimum standard within the first month received a verbal warning from her supervisor, which was documented and kept on file. If this minimum standard was not met within the second month, the employee received a written warning from her supervisor, which was also forwarded to the Personnel Department. After the verbal and written warnings were received, if the minimum rate was still not met, the employee was placed on a 30-day probation status, during which training and assistance were offered. The employee was terminated if no progress was made.

To summarize, the old incentive system was based on a monthly fixed ratio schedule that provided little knowledge of results and a 1-month delay before rewards were delivered. This system included an upper limit on the amount of reinforcement that could be earned. The proof operators received no feedback on the quantity or the accuracy of their performance before the end of the monthly interval and were punished with the threat of termination if the minimum was not met. Employees were given the most attention when they failed to meet the minimum standard rather than when they exceeded it.

To improve the productivity of the bank's proof operators, a new incentive plan was implemented in three units, each of which consisted of eight proof operators and one supervisor. As in the Arkansas banking project, baseline data were obtained by using clocks in the keypunch machines in order to measure the rate that items were encoded per hour that the machine was on, rather than on a number-of-hours-worked basis. When this performance rate was measured on the old system by dividing the rate of items encoded by the total hours worked, the baseline measure was 950 items per hour. The more accurate measurement, calculated by dividing the daily total by the number of hours the keypunch machine was on, averaged 1,465 items per machine hour. In addition to the baseline data, an upper limit was obtained by having one button on the keypunch machine pressed continually for a period of 1 hour. The maximum estimate of possible items keypunched was calculated to be 3,600 items.

To introduce the new incentive system to the proof operators and quickly shape high response rates, rate games called "hourly specials" were implemented in which these employees immediately received points for exceeding their preceding hourly rate of items processed on the keypunch machines. Each point was worth $.25. A variety of "hourly specials" were implemented. Those aimed at low performers were based on their own performance rate, while those aimed at high performers provided extra points for the highest hourly performance rate. Middle performers were similarly rewarded for beating the group average. These "hourly specials" were continued while the new incentive system was in effect. Although hourly rates increased as a result of these specials, it was noticed that the proof operators were processing items more quickly, but not proving more items per day. Therefore, they had to be decreasing the number of hours the keypunch machines were on. In order to encourage the proof operators to focus both on their hourly rates and on the total items processed each day, the specials were changed to include rewards for hourly rates as well as the total number of items processed daily. Reversal data was obtained when these daily specials were intermittently removed as shown in Figure 19.2.

The goal for each proof operator was to increase the baseline rate of 1,465 to a new standard of 2,200 items per machine hour. Each operator was given a daily feedback form

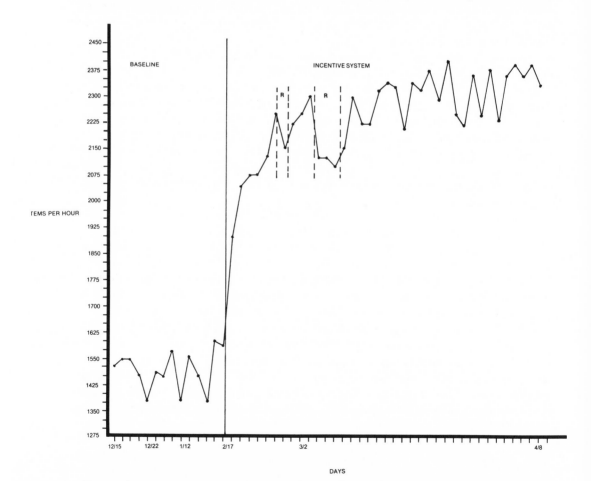

Fig. 19.2. Group Rates of Proof Operators at Virginia National Bank. Pre and Post Treatment Including Reversal Days on Hourly Specials.

on which she recorded her daily rate of performance. These employees received anywhere from one to eighteen points per day, depending on their rate of performance. This in turn was multiplied by the number of machine hours worked to determine daily totals. A single point was worth $.25. As in the Arkansas Banking project, employees were placed on a shifting ratio schedule of reinforcement, with higher levels of performance rewarded with an increasing number of points. A response cost measure was included in which proof operators were penalized for avoidable errors. All types of encoding errors received one penalty point, while forced balancing of daily totals received twenty penalty points. Each day, each operator's avoidable errors were tallied and points were subtracted from the total.

Base pay and incentive pay for points accumulated were to be awarded on a fixed time schedule of every 2 weeks. However, within the first 7 days, the proof operators averaged the rate of 2,250 items per machine hour, which exceeded the new standard goal of 2,200. Some individual hourly rates exceeded 3,000. One proof operator actually beat the earlier maximum estimate of 3,600 items per machine hour! Not only did the quantity of performance increase, but the quality of performance improved as measured by a marked decrease in the frequency of errors.

The subsystem of proof operators did not exist in a vacuum. Increasing productivity in the proving area was in part dependent on the timeliness with which bundles of checks were delivered from the tellers at the various branches. Unless checks were there to be proved, it would be impossible to increase proving rate. The interplay between the teller and proof operator subsystems was not direct. Rather, couriers picked up the bundles of checks and deposit slips from the tellers and delivered them to the proof operators. Unless these couriers were prompt in their pick-ups and deliveries, any increase in proving rate was limited.

To increase the frequency of batches of deposit slips and checks delivered to the proving department "on time," twenty-five couriers were placed on a feedback system for a 1-month period. In order to obtain baseline data, couriers were individually timed for each run made in delivering batches over a 5-week period. They averaged approximately three runs daily. "On time" was operationally defined as ranging from 5 minutes early to 5 minutes late on scheduled runs. Baseline data indicated that the couriers were delivering only 21% of the batches "on time." The feedback system consisted of providing the couriers with group performance rates which were posted on a daily basis.

In order to strengthen this system, a variable ratio schedule of reinforcement was introduced in the form of a lottery system. Each courier received one "B.E.S.T." coupon per successful run. These were accumulated and subsequently placed in a fishbowl at the end of the week. Weekly drawings from the fishbowl awarded couriers whose names were picked with a $10 gift certificate. Three gift certificates were awarded per drawing, and the bowl was emptied after each drawing was completed. Thus, the coupons served as secondary reinforcers for each courier. The chances for the back-up generalized reinforcement ($10 gift certificates) increased as the number of on-time daily runs increased. Within the first 10 weeks, including the initial month on feedback alone, the number of batches delivered to the proving department on time increased from 21 to 57%. At 34 weeks, the number of batches delivered on time was 65% (See Figure 19.3).

Having implemented programs to improve the item processing rate and increase the timeliness of the couriers, it became necessary to extend the project to the source of the task, the subsystem that dealt directly with the customer. If the tellers were delayed in "batching" the incoming checks and deposit slips, no program would be effective in increasing the timeliness of courier performance.

A feedback system was implemented for a group of forty tellers for a period of 15 weeks. Previously, tellers were measured on the accuracy of balancing daily totals. In order for them to balance accurately, work was held for later checking rather than given to the couriers. The result was that many checks and deposits missed courier runs, therefore increasing float. As noted in the Union National Bank Project, "float" was defined as those checks or deposits not available to loan or for the receipt of federal credit because they were not processed.

The teller feedback system was installed in three test branches and measured the four major outputs of tellers, which included transaction rates, referrals, differences in daily totals, and the frequency of batches of deposit slips and checks given to the couriers on time. Baseline data consisted of the dollar value missing from courier runs over a 2-week period. An average of $65,805, $108,740, and $9,164 per day were missing from the three branches, respectively. Tellers were given a summary feedback form on which the frequency of each output area was tallied on a daily basis, and points were awarded at the end

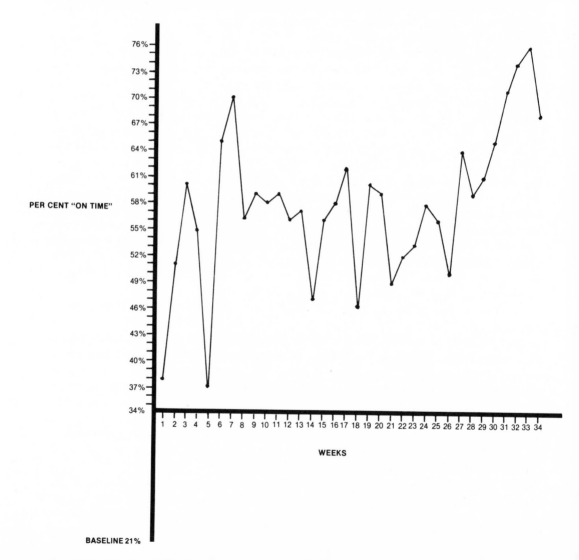

Fig. 19.3. "On Time" Performances of Couriers Following Lottery Incentive Intervention.

TABLE 19.1. Dollar Value Missing From Courier Runs From Baseline Through Feedback Intervention.

	Baseline (daily dollars missing from courier runs)	Feedback (daily dollars missing from courier runs)	Percent Improvement
Branch 1	$ 65,805 per day	$2,367 per day	96%
Branch 2	$108,740 per day	$9,062 per day	92%
Branch 3	$ 9,164 per day	$2,618 per day	71%
	2 weeks	4 weeks	

of each day for those rates above the minimum standard. Managers gave tellers time-off as a reward for decreasing the amount of dollars missing on courier runs. The results at the end of 4 weeks are presented in Table 19.1.

All comparisons were significant at the p. 05 level by t-tests for related measures. Thus, the feedback forms provided the bank tellers with continuous reinforcement for increased rate of performance in all four output areas, which was immediately and contingently reinforced by points serving as conditioned reinforcers. Instead of cash rewards, time-off appeared to be a potent back-up reinforcer for this group.

Checking is not a bank's only function. At the Virginia National Bank, every subsystem has been or is currently being incorporated into a feedback model based on Behavioral Engineering Systems Training (Performance audit, 1972). The following sections present preliminary data from six different subsystems encompassing a variety of banking responsibilities.

Forwarding Clerks

A major banking function involves the transfer of money both within the bank and to external sources. The data in Table 19.2 summarizes the performance of three groups of Forwarding Clerks from baseline through intervention. The Return Item Clerks have the necessary job of returning checks that cannot be honored by the bank for one reason or another. The more quickly these "bounced" checks are returned, the more quickly the customer receives the information that his or her checking account has insufficient funds. The function of the Wire Room Clerks is to wire money from one bank to another or to the federal reserve. The function of the REG-E Clerks is to respond by letter within the federal regulation time limits to special problems of customers involving cash flow.

Customer Information and Relations

Another major banking function is to assure customer satisfaction through providing efficient services and informational resources. The data in Table 19.3 summarizes the performance

TABLE. 19.2. Output Performance of Forwarding Clerks From Baseline Through B.E.S.T. Intervention.

	Output	Baseline	Goal	Actual
Return Item Clerks	% checks returned by 5:30	15.4%	100%	57%
Wire Room Clerks	% wires transmitted by federal deadline	76%	90%	100%
REG-E Clerks	% REG-E letters written within 3 days	23%	100%	100%

TABLE 19.3. Output Performance of Customer Information and Relations Clerks From Baseline Through B.E.S.T. Intervention.

	Output	Baseline	Goal	Actual
Customer Relations Clerks	% customers inquiries resolved on time	89%	98%	99%
	% deposits cleared on time	60%	85%	68%
Customer Information Filing Clerks	% customer calls completed of those received	76%	100%	84%
Teller Information Filing Clerks	% teller calls completed of those received	78%	100%	91%
Maintenance Clerks	% maintenance journals updated on time	59%	100%	79%
Cross Index Clerks	% cross index journals updated on time	54%	100%	88%

of five groups of Customer Information and Relations Clerks from baseline through intervention. The Customer Relations Clerks serve the function of assisting customers through resolving their inquiries. These clerks also have the responsibility of clearing customer deposits as quickly as possible. The Customer Information Filing Clerks and the Teller Information Filing Clerks are phone operators who respond to both customer and teller phone inquiries, respectively. In order to maintain correct demographic data on all banking customers, the Maintenance Clerks update all current account files with new addresses, changes in marital status, etc. The function of Cross Index Clerks is to keep both the customer and the bank informed of the balance in a customer's savings and checking accounts at any given time.

Telephone and Correspondence

In order to systematize the telephone communications within a banking organization, telephone calls must be regulated through a central operating office. Telephone Operators serve the important function of regulating both incoming and outgoing calls, as well as being responsible for updating the bank's telephone directory. Telephone Billing Clerks, on the other hand, have the responsibility of allocating telephone bills to employees and paying bills accrued by the banking organization (See Table 19.4).

TABLE 19.4. Output Performance of Telephone Operators and Correspondence Clerks From Baseline Through B.E.S.T. Intervention.

	Output	Baseline	Goal	Actual
Telephone Operators	Telephone Directory updated accurately	96%	99%	96%
Telephone Billing Clerks	Bills paid on time	60%	93%	79%
	Bills allocated on time	61%	93%	79%

TABLE 19.5a. Output Performance of Mail Clerks From Baseline Through B.E.S.T. Intervention.

	Output	Baseline	Goal	Actual
Mail Clerks	Internal mail delivered	50%	95%	75%
	Priority mail processed	82%	95%	68%

TABLE 19.5b. Output Performance of Procedure Writers and Press Machine Operators From Baseline Through B.E.S.T. Intervention.

	Output	Baseline	Goal	Actual
Procedure Writers	% circulars written on time	18%	95%	100%
Press Machine Operators	Average days to print jobs	33 days	25 days	21 days

Office Services

Just as telephone communications are systematized through a central operating office, the process of communications through mail is also made more efficient through a central office of operations. Mail Clerks serve the function of delivering interoffice mail and processing priority mail as promptly as possible (See Table 19.5a).

Each subsystem of a banking organization is specialized, with its own purposes and contributions. However, general banking procedures are incorporated into the functioning of these subsystems on an organizational level. Procedures and updated regulations are communicated among these subsystems through the services of Procedure Writers and Press Machine Operators, who also have the job of developing circulars and brochures to be distributed to the customer. Table 19.5b summarizes the performance of these groups.

Maintenance

The physical appearance and upkeep of bank branch buildings is also an important aspect in providing customer satisfaction. Bank appearance can communicate bank prestige and

TABLE 19.6 Output Performance of Properties Maintenance Servicemen From Baseline Through B.E.S.T. Intervention.

	Output	Baseline	Goal	Actual
Properties Maintenance	(Tidewater Group) miles per maintenance run	9.5 miles	9 miles	5.6 miles
	labor hours per maintenance run	21.6 min.	18 min.	20.3 min.
	(Peninsula Group) miles per maintenance run	8.4 miles	7 miles	7.7 miles
	labor hours per maintenance run	54 min.	45 min.	52 min.

TABLE 19.7. Output Performance of Operations Department Personnel Within the Credit Card Division From Baseline Through B.E.S.T. Intervention.

Operations Department	Output	Baseline	Actual
Preparatory	# payments processed per hour	385/hr.	530/hr.
	# payments audited per hour	438/hr.	700/hr.
Audit	# items audited per hour	73% of standard	82% of standard
Input	# payments posted per hour	523/hr.	760/hr.
POS	% POS batches audited accurately	97%	99.7%
Settlement	% settlements completed by 3:30 pm	57%	100%
	% reconcilement entries completed by noon	57%	87%

credibility to the customer. Properties Maintenance Servicemen are responsible for the maintenance and upkeep of bank branches, which are separated into territories surrounding the five cities around the Norfolk area. Table 19.6 summarizes the performance of Properties Maintenance Servicemen measured in distance and time required for maintenance tasks to be completed in two of these territories.

Credit Card Division

Finally, the Credit Card Division will be mentioned as a subsystem of the Virginia National Bank presently utilizing the B.E.S.T. feedback model. The Credit Card Division in a banking organization can be divided into the three following major departments: the Operations

TABLE 19.8. Output Performance of the Consumer Department Within the Credit Card Division From Baseline Through B.E.S.T. Intervention.

Consumer Department	Output	Baseline	Actual
Input	Applications entered, address changed, status changed, computer letter entered, pts. given/ standard time required	1.08 pts/ min.	1.4 pts/ min.
	% applications entered accurately	91%	97%
	% other work entered accurately	98%	97.5%
Customer Services	% original letters to customers written to model	78%	91%
	% chargebacks completed accurately	92%	95%

Department, the Consumer Department, and the Recovery and Credit Department. The primary function of the Operations Department is to process credit card payments received from customers and make adjustments or audits on those payments requiring additional paperwork. Employees in this department also deal directly with the merchants who send batches of bills of sale (POS batches) from customers whose accounts must receive debits for the amount owed the bank. Customer settlements in the form of finance charges are calculated through this department for bills not paid within 30 days. Table 19.7 summarizes the performance of employees in sections within the Operations Department from baseline through intervention.

The function of the Consumer Department is to update credit card application data and keep a log of all applications submitted, whether approved or not. Through this department, letters are sent to those customers who have missed credit card payments. Credit is also given to customers who have returned store items initially charged on credit cards, and the Consumer Department subsequently charges the merchant for the payment previously made for the returned item (chargebacks). Program effects in this area are shown in Table 19.8.

The function of the Recovery and Credit Department is to recover actual credit card payments and to make arrangements with those customers who can only pay in monthly installments. Credit card applications are approved or denied through this department within 10 working days on the basis of credit rating, and the appropriate letters are forwarded to the applicants. Performance increments in these functions are shown in Table 19.9.

The total contingency management system at the Virginia National Bank is still in its infancy, yet the trend in the results is clear. Over 95% of the interventions that have been initiated to date have resulted in performance increments in measureable outputs across a wide variety of tasks. While an occasional measurement problem remains and chosen rewards once in a while turn out not to have been reinforcing, immediate performance increases have been the rule and lack of impact the rare exception.

Since it is impossible to begin a program in all subsystems of a large organization at the same time, some interventions have to wait for improvements in other subsystems before their impact can be determined. Evaluation of the program at the Virginia National Bank must proceed cautiously because of these limitations. Nonetheless, the overall success of the B.E.S.T. program in almost every aspect of this financial institution suggests that it is possible to implement feedback and reinforcement interventions that will improve productivity organization wide.

TABLE 19.9. Output Performance of the Recovery and Credit Department Within the Credit Card Division From Baseline Through B.E.S.T. Intervention.

Recovery and Credit Department	Output	Baseline	Actual
Recovery	$ recovered monthly	$3548/mo.	$3780/mo.
Word Processing	# letters with errors /week/operator	14	5.6
Credit	# lines typed/day/operator	582	1287
	% letters proofed and filed accurately	89%	96%
	% applications approved or denied within 10 working days	44%	72%

REFERENCES

Andrasik, F., Heimberg, J. S., & McNamara, J. R. Behavior modification of work and work-related problems. In M. Hersen, R. M. Eisler, & P. M. Miller (Eds.), *Progress in behavior modification*. New York: Academic Press, in press.

Malott, R. W. A behavioral systems approach to the design of human services. In D. Harshbarger & R. F. Maley (Eds.), *Behavior analysis and systems analysis: An integrative approach to mental health programs*. Kalamazoo, Michigan: Behaviordelia, 1974.

Performance audit, feedback and positive reinforcement. *Training and Development Journal*, 1972, **26** (11), 8-13.

Reynolds, G. S. *A primer of operant conditioning*. Glenview, Ill.: Scott, Foresman, 1975.

Part V:
Broader Perspectives

Introduction

Up to this point we have considered various techniques that are currently being used in industrial behavior modification and presented some results that have been achieved through their application. But there are several broader issues that should also be discussed as we consider the continuing growth of the field. As industrial behavior modification gains wider acceptance in the business setting we must concern ourselves with staffing and manpower needs. How are practitioners in the field currently being trained and what would optimum training consist of (Chapter 20)? Secondly, in spite of their obvious effectiveness, behavior modification techniques may be resisted because the underlying assumptions seem to conflict with widely held beliefs about human nature. Is this, in fact, a real conflict? And just as importantly, how can the ethical problems which arise from these assumptions be analyzed and confronted (Chapter 21)? Finally, where do we go from here? What can we say at this time about the future direction of industrial behavior modification (Chapter 22)?

While this volume most properly ends with a discussion of the emerging trends, we will consider Chapter 22 first, as it represents a logical extension of the previous articles. Current applications necessarily set the stage for future extensions. Yet other factors will contribute to the direction that the field will ultimately take. It is quite clear that organizations do not exist in a vacuum, but are a part of the larger social system. As society changes, organizations will also change. These changes will in turn influence the direction and scope of industrial behavior modification.

Forecasting the future is a difficult task, especially in a rapidly changing society, but it is safe to say that some techniques will continue along present lines of development because they remain useful, while others may decline in use or change to meet new requirements. Entirely new aspects of this technology can also be expected to develop as a function of requirements not presently represented in industry. Andrasik and McNamara consider these issues by first describing changes in the work setting that can be expected on the basis of societal changes currently underway. They then provide a detailed treatment of expected developments in the industrial behavior modification field, first from the perspective of current practitioners and researchers, and then in terms of their own analysis of the major areas within the field.

This information should prove particularly useful to practitioners who have options with regard to the allocation of their efforts and resources and who wish to take a lead in meeting these new challenges. It shold also be of great interest to students and teachers who must by necessity be concerned with the future. This then brings us to the issue of industrial behavior modification training, as described by Duncan and Lloyd in Chapter 20.

The application of behavior analysis techniques in the business arena has expanded rapidly in the past several years, and as these techniques continue to gain acceptance the market for skilled practitioners will grow. What should practitioners be able to do? Who should do the training? Where should training take place and for how long? Duncan and Lloyd provide a thorough and detailed consideration of such issues, respecting the viewpoint of those in the business world as well as those of the academician. The value of their analysis is further enhanced by the examples provided and the specificity and practicality of their recommendations.

Many managers will find this chapter enlightening because of the insights it provides regarding the strengths and weaknesses of industrial behavior modification practitioners that they may hire or be allied with. They can also use it to assess their own skills with respect to some of the practical problems that confront them within their organizations. Further, since an essential portion of education for practitioners must take place within the business setting, the chapter also provides the manager with a basis for active participation in this training.

University teachers and students will find the chapter especially meaningful for the opportunity it provides to assess the strengths and weaknesses of their own programs. General curriculum design, the method and content of specific courses, and the essential characteristics of practicum and internship experiences can all be derived from Duncan and Lloyd's treatment.

Finally, although the chapter was included in this unit because of its relevance for training practitioners in industrial behavior modification, the last half presents principles and techniques that are applicable to all types of training. This material will be useful in the early stages of the development of any training program and can provide a basis for the choice of specific training materials and procedures. Training alone, however, does not insure adherence to behavior analysis principles after the training program concludes. In Chapter 21 Berthold suggests that the acceptance of the assumptions which underlie behavioral techniques will increase the likelihood that practitioners will continue to apply the skills they acquire during training.

Behavioral approaches are based on assumptions that appear to conflict with some deeply ingrained traditional views of human nature. Failure to recognize this seeming conflict and deal with it prior to the application of specific techniques may result in resistance to such application. These issues are usually thought of as ethical or value questions. Berthold shows that the assumptions underlying behavioral approaches are, in fact, quite consistent with essential features of the field of management; that management would not be management if it did not firmly adhere to the same assumptions. This treatment provides reassurance for any reader with doubts along these lines as well as an excellent basis for dealing with such issues when raised by others.

Nevertheless, as with any new technology, a number of questions are likely to arise for which well-developed "ethical" views or guidelines are unavailable. In the last half of his chapter, Berthold presents some very useful "rules of thumb" for minimizing conflict regarding such issues. Many of the same questions have already been dealt with in other areas of application, such as education, mental retardation, and the criminal justice system, and Berthold gives us this information as well. Such information should prove useful in addressing the ethical concerns of business associates.

Although these last three chapters do not offer any specific practical techniques, they are essential to our coverage of behavioral applications in business and industry. They offer us challenges and new directions for growth. It is now up to us to take action with regard to this material to further advance this developing technology based on a science of behavior.

Alyce M. Dickinson
Western Michigan University

20

Training Format in Industrial Behavior Modification

Phillip K. Duncan and Kenneth E. Lloyd
Drake University

Industrial behavior modification has clearly become an area of interest for behavioral psychologists and as yet to a lesser extent for working managers. The growth of organizational behavior management interest groups in professional associations such as the Association for Behavior Analysis and the Association for the Advancement of Behavior Therapy witnesses this interest. One journal (*Journal of Organizational Behavior Management*, 1977 to present) and one conference (the Second Drake Conference on Professional Issues in Behavior Analysis: Organization Behavior Management, 1979) exemplify the growth of organizational behavior management from the relatively isolated interest of a few to the national interest of academics and practitioners.

Despite the growth of this area, industrial behavior modification does not yet appear to constitute a field of study in which degrees may be earned. University training in industrial behavior modification is typically housed in programs designed for different training purposes, and non-academic training is for practical purposes quite circumscribed in the theoretical basis for organizational behavior management.

MINIMAL REPERTOIRES

Regardless of where training is housed, there appear to be three response repertoires that are recommended for training practitioners.

Behavioral

Behavioral repertoires are necessarily the most critical to a practitioner. The behavioral analytic methodology sets this person apart from all others in the management field. There is some debate about the particular structure of behavioral training, but three general sorts of training experiences seem reasonable.

Theoretical/conceptual. The initial basis for the Experimental Analysis of Behavior, Applied Behavior Analysis, and Industrial Behavior Modification is the philosophy of behaviorism described by Skinner (1938, 1953) and others in a variety of sources (i.e., *Behaviorism*, 1972 to present). At the heart of this philosophy is the assumption that behavior is a naturally-occurring phenomenon, and is therefore the reasonable subject matter for a science. A second assumption holds that behavior is related in orderly and predictable ways to environmental events, and that a study of these relations will lead to prediction and control of behavior. Were there no orderly relations between behavior and the context in which it occurs, attempts to understand or influence behavior would be pointless.

Experimental. The philosophical assumptions of behaviorism led to research that identified the nature of the relations between behavior and environment. This research, begun by Skinner (1938), and carried on by others (*Journal of the Experimental Analysis of Behavior*, 1958 to present) has led to the identification of basic principles of behavior. These principles, such as reinforcement, punishment, stimulus control, generalization, discrimination, and the conditions which control them, form the basis for our understanding of how behavior functions and changes.

The value of theory and experimental analysis is not always acknowledged by practitioners in any field. The theories and findings that indicate that the human body will float at rest are of little interest to the novice swimmer struggling furiously to keep from sinking. Similarly, the manager struggling to meet the acute demands of the day may give little credence to theory, preferring tried and familiar (if not true) methods of behavioral control. In each case, solutions may be available, but ignorance of the science prevents implementation of the solutions.

Applied. The ultimate utility of theoretical and experimental knowledge is their provision of a basis for application to "real world" problems. The importance of experimental chemical research becomes apparent when the consumer realizes that the dose of his drug prescription is based on the change the drug affected in laboratory animals. The importance of basic behavioral research becomes apparent when the manager realizes that employees produce well or poorly, depending on the amount and pattern of feedback given them. Therefore, to be useful theory and research must suggest practices that make a readily observed difference in the work place.

Behavioral principles have guided behavioral applications, and the resultant behavioral technology (applied science) has been used in many fields, including education, mental health, and management. The forms of the technology may differ (i.e., a token economy in a classroom and a production feedback chart in a factory), but the underlying principles remain the same. The applicability of this common technology to a variety of situations makes it particularly appealing. The technology applies to line workers and supervisors, nonexempt and exempt employees.

Finally, it is imperative that philosophy, research, and application be understood as inseparable. Without acknowledging the importance of experimentation, the technologist has no source for new information; without eventual ties to application, the theorist erects a sterile ivory tower (Miller, 1978). And without assuming discoverable order in the behavior of people, neither experimenter nor technologist should pursue their activities at all.

The appreciation of basic experimental and theoretical findings is of most concern at the present time. The technologist who is ignorant of the basic science is like the novice firefighter who tries to stifle a chemical fire with water – the results may be disastrous due to scanty knowledge about what causes and maintains various fires. The behavioral technologist may make analogous blunders by "reinforcing" a child's withdrawn behavior in order to demonstrate to the child that he/she is loved. The supervisor may make the same sort of mistake by ignoring poor work or by indiscriminantly praising workers in an effort to create a "pleasant" work environment where production will improve. There is, of course, no reason to expect these techniques to have any desirable effect, for they are applied without an understanding of the nature of reinforcement contingencies.

Whereas training in behavioral procedures is paramount for the industrial behavior modification practitioner, there are knowledge areas in business that are likely to be valuable. Just as the mental health worker should know something about the nature of schizophrenia and the special educator something about the characteristics of various syndromes, the behavioral practitioner should have some understanding of the issues that confront business and industrial organizations. There is not unanimity about the emphasis placed on non-behavioral experiences in an essentially behavioral training program. Michael (1980) has argued that non-behavioral coursework should be held to a minimum, while Hall (1979) has urged broad exposure to non-behavioral writing, and Duncan (1980) has described a behavioral training program that combines both behavioral and non-behavioral components. The following constitute broad knowledge areas about which the organizational behavior management practitioner should acquire at least a rudimentary understanding (See Goldstein & Sorcher, 1973 for a list of skill areas).

Business

Person management. For several decades programs of study related to the management of persons in the workplace have included a variety of courses about human conduct based on social psychological theories of motivation and personality (e.g., Maslow's needs theory, Herzberg's Motivation Hygiene theory, Cognitive Disonance). The considerable drawbacks to these theories as practical management procedures have been discussed elsewhere (Miller, 1978; Nord & Durand, 1978; Gilbert, 1978). Nevertheless, many managers have been trained in these theories, and the organizational behavior management practitioner should be sufficiently familiar with them to point out their difficulties and suggest alternative strategies.

Another area within person management deals with working relations between union and management. The practitioner is certain to confront labor-management issues, either in working to introduce or stop unionization or to effect smooth relations between union and management. Behavior analysis provides tested guidelines for contingency contracts, but familiarity with labor laws and the conventions of union-management interactions would be difficult to replace or duplicate.

The official and actual chain of command constitutes an important aspect of person management. Companies may have quite structured procedures for proposing and receiving feedback about programs. In addition, the titular leaders may not be those who actually make program decisions. The organizational behavior management practitioner who overlooks the chain of command may do so at considerable peril to both programs and job.

Production management. The actual production of goods or services in a cost-effective manner is the ultimate goal of business. The behavioral manager would be wise to learn the process by which materials become products. This knowledge is not intended to prepare the behavioral manager to supervise production, but rather to familiarize him/her with the variables that constrain production supervisors.

Finance and Accounting. The general flow of money in an organization is also an area about which the behavior manager should have some knowledge. Company policy, union contracts, and other regulations may limit the extent or ease with which money can be introduced as a variable for behavior control.

Current Events. Less formal, but still useful, is a familiarity with the events that influence the business world on a daily basis. These might include stock market trends, national monetary policies, and events that have a more specific impact on the particular industry in which the practitioner is working. Again, knowledge in these areas is not to be the principal focus for the industrial behavior modification practitioner, but failure to be aware of issues in these areas may significantly reduce his/her credibility and effectiveness.

Social

The industrial behavior modification practitioner may have vast knowledge in behavior analysis and familiarity with traditional management areas, but without certain social skills he/she will seldom see them put into practice. Although there is much less formal training involved in social skills development, a variety of writers have deemed such skills crucial to the effective delivery of behavior change programs (Hall, 1978; Lloyd & Whitehead, 1976; Miller, 1978).

Manager as reinforcer. A particular interpersonal skill that can facilitate the work of the industrial behavior modification practitioner involves the routine delivery of praise, feedback, and other appropriate positive consequences for good or improved work. This technique, simple as it seems, is not widely practiced. When carried out, it has the effect of improving or maintaining performance, and just as important, establishing the workplace and the manager as situations which are associated with reinforcement. Having established the consequences within his/her control as reinforcers, the manager can then manage the variety of tasks for which he/she is responsible.

A second kind of social skill involves the manager's arranging for coworkers to receive reinforcers from other sources in the business. The manager can do this in a variety of ways, such as giving "credit" to colleagues and subordinates for their part in effective programs and by describing the efforts of these coworkers to supervisors who control reinforcers. Again, this practice maintains desirable behavior and establishes upper level company management as a source of reinforcement.

Modeling enthusiasm. Behaving as though problems can be solved is a useful way to provide the occasion for the solution as well as reinforcer for the solution. Such behavior is called enthusiastic, optimistic, or positive, and involves such activities as saying that there are ways to address the issue, describing the solutions and their benefits to the company, and actually instituting the programs.

Flexibility. There may be a variety of sound behavioral solutions to a particular performance problem. One social skill that may be of value to the practitioner is the consideration of reasonable ideas from any source. The benefits here are to reinforce sound creative problem solving from different members of the management team and to make a problem situation the occasion for problem solving from as many informed persons as possible. Note that the organizational behavior management practitioner does not support any proposed program, rather he/she should support those that are behaviorally sound. Gilbert (1978) points out that there are many useful technologies that can contribute to the solution of performance problems, such as those of human factors specialists or industrial engineers.

Information flow. A final social skill involves keeping all persons involved in an organizational behavior management program informed of the program's progress. Decisions about how much information must be shared with which individuals can be made on a need-to-know basis. It is only good sense to tell an executive whether or not an expensive program is working, just as it makes good sense to tell a line worker that he/she is achieving 100% of the goal. Giving such information provides the opportunity for reinforcing participation of all involved and once again allows the practitioner to acquire reinforcing properties.

These categories are only broad areas within which more specific tactics can be employed. Whereas these social skills derive as contingency shaped behaviors, they have been identified more through practitioner experience than through empirical research. Despite the paucity of research in this area, the practitioner is advised to consider these categories as the basis for establishing rule-governed repertoires which the organizational community may then shape.

PROGRAMMATIC STRATEGIES FOR INDUSTRIAL BEHAVIOR MODIFICATION TRAINING

Within the relatively few sources for training in industrial behavior modification, there appear to be two major training formats. One of these is university-based, and leads to a graduate degree, usually in psychology, and the other is industry-based and usually leads to designation by the training corporation as a behavioral consultant. Each of these formats entails quite different practices and therefore addresses the minimal repertoires for industrial behavior modification practitioners in quite different ways. The following section discusses how university-based and industry-based training practices address these repertoires, as well as a number of other variables related to the training of the practitioner.

Length of Training

One of the most obvious differences in training programs is the time taken to provide the training. Didactic industry-based training is generally accomplished in a matter of weeks or months, whereas academic training, leading to a Master of Arts or Master of Science academic degree, usually requires at least 2 years. Differences in training time may be attributable in part to quite different contingencies operating in the training agencies. Industry-based programs expend money as part of the training program, with one of the expenses being the salary of the trainee. At the same time the trainee provides little if any financial benefit to the company. Thus contingencies that decrease training costs and increase monetary benefits to the company are likely to operate. Such a contingency easily translates into relatively short training programs. (See Gilbert, 1978 for exceptions to this point.) The contingencies operating in a university are quite different. University-based programs receive money from the trainee in the form of tuition, which ceases when the trainee graduates. Contingencies which maximize income to the university are those which lengthen training programs.

Theoretical/Experimental Emphasis

Because of the constraints which exist in the business world (i.e., getting personnel into productive activities as soon as possible), relatively little stress is placed on behavioral theory or research. But the writings of Skinner and others on behavioral theory cannot be skimmed, nor can the techniques of basic research and their relation to theory be taught in a workshop of a few days or weeks. These factors combine to produce a perspective which on one hand acknowledges that behavioral theory and research have led to a technology, but which on the other suggests that the technology can be effectively applied without training in theory and research. What industry needs is organizational behavior management practitioners, not researchers and theorists.

Not surprisingly, the academic perspective on theory and research is quite different. Academia is the primary locus of theory and research, and contingencies within academia operate not only to reinforce but to require theoretical and research activities. The pronounced view in academia is that behavior *analysis*, rather than behavior *modification*, is the center of any behavioral training program, including organizational behavior management programs, and that there must therefore be considerable emphasis placed on behavioral theory and research (Krapfl, 1980; Michael, 1980). What is needed are practitioners who understand the underpinnings of their technology, not technicians who do not realize where their techniques came from or why they work.

Applied

The application of behavioral principles is the goal of the industrial behavior modification practitioner, regardless of his/her training. For the practitioner trained in industry, this is the near exclusive aspect of training. Possessed of behavior and management skills, the trainee-practitioner seeks to effect changes in worker productivity. Verifying the effect of independent variables through single subject research designs is acceptable, but not required. Creativity and progress involve identifying new behaviors which are amenable to control by the basic principles. The dependent variable is of prime interest.

Of course, application of behavioral principles is also important to the university trained practitioner. However, the approach to applications may be somewhat different. Interest may be not only in effecting changes in the dependent variable, but also in the contribution to those changes made by different values or forms of the independent variable. Forms of independent variables more complex than the basic reinforcement relation may come into play. New understanding or progress from this view would involve identifying and applying complex behavioral relations as well as effecting changes in the target response. The independent variable occupies a key role.

Business Issues

Attention to traditional business issues varies both within and across programs. As mentioned earlier, there is a view in academic behavioral training programs that business and traditional systems issues should be addressed within training programs established primarily to teach applied behavior analysis skills. The recent merger of West Virginia University's Systems Analysis Psychology program into its Behavior Analysis program is an example of the implementation of this view. Similarly, Drake University's training program in Behavioral Systems Administration, while requiring management/administrative coursework, retains a core of behavior analysis training as the basis for its students. In summary, training is focused on behavioral repertoires with acquaintance with business issues as a second knowledge area.

Behaviorally-oriented businesses seem to take differing views on the weight given to behavioral and business repertoires. For example, Tarkenton & Company formerly hired persons whose primary training was in behavior analysis. Recently, however, this company has elected to hire persons trained primarily in business skills, assuming that the company could teach the behavioral skills necessary for work in the company (Hall, personal communication, 1979).

A similar firm, Performance Systems Improvement, seems still to be hiring persons trained primarily in behavior analysis. This firm also clearly indicates interest in business knowledge (Rhoton, personal communication 1979) but the emphasis appears to be quite different from Tarkenton & Company.

Edward J. Feeney Associates (Staelin, personal communication, 1981) looks for people who have demonstrated some quantitative behavior change in their previous work. The key for this consulting firm is to get individuals who have in the past attained measurable behavior change. Although training in behavior modification is considered desirable, an orientation toward working with measurable behavior is more crucial than sophistication in behavioral terminology. Experience in training or sales, a business or organizational background, familiarity with statistics and accounting, and marketing or manufacturing experience for related familiarity with management jargon, are also deemed desirable. Nonetheless, individuals must be able to demonstrate that they have actually accomplished something in an organizational setting. This does not eliminate those coming directly out of a graduate program in applied behavior analysis if these academic experiences included work that achieved meaningful results in an oganizational setting. Generally speaking, acquaintance with rather than fluency in general business issues seems to be the rule. Clearly, however, there are exceptions.

Although they are not a part of a formal academic discipline, both industry and university-based behavioral training programs regularly evaluate the interpersonal skills of trainees (Hall, 1979; Lloyd & Whitehead, 1976). These evaluations are generally conducted by surveys or rating scales over a range of categories, from grooming habits to verbal fluency. With the relatively shorter training time in industry, there may be more of a tendency to select trainees who possess acceptable social skills, since teaching these can be a long-term undertaking. In the academic setting, organizational behavior management trainees who do not exhibit appropriate social behavior are generally not terminated from training, but receive instruction and continued feedback about deficient repertoires. Eventually, of course, the practitioner must emit the proper social responses or his/her effectiveness as a change agent will be jeopardized.

Access to Training Sites

In applied fields such as industrial behavior modification, access to real world settings is critical to the training process. Such sites permit the trainee to practice skills acquired in other training components and to gain additional skills that are necessary for successful performance in real world settings but are difficult to obtain in the artificial environment of a classroom setting. Academic and industry based programs differ with respect to the kinds of real world experiences that are available and the degree to which trainees have access to on-site settings.

To a large extent, industry-based training comes with built in practice sites. Organizational behavior management counseling firms such as Tarkenton & Company and Performance Systems Improvement generally assign practitioners to selected, current accounts. Corporations which contain in-house organizational behavior management staff, such as J. P. Stevens and National Semiconductor, generally target individual facilities existing within the company for practicum training.

Acquisition of practicum sites for university-based programs can be somewhat more challenging. Business sites do not come built-in, and therefore must be generated. This generation may occur in several ways.

Consulting

One method is for academic trainers to establish consulting relations with businesses where trainees may then work. This method is not unlike establishing a strictly "for profit" consulting relation, as is done by management consulting firms, but being university-based, it clearly entails a student training function which some businesses may wish to avoid in favor of a full-time, exclusively "for profit" consultant.

Internships

A second approach for academic trainers is to establish internships with business and industry. Internships allow a business to retain a full or part-time organizational behavior management trainee who can remain on-site, working on company issues and applying his/her training under both academic and business supervision.

Industrial Behavior Modification Courses

A form of access to business sites can be generated by offering an industrial behavior modification course for working managers through university evening classes. Part of the class can involve applying behavioral principles, and trainees can assist the managers with the projects.

Evaluation

In determining an optimal training approach, consideration must be given to the value placed on the various components of the minimal industrial behavior modification repertoire and the adequacy with which training establishes those repertoires. Industry and university-based programs offer very different training.

Technicians. If training is viewed primarily as a means of producing persons capable of applying a set of techniques that can change behavior, their industry-based practices may be adequate. Stress on theory, research, and issues involving the independent variable are discounted. The short-term benefits include a practitioner who can return money to the company by remedying current problems.

Analysts. If industrial behavior modification training is viewed as a means of producing technically capable persons who can relate technique to theory and research and investigate alternative forms of independent variables, then academically-based practices appear superior. The short-term effect of university-based training is not a quick return on investment – the practitioner is still a trainee. The long-term contingencies may determine the ultimate worth of training, and these favor the kinds of training offered in universities.

Many industries involved in manufacturing, such as chemical and pharmaceutical companies, retain large research staffs who perform both "applied" and "basic" research. This research, combined with information gathered in university laboratories, provides the basis for the development of new and presumably better products. The analogy to the business of human behavior is direct. Complete answers to sources of behavioral control do not currently exist. For the industry which relies on effective methods of managing behavior to discount theory and research or to leave it exclusively in the hands of academics, is to forego progress for the sake of current, temporary gain.

INDUSTRIAL BEHAVIOR MODIFICATION TRAINING FORMATS

Within any training program, industrial behavior modification repertoires may be taught in a variety of ways. The following section describes the most typical of these methods and identifies steps that appear to be minimally necessary to constitute effective training.

Industrial training has apparently taken a wide variety of forms. A consultant from a nearby university may offer a 4-hour workshop at an industrial site on some desirable aspect of performance, such as motivation, incentives, memory, or productivity. The consultant may approach the topic so generally that it could be taught at any of a number of industrial plants or may approach it specifically to the group of trainees or students at hand. The latter approach requires a knowledge of the specific tasks and problems involved in the particular industrial site so that examples of concepts being taught can be illustrated from the day-to-day lives of the trainees. A generally accepted recommendation is that training problems be as specific as possible to the situations at hand. Deviations in training from the immediate situation require the students to generalize from the training situation to their own work. Generality of training may be arranged so that students are as effective on the job as they are in training. Stokes and Baer (1977) and Johnston (1979) have discussed conceptual and practical issues related to insuring the generality of successful training.

An alternative training format might be to enroll students from several different industrial sites into one training program possibly offered by a nearby university. Faced now with a heterogeneous group of students, the instructor must resort to generalities in attempting to explicate the concepts he hopes the students will acquire. Any efforts at treating specific issues will mean considerable attention to single or small groups of students. This is not to say that other students from different work environments may not offer potentially helpful suggestions, but such suggestions are likely to vary widely in their applicability or usefulness. Such a situation would not be unlike that of the typical university classroom which is filled with students whose major vocations remain as yet largely unknown. Any skills acquired in the classroom must perforce be general since there is no way of predicting the future problems that the students will eventually encounter.

Perhaps a more common training format occurs wholly within and between the employees of the industrial site. A training department may have been established within a business. New and/or old employees may be selected or may volunteer for a given training program, which once again may be characterized by a broad or specific orientation, although the opportunities for highly specific training programs should now be large — a characteristic which would highly recommend this training format at the outset. We have already cautioned the reader about relying upon "automatic" generality from classroom to job even when the content of the training program may appear to be identical to that of the actual job. Formal similarities in such situations can be misleading. It is not only necessary to measure a student's performance on the materials in the training program itself, but also the trainee's change, if any, in performance of the job. The early recognition of this potential difference between performance in a training program and that on the job will be a major step in improving any training program.

Common sense suggests that the trainee who will skillfully describe verbally how a job may optimally be performed should also perform the job optimally. This suggestion is not one upon which one can rely. A problem arises in those frequent situations where one set of variables controls the trainee's behavior in the training program (e.g., performing well for the instructor), and another set of variables controls the trainee's behavior on the job (e.g., performing at a level acceptable to his/her supervisor or at a level just discriminably above that of a competitor).

Training programs may best be viewed as three-stage affairs. First, trainees must encounter some types of materials that somehow change their behavior in a desirable direction. Second, this behavior change measured during the training program must persist on the job after the end of the program. In other words, variables that will maintain this behavior change must be present in the work situation. Third, this on-the-job behavior change must result in some outcome which is itself judged desirable. A hypothetical example may be helpful to illustrate the three stages. A superintendent of a state psychiatric hospital hopes to introduce a training program for the direct care staff working on four wards, each of which houses 45 patients diagnosed as chronic schizophrenics. A previous training program which stressed personality theories of schizophrenia had been of considerable interest to the trainees who soon after, however, appeared to have forgotten their lessons or at least did not seem to put them into practice. Now the superintendent is seeking a more outcome-oriented, accountable training program. She/he selected a programmed package of instructional materials which required the trainees to read short passages of written descriptions of behaviors of chronic hospitalized patients and descriptions of how these behaviors were changed by hospital staff working directly on the hospital wards. After reading each short passage the trainee answered several questions taken from the material. After reading and correctly answering questions from four to six of these short passages or units, the trainee was asked to demonstrate with another trainee what he had learned and was given a review test consisting of questions from the prior units. All trainees were required to answer all sets of questions at a 90% accuracy level. If they failed to do so at the first attempt at answering a set of questions, they would then reread their materials before attempting a second set of questions over the same materials.

The training program director(s) graded all answers by the trainees, gave occasional short lectures in class, and observed and scored all demonstrations. Concurrently, the training director(s) also periodically observed and scored the trainees while they were working on their wards. The supervisors of the trainers were aware of the goals of the training program and had been instructed to praise the trainees with words of encouragement whenever the trainee behaved in accordance with the goals of the training program. The training program director(s) observed and recorded the supervisors' behavior to learn if they were following instructions.

The ultimate goal of the training program was to improve the social interaction skills of the patients. The final observations and recordings made by the training program directors were directed at the patients themselves to see if indeed there was any change in their social interaction skills. The ultimate criterion would be a change in the desired direction of the social interaction skills of the patients. If such a change did not occur, then some revision in part or all of the training program is required. The reading materials may require revision, the supervisors may require additional instructions to induce them to more volubly praise the appropriate behaviors of the trainees, or the training may need to be expanded to encompass the entire staff (supervisors, direct care staff, medical staff, all three working shifts) of the four wards. Only an empirical trial and error procedure will identify those elements of the training program which require revision. However, if a change in the desired direction of the social interaction skills of the patients actually did occur, then the training program director(s) may pause momentarily to enjoy their feelings of satisfaction, but only momentarily, since they only know that success was achieved with the use of a complex package of reading materials, test questions, review tests, demonstrations, lectures, supervisor praise, as well as many other unknown variables. They cannot yet know the necessary elements of their training program; some of the elements included may be superfluous. Generally some refinement would be judged reasonable. Extensive refinement may be limited by the interests and budget of the hospital superintendent. The money that could be spent on further refinement might better be spent on training more staff with the extant training program.

Another concomitant of a successful program is worthy of comment. It was stated previously that the ultimate goal of the training program had been to improve the social interaction skills of the patients. No level of improvement or criterion of acceptable change in skills for some specified period of time was established. In order to detect even a minimal change in patient behavior after or during the training program, it would be necessary to have available a measure of patient social interaction skills before the training program began. Changes due to the effects of the training program could then be evaluated with reference to this baseline measure of skills. Program success could be stated in terms of a percent change measure (immediate post-training skills divided by baseline skills times 100). A successful training program could be defined as one whose immediate percent change measure equaled or exceeded some minimal percent (for example, 20%). If our first training program improved immediate patient social skills by 25% (from a baseline score of 10 skills per hour displayed by 45 patients to a post training skills per hour score of 12.5), then at least two decisions about future research on the training package might be stated. One might be: 25% improvement is okay. Another might be: 25% is fine, let's try for 40% improvement. Similarly, we could compute a post-training percent change measure over a time period of 1 month or year. In either case a decision to refine the training program components might be positive or negative depending upon other considerations.

This lengthy and hypothetical illustration of a training program was intended to illustrate the three stages of a specific training program: study materials, persistent effects on the job, and a desirable outcome (See Connellan, 1978, p. 87). The hospital setting was chosen since some research has already been completed in that setting. Some actual, industrial examples will also be presented in order to match more closely the specific interests of the intended readers of this chapter.

One example illustrates a possible problem when only some of the three stages receive attention. A company instituted a training program in the proper ways of lifting heavy objects (Connellan, 1978, pp. 77-78). At the end of training, the trainees were indeed lifting heavy objects appropriately. Observations of these behaviors on the job resulted in low scores, however, for the ways they were lifting heavy objects. Further observations seemed to indicate that the supervisors of the trainees generally failed to attend to or comment upon the ways trainees lifted. Some support or reinforcement in the form of friendly comments from supervisors may often be necessary in order to maintain behaviors newly acquired in a training program once trainees are back on their jobs. In the present example a prior training program for supervisors emphasizing the importance of their consequenting in some or several ways the correct behaviors of their subordinates would seem indicated (Goldstein and Sorcher, 1973). On the other hand, the company could establish an incentive system for behaviors associated with safety on the job. In either case some procedures for insuring on-the-job maintenance of behaviors acquired in a training program have been attempted.

In the present example, measurement was restricted to observing the frequency of correct lifting behaviors on the job. While the measurement of these behaviors could be used to evaluate the efficacy of the training procedures, the objective of the training program was no doubt not to simply increase the frequency of correct lifting behaviors but to reduce the number of reported accidents, increase productivity, or to increase some assessment of job satisfaction. In other words, the objective of the program was to affect the results of lifting behaviors, not just to influence the frequency of correct lifting behaviors. Yet no effort was made to measure the results. Measurement of one or more of these results would have either justified the training program or, just as importantly, pointed out the necessity for revision. As it was, justification of the training program could only be based on the humanitarian notion that employees should be trained in safety procedures (a notion that is responsible for the continuation of many "humane" yet ineffective training programs).

Another example will elaborate upon a textile company which employed consultants to attempt to establish a behavioral mangement system to increase the frequency with which its 195 long-haul and inter-mill truck drivers purchased diesel fuel at company-owned outlets versus commercial outlets and to increase the miles per gallon of fuel consumed while driving the trucks (Runnion, Watson & McWhorter, 1978). The consultants introduced a complex package of instructions, prompts, and public feedback to induce drivers both to purchase fuel at company outlets and to reduce fuel consumption. Fuel consumption was measured by obtaining fuel tickets from the drivers and by odometer readings from the trucks. These outcome measures were obtained during a 1-week baseline period and during all subsequent conditions. Two distinct intervention strategies were instituted for 1 year each. In the first year the miles per gallon program was announced to drivers in a letter which also contained a list of ways to attain more miles per gallon (decrease engine idling time; drive in the correct gear for a given speed; drive less than 55 miles per hour; brake appropriately for stops; purchase fuel at appropriate locations and in quantities just sufficient to allow the driver to reach a company fuel terminal before filling up). In addition, graphs indicating miles per gallon for the fleet and for each individual driver were posted publicly daily and weekly in the drivers' room at each terminal (See also DeSeve, 1971). On a random basis personal letters were sent to drivers commending them for improved performance. Unscheduled social praise for improvement was provided by dispatchers and terminal managers. Peer competition was another unscheduled influence. The second year intervention involved all of the above plus a weekly lottery and a free dinner. Lottery tickets were awarded to each driver on any day he exceeded six miles per gallon fuel consumption. The free dinner was provided to drivers and their wives who performed best over a period of several weeks.

Miles per gallon by long-haul drivers increased from a baseline of 4.80 to 4.90 and 5.23, respectively, during the first and second years of the program; miles per gallon by inter-mill drivers increased from a baseline of 5.73 to 6.02 and 5.97, respectively, during the first and second years. The approximate improvements of 5% become highly significant when it is recognized that one-hundredth of a percentage point translates into substantial dollar savings (Runnion et al., 1978, p. 180). Fuel purchases at company terminals increased from 30% to 48% during the year.

After 60 weeks the feedback procedures were eliminated entirely for 4 weeks. It had been suggested that the prior decreases in consumption were attributable to wind deflectors installed on some truck cabs. As miles per gallon decreased from over five to less than five, company personnel were convinced of the success of the intervention procedures and immediately reinstated the feedback system. During the second year the company had saved enough fuel to operate its entire fleet at no cost for 1 month.

In this textile mill illustration no direct observations were made of the behavior of the drivers either during a training program or on the job. Instead, these first two training program stages were omitted in favor of an outcome measure. Thus the third stage of a training program was immediately available. Since the outcome was desirable, everyone was pleased.

It should be noted that when outcomes are judged to be of low desirability, and if outcome measures rather than direct measures of behavior have been employed, then the trainer lacks specific measures of responses that failed to occur or that occurred but contributed to the undesirable outcome. This is a potential disadvantage of procedures that obtain only outcome measures as opposed to behavioral ones: if the method fails, the trainer has learned very little about the reasons for failure. It may not be important in a particular case to understand the reasons for the success or failure of a program, but if it is desired to be used again or is assumed to possess generality, then more detailed analyses are needed.

At the end and/or during any of the three stages of specific training programs, subjective measures of satisfaction with the training program may be obtained (Wolf, 1978). Simple, short attitude questionnaires can be completed by the trainers, their supervisors, higher level managers, and/or by any class of persons who may be making verbal judgments about the training program (i.e., customers, creditors). Subjective measures never replace objective measures, but they can alert the trainer to reactions to his/her training program which may or may not agree with the actual objective data. The trainer may need to explain the training program in greater detail or justify objectively certain components. Subjective measures obtained early on in a program may increase the likelihood that judges will respond favorably; that is, the judges will include people who have probably been instrumental in starting the training program in the first place and their initial reactions may be favorable due to their satisfaction in actually seeing the planned program underway. Any initially favorable judgments cannot help but bolster the trainer's motivation to continue and may be of considerable value if problems develop later. It will be valuable to have some people supporting the program at all times.

Finally, it must be pointed out that in the last analysis even a training program that is successful both in respect to all three stages and to social validation may be quickly abandoned by an unpredictable management. The most highly documented example of this state of affairs may be seen in Paul and Lentz (1977). This book describes a 6-year comparative study of the behaviors of chronic mental patients on three types of wards in a state psychiatric hospital system. One type of ward was operated on social learning principles (emphasizing feedback), another was operated on milieu therapy principles (individualized attention), and the third type served 25 typical control types of wards. All measure of behavior over the years indicated continual superiority for the social learning wards. These measures included social interactions, personal hygiene and grooming, work habits and success following discharge. At the end of the 6-year project, budgetary decisions from the state capital ordered discontinuance of the successful programs.

THE THREE STAGES OF TRAINING PROGRAMS

Study materials and didactic training efforts have been directed at the first stage, although even these efforts have been described as only a beginning (Gardner, 1973). The most well-known and most evaluated training system (Keller, 1968) has been employed in university classrooms (Lloyd, 1978) as well as more down-to-earth settings (Lloyd & Whitehead, 1976; Kazdin & Moyer, 1976). As originally conceived, this training system consisted of five features (Lloyd, 1978, p. 494 ff).

The first feature, self-pacing or student-pacing, meant that the student decided when to complete course assignments. Several investigations reporting cumulative number of assignments completed as a function of time intervals during the course indicated that students completed few assignments early in the semester and many assignments late in the semester (Burt, 1975; Lloyd & Knutzen, 1969; Sheppard & MacDermott, 1970). Most courses today invoke some form of instructor-pacing (Bitgood & Segrave, 1975; Malott & Svinicki, 1969).

The second feature, unit mastery, specified that the student could proceed to new course material only after passing a test over assigned material at some specified criterion level (Johnston & O'Neill, 1973). In a traditional course a student who answers 60% of the test items correctly, for example, may receive a C; in a Keller course that same student would be required to restudy the material until correctly answering 85-100% of the test items. Instructors typically provide students with study questions covering the reading assignment for each unit test to alert the student to the most important parts of the assignment.

The third feature concerned lectures that were viewed as reinforcers for completing prior tests rather than as a means of imparting information about forthcoming tests, i.e., only students who had completed certain assignments were permitted to attend lectures. Research has not supported this notion (Lloyd, 1978, p. 514 ff).

Nevertheless, there is an emphasis shift for the fourth feature from the student as passive recipient of the teacher's lectures to one in which the student is actively reading, studying, and writing on his own while the teacher acts as planner, coordinator, manager, and occasional lecturer.

Finally, for the fifth feature, the teaching staff was expanded to include student peers who had previously passed the course with an excellent grade. Generally the literature indicates that peer proctoring facilitates student performance and also benefits proctors (Lloyd, 1978, pp. 516–518).

At least 29 comparisons of performance of a Keller class with a traditional class on a common criterion measure (e.g., a final examination) have been reported. Seventeen studies indicated higher criterion scores for the Keller method based upon a statistical analysis, four obtained results partially showing higher scores for the Keller section, and eight reported no statistical differences between the classes. None indicated a superiority for the traditional method. Testing occurred much more often in Keller sections than in traditional sections. This factor by itself may account for the superiority of the Keller system. Some studies retested students after an interval of several months; they reported continued superiority for the Keller system. Students overwhelmingly preferred the Keller method to traditional courses.

Some form of the preceding system can be confidently recommended as a starting point for any training program; a successful outcome is highly likely since, given the amount of research already published, specific recommendations can be made. Recommendations for carrying out the second and third stages of a training program cannot be stated with as much confidence due to a general lack of research either on how well trainees perform on-the-job or on how desirable the eventual outcomes actually are or are judged to be (Prue, Fredericksen & Bacon, 1978, pp. 247–250).

ON-THE-JOB PERFORMANCE OF TRAINEES

The available research on changes in on-the-job behavior subsequent to a training program (i.e., follow-up research) has often been disappointing (e.g., Fielding, Errickson & Bettin, 1971; Katz, Johnson & Gelfand, 1972). More often follow-up data are unavailable (Gardner, 1973; Kazdin & Moyer, 1976; Loeber & Weisman, 1975; Mazza & Pumroy, 1975). These studies are derived from employment situations within the mental health field. As Burg, Reid and Lattimore (1979, p. 364) point out "the maintenance of the change in staff behavior following termination of the formal investigation . . . (has been neglected) . . . although its importance has been well discussed . . . " This issue has also been addressed by Kazdin (1973).

Two recent studies have reviewed the literature in this field (thus providing the interested reader with a reading list) and have reported more complete research paradigms. In one study the trainees, the eight day-shift attendants on one ward of a state residential facility for the developmentally disabled, were trained in the use of a self-recording device to count social interactions between themselves and residents on the ward (Burg et al., 1979). On-the-job measures of the interactions of attendants and residents were made for 11 weeks during the training period and during the eighteenth and twenty-second weeks after the training period. In addition observations of ward cleanliness, resident cleanliness, resident aggression, and resident self-stimulation were recorded by the trainers. The use of the self-recording devices increased the number of observed interactions between attendants and residents, (i.e., the training program changed on-the-job performance both during and after the training period). As the number of attendants making self-recordings increased from zero to two and as there was a concurrent increase in the number of interactions between residents and attendants, ward and resident cleanliness increased, and resident aggression and self-stimulation decreased. In other words, not only did attendant self-recording behaviors increase, but desirable outcomes for the residents were realized. Thus, the evaluation of program success was based not only on measures of behaviors, but also on the attainment of desirable outcomes. No subjective measures of satisfaction with the training program were collected for residents, attendants or supervisors.

In another study the trainers again selected social interaction between ward attendants and residents as the behavior to train (Adams, Tallon & Rimell, 1980). The trainees were 15 aides from one cottage in a public facility for the mentally retarded. Lectures on social interactions were provided for two groups of trainees. One of these groups also received role-playing experience in social interactions. Training was completed when the trainees attained test scores of 80% correct. For 9 weeks both before and after the training program, measures of on-the-job responses to residents by the attendants were obtained; the number of responses by attendants to residents was greater after the week of training than before the training period. In this study no outcome measures of resident behaviors were obtained nor were any subjective satisfaction measures taken. Both of these studies (Burg et al., 1979; Adams et al., 1980) are highly recommended reading for anyone contemplating a training program.

OUTCOME MEASURES OF TRAINING PROGRAMS

Typically behavioral or subjective measures are obtained even though an outcome measure of behavior serves as the stated dependent variable in the training program (See Runnion et al., 1978). A notable exception is the Burg et al. (1979) study just described. Outcome measures do not guarantee that a good program will be continued by management (Paul & Lentz, 1977), but they must be a necessary step if management is to know whether trainees are achieving the missions of their job. Indeed, Gilbert (1978) points out that management attention to behaviors rather than outcomes may in fact guarantee that a poor program be continued and a good one terminated.

Social Validation

Individuals employed in training departments need to be skilled in devising procedures that will quickly change the behaviors of the novice so that they resemble the behaviors of the skilled expert. However, knowing *how* to change behavior and knowing *what* to change are two separate issues. If the trainer observes the performance of a skilled employee in order to ascertain the behaviors which should be taught to the novice, he/she may well detect some of the necessary behaviors for successful performance but will no doubt miss some important ones or assume that some behaviors are critical when in fact they are not. Trainers must consult with experts in the particular performance area in order to determine what the content of the training program should include. This social validation process is introduced, in part, to guard against the errors of omission (of important behaviors) and commission (of unimportant behaviors).

Social validation also plays a role in the evaluation of the training program. Trainers must seek the assistance of knowedgeable judges in the performance area to evaluate the adequacy of the performance of trainees and to evaluate the adequacy of the course materials (Jones & Azrin, 1969; Wolf, 1978). Subject matter experts should also be employed to ascertain the worth of the entire training program. While decisions about behavior change procedures must be left in the hands of the trainer, the evaluation of the importance of the training program, the specification of the desired outcomes of the program and the evaluation of the success of the training program is best left to the consumers of the program. Such judgements are usually subjective.

Wolf (1978) has suggested that "society (the consumers) would need to validate (the trainer's) work on at least three levels. The social significance of the goals . . . The social appropriateness of the procedures . . . The importance of the effects. . . . [p 207]." In defense of the subjective judgements which comprise any social validation process, Wolf (1978) states that it seems "clear that a number of the most important concepts of our culture are subjective, perhaps even the most important [p 210]."

In considering the present emphasis on social validation, no reader should assume that subjective judgements can replace objective measures or that subjective measures will necessarily agree with objective measures. A program may be judged by the consumers and society as successful even though objective measurement shows that the program was ineffective in developing or maintaining the desired behavior changes. On the other hand, it is entirely possible that a clearly effective program (one that results in changing the behavior of trainees) may be judged as a failure by the consumers or society. In the first case, it is the responsibility of the trainer to implement more effective behavior change techniques. In the latter case, the trainer must consult with the subject matter experts in an attempt to reconcile the differences in the subjective and objective measures. Such a reconciliation may require changes in the goals of the program, the effects of the programs, or in the procedures to make the procedures more socially acceptable.

CONCLUSIONS

We have outlined in this chapter a generally accepted set of repertoires with which the industrial behavior modification practitioner should be equipped. That these repertoires have been derived primarily from practical experience rather than systematic research suggests that a productive area of research would be to identify those repertoires which in fact contribute to significantly more success as an organizational behavior manager.

That there are clear differences between the nature of industrial behavior modification training received from business and universities is indisputable. The person interested in industrial behavior modification positions must therefore carefully consider the nature and depth of training that is generally available from each source.

REFERENCES

Adams, G. L., Tallon, R. J., & Rimell, P. A comparison of lecture versus role-playing in the training of the use of positive reinforcement. *Journal of Organizational Behavior Management*, 1980, **2**, 205-212.

Behaviorism. Reno, Nevada: University of Nevada, Department of Psychology, 1972.

Bitgood, S. C., & Segrave, K. A comparison of graduated and fixed point systems of contingency managed instruction. In J. M. Johnston (Ed.), *Behavior research and technology in higher education*. Springfield, Illinois: Charles C. Thomas, 1975.

Burg, M. M., Reid, D. H., & Lattimore, J. Use of a self-recording and supervision program to change institutional staff behavior. *Journal of Applied Behavior Analysis*, 1979, **12**, 363-376.

Burt, D. W. Study and test performance of college students on concurrent assignment schedules. In J. M. Johnston (Ed.), *Behavior research and technology in higher education*. Springfield, Illinois: Charles C. Thomas, 1975.

Connellan, T. K. *How to improve human performance*. New York: Harper & Row, 1978.

DeSeve, K. L. Feedback as a reinforcer in industry. Unpublished thesis, 1971, Washington State University, Pullman, Washington.

Duncan, P. An interdisciplinary approach to behavioral systems administration. Paper presented at the Association for Behavior Analysis, 1980, Dearborn, Michigan.

Fielding, L. T., Errickson, E., & Bettin, B. Modification of staff behavior: A brief note. *Behavior Therapy*, 1971, **2**, 550-553.

Gardner, J. M. Training the trainers: A review of research on teaching behavior modification. In Rubin, D., Brady, J. P., & Henderson, J. D. (Eds.), *Advances in behavior therapy*. Vol. 4. New York: Academic Press, 1973.

Gilbert, T. *Human competence. Engineering worthy performance*. New York: McGraw-Hill, 1978.

Goldstein, A., & Sorcher, M. Changing managerial behavior by applying learning techniques. *Training and Development Journal*, 1973, **27**, 36-39.

Hall, B. Personal Communication, 1979. Tarkenton and Company.

Hall, B. Invited Address, Second Drake Conference on Professional Issues in Behavior Analysis: Organizational Behavior Management, 1979, Drake University, Des Moines, Iowa.

Johnston, J. M. On the relation between generalization and generality. *The Behavior Analyst*, 1979, **2**, 1-6.

Johnston, J. M., & O'Neill, G. W. The analysis of performance criteria defining course grades as a determinant of college student academic performance. *Journal of Applied Behavior Analysis*, 1973, **6**, 261-268.

Jones, R. J., & Azrin, N. H. Behavioral engineering: Stuttering as a function of stimulus duration during speech synchronization. *Journal of Applied Behavior Analysis*, 1969, **2**, 223-230.

The Journal of the Experimental Analysis of Behavior. Bloomington, Indiana: Society for the Experimental Analysis of Behavior, 1958.

Journal of Organizational Behavior Management. New York: Haworth Press, 1977.

Katz, R. C., Johnson, C. A., & Gelfand, S. Modifying the dispensing of reinforcers: Some implications for behavior modification with hospitalized patients. *Behavior Therapy*, 1972, **3**, 579-588.

Kazdin, A. E. Issues in behavior modification with mentally retarded persons. *American Journal of Mental Deficiency*, 1973, **78**, 134-140.

Kazdin, A. E., & Moyer, W. Training teachers to use behavior modification. In Yeu, S., & McIntire, R. W. (Eds.). *Teaching behavior modification*. Kalamazoo: Behaviordelia, 1976, pp. 171-200.

Keller, F. S. Goodbye teacher. *Journal of Applied Behavior Analysis*, 1968, **1**, 79-89.

Krapfl, J. The relation of systems analysis to the basic sciences. Paper presented at the Association for Behavior Analysis, 1980, Dearborn, Michigan.

Lloyd, K. E. Behavior analysis and technology in higher education. In Catania, A. C., and Brigham, T. A. (Eds.), *Handbook of applied behavior analysis: Social and instructional processes*. New York: Irvington/Halstead Press, 1978, pp. 482-521.

Lloyd, K. E., & Knutzen, N. J. A self-paced programmed undergraduate course in the experimental analysis of behavior. *Journal of Applied Behavior Analysis*, 1969, **2**, 125-133.

Lloyd, M. E., & Whitehead, J. S. Development and evaluation of behaviorally taught practica. In Yeu, S., & McIntire, R. W. (Eds.), *Teaching behavior modification*. Kalamazoo: Behaviordelia, 1976, pp. 113-144.

Loeber, R., & Weisman, R. G. Contingencies of therapist and trainer performance: A review. *Psychological Bulletin*, 1975, **82**, 660-688.

Malott, R. W., & Svinicki, J. G. Contingency management in an introductory psychology course for one thousand students. *Psychological Record*, 1969, **19**, 545-556.

Mazza, J., & Pumroy, D. K. A review and evaluation of behavior modification programs. *Psychological Record*, 1975, **25**, 110-121.

Michael, J. L. Flight from behavior analysis. *The Behavior Analyst*, 1980, **3**, 1-21.

Miller, L. *Behavior management*. New York: John Wiley and Sons, 1978.

Nord, W., & Durand, D. What's wrong with the human resources approach to management? *Organizational Dynamics*, 1978, Winter, 13-25.

Paul, G. L., & Lentz, R. J. *Psychological treatment for chronic mental patients: Milieu versus social learning programs*. Cambridge, Massachusetts: Harvard University Press, 1977.

Prue, D. M., Frederiksen, L. W., & Bacon, A. Organizational behavior management: an annotated bibliography. *Journal of Organizational Behavior Management*, 1978, **1**, 216-257.

Rhoton, W. Personal communication, 1979. Performance Systems Improvement.

Runnion, A., Watson, J. O., & McWhorter, J. Energy savings in interstate transportation through feedback and reinforcement. *Journal of Organizational Behavior Management*, 1978, **1**, 180-191.

Sheppard, W. C., & MacDermott, H. G. Design and evaluation of a programmed course in introductory psychology. *Journal of Applied Behavior Analysis*, 1970, **3**, 5-11.

Skinner, B. F. *The behavior of organisms*. New York: Appleton-Century-Crofts, 1938.

Skinner, B. F. *Science and human behavior*. New York: Macmillan, 1953.

Staelin, J. R. Personal communication, 1981. Edward J. Feeney Associates.

Stokes, T. F., & Baer, D. M. An implicit technology of generalization. *Journal of Applied Behavior Analysis*, 1977, **10**, 349-367.

The Second Drake Conference on Professional Issues in Behavior Analysis: Organizational Behavior Management, 1979, Drake University, Des Moines, Iowa.

Wolf, M. M. Social validity: The case for subjective measurement or how applied behavior analysis is finding its heart. *Journal of Applied Behavior Analysis*, 1978, **11**, 203-214.

21

Behavior Modification in the Industrial/Organizational Environment: Assumptions and Ethics

Howard C. Berthold, Jr.
Lycoming College

Organizations are becoming increasingly complex. Companies have grown in size and scope. Competition, both at home and abroad, is greater than ever before. The whole tempo of the work place has increased dramatically as a result of sophisticated telecommunications, computers, and mechanical, robot-like assembly line processors. All of this has placed ever greater burdens on management and human resources.

People must themselves develop increased skills to cope with the technical and competitive pressures. One indication of this need is the amount of money spent by industry in training personnel. Bell Telephone, for example, spends more than $700 million a year on training, over three times the budget of The Massachusetts Institute of Technology (Jacobs & Phillips, 1979). Other companies do likewise.

What are the implications for management? Obviously, managers need to become more effective, and to do so they will have to utilize more effective methods. Since behavioral psychologists are specialists in the modification of human behavior, it would make sense for organizations to turn to them for help. But will managers be willing to accept such help? At first blush, this might seem an absurd question in the face of such demonstrable need. On the other hand, there is some evidence that these techniques will be rejected, that managers will prefer ineffective methods to effective ones.

The reason for such an illogical choice lies in the very assumptions we make about human nature and the ethics of control. This is an issue that many behavior modifiers prefer to ignore. They would rather spend their time devising a new strategy of behavioral control than dwelling upon the ethics and implications of such control. The trait is common to research scientists in all fields: "Let others worry about how and whether to use some method, I just want to discover how nature operates."

If behavioral methods are to be used in industrial/organizational settings, and if they are to be used ethically, then those who know the techniques must do a better job of communicating with those who could use them. This communication must transcend mere descriptions of the techniques, as many of the articles in this book have done. Behavior modifiers must also be explicit about what assumptions underlie the techniques and what ethical implications ensue. Managers, on the other hand, must understand these assumptions and ethical considerations and be willing to confront the issue of what they really want when they ask a behavioral psychologist for help. These are the issues that will be developed in this chapter.

ASSUMPTIONS UNDERLYING BEHAVIOR MODIFICATION *

Psychology as a Science

Behavioral psychologists utilize the scientific method in studying behavior. Some critics argue that this is merely blind faith in a method that has proven useful in the physical sciences. Granted, there is a certain amount of faith involved. Someone who rejects this approach is, however, also expressing a type of faith – namely that the scientific approach won't work. Neither can be absolutely certain they are correct. No matter what one believes, however, one must start somewhere. Assumptions must be made. Why do behavioral psychologists begin with the assumption that the scientific approach will enable them to understand behavior? Although assumptions may never be unequivocally verified, there are almost always good reasons for selecting the ones we do. In the case of psychology and (as we will see) management, the scientific approach dictates certain strategies and goals which coincide closely with what we want to accomplish as psychologists and managers.

Emphasis on Observable Behavior

One of the primary tenets of the scientific approach is that it deals with observable behavior or behavior that can be defined in terms of observable behavior. This is precisely what behavioral psychologists and managers need to deal with, too. To demonstrate this point, let us consider an example of something that may seem unobservable: unhappiness. Suppose an employee was very unhappy. Should a manager say he or she didn't care about this if it never showed itself in any overt way? Suppose it was the manager's husband, wife, boyfriend, or girlfriend. Should the manager say that such unhappiness doesn't matter to him or her? No, not at all. That would be tragic. But if this unhappiness was in fact never observable – not through actions, words, or even through medical or research instruments, then how would anyone except that person ever know of its existence? For others to know there would have to be some observable signal, perhaps something extremely subtle, but nevertheless observable. Hence, psychologists study observable behavior, not because unobservable behavior may not exist, but because they can't know about it unless it is observable.

Note that the preceding example used a term which isn't behavior *per se*. One doesn't see unhappiness. One sees behavior that is interpreted as unhappiness: complaints, frowns, crying, lowered eyes, etc. This is what is meant by the statement that psychologists study behavior that is observable, or unobservable behavior, like unhappiness, which is defined in terms of, or made known by, the observable. The important point, however, is that as a manager or a person in some other role, you too have to work with what is observable in other people or what you can make observable, because that is also all you know.

Many management texts emphasize the importance of empathy. Some suggest that behavior can be studied by trying to feel the same way as another person when that person engages in certain types of behavior. The problem, of course, is that we can never know if we have succeeded. We can never be certain that we feel the same way as another person, any more than they can be certain they feel the same way as we. Validation is simply impossible without direct observation. Thus, one of the primary tenets of the scientific approach coincides very nicely with the approach that seems most logical for both psychologists and managers: always deal with observable behavior.

There are other reasons why it seems logical to pursue the scientific approach in study-

---

*The content of this section is based upon an article by Berthold (1975).

ing psychology. One of these is the compatibility of methods and goals between science, psychology, and, incidently, management.

Goals and Methods of Science

What psychologists want to do when they study behavior, and what managers want to do when they use psychology in their organization, is explain, predict, and perhaps even control observable behavior. Physical scientists aspire to the same goal. The way that scientists achieve this goal is through the discovery of laws. Laws can be defined as statements of relations between two or more independently and properly defined objects or events. Laws frequently take the following form: *If* one does X, *then* Y will follow. Some simple physical laws are as follows:

If water is heated to 100°C at sea level pressure, *then* characteristics result which we term boiling. *If* an object in a vacuum on earth is dropped, *then* it will fall a distance expressed by $\frac{1}{2}gt^2$.

Analogously, some simple laws in psychology are as follows:

If an SST passed overhead right now at top speed, *then* people on the ground would show a startle response. People would jerk, take a quick short breath and stoop over slightly at the sound of the sonic boom. *If* a person makes his or her opinions known to others, *then* the person's views will be harder to change than if his or her opinions were held privately.

It should be noted that many of these laws are potentially complex when they are applied to different settings, and this is just as true in the physical sciences as in the behavioral sciences. The law governing the behavior of a falling object in a vacuum seems simple enough, but what scientist would dare predict the exact behavior of a feather released from atop the Washington Monument? Similarly, the seating habits of students in a classroom are easily predicted after a few class sessions, but their seating at a concert in a huge auditorium might be more difficult to predict.

How far can one go with the analogy between inanimate objects and the physical sciences and humans and the behavioral sciences? After all, don't people have free will? Doesn't this mean that people's behavior isn't determined in the same sense that the behavior of inanimate objects is determined? The issue of free will and determinism is a complex one. Obviously, it won't be resolved in this paper. We can, however, make a strong case for assuming determinism rather than free will. To do so, let us return to the realm of inanimate objects.

Suppose we began dropping a steel ball in a vacuum. Suppose that the first time it fell a distance of $\frac{1}{2}gt^2$, the next time it fell a distance of $\frac{1}{2}gt^4$, the third time it hung in midair, and the fourth time it went straight up. Where would physics be then? Would it make sense to study the behavior of falling objects if they did whatever they pleased, one thing this second, something else the next, and never exhibited any demonstrable regularity? Would it make any sense for a group of manufacturers to ask a physicist how steel balls will behave in a given product if such balls didn't follow consistent laws?

Let's pursue the analogy even further. Suppose the balls usually fell a distance of $\frac{1}{2}gt^2$, but sometimes fell a different distance. Perhaps we could build a science and a technology on what usually happens. In fact, some areas of theoretical physics are based upon statistical rather than absolute regularity, but even there the variations must follow well-defined patterns. The distribution of "random" events must be predictable if our science and technology are to succeed. Moreover, we are talking here of very simple laws governing the behavior of simple objects in well-defined situations. If there is no regularity at this level, either statistical or absolute, how could one ever hope to predict outcomes in a more complex situation where several such laws and objects interacted? Furthermore, how would we ever know whether apparent violations of a law were not in fact violations but lawfully determined phenomena due to factors which we had not considered, such as air pressure, wind velocity, or density of the object in relation to the air around it?

Consider the example of boiling water. Suppose some people first tried an experiment involving heating water at a laboratory at the base of a mountain. Suppose they then went to a field station atop a high mountain and discovered that the boiling temperature differed markedly. If the people assumed at that point that water simply behaved any way it wished, it isn't likely they would continue to study the behavior of water. Why bother? On the other hand, if they assumed that the behavior of water follows consistent laws, they would continue to search for other factors that might have caused the different results. In this case, of course, the people would eventually discover the importance of atmospheric pressure.

Scientists always assume that there is a reason for failures to follow established laws. When the side of Apollo 13 blew out as it headed toward the moon, scientists didn't say, "Well, there go the laws of nature changing on us again." Rather, they looked for causes within the laws of nature, known and unknown, and they found them! A pipe had cracked during the pumping of oxygen in and out of the rocket during a long delay.

Returning to people, what assumptions should psychologists and managers make when they try to predict the behavior of people? Don't they have to make the same ones as the physical scientists? If human behavior isn't predictable, reducible to consistent laws, determined if you will, then what use is there in studying it? It won't do to say that we only expect to discover laws about the part of behavior that is determined, well-ingrained habits for example, so that we can make a good bet about behavior when people aren't using their free will in tricky ways. If one says that about simple laws, then is there any hope of making molar predictions about the complex behaviors that really interest us in management and other areas of life? If all the basic laws of human behavior are constantly changing, how can we ever hope to explain behavior that rests on many such laws? Further, if we assume that people have some freedom to modify basic laws of behavior, how would we ever know when we had discovered all the laws up to the point where their free will takes over? Obviously, we must continue to search for laws of behavior anyway, just in case we have overlooked some obvious explanation as in the case of the boiling water and Apollo 13. Neither had exercised free will. They operated in precise correspondence with laws that scientists had overlooked.

In most cases in everyday life, human behavior is influenced by an incredible number of factors. The example of predicting the landing point of a feather dropped from the Washington Monument is a closer analogy to the kinds of predictions psychologists are asked to make than predicting the distance traveled by a steel ball. Nevertheless, as difficult as the task may be, if human behavior follows natural laws in a clear, reliable manner, then there is hope of prediction, explanation, and control. Psychologists must assume such regularity in human behavior, or there is little sense in trying to study it. Managers must assume such regularity, or there is little hope in trying to manage behavior. The assumptions of science regarding determinism and the presence of laws are necessary ones for the study of psychology and the practice of management. This is why it is reasonable for both groups to adopt this approach.

Do Managers Really Want to Know?

A willingness to accept the assumption that laws of human behavior exist is only the first step practicing managers must take if they are to benefit from the information known by behavioral psychologists. The next step is deciding to actually use such laws. Why wouldn't managers want to use them? One reason is that the concepts of prediction and control of human behavior run counter to deeply ingrained beliefs about free will. Managers are caught in the dilemma of wanting to predict and control behavior while simultaneously retaining the popular concept of free will. Managers want results in terms of changes in behavior, but they don't want to believe that all behavior can be changed.

Many of the earlier management theories were able to disguise this dilemma by using vague language and socially acceptable jargon. Behavioral psychologists, on the other hand, come directly to the point: if one is able to predict and control behavior, then behavior must be predictable and controllable, i.e., have causes and be determined.

Stated so bluntly, most managers *say* they don't believe it, but they *act* like they do. Ample evidence can be found in any business magazine or book devoted to human relations in business. With only minimal effort, one can translate most of the concepts found in these sources into the paradigm for laws of behavior: if the manager follows certain rules such as enhancing two-way communication, establishing certain kinds of communication networks, delegating greater responsibility, encouraging team management, etc., then the effectiveness of the manager and the work group will increase. To the extent that such techniques are valid, they are simply conveying accurate laws of human behavior. Managers want effective laws like these, but they don't want the assumption upon which successful laws must be based – that behavior is caused or determined by antecedent conditions.

Perhaps behavioral psychologists should follow the practice of previous writers and ignore such paradoxical thinking. One writer (Lefcourt, 1973) noted that it might be necessary to maintain the illusion of freedom of choice even if it doesn't exist. This argument parallels another which states that if there were not a God, it would be necessary to invent one; otherwise, released from their fear of God, people might become little devils or worse, real villains. In a similar manner, people who believe their lives are completely determined might become unproductive, introverted, or depressed.

Maintaining the illusion of freedom would be acceptable, provided it didn't prevent the discovery and application of laws. Unfortunately, reluctance to believe that laws of behavior exist probably does interfere with the willingness of some managers to utilize them. For this reason, managers need to confront this issue directly. It cannot be ignored, as writers have tried to do in the past.

Perhaps even greater obstacles to the widespread utilization of behavioral techniques in business are the problems of how and when such laws should be utilized once they are known, the reactions people may have when they are used, and the form such laws may take. An extreme example illustrates the point. Several years ago a popular movie entitled "Clockwork Orange" appeared at theaters throughout the nation. It depicted a gang of violent youth in a futuristic society who raped, murdered, orgied, stole, and assaulted at will. One of the gang was eventually apprehended and sent to prison. He volunteered to undergo psychological procedures designed to make him ill at the sight of violence and indiscriminate sex. The procedures worked. He was released and through an extraordinary set of coincidences ran into the very people who hated him most. In the end, the government apologized for so mistreating him and initiated procedures that would return him to his formerly violent ways.

The most interesting aspect of the movie for many psychologists wasn't the plot or even the psychological techniques; it was the audience reaction. The reactions were always the same, and they mirrored the reactions of columnists who reviewed the movie: wild applause when the poor fellow was returned to his "naturally" violent state from which the psychologists had changed him.

One need not go to the movies to see a similar drama unfold. In real life, behavior modification has been used in prisons, and the same sort of negative reaction has followed. In the mid seventies, about the same time as the movie, the Law Enforcement Assistance Administration ordered federal support for behavior modification programs in correctional institutions curtailed. Congressional committees were called to examine the situation.

What kind of programs caused such an uproar? One such program was described by Trotter (1974). Participation was voluntary, and only those who were least likely to respond favorably to traditional treatment programs were permitted to enroll. Why would anyone object to such a program? It wasn't because it involved aversive techniques. Punishment wasn't used. The program incorporated only positive reinforcement: praise, credits to buy or rent what one wanted, etc. It couldn't have been because the program was ineffective, because if that was the only problem, it wouldn't have elicited the degree of controversy it did or explain similar attacks on other programs, some of which clearly worked.

A more likely explanation lies in the terminology utilized in behavioral programs. Many of the laws upon which behavior modification is based were initially discovered in laboratories by psychologists working with animals. When it was later found that the techniques worked in modified form with humans, the cold, scientific-sounding terminology remained. Terms like behavior modification, control, reinforcement, engineered settings, contingency management, schedules of reinforcement, shaping, generalization, and so forth have an unfamiliar and somewhat ominous sound to the person who doesn't know what they mean.

Asher (1974) made this point some time ago, when he said: "Yet Krasner believes many behaviorists (including himself) have asked for trouble by remaining insensitive to the social consequences of their theories and slogans [p. 3]." Asher suggested that a new terminology be developed so people wouldn't confuse the aversive chemical methods of "Clockwork Orange" with the non-aversive, positive methods used in most current programs.

A change in terminology might help. Other management theories and techniques certainly have a more pleasant ring to them. Consider some of the topics in the traditional management literature: The Psychology of Success and Failure; The Human Side of Enterprise; Managerial Behavior and Interpersonal Competence; Interpersonal Communication; Organizational Leadership; New Patterns of Leadership for Tomorrow's Organizations, Is Help Helpful?; The Ideal of Individualism and the Reality of the Organization; Job Enlargement, Individual Differences and Worker Responses; Employee Reactions to Job Characteristics; and What Makes the Other Guy Tick?

All of these titles sound innocent enough, but isn't the point in every case, *if* the manager follows the advice given in this article, *then* the behavior of the employee will be changed in the desired direction? If, in fact, these techniques really proved to be successful, would employees continue to believe that their behavior wasn't being controlled? Sooner or later the semantic cover on any truly effective method of behavioral control is likely to be blown.

So long as the advice that psychologists gave the business world was only mildly effective or ineffective, there was no problem. Now, however, books like this one are beginning to provide advice and demonstrate through tangible data that there are methods that actually work. Psychologists will increasingly be able to go to organizations and state that they can change the behavior that concerns managers. They will ask for the opportunity to change the organization in the light of cold, hard facts supported by data. What will be the reaction of managers? Do they really want to know?

ETHICS OF BEHAVIOR MODIFICATION

The question of whether managers really want to know how to control behavior takes us from the issue of assumptions to the issue of ethics. If behavior modification achieves its apparent potential, managers and psychologists in industrial/organizational settings will encounter ethical issues they could pretty much ignore in the past. Effective methods of control are more threatening then ineffective methods. Moreover, as practically every writer of a behavioral text notes, there exist fairly widespread misconceptions about what behavior modification is and how it is usually applied.

There are numerous past instances in which application of behavioral principles to mental health facilities, prisons, and schools prompted strong negative reactions and even the banning of funds. Just recently the director of a federal program advised this writer to avoid any use of the term "behavior modification" on an application, even if it meant deleting information about relevant research or experience. Similar reactions could easily occur in business settings, where governmental regulation of practices and policies is extensive. It seems probable that legal issues will also be raised, just as they were when behavior modification was applied to other institutions (see Budd & Baer, 1976 and Friedman, 1975 for extensive discussions on legal issues in other settings).

One approach to such problems is to answer "No" to the question: "Do managers really want to know?" In the long run, however, the strategy of avoidance is unlikely to work. In general, ignorance is not preferred over knowledge, and knowledge once gained will be applied. The real question is what can be done to insure that the application of behavior modification to industrial/organizational settings will be done in an ethically acceptable manner. Part of the task involves correcting misconceptions about behavior modification so that people will begin discussing real issues rather than phony ones.

Common Misconceptions

It is beyond the scope of this paper to catalog the many issues and misunderstandings that are relatively easily answered by behavior modifiers. A few will be presented to give some idea of the form they take and the answers that are given.

Isn't it unethical to modify another individual's behavior? Behavior modifiers note that we modify the behavior of other people all the time, both in our personal and professional lives. Parents influence their children, and children influence their parents. Friends modify each other's behavior in countless ways. Educators utilize assignments to enhance the educational development of children and rules and regulations to influence their social behaviors. Clubs and organizations utilize social pressure to alter behavior, even to the extent of persuading members to espouse various doctrines and wear unusual attire. Ask any manager for the best way to get employees to do their work, and you are sure to get a ready answer. Even in what we term a free society, our government exerts strong controls through licensing, fines, tax laws, traffic laws, criminal and civil codes, mandatory schooling, and countless other regulations and restrictions.

The need for such attempts to modify behavior is stated nicely by Schein (1980): "First of all, it is important to recognize that the very idea of organizing stems from the fact that the individual alone is unable to fulfill all of his or her needs and wishes. . . . The largest organization, society, makes it possible, through the coordination of the activities of many individuals, for all of its members to fulfill their needs (pp. 12-13)." Stated this way, it becomes obvious that some degree of control is not only present in most activities, but desirable. Indeed, it is difficult to imagine how anyone could avoid influencing others or being influenced by others. Even a hermit is likely to find that sooner or later someone will decide to do something to the land the hermit occupies. The issue of modifying behavior is not unique to behavior modification. We live with it daily and accept it.

Isn't behavior modification worse than some other methods because it is planned rather than unplanned – intentional rather than unintentional? Many ways in which we influence the behavior of others are indeed unintentional. Leaders of a social organization, for example, may not plot the methods by which they get members to accept certain values or life styles, but the end result may in fact be strict adherence to certain modes of behavior. Does the lack of understanding about the methods by which behavior is being modified make them more acceptable? On the surface, it may seem so. We prefer to believe that we behave in certain ways because we choose to do so and not because someone else has made the decision for us. But if the methods used by others are effective in changing our behavior, do we really have any greater choice if they were unknown to these people than if they were known? Obviously not.

One of the ethical guidelines which has been established for behavior modification in treatment settings is that the patient be aware of the type of treatment and its goals before it is applied (Stolz and Associates, 1978). If anything, behavior modification applied in this manner is more honest and open because it is intentional. Unintentional methods of changing behavior that are effective may actually pose a greater threat because we aren't aware of how we are being changed and what the end result will be. Moreover, at the organizational level such as in government, institutions, and business, planned change has always been the goal. Laws and regulations are made with the intention of modifying behavior. Traditional business practices are established with the intention of influencing behavior. Behavior modification differs little in terms of planning or intention, except perhaps in more openly admitting what it is doing.

Aren't the techniques of behavior modification more objectionable than the techniques associated with other methods? This concern arises primarily from popularized accounts of some applications (and misapplications) of behavior modification. Newspapers, magazines, and books tell of electric shock, aversive drugs, whippings, starvation, consignment to bleak rooms, and the like. Make no mistake, such incidents have occurred under the guise of behavior modification, though they are rarer than the proportion of press coverage might lead one to believe. It should be noted, however, that such incidents have occurred under the name of many other psychological methods as well. Behavior modification hardly has a corner on the market of aversive techniques, nor has it been misapplied to greater extents than other methods. The fact is that the vast majority of programs utilizing behavior modification emphasize pleasant methods for altering behavior. The basic principle underlying most behavior modification programs is that people behave in certain ways because of what they get out of it, and most programs are designed to insure that people achieve what they want. One reason people in industry have not accepted behavior modification as rapidly as they might is because industry, by and large, is based on aversive practices: threats of job loss, lowered pay, lack of promotion, criticism, and the like.

Behavior modification emphasizes positive practices: praise, recognition, positive feedback, promotion, etc. It has been difficult to persuade managers who are accustomed to barking orders and complaining about mistakes to turn around and praise peoples' efforts and design conditions for success. The kinds of techniques most frequently used in behavior modification programs are certainly no more objectionable than other methods, and this is particularly true in the case of applications to industrial/organizational settings. One final point: perhaps the most objectional method of all is one that promises an employee or employer a better life, but fails to achieve it. To the extent that behavior modification works, it should be seen as a better method than those that offer only empty promises.

Wouldn't a successful program of behavior modification cause people to lose their individuality? The ultimate goal of any scientific endeavor is complete understanding of the laws governing the behavior of a certain set of objects or events. As noted previously, explanation, prediction, and control all hinge on knowing relevant laws. Prediction differs from explanation in that one must know the laws and antecedent conditions before an event occurs. Control is even more difficult, because in addition to being able to predict, one must be able to change the antecedent conditions in such a way that the appropriate laws will operate.

The concern about loss of individuality, or what some critics refer to as the creation of "robot people," may be valid from some abstract, theoretical standpoint, but it hardly coincides with what behavior modifiers can do or want to do either now or in the foreseeable future. The issues of what behavior modifiers can do and want to do are so important that they will be analyzed separately.

What behavior modifiers can do. The experimental approach to the study of human behavior is barely a century old. Despite impressive gains, it would be foolish to believe that the current level of knowledge is anything more than primitive compared to what will be known after another century of study. Practically speaking, this means that current methods for producing the kind of rigid control some people fear simply don't exist. Even if one disagrees with this premise and believes we have discovered all the necessary laws and their subtle variations, there is another important factor which would prohibit strict control; we often don't know or can't control all the antecedent conditions.

Consider once again the plight of the physicist who wants to predict (much less control) the point of landing of a feather dropped from the Washington Monument. In this case, the physicist almost certainly knows all the relevant laws affecting its flight. The physicist can even measure many of the antecedent conditions like surface area, weight, and structure of the feather, as well as direction and velocity of the prevailing wind, distance from the ground, and the exact point and nature of the release. Nevertheless, a perfectly accurate prediction would be close to impossible due to the sheer number of antecedent conditions and their mode of interaction as the feather drops.

The behavioral scientist is confronted with an analogous situation when it comes to predicting and controlling much of behavior. The antecedent conditions are so vast and variable that precise prediction and control are seemingly impossible.

In the face of such complexity and resultant uncertainty, one might question whether the term "control" should be used at all. Instead, terms like "influence," "modify," and so forth might seem more appropriate. They better convey the fact that predictive accuracy is by no means absolute, that antecedent conditions or laws that are unknown or haven't been considered may intervene to alter the predicted result.

Despite the fact that most behavior modifiers would agree with the preceding argument, there is a widespread tendency for writers to use the term "control." The reason for this is probably because they don't equate control with absolute control. In everyday life, we talk of controlling all sorts of inanimate objects from automobiles to typewriters, yet they sometimes behave in ways that differ greatly from our expectations. The degree and precision of control can vary widely, and everyone recognizes this. Still, somehow, when the term "control" is shifted from inanimate objects to humans, there arises a sense of discomfort. For this reason, writers of behavioral literature should probably try to substitute terms like "influence" for "control." This should help alleviate some of the irrational concerns some people have about the possibility of control in any absolute sense or the image of robot people. In addition, writers should attempt to educate readers to what the term really means when it appears in behavioral writings and to be clearer about the degree to which behavior can be influenced.

What behavior modifiers want to do. The preceding assurances that behavior modification can influence behavior but not control it completely may be small comfort to some. The fact that these techniques appear to be more powerful than any utilized previously and their apparent potential for exerting even greater influence are enough to bother some people. In response to this, it can be noted that even if fairly precise control were possible, there would be little reason to significantly alter most of the behavior that results in people's individuality. Consider the quality control standards at a plant that manufactures cheap plastic model airplane engines as compared to one that produces real engines whose performance determines the safety of hundreds of people. In the latter case, tolerances have to be very precise, and considerable amounts of money are spent to insure they are. In the former case, it would be foolish to worry about such precision.

Successful management is in an analogous position. Some behavior must follow rather exacting standards, but it would be foolish to try to influence many other kinds of irrelevant behaviors, even if one could.

Consider another example based on an actual case. A district manager of gasoline stations wanted to stop declining sales. He felt that the key was to insure that customers received prompt service. He began by giving the attendants a pep talk. When this failed, he went the opposite direction and chewed them out. When service failed to improve, he instituted rules prohibiting attendants from socializing, reading, eating, and talking on the telephone. He began spying on attendants from several blocks away through powerful binoculars and firing those he caught breaking the rules. Still he heard complaints about poor service. Sales continued to drop.

Suppose the manager had used instead a method based upon behavior modification incorporating positive reinforcement. The simplest method might be to devise a simple feedback sheet upon which attendants checked sales and evaluated their performance against a standard. If sales increased by a certain amount, they would receive a bonus. This should increase such behaviors as fast and friendly service which were relevant to the goal.

Which system permits the greater freedom for the expression of individual behavior? In the first case, the employee had the option of sitting at a desk and doing nothing until a customer appeared or being fired. In the second case, the employee had the freedom to do anything, but received positive reinforcement for behaviors that were essential to the goal.

The effective management of behavior need not restrict individuality. It does require greater attention to what behaviors are important and what are not. This involves both practical and ethical considerations and will be discussed in greater depth later. The important point here is that behavior modification *per se* should not lead to less individuality. Indeed, successful methods for influencing behavior are likely to produce greater individuality. Imprecise methods are the ones that force managers to alter a whole range of behaviors, including many behaviors irrelevant to the goal.

Can't behavior modification be misused? Any method that is effective in changing behavior can be misused. The real question is whether there is something inherent in behavior modification that makes it more of a threat than other methods. One might argue, for example, that to the extent that behavior modification is more effective than other methods, it has greater potential for misuse. There are several reasons why this argument should be rejected.

In the first place, in a situation where behavioral management is clearly warranted and necessary, ineffective methods represent a far greater threat than effective ones. For example, in the industrial setting, people's jobs and standard of living depend upon the successful functioning of the company, which in turn depends upon effective methods of behavioral management. Ineffective methods are a threat to the survival of the company and to the people who depend upon the company for their livelihood.

Second, behavior modification is a two-way process. Workers can modify the behavior of supervisors by using the same techniques that are used toward them: praise, work output, feedback, etc.

Third, good behavior modification programs do not require secrecy. Quite the opposite, the most effective programs are those in which the contingencies, goals, and consequences are clearly explained in advance. This further weakens the potential for misuse.

Finally, the emphasis on positive reinforcement as opposed to punishment further insures that, if anything, there will be less misuse within behavior modification programs than within many current practices that seem based upon fear, threats, arbitrary use of power, and criticism.

The Bottom Line on Popular Misconceptions

The preceding five questions typify the kinds of concerns many people express toward behavior modification. For these and others, writers in the field have developed fairly standard answers (see, for example, Grunbaum, 1952; Kaufmann, 1968; Luthans & Kreitner, 1975; Rogers & Skinner, 1956; Skinner, 1955-56; 1973). The bottom line to most of these concerns is that the ethical questions directed at behavior modification turn out upon analysis not to be unique to this approach at all, but are issues that should be raised when any technique is applied to the sphere of management. There remains, therefore, only one real question, and that is how one insures that any approach, regardless of its name or methods, is ethical. The remainder of this paper is devoted to this question.

Six Ethical Principles

Philosophers have debated the topic of ethics for centuries. In some ways it seems we are no closer to universal agreement than we were at the beginning. Some claim that statements of value can be grounded in empirical fact. Others opt for the view that ethical judgements are completely relative. Some suggest that majority rule should dictate ethical standards. Others suggest that a truly ethical system is one that protects the minority from the majority. And so it goes.

This paper makes no claim for a resolution to these fundamental issues. What it will do is try to outline some practical guidelines that seem to be consistent with currently accepted ethical standards.

During recent years, much has been written about ethical practices underlying the application of behavior modification to such settings as prisons, schools, and mental health facilities (see, for example, Krasner, 1976). Less has been written about the ethics of behavior modification in business settings, but the former can serve as a guide for the latter.

This is the approach to be taken in this paper. Six principles will be presented which, if followed, should help avoid some ot the ethical concerns which arose during previous applications of behavior modification to other settings.

Principle #1. The use of behavior modification appears to be least controversial when it makes use of positive rather than negative techniques, and when the techniques are applied to behaviors for which there is widespread agreement that behavioral management is justified.

A clear statement of this principle is contained in a set of guidelines established by May, Risley, Twardosz, Friedman, Bijou, and Wexler in 1976. The writers were members of a panel established in response to adverse publicity emanating from a token economy program for mentally retarded, delinquent, and disturbed boys. Under the ruse of using behavior modification techniques, the boys were subjected to fairly extreme deprivation, forced sexual acts, and various forms of severe physical punishment. The panel developed a three level system which varied according to the degree of controversy surrounding various techniques and the degree to which change might be questioned. The first level included techniques which posed little threat to the patient, for example positive reinforcement used to alter behavior in ways that were clearly in the patient's self-interest. The third level included aversive techniques such as electric shock for behaviors that may or may not have benefited the patient depending upon one's point of view. The second level covered techniques and changes in between the two extremes. The higher the level, the greater the ethical concern and need for controls which would insure ethical behavior by practitioners.

Applying these distinctions to the use of behavior modification in industry, it is clear that current techniques, as exemplified by the readings in this book, are based upon widely accepted, positive methods of control such as praise and feedback. This is not to say that unethical practices could not occur. Child labor laws, minimum wage, OSHA regulations, affirmative action guidelines, and so forth provide testimony to alleged abuses in the past. To the writer's knowledge, serious allegations of abuse have not been directed at the utilization of behavior modification in industry. Lest we feel smug at this point, it is important to note that this may be partially due to the fact that the explicit use of behavior modification in business settings is relatively new. Certain kinds of incentive systems, which are consistent with behavioral principles but weren't identified as behavior modification, have been opposed by managers, workers, and unions.

The message from problems arising in other facilities is clear. If we want to insure that our applications remain within clearly acceptable ethical standards, we must continue to rely on those techniques that are positive, widely accepted, and routine. Happily, applications of behavior modification to industry are almost always seen as being even more positive than many current techniques.

We must also insure that the techniques and benefits are in the self-interest of the people who are exposed to them. Increasing the productivity of workers through contingent use of praise and feedback would be seen as benefiting the workers if the praise led to more positive emotional responses than criticism, for example, if there was a greater sense of accomplishment as a result of seeing that reasonable goals were being achieved and if greater job security was obtained through the knowledge that the company was now more competitive with other firms. Sharing monetary gains is another way to insure that the benefits are in the self-interest of workers. Hamner and Hamner (1976) describe one such system in the city of Detroit. Sanitation workers were offered bonuses for increased efficiency. Savings due to the increased efficiency were split between the city and the workers.

On the other hand, if achievement of a particular goal simply adds to the amount of work and the setting of even higher goals, if job security is reduced by the need for fewer workers to accomplish the same output, and/or if increased profits or other gains are not filtered down to those who are responsible for them, then one must question whether the techniques are being used in an ethical way. The writer knows of one case where a supervisor attempted to reduce the length of coffee breaks through behavioral techniques. The supervisor's superior put an end to the project because the savings in time benefited neither the workers nor the company. It is important for people using behavioral techniques to consider both the kinds of techniques being used in order to insure that they bring about positive consequences to workers, and the behaviors being changed in order to insure that it is reasonable to have people behave in a certain way.

Principle #2. Behavior modification appears to be least controversial when participants in a program have full knowledge of the methods and goals, and when they have the opportunity to accept or reject such techniques.

There has long been a widespread tendency to distrust psychologists, to assume they are trying to change people without their knowledge. Early books like Vance Packard's (1957) *The Hidden Persuaders* and Martin Gross' (1962) *The Brain Watchers*, as well as countless others probably helped to forge and sustain such a belief. Like most popular beliefs, there is probably a kernel of truth to the charge. The APA (1979) *Ethical Standards of Psychologists* specifically addresses this topic, an admission that there is legitimate cause for concern. Research on attitudes has shown that warning a person of manipulative intent is likely to reduce the likelihood of attitude change, the implication being that people should not be forewarned of such efforts (Zimbardo, Ebbesen, & Maslach, 1977). On the other hand, some have argued that in order for behavioral techniques to be effective, people must be aware of the contingencies (Brewer, 1974).

Whatever the practical considerations of actually achieving change, one ethical guideline seems fairly clear-cut: techniques based upon full knowledge and unconstrained consent of people on whom the techniques are used are ethically acceptable.

Translating this to the business setting, the guideline is least problematical in the case of people who are applying for a job. They can either accept or reject an offer of employment based upon whether or not they are willing to participate in such a program. Such factors are always taken into consideration by applicants, only in this case the rules of the work environment happen to be based on behavior modification rather than some other approach.

For current employees, the best approach would be one in which there was actual participation in the design of the program. Another approach is that of contracting. The term itself probably originates from the business practice of precisely stating each party's roles and obligations. A behavioral contract specifies the conditions, goals, and procedures that will be utilized (DeRisi & Butz, 1977). The method has not received widespread attention in behavioral approaches to business, but it should, not only because it may be an effective tool, but because it is an excellent procedure for promoting ethical practices (Kazdin, 1980). Both employees and employers are provided the opportunity to discuss and negotiate their commitments to each other. There is not only full knowledge of the methods and goals, but the opportunity to accept or reject a specific contract. It is important, of course, to insure that all parties have equal bargaining power (Redd, Porterfield, & Anderson, 1979). If one side has no meaningful choice or alternative, then this ethical principle has not been met.

There is a common misconception that sound ethical practices while desirable in terms of some vague social ideal, actually work against the good of upper level management, investors, or the firm. One hears of unscrupulous practices which result in enormous wealth for given individuals or firms. While this may hold true in certain highly publicized cases, it is not true overall. Consider, for example, a typical manufacturing firm which suddenly lands a lucrative new account that demands substantial increases in the number of units produced. Suppose further that limitations in equipment and space prohibit adding new workers, but that substantial evidence indicates that present workers could meet the new demand if their work efficiency increased.

One method for achieving the new goals might be to shift workers from an hourly wage scale to a piece rate scale that would offer them the same wages if the new output was reached. This is consistent with the behavioral principles of immediate feedback and reinforcement for specific output. Chances are, however, that workers would oppose such a unilateral move. Management might be left with no alternative but to fire those who weren't willing to comply.

Such an approach would not be consistent with the second principle. In the first place, workers were not told why the company changed its methods or the reason behind the new goals. More importantly, workers did not have the opportunity to reject the new system.

A better approach would be to inform the workers or their representatives of the new account, and discuss alternative methods for responding to it. One alternative might be to reject the account, but this would probably not benefit the company or the individuals and might eventually lead the company to a state where it was no longer competitive with other firms. Another alternative might be to add a bonus system or a stock option system to the hourly wage scale. Yet another alternative would be to move to a piece rate system of compensation, but one which would raise the amount of compensation workers currently received in proportion to the increases in productivity. The latter two alternatives would cost the company more money, but is there any reason why the workers should not join other constituents who share some of the increased profits? Stated this way, it seems likely that workers would be willing to accept a new system and do what they could to make it work.

The cornerstone of all ethical practice is fairness. If what management proposes is perceived as fair, it is likely to be accepted by workers. The cornerstone of effective behavioral programs is finding consequences that are truly reinforcing. Fortunately, this is also the cornerstone of the ethical practice delineated by the second principle. Because of this, there is no reason to be secretive about what one is trying to do or to embark on methods unacceptable to workers. Sound ethical management is also sound behavioral practice.

Principle #3. Behavior modification appears to be least controversial when there is a clearly established need or reason for using it.

Homme and Tosti (1971) stated: "Either one manages the contingencies or they get managed by accident (p. 1-4)." Most often statements of this kind are used as arguments for increasing the frequency of use of behavior modification, but they may overstate the case. Our behavior is modified in countless ways, through rules, traditions, habits, laws, lines of authority, social status, etc. Granted, these modifications have not evolved in the planned, systematic, empirically-based fashion that a program in behavior modification might, but neither are they entirely accidental. Most of us lead reasonably well-organized lives without continual reference to behavioral principles. We may even take some comfort in the fact that a relatively wide range of behavior is possible due to the diversity of influencing factors and the relative inefficiency with which influence from any given source is exerted.

One sometimes gets the impression from the behavior modification literature that specific, planned influence is always better than the less structured kind we currently have.

Concern over the ethics of modifying behavior, particularly in institutionalized settings, has led to a different viewpoint, however. One now hears such statements as: "Patients should be provided the highest quality of life in the least restrictive environment." It seems likely that if behavior modification becomes widely practiced in industrial/organizational settings, a similar kind of principle will be adopted here as well. Ethical positions that have become well established in one area tend to generalize to emerging applications in other areas.

The example cited earlier of the supervisor who attempted to reduce tardiness following coffee breaks is relevant here. The few extra minutes that could be gained were of little benefit to the organization. The lack of specific behavioral control had no adverse effects in this case, nor are there any in countless other situations.

The third ethical principle is compatible with some of the so-called humanistic approaches to the study of people and certain aspects of what in the management literature is termed the human relations approach. These approaches often begin with the assumption that people are basically good, and that external methods of control should be avoided. Behaviorists reject the assumption of basic goodness and are more likely to begin by assuming that changes in an established program will be beneficial. From an ethical standpoint, perhaps it is fortunate that such a powerful method for changing behavior has arisen concurrently with schools of thought that are critical of external control. Behaviorists may reject ambiguous methods and jargon, but the starting point is a good one. In the industrial/organizational setting, the first question should not be, "How can behavior be changed?" but rather, "If there a problem that requires behavioral change?"

Consider an example which occurred recently in a hospital setting. The hospital sponsored a program in which volunteers, called candy stripers, donated several hours of their time each week to help patients. Most of the candy stripers were high school students who were interested in helping people or wanted to know more about the health professions. Their primary duties included talking to patients, bringing flowers to rooms from the lobby, and supplementing normal care in whatever ways they could.

In one unit of a hospital, the head nurse discovered that candy stripers sometimes arrived on the floor as much as half an hour late. In most cases, the tardiness was caused by unavoidable delays at school or having to do chores at home before coming to the hospital. As a rule, when candy stripers arrived late, they extended their hours, and indeed, many did so anyway, regardless of when they arrived.

The occasional tardiness apparently upset the head nurse, and she discovered a way which she felt would stop it. Off the lobby was an old punch clock that was still in working order. The candy stripers were given cards and told to punch-in when they arrived. Those who were late received a verbal thrashing. Unfortunately, the program didn't work as intended. All the candy stripers either quit or transferred to another unit.

Had the head nurse been more skilled in behavioral management, she might have utilized a positive method for reinforcing promptness and had more success, but the method *per se* isn't the important issue. The real issue is whether a program was needed at all. If the candy stripers performed some essential service that was affected by their occasional tardiness, or if late arrivals disrupted the routine of other personnel, then there would be reason to implement a program of behavioral change. On the other hand, if the occasional tardiness had little or no effect on the operation of the unit, then a program to modify behavior would be open to question.

The case illustrates a violation of the third principle. One could, no doubt, think of far more serious cases in which behaviors were changed simply because the techniques for change were available, or someone had personal preferences totally unrelated to the work which needed to be done. In some ways, though, the more minor the reason for attempting to change behavior, the worse it is from an ethical perspective. Once again, the congruence between ethical and practical considerations is apparent. Needless or capricious change is likely to arouse resentment, as the example shows. Necessary or reasonable change is likely to be accepted.

How does one decide when a behavioral program is necessary? This reduces to a comparison of alternatives. The important point here is that the option for change should be the one for which a case must be made rather than the reverse. The concept of comparing alternatives can be generalized even further and serves as the basis for the next major principle.

Principle #4. Behavior modification appears to be least controversial when all reasonable alternatives have been specified, and there is general agreement that a given alternative is best.

Sir Winston Churchill is purported to have said: "We conferred endlessly and futilely and arrived at the place from which we started. Then we did what we knew we had to do in the first place and we failed as we knew we would." The ethical nature of decisions cannot be judged in isolation. As the quote by Churchill acknowledges, even undesirable courses of action may prove necessary when viewed in terms of the alternatives. The well-known life boat game, which is used in courses to stimulate discussion and demonstrate group processes is an example of this concept. The game begins with the assumption that all the people in the group are on a life boat, and due to scarcity of supplies one must leave or everyone will die. Most groups choose the former alternative, whereupon the brunt of the discussion focuses upon what criteria to use in deciding who should leave and therefore face certain death. Neither alternative is acceptable in an absolute sense, but most groups reach the conclusion that one is more acceptable than the other.

In business, situations also arise where a given course of action becomes ethically acceptable only because the alternatives are worse. One would only rarely want to lay off workers, but if the alternative is failure of the business and loss of everyone's job, then it might become the most ethically acceptable alternative. No one likes to fire a person, but if the person's performance endangers the welfare, livelihood, or morale of significant groups of other people, then it may be the best course of action. Employees may strike, not because they prefer to be out of work, but because the alternative of unsafe conditions, low salary, or whatever is seen as even worse. Auto workers obviously don't want a freeze in salary, but if the alternative is failure of the business and loss of everyone's job, then they are likely to accept it. The decision to utilize a behavioral program in a given business setting is seldom made under the stress of such dire alternatives, nevertheless the principle of selecting the best available alternative in any situation is the same. It is important to realize that making no change at all can be as much of an ethical decision as changing current practices. For this reason, it is continually necessary to specify alternatives. Identification and selection among alternatives is the cornerstone of the ethical decision-making process.

Consider a situation in the hardware/outdoors department of a large retail store. Based on a complex formula including past sales at the present and similar stores, market conditions, etc., the central office sent figures of expected sales during the year for each department to the store manager, who relayed them to departmental supervisors.

In this case, a new supervisor had just replaced one who had been unable to achieve the expected sales. The primary reason appeared to be lack of effort in sales and service by the employees of the department. The new supervisor was confident of success because he felt he could establish a much friendlier relationship with the employees than the previous supervisor, and that this would motivate them to work harder. After several months, however, sales continued to fall increasingly below the quotas sent by the central office.

In order to follow the fourth ethical principle, the supervisor must consider the various alternatives. One alternative would be to do nothing. A second might be to check with the central office to make sure their expected sales figures were fair and accurate. A third might be to establish an effective behavioral program.

A simple behavioral program might consist of hanging a large chart in the staff lounge area. The chart could contain three lines: actual sales, company expectations, and goals set by the department. Each week the manager could meet with the employees to review the chart, note progress, discuss goals, and devise new methods for achieving goals. As an added incentive, employees who met or exceeded individual goals could be given state lottery tickets in proportion to their weekly contribution. The tickets would be more reinforcing than their purchase price because of the possibility of winning even larger amounts of money.

In considering the three alternatives, doing nothing is perhaps the least acceptable from an ethical standpoint. One supervisor has already been fired for failing to meet the stated sales quota, there is little reason to believe the same fate wouldn't greet the current supervisor for similar failure, and the jobs of the other employees would eventually be jeopardized as well, either due to policies by a desperate supervisor or perhaps by action of the store manager. In the long run, doing nothing places the jobs of all the employees at considerable risk. It does not seem to be an ethically acceptable choice.

The second alternative appears to be the least disruptive and controversial. It should probably be pursued first. If the central office is in error, then the problem may be solved. If it is not, then this information provides additional support for the need to institute a program of behavioral change, alternative three. Granted, the employees would have to work harder, but in return they would gain increased job security, a greater sense of participation in the establishment and maintenance of departmental goals, more immediate reinforcement in the form of lottery tickets, praise, recognition, increased feedback, and a greater sense of accomplishment as they meet short term goals.

In an actual case like the one described, the goals set by the central office were met for the first time in over a year during the first month of operation of a behavioral program similar to the one described. During each of the subsequent 6 months, the goals were exceeded by increasing amounts, and the department received special recognition from the company. The supervisor was promoted and transferred to a larger store. Although specific data are unavailable for what happened after the supervisor left, the present writer noted that during the subsequent year there was a rapid turnover in supervisors and employees in the department. Apparently the new supervisors discontinued the behavioral program with the result that sales and service again dropped to unacceptable levels. The correspondence between ethical and practical considerations is evident once again.

Principle #5. Behavior modification appears to be least controversial when the people who practice it are well informed about the ethical issues involved, can discuss the issues in an intelligent way, and strive to follow the established guidelines of their profession.

Any application of new knowledge can generate new ethical concerns. This seems particularly true of behavior modification. Hilts (1974) describes an incident in the Montgomery County, Maryland, school system which illustrates this point. One year after the institution of a program in one of the public schools, the *Washington Star* ran an article which said the program involved behavior modification. The program had passed easily under a different name, but once the label "behavior modification" was applied, a public outcry ensued. The school board began an intensive investigation which included public hearings for concerned parents. Eventually the program was permitted to continue because directors of the program were able to adequately address the ethical issues and show the program had merit.

This is not an isolated phenomenon. Stories abound among professionals about similar reactions to programs incorporating principles of behavior modification. Even if they want to do so, psychologists can no longer simply ignore ethical questions directed at their work. As Krasner (1964) warned us some time ago, "it is the psychologist-researcher who should undertake the task of contact with the public rather than leaving it to sensationalists and popularizers [p. 204]."

Psychologists must be able to respond to ethical concerns and take them into consideration before beginning their programs. Recognition of this principle is seen in the fact that most texts on behavior modification now include chapters on ethical issues. Graduate programs in psychology are increasingly adding courses on this topic. In a recent poll of APA-approved clinical psychology programs, Tymchuk, Drapkin, Ackerman, Major, Coffman, and Baum (1979) found that 67% offered formal courses in ethics compared to only 9% 22 years earlier. Over the last 15 years, the American Psychological Association issued several important documents on ethical standards (APA, 1967, 1973, 1974, 1977, 1979). A recent set of criteria for accreditation by the Council of Representatives of APA mandates instruction in professional ethics for every student in programs of professional psychology (APA Council of Representatives, 1979).

Some movement is also apparent in the business field. Although separate chapters on ethics are still relatively rare among texts in industrial/organizational psychology unless they are specifically oriented toward the behavior modification model, there is a perceptible increase in the number of statements about ethical and legal matters in the more traditional chapters. There are a number of recent texts specifically dealing with ethical issues in the business setting (Barry, 1979; Beauchamp & Bowie, 1979; Davis & Blomstrom, 1977; DeGeorge & Pichler, 1978; Donaldson & Werhane, 1979; Luthans, Hodgetts, & Thompson, 1976).

While few business schools offer courses in ethics at the present time (Donaldson, 1978), efforts are underway to rectify this situation. *The Philosophy Teacher's Handbook* has recently initiated a column/newsletter component entitled *Teaching Business Ethics*. Dill, Donaldson, Goodpaster, and May (1979) discuss preparation of syllabi for courses in management ethics, and The National Endowment of the Humanities has funded several similar projects.

All of this demonstrates increasing concern within both psychology and business over ethical matters. The increased discussion, study, and training should in itself help to insure that as behavior modification is increasingly applied to the industrial/organizational setting, it will be done with due consideration to important ethical questions.

While extensive, far reaching public concern has not yet arisen over the application of behavior modification to industrial settings, it is not difficult to imagine a situation in which it could occur. Consider a hypothetical example in the small computer industry. Prior to the spring of 1981, three companies (Tandy, Apple, and Commodore) had cornered a vast share of the market. Beginning in the spring of 1981, several Japanese firms began entering the field in a decisive way, providing stiff competition for the established firms and others based in the United States which are contemplating entering the market. The key to meeting this challenge may well rest on improved management techniques. Such techniques may have to be radically different than those used in the past.

Suppose a firm decided to meet the challenge by embarking on an ambitious program involving behavior modification. The details of such a program will not be discussed, however they would certainly want to include the Premack Principle, transitional contingency contracting, feedback, recognition, praise, and possibly an incentive system with monetary or monetary based reinforcement. Such a program would represent a major shift in traditional management practice. It would hardly go unnoticed by those involved in it or the media, particularly if it was labeled behavior modification. Management would not have the option of ignoring the ethical issues that would be raised. It would have to respond in clear, sensible, reassuring ways. Managers would need to know and be able to express not only the technical principles underlying behavior modification, but why they are compatible with good ethical practice. If behavioral psychologists aren't prepared to train managers to cope with the ethical issues, then there is little likelihood that behavioral programs of this scope will commence or continue for very long.

Principle #6. Behavior modification appears to be least controversial when it advances and supports personal and social ideals held by people.

Early in this paper, mention was made of the semantic problem confronting behavior modifiers. The language used to describe many of the ideals upon which our society is based defies simple translation into observable, behavioral events. Skinner (1971), in part, attempted such a task in *Beyond Freedom and Dignity*. Rather than allaying fears and apprehensions among non-psychologists, he seems to have increased them. People at both ends of the political spectrum, from conservative politicians to antiwar activists, united in their criticism of this work. The criticism itself could be explained using behavioristic jargon by alluding to conditioned emotional reactions to certain phrases and words. Unfortunately, such an explanation, even if it is valid, doesn't necessarily reduce the discomfort people feel. Likewise, it seems unlikely that behavioral psychologists will to able to produce rapid, radical changes in the way people utilize and react to such words. Concepts like human rights, freedom, liberty, equality, justice, dignity, self-worth, and respect are not going to be replaced by words and phrases like schedules of reinforcement, contingencies, generalization, goal gradients, discriminative stimuli, and so on. The great speeches and statements like The Gettysburg Address, The Declaration of Independence, and The Bill of Rights are not going to be translated into terms that are definable by observed entities and events. People may not know exactly what abstract concepts mean, but they do know how they feel about them, and in many cases are even willing to pay the ultimate individual price in their defense.

It is quite possible that behavioristic methods will never be accepted and utilized extensively in industrial/organizational settings unless its practitioners can rise above their own language and technical precision. They may need to say the things they feel – that they care about people, value their individuality, and respect their dignity, goals, and aspirations – even if these terms defy easy or precise definition.

Krasner (1976) was correct in pointing out how unfortunate it is that behaviorists haven't more strongly resisted the dichotomy some writers have established between behaviorism and humanism. In their concern for precision, behavioral psychologists have conveyed the impression that humans *per se* aren't that important; they simply have more advanced motor skills than rats or pigeons. A larger perspective is needed. There is no point to increasing efficiency in the work place or the amount of positive reinforcement in the environment if in the process we lose that indefinable sense of our humanity. People distrust any system or theory that denies the reality they feel inside, because for them that is the only true reality. It is the only reality they directly sense.

All of this may sound unbehavioristic, and perhaps it is. Let us not forget, however, that the scientific method is simply a tool, an extremely effective one, but still a tool for understanding our environment and determining our fate. Science isn't people. It is a creation of people to achieve their ends. Psychologists and managers must use the science of behavior modification to enhance the quality of human life, not to demean, denounce, or devalue our humanness.

The goals and ideals relating to industrial/organizational settings are difficult to define. On the one hand, there are pronouncements like that of Charles Wilson, former Secretary of Defense: "What is good for business is good for the country." The emphasis in such statements is on what the individual can and should do for business. On the other hand, some writers emphasize what business can and should do for the individual (Elbing and Elbing, 1967), and how individuals can satisfy their own goals while working within a company (Schoonmaker, 1968). Behaviorism does not really take a stance on such issues, but behaviorists must. Behaviorism provides the tools for achieving ends. Behaviorists, as managers or managerial consultants, must take positions on those ends.

There is nothing inherent in behaviorism which prevents practitioners from being concerned about personal and social ideals. Sloane, Staples, Cristol, Yorkston, and Whipple (1975) reported an interesting comparison between behavior therapists and psychoanalytically-oriented psychotherapists. On a series of standard scales scored by independent raters, behaviorists were found to demonstrate equal degrees of warmth or unconditional positive regard as the psychotherapists. On several other scales, behavior therapists actually scored significantly higher than the psychoanalytically-oriented psychotherapists, including those for accurate empathy and interpersonal contact. Behavior therapists also conveyed more genuine feeling and a greater sense of meaning what they said.

Such findings contradict public stereotypes of behaviorists as people who see others as automatons or objects to be manipulated. There is no reason to believe behaviorists in industrial/organizational settings would demonstrate any lesser concern for individuals and their personal and social beliefs. In this respect, it is important for behaviorists to have a good understanding of the environment in which people work and the commonly accepted goals and ideals of people in an organization. It means understanding the language that people and organizations use to describe their values and aspirations. It means seeking ways to integrate such concepts, attitudes, and feelings into programs. If this can be done, it will provide clear evidence that our behavioral programs seek to follow high ethical standards.

SUMMARY AND CONCLUSIONS

Despite changes in emphasis through the years, the task of management has always been the modification of human behavior. From this standpoint, behavior modification raises few ethical concerns that should not have been raised about any of the past techniques for behavioral management. Nevertheless, experience in other settings suggests that the application of behavior modification to industrial/organizational settings will generate increased concern over ethical issues, partly because of negative associations in the general public's mind regarding behavior modification, partly because behavior modification raises the question of control in more specific terms than some of the older methods, and partly because even its critics admit that behavior modification may be more successful than most previous methods in actually producing planned behavioral change.

In light of this situation, managers will be forced to confront the question, "Do you really want to know how to control behavior?" In some cases the answer is likely to be "No." Managers will prefer outmoded and less effective methods simply because they raise less controversy. On the other hand, history tells us that the acquisition of new knowledge continues despite society's objections and fears. Indeed, acquisition of knowledge appears to be one of the most fundamental qualities underlying human nature. It seems equally apparent from a historical perspective that once knowledge is gained, it is used. Hence, whatever answers individual managers may give at present, in the long run, if behavior modification achieves its apparent potential, its use in industrial/organizational settings will continue to grow. The need for ethical standards to guide such usage will also increase.

Currently, chapters on ethical concerns in the application of behavior modification to industrial/organizational settings seem to be directed primarily at correcting common misconceptions about the method and its typical applications. Once this is accomplished, the task for the future will be to establish guidelines and procedures that can direct new programs. This task has already been undertaken in some other settings, but is only just begun in the industrial/organizational area. Eventually, rather detailed and specific principles are likely to appear. The present paper represents a modest beginning for such efforts.

Six recommendations have been introduced: (1) using relatively routine procedures which emphasize positive rather than negative types of control; (2) assuring that all participants in programs are fully aware of the procedures and goals and have the opportunity to accept or reject participation; (3) beginning any program with the question of whether there is a clearly established need or reason for using it; (4) specifying all reasonable alternatives and reaching general consensus that a given alternative is best; (5) increasing the ability of practitioners to analyze the ethical questions inherent in such applications; and (6) being sensitive to how programs advance and support personal and social ideals. If these are followed, current and future applications of behavior modification in industrial/organizational environments should avoid many of the controversies which arose in other settings. Properly utilized, behavior modification offers great hope and promise to industries and organizations in achieving their goals and to individuals in achieving a higher quality of life in the work place.

REFERENCES

American Psychological Association. *Casebook on ethical standards of psychologists.* Washington, D.C.: Author, 1967.

American Psychological Association. *Ethical principles in the conduct of research with human participants.* Washington, D.C.: Author, 1973.

American Psychological Association. *Standards for educational and psychological tests.* Washington, D.C.: Author, 1974.

American Psychological Association. *Standards for providers of psychological services.* Washington, D.C.: Author, 1977.

American Psychological Association. *Ethical standards of psychologists.* Washington, D.C.: Author, 1979.

APA Council of Representatives. *Criteria for accreditation of doctoral training programs and internships in professional psychology.* Washington, D.C.: American Psychological Association, 1979.

Asher, J. 'Behavior Mod' defiled. *APA Monitor*, 1974, **5** (9 & 10), 3.

Barry, V. *Moral issues in business.* Belmont, CA: Wadsworth, 1979.

Beauchamp, T. L., & Bowie, N. W. (Eds.) *Ethical theory and business.* Englewood Cliffs, N.J.: Prentice-Hall, 1979.

Berthold, H. C. What makes the other guy tick? Do you really want to know? *Quality Progress*, 1975, **8** (6), 20-21, 34.

Brewer, W. F. There is no convincing evidence for operant or classical conditioning in adult humans.

In W. B. Weimer & D. S. Palermo (Eds.), *Cognition and the symbolic processes.* Hillsdale, N.J.: Erlbaum, 1974.

Budd, D. C., & Baer, D. M. Behavior modification and the law: Implications of recent judicial decisions. *Journal of Psychiatry and Law,* 1976, **4**, 171-244.

Davis, K., & Blomstrom, R. *Business and society: Environment and responsibility.* New York: McGraw-Hill, 1977.

DeGeorge, R. T., & Pichler, J. A. (Eds.) *Ethics, free enterprise, and public policy: Original essays on moral issues in business.* New York: Oxford University Press, 1978.

DeRisi, W. J., & Butz, G. *Writing behavioral contracts: A case simulation practice manual.* Champaign, IL: Research Press, 1975.

Dill, D. D., Donaldson, T. J., Goodpaster, K. E., & May, W. W. *Syllabi for the teaching of management ethics.* New Haven, CT: Society for Values in Higher Education, 1979.

Donaldson, T. Ethics in the business schools: A proposal. *National Forum,* 1978, **58** (3), 11-14.

Donaldson, T., & Werhane, D. H. *Ethical issues in business: A philosophical approach.* Englewood Cliffs, N.J.: Prentice-Hall, 1979.

Elbing, A. O. *Behavioral decisions in organizations.* (2nd ed.) Glenview, IL: Scott, Foresman, 1978.

Elbing, A. O., Jr., & Elbing, C. A. *The value issue of business.* New York: McGraw-Hill, 1967.

Friedman, P. R. Legal regulation of applied behavior analysis in mental institutions and prisons. *Arizona Law Review,* 1975, **17**, 39-104.

Gross, M. L. *The brain watchers.* New York: Random House, 1962.

Grunbaum, A. Causality and the science of human behavior. *American Scientist,* 1952, **40**, 665-676.

Hamner, W. C., & Hamner, E. P. Behavior modification on the bottom line. *Organizational Dynamics.* 1976, **4** (4), 8-21.

Hilts, P. J. *Behavior Mod.* New York: Harper & Row, 1974.

Homme, L., & Tosti, D. *Behavior technology: Motivation and contingency management.* San Rafael, CA: Individual Learning Systems, 1971.

Jacobs, F., & Phillips, D. Beyond the little red schoolhouse. *Change,* 1979, **11** (5), 5-15.

Kaufmann, H. *Introduction to the study of human behavior.* Philadelphia: Saunders, 1968.

Krasner, L. Behavior control and social responsibility. *American Psychologist,* 1964, **17**, 199-204.

Krasner, L. Behavioral modification: Ethical issues and future trends. In H. Leitenberg (Ed.), *Handbook of behavior modification and behavior therapy.* Englewood Cliffs, N.J.: Prentice-Hall, 1976.

Kazdin, A. E. *Behavior modification in applied settings.* (Rev. ed.) Homewood, IL: Dorsey Press, 1980.

Lefcourt, H. M. The function of the illusions of control and freedom. *American Psychologist,* 1973, **28**, 417-425.

Luthans, F., Hodgetts, R. M., & Thompson, K. R. *Social issues in business.* New York: Macmillan, 1976.

Luthans, F., & Kreitner, R. *Organizational behavior modification.* Glenview, IL: Scott, Foresman, 1975.

May, J. G., Risley, T. R., Twardosz, S., Friedman, P., Bijou, S. W., & Wexler, D. *Guidelines for the use of behavioral procedures in state programs for retarded persons.* Arlington, Texas: National Association for Retarded Citizens, 1976.

Packard, V. *The hidden persuaders.* New York: McKay, 1957.

Redd, W. H., Porterfield, A. L., & Anderson, B. L. *Behavior modification: Behavioral approaches to human problems.* New York: Random House, 1979.

Rogers, C. R., & Skinner, B. F. Some issues concerning the control of human behavior: A symposium. *Science,* 1956, **124**, 1057-1066.

Schein, E. H. *Organizational psychology.* (3rd. ed.) Englewood Cliffs, N.J.: Prentice-Hall, 1980.

Schoonmaker, A. N. Individualism in management. *California Management Review,* 1968, **11** (2), 9-22.

Skinner, B. F. Freedom and the control of men. *American Scholar,* Winter 1955-1956, **25**, 47-65.

Skinner, B. F. *Beyond freedom and dignity*. New York: Alfred A. Knopf, 1971.

Skinner, B. F. Answers for my critics. In H. Wheeler (Ed.), *Beyond the punitive society*. San Francisco: W. H. Freeman, 1973.

Sloane, R. B., Staples, F. R., Cristol, A. H., Yorkston, J. J. & Whipple, K. *Psychotherapy versus behavior therapy*. Cambridge, Mass.: Harvard University Press, 1975.

Stolz, S. B. and Associates. *Ethical issues in behavior modification*. San Francisco: Jossey-Bass, 1978.

Trotter, S. ACLU scores token economy. *APA Monitor*, 1974, **5,** (8), 1;7.

Tymchuk, A. J., Drapkin, R. S., Ackerman, A. B., Major, S. M., Coffman, E. W., & Baum, M. S. Survey of training in ethics in APA-approved clinical psychology programs. *American Psychologist*, 1979, **34,** 1168-1170.

Zimbardo, P. G., Ebbesen, E. B., & Maslach, C. *Influencing attitudes and changing behavior*. (2nd ed.) Reading, Mass: Addison-Wesley, 1977.

22

Future Directions for Industrial Behavior Modification

Frank Andrasik   and   **J. Regis McNamara**
State University of New York   *Ohio University*
at Albany

Even though behavioral applications to organizations in the public and private sectors have been increasing since Aldis (1961) first suggested the potential for this approach, the area is still in an early phase of growth and development. The earliest beginnings of industrial behavior modification or organizational behavior management (OBM) were characterized by the straightforward applications of learning theory to conventional organizational problems. Case studies, within group manipulations, and an occasional well-controlled factorial project were representative of these early endeavors. These early projects served two major functions: (1) to increase awareness about the area, and (2) to provide an empirical and conceptual knowledge base upon which more sophisticated interventions could build. Recent content (Andrasik, Heimberg, & McNamara, in press; Babb & Kopp, 1978) and methodological reviews (Andrasik, 1979) of the OBM literature, as well as the chapters contained in this volume, indicate that the area has been born, is doing as well as can be expected for its age, and gives every indication of having a bright and promising future. In this chapter we discuss some of the directions OBM might travel in the future.

Developments in the near term are the most clearly discernible because they can be inferred from the amount of emphasis placed on current research activities. Literature reviews coupled with the prognostications of experts provide the means of looking into the future and anticipating what it will contain near term. Longer range predictions for OBM, however, are not firmly rooted in the present and require more of a sense of what is desirable or possible in the future. Both near and long range forecasts are speculative in nature, although short-term predictions are largely extensions of the present. As such, they require only a knowledge of the field and a sense of where it is likely to go. Longer range forecasts rely more on a sense of personal vision to construct tomorrow and are likely to be more similar to the work of futurologists or science fiction writers. The reason is that the activities of organizations in the long term will be influenced by many factors outside of the immediate confines of the organization. Several general factors need to be considered before future directions and issues directly associated with OBM are explored. First, OBM is but a small subset of the larger field of applied psychology. Applied psychology, as both science and profession, is intertwined with larger economic and sociopolitical areas of our society. Thus, before considering a possible tomorrow for OBM, some basic issues related to future industrial-organizational developments and current concerns of the industrial behavior modification field should be examined.

FACTORS INFLUENCING FUTURE DEVELOPMENTS

Increased Internationalization

Views on the future of America range from the extremely optimistic (Kahn, Brown, & Martel, 1976) to the very pessimistic (Meadows, Meadows, Randers, & Behrens, 1972). However, one area that will need to be addressed seems reasonably clear. Over the next 10 to 20 years the economic metaproblem that we will face as a nation is how to cope with and manage a "worldwide super-industrial economy" (Kahn & Phelps, 1979). This problem will most certainly create greater worldwide economic interdependence and increase the internationalization of American business.

As American-based multinational corporations develop or expand foreign-based operations, they will likely bring with them the motivation and management systems that seemed to have produced results in the United States. If OBM is one such system that is transported to a foreign operation, then special cultural considerations need to be given to the design and implementation of the OBM approach for that foreign country. Such an alteration is particularly important to consider in light of recent research which has found that elements of national culture influence the response to and effectiveness of management systems as they relate to such dimensions as incentives and promotions (Hofstede, 1980).

Technological Changes and Challenges

The widespread application of science and technology to our lives has undoubtedly affected the way we live and the quality of our lives in ways that were undreamed of 100 years ago. Although major improvements in our standard of living have been achieved, certain social costs have been evidenced also. Several technological innovations and solutions that were developed to solve problems have produced delayed negative effects or unanticipated consequences years and even decades later. Only recently, however, has awareness of the paradox between technological advance and its associated costs begun to be actively debated and studied.

At a federal level, the Office of Technology Assessment attempts to assess the potential impacts of selected new scientific applications early in their development. It does this in order to better understand and facilitate positive impacts, while attempting to inhibit the growth of negative consequences for that technology (Peterson, 1979). Other groups are similarly concerned about forecasting the usefulness and benefit of technological innovation. Nowhere is this attempt more evident than in a recent book that attempts to examine some of the forces that will shape and influence the world of work in the next century (Sheppard & Carroll, 1980).

OBM will be faced with several opportunities as well as challenges during the next decade of marked technological growth in business and industry. The need to develop educational and reinforcement systems which facilitate the introduction and appropriate use of high technology systems into an existing work force is already apparent. The very introduction of this technology, however, will likely displace a segment of the work force. The socially responsive behavioral manager needs to be aware of this likelihood and attempt through counseling, retraining, severance allowances, and/or outplacement employment services to assist the employee in overcoming the associated personal and economic distress.

Much of the current emphasis on improving productivity in the work place via behavioral means relies almost exclusively on increasing the output or effectiveness of the worker (Latham, Cummings, & Mitchell, 1981). In the future, increased automation and rapid advances in microelectronic technology will require greater consideration of ways to secure the most optimal interface between persons and machines. As such, behavioral psychologists and managers will need to work more directly with human factors, and systems engineers will need to better manage productivity.

Work and Work Force Changes

We are in the midst of a radical change in the way people earn and will earn a living. Most of the work force lived on farms 100 years ago. Today, fewer than 4% of the American people earn their livelihood this way. Over the last 50 years automation in the manufacturing and industrial sectors has produced declines in that labor force also. However, major increases in people working in the service and information sectors of our economy have been noted (See Kahn & Phelps, 1979). These trends are being accompanied by certain changes in the composition of the work force. Increased numbers of women, more highly educated workers, more professionals, technicians, and managers are likely to be part of the work force in the 1980s and beyond (Bass, 1972).

OBM may have several important roles to play with this new work force. Historic problems of sexism in the work place will need to be overcome for men and women to cooperate and participate fully in the organizational life of the future. Although discrimination remains a difficult social and organizational problem to manage, social learning models do exist (O'Connor, 1977) to guide future organizational interventions in this area. The presence of many highly trained and educated workers may also pose some interesting personnel problems for future organizations. It may well be that organizations will need to create stimulating and personally fulfilling work experiences in order to retain and utilize these human resources to their fullest. OBM could become involved in such a process by designing projects or task goals that would suit these workers' needs as well as those of the organization.

Acceptability and Accountability of OBM

A growing number of managers are becoming acquainted with the techniques and principles associated with the OBM approach. However, OBM is neither understood nor practiced in many sections of the business community. Factors that seem to account for this are the relative newness of the field and the strong competition from other practitioners and approaches in the marketplace. Acceptance of the approach has been further limited by the biases and misperceptions that have arisen about behavior modification itself.

As more individuals are trained in OBM and more firms offer consulting services that are behavioral in nature, better overall familiarity with the field can be expected. Biases and criticism of the field are likely to remain, however. One factor accounting for such bias seems to involve an interaction between pre-existing negative attitudes and the way in which behavior modification procedures are described (Barling & Wainstein, 1979). In order to remove or attenuate such reactivity to the terms of OBM, one set of behavior managers are simply replacing the labels "behavior," "punishment," "consequation," and "reinforcement" with the less emotion-laden terms "performance," "correcting," "follow-up," and "payoff and payoff analysis" (Rhoton, 1979). Assessing the receptivity of the target person or group toward OBM principles and terms seems like a prudent initial step to take in any future OBM intervention.

One of the strong suits of OBM has been its reliance on empirical analysis as a basis for program change and intervention. This among many other features of the approach has made it highly attractive to managers who are interested in objectively knowing about the usefulness of a given procedure. Several OBM programs have produced good outcomes at favorable cost-benefit returns to the organization (Adam, 1975; Bourdon, 1977; Emmert, 1978; Latham & Dossett, 1978). However, a persistent concern that has been articulated in both earlier (Schneier, 1974) and more recent (Andrasik et al., in press) OBM literature reviews is the need to document the comparative effectiveness of OBM with alternative organizational procedures. Only until such research is done will it be possible to determine the differential costs, benefits, and overall utility of the OBM approach to the organization.

FUTURE DIRECTIONS OF OBM

Perspectives of Individuals Within the Field

Two opinion polls providing views of the future of OBM have recently been reported in the literature. One of these was conducted by the present authors (Andrasik, McNamara, & Edlund, 1981) who solicited predictions from members of the editorial board of the *Journal of Organizational Behavior Management* and a small number of individuals actively engaged in research in behavior management (N = 37) – a sample judged to be "in the know." Respondents were specifically asked to identify the future needs of business and government and the kinds of approaches likely to meet these needs. When tabulating the survey results we lumped specific interventions or applications identified by respondents under more general category headings and presented only these general areas of application in the manuscript. Since the second opinion poll (to be discussed in a moment) listed specific areas of applications, we have re-examined responses to our survey and present them here in specific fashion so they can be compared more directly to the second survey. The specific areas for future application drawn from Andrasik et al. (1981) are presented in Table 22.1 in the rank order of their mention; applications assigned identical ranks were listed by the same number of survey respondents.

Frederiksen and Lovett's survey (1980) inquired about various areas and was administered to a larger number of individuals (159 members of OBM special interest groups within the Association of Advancement of Behavior Therapy and the Association for Behavior Analysis). One section of the questionnaire asked respondents to specify further opportunities for applying OBM in their respective work settings and, thus, is of interest here. Since participants were instructed to restrict their responses to their present work settings, the response generated may be somewhat constrained. Nonetheless, subject responses do provide some additional insights into areas for future in-roads and are reproduced by rank order in Table 22.1 along with the results from the Andrasik et al. (1981) survey.

One conclusion is readily apparent from examination of the survey responses – the areas predicted to be of importance for tomorrow are occupying much of the field's attention today. The statement, "the best predictor of future behavior is past behavior," again holds. Respondent personal biases notwithstanding, we believe most of the areas identified will continue to be actively studied by individuals within the field of OBM. Many of these areas identified for continued application and development are the subject of chapters in this text and need no further discussion here. A few emerging areas of application not covered in previous sections of this text merit further, albeit brief, discussion here. These include behavioral self-management, energy conservation, customer service behavior, occupational safety, and worker and employee theft.

Perhaps the most recently developing area concerns application of behavioral principles to oneself. Two articles have recently appeared in the literature on this topic, and

TABLE 22.1. Future Applications of OBM: Comparisons Between Two Surveys on the Basis of Rank Order.

Application	Andrasik, McNamara, & Edlund (1981)	Frederiksen & Lovett (1980)
Increase individual employee productivity	1	1
Improve employee training procedures	2	3
Help produce and direct organizational change	3	3
Improve employees' abilities to self-manage	5	–
Train specialists in OBM	5	–
Modification of anti-health behaviors	5	–
Increase conservation of energy	8.5	–
Improve the climate of organizations	8.5	–
Increase staff communication with management	8.5	7.5
As a basis for job descriptions/job evaluations	8.5	3
Increase consumer satisfaction	14.5	9.5
Increase use of safety precautions	14.5	11
Establishment of cost control procedures	14.5	5
Increase the productivity of the entire organization	14.5	6
Assist employees in developing satisfying leisure-time activities	14.5	–
Increase employee morale	14.5	9.5
Provide behavioral counseling to employees with personal problems	14.5	–
Improve customer service behavior	14.5	–
Increase attendance/reduce tardiness	–	7.5

although the articles have much in common, each points out somewhat different reasons for bringing self-management technology into the workplace. Manz and Sims (1979) suggest that development of effective self-management by subordinates can serve as a "substitute for leadership" (Kerr & Jermier, 1978) for the manager. Luthans and Davis (1979) view behavioral self-management as the "missing link in managerial effectiveness" and thus place more emphasis on the gains directly accrued by the manager who applies self-management strategies in his or her daily work routine. Even though there is limited support for the utility of this approach (Lamal & Benfield, 1978), the potential uses of behavioral self-management are many (see Andrasik & Heimberg, in press, for discussion of ways to use self-management procedures at work).

The literature is similarly just beginning to reveal a concern with energy conservation, and prudent use of resources will certainly continue to be important in the future because of our depleting global energy reserves and the associated increasing acquisition expenses. Runnion, Johnson, and McWhorter (1978) describe one successful behavioral attempt at reducing petroleum usage by freight haulers. The success of behavioral procedures in reducing residential consumption of fuel oil (Seaver & Patterson, 1976), natural gas (Winett & Nietzel, 1975), and electricity (Hayes & Cone, 1981) suggests these behavioral procedures may be of considerable value to organizations as well.

Customer service behavior is yet another area in which behaviorists are beginning to make important advances. Interventions by Komaki and her colleagues (Collins, Komaki, & Temlock, 1979; Komaki, Blood, & Holder, 1980) and Brown, Malott, Dillon, and Keeps (1980) have shown a variety of behavioral procedures to be effective for improving customer approach and greeting behaviors and the quality and quantity of specific services provided to customers.

Researchers are increasingly investigating ways to improve occupational safety by behavioral procedures, which constitutes a marked departure from traditional approaches of modifying the work environment and task variables and educating workers about important aspects of safety. Behavioral interventions have been successful in a variety of work settings (for example, coal mine, research laboratory, and vehicle maintenance division) for decreasing safety violations and other work hazards as well as lost-accident time (Komaki, Barwick, & Scott, 1978, Komaki & Collins, 1979; Komaki, Heinzmann, & Lawson, 1980; Rhoton, 1980; Sulzer-Azaroff & de Santamaria, 1980; Zohar, 1980).

One final area, unmentioned in either survey, but one which behaviorists are successfully tackling, concerns theft by employees and customers, which still constitutes one of the major profit killers for retailers. The success of several recent interventions is encouraging and should inspire additional research (Carter, Hansson, Holmberg, & Melin, 1979; McNees, Gilliam, Schnelle, & Risley, 1979).

All of the recently developing areas of application reviewed here are in the very early stages of development (see Andrasik et al., in press, for more indepth coverage of these new developments). Much additional well-controlled research is needed to document that these OBM approaches can produce effects which endure over the long term (the behavioral literature is replete with examples of "effective" demonstration projects that for one reason or another have soon fallen by the wayside) and constitute meaningful alternatives to existing non-OBM approaches with regard to differential costs, feasibility, and effectiveness. Increased dissemination of OBM coupled with training of OBM specialists will be helpful in accomplishing these research objectives.

Integrating OBM With Other Areas of Organizational Behavior

Over the years a number of theoretical perspectives and approaches have come to dominate the field of organizational behavior, most of which center on trait and traditional personality theories, internal motivational states, and the like. Having evolved from the applied behavior analysis tradition, the behavior management approach differs considerable in theory and substance from mainstream orgaizational behavior. The features which set OBM apart from classical organizational behavior approaches are: (1) its focus, which is applied, behavioral, analytical, and technological; (2) its underpinnings, which are empirical and grounded in operant psychology; and (3) its concern for pragmatics, which demands that behavior change be of general and practical utility (Baer, Wolf, & Risley, 1968). Recently a number of individuals have suggested that many of the traditional areas of organizational behavior could be improved by integrating OBM with them because of the above identified features. We have previously encouraged researchers to extend behavioral concepts and methodologies to all important areas of organizational research (McNamara & Andrasik, in press). The integration of OBM and management by objectives (MBO) proposed by Ritschl and Hall (1980) is representative of the form such integrations will take and is briefly presented here for purposes of illustration.

As pointed out by Ritschl and Hall (1980), MBO goes by many definitions, with the one most frequently quoted being:

> the system of management by objectives can be described as a process whereby the superior and subordinate managers of an organization jointly identify its common goals, define each individual's major area of responsibility in terms of the results expected from him and use these measures as guides for operating the unit and assessing the contribution of each of its members [Odiorne, 1965, pp. 55-56].

Even though MBO dates back to the mid fifties (e.g., Drucker, 1954; McGregor, 1975), the many years of study and numerous application attempts have garnered little solid empirical support for MBO. Ritschl and Hall's (1980) survey of the MBO literature lead them to conclude:

> Of all articles reviewed, only two investigators utilized performance measures to assess the effects of MBO. The remaining articles/studies primarily consisted of testimonials, anecdotal reports, position papers, and studies using satisfaction and/or attitudinal measures to assess the effects of MBO. Furthermore, these studies, although employing statistical analyses, failed to achieve experimental control or manipulation of the variables in question. Thus, they point out that there is a lack of rigorous scientific research of MBO programs in the professional literature [p. 271].

In Ritschl and Hall's (1980) proposed integration, the form of MBO remains relatively intact. Thus, the goal in their integration is to improve rather than replace this management approach by restricting its focus to observable/measurable behaviors, establishing behavioral objectives and pinpointing the activities that will lead to their accomplishment, incorporating behavioral measurement technologies, and subjecting the approach to behavioral evaluation strategies.

Bourdon (in press) proposes a wedding of OBM and Human Resource Management (HRM) broadly defined by Bourdon as "any area where human beings are involved which literally taps every aspect of most organizations." Some of the areas of interface identified by Bourdon are being actively pursued at present: training, developing managerial skills, utilizing behavioral technologies to meet an organization's educational and instructional needs, and improving performance. However, many areas of HRM remain somewhat virgin territory for OBM: recruitment of personnel, selection of employees for advancement opportunities, development of viable and suitable career ladders for employees, improvement of the organizational climate and organizational life, promotion of organizational change, and improvement of systems of operation. Here, as in the model advanced by Ritschl and Hall (1980), the techniques and skills of the behavior analyst are seen as being useful for improving the functioning of the human resource manager.

Leadership is a topic for which several behavioral models have been advanced. The first behavioral models of leadership, as pointed out by David and Luthans (1979), employed one-sided conceptions of the leader-subordinate relationship. Thus, Sims (1977) stressed the role of the leader as a dispenser of contingencies; Scott (1977) discussed the contingencies operating on the leader; and Mawhinney and Ford (1977) described the leader's role as one of cuing or prompting desired employee behavior. Davis and Luthan's (1979) model of leadership is more complex, taking into account the effects that subordinates exert on the leader, the resulting interaction of effects, and the role that cognitive factors play. Thus, behavioral examinations of leadership have called for increasingly more substantive changes to traditional organizational behavior approaches.

Synergistic technologies (McNamara, in press) represent another form of integration that hold much potential for the future. In a synergistic intervention, the principles and technologies of two or more separate approaches are combined in such a manner that the effect produced is larger than either is capable of producing by itself; the whole is truly greater than the sum of its parts. The best example of the enriched yield capable of being harvested from synergistic technologies in organizational settings remains the behavioral engineering model of human competence articulated by Gilbert (1978). Behavioral fusion systems will likely become more commonplace in organizational settings and are expected to markedly impact the field.

Training

Many private corporations and most government agencies have some sort of training department. The scope of activities pursued in these departments is indeed broad, and ranges from scientific-technical training to human relationship enhancement endeavors. Training personnel have to date found the programmed instruction and interpersonal skill training approaches of OBM to be most useful. Programmed instruction techniques are being successfully used with employees to develop knowledge and performance proficiency in various facets of job demands (Babb & Kopp, 1978). Interpersonal skill training more typically deals with improving supervisory effectiveness around subordinates (Goldstein & Sorcher, 1974; Latham & Saari, 1979). Both of these OBM application areas are likely to continue to expand in order to train and upgrade the knowledge and skill base of tomorrow's work force.

OBM may also be able to contribute in an important way to several emerging concerns in the training field. Goldstein (1980), among others, has emphasized that the next major task of training directors is to develop more appropriate needs assessment procedures which incorporate elements of the task, person, and organization. Most current training needs assessment procedures rely almost exclusively on questionnaire answers and interview responses for guidance as to the type of training the organization requires. All too frequently organizational stereotypes emerge from such an analysis, but nonetheless serve to guide the development of training programs. OBM assessments can provide more valid data as to the "real" training needs by conducting observations in the organizational environment and documenting what educational and skill deficits exist among various organizational groups.

Conducting more behaviorally-based needs assessments before training may force the entire training enterprise to focus more intensely on the job relevance and direct work application of training. Such an emphasis will require the construction of training programs that will show carry-over effects to the work environment. In order to more successfully design such programs, trainers will need to incorporate aspects of generalization technology (Stokes & Baer, 1977) within a transfer of training system (McNamara, 1980).

Performance Improvement Approaches

Utilizing behavioral techniques to enhance performance has been the major focus of most OBM interventions. The components that have been found to be particularly important in facilitating such performance improvement are: administrative policy, goals, instructions, monitoring, modeling, social and material reinforcers, contingency arrangements, and performance feedback (Andrasik et al., in press). Each one or combination of these factors seems to have differential utility depending on task, situational, and/or worker characteristics. How each precisely contributes to performance improvement will be better understood in the future. Two of these components may play particularly important roles in the future.

Incentives. Several major factors such as pay, security, hours, fringe benefits, and working conditions have historically been viewed as the principal incentives that could be used to motivate workers (Luthans, 1973). Some of the structural changes in the composition of the work force, as well as the type of work that will be done, may necessitate greater experimentation with incentive conditions than is currently the case. New pay practices which have potential of becoming more widely utilized in the future are: cafeteria-style fringe benefits, lump-sum salary increases, skill-based evaluation salaries, open salary information, and participative pay decisions (Lawler, 1977). Even more innovative systems are in the offering as evidenced by Pedalino and Gamboa's (1974) lottery program with money, which has been used to reduce absenteeism. Although money and other tangible rewards along with social praise seem to be used most frequently in current programs, the knowledgeable worker of the future may require a different system. For instance, activity menus of challenging or stimulating tasks could be used in a Premack fashion to reinforce the more mundane, but immediately necessary work of the organization.

Monitoring Systems. Behavioral assessment is becoming more widespread as a method to collect reliable and valid information in the work setting (Komaki, Collins, & Theone, 1980). Self-recording programs as well as external monitoring systems, typically associated with feedback and consequation, have been important features of the performance improvement area. More recently, performance appraisal systems themselves are being viewed as a major vehicle by which to influence the productivity of employees (Latham & Wexley, 1981). In this area, the development of behavior observation scales (BOS) (Latham & Wexley, 1977) represents an important method of obtaining data about employees, which can then be used as a basis of performance review with them. Positive behavior change attendant to the use of BOS in performance appraisal situations has been noted when combined with explicit performance feedback and the establishment of specific goals (Latham & Wexley, 1981). Such a system when combined with a larger evaluation environment, such as a behaviorally based assessment center, may usher in a new era of how we look at, as well as better manage, performance-based problems.

Integrating People, Technology, and Work

According to Toffler (1980) we are in the midst of a great era of change, which may be unlike anything previously experienced. Nowhere is the leading edge of this technological change more visible than in the corporate sectors of the nation. Probably the single most important element that has produced a technological revolution of sorts has been the introduction of microelectronics into the work place.

Microelectronics are already demonstrating their potential to save labor and increase productivity during a period when the rate of economic growth is expected to slow. As a result, the prospects for unemployment in certain sectors of the economy seem likely. Some early casualities, such as the typesetters in the newspaper industry, have already started to experience occupational displacement as a result of the introduction of electronic automation to their industry. Many of these individuals are finding it difficult or impossible to secure comparable new employment elsewhere (Gilchrist & Shenkin, 1981). OBM may be able to help labor and management alike by advising them about the possible consequences of the introduction of this new technology and assisting them in the development of recycling programs for the affected workers.

The introduction of word processors, computers, robots, and other intelligent-like machines is fundamental to the growth of the automated work place (Norman, 1981). The current generation of computers seems to be used mainly for purposes of job enlargement (Kearsley, 1981); this role will likely expand in the future. The storage capacity and operating efficiency of the computer will increasingly be used to handle most of the information processing and some of the decision-making functions of the organization of the future.

One potential area of interface between OBM and this computer-based automation is in the field of robotics. The current generation of industrial robots has largely taken dangerous and unpleasant jobs away from humans. OBM along with human factors analysts can facilitate such a process by determining whether organizational job demands, within certain parameters of safety, productivity, etc., can and should best be done by humans or robots.

New highly automated work environments will be gradually replacing the older more labor intensive ones. This change will create new opportunities and challenges for workers, managers, and researchers. Historically, OBM has directed its efforts at understanding and managing fairly discrete aspects of the work environment. Given the influence that technology will exert on the total work setting, organizational behaviorists may have to focus on studying and assisting with change in larger ecological units of the organization. One of the major strengths of this orientation would be the creation of work settings with high positive reinforcement values associated with them (McNamara & Andrasik, in press). Such an approach would likely assist in improving the overall quality of the work environment in more basic ways than the current generation of behavior modification programs has been able to accomplish.

REFERENCES

Adam, E. E., Jr. Behavior modification in quality control. *Academy of Management Journal, 1975,* **18**, 662-679.

Aldis, O. "Of Pigeons and Men." *Harvard Business Review,* 1961, **39** (4), 59-63.

Andrasik, F. Organizational behavior modification in business settings: A methodological and content review. *Journal of Organizational Behavior Management,* 1979, **2**, 85-102.

Andrasik, F., & Heimberg, J. S. Self-management procedures. In L. W. Frederiksen (Ed.), Handbook *of organizational behavior management.* New York: Wiley, in press.

Andrasik, F., Heimberg, J. S., & McNamara, J. R. Behavior modification of work and work-related problems. In M. Hersen, R. M. Eisler, & P. M. Miller (Eds.), *Progress in behavior modification.* New York: Academic, Vol. XI, in press.

Andrasik, F., McNamara, J. R., & Edlund, S. R. Additional future directions for OBM. *Journal of Organizational Behavior Management,* 1981, in press.

Babb, H. W., & Kopp, D. G. Applications of behavior modification in organizations: A review and critique. *Academy of Management Review*, 1978, **3**, 281-292.

Baer, D. M., Wolf, M. M., & Risley, T. R. Some current dimensions of applied behavior analysis. *Journal of Applied Behavior Analysis*, 1968, **1**, 91-97.

Barling, J., & Wainstein, T. Attitudes, labeling bias, and behavior modification in work organizations. *Behavior Therapy*, 1979, **10**, 129-136.

Bass, B. M. Organizational life in the 70's and beyond. *Personnel Psychology*, 1972, **25**, 19-30.

Bourdon, R. D. A behavioral proposal on human resources management: An invitation to a wedding. *The Behavior Therapist*, in press.

Bourdon, R. D. A token economy application to management performance improvement. *Journal of Organizational Behavior Management*, 1977, **1**, 23-37.

Brown, M. G., Malott, R. W., Dillon, M. J., & Keeps, E. J. Improving customer service in a large department store through the use of training and feedback. *Journal of Organizational Behavior Management*, 1980, **2**, 251-265.

Carter, N., Hansson, L., Holmberg, B., & Melin, L. Shoplifting reduction through the use of specific signs. *Journal of Organizational Behavior Management*, 1979, **2**, 73-84.

Collins, R. L., Komaki, J., & Temlock, S. Behavioral definition and improvement of customer service in retail merchandising. Paper presented at the meeting of the American Psychological Association, New York, September 1979.

Davis, T. R. V., & Luthans, F. Leadership reexamined: A behavioral approach. *Academy of Management Review*, 1979, **1**, 237-243.

Drucker, P. F. The practice of management. New York: Harper & Row, 1954.

Emmert, G. D. Measuring the impact of group performance feedback versus individual performance in an industrial setting. *Journal of Organizational Behavior Management*, 1978, **1**, 134-141.

Frederiksen, L. W., & Lovett, S. B. Inside organizational behavior management: Perspectives on an emerging field. *Journal of Organizational Behavior Management*, 1980, **2**, 193-203.

Gilbert, T. F. *Human competence: Engineering worthy performance*. New York: McGraw-Hill, 1978.

Gilchrest, B., & Shenkin, A. The impact of computers on employment. *The Futurist*, 1981, **15** (1), 44-49.

Goldstein, A. P., & Sorcher, M. *Changing supervisor behavior*. New York: Pergamon, 1974.

Goldstein, I. L. Training and organizational psychology. *Professional Psychology*. 1980. **11**, 421-427.

Hayes, S. C., & Cone, J. D. Reduction of residential consumption of electricity through simple monthly feedback. *Journal of Applied Behavior Analysis*, 1981, **14**, 81-88.

Hofstede, G. Motivation, leadership, and organization: Do American theories apply abroad? *Organizational Dynamics*, 1980, **9**, 42-63.

Kahn, H. Brown, W., & Martel, L. *The next 200 years: A scenario for America and the world*. New York: William Morrow, 1976.

Kahn, H., & Phelps, J. B. The economic present and future: A chartbook for the decades ahead. *The Futurist*, 1979, **13** (3) 202-222.

Kearsley, G. Software psychology: Plugging into human performance in computer systems. *APA Monitor*, 1981, **12** (4), 15; 54-55.

Kerr, S., & Jermier, J. Substitutes for leadership: Their meaning and measurement. *Organizational Behavior & Human Performance*, 1978, **22**, 375-403.

Komaki, J., Barwick, K. D., & Scott, L. R. A behavioral approach to occupational safety. Pinpointing and reinforcing safe performance in a food manufacturing plant. *Journal of Applied Psychology*, 1978, **63**, 434-445.

Komaki, J., Blood, M. R., & Holder, D. Fostering friendliness in a fast foods franchise. *Journal of Organizational Behavior Management*, 1980, **2**, 151-164.

Komaki, J., & Collins, R. L. Attaining intermediate goals using the behavior analysis approach: Measurement and improvement of preventive management. In M. R. Blood (Chair), Applied behavior analysis research and applications in organizational settings. Symposium presented at the annual meeting of the Institute of Management Science, Honolulu, June 1979.

Komaki, J., Collins, R. L., & Thoene, T. J. F. Behavioral measurement in business, industry, and government. *Behavioral Assessment*, 1980, **2**, 103-123.

Komaki, J., Heinzmann, A. T., & Lawson, L. Component analysis of a behavioral safety program: Effects of information and feedback. *Journal of Applied Psychology*, 1980, **65**, 261-270.

Lamal, P. A., & Benfield, A. The effect of self-monitoring on job tardiness and percentage of time spent working. *Journal of Organizational Behavior Management*, 1978, **1**, 142-149.

Latham, G. P., Cummings, L. L., & Mitchell, T. R. Behavioral strategies to improve productivity. *Organizational Dynamics*, 1981, **9**, 5-23.

Latham, G. P., & Dossett, D. L. Designing incentive plans for unionized employees: A comparison of continuous and variable ratio reinforcement schedules. *Personnel Psychology*, 1978, **31**, 47-61.

Latham, G. P., & Saari, L. M. Application of social-learning theory to training supervisors through behavioral modeling. *Journal of Applied Psychology*, 1979, **64**, 239-246.

Latham, G., & Wexley, K. N. Behavioral observation scales for performance appraisal purposes. *Personnel Psychology*, 1977, **30**, 255-268.

Latham, G., & Wexley, K. N. *Increasing productivity through performance appraisal*. Reading, Mass.: Addison-Wesley, 1981.

Lawler, E. E. New approaches to pay administration. In J. R. Hackman, E. E. Lawler, & L. W. Porter (Eds.), *Perspectives on behavior in organizations*. New York: McGraw-Hill, 1977.

Luthans, F. *Organizational behavior*. New York: McGraw-Hill, 1973.

Luthans, F., & Davis, T. R. V. Behavioral self-management: The missing link in managerial effectiveness. *Organizational Dynamics*, 1979, 42-60.

Manz, C. C., & Sims, H. P., Jr. Self-management as a substitute for leadership: A social learning theory perspective. *Academy of Management Review*, 1980, **5**, 361-367.

Mawhinney, T. C., & Ford, J. C. The path-goal theory of leader effectiveness: An operant interpretation. *Academy of Management Review*, 1977, **2**, 398-411.

McGregor, D. M. An uneasy look at performance appraisal. *Harvard Business Review*, 1957, **35**, 89-94.

McNamara, J. R. Why aren't they doing what we trained them to do? *Training*, 1980, **17**, 32-3, 36.

McNamara, J. R. Behavior therapy in the seventies: Some changes and current issues. *Psychotherapy: Theory, Research, and Practice*, in press.

McNamara, J. R., & Andrasik, F. Behavioral intervention in industry and government. In L. Michelson, M. Hersen, & S. Turner (Eds.). *Future perspectives in behavior therapy*. New York: Plenum, in press.

McNees, P., Gilliam, S. W., Schnelle, J. F., & Risley, T. Controlling employee theft through time and product identification. *Journal of Organizational Behavior Management*, 1979, **2**, 113-119.

Meadows, D. H., Meadows, D. L., Randers, J., & Behrens, W. *The limits to growth*. New York: Universe Books, 1972.

Norman, C. The new industrial revolution: How microelectronics may change the workplace. *The Futurist*, 1981, **15** (1), 30-42.

O'Connor, R. D. Treatment of race and sex discriminatory behavior patterns. In G. A. Harris (Ed.), *The group treatment of human problems*. New York: Grune & Stratton, 1977.

Odiorne, G. S. *Management by objectives*. New York: Pitman, 1965.

Peterson, R. W. Impacts of technology. *American Scientist*, 1979, **67**, 28-31.

Pedalino, E., & Gamboa, V. U. Behavior modification and absenteeism: Intervention in one industrial setting. *Journal of Applied Psychology*, 1974, **59**, 694-698.

Rhoton, W. W. Personal communication, November 6, 1979.

Rhoton, W. W. A procedure to improve compliance with coal mine safety regulations. *Journal of Organizational Behavior Management*, 1980, **2**, 243-249.

Ritschl, E. R., & Hall, R. V. Improving MBO: An applied behavior analyst's point of view. *Journal of Organizational Behavior Management*, 1980, **2**, 269-277.

Runnion, A., Johnson, T., & McWhorter, J. The effect of feedback and reinforcement on truck turnaround time in materials transportation. *Journal of Organizational Behavior Management*, 1978, **1**, 110-117.

Schneier, C. E. Behavior modification in management: A review and critique. *Academy of Management Journal*, 1974, **17,** 528-548.

Scott, W. E. Leadership: A functional analysis: In J. G. Hunt & L. L. Larson (Eds.), *Leadership: The cutting edge*. Carbondale, Ill.: Southern Illinois University Press, 1977.

Seaver, W. B., & Patterson, A. H. Decreasing fuel oil consumption through feedback and social commendation. *Journal of Applied Behavior Analysis*, 1976, **9,** 147-152.

Sheppard, C. S., & Carroll, D. C. (Eds.) *Working in the twenty-first century*. New York: Wiley, 1980.

Sims, H. P. The leader as a manager of reinforcement contingencies: An empirical example and a model. In J. G. Hunt & L. L. Larson (Eds.), *Leadership: The cutting edge*. Carbondale, Ill.: Southern Illinois University Press, 1977.

Stokes, T. F., & Baer, D. M. An implicit technology of generalization. *Journal of Applied Behavior Analysis*, 1977, **10,** 349-367.

Sulzer-Azaroff, B., & de Santamaria, M. C. Industrial safety hazard reduction through performance feedback. *Journal of Applied Behavior Analysis*, 1980, **13,** 287-295.

Toffler, A. *The third wave*. New York: William Morrow, 1980.

Winett, R. A., & Nietzel, M. T. Behavioral ecology: Contingency management of consumer energy use. *American Journal of Community Psychology*, 1975, **3,** 123-133.

Zohar, D. Promoting the use of personal protective equipment by behavior modification techniques. *Journal of Safety Research*, 1980, **12,** 78-85.

Author Index

Subject Index

About The Editors and Contributors

THE EDITORS

Richard M. O'Brien is an Associate Professor of Psychology at Hofstra University where he has developed an undergraduate practicum course in industrial behavior modification. He received his doctorate in clinical psychology from West Virginia University. Dr. O'Brien's current research interests are in behavior modification in industry and sports. He has been involved in productivity improvement programs in transportation, manufacturing, and municipal government settings as well as with professional and college athletes. He has recently published a book with Tom Simek that uses behavioral approaches to help golfers lower their scores (*Total Golf*, Doubleday, 1981).

Alyce M. Dickinson received her Master's Degree in Industrial Psychology from Fairleigh Dickinson University. She continued her interest in behavior modification in her work in personnel selection, placement, evaluation, and productivity improvement first at the Port Authority of New York and New Jersey and later at the New York State Office of Court Administration. She is currently at Western Michigan University pursuing a Ph.D. in Applied Behavior Analysis with an emphasis in Behavioral Systems Analysis.

Michael P. Rosow has been a consultant to the Work in America Institute since its creation and assumed responsibility as director of the Institute's Education and Training Division in 1980. As vice-president of the Institute's Education and Training Division, his present responsibilities include development and management of the Institute's new service, "The Productivity Forum"; supervision of research and writing for the continuing "Studies in Productivity" series; direction of research and demonstration projects, Job Development Training, symposia, conferences, and workshops. Dr. Rosow holds a Ph.D. from Hofstra University. He is listed in *Who's Who in the East (1979)*, *Men of Achievement (1979–1980)*, *Dictionary of International Biography (Volume XVI)*, and *The American Registry Series*.

THE CONTRIBUTORS

William B. Abernathy (Project Director, Edward J. Feeney Associates, Redding, Connecticut). Since joining Edward J. Feeney Associates, Dr. Albernathy has worked with a number of banks and one of the nation's top restaurant chains. He completed his Master's Degree at George Peabody College and holds a doctorate in Psychology from Ohio State University.

Beverly S. Adler (Doctoral Candidate, Hofstra University). Ms. Adler holds a Master's Degree in Applied Behavior Analysis from Western Michigan University. Her current research interests are in feedback and the role of goals as discriminative stimuli and secondary reinforcers for industrial tasks.

Frank Andrasik (Assistant Professor of Psychology, State University of New York at Albany). Frank Andrasik received his doctorate in clinical psychology from Ohio University in 1979. His research interests include staff development and training and the treatment of stress related disorders.

Teodoro Ayllon (Professor of Psychology and Special Education, Georgia State University). Dr. Ayllon is co-author of *The Token Economy* (with N. Azrin) and *Correctional Rehabilitation and Management* (with M. Milen, M. Roberts, & J. McKee). His interests are in the applied analysis of human behavior, and he holds a Ph.D. in psychology from the University of Houston.

Howard C. Berthold, Jr. (Chairman and Associate Professor of Psychology, Lycoming College). Dr. Berthold has taught industrial-organizational psychology at four different colleges and has done extensive consulting work with both public and private organizations. He holds a doctorate in psychology from the University of Massachusetts. His current interests include integrating behavioral techniques with human relations approaches to management.

Daniel D. Brand (Performance Analyst, United States Department of Housing and Urban Development, Washington, D.C.). Mr. Brand has served as a performance analyst with Edward J. Feeney Associates and the federal government. He holds a B.A. in Psychology from the University of Louisville and advanced degrees from the Institute Oecumenique de Celigny in Geneva and the Institute Oecumenique Orthodoxe in Paris.

Dale M. Brethower (Associate Professor of Psychology, Western Michigan University). The author of the first textbook in industrial behavior modification, Dr. Brethower has been active in this field since the early 1960s. He currently heads the Industrial Psychology Master's Committee and teaches behavior management and behavioral systems analysis at Western Michigan. His degrees are from the University of Kansas (A.B.), Harvard University (A.M.), and The University of Michigan (Ph.D.).

William P. Brittain (Senior Psychologist – Caress, Gilhooly & Kestin, Inc., New York). Dr. Brittain holds a Master's Degree in human factors from Wichita State University and a doctorate in experimental psychology from Texas Christian University. He is an experienced outplacement consultant who has taught at a number of colleges in the Northeast.

Fred E. Bushhouse, Jr. (Project Director, Edward J. Feeney Associates, Redding, Connecticut). Before joining Edward J. Feeney Associates, Mr. Bushhouse had twenty years of experience in the fields of personnel management and labor relations. He holds an M.B.A. in industrial and labor relations from Cornell University. He has directed a broad range of successful interventions with the Feeney organization.

Richard M. Carlson (Director, Behavior Dynamics Inc., New York). Since 1970, Mr. Carlson has been involved in behavioral consultation to the business world in such diverse areas as productivity improvement, interpersonal relations, communication skills, and labor relations. He received his Master's Degree from Georgia State University in Atlanta where he had conducted some of the early behavioral work on controlling absenteeism with Dr. Ayllon.

Robert L. Collins (Research Scientist, Engineering Experiment Station, Georgia Institute of Technology). Dr. Collins has a number of publications on applying behavior analysis techniques to customer service, maintenance, and increasing productivity. While at Georgia Tech he has conducted research in both governmental and profit making institutions. He earned his doctorate from the University of California at San Diego in 1975.

William J. Crawley (Project Director, Edward J. Feeney Associates). Mr. Crawley has conducted management coaching and sales training programs for Edward J. Feeney Associates in a variety of fields including heating and air conditioning, trucking and furniture sales. He received his Master's Degree in organizational behavior from the University of Massachusetts.

Elaine M. Duffy (Doctoral Candidate, Hofstra University). Ms. Duffy holds a bachelor's degree in psychology from Canisius College and a Master's Degree from Hofstra University. She has served as a graduate teaching assistant in industrial behavior modification and has research interests in outplacement, employee productivity as a function of reinforcement schedules, and behavioral health psychology.

Phillip K. Duncan (Assistant Professor of Psychology, Drake University). As Director of Drake University's M.S. program in behavioral systems administration, Dr. Duncan's interests are in the measurement of human behavior and industrial behavior modification. He received his doctorate in the experimental and applied analysis of behavior from the University of Florida.

Edward J. Feeney (President – Edward J. Feeney Associates, Redding, Connecticut). As vice-president of Systems Performance at Emery Air Freight, Mr. Feeney installed behavioral systems that produced a two million dollar increase in annual profits for that company. Since establishing his own consulting firm, he has extended behavioral programs and systems to the task of improving performance in key payoff areas for numerous organizations. His work has served as case history material for the business schools at both Harvard and Dartmouth and his film with B. F. Skinner has been influential in popularizing industrial behavior modification.

Robert W. Figlerski (Doctoral Candidate, Hofstra University). Having completed a bachelor's degree in psychology at Lycoming College, Mr. Figlerski attained a Master's Degree at Hofstra University. He is currently working on his doctoral dissertation which involves research on the reinforcing effects of feedback and goal setting among industrial employees.

Steven R. Howard (Doctoral Candidate, Hofstra University). Mr. Howard has his bachelor and Master's Degrees in psychology from Hofstra University. His research interests are in the fields of industrial psychology and clinical psychology.

David J. Kolko (Doctoral Candidate, Georgia State University). Mr. Kolko is in the process of completing his doctorate in clinical psychology. His area of specialization is behavior analysis and therapy and he has a number of publications and presentations in these fields.

Judi Komaki (Principal Research Scientist, Engineering Experiment Station, Georgia Institute of Technology). Dr. Komaki has demonstrated successful behavioral interventions in government, major corporations, and small business. She has numerous publications and presentations in applied behavior analysis including such difficult to monitor areas as preventive maintenance, occupational safety, and customer service. She is also on the editorial board of two major journals in applied behavior analysis. Dr. Komaki received her Ph.D. from the University of Illinois.

Kenneth E. Lloyd (Professor of Psychology, Drake University). Dr. Lloyd has been a member of the teaching faculties at the University of Virginia, Washington State University, and presently Drake University. He received his doctorate at Ohio State University and is a fellow of the American Psychological Association. His major interests are in social behavior, environmental psychology, and educational psychology.

Renee R. Mawhinney (Associate – Barnes, & Thornburg, Indianapolis, Indiana). Following her Master's Degree at the University of South Florida, Renee Mawhinney obtained a J. D. from the Indiana University School of Law. She has served as Editor-in-Chief of the Indiana Law Journal.

Thomas C. Mawhinney (Associate Professor of Personnel and Organizational Behavior, School of Business, Indiana University, Bloomington). Dr. Mawhinney has published both theoretical and empirical research articles relating operant terms, concepts, and methods to leadership and intrinsically motivated behavior. He completed his doctorate in business administration at Ohio State University after having attained a Master's Degree in management from the University of South Florida.

J. Regis McNamara (Associate Professor of Psychology, Ohio University). Dr. McNamara is Associate Director for Training and Program Development for the Institute of Health and Behavioral Sciences at Ohio University. His interests include the development and evaluation of behavior change systems in a variety of organizational settings. His doctorate is from the University of Georgia.

Richard L. Miller (Professor of Psychology, Western Kentucky University). As a licensed psychologist, Dr. Miller provides individual stress management training and training seminars for a wide range of business community. He holds a doctorate in physiological psychology from the University of Houston.

Robert Mirman (Director, Performance Systems Department, General Mills). Prior to joining General Mills, Mr. Mirman was a senior management consultant for Tarkenton and Company. He is currently completing his doctorate in behavioral psychology at the University of Kansas.

William F. Pfohl, Jr. (Assistant Professor of Psychology, Western Kentucky University). Dr. Pfohl is a graduate of the Psy.D. program at the Graduate School of Applied and Professional Psychology at Rutgers University. He has worked at the Rutgers Medical School Behavior Therapy and Pain Clinic and has conducted workshops in stress management in a variety of industrial settings.

Diana R. Richman (Staff Psychologist, The Institute for Rational Living, New York). Dr. Richman holds an M.Ed. in counseling from Tufts University and a Ph.D. in School-Clinical Psychology from Hofstra University. For over ten years she was employed as a consultant and employment counselor for the New York State Department of Labor where she worked with work incentive programs for the hardcore unemployed. Her interests are in psychological approaches to career planning and development as well as stress management.

William A. Sperduto (School Psychologist, Farmingdale, New York). In addition to his work as a school psychologist. Dr. Sperduto has worked with Behavior Dynamics and is currently Associate Director of Health Psychology at the Hofstra Health Dome. He received his doctorate in psychology from Hofstra University where he served as the graduate teaching assistant for an undergraduate course in industrial behavior modification. Dr. Sperduto has a number of publications and presentations in behavioral medicine and industrial behavior modification.

John R. Staelin (Vice President for Client Services, Edward J. Feeney Associates, Redding, Connecticut). Mr. Staelin has worked extensively with companies in the fields of banking, manufacturing, transportation, and retail sales. He is a frequent speaker throughout the country on implementing behavioral techniques to improve productivity. Mr. Staelin received his MBA from the University of Michigan.

Date Due